THE PROFESSIONAL MODEL'S HANDBOOK

A Comprehensive Guide to Modeling and Related Fields

by Linda A. Balhorn

Bobbi Ray Madry
Senior Editor/Curriculum Specialist

Milady Publishing Company
(A Division of Delmar Publishers, Inc.)
3 Columbia Circle Drive, Box 15015
Albany, New York 12212-5015

NOTICE TO THE READER

Milady Staff:
Author: Linda A. Balhorn
Editor: Bobbi Ray Madry
Editorial Director: Mary Healy
Production Manager: Jan M. Lavin
Art Director: John P. Fornieri
Graphic Artists: Pat Miret, Pat Genova, Mark Stein
Illustrations: Janet Asbury
Cover Credits:
Live Fashion Modeling/Runway (upper left): Photographer: Philippe Costes; Location:
Yves St. Laurent Collection, Paris; W. Fairchild Publications. By permission of Fairchild Syndication.
Electronic Media/Television (upper right): Photographer: Michael Roberts, Chicago; Stylist: Tricia Schneider; Makeup/Hair; L. Balhorn; Talent (clockwise); Larry Sherwood, Janet Kauss, Paul Cook, Eric Sherwood. A-Plus Talent, Chicago.
Live Promotion/Trade Show (lower left); Photographer: Michael Roberts; Models: SusanMarie Maveety, Kevin Goulet, A-Plus Talent, Chicago. Location: Modulex Inc. Creative Sign systems showroom, Chicago. Designed by Evamaddox and Associates. Location permission, Pierre Husson, President, Modulex, Inc.
Print/Editorial (lower right): Photographer: Gordon Munro, New York. Originally commissioned by *Madame* magazine, Munich, Germany.

Printed in the United States of America
7 8 9 10 X X X 03 02 01 00 99

For more information, contact Milady, 3 Columbia Circle, PO Box 15015, Albany, NY 12212-0515; or find us on the World Wide Web at http://www.Milady.com

Library of Congress Cataloging-in-Publication Data:
ISBN: 0-87350-376-7

About the Author

Linda Balhorn has helped hundreds of individuals realize their potential as professional models. Utilizing her unique combination of photography, makeup artistry, styling, graphic arts and promotional skills, she develops and counsels aspiring models and acts as an independent model scout for several top American and European model agencies.

Linda's own experience has covered all facets of the industry. While in college she worked for an advertising agency, specializing in radio and television productions. Later, she was selected on the merit of her writing skills as a guest editor in the Beauty Department of *Mademoiselle* magazine.

After graduation, she began her modeling career which spanned seven years and included assignments in New York, Milan, Paris, Zurich, Munich, Tokyo and many other international locations. During her four year stay in Europe, she became a partner in the Model Team Agency in Zurich, where she began photographing and promoting new faces.

After returning to the U.S. she opened her own photography studio in Chicago and began work on several publishing ventures.

Linda is also the author of the best selling *Beauty Trade Secrets,* a book of tips on makeup application and hairstyling gathered from well known models and beauty professionals.

Foreword

THE PROFESSIONAL MODEL'S HANDBOOK is a comprehensive guide for anyone interested in becoming a model or pursuing a related career. You will find this guide to be an invaluable source of information for determining your own qualifications for becoming a professional model, and for exploring your competitive advantages and opportunities in this glamorous field.

THE PROFESSIONAL MODEL'S HANDBOOK is divided into six parts of study: The first part deals with exploring the fields of modeling and determining where there are needs in the industry for your looks, skills and talents. An important part of this process is developing your own special look through self-analysis, grooming, physical presentation, makeup artistry, hairstyling, wardrobe and personality projection.

The second part deals with approaching modeling as a business. Finding an agent and establishing your business are covered in detail. In the third part, you will learn step-by-step techniques in how to assemble professional tools such as a portfolio and composite for promoting your talents, skills and looks to those who may be in a position to employ you.

The fourth part explains in detail on-the-job procedures and helps you to polish your skills in the four fields of modeling: print media, electronic media, live promotions and live fashion showings.

The fifth part explores modeling opportunities around the world, from New York City to cities in Europe, Japan and other countries.

The final part explores the many varied careers related to modeling for those who find that their interests and potential are better suited for jobs behind the scenes.

The information presented in THE PROFESSIONAL MODEL'S HANDBOOK is applicable no matter what your type, where you plan to model, or at what level you plan to pursue your career. Models of all types, from fashion to commercial, to character models of both sexes and all ages, are addressed throughout the book. In addition, the information is geared to minor as well as major markets throughout the United States, with chapters addressed specifically to modeling in New York City, and modeling outside of the United States.

While THE PROFESSIONAL MODEL'S HANDBOOK is an important guide for the aspiring model, it is also an essential teaching and reference tool for modeling instructors, agents, photographers, stylists, fashion coordinators, casting directors, and others who employ models.

Even people who are not seeking a career in modeling can benefit from the information contained in THE PROFESSIONAL MODEL'S HANDBOOK. Both men and women can improve their appearance and the way they present themselves by learning the trade secrets successful models have known and used for years. In addition to improving your image, you will gain an understanding of how to promote your skills to others and how to conduct yourself in a professional, polished manner, no matter what business or career you pursue.

Acknowledgments

*The author and publisher of THE PROFESSIONAL MODEL'S HAND-
BOOK wish to thank the following people for their contributions to
this textbook; including photographs, permissions and much valued
information:*

MODELS AND THEIR ASSISTANTS

Christie Brinkley, Claire Mercuri, New York; research and
permission.

Brooke Shields, Lila Wisdom, New York; research, contribution and
permission for photograph; information.

Beverly Johnson; New York; permission for photograph.

Naomi Sims, Donna Italiano; New York; permission for photograph.

Dorian Leigh Parker, Georgia; permission for photograph.

Mrs. Bradford Dillman (Suzy Parker), California; permission for
photograph.

Jan Leighton, New York; permission of composite and photograph.

Candy Jones, New York, information on history of modeling.

Mary Hardt, Chicago; permission and contribution of composite.

Debbie Lemons, Amy Roskelley, Chicago; permission for composites; Rochelle Susanne, contribution of promotional model's
resume.

Models for illustrations: Cyndi Wyatt, Jacqui Stokes, Renee Prejean,
Joan Almaguer, Debora Ford, Patrick Hickey;

Models for photographs: Suzanne Kelsey, Angela Stanley, Bill
Carico, Dawn Carlson, Katie Lehnerd, Chris Lehman.

PHOTOGRAPHERS AND THEIR ASSISTANTS:

Horst, Richard J. Tardiff, New York; contribution and permission of
Lisa Fonsagrieves and Jean Patchett photographs.

Barry Lategan, London; contribution and permission for Twiggy photographs; information.

Patrick Demarchelier, New York; permission for Brooke Shields
photograph.

David Bailey, Nicole Jacob, London; Jean Shrimpton information.

Stan Malinowski, Chicago; consultation on cover design.

Bert Stern, New York; permission for Wilhelmina photograph.

MODEL AGENTS

Elite Models, New York, Monique Pillard, President; contribution and
permission for Elite model composites.

Ford Models, New York; Eileen Ford, President, Marion Smith, Joe
Hunter, information.

Cuington Models, New York, Phyllis Cuington, President; information.

Click Model Management, New York; Frances Grill, President; contribution of composites and information.

Big Beauties, Mary Duffy (Ford Models), New York; Information.

Pauline's Model Management, New York; Pauline Bernatchez, President; Judy White, Director of Recruiting and Promotion; contribution

of composites and information.

Wilhelmina Models, New York, Jan Kaplan, booking agent; research and contribution of Beverly Johnson photograph.

Mannequin I.M.G., New York; Joan Donovan; information.

Arlene Wilson Models, Milwaukee; Arlene Wilson, President; information.

Talentplus, St. Louis; Sharon Lee, President; information.

Model Team, Zurich; Heidi Von Munchofen, President; information.

A-Plus Talent Agency, Chicago; Sharon Cooper-Wottrich, President, Katherine Tenerowicz, vice president, Andy Westerman and Becky Mandolini, booking agents; information and assistance.

Rascals, New York, Deirdre Gentile; contribution and permission for child model composites.

Zoli Management, Inc., New York; Gail Morgan, Eleanor Lange, information.

PUBLISHERS Anthony Mazzola, Editor-in-Chief, Harper's Bazaar, Melissa Bedolis, assistant to the Editor; Permission on Harper's Bazaar photographs.

Isabel Summer; Fairchild Syndications, New York; permissions on Women's Wear Daily photographs

Diana Edkins, Conde Nast Publications, New York; research on rights and clearances of Vogue photographs.

OTHERS Bryan Bantry, Photographers' Representative, New York; permission on various photographs.

Julian Bach, Edward Steichen Estate, permission for photograph.

Mrs. Joanna T. Steichen; information on Steichen photographs.

George W. Feld; Revlon, NY; research on advertisements rights and clearances.

Robert Bibbee; Chicago Public Library; special permissions on library materials.

Richard A. Giangiorgi; Trexler, Bushnell, Giangiorgi and Blackstone, Ltd., Chicago; legal cousel on rights and clearances information.

Stuart Kahan, American Society of Magazine Photographers, New York, permissions for model release forms, information.

Sylvia Wolf, Colin Westerbach, Peter Iska, The Art Institute of Chicago, Chicago; Steichen print.

Dr. Marianne O'Donoghue, dermatologist, Chicago; information.

Camille O. Hoffmann, information and assistance.

Bill Coyer, Innovative Designer Products, New Jersey; information.

Mary Lou Bilder, Public Relations, Sears, Chicago; information.

Talent and Residuals, Chicago.

Stephanie Young, Health and Fitness Editor, Glamour Magazine, assistance.

Dorothy Fuller, President, Apparel Mart, Chicago; information.

SAG, AFTRA; Chicago and New York offices.

CONTENTS

PART 1 MODELING AS A PROFESSION

Chapter 1 Introduction to Modeling

THE HISTORY OF MODELING

Marie Vernet Worth is regarded as the first live model. A great beauty with a perfect figure, she inspired and modeled clothing designed by her husband, Charles Worth. Worth was one of the great French couteriers in the mid-1800s and is said to have invented the crinoline. He also possessed publicity skills. Instead of displaying his fashions on tailor's "dummies" as was the custom of other salons, he employed attractive shopgirls as house models to show clothing to customers in the salon and to circulate at events where rich, fashionably dressed women congregated. Essentially the first models were similar to the house models and informal models that exist today.

Before the mid-1800s, dresses were shown in scaled-down versions on dolls. These "model dolls," as they were called, were first used by Rose Bertin, a sixteenth-century clothing designer from Versailles. In order to secure orders for her designs, she would send dolls demonstrating her fashions to customers throughout Europe.

In 1914 the first fashion show using live models was held in Chicago, which at the time was the center of the garment industry. It was called "The Greatest Style Show in the World" and employed 100 models to show 250 garments to an audience of 5000 people. The extravaganza presented the finest fashions of the day, most of which were manufactured in Minneapolis, Detroit, Chicago, and surrounding cities. This fashion show was filmed and shown in cinemas throughout the country.

In the early days, live fashion modeling was not considered a proper profession for a woman. Most models also worked as shopgirls, showgirls, or part-time actresses. This concept began to change when the Paris fashion designer Jean Patou initiated a search for well-bred, intelligent, and attractive young women to model in his salon in France. With the cooperation of *Vogue* magazine in America, a search was conducted, and six young women were chosen to set the standard for latter-day models. This brought wider acceptance of the modeling profession.

Photographic modeling did not begin until the 1920s. Although fashion magazines existed and newspapers used photography to document news events, fashions were still depicted in beautiful, creative illustrations. Edna Woolman Chase, the editor of Paris *Vogue,* was the first to use photographs of live models. As fashion photography began to develop, the demand for models increased and brought about the first agency to organize models and handle book-ings. The first modeling agency was founded in the United States in 1928 by John Robert Powers, a New York actor, who began by employing his actress and starlet friends as models. The "Powers Girl" with the natural look was the prototype for today's model.

In New York the modeling business grew and became more sophis-ticated. Harry Conover, a former Powers model, started his own mod-eling agency in 1938, followed by the millionaire Huntington Hartford in the 1940s. Hartford was the first to institute the voucher system, which allowed models to be paid in a regular, more business-like man-ner than had previously existed. In 1946 the Ford Agency was estab-lished by a New York photographer's stylist and former Conover employee named Eileen Ford and her husband, Jerry Ford. The Ford Agency is responsible for developing many of the business practices that exist in the profession today, including many model scouting and training procedures. As the value of models in advertising increased, modeling agencies were formed in every major American city.

Modeling agencies did not exist in Europe at this time mainly because of postwar legislation prohibiting employment agencies. Therefore, most professional photographic models were imported from America. In the early days in Europe when a photographer needed a model, he would select a few pretty girls off the street and ask them to arrive at his studio at a specified time. Hopefully, one of them would appear and the session would be a success. However, this was a difficult way to conduct business, and with the quantity of great fashion being created in France, there was a definite need for professional photographic models. In 1957 Dorian Leigh, one of the most famous American models of the period, opened the first mod-eling agency in Paris. Subsequently other agencies were formed throughout Europe.

John Casablancas, who founded the Elite Agency in Paris in 1974, was the first to establish a worldwide network of modeling agencies.

Beginning in the 1970s acceptance of a wider variety of model looks evolved. Prior to this time the classic-looking model described earlier prevailed. In 1975 the Wilhelmina Agency introduced the first freckle-faced beauties to become Vogue cover models (Patti Hansen and Shaun Casey). Until this time freckles were considered a beauty blight, not an asset. In 1977 the first large-size (over size 10) models appeared, introduced by Mary Duffy, founder of The Big Beauties Agency in New York. In 1981, Frances Grill founded Click Model Management, expanding the field of fashion and beauty photography to include models with ethnic and highly individual looks. During the 1980s the first models over the age of 40 appeared in fashion spreads and advertisements in response to changing demographics.

The late 1980s brought about greater specialization in the modeling industry. Smaller, boutique-type agencies specializing in specific model looks appeared, while large, established agencies departmen-talized to better represent models of differing age groups, sizes and looks. Today modeling is a multifaceted, multimillion dollar field that encompasses the globe.

1920s and 1930s. *During the
1920s fashion illustrations
predominated in magazines
because photographic
reproduction techniques were
not yet perfected. Throughout
the 1930s actresses and
socialites appeared in fashion
photographs and ads. Starlets
who modeled for ads were paid
around $3 to $5 per hour to pose
for the camera. Portraits of
society hostesses for* Vogue
*were among the first editorial
fashion photographs.
Photograph by Edward
Steichen, 1930. Reprinted with
the permission of Joanna T.
Steichen.*

1940s. *Swedish-born Lisa
Fonsagrieves was one of the
greatest models of all time. Her
striking profile and elegant
movements established her
reign as a top model in Paris in
the 1930s, and in New York in
the 1940s and 1950s.
Photograph by Horst. By
permission of Horst.*

1950s. *Dorian Leigh was chosen
as the first "Revlon Girl" and
was an ever-present model in
fashion spreads. Her private life
was equally dazzling as she is
said to have been the inspiration
for Truman Capote's Holly
Golightly character in* Breakfast
at Tiffany's. *Photograph by
Richard Avedon. Copyright ©
1952, by permission of Revlon,
Dorian Leigh.*

1950s. Jean Patchett was the top model in the early 1950s. Her trademark was her beauty spot above her right eye. Her pale, pancake made-up face, highly arched brows, tiny waist, and aloof expression epitomized the beauty ideal at the time. Models' rates in the early 1950s were $25 per hour. Photograph by Horst, 1950. By permission of Horst.

1960s. Suzy Parker was Dorian Leigh's younger sister and one of the most famous models of all time. Although the going rate for models was around $35 to $45 per hour, superstars like Suzy commanded $125 per hour fees. Photograph: Springer, The Bettmann Archive. By permission of Mrs. Bradford Dillman (Suzy Parker).

1960s. The late Wilhelmina had appeared on 285 magazine covers before she retired from modeling to open her own successful New York modeling agency. She appeared in high-fashion photographs throughout the sixties and was known for her sculpted, sophisticated look. Photograph by Bert Stern. Courtesy Vogue. *Copyright © 1964, by the Conde Nast Publications.*

1960s. Raised on a Buckinghamshire farm in Britain, Jean Shrimpton had never considered a modeling career. At 17 she was discovered by a young British photographer named David Bailey. Three years later their partnership would make the "Shrimp" take the fashion world by storm. Her waif-like figure (5'9", 33-22-34), exquisite, feminine face and chameleon like ability to adapt her look from childlike to sophisticated made her an international star. Photograph by Richard Avedon. Copyright © 1965, The Hearst Corporation. Courtesy Harper's Bazaar.

1960s. Twiggy was a skinny cockney girl plucked from obscurity and created almost overnight by her boyfriend/manager. Her short haircut, huge eyes, and boyish figure were her trademarks. Photograph by Barry Lategan. Copyright © 1966, by permission of Barry Lategan and Twiggy.

1960s. A six-foot, one-inch-tall German-born baroness, Verushka represented a modern, psychedelic look in the late sixties and early seventies. Her innate sense of style and creative approach to modeling established her as an editorial superstar. Photograph by Richard Avedon. Copyright © 1965, The Hearst Corporation. Courtesy of Harper's Bazaar.

1970s. Naomi Sims was the first black model to achieve superstar status. She appeared in leading fashion magazines and was the subject of a Life magazine cover. She went on to become an author, lecturer, and successful businesswoman. Photograph by Alexis Waldeck. Permission by Naomi Sims.

1970s. Lauren Hutton was a characteristic beauty with a drifting eye and a gap between her front teeth. She made imperfection fashionable. Her uninhibited style mirrored the changing feminine ideals of the women's liberation movement. Photograph by Bill King. Copyright © 1972, The Hearst Corporation. Courtesy of Harper's Bazaar.

1970s. Cheryl Tiegs brought the all-American, tanned California-girl look into fashion in the late seventies. She pioneered the way for models in the area of licensing when she signed a contract with Sears, guaranteeing her a percentage of sales on the clothing line that bore her name. Photograph by Marco Glaviano. Copyright © 1978, The Hearst Corporation. Courtesy of Harper's Bazaar.

1970s. Beverly Johnson was the first black model to appear on the cover of Vogue magazine. Photograph by Roger Prigent. Permission by Beverly Johnson.

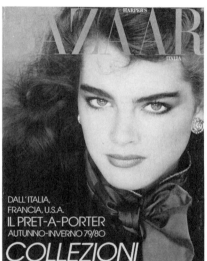

1980s. At age 14 Brooke Shields appeared on the cover of Vogue in grown-up clothes and makeup bringing in the "pretty baby" look and a trend toward younger models. Photograph by Patrick Demarchelier. By permission of Brooke Shields. Demarchelier, Italian Harper's Bazaar.

1980s. Iman originates from the Somali tribe in Africa where she was discovered by an American photographer. Her fine-featured look, lanky body, and graceful way of moving established her as an international star in the runway and print areas of modeling. Photograph by Francesco Scavullo. Copyright © 1982, The Hearst Corporation. Courtesy of Harper's Bazaar.

1980s. Christie Brinkley's athletic figure and healthy look established the ideal for active, fitness-conscious women of the early 1980s. Top models at this time earned in excess of $2500 per day. Photograph by Steven Meisel. Permission by Christie Brinkley.

1980s. Paulina Porizkova, a Czechoslavakian beauty, represented the trend toward natural, feminine beauty and a more voluptuous shape (5' 10", 35-23½-35½). In 1988 Paulina achieved one of the top prizes in the modeling business—a cosmetics contract. Signed to a multimillion dollar arrangement, she represents Estee Lauder Cosmetics. Photograph by George Chinsee for Women's Wear Daily. Permission Fairchild Syndication.

Gallery of Models Then and Now

The models shown in Figures 1 to 18 were all superstars and trend-setters whose looks mirrored the changing ideals of beauty. These photographs by no means show all the numerous faces who graced the covers and pages of leading magazines. They are representative of the model looks that were popular from the 1920s when photographic models first appeared to the present day.

THE FOUR TYPES OF MODELING WORK

Anyone with ideas and products to sell continually searches for ways to promote them and to increase their popularity with consumers. Originally, models were employed primarily to promote fashions. Today they promote every product or service imaginable. The concept is that a model presents an image worthy of attention, admiration, or imitation. The model draws interest and shows the merchandise at its best, stimulating the potential customer's desire to own the item or obtain the service. Because so many types of media have developed, modeling has become a diversified field. Anyone considering a modeling career should be aware of all the facets that exist.

1. *Print.* Print work refers to photographs or illustrations in printed media, such as newspapers, magazines, catalogs, brochures, weeklies, direct mail flyers, books, posters, billboards, and packages.

2. *Electronic media.* Electronic media work appears on radio, television, videotape, film, slide programs, and other audio and/or visual presentations made for advertising, promotional, feature or entertainment, industrial, public relations, educational, or direct sales purposes.

3. *Live promotional.* Live promotional modeling refers to the model making appearances or presenting products. This work is done at conventions, sales meetings, or exhibitions for purposes of advertising, entertainment, promotion, public relations, education, and direct sales. Live promotional modeling is sometimes referred to as *live industrial modeling.*

4. *Live fashion.* Live fashion modeling entails showing fashions in person for a single individual or a group, either in a formal, structured show or in an informal presentation. Models are also employed by designers and manufacturers as fitting models to establish designs and sizes for garments. Models show fashions in stores, in designer salons and showrooms, at entertainment functions, and on television.

Types of Work in Print Modeling

Photographs or illustrations in which models depict an idea or the use of a product or service are published in printed media. The four types of work in the area of print modeling are:

1. *Editorial.* Editorial print work refers to the pages of magazines that are produced by the magazine staff or its assigns, not the advertisers.

2. *Catalog.* Catalog work refers to modeling for catalogs that are produced by a manufacturer or distributor to sell items.

3. *Advertising.* Advertising work or print ads utilize models to wear, hold, demonstrate, accompany, or represent a product or service. The ad may be a page in a magazine or a flyer, brochure, billboard, sales display, or packaging.

4. *Publicity/public relations.* Publicity and public relations photos are distributed to news services, newspapers, or magazine editors and the like in hopes that the publication will include the photos along with information about the sender in its editorial content. This is sometimes referred to as *free advertising.*

Types of Work in Electronic Media

This is an important area of work for models, and most modeling agencies have divisions specifically devoted to it. Models are booked to model, act, or lend their voices for basically seven types of audio and/or visual productions.

1. *Advertising.* Models appearing in television commercials advertise all types of products. Models whose looks fall into the character and straight commercial or product categories are most often used to advertise products. Fashion models are usually used in commercials for glamour (cosmetics, clothing) and glamourized (cars, travel) items. Specialty models, especially hand models, earn the largest percentage of their income from television commercials.

2. *Promotional.* Promotional videos and films are extended advertisements used to promote a product or service. Cosmetic companies often produce promotional videos to be used at the point of purchase that demonstrate how a cosmetic is used. A fashion designer may videotape his collections showing and distribute copies of the tape to stores in which his products are sold to draw interest and to show the consumer how the clothing is to be worn.

3. *Feature.* Models may be booked to appear in entertainment feature film and videotape productions, such as soap operas, motion picture films, and videocassettes. Models may be cast as principal players or as extras to lend atmosphere.

4. *Industrial.* Industrial films are produced by companies to train employees, analyze working techniques, keep customers and staff informed and enthusiastic, recruit staff, and for a variety of other reasons. Industrial films are often made for use at trade shows or exhibitions in which the company participates. Models are used in industrial films in addition to professional actors and company employees to draw attention or to act out the script.

5. *Publicity/public relations.* Publicity films are made by companies to distribute to editors and others who are in a position to publicize an idea or product. For example, a designer may make a videotape or film showing the highlights of his new collections. He sends the film to television stations in hopes that it will be featured in a news or current affairs program.

6. *Educational.* Models are occasionally employed to appear in educational films and videos. For example, a model may be used to demonstrate the exercises presented in a videocassette based on a book.

7. *Direct sales.* Direct sales involves marketing to an individual through the use of videocatalogs on television or videocassettes in which the viewer can use his phone or home computer to order items presented on the screen.

Types of Work in Live Promotion

Models appear in person at conventions, trade shows, exhibitions, sales meetings, in stores, at publicity events, and elsewhere to promote products and services. They work in six capacities.

1. *Hosting or hostessing.* Models are hired to attract attention to an exhibit. They may greet and direct visitors or lend a friendly or attractive appearance to an exhibit. Models may also be used to fill out forms to register visitors, enter them in contests or special promotions, take down addresses for mailing literature, or take orders for products.

2. *Demonstrating.* A model may perform a routine showing how a product or service is used.

3. *Narrating.* A model may give an informal talk, a speech, or technical narration explaining a product and its uses, attributes, or promotional attractions.

4. *Performing.* A talented model may be hired to attract attention to an exhibit by singing or dancing, acting out a skit, or performing a special presentation such as pantomime, magic, and the like.

5. *Sampling.* Sampling refers to distributing samples of a product to potential customers. For example, the model may offer samples of cologne to customers in a department store.

6. *Platform modeling.* A platform model is the model on whom a product, service, or technique is demonstrated. For example, a model may appear on stage at a trade show exhibit so that a hairstylist can demonstrate a haircutting technique or a hairstyling product.

Types of Work in Live Fashion Modeling

There are basically five types of work that live fashion models do:

1. *Fit modeling.* Fitting models can be divided into two types: those on whom the clothes are designed, a procedure that results in a finished design or model sample, and those on whom the standard sizes for a design line are established, which results in the creation of a production sample.

2. *Showroom modeling.* A showroom model shows garments to buyers in a designer's or manufacturer's showroom. She may have a full-time position that includes secretarial and sales tasks in addition to modeling during market weeks or for informal showings to buyers who may stop by. She will also model in scheduled collections showings, along with other free-lance models. Showroom modeling is sometimes called *wholesale modeling.*

3. *Salon or house modeling.* A salon or house model is the model on whom a hairstylist, designer, or other creative individual experiments with new looks, creates new designs, and exhibits them for customers. A fashion designer's house model is often the model on whom the fabrics are draped and the clothes designed. She may participate in collection showings, which can be trunk shows that travel around the country or one-time publicity events. This model also gives private showings in the salon for the designer's most important customers.

4. *Informal or floor modeling.* Informal or floor modeling occurs when the model strolls through a store, tearoom, or restaurant affording potential retail customers a close look at a garment she is showing.

5. *Runway modeling.* A runway model may be employed by a fashion designer, department store, or any concern hosting a fashion show to model garments before a group of people who may be consumers, editors, members of an organization, or the like. When runway shows are conducted for groups of consumers, it is sometimes referred to as *retail modeling.*

TYPES OF MODELS
Female Fashion Models

Fashion models show, represent, or sell fashion and beauty-related ideas, services, and products. They are employed mostly in print work and fashion shows but also model in electronic media productions.

There are basically seven types of fashion models, with variations in each category. These categories are not rigid. Many models are versatile enough to work in two or more categories simultaneously. Some models develop over the years, graduating from one category to another, such as a young model who starts as a junior and later becomes a high-fashion model.

High-Fashion Models

High-fashion models are often seen in the editorial pages of *Vogue, Harper's Bazaar,* and other high-fashion magazines as well as on runways modeling in haute couture or designer-collections showings. They are also seen in catalogs, print ads, and television commercials for high-fashion designer and glamourous or trendy products.

High-fashion models are usually distinguished by their extreme, unique, sophisticated, or exotic looks. There are different extremes within this type. Some high-fashion models have such unusual looks that they are rarely seen in ads, catalogs, or on magazine covers, especially in the United States. European markets tend to favor more extreme looks. These ultra-high-fashion models may have a distinctly European look or one that is trendy or avant garde. They appeal to a very select, fashion-conscious group of consumers.

Other high-fashion models have a less extreme, more commercial look. This model has an individual look that has international appeal.

This model's looks fall between the ultra-high-fashion look and that of the general-fashion model described later. She may possess a single feature, such as a square-shaped face, full lips, or almond-shaped eyes, or a combination of features that give her a memorable look. This less extreme type of high-fashion model appears in all kinds of media. She can achieve both editorial and commercial stardom. She may appear simultaneously on magazine covers ranging from *Vogue* to *Glamour* to *Cosmopolitan*. Many of the models in this category become celebrity models because they have such wide appeal.

High-fashion models tend to be taller than other types of models and are usually between 5'8" and 5'11" in height. They usually wear Misses sizes 8–10. Most high-fashion models are between the ages of 18 and 25; however, some models in this category have been as young as 13 or 14 and as old as over 45.

General-Fashion Models

General-fashion models are characterized by their universally appealing good looks. The pretty, all-American, blue-eyed blonde is an example. These models are seen most often in print ads, television commercials, and catalogs. Their looks are not high fashion or unique enough to appear in high-fashion editorials yet they may appear in magazines such as *The Journal, Redbook,* and *Good Housekeeping.* General-fashion models do a lot of the day-to-day, catalog work, which, because of its steadiness and longevity, can be very lucrative. Some are also seen in retail fashion shows and work as promotional models. Most general-fashion models are between the ages of 18 and 25. Also within this category are Contemporary Woman models, who are between 28 and 44 years of age, and Classic Woman models, who are over 45.

Junior Models

Junior models look to be in their teens and wear Junior-sized apparel. They are seen editorially in magazines such as *Teen* and *Seventeen.* They are often seen in print ads and catalogs as well as in television commercials. In runway work, they are most often seen modeling Junior clothing in retail shows. They are rarely employed for promotional modeling because most promotional work requires maturity. Junior models are usually between the ages of 13 and 19 and are between 5'6" and 5'7" tall. They usually wear Junior sizes 5–7.

Large-Size Models

Large-size models wear clothing that is Misses size 12 or larger. The majority wear sizes 14–16. They are usually between 18 and 28 years of age. Large-size models most often appear in catalogs. They also appear in fashion shows where they model larger-sized apparel. Large-size models range in looks from wholesome to sophisticated.

Petite Models

Petite models wear clothing that is size 3–7 Petite, and they are approximately 5'2" to 5'6" tall. These models are usually between 18 and 25 years of age, though there are some exceptions. In addition to modeling fashions, petite models with outstanding faces model beauty products. They might also appear in television commercials modeling products in which height is not a factor. Petite models often appear in catalogs and occasionally in print ads and fashion editorials where they model Petite size clothing. Their looks range from junior to high fashion.

Male Fashion Models
High-Fashion Models

The information given for female models also applies to males. High-fashion male models are seen in high-fashion men's magazines, such as *Gentleman's Quarterly,* and high-fashion women's magazines where they accompany female models. They are also seen in print ads, television commercials, and on runways. Generally they model designer menswear and glamourized products. Most high-fashion male models are between 21 and 35 years of age.

General-Fashion Models   There is a broad range of looks found among male models. The youngest type of male model is the collegiate type or slightly older, ranging from 18 to 28 years of age. Models with this look and age range are more often called for modeling underwear and bathing suits than are other types of models. Male models most commonly seen look as if they are between the ages of 25 and 35 and model garments ranging from sportswear to formal wear. Male models who look between the ages of 32 and 45 are often seen modeling business clothes.

Big and Tall Models   Big and tall male models wear a size 44 Long suit and up. They usually exhibit looks similar to the general-fashion model.

Child Models   Child models are primarily used to promote clothing and accessories for children. Babies are up to 18 months. Young children up to 4 years of age are called toddlers; 5- to 12-year-olds model school and play clothes and are most commonly seen in catalogs, television commercials, and fashion shows.

Product/Commercial Models   Product/commercial models show, represent, or sell products other than items associated with beauty and fashion. They are employed in print ads, packaging, sales displays, product catalogs, and live promotional work. They are most visible in television commercials. A wide range of ages, physical features, and types are found among product/commercial models. Because fashion is not being featured, there are no specific height or figure requirements. Product/commercial models can be divided into two basic types: straight and character.

Straight. Straight product/commercial models are most often seen in television commercials and print ads. They also appear in product catalogs. They range in looks from average (real people) to attractive types. Straight commercial models are most often employed because they appeal to a client's base of customers.

Character. Character models most often appear in print ads and television commercials for products. Character models include funny-looking or off-beat characters. They have looks that are neither fashion-like nor average. They are often exaggerated versions of reality. Character models also include those who impersonate famous people or imaginary characters such as Santa Claus.

Special Types   This category includes parts or specialty models, nude or figure models, and celebrity models. They appear in print editorials and advertisements and electronic media and promotional assignments.

Parts or Specialty Models   These models specialize in modeling only one or two characteristics, for example, hands, feet, legs, or facial features. Work for this type of model is limited simply because photographers most often prefer to work with models who can do specialties in addition to other types of work. A few hand models do make substantial amounts of money modeling for advertising in print and television.

Nude or Figure Models   Nude or figure models are employed mostly in print work, videos, and films. These models range in age from 18 to 24, with some exceptions. An excellent figure with a well-developed bustline is most often preferred. A pretty face and excellent skin are also important. Unlike fashion models, the preferred looks of figure models do not vary from season to season. Looks ranging from wholesome to sexy to mildy exotic are usually in demand.

Nude or figure modeling no longer has the stigma that was once attached to it. There are still different categories of this type of modeling that range from pornographic at the low end of the scale, to nude modeling for major men's magazines, to modeling in the nude for art photography and fashion magazines. Several top fashion models have been artistically photographed for major fashion and special interest magazines; however, exposure in raunchy, pornographic publications rarely, if ever, benefits a would-be or established fashion model.

Modeling for a mainstream men's magazine often offers greater career and income opportunities for some young women than does fashion modeling. In former times, girls who modeled for these types of magazines might have never been considered for other types of modeling, but today women appearing nude in such publications often continue to have successful modeling careers. Sometimes exposure in such magazines is the stepping stone for women who aspire to careers in entertainment. In general, a fashion-oriented magazine would not grant these women exposure because they are too sexy or do not have the right look or figure for modeling fashions.

Nude or figure models also work as bathing suit and lingerie models and are seen in catalogs and print ads. They may also be seen in television commercials and fashion shows and may work as promotional models.

Nude modeling opportunities exist in all major markets but are greatest on the West Coast or in the Los Angeles area. In these areas a figure model may be represented by a modeling agency specializing in nude or figure modeling work.

Celebrity Models   A celebrity model is employed to draw attention and create an image for a company and its product or service. In addition, he or she may have some input into the design, development, or marketing of the item. Two types of celebrity models are superstars from other various fields, and superstar models who become celebrities.

Celebrities who are superstars from many fields such as athletics, the entertainment field, business, and the arts are often chosen by advertisers to promote products and services. Also included in this group are relatives of famous people including royalty and political figures.

Models who become superstars within the modeling field can become celebrities in their own right. Suzy Parker in the 1950s, Twiggy in the 1960s, Cheryl Tiegs in the 1970s, Christie Brinkley and Brooke Shields in the 1980s are all examples of celebrity models. These models are unlike other models in that they are known to the public by their names as well as their faces and figures. A celebrity model has a public that follows her private life and public activities as they are recorded in national magazines, in newspapers, and on television. The celebrity model is used by advertisers because her fame and visibility attracts the attention and admiration of the public. The celebrity model commands the highest fees of all models, and every assignment is individually negotiated through an agent. He or she usually has exclusive contracts with several companies.

MODELING CLASSIFICATIONS AND REQUIREMENTS
Age Group

When a client calls a model or talent agency, he or she will request an individual as defined by the following classifications.

The model's actual age or the age he or she looks will partly determine the products he or she will model. Fashion and product/commercial models are of all ages, but certain age groups do predominate. The following is a list of the most commonly requested models by type and age. (Consult preceding information regarding age groups for fashion model types.)

Commercial/Product Models	General Age Categories
Infants	Less than 6 months
Babies	Up to 18 months
Toddlers	1–4 years
School ages girls/boys	5–12
Preteens	12–13
Teens	13–18
College Kids	18–22
Young Adults	18–24
Young Mothers	22–27
Homemakers	25–40
Young Fathers	25–30
Fathers	28–55
Husbands	28–45
Businesswomen/career women	25–45
Businessmen/career men	35–55
Grandmothers	50 and up
Grandfathers	50 and up

Coloring of Eyes, Hair, and Skin

The color of eyes, hair, and skin may also determine the model's type to some extent. Fashion models booked in groups usually exhibit a variety of color types so that fashions and makeups of all colors can be displayed. Different skin, hair, and eye colors help to show off clothing colors to better advantage. Casting directors pay attention to color types when grouping models for family parts.

Size and Figure Type

Size and figure type are important in some areas of modeling and irrelevant in others.

Print Models

Product/commercial models for print advertisements can be nearly any size or figure type depending on the product or preferences of the client.

Print fashion models must be able to fit into sizes of clothing commonly supplied at photo shootings. In general, a print model having a figure that is long all over—long legs, long hands, long neck—is most photogenic. Balanced proportions, shoulders that are not rounded or sloping, and attractively shaped, slim legs with long calves are also important. Ideal figure types vary with fashion. At one time the trend may be toward a shapely figure, while at another time a slim, delicate figure may dominate. The styles of clothing being designed will dictate the type of figure they will look best on. The most common fashion model sizes are listed in Table 1.

Print fashion models who model lingerie and bathing suits must have attractive, well-proportioned, slender, firm figures. When modeling bras, usually a full B cup is required. Bathing suit models usually exhibit figures that are slightly rounder or more athletic looking than the typical fashion model figure. Smooth contours are most important when modeling bathing suits or lingerie as protruding bones or fleshy bulges detract from the items being modeled.

TABLE 1   Common Fashion Model Sizes[a]

Fashion Model Type	Sizes	Measurements (inches)	Weight (pounds)	Figure Characteristics
Junior	7 Jr.	B 32–34 W22–24 H 32–34	105–116	5'7" tall; youthful looking figure with slightly higher bustline, narrower hips, less defined waist than Misses
Petite	3–5P 3– 5JR. 5 JP 2 M	B 31–33 W 21–23 H 32–33	90–110	5'2" to 5'6" tall; slightly higher waist and smaller shoulders than other figures
High fashion	8–10M	B 32–34 W 22–24 H 34–35	115–130	5'8" to 5'11" tall; usually slimmer and longer boned
General fashion	6–7–8	B 32–35 W 22–24 H 34–35	110–125	5'6" to 5'8" tall; should be able to fit into retail sizes
Large size	12–16	B 36–42 W 26–32 H 36–44	140 and up	5'8" to 5'10" tall; larger overall, well proportioned, firm figure
Male models (high fashion and general fashion)	40 R	Shirt 15–15½ 34–35 Waist 32–34 Inseam 32–34 Chest 38–40	145–165	5'11" to 6'1" tall

[a]*Abbreviations: B, bust; W, waist; H, hips; Jr., Junior; P, Petite; JP, Junior Petite; M, Misses; R, Regular.*

Child Models   There are child models of all sizes, but most jobs call for children between the ages of 5 and 12. Children who are large for their age will find modeling opportunities limited. On the other hand, children who look young and are small for their age are often preferred because they are more mature. A child model should wear the size he or she appears to be in age. For example, a child who looks six years old should wear size 5 to 6.

Electronic Media Models

There are no strict size requirements for models who appear in television commercials. The only qualification is that the model fit the image of the age and character he or she portrays. For fashion-related commercials, fashion model measurements and sizes apply.

Promotional Models

For promotional modeling assignments, models need not be tall and thin like fashion models, but they should have attractive figures.

Fashion Show Models

Fashion show models wishing to participate in collections showings and wholesale modeling must be able to fit into sample sizes easily. The exact measurements of the sample size are dictated by the designer who employs the model. Each designer has a certain figure type in mind. Sample sizes are usually based on a model's figure rather than an average person's figure.

For runway modeling the ideal body is 5'9" to 5'11" tall with measurements similar to those of print fashion models. A narrow body with hipbones that are narrower than the shoulders is a must. Shoulders are very important because they determine the way a garment hangs and moves on the body. Squarish, "coat hanger" shoulders and a body that is built like an inverted triangle is the ideal. Legs that are long from the knees down (high knees) and a long neck show off garments more attractively. Fashion show models employed for consumer or retail fashion shows must fit into retail sizes with no alterations necessary.

Fitter's models for design samples must maintain the exact measurements dictated by the designer for whom they work. The fitter's model employed by a manufacturer for production samples must have a figure that represents sizes worn by the general public.

Look or Type

Look or type may be defined by age, personality, mannerisms, skin, hair and eye coloring, facial features, size, figure characteristics, and nationality.

Print Models

Models of a variety of types are needed for print advertisements because they must appeal to markets defined by consumer age, marital status, income, and other factors. A straight product/commercial model with a face that is conventionally attractive, yet sincere, can have great success on Madison Avenue. Fashion models who have beautiful hair and attractive smiles can earn substantial amounts from hair and tooth product accounts. Real people, character models, and celebrities also appear in advertising.

The looks of models needed for print fashion editorials are dictated by continually changing fashion trends. For more information on fashion model characteristics, consult preceding section on types of fashion models.

Fashion Show Models

The ability to move with grace and authority, a figure that shows off clothing optimally, and the ability to fit into sample or retail sizes are more important than any particular facial features. Runway models should have interesting or attractive faces that enhance or work with the designer's or client's clothes and current fashion philosophy. At collections fashion shows where models are extensively photographed and videotaped, print editorial fashion models who are adept at runway modeling are often employed. These models are preferred because they are very photogenic.

Promotional Models

Promotional models' looks will vary according to the needs of the company that employs them. The three most commonly requested looks are: a businesslike, professional look to represent a conservative firm; an all-American look to represent a firm with a wholesome, family-oriented image; and a glamourous, sexy look to represent a firm that has a less conservative image.

Skills and Talents   The client may specify that a certain talent or skill is required. For example, in a television commercial the model may be required to swim to demonstrate a waterproof cosmetic. Promotional models are often hired because they can act, sing, or dance and therefore can attract attention to an exhibit. Fashion show models are often given preference if they can dance because of the choreography used. Print assignments, such as those for a specialized catalog, may need models who can portray a sport realistically. For example, if a boat is being shown, the individual who can waterski, swim, or drive the boat would be preferred. Being a contact lenses wearer might even be an advantageous skill if you were called upon to model contact lenses.

Special Features   Sometimes an assignment may require that a model in addition to meeting other classifications, possess a specific type of feature. For example, a cosmetic company advertising mascara would need a model having long, thick eyelashes. A client showing a typewriter will need a model with excellent hands. In addition to excellent hands, special features often required for modeling assignments are excellent legs, feet, teeth/smile, beauty/skin/hair, and figure (lingerie and bathing suit models).

Hands   Hands may be selected according to how well they go with another person's face. The hands you see along with actors and actresses in commercials and with beautiful faces in cosmetic ads often belong to a hand model. Most hand models have attractively shaped, smallish hands with no blemishes or skin problems. Nails that have a healthy color, curve neither upward nor under, have no ridges or other blemishes, and perfect cuticles are necessities for hand models. Models who must wear sculptured nails are usually not selected for hand modeling assignments. Natural nails are preferred, especially for closeup photography. Most hand models wear a size 6½ to 7½ glove and a size 4½ to 5½ ring. Male hands wear an 8½ to 10 glove size. Hands that exhibit long, tapering, graceful fingers and long nails are often referred to as *cosmetic hands* and are used to model fashion-oriented and glamourized products. Hands that are attractive, yet have a more utilitarian or average look are referred to as *noncosmetic hands* and are used to model household products and other items not associated with fashion and beauty. Dexterity and steady hands that do not shake in even the most nerve-racking situations are also musts for successful hand models.

Legs   Models with beautifully shaped, straight, slim, long legs are used to model pantyhose, grooming products, and other items made for the legs. Skin on the legs must show no veins, scars, or other blemishes. Attractive feet that aren't too large are also necessary.

Feet   Female models with graceful, flawless feet usually wear size 6 narrow or medium, the shoe sample size used in ads. Feet that are well shaped and have no blemishes or protruding veins are needed to show shoes, stockings, and grooming items for the feet. Attractive ankles and lower legs are also important.

Teeth/Smile   A model who possesses perfectly straight, white teeth with an ideal size and shape and a beautiful smile will be eligible for advertising oral hygiene products. Healthy, pink gums that are not overly obvious when the model smiles and attractive lips are important.

Beauty   Very few models are able to make a living solely from modeling their faces. The majority of models who are signed to high-paying cosmetic contracts are successful fashion models who model a variety of products. An attractive, well-proportioned face with even features and good bone structure is necessary for beauty modeling. Flawless skin that possesses fine, nearly invisible pores and no blemishes is essential. Also there should be no circles or darkness under the eyes, which may be difficult to conceal with makeup and retouching. Expressive, beautiful, wide-set eyes, a long slim neck, lips that are neither too thin nor overly full, and a face that takes well to makeup are desirable characteristics.

Healthy, thick, easy-to-manage hair and attractive hands are big pluses, as hand, nail, and hair care products are also usually made by cosmetic manufacturers. When casting models for hair products, clients usually prefer models with thick, shiny, easy-to-manage hair. A versatile hair length and cut and virgin hair (no coloring, perms, etc.) is also usually needed to provide more options. Very dark haircolors are often not desired because they tend to be difficult to photograph.

Many of the same points mentioned above apply to male models who show products for the face. In addition, a strong jaw and an even hairline are often necessary characteristics for such models.

Lingerie Models   An attractive figure with a full 34B bust is usually required. It is also very important that the model have excellent flawless skin on the body. An abundance of body hair, freckles, or prominent scars or moles will prohibit a lingerie model's success. A suntan is usually not desired for lingerie models. It is also important that the model's bones especially in the rib and chest area do not protrude. A very muscularly developed body is also not preferred.

Bathing Suit Models   An attractive slender figure with a 34B bust is usually preferred. Also a model with naturally darker skin or a light tan usually shows off swimwear best. Smooth, attractive contours are also important. Bony or angular shoulders, rib cage, or hipbones are usually unattractive. A well-toned figure that is completely cellulite free and not overly muscled is usually desired.

EVALUATING YOUR POTENTIAL AS A MODEL   Over the years modeling has evolved so that a model must no longer look a specific way in order to succeed. The definition of beauty continues to widen and include more types of faces, figures, and looks—many of which would not have been considered attractive a decade ago. As people's life-styles change, so do trends in advertising. As new ways of living emerge, so do new roles in television commercials, print ads, and fashion literature. Socioeconomic trends and other factors will always play an important role in determining which individuals' looks will be most in demand at different times.

Judging an individual's potential for success in the field is difficult. Certainly specific qualifications must be met for each division. Modeling and talent agents decide which models to represent based on what their clients are currently demanding; however, even experienced, successful agents sometimes overlook faces that later become famous.

Each assignment has certain qualifications that a model must fulfill. In addition, clients, photographers, art directors, and other decision makers have their own preferences and ideas about how a model should look. Other factors may enter into determining which model is chosen for an assignment. For an advertisement, to appeal to the largest group of people, the client may need an individual with certain features. On the other hand, for an editorial shot, the best model may not be the one with perfect features, but the one who inspires the photographer or editor at that particular moment.

Often times, more important than any physical feature is the attitude, personality, or spirit that an individual projects for the camera or the audience. A sparkle in the eyes or a graceful or interesting way of moving that projects something interesting about the person will always inspire decision makers in the modeling business and ultimately the consumer.

Physical presentation (facial expressions, walk, posture, mannerisms, etc.), makeup, hair, wardrobe, verbal presentation, and personality are the aspects with which a model conveys an individual style, class, intelligence, charisma, sex appeal, or creativity—commodities that translate an image on a printed page, a runway, a film, or videotape into dollars and cents for her employer. These unique aspects are important no matter what type of work the model does. From the cute granny in a television commercial to the aloof, high-fashion model in *Vogue,* all must transmit something that catches the viewer's attention and therefore makes him or her remember the idea, product, or service that the model is promoting.

The modeling field is very diversified and utilizes people of many different looks and talents. Electronic media, print, live fashion, and promotional modeling all require a vast variety of skills, personalities, and physical features. Most often a model's success is greatly dependent on developing his or her best look and finding the perfect market for it. Persistence and professionalism are also keys to success.

Now that you have read about the different areas, classifications, and requirements in modeling, consider where you might fit into this exciting, diversified business. Study the following pages to determine what your special qualities are.

DISCOVERING YOUR COMPETITIVE ADVANTAGES

It may be difficult to look at yourself objectively, but it is necessary if you want to become a professional model. Your face, body, talents, and personality are the commodities from which you will derive your income. As with any individual in business, research and development are involved before the product or service can be sold. You have to know your assets and liabilities to be able to market yourself and your looks to agents and clients. If you were a salesperson for any other product, you would have to know that product backward and forward from its limitations to its possibilities.

Everyone has a look, but a model's look differs from the average person's in that he or she must present a total, professional, and marketable image. In modeling, finding your look means finding what will look best to prospective clients. If you look good, but do not have the type of look that advertisers use to promote their products, you won't be a successful model. You must set aside your personal feelings and preferences and those of your friends and family and concentrate on developing an image that clients will respond to. The right image will be determined by where you will be modeling, the types of clients and products represented in your area, current trends, and several other factors. An agent can guide you, but no one person can formulate your style for you—that is up to you. Consider the following questions and use them as a starting point.

• What types of models are currently being presented in advertising and fashion? Look at models in magazines, television commercials, and fashion shows to see what images prevail. Consider both national and local examples.

- What physical features, skills, or talents do I have to offer that other models do not? What can I play upon that will set me apart from the competition?
- Do I resemble a famous person, movie star, celebrity, etc., and could I capitalize on this? (If you look just like a currently popular model, this will probably be a hinderance.)
- What fashions in makeup, hair, and clothes look best on me and why?
- What area of modeling do I want to aim for and why? For what area am I best qualified?
- What is my age? How old do I look? How young or old can I look?
- How would I describe my look or image? Do I have a definite look, style, or image?
- What types of characters can I portray with my looks, movements and personality?
- Which magazines best express my style or image? What television commercial characters could I realistically see myself portraying?

When formulating your look, your best sources for information and criticism will be experts currently working in the field. These include modeling and talent agents, makeup artists, hairstylists, fashion stylists, fashion designers, potential clients, experienced models, photographers, fashion and beauty editors, or anyone in the business who might require your services or with whom you might be working. Encourage their advice. Record their comments and study and act on them. Survey a variety of experts because each has his or her own area of knowledge or specialty. For example, a television commercial agent may have lots of good suggestions for you, whereas a fashion modeling agent may have no recommendations or interest in your look.

Taking your own description and the comments of others in regard to your physical and nonphysical characteristics, try to pinpoint your look by describing it in a few words. Look at other models and describe their looks in a word or two. Where do you fit in? Ask agents what type they see you as and in what direction you should go. You will save time, energy, and money if you have a specific direction or concept.

You should consider also that each model has several different looks within the framework of her type. Search out these variations and find the extent to which you can go within that type. Experiment with makeup and hair and then take Polaroid shots, make a videotape, or have test shots taken. Seeing your look this way will help you to judge more objectively what is right for you and what can be improved. Capitalize on the looks that work best for you, then direct your efforts toward fine-tuning them. While versatility is an asset, presenting too many widely divergent looks will only confuse prospective clients. They will want to know that they can count on you to present certain predictable images. It is important to realize that you can't be all things to all clients. However, you should learn how to be flexible and how to adapt your look to the client's situation and product. Presenting an image that really sells the product or clothes, whether in a photo, on the runway, at a promotion, or on television, is what modeling is all about.

PART 2 CREATING YOUR IMAGE
Chapter 2 Making the Most of Your Appearance

The foundation of a model's or anyone's appearance is based on four important factors: health, figure control, grooming, and physical presentation.

GOOD HEALTH. . . THE FOUNDATION FOR GOOD LOOKS

Good looks begin with good health. No amount of skillful makeup artistry, photography tricks, or treatment products can compensate for or camouflage eyes that lack sparkle or skin, hair, or nails that look dull and unhealthy. Your skin, hair, and eyes are the first features to mirror internal problems. Good looks come from within. Paying strict attention to your health is necessary before going on any appearance improvement program. Listed here are the keys to maintaining your health and good looks.

Healthy Environment

Consider your environment. An unhealthy environment can promote the spread of germs and affect your health, which will in turn affect your looks. Your home or apartment when overheated or over-air-conditioned can dehydrate your skin, giving it a dull appearance. A humidifier will help to achieve good moisture balance in the air. In addition, try to get some fresh air daily.

Balanced Diet

A balanced diet is important for maintaining a healthy body. Eat foods from the four food groups daily to be sure you are getting the right amount of vitamins and minerals in your diet. The four basic food groups are:

1. *Dairy.* Major sources include milk, cheese, butter, and yogurt.
2. *Cereals.* Major sources include grains, whole grain bread, and rice.
3. *Protein.* Major sources include meat, fish, eggs, and nuts.
4. *Fruits and vegetables.* This includes both green and yellow varieties.

Avoid eating foods high in calories and low in nutritional value and those containing possible allergens and irritants. Avoid foods or beverages that you know will affect your skin. Although no particular food may be to blame for an outbreak of blemishes, too much chocolate, fried food, snack food, colas, coffee, tea, sweet drinks, and alcoholic beverages should be avoided. Cut down on sugar, salt, fat, and highly processed or refined foods. Instead eat the foods you know to be rich in nutrients, such as vitamin A, B complex, C, D, and E. Opt for fresh, raw vegetables, and fruit and other sources of vitamins and minerals. Drink lots of water. Drinking up to eight glasses of pure, bottled mineral water daily will improve your general health.

Proper Body Functions   Proper body functions are important. Regular elimination is a must. Bowel movement habits differ among individuals, ranging from once a day to once every three days. Constipation can affect your appearance and your sense of well-being. Preventative measures such as eating fiber foods (whole grains, fresh fruits and vegetables) and drinking plenty of water daily are best. Drinking a glass of warm water into which you have squeezed the juice of a lemon wedge will help to overcome minor elimination problems, especially if taken before breakfast.

Water retention is best prevented by avoiding salt. Minor problems can be helped by using a diuretic, which is a substance that increases the flow of urine and lessens water retention in the tissues. Certain herbal teas have been proven to be mild, yet effective, diuretics.

Regular menstruation (approximately every 28 days) and hormonal balances are important to health.

Proper breathing from the diaphragm will ensure adequate oxygen and will improve your sense of well-being.

Exercise   Exercise is important because it keeps the body in shape and increases the flow of nutrient-rich blood to the skin. Vigorous activity for 20 minutes a day, in addition to walking, climbing stairs, and other activities, should be your aim. If you can participate in sports, such as swimming, tennis and dance, or exercise classes, so much the better.

Adequate Rest   Getting plenty of rest is important, and sleeping eight hours a night is recommended. Enough rest is an absolute necessity for attractiveness, because skin cells do most of their growing and replenishing when the body is at rest. Getting lots of sleep will ensure that dark circles or puffiness around the eyes are kept to a minimum.

Medical and Dental Checkups   Regular medical and dental checkups to ensure good health are always important. Yearly checkups as well as regular, periodic self-examinations such as breast exams, are necessary for preventing and treating health disorders.

Personal Hygiene   Personal hygiene is important to prevent problems that may occur because of the spread of bacteria. Keep your body clean by bathing daily and by periodically removing dead skin cells with a skin brush, natural sponge, or loofah. This will aid your skin's renewal cycle. Keep your teeth clean by brushing after meals and using water or toothpaste that is fluoridated to inhibit tooth decay.

Healthy Habits   Establish good, healthy habits. Avoid such health and appearance destroyers as smoking, drugs, alcohol, and caffeine. Establish good habits by not touching, picking, or otherwise irritating the skin. Be aware of any facial expression habits you have that could contribute to the formation of wrinkles or lines that may detract from your appearance, such as biting your lips, making facial grimaces, leaning your face on your hands, and the like. Never bite your fingernails or chew your cuticles. Observe proper posture when standing and sitting. Poor posture can affect the proper functioning of internal organs and contribute to fatigue.

Good Mental Attitude   One of the most important keys to good health is maintaining a good mental attitude. Making up your mind to have a positive outlook, to be content no matter what the circumstances, to maintain your sense of humor, and to not take yourself too seriously will help you to deal with stress and pressure. A model must especially be aware of not becoming obsessed with her appearance, so much so that it detracts from her normal, natural, most attractive self.

FIGURE CONTROL   In addition to maintaining a healthy diet, a model must be concerned with figure control. A model must achieve a figure that fits her image and meets the qualifications for the types of work she hopes to obtain. A model tends to be thinner than the average person, but there are no strict weight requirements. The camera tends to add the appearance of more weight, and a slender figure shows off clothing better. Also, it is easier to pin in a garment to be modeled that is too large than to let out one that is too small.

Figure types change with fashion concepts, and it is possible to be too thin. Weight can be deceiving depending on an individual's bone structure and muscle tone. Attractive distribution of the weight is most important. Other factors may be involved. For example, a model with a slender body but a face that appears too full may be able to enhance her cheekbones and slenderize her face by losing a few pounds. Establishing an ideal weight and figure proportions for yourself and for modeling and then maintaining your ideal weight is important to your success as a model.

Not all models have weight problems, but those who do fall into two basic categories: those who lose weight and keep it off by using a sensible approach, and those whose weight goes up and down because they try every new diet that comes along. The best way to achieve your ideal figure is to eat less and eat foods with fewer calories while exercising more. Listed below are some foods that models tend to favor because they are high in nutritional value and low in calorie content.

Protein-rich foods are necessary for a balanced diet; however, many tend to be caloric. Choose foods such as broiled chicken or fish and clear broths made from chicken or beef. Avoid red meats as they tend to be higher in calories. Eggs either soft boiled or poached, cottage cheese, plain yogurt, and low-fat milk are also good protein sources, but consumption of these foods should be limited due to their calorie count.

Models know that vegetables (especially eaten raw) are full of vitamins, and they help to appease hunger. Celery, zucchini, cabbage, tomatoes, green peppers, spinach, cauliflower, broccoli, radishes, mushrooms, sprouts, and carrots are great for weight control. They can be steamed, combined, and prepared different ways, but beware of loading them with high-calorie sauces, butter, and dressings. Learn to like your salads with lemon juice or vinegar only. Vegetable broths are nutritious and low in calories.

Fruits and juices keep you healthy while keeping you trim. Low-calorie juices include grapefruit and tomato. Higher-calorie, yet nutritional, juices such as grape, cranberry, and apple can be diluted with equal parts of sparkling water. The mixture tastes refreshing and cuts calories.

Grains are high in vitamin E and provide fiber. The best sources are raw nuts, seeds, whole grain bread, bran, or wheat germ cereal. However, eat only small amounts because grain products tend to be high in calories.

If you want to be slender and energetic, avoid salt, sugar, sweets, and alcoholic beverages. Substitute water for tea, soda, coffee, and sweet beverages. Do not rely on pills, fad diets, and periods of unsupervised fasting to keep trim. When dieting it is best to lose weight gradually. Your objective should be to lose not more than two pounds per week. Losing weight too quickly and improperly will adversely affect your looks and health.

Trimness is not the only key to achieving an ideal figure. Obtaining a firm, well-toned appearance is also necessary. Use the Self-Improvement Record found at the end of this chapter to decide where your problems (if any) lie, then embark on a fitness program. It may be worthwhile to work out with a fitness trainer who can personalize your exercise routines. Books, magazines, and videotapes are also good sources for exercises designed to attack your specific problem areas. Regardless of the exercise program you decide to use, always do a combination of aerobic and toning exercises for best results. Keep a notebook for magazine clippings, sketches, and written descriptions of your favorite exercises, and consult it to vary your fitness routine from time to time. It is important that your fitness routine be performed regularly over a long period of time in order to achieve the desired results.

GROOMING

Any person makes a better impression with faultless grooming, but a model's entire existence depends on it. Good grooming is fundamental. It is the foundation upon which the model builds his or her look and maintains a career. The model who always strives for perfection in personal grooming increases his or her chances for success. One minute detail, such as a ragged cuticle, can make an otherwise ideal closeup photo unattractive. Grooming is a personal subject and usually agents, photographers, and clients will feel too uncomfortable to mention a problem. They will just overlook the model and eventually bookings and opportunities will dwindle.

Cleanliness

Clean skin, hair, and body are absolute musts for a model. You must bathe or shower everyday. It may also be necessary to shampoo your hair every day. Hairstyling products, the environment, and constant manipulation, all of which are a part of modeling, contribute to lackluster hair. Always remove your makeup completely before going to bed, and always start your makeup application with clean, moisturized skin. Clean clothes and undergarments are a must, as is cleanliness in the items you use, such as makeup and hairbrushes.

Dental Hygiene

An attractive smile is important to a model. Your smile should consist of healthy gums and shiny white teeth. You must have regular checkups (about every six months) to correct any disorders and to have your teeth cleaned professionally. Your daily dental care should include brushing and flossing. A model works closely with others and should avoid offensive breath by using a good mouthwash and by avoiding foods (garlic, onions, etc.) that cause breath odor. Also people who smoke must be careful of "smoker's breath."

Hair Removal

For male models, a clean-shaven face and neck and trimmed sideburns is usually all that is necessary. Male models should experiment with various shaving products and techniques to achieve best results. For women, there are more areas that require attention. A model should pay attention to the following:

Upper lip. A lot of women have "mustaches." In a photograph, hair above the upper lip will appear as a shadow or blotchy areas and will be very noticeable. Use a cream depilatory, wax, or bleach to eliminate or subdue facial hair.

Between brows. Stray hair between the eyebrows may be a problem for both males and females. Make sure the area between your brows is hair-free by tweezing out strays. Male models may find that removing a few stray eyebrow hairs between brows gives a cleaner look.

Nose. Tiny hairs growing from the nose may not be noticeable to you, but they will stand out in a photograph. Check every week or so and if there are hairs, trim them with a special pair of scissors made for this purpose, or use small, sharp manicure scissors.

Sides of face. Some women have hair on the sides of their faces. If it is dark and fine it can be bleached. If it is light or dark but quite heavy, it may be best to remove it with facial depilatory or wax. A lot of hair on the face can reflect light and give the appearance of a beard. Also too much hair tends to matt when foundation or other makeups are applied.

Underarms. Underarm hair is considered unsightly, so make sure that all hair is removed from the underarms before each booking. You never know when you may be called upon to model sleeveless outfits or other revealing garments. Shaving or depilatory cream works best; hair removal should be done once or twice a week.

Forearms. If hair on your arms is dark or thick, it should be bleached because it will be unattractive in photographs. If you do hand modeling, it may be necessary to remove or bleach hair on your wrists.

Legs. Shaving, waxing, or using depilatory cream on the legs is necessary and should be done when the slightest stubble outgrowth is visible. Remove hair on upper inner thighs and around the bikini line. This is especially important when modeling bathing suits or lingerie.

Methods of Hair Removal   Models differ as to the preferred method of hair removal. Select a method by considering the size of the area where hair grows, the amount and type of hair, and how fast it grows. Experiment with the following methods until you find the ones that work best for you. Regardless of the method you choose, hair removal should be done a day or two in advance of an important assignment to allow any redness or slight swelling to subside.

Tweezing works best for removing a limited amount of coarse hairs. For example, eyebrow hairs are best removed by tweezing. To make tweezing easier, apply a hot, damp towel to the area to be tweezed. Apply a small amount of cream or lotion then tweeze the brows out in the direction of the hair growth. When done consistently, tweezing pain eventually subsides or lessens.

Waxing gives the smoothest look of all but requires some outgrowth of hair before it can remove the hair effectively. Best results are achieved when waxing is done in a salon by a professional. Waxing works particularly well for removing facial hair and hair in the bikini area.

Shaving is quick, easy, and gives good results because it removes dead surface cells from the skin. It is preferred for removing hair on legs and underarms. Always use a clean, sharp safety razor, and be careful not to scrape or nick the skin. Such blemishes are difficult to conceal with makeup. Use a shaving cream to achieve a close shave. It is a good idea to carry a safety razor in your totebag, just in case you need to smooth certain areas. Male models should always carry a shaving kit.

Depilatory creams are a good alternative to waxing and shaving; however, they are more time-consuming and less convenient to use. Also some women experience allergic reactions to certain ingredients used in depilatories. Always follow package directions and do a patch test first before using a new depilatory cream.

Bleaching works well for subduing the appearance of hair growth. Use it to lighten hair on forearms, thighs, and face. Purchase a bleaching cream designed to be used on the face or other areas and follow directions closely.

Trimming the hairs with small manicure scissors should not be used in place of other hair removal methods because it doesn't get close enough. Reserve trimming to clip a few hairs that may sprout from a mole. Use trimming when other hair removal methods should not be used such as on areas where the skin shows signs of eruption, abrasion, or inflammation.

Electrolysis is the process of removing hair permanently by means of electricity. It should be done by a trained and licensed electrologist. This is the method often used for eliminating excessive facial hair. Do not use electrolysis on the eyebrows because fashion may dictate more or less hair and will preclude your options.

Perspiration Control   After a model wears a client's clothes, they are usually retagged and put back in stock. After shows and informal modeling, garments are often cleaned before being returned to the store. For some jobs such as showroom modeling, only samples are used. These garments may be sold at a discount when they are no longer needed. Whatever the situation, it is important to protect the clothes from perspiration to maintain them in their original condition. Also, because you will be working in close proximity, it is important to use a deodorant and/or antiperspirant to avoid offending others.

An antiperspirant contains ingredients that inhibit perspiration but may be drying to skin, whereas a deodorant, which is milder, may not be as effective as it merely masks perspiration odor. Use a deodorant/antiperspirant several times during a long session. If you are perspiring heavily, blot the area first with a tissue, then apply deodorant and follow with talcum powder or cornstarch. A good, basic, fragrance-free deodorant used by models is 2 teaspoons of alum dissolved in a pint of warm water. This solution can be transferred to a small spray bottle.

It is also helpful to apply antiperspirant before going to bed at night because it has a better chance to work when you are in a cool, relaxed state. Reapply it in the morning. Alternating products from time to time may be helpful.

Use fragrance lightly. Too much or too strong a fragrance may be disturbing to other people who have to work close to you.

Skin Care   Good skin from head to toe is a must for a model. Always be sure that body skin has the proper balance of moisture, healthy color, and smooth texture. Get rid of dark, rough skin on elbows, heels, and other areas by using a pumice stone and by massaging these areas with a lemon half. Use a synthetic skin buffer to exfoliate scaly, bumpy areas that might exist on backs of upper arms or on your knees. Use a lightweight, nongreasy moisturizer after you bathe.

Avoid dark tans if you want to model. Tanning ages the skin prematurely and makes it appear coarse and leathery in a photograph. A light tan is often preferred for modeling bathing suits and summer fashions; however, take precautions to avoid tan lines. Also, avoid peeling skin on your face or body as it is nearly impossible to cover with makeup. Always consult with your agent before you attempt to get a tan.

For facial skin, find a good skin care system that works for you. If you are prone to problem blemishes, see a dermatologist. Try some of the basic skin care routines listed in this chapter. Make certain that your lips are never chapped and scaly. Apply petroleum jelly or lip conditioner every night and take care not to moisten your lips when you are out in cold, windy weather. If you need a quick lip fixer, apply glycerin several times, and your lips will soon regain their soft, smooth condition.

Understanding Skin Types   Understanding your skin's characteristics and type is important before any program of skin care can be undertaken. Consistent skin care must become a major part of your daily grooming ritual. To determine how to take care of your skin, observe it without makeup at different times of the day. Note whether oiliness develops during the day and in which areas, and if there is flakiness or dryness. Examine your skin for pore size, discolorations, sun sensitivity, hair growth, and other characteristics. Look at your parents' skin types to see if you have inherited any of their particular skin traits.

Take into consideration your complexion, hair, and eyes. Olive or melanin-rich (dark pigmentation) skins tend to be on the oily side, whereas fair-skinned blondes and redheads usually have drier, more delicate skins. Oily hair usually indicates oily or combination skin; dry hair usually indicates dry or combination skin.

Oily skin is characterized by overproduction of sebum (oil) by the sebaceous glands. Eruptions, blemishes, and acne often accompany oily skin. Dry skin is skin that is lacking in sufficient oil and moisture. Combination skin exhibits both dry and oily characteristics. Nearly everyone has combination skin; that is, some areas of the face are drier (cheeks) or oilier (forehead, nose, and chin) than others. All skin types may exhibit dry or oily conditions as a result of substances taken internally or external conditions. A good skin care system is composed of basically four procedures: cleansing, toning, moisturizing, and exfoliating.

1. *Cleansing.* The removal of soil, makeup, dead surface cells, etc.
2. *Toning.* The removal of residue from cleansing products and excess skin oils. Toning also restores the natural acid balance of the skin. Fresheners and astringents are toners.
3. *Moisturizing.* The application of products to help retain or add moisture to the skin and lubricate it with oils.
4. *Exfoliating.* The periodic removal of congealed oils and dead skin cells.

One good skin care habit that you should observe is to remove all traces of makeup before going to bed. Rest periods are the times when your skin rejuvenates itself.

To remove makeup, models use oil to melt the makeup and then cleanse the face with an appropriate cleanser or soap and water. Of the three types of oils, animal (codliver, lanolin), vegetable (almond, safflower), and mineral (baby oil), animal oils seem to be best for the skin because they most closely resemble sebum, the skin's own natural oil. However, vegetable oils have greater lubricity and are often easier to use.

To remove heavy theatrical makeup, solidified mineral oil, such as abolene cream, is an old standby. The best way to use cream or oil is to smooth it on, tissue it off, repeat as necessary, and then follow by cleansing the skin with a good soap or cleanser. Be sure to rinse well after cleansing.

Skin Care Program for Normal Skin Normal skin should be
cleansed in the evening to remove makeup and debris that has collected during the day. Cleansing skin again in the morning is optional.
Many models with normal skin simply splash clean warm water on the
face in the morning.

Step 1: *Cleanse.* Remove makeup or soil by applying oil and using
your fingertips to smooth it over your face. Remove oil with cotton
balls, pads or swabs. Use a pure, gentle, unscented, undyed, pH-neu-
tral soap. With the pads of your fingers, use gentle circular motions
to loosen dirt and dead cells. If you prefer to use a milky cleanser,
select one that is designed to be easily removed with water. Cleansers formulated to be tissued off tend not to cleanse as well and may
leave a film on your skin. Rinse your face well with warm water (about
20 splashes). Gently pat dry.

Step 2: *Tone.* Saturate a cotton ball with a commercial freshening
product and spread all over face. If you prefer, substitute with a basic,
homemade freshener by diluting 1 part apple cider vinegar with 1 part
mineral water. Or combine 1 cup witch hazel with 1 teaspoon of alum.
Shake well before using. Store the solution in the refrigerator.

Step 3: *Moisturize.* Use a good moisturizer such as pure aloe vera gel
(available at health food stores). Apply generously on the undereye
area. Use a lip balm (anhydrous lanolin works well) to prevent
chapped lips.

Step 4: *Exfoliate.* Once a week use scrubbing grains or a mask to
remove dead skin cells that tend to dull the skin. You can create your
own scrubbing grains by adding a teaspoon of yellow cornmeal to
your milky cleanser.

Skin Care Program for Oily Skin Oily skin may benefit from frequent cleansing, up to three times per day, to control bacteria. Oily
skin is often accompanied by blemishes and other disorders. Keeping
hair such as bangs off the face and using a strong, detergent shampoo will inhibit the spread of bacteria. Oil-free skincare and makeup
products are preferred over oil-based products that may clog the
pores and cause the skin to break out. To control oiliness and absorb
oil flow throughout the day, use an oil-blotting lotion or astringent
before applying makeup.

Astringent-type and water based makeups are best for oily skin.
When a heavier cream, pancake, or panstick makeup is used for modeling assignments, remove it as soon as possible after the job is completed. Avoid overuse of masks, abrasive cleansers, or saunas
because these tend to compound rather than solve problems.

Step 1: *Cleanse.* Use an oil-saturated cotton swab to remove makeup
around eyes and on lips. Remove heavy makeup with an oil-free
makeup remover, or cleanse your face twice to remove all traces of
makeup. Use a mild, neutral soap. Avoid deodorant soaps or those
containing oils or perfumes. Use circular motions with your fingers or
a soft washcloth when washing your face. Rinse your face with warm
water, then pat dry with a soft paper towel.

Step 2: *Tone.* Apply an astringent. You can make a mild, effective
astringent by combining ½ cup witch hazel, ½ cup alcohol, and 1 teaspoon alum. Shake well before applying, and keep the solution in the
refrigerator.

Step 3: *Moisturizing.* Apply an oil-free moisturizer on dry areas especially under the eyes. Use a lip balm for the lips. Apply a drying agent
such as rubbing alcohol to oily areas that are prone to breakouts
(nose, forehead, chin).

Step 4: *Exfoliate.* Use scrubbing grains or a mask about twice a week to remove dead cells and congealed oils. There are several effective granulated, medicated cleansers that your pharmacist or dermatologist can recommend. A good anti-oil mask is a clay mask that is made by mixing a paste of 2 tablespoons alcohol with 1 to 1½ tablespoons Fuller's earth. You will find these ingredients at most drug stores. Apply the paste to your face in a thin, even layer. Allow it to dry. Saturate a washcloth with hot water, wring out excess water, and apply the cloth to your face to steam out impurities. Rinse your face with warm water to remove all traces of mask.

Skin Care Program for Dry Skin

Step 1: *Cleanse.* Apply oil all over your face to remove makeup or soil. Apply a mild cleanser. Use gentle circular motions with the tips of your fingers. Rinse face well (about 20 splashes) with lukewarm water.

Step 2: *Tone.* Apply a mild freshener or try this homemade preparation. Combine 1 cup distilled or mineral water plus ½ cup witch hazel. Shake well. Saturate a cotton ball with the solution and apply all over face. Store the solution in the refrigerator.

Step 3: *Moisturize.* Apply moisturizer all over your face concentrating it under the eyes, around the mouth, and on the forehead. Apply lip balm to your lips.

Step 4: *Exfoliate.* Use a mask of cleansing grains once a week or try an egg white mask. Beat an egg white until stiff peaks form. Spread on face and and allow to remain 5 minutes. Rinse well.

Dealing with Skin Disorders

It may be necessary to consult a dermatologist when you have persistent skin problems such as pimples, whiteheads, acne, blackheads, allergies, or other conditions that may be caused by any number of factors. You may have a hormonal imbalance or an allergic reaction either to something in your diet or to medication you may be taking. Your skin may be reacting to stimulation (touching) or the cleansing method or makeup you are using. If your problem does not respond to over-the-counter drugs, consult a dermatologist before further complications such as scarring develop. A dermatologist will know how to treat your specific condition. Do not use a friend's medication or attempt to treat a severe problem yourself.

Dry, flaking skin is often more difficult to care for than blemished skin. Small blemishes can be concealed with makeup, but it is almost impossible to conceal peeling skin; makeup only tends to accentuate the problem. Model agents can usually recommend a dermatologist whom their models consult. Professional skin care, such as facials given by a skin care specialist, may be helpful but should not replace treatment by a dermatologist when skin abnormalities exist.

Hand Care

Beautiful hands are not an absolute must for a model, but attractive, well groomed hands enhance the model's appearance and increase the types of jobs he or she is qualified to do. Excellent hands can make a model eligible for modeling various products. Of course, if your nails are bitten and your cuticles raggedy, you must make an effort to correct this bad habit if you want to model professionally. If you do not have great nails, synthetic nail tips or sculptured nails may be the answer. Of course, with special techniques, cost, time, and upkeep must be considered.

A monthly professional manicure is a must for any working model, male or female. Twice-weekly at-home manicures to maintain the health and shape of the nails, cuticles, and hands are important. If you wear polish or if a client requests polish on assignments, daily touchups will be required. Whenever possible, avoid using nail polish remover more than once per week. The chemicals it contains weaken the nails and irritate the skin.

Most models wear clear polish or light pink or beige shades that closely match the color of the skin for everyday use and alter the color as the situation demands. A well-prepared model carries several shades of polish in her totebag including a basic clear red, a neutral pink or beige, an orange-toned coral or rust color, and colors that are currently in fashion. Nailcolor remover in foil packets is also a must. An emery board to smooth jagged edges or to reshape a broken nail (and a nail repair kit) should be included.

Basic Manicure

1. Remove old nailcolor with cotton balls saturated with oily polish remover.
2. Shape nails using an emery board, filing in one direction.
   Shapes of nails often change as fashion changes (Figures 1–8). Your hand and finger shape will also determine what will look best. The oval is a good shape for nails, with the tip of the nail matching the shape of the base of the nail. The length of the nails is influenced by fashion trends and also by the characteristics of your hands and fingers. Longer fingers can accomodate longer nails. Most important is that the length and shape of your nails work with the image you are trying to project. For example, a young-looking junior fashion model would have shorter, more natural looking nails than would a very sophisticated high-fashion model.

   It is also important that your nails be consistent in length. You can use nail tips to make one or two broken nails match the length of your other nails. If two or more nails are broken or shorter than the others, file the longer nails to a shorter length, so the difference in length will not be so obvious.

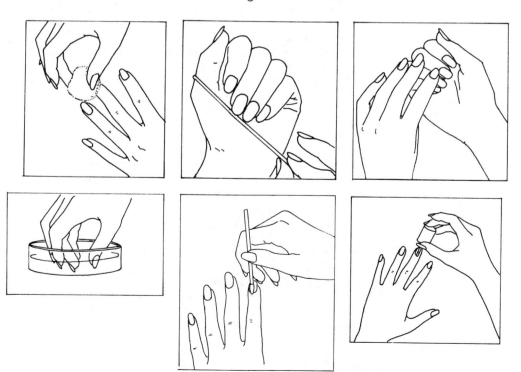

Male models' nails should reach the tips of the fingers. The shape of the nail at the tip should conform to the shape at the base of the nail.

Clean stains on nails with diluted household bleach or hydrogen peroxide using a cotton swab. Rinse well.

3. Apply petroleum jelly to cuticles.

4. Soak cuticles in ½ cup warmed cuticle cream, baby oil, or olive oil for 5 minutes.

5. Wipe off oil or cream with a soft towel. Push cuticles back gently using an orangewood stick wrapped in cotton. Clip off hangnails, but do not clip cuticles. Cuticles are best maintained by pushing them back daily with a towel or small cloth after bathing.

Massage the nails, hands, and arms with moisturizing lotion.

6. First, apply the base coat. Then apply at least two coats of nail-color. Begin by dabbing some polish on the nail tip then coat the entire nail. Be very exacting when applying nailcolor. It should not overlap onto the cuticles. Use a toothpick to remove stray polish.

Apply a protective topcoat.

Male models should follow these procedures, but omit nail color or use colorless nail polish. For a more natural look, male models buff the nails to a shine and use a nail white pencil under the tips of nails to whiten.

MODEL'S TIP: *Every other week apply petroleum jelly to your hands and wear lightweight cotton gloves overnight to condition the skin and to improve the moisture retaining ability of the nails and cuticles.*

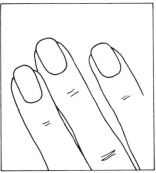

Figure 1. Classic oval shape. Shape at base of nail and at tip match. Length is short.

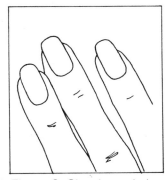

Figure 2. Classic oval shape, medium length.

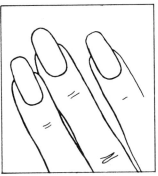

Figure 3. Classic oval shape, long length.

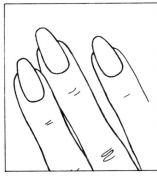

Figure 4. Rounded oval. Tips are narrowed.

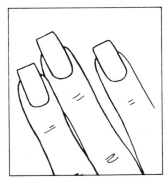

Figure 5. Squared tips.

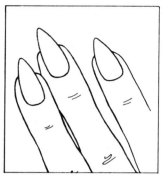

Figure 6. Pointed tips.

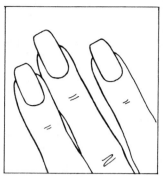

Figure 7. Squared oval.

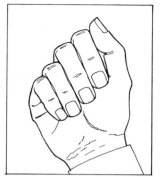

Figure 8. Male model's nails.

Foot Care   Healthy, strong feet are a must for models. A model spends a great deal of time walking to and from appointments and is constantly standing during assignments. Attractive feet are important when modeling garments that require bare feet. For example, you may be required to model bathing suits, lingerie or sleepwear, or open shoes or sandals. Also a model is often called upon to wear shoes that are a size too small or in some way hard on the feet. Therefore, proper foot care to compensate for such problems is important.

Any major foot disorders should be taken care of by a podiatrist or dermatologist. To prevent foot infections, wipe out your shoes frequently with an alcohol-saturated cotton ball. Keep your feet dry by using a foot powder or spray. To soothe and revive tired feet at the end of the day, use the ballet dancer's method: Immerse the feet in baths of contrasting temperatures, alternating from hot to cold and back to hot.

The Basic Pedicure   1. Start the pedicure with clean, dry feet. Use a corn and callous file or pumice stone to soften rough, dry skin.

2. Apply an abrasive cream, such as ground pumice in moisturizer, to your feet. Massage it into the skin giving special attention to heels, soles of the feet, and toes.

3. Use a toenail clipper to trim the nails straight across. Soften and smooth edges of toenails with an emery board.

4. Apply dabs of petroleum jelly to cuticles. Soak feet in warm, soapy water to which you have added bath oil. Soak for about 10 minutes.

5. Dry feet with a soft towel. Push back cuticles of the toenails with the blunt end of an orangewood stick.

6. Use pumice stone again to slough off dead skin. Brush off flakes of skin with a stiff nail brush.

7. Saturate a cotton ball with witch hazel, and pat it all over feet.

8. Massage the feet, ankles, and legs with moisturizer.

9. Apply a basecoat to toenails and then two coats of a polish that harmonizes with the fingernail color. Apply a topcoat. Male models usually buff toenails.

MODEL'S TIP: *For a supersoftening once-a-month foot conditioner, apply petroleum jelly to feet and put on lightweight cotton socks. Leave on overnight.*

PHYSICAL PRESENTATION   A model's physical presentation, also referred to as visual poise, is a very important factor in the effectiveness of her appearance. Physical presentation includes the following aspects:

- Posture.
- Standing.
- Walking.
- Sitting.
- Stooping and bending.
- Movements of the hands.
- Mannerisms.
- Facial expressions.

Often these nonverbal aspects are called "body language." Physical presentation often tells more about an individual than any other aspect of his or her appearance. You can sense a person's intelligence, level of education, social standing, general attitude toward life, economic status, and upbringing just by the way he or she performs these activities.

Effective physical presentation is an aspect of appearance that often takes the beginning model longest to acquire. Some models have innately attractive grace or style in their posture and movements. Other models need to make minor refinements or improvements. Still others must be made aware of their shortcomings and must work on developing more effective physical presentation gradually.

You may notice that the difference between a beginning model and her more experienced counterpart is not only in fashion, makeup, and hair, but in the model's outward projection of confidence and style. The way an individual presents herself can make the difference between someone who is attractive and someone whose physical appearance makes a real impact. Modeling is a business based on images. A model needs effective physical presentation in order to draw people's attention to her in a positive way.

Understanding the importance of effective physical presentation is vital to a model's success. Many aspiring models fail because they lack this nonverbal style or awareness. This is because in modeling experts can see to it that a model's makeup, hair, and clothing look ideal, but only the model herself can project an attractive individual style or attitude with movement, facial expression, and deportment. Photographers, fashion designers, choreographers, acting coaches, and directors cannot do this for you, although they can give you valuable suggestions.

In addition to expressing a certain style or an air of confidence in the way she moves, a model must learn how to present her physical self in the most appealing manner. No model is physically perfect, but a good model is a master of illusion. A good model knows that it is not only the actual physical appearance of the body or facial features that matters; it is the way she presents herself that makes the difference. Learning a few illusory tricks can make it possible to make less than ideal legs look attractive or a smile that is too toothy appear less so.

Natural grace is what all models strive for. Being affected or overly concerned with movement and expression is as undesireable for a model as it is for the average person. Artificial movements that are too proper or posed should always be avoided, unless they are appropriate for a special effect in a photograph or on the runway.

Good health, figure control, meticulous grooming, and effective physical presentation are all essentials to a model's successful appearance. After acquiring these basics, a model's success will depend on his or her creativity, professionalism and whether he or she has the look or image that is currently in demand.

Posture   Good posture is the starting point, whether it is for modeling or any form of personal contact. Proper body alignment is vital to an attractive appearance. Good posture improves the contours of the body and makes you appear taller, slimmer and more graceful. Good posture imparts importance and status to yourself and to the clothing you model or wear for other occasions.

Posture alignment is concerned with the following five areas of the body: the feet, knees, hips, shoulders, and head.

The feet. Good posture begins with the feet because this is where the weight of the body is concentrated. If you have ever injured a foot or if you wear high heels, you can understand how the feet can throw the body out of alignment. To begin your search for your own perfect posture, make sure that your weight is evenly distributed on both feet, with the same amount of weight on the heels and balls of the feet. Toes should be pointed straight ahead for proper walking; ankles should be held firm and straight, turning neither inward nor outward. Improper placement of weight on the feet will often show up in the heels of your shoes where the inner or outer portion of the heel will be more noticeably worn or where there is heavier callousing on the soles, balls, or heels of your feet.

The knees. The knees carry the next largest burden of weight. Knees should be straight (relaxed, not stiff), and they should appear as if the weight has been lifted upward from them. Allowing too much weight to settle into the knees causes undue strain and will result in a knock-knee or concave-knee appearance.

The hips. The hips should follow the line of the legs. The buttocks should neither indent nor protrude. The most common posture mistake, other than hunched shoulders, is allowing the weight to settle into the hips. This gives your body a collapsed look by causing the abdomen to protrude, and the chest to appear hollow. It is important to always be aware of elongating or stretching the body upward, bringing the weight up and out of the hips. This is especially important for models because it makes the waist appear smaller and prevents sags and wrinkling in the bodice of garments being worn or modeled. Stretching upward is especially important when you are in a sitting position.

The shoulders. The shoulders, being situated directly over the hips, should follow the line of the legs and hips. Shoulders are very important to the model because basically all garments hang from them. Shoulders should be held neither too high nor unevenly (with one higher than the other); they should not show tension. Hunched shoulders or shoulders that curve inward create a hollow chest or caved-in look and appear to be too relaxed. Your objective is to hold the shoulders back to lessen the protrusion of the shoulder blades yet keep them as far down as possible to elongate the neck.

The head. The head should be in line with the body, neither preceding nor following it. The neck should be lifted out of the shoulders so as to create a long look that enhances any garment. The head and neck should never look rigid or fixed but should retain a natural line with the body. Reaching upward with the crown of the head as well as keeping the chin parallel to the floor is important in achieving a poised, graceful look.

Posture Correction   Posture problems due to carelessness can be corrected once you are aware of the importance of good posture to health and a more attractive appearance. Serious posture problems, such as curvature of the spine, should be treated by a physician. The model should remember that poor posture, especially swayback (lordosis) and round shoulders (kyphosis), affects the way clothing hangs on the body. Skirts and pants will hike up in certain places, whereas jackets and dresses will hang unevenly. Clothing is not designed to compensate for these posture problems. Study Figures 9 to 17 to determine any posture problems you may need to correct.

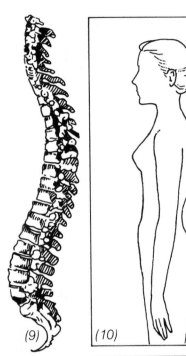

(9)

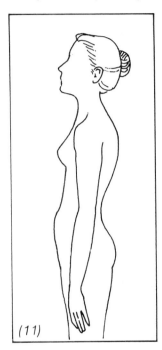

(10)   (11)

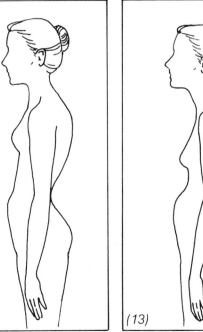

(12)   (13)

Figure 9. This is a diagram of the spine showing the cervicals, the first 7 vertebrae; the thoracic, the middle 12 vertebrae; and the lumbar, the lowest 5 vertebrae.

Figure 10. This is an example of correct posture and body alignment. The body is held erect but relaxed.

Figure 11. When the head is held too far backward, it affects the cervicals. This is a posture problem common to men. This posture problem may be the result of nervousness or may occur when the body is held in an unnaturally relaxed or self-conscious position. Good posture is poised yet comfortable.

Figure 12. Lordosis or swayback is caused by slumping the shoulders and allowing the weight to concentrate in the hips. This contributes to fatigue. Practice pulling your hips under as you pull your pelvic bone upward and forward. This movement helps to align the spine and correct swayback. Practice standing and walking with good posture until it becomes natural to you.

Figure 13. Kyphosis is problem posture indicated by round shoulders. The chest is caved in, and the waist appears thick in proportion. Weight concentrates in the hips and gives a sagging appearance to the body. If you have this problem, practice pulling your head up and keeping your chin level as you walk and stand. Do exercises to keep your muscles flexible and strong.   37

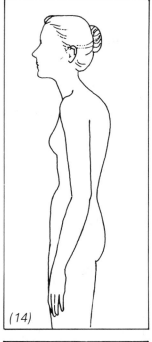

(14)

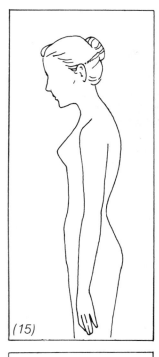

(15)

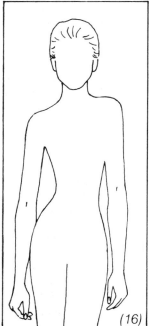

(16)

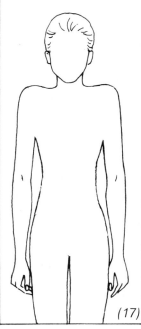

(17)

Figure 14. Posture characterized by a caved-in chest and buttocks that are tucked under often occurs in men. Women sometimes adopt this posture when attempting to make the buttocks appear smaller. However, the best solution to this problem is to hold the chest and head high while tucking the buttocks in very slightly. This will result in a healthy, confident-looking posture.

Figure 15. Posture characterized by a drooping head may result if you are always looking down to see where you are going. You may have noticed that a model keeps her head up (even when descending stairs) and will glance down when it is necessary to see where she is going. Concentrate on looking ahead, not down, when you are walking or standing.

Figure 16. Unbalanced posture develops when a person habitually carries a heavy object, such as a totebag or handbag, on the same shoulder. Gradually one shoulder may become higher than the other, causing a lopsided appearance. Correct this habit by carrying heavy objects on alternate sides.

Figure 17. Tension often shows in shoulders that are held unnaturally high. This causes the head to jut forward. Avoid this stiff, rigid posture by relaxing your shoulders. Roll them backward and downward and allow your arms to relax naturally.

More Tips to Improve Posture

Aligning your back against a wall and walking with a book on your head may give you some indication of what you need to do to correct your posture, but such exercises alone will not produce the desired results. Constant reinforcement of the above principles and awareness of your posture will achieve results. Posture exercises and activities that require attention to body alignment, such as ballet, fencing, and skating, naturally and unconsciously will help you to develop good posture.

Standing   Good posture is also the basis for standing attractively. Paying attention to the placement of your feet when standing will make you appear more attractive. In all stances it is important to determine where your weight will be centered. The weight of the body can be evenly centered over both feet to provide steady footing, or it can be shifted to one foot or the other. When the majority of weight is centered over one foot, this foot is called the base foot. The foot carrying very little or no weight is called the free or working foot. The position of the free (or working) foot is often altered to vary the appearance of the legs. Figures 18 to 21 show natural-looking, basic stances that models or anyone can use to stand more attractively.

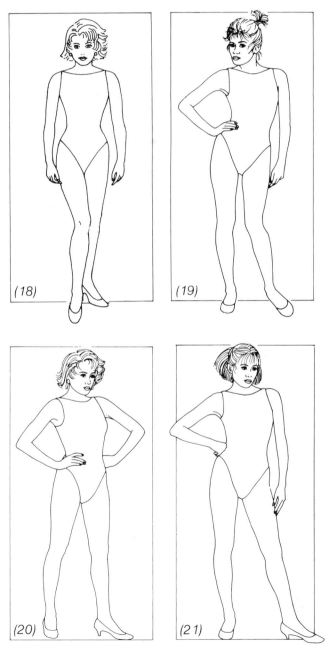

(18)

(19)

(20)

(21)

Figure 18. The model's basic stance (closed) is the one most frequently used by women because it makes legs appear more attractive. To practice this stance center your weight over both feet. Keep your back foot at an angle to the forward foot. The forward foot should be placed straight forward with the heel at the arch of the back foot. The knees should be slightly flexed, with the forward knee flexed slightly more. Your hips should be turned at an angle to the viewer.

Figure 19. The model's basic stance (open). This is an attractive variation of the basic stance. Maintain the same basic angle of your feet but spread your feet apart shoulder width or wider.

Figure 20. The model's wide stance (symmetrical). This stance is considered casual, yet aggressive. Male models often use this stance. It works best with sportswear. Your weight should be centered evenly on both feet. Feet should never be pointed inward. Knees should be straight, but not rigid. Also, female models' legs appear more attractive if one or both toes are pointed slightly outward.

Figure 21. The model's wide stance (asymmetrical). This stance is also a casual stance. It is the same as the wide stance, but the weight is shifted so it is centered over one foot. The hips shift slightly toward the weighted side.

39

Movement of the Hands   The way you move your hands is important to your physical appearance. (See Figures 22 to 30.) If you have attractive hands, you will want to make them a focal point. If your hands are less than ideal, you will not want to hide them but you may want to confine your gestures and move your hands in a way that will make their unattractiveness less apparent. You may have noticed that the most graceful and widely used hand and foot positions in modeling are loosely based on those found in classical ballet. Studying ballet will help you to become more aware of your hands and feet.

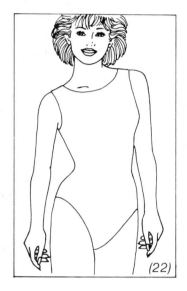

(22)

(23)

(24)

Figure 22. The normal hand position. The normal hand position that you will apply for most situations is relaxed, yet poised. Very limp or very stiff hands are not attractive. Movements of the hands should always involve smooth motions beginning from the forearms, rather than the wrists. To master this hand position, use the pencil trick. Hold a pencil as you normally would, then relax your hand and remove the pencil. This is an ideal hand position.

Figure 23. Folded hands. Cup the palm of one hand over the back of the other hand. Folding your hands yields an attractive yet natural look. Doing so will also help you to keep your hands still when in an interview situation or when in front of a group of people. This hand position looks equally well for men and women, whether they are in a sitting or standing position.

Figure 24. Interlaced fingers. Another way to fold your hands is by interlacing your fingers gently. Hands and fingers appear longer and more attractive when crossed at the knuckles, rather than at the base of the fingers. When adopting this hand position, nails should be well manicured.

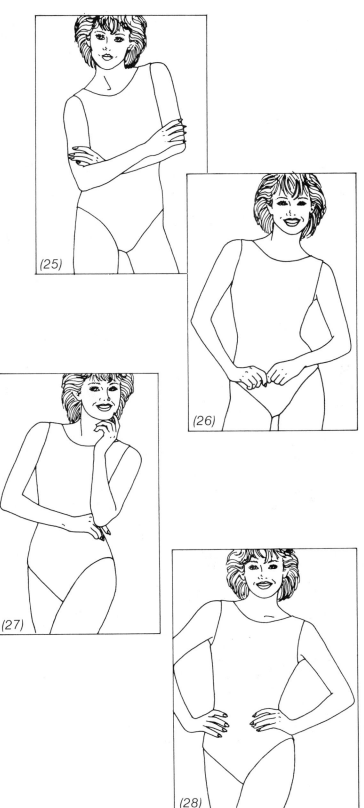

(25)

(26)

(27)

(28)

Figure 25. Crossed arms. Crossed arms are attractive but may give the illusion of being unapproachable. Models must pay attention that when crossing the arms they do not cover important details of the garment being modeled. They must also be sure their hands look attractive.

Figure 26. Poised hands and hand position for holding an object. This is an attractive position for holding the hands in front of the body or for holding a small object. It enhances the waistline and arms. To find the right position, hold a pencil horizontally in both hands. Hands should be touching, elbows should be comfortably bent. Remove the pencil, keeping the hands in position.

Figure 27. Hands touching face. When placing a hand on your face, use the basic hand position shown in Figure 22. You may also want to straighten your fingers for a different effect. Always place your hand gently on your face so that it does not push the skin, and do not allow it to cover your face. Keeping the hand in profile is also preferred. Bending the wrist only slightly backward or forward usually looks better than an exaggerated bend.

Figure 28. Hands on hips. Put one or both hands on your hips. For dresses and skirts, place hands gently on hips with the fingers tapering and slightly spread. Men should use the loose fist position when placing hands on hips.

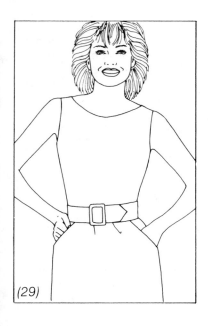

(29)

(30)

Figure 29. Hands in pockets. Placing hands in pockets looks relaxed and confident. Models often do this because pockets are a selling point for any garment. Keep the hands flat inside the pockets, not in fists, as fists inside pockets tend to cause the hips to appear wider. When wearing tight garments, it is best to put only the fingers, not the whole hand in the top of the pocket.

Figure 30. The normal hand position for men. Men's hands usually appear most attractive when held in a loose fist. Hands should not look limp, nor should they appear tense or clenched. Women sometimes use this hand position when a casual, aggressive, or sporty look is desired. For example, when wearing jeans a model might place her hands held in fists on her hips.

Walking The following guidelines will help you to achieve a more attractive and efficient walk.

1. Good posture is essential for an attractive, controlled walk. The first rule is to keep your body and head in proper alignment at all times.

2. When beginning a step or going from one step to the next, always push with your back foot, rather than your forward foot. This propels your weight and is important for smoothness and speed.

3 When taking a step, reach with the ball of your foot. The step you take should be about the length of your foot.

4. Step as lightly as you can without inhibiting your movements. Be sure your footsteps are made in a smooth, rolling motion from heel to toe. There should be no scuffing sound, nor should your steps make a clicking noise.

5. Walk with your weight centered evenly over your feet with the most weight on the outside of the foot. The ball and heel of your foot should be in line with the line on which you are walking. To practice, picture an imaginary line. The inside edge of your right foot should be on the right side of the line. Bring your left foot forward and place it to the left of the line. Your feet should barely touch the line. Your knees should brush only slightly as you walk. Be sure your feet are parallel and that your toes are pointed ahead. Turning your feet outward or inward will not be attractive.

6. Nearly all movement should be in your legs, so lead with your legs, not your head. Avoid exaggerated movement, such as swaying or bouncing in your hips and shoulders when you walk. Keep your walk graceful and controlled.

7. Always keep your head up. Glance down only when it is necessary to see where you are going.

8. Allow your arms to swing naturally at your sides. Your arms should swing in opposition to your feet and about the length of your step. Elbows should be slightly bent and held away from your waist. Your hands should be relaxed and poised; never hanging limply at your sides.

Walking Tips for Less Than Ideal Legs

Legs look more attractive when shown in profile. When possible, show your legs at an angle to the viewer (camera or audience). Otherwise, observe the following:

Bowlegs. Walk so that your steps are slightly inside of the line described in step 5. This will enable you to cross one foot slightly in front of the other.

Thin legs. If your legs are very thin, they will appear fuller if you use a very slight crosswalk in which one foot is placed slightly in front of the other, as recommended for bowlegs.

Short legs. Short legs will appear to be longer if you take a slightly longer step.

Sitting

Although the sitting action is rarely photographed or performed on the runway, it is important to know how to sit gracefully. Rather than just plopping into a chair, you should be able to sit with a certain amount of poise and control. Sitting on a chair or piece of furniture that is firm and high off the floor, rather than on something low and soft, will make you look more attractive. However, you should have enough body control to be able to sit gracefully on a high stool, any style sofa or chair, a stair step, or the floor, as the situation may require. Practice the following guidelines.

1. To sit gracefully, walk up to a chair and pivot slowly when your leg is close enough to touch the chair. After you've turned, if you are not close enough to touch the chair, take a step back. This way you will not have to make the unattractive move of turning around to look down at the chair.

2. Lower yourself into the chair by slowly bending your knees while keeping them together. Keep your head up and your back straight. Do not reach with your buttocks. Keep your hands at your sides, and when you are almost sitting, place the palms of your hands on the seat of the chair. Raise your body slightly to allow you to slide back in the chair in one smooth motion. You should not wiggle or inch back. In most straight chairs your back will touch the back of the chair comfortably.

3. Always sit at an angle, either right or left, and keep your knees and feet together. Legs usually look best when feet are extended slightly further out from the chair than the knees. (See Figure 31.) Do not pull your feet far back under the chair. When crossing your legs, they will look more attractive if you cross them at the ankles (Figure 32). When crossing the legs at the knees, be sure you are sitting at an angle and always cross your legs away from your audience. Also keep your feet touching with your toes pointed slightly downward and outward. (See Figure 33 and 34). Legs also appear attractive when feet are positioned in a closed basic stance. Practice sitting positions before a mirror to become more aware of what your audience will see.

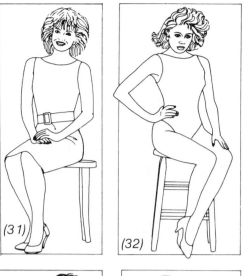

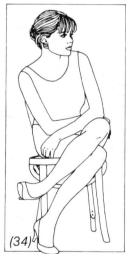

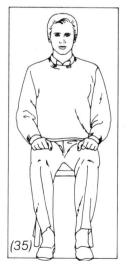

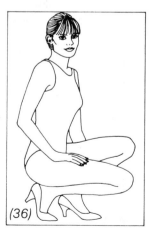

Figure 31. Basic sitting position with feet in the basic stance position and knees angled away from the viewer or audience.

Figure 32. Crossed ankles

Figure 33. Crossed legs.

Figure 34. Wrong position of crossed legs. Knees are pointed straight on, feet appear awkward because they aren't pointed downward, back is hunched and hands are placed unattractively.

Figure 35. Men's basic sitting position. Back is straight. Knees are balanced directly over feet.

Figure 36. Proper stooping and bending technique involves keeping the back straight, the head up. Only the knees bend to lower the body.

(31)

(32)

(33)

(34)

(35)

(36)

4. Remember to always keep your back straight and rested gently against the back of the chair (Figure 35). Fold your hands in your lap or keep them at your sides. Let your weight settle into your feet, rather than into your thighs. Lifting the thighs upward slightly from the chair will give them a trimmer and more elegant look.

5. When arising from a chair, first slide forward in one smooth motion, placing your hands at your sides. Place one foot forward, keeping your knees together. Use the strength of your thighs to rise from the chair, while keeping your back straight and your head up. If you are arising from a low chair or other type of furniture, use the palms of your hands to help lift your weight up and out of the chair. You should never look as if you have to struggle to rise to a standing position.

6. To sit gracefully on the floor: Assume the model's basic stance (closed) position. Keeping your knees together, lower your body by bending your knees. Keep your back straight and your head erect. When your knees are completely bent, place your right hand on the floor, followed by your right hip. This movement should be smooth and controlled. When seated on the floor, keep your knees together, or cross one knee in front of the other. Keep your legs extended, not curled up under you. Your toes should be pointed. Keep the majority of your weight centered over your hip. You should not lean too heavily on the hand that is supporting you. This causes the wrist and elbow to look deformed. Lift your weight off the hand to soften a sharp, unattractive bend at the wrist.

Stooping and Bending

Many everyday tasks and sometimes an assignment will call for stooping and bending. For example, you may be picking up something from the floor or opening a low file drawer, etc. Do not bend over from the waist, instead place one foot slightly ahead of the other, keep your knees together while bending them, then lower your body. Keep your back erect and your head up. (See Figure 36.) This position helps you control your movements; it also looks attractive and helps strengthen your muscles. This advice also applies when you are lifting a heavy object.

Mannerisms

Mannerisms are another important component of physical presentation. Because a model usually tries to portray an image worthy of imitation, she should eliminate mannerisms that detract from her physical appearance. The model may not even know that she possesses unattractive habits or mannerisms—some may surface only when she is nervous or uncomfortable. Although the unattractiveness of the mannerisms listed here seems obvious, check these points to make sure that you avoid them.

Hands present the greatest problems. Keep them still and be aware that when you move them, they should enhance your appearance. Avoid nail biting, stroking or playing with your hair, fidgeting with clothing or personal belongings, picking your nails, face or other body parts, cracking your knuckles, or scratching in the presence of others. Avoid overgesturing or awkward gestures.

The mouth presents another set of problems that can make an individual appear less attractive. Avoid biting your lips, chewing the inside of your mouth, twitching your mouth, and gum chewing. Do not eat or drink unless you are seated at a table for dining or in a situation in which others are eating or drinking. Never attempt to clean your teeth in front of other people. Avoid making sucking, gurgling, and other disturbing noises. Try to avoid sneezing, yawning, or coughing in public, and if you must, cover your mouth with a tissue. Men should avoid spitting. Always try to avoid smoking in the presence of others. If you must have a cigarette, observe attractive smoking habits. Do not talk while exhaling smoke, and don't make smoke rings or blow smoke through your nose.

Avoid twitching your nose, and making sniffling or snorting noises. Use a tissue to blow your nose and do so discreetly.

Avoid making facial grimaces that don't reflect well on your appearance. Don't mimic, squint, excessively blink, wrinkle your forehead, or frown. Avoid expression habits that cause unwanted lines to form. When talking to someone, establish eye contact and maintain it. Don't allow your eyes to drift to other people or things. Don't nervously twitch your eyes or brows.

When standing or sitting, avoid jittery movements. Don't tap your feet, shake your legs, or move to a rhythm in your head.

Don't adjust your clothing or fix your hair or makeup when you are in public places in view of other people.

Facial Expressions

A model uses facial expressions to convey her personality. In average situations a model will want to portray positive emotions to be most effective. Alertness, attentiveness, intelligence, enthusiasm, pleasantness, openness, and cheerfulness are all good expression habits for a model or anyone to capitalize on. A model avoids an expressionless face and expressions that make her appear self-conscious, bored, depressed, or artificial. A model learns to appear positive and even-tempered in business settings, rather than revealing negative emotions that she may actually be feeling.

Creative Physical Presentation

The principles of physical presentation previously described apply in all situations, from face-to-face meetings to modeling assignments. However, for modeling assignments, a model's physical presentation may have to be altered so that it is more effective for the medium in which she is working or so that it makes a greater impact. This is referred to as "creative physical presentation." For example, some of the movements previously outlined may have to be altered for the camera to appear more photogenic. For the runway, movements may have to be exaggerated to increase projection and draw attention.

The preceding information on physical presentation outlines how a model or any individual should appear in average situations. However, modeling is a creative endeavor, and when given the option of using her imagination, a model thinks of ways to alter these basic principles to adapt her physical presentation to show a garment or item. This is what modeling is all about. Any aspect of physical presentation can be exaggerated or changed to add impact to the model's appearance in a photograph, fashion show, or other type of modeling assignment. A model alters her posture, standing, walking, hand movements, and facial expressions for the following reasons:

- To correct her own physical flaws and to exaggerate her good features.
- To enhance the garments or items he or she wears by aligning or moving the body in such a way that garments hang, drape, or move on the figure more attractively.
- To express an attitude, look, character, or feeling.

A good model assesses how she can best present a product or service to be modeled and alters her physical presentation accordingly. Of course, in some modeling situations, such as in character modeling, the objective is not to look beautiful. In such instances you will have to determine the elements of physical presentation, which may not coincide with the ideals presented here, that best express the character you are to portray.

The following information gives a few examples of how a model might apply creative physical presentation to modeling. There are no hard-and-fast rules in regard to body movements or specific modeling positions that must be learned. Your objective should always be to use your own creativity.

Creative Posture for Modeling

For a model, posture goes beyond the basic principles for good posture. Modeling requires no standard "proper" posture that is employed for all situations or for all items that an individual models. Good posture for modeling does not necessarily mean "shoulders back and head up." A model varies his or her posture as the situation or the items to be modeled demands.

Although there are several different postures a model may adopt, Figures 37 to 40 show the four basic postures models use to enhance their bodies and the items they wear.

(37)

(38)

Figure 37. Arched. An arched posture is indicated by an inward curve of the spine.

Figure 38. Forward curve. A forward curved posture is the opposite of an arched posture. A forward curve is indicated by an outward curve of the spine.

(39)

(40)

Figure 39. Asymmetrical. An asymmetrical posture occurs when one shoulder and the opposite hip are raised forming the body in an S curve. This accentuates the waistline.

Figure 40. Twisted. A twisted posture occurs when the upper half of the torso turns in opposition to the lower half of the torso. Models often twist their hips away from the camera to create a slimmer look.

Other Aspects of Creative Physical Presentation

Figures 41–51 are other aspects of creative physical presentation.

(41)

(42)

(43)

(44)

(45)

(46)

Figure 41. Creative standing. When on a runway or in front of a camera, models think of lots of creative ways to stand that would look out of place in normal situations. The model's exaggerated stance (closed) shown here is commonly used by models when posing for photographs. It accentuates the waist giving an interesting line to the body, while making the legs appear graceful. To accomplish it, the model follows the same instructions as for the basic stance, however, she places nearly all her weight on one foot (the base foot), while resting on the side of the ball of her working foot. The knee of her working leg automatically curves inward toward her base leg. The model varies her hand and arm position to enhance her garment.

Figure 42. Creative hand movements. A good model is never puzzled as to what to do with her hands. She may hold them down at her sides or place them in her pockets or on her hips. For a creative hand movement, the model may hold one or both hands poised in midair as in this illustration.

Figure 43. Another creative hand movement such as this attractively shows off the shape of a garment's sleeves.

Figure 44. Another variation shows an important detail of the model's outfit—in this case, her movement highlights the gloves.

Figure 45. Creative walking.

Figure 46. Another variation of creative walking. In order to make a full skirt sway attractively, a model may adopt a walk with a longer than normal stride. To accentuate the waistline, she twists her torso.

(47)

(48)

(49)

(50)

(51)

Figure 47. Creative sitting. A clever model can think of lots of imaginative ways to sit on a chair. One of the most common ways that models sit for photographs is shown here. This sitting position enables the viewer to see the front of the model's garment more easily. To accomplish it, when sitting in profile to the camera, the model rolls her weight onto the hip closest to the camera. She is careful to arrange her legs, arms and hands in attractive positions.

Figure 48. Another variation of creative sitting. In this instance the model sits on the floor.

Figure 49. The article on which the model sits can influence her sitting position. This model adopts a casual sitting position when seated on a stool.

Figure 50. Creative stooping and bending. A model sometimes stoops, bends, or kneels to create a pose for a photograph. When doing such movements she is careful to keep her back straight and to achieve attractive positions with her legs and feet.

Figure 51. Sometimes a model will lean against a wall or a part of the set. Notice how this model's pose highlights the design details along the side of her top.

Creative Mannerisms   Sometimes a model will portray a mannerism to give style, impact or familiarity to her presentation. For example, if a model is given a cigarette she may pretend to smoke it in either a very stylized, almost theatrical manner or in a realistic, normal way.

Creative Facial Expressions   A model learns to express herself and to express the mood of an item she is modeling by altering her facial expressions as an actress does. For example, she may slightly raise one eyebrow to create a subtly sexy look when modeling a sexy, tousled hairstyle. A model also learns how to manipulate her face to make it appear more attractive. For example, if too much of the model's gums show when she smiles normally, she learns how to slightly alter her smile naturally to make this problem less obvious. If the model unconsciously tucks her chin under when she smiles, creating a double chin, she learns to become conscious of attaining a more attractive line for the chin and jaw.

HOW TO USE THE SELF-IMPROVEMENT RECORD   Use this chart to identify the aspects of your appearance that you need to correct and to outline how you will make improvements. Recording this information will help you to see yourself objectively and to keep track of your progress. Use the guidelines below to take your measurements. For accuracy, take all measurements wearing only undergarments and no shoes.

Height:	Stand as you normally do because this is how you appear to others. As you improve your posture and learn to stand taller, you'll find there will be no difference between your normal posture and the posture you adopt when you are having your height measured.
Bust:	Wearing a normal bra, measure the fullest part of the bustline.
Chest:	Men should measure the fullest part of the chest.
Waist:	Measure the slimmest part.
Abdomen:	Measure fullest part.
Hips:	Measure the fullest part, approximately 7 inches below waistline.
Upper thigh:	Measure fullest part of both thighs and record each.
Mid thigh:	Measure midway between knee and crotch of each and record.
Knee:	Measure fullest part of each and record.
Calf:	Measure fullest part of each and record.
Ankle:	Measure slimmest part of each.
Upper arm:	Measure fullest part of each.
Wrist:	Measure slimmest part.
Shoulders:	With arms down at sides, measure fullest part around shoulders, back, upper chest, and arms.

Self Improvement Record

FIGURE CHART

© THE PROFESSIONAL MODEL'S HANDBOOK

MODEL _____   DATE _____   HEIGHT _____

MEASUREMENTS	INITIAL	Checkpoint 1		Checkpoint 2		Checkpoint 3		Checkpoint 4		Checkpoint 5		Checkpoint 6		IDEAL
		Actual	Goal	Actual	Goal	Actual	Goal	Actual	Goal	Actual	Goal	Actual	Goal	
DATE														
Weight (Without Clothing)														
Bust (Females)														
Chest (Males)														
Waist														
Abdomen														
Hips (Females)														
Upper Thigh														
Mid. Thigh														
Knee														
Calf														
Ankle														
Wrist														
Shoulders														

Self Improvement Record

PERSONAL CARE CHART

Characteristics	Improvements Needed	Course of Action
■HAIR □Color □Texture □Condition □Cut		
■SKIN □Color □Texture □Condition □Other		
■HANDS □Skin Condition □Nails □Other		
■FEET □Skin Condition □Nails □Other		
■EYES		
■LIPS		
■DENTAL		
■POSTURE		

Chapter 3 The Model's Guide to Professional Makeup Artistry

Makeup is a very important factor in modeling. A model must have a good understanding of the art of makeup for three reasons:

1. To correct imperfections in the skin, facial structure, and features so they will not detract from the item being modeled.
2. To enhance the skin and features so that the model appears as attractive as she or he can be and to make the model appear most attractive for various media.
3. To change the model's look to create the character he or she is to portray based on the items being modeled.

A model who really knows how to use makeup will always have an advantage over the one who doesn't. A model cannot always rely on having a professional makeup artist available. Makeup artists are usually selected and employed either by the model's client or by the photographer, when the client's budget allows and when the model's makeup is important to the success of the job. Outside of major modeling markets, makeup artists are employed less frequently. In addition to assignments, models must know how to apply their own makeup when interviewing with clients and photographers for prospective modeling opportunities.

Most models learn how to apply makeup by watching other models, by having their makeup applied by different makeup artists, and by experimenting on their own. Photographers, modeling agents, and clients can also provide valuable information. Photographic testing and videotaping are helpful for giving the model instant feedback. Experimentation is a key to learning how to apply makeup effectively.

The way in which models use makeup changes with the course of fashion. In the 1940s and 1950s models painted on their faces, starting with pale pancake foundation and drawing in dark, highly arched brows. In the 1960s models, such as Twiggy, wore several pairs of false eyelashes and used white lipstick. Although the look of recent years has allowed for less dramatic changes, creative makeup artistry is still often used in high-fashion modeling. The "natural look," even though it may take a variety of cosmetics to achieve, is the one used for most modeling assignments.

Success with makeup is dependent upon good skin and a healthy appearance. No amount or type of makeup can cover bad skin and lackluster eyes. Proper skin care and good health maintenance habits are essential.

Use this chapter as a beauty primer to help you learn the basics as well as all the possibilities that exist beyond the fundamentals. Try all the tips found in these pages to find which combinations are just right for your features, life-style, tastes, and prospective modeling opportunities. Experiment with lots of different looks, and keep a record of them by having a friend take a Polaroid or regular photo. Diagram and take notes on applications and products makeup artists have used on you. Record the information on the Makeup Notes form. It is also a good idea to keep a notebook to store magazine photos and sketches of makeup looks you like and want to try.

There are five steps in mastering makeup techniques for modeling:

1. Analyzing your skin and features.
2. Assembling professional makeup tools and the right cosmetics for you.
3. Utilizing corrective makeup techniques to solve your beauty problems.
4. Experimenting to create different looks.
5. Understanding the effects of various media in relation to makeup.

ANALYZING YOUR SKIN

Good health and proper skin care are essential. Healthy, flawless skin is one of the most important assets a model can possess. The camera tends to coarsen the skin and exaggerate imperfections. Examine your skin to determine whether you need the assistance of a dermatologist, cosmetic surgeon, or other professional or whether your problems can be helped by using makeup techniques.

Analyze your skin by looking at it closely in a mirror in direct daylight. Identify where your problems lie, and consider how the specialists listed here may be able to help you.

Cosmetic surgeon. Moles, scars, surface wrinkles, and broken capillaries can all be eliminated or diminished by the skills of a cosmetic surgeon. However, always obtain several opinions before undertaking surgery, and ask for references of doctors from your agent. He or she usually knows of several qualified individuals who have helped other models with similar problems.

Dermatologist. A dermatologist is medically trained to treat skin disorders. A dermatologist is often a model's best friend. Seeing a dermatologist on a regular basis and practicing preventive medicine are usually the best ways to stave off problems. Finding the best dermatologist is the key. Your agent or other models may be able to recommend a good dermatologist.

Skin care expert. An esthetician is a licensed professional who specializes in the care of skin but does not treat skin disorders. If your skin is clear or your problems are very mild, you may benefit from occasional or regular visits to an esthetician. He or she will administer facials and other treatments that will improve your skin's appearance. However, never have a facial the day before an assignment or important interview, as redness or other temporary problems may exist.

Electrologist. An electrologist is a licensed professional who employs techniques to permanently remove superfluous hair on the face and body.

Cosmetologist. A cosmetologist is a licensed professional who is trained in a number of personal services. Most specialize in haircutting, styling, and coloring. However, they are also trained in such areas as manicuring, pedicuring, and temporary hair removal (waxing, tweezing) and bleaching techniques to make facial hair less noticeable.

Corrective Makeup Techniques for Skin Flaws

For problems that can't be corrected with any of the above treatments, the only answer may be corrective makeup. Practically any skin problem can be diminished or camouflaged by skillful use of makeup. Consult Table 1 under "Corrective Makeup Techniques for Skin Flaws" in this chapter.

ANALYZING YOUR FACIAL STRUCTURE AND FEATURES

Aside from correcting imperfections of the skin, an individual may need to correct, minimize, or define certain aspects of his or her face. This can be accomplished by using the principles of highlighting and contouring.

If you have read or heard beauty advice and have been confused as to whether your face is heart, pear, round, rectangular, square, or oval shaped or whether your eyes are wide or narrow set, this exercise may help you to see yourself objectively. Trying to fit your facial elements under labels usually leads to uncertainty and incorrect conclusions. A human face is made up of a combination of characteristics, and each is unique. Finding your own facial characteristics and determining whether your look or the look you wish to have benefits from exaggerating or downplaying those aspects will be your objective. Understanding the shape, size and proportion of your facial characteristics will aid you in the correct use of makeup.

Step 1: *Black and white photos.* You will need 4 x 5-, 5 x 7-, or 8 x 10-inch black and white photographs of your face. Wear no makeup or jewelry. No blouse or top should show in the photo. Your hair must be pulled straight back and smoothed down as closely to your head as possible. The photo must be shot using even, shadowless lighting that can either be reflected or direct and undiffused. The texture of your skin should show. Have a friend or photographer take these photos using a 35-mm camera with a portrait (85- to 180-mm) lens. A longer or shorter lens may distort the actual appearance of your face. A flash placed right on the camera will yield flat, simple lighting. The three types of shots you will need will be (1) straight on with your face and eyes aimed straight into the lens, (2) a left profile, and (3) a right profile. In all of these pictures you should have no expression, your lips should be closed, and your chin should be neither raised nor lowered. For several shots, very slightly raise and lower your chin and turn your head to ensure that you get good symmetrical shots. Sharp focus is a must.

Step 2: *Charting your face.* You will need a straight edge or ruler, a pencil with a sharp point, an eraser, and a few sheets of ultratranslucent tracing paper. You should also make several photo copies of your photo. Observe the elements of your face by drawing the lines and taking the measurements explained on the following pages.

Step 3: *Drawing conclusions.* Use the information you have obtained to determine the aspects of your face that should be accentuated as well as the aspects that should be corrected or subdued. However, always be flexible. Retain an openness for seeing your face in new ways and for utilizing techniques for projecting different looks. Avoid regarding irregularities in your face as undesireable characteristics. These aspects may give your face an individual look and can be your greatest assets.

Step 4: *Experimentation.* Using the photocopies you have made, or by placing a sheet of tracing paper over your photograph, shade different areas with a soft leaded pencil to show the effects of different contouring and highlight applications. Employ the techniques explained in Figures 6 to 37 to accentuate the positive features and subdue the negative ones. Consult the charts in this chapter for experimenting with various ways to apply eyebrow makeup, eyeshadow, eyeliner, mascara, cheekcolor, and lipcolor. Assemble these tracings along with sketches and magazine pages in a makeup notebook. This will provide you with a personalized beauty scrapbook from which you can select ideas that work best for you in a variety of situations.

The concepts that follow are simply points of analysis. There is no one facial ideal. However, by being aware of these points, you will be able to better establish objectives for applying your makeup to best project the look or looks you desire.

Finding Your Face Shape   Place a sheet of tracing paper over your photograph and draw the outline of your face following the line of your hairline, the sides of your face, and the contour of your jaws and chin. Remove the tracing paper and place it on a sheet of clean white paper (see Figure 1). Does the shape that you drew resemble an oval, square, heart, pear, upside-down pear (triangular), diamond, round, or rectangular shape? If you can't decide, ask someone else to judge the shape of your drawing.

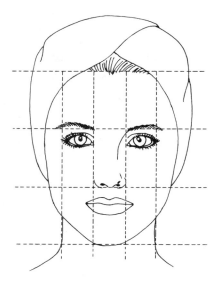

Figure 1. Facial proportions.

Comparing the Sides of Your Face   Place tracing paper over your photograph, and draw a line down the center. Does one side look happier? Are the features more balanced on one side? Is your jaw fuller, squarer, or rounder on one side? Is your nose straighter on one side? Compare your left eye to your right eye, the right side of your mouth to the left side. Now compare your left and right profile shots, asking the above questions. Do you prefer one side of your face to the other?

Finding Your Lengthwise and Widthwise Facial Proportions   The ancient Greeks devised a method for determining ideal facial proportions. These ideals were used by artists and sculptors to obtain symmetry when depicting the human face. You can use these principles to determine how closely your face approaches these ideals. Remember, these measurements are approximate.

Length   Draw a horizontal line at your hairline, another through the brows, another at the base of the nose, and another at the bottom of the chin. Using your ruler, measure the distance between the lines in each third. If the top two-thirds are equal, but the bottom third is longer, this indicates that you probably have a chin that is a bit long.

Width   Measure the width of each eye from the tearduct to where the outermost lash takes root. Are both eyes equal? If not, using an average between the two, divide the face into five widths using this width, starting at the center. Are your eyes wide, narrow, or normal set. Are your temples wide or narrow? Does the widest part of your nose fit within the lines?

Eyebrow Measurements

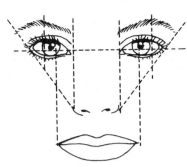

Use these checkpoints to determine whether you need to improve the shape of your eyebrows. Refer to your straight-on photograph for aid in observing these aspects (Figure 2).

- Does your eyebrow start at a point aligned with the inner corner of your eye?
- Is the arch of your eyebrow in line with the outer edge of your iris?
- Does the taper of your eyebrow end just beyond the outer corner of the eye?
- Draw a horizontal line through your brows from the end of one to the end of the other. Is one brow higher or more arched than the other?

Figure 2. Eyebrow measurements.

Eye Measurements

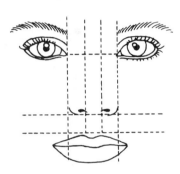

- Are your eyes in a straight line? Draw a straight line intersecting the inner and outer corners of your eyes. (See Figure 3.) If it is not possible to draw a straight line, one or both of your eyes may droop at the inner or outer corners. This line will also tell you if one eye is lower or higher than the other.
- Compare your eyes to see if they match in shape. Is one eye rounder, smaller?
- Check the lids of your eyes. How much of the lid is showing on each eye? Are the lids prominent, not visible, uneven?
- Check the distance between the eye and the brow. Are brows high above eyes or close to eyes?
- How deeply set are your eyes?

Figure 3. Eye measurement.

Lip Measurements

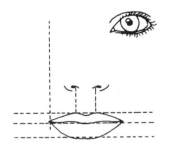

- Are the points of your upper lip in line with the center of each nostril? (See Figure 4.)
- Is the fullest part of your lower lip in line with these two points?
- Are the corners of your lips in line with the irises of your eyes?
- Do your lips match in thickness or is your upper lip or lower lip thinner or thicker?
- Are your lips straight? Draw a straight line through the opening of the lips. Does one or both corners droop or turn up?

Figure 4. Lip measurement.

Nose Measurements

- Hold an orangewood stick vertically in line with the inner corner of your eye. Is the bridge of your nose about the same width or slightly narrower or wider than the bottom of your nose?
- Look at the measurements you took using thirds of the face. Is your nose too long or too short?
- Look at your profile. Is your nose straight or does it curve upward or downward?
- Is there a ball, pointed tip, or indentation at the end of your nose? Are there protrusions or indentations on the length of your nose?

ASSEMBLING A PROFESSIONAL MODEL'S MAKEUP KIT

One of the most important necessities of the trade is a model's makeup kit. Use these checklists to assemble everything you will need. Keep these items in a case that keeps your makeup organized, maintains it in good condition, and looks neat. Your makeup kit will have two important types of items: beauty tools and beauty products.

Beauty Tools

The tools you use to apply your makeup partly determine the results you will achieve. Select high-quality, professional tools. It is not important that you have a wide variety of brushes. You may find you like to use certain types of brushes and will want to have several of each. The tools listed here are the ones makeup artists most often prefer (See Figure 5).

It is also important to take good care of your beauty tools. Dirty brushes, sponges, and applicators can spread infection and impair makeup application. Makeup, skin oils, and other debris left in brushes and sponges can also speed their deterioration. Therefore, clean brushes weekly. Makeup sponges should be cleaned after each use. Wash with a mild shampoo, rinse well with warm water, and allow to dry overnight.

Beauty Tool Checklist

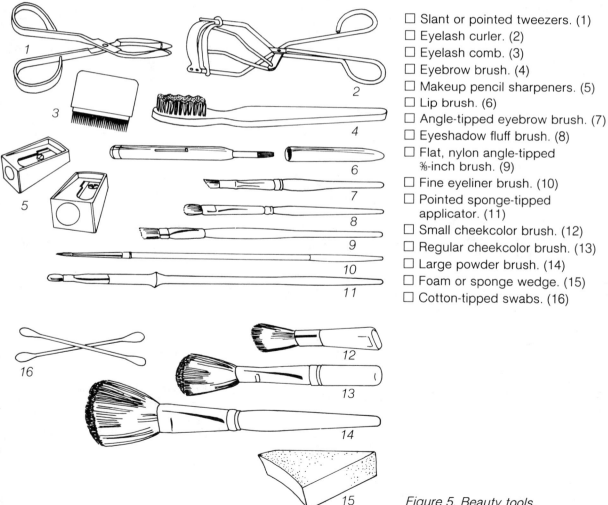

☐ Slant or pointed tweezers. (1)
☐ Eyelash curler. (2)
☐ Eyelash comb. (3)
☐ Eyebrow brush. (4)
☐ Makeup pencil sharpeners. (5)
☐ Lip brush. (6)
☐ Angle-tipped eyebrow brush. (7)
☐ Eyeshadow fluff brush. (8)
☐ Flat, nylon angle-tipped ⅜-inch brush. (9)
☐ Fine eyeliner brush. (10)
☐ Pointed sponge-tipped applicator. (11)
☐ Small cheekcolor brush. (12)
☐ Regular cheekcolor brush. (13)
☐ Large powder brush. (14)
☐ Foam or sponge wedge. (15)
☐ Cotton-tipped swabs. (16)

Figure 5. Beauty tools.

Beauty Products   There are seven basic types of makeup products you will need: concealer, foundation, contour/highlight makeup, face powder, cheekcolor, lipcolor, and eye makeup (eyebrow makeup, eyeliner, eyeshadow, and mascara). Select these products carefully. Experiment with several and don't scrimp on quality. Consult the Beauty Products Guide in this chapter for selection and application tips.

Model's Makeup Kit   Skin care supplies   ☐ Makeup remover.
Checklist   ☐ Moisturizer.
                                                 ☐ Astringent.
                                                 ☐ Cleanser.

Beauty products   ☐ Foundation (three shades: one perfectly matched to skintone, one a shade lighter, and one a shade darker).
                   ☐ Concealer.
                   ☐ Concealer pencil for quick touch-ups.
                   ☐ Undertoner or skintone neutralizer.
                   ☐ Contour/highlight cream or powder.
                   ☐ Face powder (translucent, matte, skintoned in a light, medium, and dark shade).

Cheeks   ☐ Cheekcolor (powder or cream in a basic wardrobe of colors: red tones, orange tones, violet tones, brown tones, and gold; a soft pink to simulate the natural blush of cheeks is important; include any other colors that are fashionable and flattering).

Lips   ☐ Lipcolor (same shades as above but also include matte white, frosted gold, and frosted silver to lighten, warm, cool, or add frost to all colors).
        ☐ Clear lip gloss or petroleum jelly.
        ☐ Lip pencils (auburn or natural lipcolor plus shades to match lipcolors).

Eyes   ☐ Mascara (black, brown, navy).
        ☐ Eyeshadows (matte, neutral shades, such as brown, navy, charcoal, beige, flesh pink, and cream; frosted highlighter in white or light gold to add frost to any eyeshadow; also include colors that are fashionable and flattering).
        ☐ Eyeliner pencils (brown, black, navy, white, light blue plus fashionable and flattering colors).

Beauty tools   ☐ Eyelash curler, eyelash comb, eyebrow brushes, lip brush, eyeshadow fluff brush, nylon ⅜-inch brush, fine eyeliner brush, small cheekcolor brush, regular cheekcolor brush, large powder brush, foam or latex sponge puffs, wedges and applicators, makeup pencil sharpeners, slanted or pointed tweezers.
                ☐ Cotton balls and swabs, facial tissues, powder puffs.

Miscellaneous   ☐ Eyedrops   ☐ _____

**Beauty Product Guide:
Types of Cosmetics,
Functions, How to
Select, and How to Apply**

In order for a model to use makeup effectively to achieve her own best looks, it is important to understand the types of cosmetics available, their functions, and how to select and apply them. Preparation of the face for makeup (cleansing, toning, moisturizing) is covered in Chapter 2.

CONCEALER

Functions

Concealer is used to cover such imperfections as blemishes, scars, skin discolorations, and undereye circles.

Types Available

Concealers are available in different consistencies ranging from creamy liquids to thick, cakey creams. Those with a thick consistency provide heavy coverage, whereas those with a thin consistency provide sheerness and minimal coverage. One of the most useful makeup products is concealer in pencil form. Concealer pencils are used to retouch small areas that may need additional coverage after makeup has been applied. Concealers are made in a wide range of fleshtones as well as white (to dramatically lighten areas), yellow (to cancel red or brown areas), mauve (to combat grayish areas), lavender (to conceal yellow areas), and green (to combat red areas).

How to Select

For general use, select a concealer that is nearly opaque and half a shade lighter than your complexion. Select one that is neither greasy nor dry.

Application Tips

• For precise, adequate coverage, apply concealer with a flat, nylon angle-tipped brush. For sheerer coverage use a foam sponge wedge.

• For heaviest coverage with concealer, stipple it onto the area using fingertips. Use pressing motions to blend, not strokes.

• Always confine concealer to the objectionable areas and blend well.

• Concealer application should never be detectable. Always dab lightly over applied and blended concealer with foundation to ensure one even complexion color.

FOUNDATION

Foundation is used to create attractive skintones, even out the texture and color of the complexion, conceal imperfections, set a base for the rest of the makeup, and protect the skin.

Types Available

Foundations are available in different forms and consistencies. They range from thin, watery liquids to creams, foams, powders, gels, sticks, cakes, and pancake. The opacity or covering ability of a foundation is also important to consider. The different degrees of coverage range from heavy to medium to sheer. Finish is another distinguishing characteristic. A matte foundation gives a soft, powdery, no-shine finish. A glossy foundation gives a dewy or shiny look. Semimatte foundations appear neither shiny nor powdery. The contents of a foundation also have an effect on the skin and the appearance created. Most foundations have either an oil or water base. Oil-based foundations tend to be richer and more beneficial to dry skin. Water-based foundations create a very sheer look and work well on oily skin.

How to Select

Foundations are available in a wide range of flesh tones and selecting the right one is vital. Always check colors in natural light. Apply to skin on cheek above jaw and match to the skin on the neck. Usually beige-toned foundations look most attractive; those with reddish or orangey tones often look unnatural. If your skin has golden or warm undertones, select a beige foundation with a hint of peach, gold, creamy yellow, or tawny color. If your skin has blue, pink, or cool undertones, select an ivory foundation or one with a hint of pinkish color. It's most important that you don't deviate too far from your skin's natural coloring or intensity. Once you have applied foundation to the face, there should never be a noticeable difference between the skincolor of the face and neck. Also be aware that the foundation color you choose should work well with the garment you will be wearing and the eye, lip, and cheek makeup colors you select. It may be necessary to combine two or more shades of foundation to arrive at the perfect match for your skin.

Application Tips
- To achieve medium coverage, apply foundation with a foam sponge wedge.

- For sheer coverage, apply foundation with a damp silk or natural sea sponge. When using water based foundation, dampen sponge with water. If using oil-based or cream foundation, dampen sponge with moisturizer.

- To achieve heavy coverage, apply foundation with your fingertips. Press foundation into skin. Apply several thin layers until you build up the coverage desired. Allow each layer to dry before applying the next.

- Always blend foundation well into hairline and under jawline. There should never be a line of demarcation.

- Finish foundation application by using downward strokes to make facial hair unobvious.

POWDER
Functions
Powder is used to smooth and refine the skin, add coverage to the foundation, create a base for application of powdered makeups (cheekcolor, eyeshadow), and give a matte finish. It is most useful for diminishing unattractive shine caused by oil and perspiration, especially on the nose, forehead, and chin. It is also used as a final step in a makeup routine to blend and soften applied makeup and to set makeup so that it won't move, fade, or change color.

Types Available
Powder is available in two basic forms: loose or compressed. Loose powder is applied with a large, fluffy powder brush and provides sheer or heavy coverage. It gives a smooth, even finish. Compressed or pressed powders are packaged in compacts and are convenient for touchups. They are applied using a powder puff.

Powder is available in light, medium, and dark fleshtones as well as white, pink, peach, and lavender. Metallic flecked powders are also made for a glamourous or evening makeup. Powder is available in three degrees of opacity: opaque, translucent, and transparent.

How to Select
For most occasions, select a matte, translucent face powder that matches your foundation. If you want to achieve special effects, select white to make skin appear lighter or for a porcelain look. Use peach, pink, or mauve to enliven a dull or greyish skintone. Select lavender to tone down sallow skin.

Application Tips
- For sheerest coverage, apply powder using a large, fluffy powder brush. Dip brush into powder, then remove excess by tapping the brush, blowing into the bristles, or flicking them with your fingers.

- For extra coverage with powder, apply it using a powder puff. Pick up a quantity of powder on puff and shake off excess. Use rolling motions to apply powder.

- Apply very thin films of powder until you achieve the desired coverage and texture. Powder should be concentrated on nose, chin, and forehead, which are usually the oiliest areas.

- To avoid streakiness, apply powder over foundation that is perfectly blended and dry. Don't use back and forth strokes with your brush or puff. Dab powder on softly.

- If you apply too much powder, dab over it lightly with a slightly damp sponge.

CONTOUR/HIGHLIGHT MAKEUP

Functions

Contour makeup defines, minimizes, or exaggerates the bone structure and facial features. Contour makeups are darker and duller than the complexion. Dark or dull colors make areas where they are applied appear to recede.

Highlight makeup emphasizes, enlarges and brings forward areas where it has been applied. Highlight makeups are lighter, brighter, or shinier than the complexion.

Types Available

Contour and highlight makeups are available in cream or powder form. Contour makeups are available in a wide range of dark flesh-tones as well as a dull bluish-gray color. Cool-toned, matte makeups tend to contour best.

Highlight makeups are available in a wide range of light fleshtones as well as white, light yellow, light pink, and pearlized or metallic gold or silver.

How to Select

For very subtle contouring and highlighting, use foundation or face powder in a shade darker than your complexion to contour. Select foundation or powder in a shade lighter than your complexion to highlight. Note that contour and highlight products should not have obvious red or orange tones.

For more dramatic effects (for example, photography, stage, etc.), select a contouring (or highlighting) foundation, cream, or powder up to three shades darker (or lighter) than your skintone.

For special effects, a contour color need not be a deep fleshtone; a highlight color need not be a light fleshtone. Any makeup that's duller, darker, or cooler than your other makeup colors will make the areas in which it is applied seem to recede. Any makeup that is shinier, frostier, brighter, warmer, or lighter in color will act as a highlighter, making areas come forward. For example, use a matte mauve cheek-color to contour cheekhollows, a frosted mauve cheekcolor to highlight tops of cheekbones.

In general, select cream contour/highlight products for dry skins, powder contour/highlight products for oily skins.

Application Tips

- Contouring or highlighting should never be obvious. Always use it sparingly and blend well.
- Use a sponge wedge to apply contour or highlight creams to the cheeks, jawline, and forehead. Use a contour brush to apply contour powder in these same areas. Use a fan brush to apply highlight powders.
- To contour the nose with contour cream, use a sponge-tipped applicator or the index finger and thumb of one hand. To contour the nose with contour powder, use an eyeshadow fluff brush.
- To highlight the bridge of the nose, the lips, or other small areas, use the pad of your index finger to apply creams or a sponge-tipped applicator with either powders or creams.
- Always finish contour/highlight application by dabbing over it lightly with a sponge that contains a trace of your foundation and a powder brush containing a trace of your translucent powder.

CHEEKCOLOR

Functions

Cheekcolor gives a healthy glow or accents cheeks to coordinate with fashions being worn or modeled.

Types Available

Cheekcolor is available in liquid, cream, cake, gel, powder-cream, and powder forms. Cheekcolors are available in a variety of shades of red, pink, orange or coral, purple or plum, blue-red, brown, and gold. They are also available in different finishes; matte, unfrosted, frosted, glossy, and lightly pearlized.

How to Select   Select powder cheekcolors for oily skins. Select cream cheekcolors for dry skins or for a very natural look. Gels are best for flawless, young skin and are most effective when used on bare skin. Liquids are best used as all-over color washes or for just a hint of color. If your skin exhibits yellow or warm tones, select peach, golden, beige, coral, or tawny cheekcolors. If your skin is pinkish or has cool tones, select cheekcolors with a hint of pink or bluish pink, such as rose, plum, or fuschia. If you want to combat your natural skintone, use the reverse of these principles.

Application Tips
- Apply cream cheekcolor after foundation, using a foam sponge wedge for subtle color or fingertips for more pronounced color.
- Apply powder cheekcolor after foundation, using a fan brush for a hint of color or a cheekcolor brush for more pronounced color.
- Always apply cheekcolor sparingly and blend well. To ensure that cheekcolor is subtly blended, stroke lightly over the edges of application with a clean foam sponge.

EYE MAKEUP   Eye makeup is used to enlarge the eyes, to improve, define, or exaggerate their shape, and to enhance their color. Eye makeup is divided into four categories: eyebrow makeup, eyeliner, eyeshadow, and mascara.

Types Available   Eyebrow makeup is available in powder or pencil form. Eyeliner is available in pencils, powders, creams, liquids, and hardened cakes (to be used with water). Eyeshadow is available in cream, stick, pencil, powder (pressed or loose), and watercolor (to be used with water). Mascara is available in liquid, cream, and cake (to be used with water).

How to Select   Select eyebrow powder for soft-looking brows. Use an eyebrow pencil for more defined brows. Select eyebrow makeup to match the color of your hair, but in a slightly lighter or softer shade.

Select pencil eyeliners for most occasions, as they can be worn defined or softened. Use powder eyeliners for a soft, subtle look. Cake eyeliners produce a hard, defined line and work well for special effects. Select a natural looking eyeliner that matches the color of your lashes or is slightly darker. Blondes and redheads should select brown. For special effects, use colored eyeliners to coordinate with your eyeshadow.

Eyeshadows in pressed powder form are most effective; however, cream eyeshadows are useful for dry or wrinkled skin. Select neutral, unfrosted brown, gray, navy, beige, and soft pink for most situations in which you will want to accentuate your eyes, yet have them still appear natural. For accents and special effects include eyeshadows to enhance your eyecolor or coordinate with fashions you will be wearing.

For a natural look, select brown mascara if you are blonde or red-haired, dark brown, if you have dark blonde, light brown, or auburn haircolor. Use black mascara if you are brunette or black haired. Select a lash-thickening formula for soft, lush lashes. Navy, when layered with brown or black mascara, can give a soft look. Other colored mascaras should be reserved for special effects.

Application Tips
Eyebrow Color
- Use a slant-tipped stiff brush to apply powder eyebrow makeup.
- When using an eyebrow pencil, use short, hairlike strokes.
- For a natural look, consider using two shades of eyebrow pencil: a lighter one to fill in the shape of the brow and a darker one to define hairs.

- Always brush and groom the brows using an eyebrow brush or toothbrush after you apply eyebrow makeup.

Eyeliner
- Always sharpen eyeliner pencils prior to each use for best results.
- Rest the heel of your hand or your little finger on your cheek to anchor and steady your hand while you apply eyeliner. (Place a sponge puff between cheek and hand to prevent face makeup from smearing.)
- Line as close to lashlines as possible.
- Always smudge eyeliner on lower eyelid lashlines for a softer, more natural look. Smudge eyeliner using a cotton swab, a sponge-tipped applicator, the end of the handle of a makeup brush, or a clean eyeliner brush— all create different effects.
- Use eyelash matching pencil on the inside rim of the upper lid to make lashes look thicker.
- Use colored pencil to line the inside rim of the lower lid when fashion dictates. For natural, eye enhancing effects, use light blue to make eyewhites look whiter. Use white eyeliner pencil to enlarge the eyes.

Eyeshadow
- To make eyeshadow blend better and last longer, apply a thin film of eyeshadow base or foundation on lids and underbrow area before applying shadow.
- Always plan your eyeshadow application. Don't just layer on several colors. Instead, define your eyes consulting Figures 55–65 in this chapter.
- Apply powder eyeshadow using an eyeshadow fluff brush. Pick up a small quantity of shadow, and dab on the back of your hand to remove excess before applying to lids.
- If you apply too much powder eyeshadow, pick up excess by stroking lightly over the area with a clean cotton swab.
- After applying, add a thin film of translucent face powder using a clean eyeshadow fluff brush. This prevents shadow from settling in the crease.

Mascara
- Using an eyelash curler adds beauty to nearly all eyes because it gives an uplifting, eye-opening effect. Always curl lashes before mascara application.
- Avoid clumpy lashes that stick together by applying mascara sparingly. Apply several thin coats of mascara, allowing each to dry before applying the next.
- Position wand at the base of the lashes, and move it slowly outward toward tips of lashes, using a slight side-to-side motion. Use the tip of the mascara wand to coat lashes at outer corners of eyes, which are easily missed.
- Use a fine-toothed comb to separate lashes before mascara dries. Each individual lash should be visible. Clumpy or spikey lashes never look attractive.
- Clean up mascara smudges immediately by dabbing them with a cotton swab. For dry or stubborn smudges, moisten cotton swab with moisturizer or makeup remover.

LIPCOLOR
Functions

Lip makeup defines, corrects, or alters the natural shape of the lips and colors them to draw attention or to accent them according to current fashion. Lip makeup such as frosted or glossy lipsticks add texture to the lips to enhance their appearance.

Types Available   Lip makeup is available in four basic forms: lip pencils to outline the lips, lipsticks and lipcreams to color the lips, and lip glosses or tints to add shine or a touch of color to lips. Lip primers are also made to condition the lips and to set a base for long-lasting lipcolor.

How to Select   Select a colorless lip primer that is rich in emollients, and use it daily to prevent dryness and chapping.

Select an all-purpose lip-lining pencil in a shade to match the natural color of your lips (usually auburn or soft rose for white skins, light to medium brown for black and dark skins). Also select lip-lining pencils to match the lipstick colors you select. Don't use a lip liner that is darker or that clashes with your lipstick.

Select lipsticks and lipcreams in a variety of colors. Use warm lipcolors, such as apricot, orange, peach, tawny, coral, warm red, beige, and golden tints, to play up warm tones in skin or clothing. Use cool colors, such as reds, cool reds, blue-pinks, plums, icy-pinks, and violets, to harmonize with pinkish or cool-toned clothing. Mix foundation with any lipcolor to soften and subdue the color.

Select clear lip gloss to add shine to nude or colored lips. Also select a frosted silver or gold lip gloss to add frost to any lipcolor or to warm or cool any lipcolor. Unfrosted white lipstick is also good to have for lightening any lipcolor.

Application Tips
- Apply lip makeup to smooth, dry lips that have been covered with a light coat of foundation.
- Sharpen the lip-lining pencil, then press on the tip with your index finger to round it slightly. Pencil point should be neither sharp nor blunt.
- When lining, press lightly. Line from the outer corners of lips to center.
- After the line is drawn, stroke lightly over it with a cotton swab to soften it slightly.
- Apply lipcolor or lipcream using a lip brush. Use flat part of brush in back and forth motions. Use the tip of the brush to apply lipcolor on top of lip liner along edges of lips.
- Blot lips lightly with a tissue and repeat application of lipcolor. This will make lipcolor last longer.
- Confine lip gloss to center of lips to prevent it from bleeding or running outside of lip line.

CORRECTIVE MAKEUP TECHNIQUES   Before you apply any corrective makeup techniques, you must take a look at the characteristics of the skin and structure of your face. It is often difficult to see ourselves as others see us, but it is absolutely necessary for a model to see herself objectively. Flaws in a model's appearance can draw attention away from what she is modeling. On the positive side, a "flaw" can often be turned into a distinguishing asset.

Makeup can be used to correct, minimize, draw attention away from, or conceal detracting aspects of the skin and structure of the face. Using the proper cosmetic and technique will achieve the desired result.

Corrective Makeup Techniques for Skin Flaws   Even models occasionally have a blemish or two. If a blemish is very obvious and occurs prior to an assignment, consult with your agent immediately. If the blemish is barely noticeable or will not cause a problem in the assignment, this may not be necessary. For example, one or two pimples would not be a major problem for a full-length catalog shot, however, it would present a problem for a closeup beauty shot. The methods given in Table 1 are helpful in concealing skin imperfections.

65

TABLE 1   Corrective Makeup Techniques

Problem	How to Conceal
Pimples	Dab on concealer cake or stick using a clean lipbrush, the tip of a handle of a makeup brush, or a pointed sponge-tipped applicator. Using a sponge wedge or your fingers, press into skin, but don't rub or streak. Cover with a thin film of foundation. Repeat if necessary. For an inflamed pimple, dab green concealer on first and cover with a thin layer of powder. Next apply skin-toned concealer, then cover with foundation.
Ruddy areas, rashes, sunburn	Erase the redness by applying a green concealing cream or undertoner. Next press on a light application of skin tone-matching concealer. Apply foundation.
Ice pick scars (pit marks), pock marks, enlarged pores	Using skin tone-matching concealer cream or heavy stick or cake foundation, dab a small quantity on area. Then using the back and tip of your thumbnail, work foundation into the indentation until it disappears. If foundation doesn't fill in the indentation adequately, use flesh-colored mortician's wax (available at theatrical supply stores), specially made for this purpose.
Large pores	Large pores all over the face are best concealed by using astringent-based or specially designed pore-minimizing foundations. Follow with face powder applied using a contour brush.
Sallowy areas	Use a lavender concealing cream or undertoner over yellowish areas. Follow with concealer if area is very yellow, or foundation if only a minor color correction is necessary.
Grayish areas	Use a mauve-tinted concealing cream or undertoner over grayish areas. Follow with concealer if area is very gray or foundation if only a minor color correction is necessary.
Smile lines	Nasolabial folds or smile lines are the indentations extending from the nostril flares to the corners of the mouth. To soften their appearance, using a ¼-inch stiff brush, paint concealer into indentation. Start at the crevices around the nose and paint down. With a finger, press and blot to blend. Follow with foundation.
Dry, flaky skin	This is nearly impossible to cover effectively with foundation. In fact, foundation often accentuates the problem. The only thing that can be done to lessen the problem is to apply a thin film of oil and go without foundation or to press on only a slight amount of pressed powder or foundation.
Chapped lips	These are difficult to conceal and require time to heal. Preventive measures work best. Use a lipbalm daily. If necessary, try this emergency remedy: Massage lips lightly with toothpaste; the grittiness will exfoliate dead skin. Then apply pure glycerin to lips.
Tan lines	Using a ½-inch flat, nylon, angle-tipped brush, apply stick concealer or foundation that matches your tan only to untanned areas. Do not blend outside of the untanned area.
Indentations from elastic	Preventive measures work best. If you will be modeling lingerie or other brief garments, do not wear clothing with tight elastic bands, waistbands, and so on, to the assignment. If you must wear tight-fitting clothes, remove them upon arrival, and slip into a loose-fitting robe or smock. The redness and indentations caused by tight-fitting clothing can remain up to two hours after clothing has been removed. To expedite the process, massage the area to increase circulation, and, if necessary, cover redness with concealer or foundation.
Red eyes	If you are a contact lens wearer, remove contact lenses for at least a few hours prior to the shooting. After applying eyemakeup, use eyedrops that contain tetrahydrozoline (check the label) to constrict blood vessels.

Moles, age spots, or a large or singular freckle	Dot concealer over the spot. For staying power, use a cotton swab to place a generous dab of face powder on the spot. Let the powder remain for a minute or two then brush away excess powder.
Freckles	Use this method to cover freckles for situations in which you won't be meeting people face to face (runway or photography). Apply cream foundation in stick form, add a thin layer of powder followed by a wash of liquid makeup, which should be dabbed on. Complete the process by applying pressed powder using pressing motions. Another trick that works is to select a foundation that is between the color of your skin and the color of your freckles.
Facial hair	There is no effective way to conceal facial hair. The best way to eliminate it is to use facial hair removal cream or wax a few days before an assignment.
Five o'clock shadow	Male models may need to shave in the morning and afternoon to prevent five o'clock shadow. When it is not possible to shave, the male model may use a heavy coverage cream makeup in stick form to cover the beard.
Shaving rash	Preventive methods work best. Shave properly by using the following method. Fold a small towel or washcloth and saturate it with hot water. Wring out the towel until it is fairly dry. Place the towel over the face. Press onto the face for a few minutes to soften beard. Remove and apply a moisturizing lather. Rub the lather thoroughly onto the area to be shaved for a few minutes to condition skin. Use a safety razor to make downward strokes followed by upward strokes, according to the direction of the hair growth. When completed, rinse face with warm water. Pat dry. Apply a moisturizer or protective lotion. Avoid strong aftershave lotions and astringents.
Shaving nicks	Use a razor that is neither too sharp nor too dull to avoid shaving nicks. If the skin is nicked and bleeding, place a piece of sterile cotton dampened with cold water on the area to stop the bleeding. Pat the area with alcohol to prevent infection. Then use a styptic pencil to protect and conceal the nick.
Capillaries, veins	Use a fine-tipped eyeliner brush or a concealer pencil to paint over the capillary or vein. If there are several close together, use green concealer cream over the area followed by flesh-toned concealer.
Wrinkles	Use a fine-tipped eyeliner brush or a concealer pencil in a flesh tone or white and paint right into the crevice. Don't blend. Make certain the line is very fine and only confined to the indentation. Follow with skin-toned foundation.
Undereye bags or puffiness	Use a small brush to apply light-colored concealer only to the area that is indented (usually below the puffiness). Next, use a brush to apply pink or flesh-toned concealer a half shade darker than your foundation to the puffy part to make it recede. Follow with a thin coat of your regular foundation.
Undereye circles and darkness	Use a slant-tip brush to paint the concealer into the indentation. Concentrate on the area below the lower lid, begin at the inner corner of the eye and extend the concealer to the area in line with the iris. (Carrying foundation too far out will make the eyes look as if they have bright rings around them). When selecting the best concealer, consider that a light pink one works best if the area under the eyes is grayish; light yellow if the area is brownish or bluish; light green if the area is reddish. When in doubt, use flesh-toned concealer that is a half shade lighter than your foundation.
Open sores	Open sores should be left alone and makeup-free. If it is absolutely necessary, first apply an antiseptic, and cover with a liquid bandage product. When dry, dab flesh-toned concealer lightly to cover. Follow with foundation, then dab powder on lightly.

Makeup Techniques for Altering Facial Features and Structure

Contouring and highlighting techniques are used to correct, improve, change, or enhance the structure and features of the face. The principle of contouring and highlighting is that contouring make-ups (makeup that is darker or duller than the skintone) will make areas in which it is applied recede. Highlighting makeups (makeup that is lighter, brighter, or shinier than the skin) will make areas in which it is applied come forward. Figures 6 to 37 show the effects created when contour or highlight makeup is used in the designated areas.

Forehead

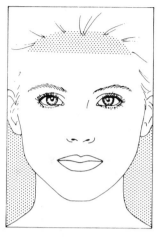

Figure 6.
Contour: Shortens a high forehead; Evens an uneven hairline when contour matches haircolor.

Highlight: Lengthens a short forehead.

Figure 7.
Contour: Rounds a square forehead.

Highlight: Gives width to a round forehead.

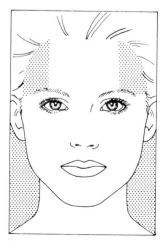

Figure 8.
Contour: Narrows a wide forehead; Elongates a short forehead.

Highlight: Widens a narrow forehead.

**Forehead
Continued**

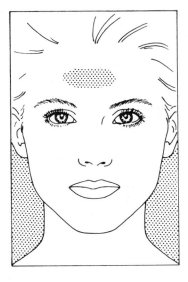

Figure 9.
*Contour: Flattens a protruding
forehead.*

*Highlight: Brings forward an
indented forehead; Enlarges
forehead.*

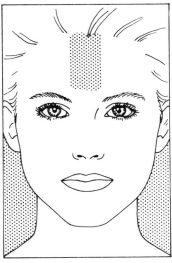

Figure 10.
*Contour: Narrows a wide
forehead.*

*Highlight: Lengthens a short
forehead.*

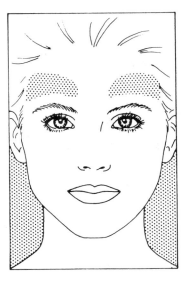

Figure 11.
*Contour: Softens a protruding
brow; Narrows a wide forehead.*

*Highlight: Broadens a too-narrow
forehead.*

Temples

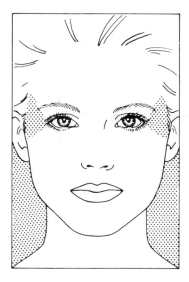

Figure 12.
Contour: Narrows wide set eyes; Adds shape to face; Gives an uplifting look to eyes; Slims a wide or round face.

Highlight: Widens narrow set eyes; Increases width of face at eyeline.

Face

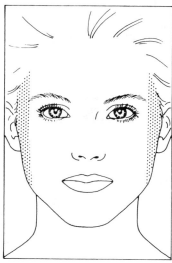

Figure 13.
Contour: Slims a wide face.

Highlight: Widens a narrow face.

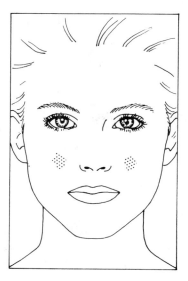

Figure 14.
Contour: Pushes back fleshy area around nose but may make nose seem more prominent.

Highlight: Gives a healthy, youthful, rounded appearance to cheeks. Highlights apples of cheeks.

Face Continued

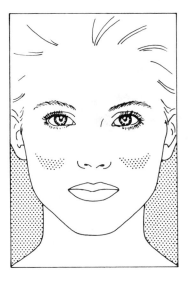

Figure 15.
Contour: Heightens cheekbones;
Slims a full face or cheeks.

Highlight: Fills out a thin face.

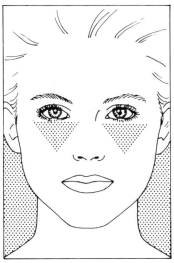

Figure 16.
Contour: Not used in this area.

Highlight: Brings cheekbones up
and forward; Emphasizes eyes;
Diminishes shadows under eyes.

Nose

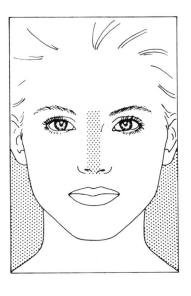

Figure 17.
Contour: Pushes back a protruding nose.

Highlight: Brings a flat nose forward; Slims a wide nose; Elongates a short nose.

71

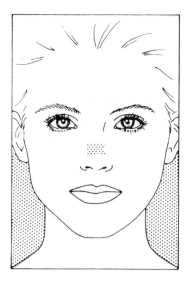

*Figure 18.
Contour: Shortens a long nose.*

Highlight: Gives the illusion of a turned-up nose.

*Figure 19.
Contour: Diminishes fullness around nose and mouth.*

Highlight: Brings out depressions around nose and in laugh lines.

*Figure 20.
Contour: Shortens a long nose; Diminishes tip on a turned-down nose.*

Highlight: Lengthens nose; Turns up tip of nose when blended upward.

*Nose
Continued*

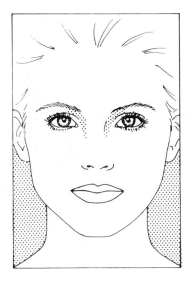

*Figure 21.
Contour: Narrows a wide nose bridge; Defines inner eye area at bridge of nose; Balances width of bridge with end of nose.*

Highlight: Widens a narrow nose bridge; Makes narrow set eyes seem wide set.

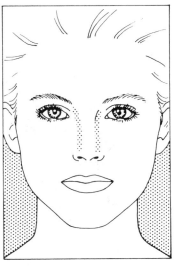

*Figure 22.
Contour: Narrows or defines sides of nose; Elongates nose; Diminishes bumps on nose when contour is applied to protrusions.*

Highlight: Widens a narrow nose; Shortens a long nose; Diminishes bumps on nose when highlighter is applied to indentations.

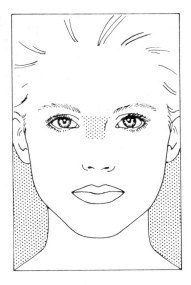

*Figure 23.
Contour: Gives shape to a flat nose; Raises or lowers a low or high nose bridge; Shortens a long nose.*

Highlight: Widens a small or narrow nose bridge; Brings forward a deep indentation at nose bridge; Raises a low nose bridge.

*Nose
Continued*

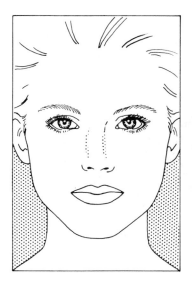

Figure 24.
Contour: Eliminates a crooked
nose. Contour side of nose that
curves outward.

Highlight: Eliminates a crooked
nose. Highlight side of nose that
indents.

Jaw/Chin

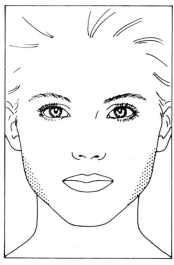

Figure 25.
Contour: Slims a wide jaw;
Rounds a square jaw.

Highlight: Widens jaw; Squares
a round or sloping jaw; Emphasizes cheekhollows.

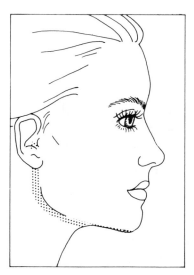

Figure 26.
Contour: Defines jaw, separating
face from neck. Shade along
jawline from earlobe to earlobe.

Highlight: Softens an angular or
bony jaw.

*Jaw/Chin
Continued*

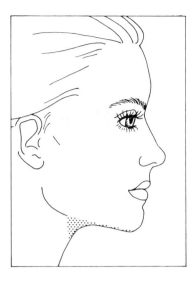

Figure 27.
Contour: Diminishes a fleshy or double chin.

Highlight: Is not used in this area.

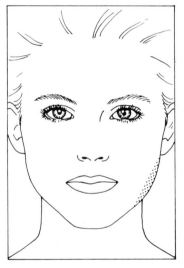

Figure 28.
Contour: Balances a lopsided jaw or asymmetrical face or lips. Apply contour to excessive side.

Highlight: Balances a lopsided jaw or asymmetrical face or lips. Apply highlight to deficient side.

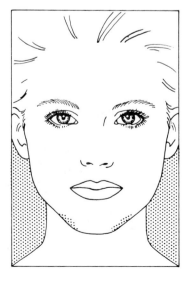

Figure 29.
Contour: Diminishes a large chin; Adds shape to a full chin.

Highlight: Lengthens a short chin.

Jaw/Chin
Continued

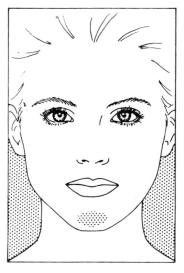

Figure 30.
Contour: Pushes back a protruding chin.

Highlight: Diminishes a cleft chin when applied just in indentation.

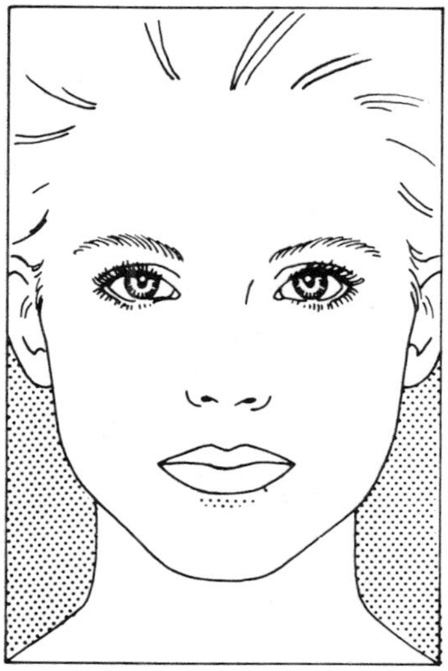

Figure 31.
Contour: Creates a slight indentation under lip to give chin more shape and shorten.

Highlight: Brings out a deep indentation under lower lip.

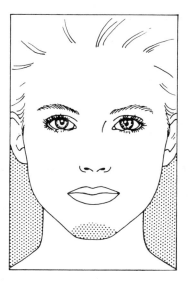

Figure 32.
Contour: Rounds a pointed chin; Shortens a long chin.

Highlight: Brings forward a receding chin.

Eyes

Figure 33.
Contour: Diminishes prominent eyelids.

Highlight: Draws attention to irises; Brings deep-set eyes forward; Enlarges upper lid.

Figure 34.
Contour: Diminishes a puffy underbrow.

Highlight: Lifts arch of eyebrow; Gives a dramatic look to brows.

Figure 35.
Contour: Reshapes brow; Brings brow closer to eye; Defines bridge of nose.

Highlight: Lifts brow, opens eye; Makes eyes seem wider set.

*Figure 36.
Contour: Diminishes under eye
bags and puffiness.*

*Highlight: Diminishes dark cir-
cles or indentations under eyes.*

*Figure 37.
Contour: Adds shape to outer
eye area and temples; Uplifts
eyes and face.*

*Highlight: Expands the temple
area; Opens up the face, yielding a brighter look.*

EXPERIMENTING WITH MAKEUP TO CREATE DIFFERENT LOOKS

In modeling, makeup is not only used to correct, enhance, or improve the appearance of the skin and facial features, it is used to change the model's face so that she can portray different looks. In one situation, a client may want the model to have a young, fresh look, whereas in another situation the client's product may dictate a more sophisticated, fashion-oriented look. The information that follows will help you to use makeup creatively to achieve different looks.

Eyebrows

Eyebrows not only show expression and frame the eyes, they are also important indicators of fashion trends. In the early 1970s, models tweezed their brows into a thin line, whereas in the 1980s fashion dictated thick, barely tweezed brows. A model must be aware of current fashion and adapt her looks accordingly, while still enhancing her own features.

Although there is no one ideal brow shape, there are a few characteristics of brows that tend to enhance the eyes and face. Your bone structure and the amount and pattern of your eyebrow hair growth will determine how you can shape your brows. It is usually best not to deviate too far from nature. Too much tweezing, coloring, or drawing on the brows looks artificial and can be distracting. To understand how the shape of your brows might be improved, consider the checkpoints outlined in "Analyzing Your Facial Structure and Features," then refer to the methods shown in Figures 38 to 45.

Fig. 38

Figure 38. For an even look. If your brows are sparse in spots, all you may need is to use a small amount of eyebrow pencil. Sharpen your eyebrow pencil to a point, and draw short hair-like strokes following the direction the hair grows. Blend using an eyebrow brush.

Fig. 39

Figure 39. To create neat-looking brows. If you have a few stray hairs between the brows or in the area under the brows, use tweezers to remove them. Waxing, shaving, or depilatory creams are not exact enough. For a natural look don't overtweeze brows so that they look "too perfect." Brush brows into desired line using an eyebrow brush or small toothbrush.

Fig. 40

Figure 40. To create tamed brows. If your brows are too thick and bushy, use tweezers to remove hairs along the lower edge of brows. To thin brows without altering their shape, brush all hairs straight up, then clip ends of hairs. Brush brows back into shape.

Fig. 41

Figure 41. To create full brows. If your brows are too thin, use powder eyebrow makeup instead of eyebrow pencil. Match it to the color of your brows, and apply it using a stiff angle-tipped brush. Follow the natural line of your brow, blending color toward the upper edge of your brow. Use a brow brush to groom brows and blend color upward.

Fig. 42

Figure 42. To create uplifted brows. Tweeze a few hairs at the ends of the brows. Using powder eyebrow makeup and a small angle-tipped brush, add color at the point where the brow should arch. Then draw ends of brow above the natural browline. This works great for brows that droop.

Fig. 43

Figure 43. To create arched brows. Straight brows can give a dramatic look; however, if your brows have no arch, or if you want a more exaggerated arch, add eyebrow pencil or powder to lower edge of brows at the inner corners of your eyes. Add pencil at the point where the brow should arch.

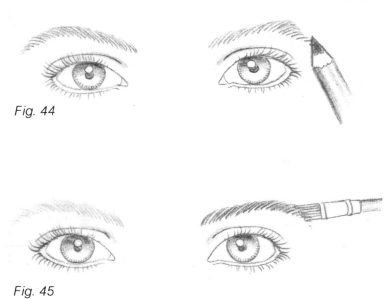

Fig. 44

Fig. 45

Figure 44. To create perfectly matched brows. No one has left and right eyebrows that are identical. If yours are so different that they detract from your appearance, determine which brow is more attractive, then tweeze and draw the other brow to match it.

Figure 45. To create brows that enhance your coloring. Check the color of your brows. In general, brows should match the haircolor exactly or be a shade darker. For a softer look, bleach your brows (use facial bleach) to make them a shade or two lighter than your haircolor. For a more dramatic look, use eyebrow makeup or comb through the hairs with mascara to make your brows a shade or two darker than your haircolor.

Eyeliner The shape of your eyes and current fashion will determine how you'll apply eyeliner. Illustrated in Figures 46 to 54 are some of the most common ways that models use eyeliner. Experiment with each method to see which ones enhance your eyes most effectively.

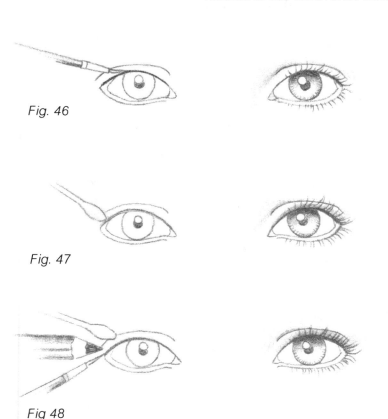

Fig. 46

Fig. 47

Fig 48

Figure 46. Defined line. A defined line will make the lashes look thick and draw attention to the eyes. For lids that are barely visible or for very deep set eyes, the line should be very thin. For more prominent lids, the line can be thicker. Cake eyeliner used with water and applied with a fine brush will create a defined line.

Figure 47. Smudged line. A smudged line defines the eye yet gives a soft look. To achieve this, use eyeliner pencil, and line close to the lashlines. Smudge the line using a cotton swab, a fine eyeliner brush, the end of a handle of a makeup brush, or a sponge-tipped applicator.

Figure 48. Defined and smudged. A line that is defined and smudged gives definition and softness. Use cake eyeliner with water and a fine eyeliner brush to create a very thin line close to the lashes. Next, use a matching eyeliner pencil to line over this line. Smudge as above.

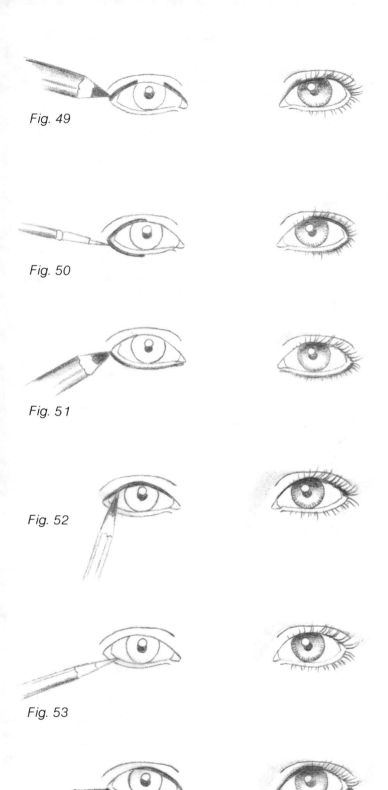

Fig. 49

Fig. 50

Fig. 51

Fig. 52

Fig. 53

Fig. 54

Figure 49. Omitting iris. With pencil liner, line the upper-lid lashline from the outer corner of the eye to the center. Skip to the other corner and line the inner stopping short of center. The line should just barely join and be thinnest above the iris. This line defines the eye, yet opens it.

Figure 50. Outer corners. Starting at the center of the lid, line the lashline of the upper lid around the outer corner of the eye and ending on the lower lid at the same point. This will make narrow set eyes seem wider apart.

Figure 51. Lower lids only. Line with pencil from inner corner of eye to outer corner along the lower eyelid lashline. Smudge the line. This always looks well on eyes with a barely visible upper lid or deep set eyes.

Figure 52. Inside rim of upper lid. Using an eyelash-matching pencil with a long point, line the inside rim of the upper lid. Look down into a mirror and tilt chin down to facilitate lining. Lining the inside the rim makes the lashes look thicker. Use this technique.

Figure 53. Inside rim of lower lid. Use an eyeliner pencil with a long point to line the inside rim of the lower lid. Use light blue to make the whites of your eyes look whiter. Use white or ivory to make your eyes look larger. Use a colored pencil that enhances your eyecolor when fashion dictates. Black can be used to make the eyes look smaller.

Figure 54. Uplifting line. Using eyeliner pencil, line the inner corner of the upper lid toward the center along lashline. Skip to the outer corner of the eye, and line the lower-lid lashline toward the center of the eye. This is attractive on all eyes and works especially well for drooping and mature eyes. When exaggerated, it yields a glamourous look.

Eyeshadow   Models know that using small amounts of makeup in just the right places can really add impact. They use eyeshadow strategically to contour, color, define, and enlarge their eyes. Experiment with all of the eyeshadow placement techniques shown in Figures 55 to 65. Try different colors with each technique. Then determine which ones create the looks you like.

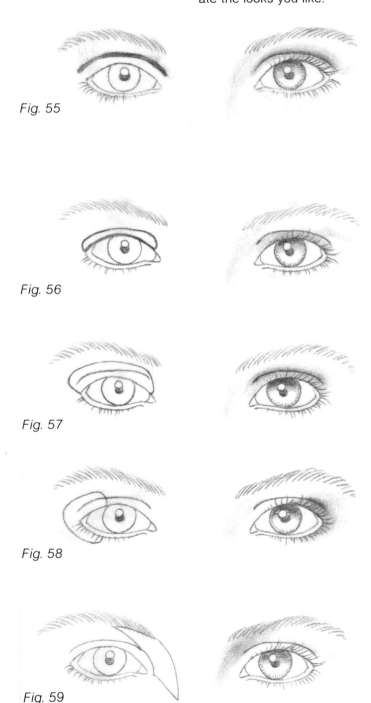

Fig. 55

Fig. 56

Fig. 57

Fig. 58

Fig. 59

Figure 55. Crease contour. Using a sponge-tipped applicator, cotton swab, or eyeshadow fluff brush, follow the contour of the eyesocket crease from corner to corner to define the shape of the eye. Blend well. Color should be darkest at the deepest point of the crease. This technique works well for most eyes and situations.

Figure 56. Upper lid. Use an accent color on the upper lid to combine with the fashion you are wearing. Or, use a darker color here to subdue prominent lids. Use a lighter color to enlarge barely visible lids or to bring out deepset eyes. Use a dot of your lipcolor or white, silver, or gold eyeshadow in the center of the upper lid to highlight the irises.

Figure 57. Eyelid and crease. Color the eyelid and crease using a medium-toned or dark color to enlarge the eyes.

Figure 58. Outer corners. Color the outer third of your eye (upper lid and crease and lower lid) using a dark or neutral color. This is flattering to normal and narrow set eyes. Use powder shadow and a fluff brush or use a soft eyepencil. When using pencil, dot several smudges on the desired area, then use a sponge-tipped applicator to blend.

Figure 59. Defined bridge. Using contour brown or a soft, subdued shade, color along the bridge of the nose upward toward brows to make eyes seem closer set. This will also slim a too-wide nose bridge. When light-colored shadow is used in the same area, it will make narrow set eyes or a too-narrow nose bridge seem wider.

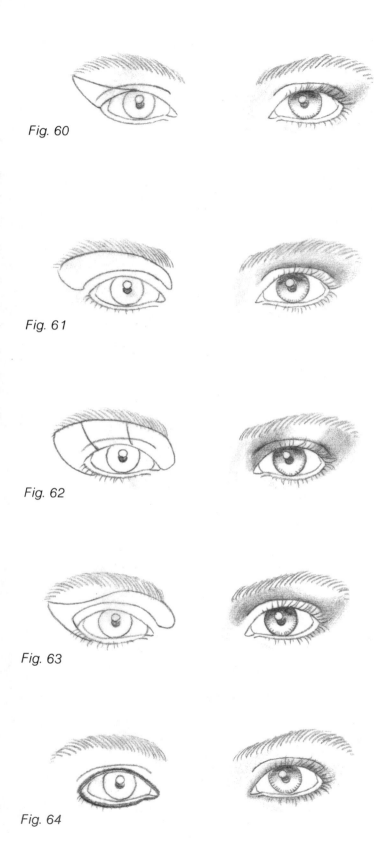

Fig. 60

Fig. 61

Fig. 62

Fig. 63

Fig. 64

Figure 60. Winged eye. The winged eye goes in and out of fashion. Starting at the crease or at the upper-lid lashline, shade diagonally toward temples. Winged eyes are flattering to normal eyes or those that slant slightly upward. This type of placement will also help to elongate or slim a wide or round face. In general, it is best reserved for a dramatic, high-fashion look.

Figure 61. Shaded underbrow. This is attractive on many eyes. It works well for Oriental eyes and for those that have very little visible upper lid. It gives a soft look for any eye. Use powder eyeshadow in soft subdued colors such as grays, browns, and beiges.

Figure 62. Rainbow eye. Use one, two, or three colors to give dimension to eyes. Oriental eyes often benefit from this placement. Shade the inner third of the eye with one color, the middle third with a second color, and the outer third with a third color. Experiment with different colors and lighter and darker tones. This yields a dramatic look and is effective on runway or when you will be seen from a distance.

Figure 63. Contoured eye. This placement is flattering to most eyes and also works well for runway modeling when you will be seen from afar. Use powder eyeshadow for best results. For a subdued look, use a touch of your cheekcolor under the arch of brow. For a dramatic look use a frosted, metallic shadow under the arch of your brow.

Figure 64. Ringed eye. Ringed eyes look well in a variety of situations. For a soft romantic look, use pink or soft blue to encircle the eye. For normal daytime wear, use a brownish contouring color. For a high-fashion, theatrical effect, ring the eyes with black, deep brown, navy, or plum. This works well for runway.

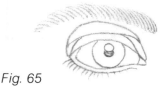

Fig. 65

Figure 65. Halo effect. The halo effect has a soft, rounding effect on most eyes. Use medium-toned, subdued colors and concentrate shadow greatest over the iris..

Mascara   Full, fluffy eyelashes are an asset to any model. To make yours their thickest and most eye enhancing, try some of the methods shown in Figures 66 to 69.

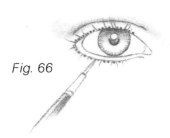

Fig. 66

Figure 66. To create an even row of lashes. Use a fine eyeliner brush dipped in clean water to moisten cake eyeliner, and draw dots where lashes are missing on lashline. Use soft mascara colors, such as gray, brown, and navy, instead of black. When lashes are sparse, a thin line of eyeliner will look better.

For the most natural look, apply individual lash clusters where your own lashes are missing. To apply, pick up lash cluster with tweezers and dip the root in lash glue. Apply to lashline. Avoid blinking for several seconds.

For a more pronounced look using artificial lashes, select strip-type lashes (the type with an invisible strip) and cut the strip into thirds. Apply glue to the strip and adhere to the upper lashline at the outer corner of your eye. Repeat on other eye.

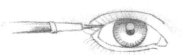

Fig. 67

Figure 67. To create rich, dark lashes. Use brown liquid eyeliner and a fine eyeliner brush to color lash roots. When applying mascara, apply black on roots, brown on the tips. Work mascara wand into roots.

Fig. 68

Figure 68. To create a wide-eyed look. Apply mascara heavier to lashes at outer corners of eyes. This technique enhances narrowly spaced eyes.

Figure 69. To create thick luscious lashes. Apply dark brown or black eyeliner pencil to inside rim of upper lid. Next apply eyeliner to lashline of upper lid, and work into roots. Use a lash-thickening mascara in the same color as your eyeliner and apply to lash roots.

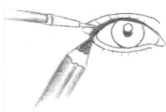

Fig. 69

Cheekcolor   The amount, color, and placement of cheekcolor varies with fashion. Pay attention to current fashion, and experiment with the techniques shown in Figures 70 to 75 to change, improve, or enhance your appearance.

Fig. 70

Fig. 71

Fig. 72

Fig. 73

Figure 70. Ideal cheekbones. To enhance ideal cheekbones, use the normal application of blusher. Apply cheekcolor on the fullest part of the cheekbone starting at the hairline and blending toward the center of the face. Cheekcolor application should end in line with the iris and the end of the nose..

Figure 71. Model cheekbones. For the look of prominent, high cheekbones, use highlighter, contour, and cheekcolor. Accentuate tops of cheekbones by using a cream or liquid highlighter to draw a triangle with these three points: inner eye corner, base of nose, and outer eye corner. Use a flat nylon brush or fingertips to fill in this area with highlighter. Next, apply contour to cheekhollows. Finish by applying cheekcolor between highlighter and contour, blending it upward and downward so there is no obvious distinction between highlighter, contour, and cheekcolor.

Figure 72. To create a sophisticated look. Slim cheeks by applying blusher in an upward slanting line. Use contour in cheekhollows. This application style will also elongate a short face and slim a round one. It works well for too round or full cheeks..

Figure 73. To create larger cheekbones. Apply cheekcolor in a horizontal line along cheekbones.This technique works well for shortening a too-long face..

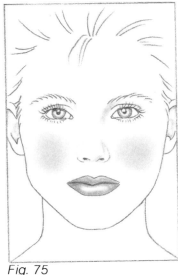

Figure 74. Suntanned look. Using a gold, tawny, or copper cheekcolor, apply cheekcolor in a line from one side of the face to the other, high on the cheekbones and across the nose. Apply a trace to top of forehead and tip of chin..

Figure 75. Youthful, natural look. For a young look, use a hint of pinkish cheekcolor on apples of cheeks. Smile and apply in soft circles on fullest part of cheeks.

Fig. 74   Fig. 75

Lipcolor   Even models don't all have perfectly shaped lips. Use the enhancement techniques to make your lips look their best. Shown in Figures 76 to 82.

Figure 76. Full-lipped look. Sketch lightly with a lip pencil on or slightly outside of the lipline. (Use a lipliner that's a shade darker than your lipstick.) Apply lipstick on top of liner, then fill in with desired lipcolor. Favor light and frosted lipcolors..

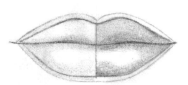

Figure 77. Slim-lipped look. Use a lipliner that matches your lipstick. Line just inside edges of the natural lipline. Powder down outer ridge and apply lipcolor. Apply a darker color to center of lower and upper lip. Favor medium-toned colors—avoid very pale, dark, or frosted lipcolors.

Figure 78. Smiling lips. Apply a little highlighting concealer underneath the lower lip at each corner. Bring the corners of the top lip up with pencil. Also, drawing the lower lip so that the fullest point is in line with the tip of the nose will give the impression of an upturned mouth.

Figure 79. To create narrower lips. Open mouth wide and apply concealer in corners of lips to cancel natural lip shape. Draw in new lip shape, lining inside of natural corners of lips. Fill in with lipcolor.

Figure 80. To create a larger mouth. Open mouth wide and apply lip liner along corners of mouth. Fill in lips with lipcolor.

Figure 81. To create smooth, satiny lips. To fill in tiny cracks on lips, smooth on petroleum jelly or pure glycerin. Conceal tiny lines outside the lip line and keep color from bleeding by applying powder to the lips and slightly beyond. Always use a lip-lining pencil. Avoid frosted and very soft glossy lipcolors. Stretch lips when applying lipcolor.

Figure 82. To create evenly proportioned lips. If your lips are unevenly proportioned, you will need to balance the shape by covering them with foundation or concealer. Draw in the new lip shape, making the thinner lip slightly fuller and the thicker lip slightly thinner. Apply a lighter lipcolor on the thinner lip, a darker lipcolor on the thicker lip.

MAKEUP FOR VARIOUS MEDIA

A model must know to apply makeup for five basic types of modeling situations:

1. Face-to-face meetings.
2. Still photography.
3. Electronic media.
4. Fashion show or stage.
5. Promotional modeling assignments.

Face-to-Face Meetings

A model almost always does her own makeup when interviewing for modeling assignments. The model's objectives in these situations should be to allow the client to see that she has all the necessary requisites for modeling (good complexion, bright eyes, etc.) as well as the ability to apply her own makeup.

In most cases, it is best to strive for the natural look. Covering trouble spots with concealer; applying a light coat of foundation that lets the skin show through; enhancing the contours of the eyes, cheeks, and lips; and grooming the lashes and brows are all that are necessary. Using natural earth tones on the eyes, such as browns and subdued grays, is best. Using a touch of subtle pink, peach, or tawny blush on the cheeks will give healthy color. Using sheer lip tints and glosses to color and condition the lips is also important. Extreme makeup colors that are the latest fashion often look too harsh for streetwear. However, using a touch of such colors as an accent can work well.

Makeup for Still Photography

We often see ourselves through our emotions and in movement. The camera is not emotional and captures only one instant in time with no regard to what motion preceded or followed that moment. Photography is a mechanical process and therefore it catches all the flaws. Makeup for photography must be very carefully applied. The slightest imperfection or poorly applied color is defined or exaggerated in a photograph. In addition, the camera lens tends to coarsen everything it sees, such as the skin and features. It also adds weight.

A model or makeup artist must be able to understand how makeup can be used to enhance the appearance of the skin and features in various photographic situations. Lighting controls makeup to a high degree. A good makeup application can be ruined or its effectiveness lessened by unattractive lighting. A good model knows how to adjust his or her makeup and movements to make the light flatter himself or herself and the item being shown. The directions the light is coming from, the quality of the light (hard and direct or diffused and nondirectional), the color of the light (warm or cool), and the amount of contrast between the highlights and the shadows are factors that must be taken into consideration when makeup is applied for photography. To gain a fuller understanding of how lighting affects the appearance of makeup, study Figure 2 in Chapter 10.

The following are objectives to achieve when applying makeup for still photography situations.

Good Skin Coloration

In most makeup for photography you will want to achieve even coloration for the skin. Discolorations tend to be exaggerated in a photograph, whether it is color or black and white. Check the skin for areas that appear more red, brown, yellow, white, or gray than other areas. Consult Table 1 in this chapter to determine how to subdue such colorations. But remember, in general a model should achieve the desired look without a lot of makeup. A masklike or artificial look is usually reserved for special effects. Most models need concealer to cover imperfections as well as a liquid foundation to provide even coloration. Panstick and pancake makeups are also very effective for photographic situations whether it is videotape, film, or still photography. Pancake and panstick makeups do not look as heavy in photographs as they do in normal wear and are used because they provide adequate coverage for any color irregularities found in the complexion. They also tend to have greater staying power than sheerer foundations.

A model must also be concerned that the color of her complexion is consistent throughout her body. The neck and hands should match the face and not appear darker or lighter in comparison. Unless after a special effect, the model should try to match concealer, foundation, and face powder makeups to her natural complexion coloring.

Attractive Texture

Shiny areas, flaky skin, enlarged pores, hairy areas, and other varying textures can be very distracting in a photo. Combating shine from oil, sweat, or the effects of different lighting is one of the most common problems in photography. Powder is a necessary cosmetic for a photographic model because it controls shininess, which is usually unattractive in a photograph. Certain types of lighting emphasize shininess or may actually bring oils and sweat to the surface of the skin. Powder also works well to blend and refine makeup application. Check your face between appearances before the camera to be sure you have applied enough powder. However, don't overdo it because too much powder will look chalky and unnatural.

Be very critical about hair on the face. Remove or bleach superfluous hair on chin, above upper lip, between brows, on sides of face, or straggly hair around hairline. Hairy areas show up as shadows or dark, dirty patches in a photograph. Excessive light hair reflects light.

Thorough Blending   When possible, check your makeup in the lighting in which you will be photographed. Bring a hand mirror to the set to preview makeup under the lights, taking care that you aren't shielding your face from the lights. If Polaroids are taken, study them to see how your makeup looks. Take into consideration that Polaroids tend to be softer than regular film. When working in video, look at the control monitor to see how the picture going out on the air looks. If none of these are possible, check your makeup in daylight facing into the direction from which the light is coming. A portable makeup mirror with different lighting settings is a good investment.

For subtle blending, select makeup colors that do not deviate too much from the colors found naturally in your complexion. For example, when applied to a fair complexion, a deep plum cheekcolor requires more careful blending than does a soft, light pink cheekcolor. A foundation that is not perfectly matched to the color of your complexion will reveal improper blending more readily than one that is perfectly matched.

To ensure subtle blending of any makeup, employ these makeup artists' techniques:

- Apply makeup to skin that is neither wet, dried out, nor oily.
- Use professional tools. Soft, high-quality brushes yield more subtle blending than stiff, poor-quality brushes.
- Apply makeup sparingly. When applying powder eyeshadows or cheekcolors, pick up a quantity from the container with your makeup brush, then dab it on the back of your hand to remove excess color and to determine how much color will be going onto the skin.
- Apply several thin layers of makeup until you achieve the color or coverage desired.
- After applying makeup, go over your application with a clean brush or sponge to pick up excess and further blend color.
- Apply face powder over applied colors to further soften and blend them.

Attention to Detail   Check that you have employed faultless grooming. Superfluous hair should be removed, and eyebrows should be groomed and brushed to coordinate with current fashion or the look you are trying to achieve. Eyelashes should be defined so that they show up well. Pay strict attention that eyelashes do not appear clumpy or that they don't stick together or have globs of mascara. Eyeliners and lip liners must be drawn with a steady hand because irregularites will be exaggerated in a photograph. The smallest imperfection can become an exaggerated flaw under a sharp camera lens.

Contouring   Defining eye and lip shapes and bone structure is often necessary because of the lack of depth in a photograph. Subtle contouring is always preferable to heavy-handed, obvious contouring. Contouring and highlighting can be used much more effectively for photography than for normal wear. A lot of effects can be accomplished with photo makeup that would look unnatural or contrived in life.

Contour and highlight makeup must be applied with a sculptor's eye in order to be believeable. Contour is applied darkest in areas that are to recede the most. Highlight is applied lightest in areas that are to come the furthest forward.

Maintenance and Repairs   Because of its nature, makeup does not stay exactly as it has been applied. It is important during an assignment to constantly check for aspects that may need repair, because such imperfections will be exaggerated in a photograph. It is also important to not touch the skin after makeup has been applied. Listed below are the most common trouble spots to check after makeup has been properly applied.

- Shiny nose, forehead, chin (oil or perspiration).
- Fading lipstick, lipstick on teeth, lipstick bleeding outside of lip line.
- Mascara smudges and globs, lashes sticking together, and flakes of mascara under eyes or on cheeks.
- Eyeshadow settling into eyesocket crease.
- Eyemakeup, especially liners, collecting in tearducts.
- Foundation and/or powder collecting in smile lines or lines around the eye area.

Be Prepared

Always find out in advance whether there will be a makeup artist. If you are to do your own makeup, find out what type of look you are to have. You will be expected to arrive with makeup in place and only finishing touches to be added. It is often a good idea to arrive with concealer, foundation, and a light application of makeup on the eyes, cheeks, and lips. This way you will have the flexibility of adding more or changing colors as the situation demands.

Bring all the makeup along that you have used and, when necessary, add makeup. It is always easier to add makeup than to reduce it. When a makeup artist is employed, you are expected to arrive with clean, moisturized skin.

Makeup for Black and White Photography

One basic difference between makeup for color photography and makeup for black and white is that in black and white, contrasts are what count, not colors. It is the lightness or darkness of a color that will affect how it appears in black and white film. Features can be emphasized by using dark or light colors to create contrast.

Understanding how various colors appear in black and white is important to the success of makeup applied for black and white photography. The most important characteristic of color in reference to black and white photography is value. Value refers to the lightness or darkness of a color. For example, the color red can have black added to it, which will make it appear deep red, or white added to it, which will make it appear light red or pink. The deeper in value a color is, the darker and closer to black it will appear on black and white film. The lighter in value a color is, the lighter or closer to white it will appear in black and white film. Shades of a color falling between these two extremes will appear in numerous gradations of gray. For example, a true red appears as a medium gray.

TABLE 2   Makeup for Black and White Photography

Foundation	Cheekcolor/Lipcolor	Eyeshadow Color	How It Appears on Black and White Film
Not applicable	Deepest red (e.g., dark burgundy)	Black or charcoal brown	Black
Deep brown	Dark red (maroon)	Dark brown	Dark gray
Medium brown	True red	Medium brown	Medium gray
Tan	Medium pink	Tawny or tan	Soft medium gray
True beige	Light pink	Beige	Light gray
Creamy beige	Ice pink	Rich ivory	Grayish white
Alabaster	White	White	White

Lighting, the type of film used, and other technical aspects of photography also influence the way colors appear in black and white, so communication with the photographer is important.

Generally, makeup in black and white is more permissive than in color. Makeup can be quite heavy yet still not appear unnatural. For most black and white photo assignments, extremes should be avoided. Extreme lipcolors, such as deep reds, burgundies, and dark plums, may appear black. Very light lipcolors such as white, light beige, or light pink may make lips blend into skin tone.

When in doubt about which colors to choose, stick to even, clean makeup that is well blended. Makeup colors that look natural to the eye usually look equally well in black and white or color photography. For example, use makeup colors that simulate, yet heighten, your natural coloring. Use foundation that is perfectly matched to your skintone. Use lipcolor close to the natural color of your lips and cheek color that simulates the natural blush of your cheeks. To create natural-looking colors for the lips and cheeks, mix a bright coral or rose-toned lipcolor or cheekcolor with brown contour cream or white highlight cream. Adjust the proportions of brown or white to best work with the darkness or lightness of your skintone. Use mascara, eyebrow makeup, and eyeliner colors that match or are slightly darker than your eyebrows and lashes.

Use basic eyeshadow, lip, and cheekcolors for black and white photography because very bright or unusual colors are often hard to predict. Matte navy, brown, charcoal, beige, and other neutrals work well for eyes. True red, coral, medium pink, and soft pink work well for lips. Peach, tawny, rose, and soft pink are good cheekcolors to select. A makeup kit containing such neutrals will be useful for applying makeup for black and white photography.

Highlighting and contouring makeups in black and white can be up to three shades lighter than skintone for highlighting or three shades darker for contouring. Careful blending of contour makeups is important to give the effect of dimension. Concentration of contour should be greatest where the indentation is deepest, and gradually diminish outward from this point. The opposite applies to highlighting makeup. To create most realistic contour and highlight effects, there must be a subtle progression from dark to light.

For black and white photos, select foundation that is matched to the overall lightness or darkness of your complexion. Foundation that is slightly lighter, rather than darker, than your complexion is often most flattering. Also, avoid foundations that have a strong reddish or pinkish cast, as the red or pink colors in them can appear gray in black and white. Whatever foundation you select, check that the neck, hands, and body do not appear darker in contrast to the face.

Matte (nonshiny) makeups tend to photograph better than shiny or frosted makeups in black and white, although there may be exceptions. Matte foundations are most attractive because greasy or frosted ones will cause unattractive shine in a photograph. Matte eyeshadows create a soft, believeable look and photograph better than highly frosted or iridescent shadows. Highly pearlized cheekcolors or face powders may make the skin appear greasy.

Use makeup to draw interest to your features. For example, if you use foundation and eye-, lip-, and cheekcolors that are close in value, your face will appear dull and uninteresting. Instead, play up one or two features. For example, use a darker makeup on the lips.

Use texture to add interest. Rather than having all the makeup on your face appear velvety, add a touch of gloss or pearlized lipcolor to the center of your lips to draw attention.

In black and white, the lines and shapes of the features or makeup placements assume much more importance than they normally do in a color image. Black and white tends to be more graphic than color. Color photography seems to be more realistic and displays dimension better than black and white, so compensating for this is important. For example, using a lip liner to define the lips looks better and will make the lips appear more realistic than an indistinct line.

Makeup for Color Photography

The basic difference between making up for color as opposed to black and white photography is that in color strict attention must be paid to the colors used and how they enhance the models appearance and the appearance of the item she is modeling.

One of the most important factors to achieving good makeup for color photography is in selecting the foundation color. Creating attractive fleshtones is very important. A model with unattractive color casts in her skin, such as sallowness, ruddiness, or grayishness, must use color correctors and foundations to cover this. A model with a dull skintone must find a foundation that closely matches the color of her skin yet slightly enlivens it. She must be careful to avoid foundations having obvious red or orange casts because these are distracting and look artificial in a photograph. For best results in general, match foundation in daylight to the skin of your neck. If you want to change the color of your skin (make it appear noticeably lighter or darker) carry the foundation down your neck, taking care that it doesn't soil collars and necklines of clothing. There should not be a great deal of difference between the skin color of the face and neck, such as a sallow neck against a white face, because this is distracting.

When contouring and highlighting is used in color photography it must be done very subtly to be believeable. When using contour makeups you will want to retain a natural, clean look. Too much or the wrong color of contour makeup can make the skin look dirty. Use contouring sparingly in the eyesocket crease, along the jawline, and in some cases along the sides of the nose and in cheekhollows. Contour colors should not be more than one or two shades darker than skin tone. Be aware also that contour colors should be dull and unfrosted. Also, cool colors tend to make areas recede more realistically than warm colors. Therefore select grayish or bluish tones of a color for contouring.

Think creatively when using contouring and highlighting. Remember that a contour makeup need not be a shade of brown. A highlighter need not be white. For example, to contour and highlight your cheeks, you could use a deeper shade of red in the cheekhollows, a bright shade of red on the cheekbone, and a very light pink to highlight the tops of cheekbones.

Although well-blended makeup is important for any look, it is critical in color photography where the slightest lack of blending is magnified. Make certain that concealer applied on blemishes or under eye shadows does not appear lighter than the foundation. Make certain that cheekcolor is well blended and doesn't appear streaky.

For jobs in which several garments will be shot in a short period of time, such as in catalog work, use a basic makeup that combines well with lots of colors. Favor neutral and classic shades like navy, brown, gray, and beige for eyeshadows; soft pinks or peaches for cheeks; true red or orangey red for lips. Create natural-looking makeup colors by custom blending different products to match your coloring. For example, if your skin, hair, and eyes are enhanced by warm-toned makeups, start with a bright orange lip or cheekcolor and add foundation or contour to lighten or darken it so it plays up the lightness or darkness of your skin. If your skin, hair, and eyes are enhanced by cool tones, select a bright rose lip- or cheekcolor and follow the same procedure.

Use charcoal gray or brown powder to line and define the eyes. Soften the lines for a natural look. Use mascara colors that match the eyeliner colors you have used. Use brown eyeshadow. Add a touch of yellow or gold eyeshadow to warm it. Add a touch of blue or gray eyeshadow to make it appear cooler. Keep your makeup as sheer and natural as possible, unless you are after a specific effect. Natural-looking makeup should not look greasy, chalky, or masklike and artifical. Adhering to these nature-enhancing basics will look well with anything you wear.

When using colored makeups, it is very important that there is harmony between the foundation and cheek-, lip-, and eyecolors used. The color of the cheeks should not clash with the lips, though they need not match perfectly. Study the language of color (see Chapter 5) to determine how you can arrive at attractive color combinations.

When using makeup on fashion assignments, you will want your makeup to harmonize with your garment. To do this most effectively, select concealer, foundation, and face powder that closely match your skin. Make up your eyes using charcoal, gray, or brown to contour the crease. To coordinate your makeup with the garment you select, add a colored eyeshadow to the lids or underbrow area. Add color to lips and cheeks that enhances the garment, while paying attention to how colors in makeup are currently being combined with fashion. For example, one season, it may be fashionable to wear bright red lipcolor with a navy blue suit, whereas the next season, a soft pink may be combined with a navy blue suit for a more played-down look. If there are several garment changes, alter your lipcolor to coordinate with a garment by blotting off old lipcolor with a tissue, applying foundation to lips and using new lipcolor. When you change your lipcolor you may also have to change your cheekcolor. To do so remove excess by using a cotton ball. Then, using a liquid foundation and a sponge, blot over old cheekcolor, apply face powder, then apply new powder cheekcolor.

When coordinating makeup to your garment, you may want to match your lipcolor to a color found in the garment, or you may want to use warm lip- and cheekcolors (rust, chinese red, peach, coral) when wearing orange, yellow, brown, and other warm clothing colors; wear pink, plum, rose, or cool red when wearing blue, violet, or gray. For single shots for an important ad or editorial work, a makeup artist is usually employed.

When shooting in color, realize that makeup colors do not necessarily photograph the way you see them in life. Test makeup colors on film, and when you find colors that work well, stick to them. Makeup colors will usually not appear as vibrant and pure as in life, so choose brighter colors than you normally would. Also note that when the lighting is very bright, brighter or more intense colors are needed. When working in a group shot, always check that your makeup is in keeping with that of the other models who are in the shot. You should not be a great deal lighter or darker than the other models nor should you have on significantly less or more makeup, unless the photographer is trying to achieve a different effect.

Makeup for Electronic Media

Usually a makeup artist is employed for television and film work, but in cases in which you must do your own makeup, keep the following in mind.

Be a perfectionist when applying makeup for video or film productions because, unlike still film, no darkroom or retouching techniques can be used. What the camera sees must be perfect. As in any type of work, it is best if you can see how you look under the lights. When on television or video assignments, after you have applied your makeup, go to the control room and ask to see the color monitor displaying the picture that will be going on the air. Check your makeup in this control monitor to see if it is too warm or cool, too light or dark, or if other adjustments need to be made. This is the best way to assess colors as the monitors in the studio probably have not been critically adjusted to display the on-the-air picture.

Television tends to be a closeup medium, that is, a majority of the picture concentrates on the area from the waist up. Extreme closeups that fill the screen with only the actor or model's face are commonly employed. Ask the director if your makeup is properly applied for closeups. The closer the camera, the more exacting application must be.

Except in cases of extreme closeups, the television image is less than lifesize. Also the TV picture is quite grainy (not possessing a high number of lines of resolution). These two factors mean that the TV image does not capture great detail, and it is not as critical in what it registers as other media. Therefore, applying more makeup to emphasize the lips and eyes is necessary. Attractive skintones and textures are also important, so use a good foundation.

In television and motion pictures several cameras may be used at one time, so makeup must be carefully applied to look equally well from all angles, Also, faces are seen from far away as well as close up, so it is important that makeup looks well from both perspectives. The success of any makeup is how well it projects the appearance of the model to the audience.

Consulting with the director on video and television productions is important to determine whether the makeup you have applied will portray the character you are depicting effectively. It may be necessary to consult with the lighting designer to determine how your makeup will appear under the proposed lighting. The lighting designer controls the total lighting effects of the production and communication with him can be helpful in arriving at the desired look.

The types of lighting setups used in video and film productions are basically the same as those used in still photography. Study Figure 2 in Chapter 10 to determine how to apply makeup most effectively for different types of lighting. As in most photography situations, using a lipliner and eyeliner to define the lips and eyes is important, particularly when a flat lighting is present. Flat lighting is used in many video productions.

Understanding how certain makeups appear on videotape is important. Greasy makeups make the skin appear oily or sweaty. Certain bright-colored or highly frosted makeups can "bloom" (appear distractingly bright or obvious) in video, so it is best to avoid them.

Lighting used in video and film productions can get quite hot, bringing oils and sweat to the surface of the skin, so frequent powder application or use of a clay-based makeup, such as pancake, to absorb oil or sweat is necessary.

Makeup for Stage and Runway

Take a more theatrical approach to runway makeup. The brighter the lights and the farther away your audience, the more intense your colors and application should be.

Frosted, iridescent, and glossy makeups are extremely effective on runway and should be used as fashion dictates. If the designer whose clothes you are modeling also has a line of makeup, use his or her cosmetics as they have been designed with the colors and textures found in the clothing line.

Use a brownish lip liner that is darker than your lipstick to add depth and make the lips "pop" out.

Go a little heavier with eyeliner and mascara to define the eyes and exaggerate their size. False eyelashes can often be used effectively to play up the eyes and exaggerate their size and will not look artificial from the audience's perspective. Extra individual lashes applied at the outer corners of eyes look natural and add emphasis.

Unless a special effect is being attempted, use vivid, well-saturated colors. Subtle coloring will wash out and look dull.

If you are doing informal, showroom, or any other type of live modeling where you will have close contact with customers, make sure makeup is clean, well blended, and not too heavy handed. In these situations, it is important that your eye and lip colors work well with your garment.

In runway modeling the time element is a consideration. If there is time for makeup changes, expedite application by uncapping lipsticks, putting eyeshadows on cotton-tipped swabs and applicators, and having powder on a large puff ready to apply.

Makeup for Promotional Modeling

The most important consideration when applying makeup for a promotional modeling assignment is that your appearance creates the right image for the company that has employed you. If you are employed by a conservative company, your makeup should include classic colors and conservative application. For a company that enlists you to project a glamourous image, your makeup should look similar to the makeup of a beauty pageant contestant. In general, for most promotional modeling situations avoid garish or extreme fashion-oriented makeup colors and techniques. Also, because you will be meeting people face-to-face, avoid heavy makeup. Use natural-looking colors that work well with the outfit you are wearing and apply makeup so it enhances your skin and features. It is also a good idea to take into consideration the lighting and other factors that are present that may affect your appearance.

When doing promotional modeling, you can telephone the electrician's office of the convention center where you will be modeling to find out the types of lighting installed. It will probably be either fluorescent, mercury, incandescent, or natural lighting.

Fluorescent

Fluorescent lighting found in most convention centers is unflattering because it is harsh and gives skin a dull, lifeless, grayish look. To combat this effect, choose colors that are warm and golden, as opposed to violet and pink. True beige foundations, toasty-toned eyeshadows in tan, beige, brown, and taupe with highlightings in apricot, peach, sand, flesh pink, and straw are great shades to choose. On lips, use clear gloss or a soft apricot lipcolor and an auburn lip-lining pencil. Also, stick to matte makeups rather than light reflective products, such as iridescent eyeshadows and lip glosses. In convention centers the light usually comes from above, making the eyes appear darker, smaller, and deeper set, so using a little extra concealer under the eyes and a touch of bright accent color on the lids directly over the iris will compensate for this fact.

Mercury

Mercury lighting tends to be greenish or greenish blue in cast. The makeup colors listed above are most effective in this light and warm pinks often work well to combat greenish tones.

Incandescent

Incandescent light has slightly golden overtones and is the type most commonly found in homes. A true beige foundation with orange-, brown-, or yellow-toned makeup colors is flattering. In some convention centers incandescent lighting is mixed with fluorescent or mercury lighting for a more flattering effect.

Outdoor or Natural Light

Bright natural light is the only type of light in which all colors show up clearly. Because of the high visibility that sunlight provides, your makeup application should be thinner and lighter than would be required for indoor wear. Heavy eyeliners, lip liners, and dark makeup will look too intense and unnatural. Stick to semimatte, translucent foundations. Powdery makeups sometimes appear dull and chalky outdoors. Be sure foundation is well matched on both face and neck because mismatches are very obvious in natural light.

Outdoor light changes in color cast throughout the day. For an hour or two around sunrise and sunset, the light is very warm having rich golden overtones. Therefore gold, coral, peach, bronze, and rust makeup shades will be especially flattering. Avoid blue-toned colors, as they seem dark and dull in this warm light. At noon or on overcast days the light is very cool, so work with cool browns, pinks, and plums. Sometimes photographers use filters over their lenses or lights to correct a blue or orange cast found in the subject, so no compensation in makeup may be needed. When applying makeup for outdoor situations, some photographers prefer a slightly heavier application of color on the cheeks, slightly lighter on the eyes.

STEP-BY-STEP PROFESSIONAL MAKEUP APPLICATION

The guidelines for applying makeup explained here (Figures 83 to 104) will create a professional look for photography, runway or stage, electronic media, and live promotional modeling. You may want to make slight variations in your application by consulting the information in "Applying Makeup for Various Media."

Before you begin your makeup application, organize and select the items you will need. Select colors that enhance your own natural coloring and the item you will be modeling. Allow 20 to 30 minutes for this makeup routine or more time if you are inexperienced or after a very specific effect. Be a perfectionist and you'll be able to obtain the same result as a professional makeup artist.

The Final Refinements

- Check that foundation is well blended. Use a foam sponge pad to even out application especially around eyes, nose, hairline, and jawline.
- Check that cheek and eyeshadow colors are well blended. Use a clean sponge, powder puff, or cotton to blend and soften.
- Brush brows to remove stray makeup and to arrive at the desired shape.
- Apply a light film of powder to ensure that there is no shininess and that all makeup colors are even and soft.
- A slightly moist sponge dabbed all over the face will set the makeup.

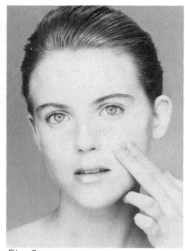

Fig. 83

Fig. 85

Fig 87

Fig. 84

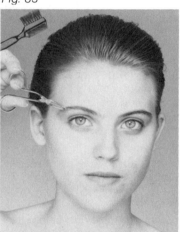

Fig. 86

Fig. 88

Figure 83. Start with a smooth complexion that is free of distracting facial hair between brows, above upper lip, on sides of face, or on chin. Apply makeup to clean skin..

Figure 84. Skin should feel and look neither oily nor dry. Set a base for your makeup by spreading on a thin film of moisturizer that is designed to be worn under makeup. Blot off excess moisturizer using a single ply of a facial tissue..

Figure 85. Shape brows by tweezing strays and brushing hairs into place..

Figure 86. Use a concealer pencil or concealer cream and a nylon brush to apply concealer to cover blemishes, under eye circles or shadows, and discolorations around the nose and mouth. Apply enough to cover the flaw, but blend well so that concealer is undetectable. Consult the chart under "Corrective Makeup Techniques for Skin Flaws" in this chapter.

Figure 87. Apply foundation evenly using the type and the method that achieves the coverage you need or the look you desire. Also cover eyelids and lips. Blend foundation well out to the edges of the face, onto the ears and slightly under the jawbone. It is also important to apply foundation over areas where concealer has been applied to create one even complexion color. When doing so, dab lightly, don't rub or streak, or concealer will be removed..

Figure 88. Next is contouring. Select the right form for your needs, and adjust your application to your situation. You may opt to avoid contouring for normal wear or you may want to use just a touch of foundation a shade darker than your complexion to define your jawline..

Fig. 89

Fig. 90

Fig. 91

Fig. 92

Fig. 93

Fig. 94

Figure 89. For modeling assignments, you may want to use contouring in cheekhollows, temples, around hairline, along sides of nose, or in any area that needs depth, definition, or minimizing. However, be careful not to overdo as too much contour makeup can give a dirty or overly made-up look. You may also want to use highlighter for a more pronounced effect. Apply it to bridge of nose, tops of cheekbones, chin, and areas you want to exaggerate or bring forward. Highlighting is optional and whether you use it will depend on the look you want to accomplish.

Figure 90. Applying powder is the next step. Use a large, fluffy powder brush to apply powder over the entire face. Concentrate the application of powder on the nose, chin, and forehead as these tend to be the shiniest areas of the face. (If cream cheekcolor is used, apply powder after cheekcolor, not before.).

Figure 91. To reach small areas, use a thin powder puff or a small clean blusher brush to apply powder..

Figure 92. Correct brows. To make eyebrows appear dramatically darker or fuller, draw several hairline strokes using a very sharp eyebrow pencil. For a softer, more natural look, use eyebrow powder applied with a slant-tipped brush. Eyebrow pencil or shadow usually looks best when it is one shade lighter than your brows..

Figure 93. Brush brows to remove stray makeup and to groom hairs into proper placement. First brush in the opposite direction of growth and then into the desired direction.

Figure 94. Use black or brown eyeliner pencil to line the inside rim of the upper lid. This makes lashes look thick and luxurious..

Fig. 95

Fig. 96

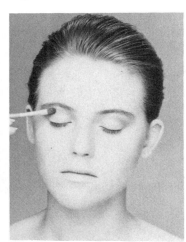

Fig. 97

Fig. 98

Figure 95. Apply eyeliner pencil that matches your mascara as close to the lashline as possible. Use a thin line for small eyelids, a wider line for thick lids. Experiment with the length, width, and shape of this line until you find application techniques that flatter your eyes and produce different looks.

Figure 96. Soften eyeliner using a cotton swab or clean eyeliner brush, working it into the lashes.

Figure 97. Using the same eyeliner pencil or one in another color that flatters your eyecolor, line the lashlines of the lower eyelids. Current fashion and the characteristics of your eyes will determine how you apply the eyeliner. Smudge this line for the most flattering effect..

Figure 98. Use a medium to dark neutral color of powder or cream eyeshadow in the crease of the eyesocket to give definition to the shape of the eye. (Defining the crease is always photogenic and looks natural. Consult the eyecharts for more ideas.) Use one or two other colors to accent and highlight the eyes. Make sure when choosing eye-, lip-, and cheekcolors that they go well with your natural coloring (skin, hair, and eye color) and the clothes you will be modeling.

Colors that work well for nearly all situations including photography are neutral brown (neither warm nor cool toned), navy, gray, and soft charcoal. Adhere to matte, not frosted colors, particularly for contouring and defining purposes. For highlighting eyes, select beige, peach, or pink. Cheekcolor can be used for highlighting the area just under the arch of the brow. In all color selections, whether for eyes, cheeks, or lips, consider the lightness or darkness of your skin. Very fair skins often look too harsh with intense colors, whereas dark skins are enhanced.

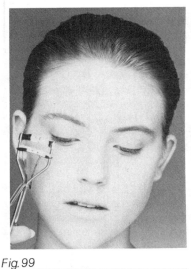

Fig. 99

Fig. 100

Fig. 101

Fig. 102

Fig. 103

Fig. 104

Figure 99. Curl lashes to open the eyes and make lashes look thicker.

Figure 100. Apply black or brown mascara, working the wand from the base to the tips of lashes. Be certain that there is no clumping or sticking together of lashes. Use a lash comb to separate lashes.

Figure 101. Apply cheekcolor. Select one that matches your natural blushing color. Warm-skinned women usually look best in peach, tawny or coral tones; for cool-toned skins, select rose and pink tones. Avoid using too much cheekcolor.

Figure 102. Line lips with a pencil that matches the natural color of your lips or the color of the lipstick to be used. Soften this line by smudging lightly with a cotton swab.

Figure 103. Fill in lips with lipcolor using a lipbrush. Load brush well and apply to center of lips. When brush is nearly free of lipcolor, extend color outward toward lipline. Color over lip liner to create a smooth even line.

Figure 104. The finished look is smooth and flawless.

MAKEUP APPLICATION TIPS FOR BLACK MODELS

Black models follow the same procedure as outlined previously. However, they should pay attention to the concepts shown in Figures 105 to 114 to arrive at the ideal look.

Fig. 105

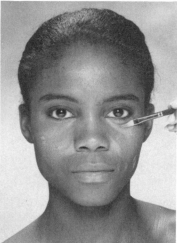

Fig. 106

Figure 105. Start with a clean, perfectly primed face.

Figure 106. Applying concealer to pimples, flesh moles, and other blemishes is important. Use a brush to apply concealer. Remove excess concealer from brush, and brush until concealer is blended.

Figure 107. Black skins often have variances in color on different areas of the face. Some areas may appear more gray (for example, between the end of the nose and upper lip and around eyes), whereas other areas appear yellow or sallow. To even the skin tone, models sometimes use undertoners or color correctors on the discolored areas before applying foundation. A lavender undertoner cancels out yellowish tones; a mauve undertoner corrects grayish tones. A green undertoner will subdue ruddy or reddish areas.

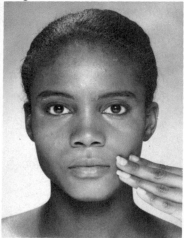

Fig. 107

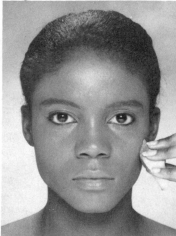

Fig. 108

Figure 108. It is very important to select a good overall skin tone-matching foundation, which is neither too orangey nor too pinkish. Match foundation to the skin on your neck and always check it in outdoor light. To obtain a perfect match, it may be necessary to mix together two shades of foundation.

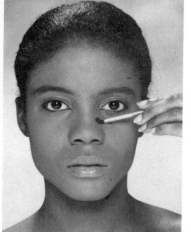

Fig. 109

Figure 109. Contouring a too wide nose is a procedure that many black models find necessary. Select a powder or cream contour in a shade of brown darker than your skin or use a dark bluish-gray cream (cool tones contour best). If using a powder, use an eyeshadow fluff brush making smooth long strokes from the bridge to the end of the nose. If using a cream pick up a small quantity on your index finger. Rub your index finger and thumb (of the same hand) together. Spread your thumb and index finger to the width of your nose or the width you would like it to be and make several long straight strokes from the bridge to the end of the nose using a light touch. You'll have two even parallel lines. With the index finger of your clean hand, pick up a quantity of highlighter or concealer and make one long straight stroke down the center of your nose from the bridge to the tip. Use a clean sponge puff to soften these lines. Check Figures 6 to 37 for other corrections.

Fig. 110

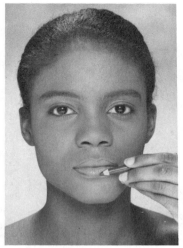

Fig. 111

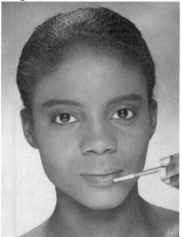

Fig 112

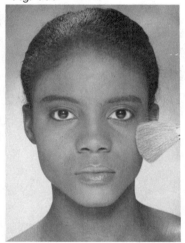

Fig. 113

Fig. 114

Figure 110. Another common beauty problem among blacks are cloudy or yellowish eye whites. To make the whites of your eyes look whiter, use a light blue, lavender, or navy eyelining pencil along the inside rim of the lower eyelid..

Figure 111. Black models often feel that their lips are too full— especially for the camera, which tends to exaggerate such characteristics. To minimize the size of the lips, use a brown lip-lining pencil or one that matches or is a shade darker than the color of your lipstick. Line just inside the lip line. Select medium-toned lipcolors, as very light, dark, or frosted ones will make the lips appear larger. Note that enlarging the eyes with makeup will draw attention away from the lips.

Figure 112. When applying makeup to black skin, color selection is important. Because of the darkness of the skin, color is absorbed. Therefore, most black models look best in very bright or very rich colors for eyeshadows, lipcolors, and blushers. Neutrals such as dark grays, charcoal and navy work well for eyes; however, they must be darker than the skin color to be most effective.

On very dark black skin few makeup colors, especially contouring colors will show up adequately. Lightening the skin with foundations and powders is also unsatisfactory because it yields a lifeless, grayish cast, and won't match the skin on the rest of the body..

Figure 113. Black skins are often prone to oiliness. To conceal excess oil, apply powder frequently..

Figure 114. The result shown here will work well for photography and other modeling situations. The heaviness of the application you choose will depend on the brightness of the lighting in which you will be seen or photographed, the distance you will be from your audience in live-modeling situations, and other specifics.

STEP-BY-STEP MAKEUP
APPLICATION FOR
MALE MODELS

Fig. 115

Fig. 116

Fig. 117

Fig. 118

Fig. 119

Fig. 120

Figure 115. Start with a clean shaven, moisturized face.

Figure 116. Use a small amount of yellow-toned or flesh-toned concealer one-half shade lighter than your skin tone to cover under eye shadows and blemishes. Dab on discolored areas.

Figure 117. Blend concealer well by stippling and pressing with your fingertip or a foam sponge.

Figure 118. To achieve an attractive, even skin tone, apply a powder-cream foundation using a sponge or powder puff. To get into tight areas such as around nose and eyes, fold the puff in half and use the tip of the fold. Select a shade that matches your skin or one with a slight bronze tone to give a glow of healthy color. Blend foundation well to cover discoloration from beard area and areas where you have applied concealer.

Figure 119. Add a touch of cheekcolor such as bronzing gel, tawny powder blush, or cream cheekcolor. Or, for a very natural look use a darker shade of powder-cream foundation. Apply it using a sponge puff along cheekbones. Blend well for a natural look.

Figure 120. Use a foundation a shade or two darker than your skin to contour the jawline. This gives a more defined look that will photograph well.

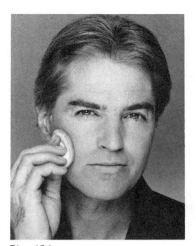

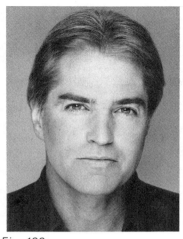

Figure 121. Apply translucent, skin-toned powder all over face, concentrating on shiny areas. Use a brush or a puff.

Figure 122. The finished face displays smooth, attractively toned skin. Brows are brushed into place using a toothbrush. A touch of colorless lip balm is applied to lips using the tip of your index finger for smooth-looking lips.

Fig. 121

Fig. 122

HOW TO WORK WITH A MAKEUP ARTIST ON A MODELING ASSIGNMENT

When a makeup artist is employed to apply the model's makeup, the model should learn how to cooperate in order to produce the desired results.

- Arrive at the booking with clean, moisturized skin. If you have a skin problem, such as pimples or a lip sore, inform your agent immediately. Never try to hide such problems from a makeup artist or client.
- Wear a button-down top or change into your first top if it is one that goes over the head. You or the makeup artist should provide a smock to protect your or the client's garment.
- If you have allergies to certain makeups, provide a selection of suitable ones from which the makeup artist can choose.
- Always bring your own foundation and face powder to ensure that the makeup artist has a perfect match for your skin. This is especially applicable to black models, white models with very light skin tones, or others with unique skin colors.
- Don't tell the makeup artist how to apply your makeup. He is a professional, has tools and products he likes to use, and knows several techniques. Allow him to use his own creativity when applying makeup, just as you like to use yours when modeling.
- Don't critique what the makeup artist has done. If you like it, of course you should compliment him. However, realize that the decision regarding how your makeup should look rests with the photographer or client, not you. You are creating an image for the product to be modeled.
- Make it easier for the makeup artist to apply your makeup by not twitching or blinking your eyes, talking when she is applying lipcolor, or holding your head down. Keep your head straight and still, and raise or lower it when she asks. Anticipate what the makeup artist wants you to do without her having to ask. For example, if she is working on your eyelids, you should close your eyes. If she is working on the undereye area, look up. It is very important that you relax while your makeup is being applied. Nervously moving your face will increase the chance of injury and make it difficult for her to do a precise, artistic makeup application.
- Avoid talking when makeup is being applied. It slows everyone down and makes it difficult for the makeup artist to concentrate.
- Don't alter your makeup after the makeup artist has finished applying it unless you get permission from him.

• Once your makeup has been applied be very careful that you don't rub or blow your nose, smile, sneeze, or scratch your face. All of these actions will disturb the makeup. Always check with the makeup artist before going on set to see if you need more powder or if corrections need to be made.

Makeup Notes

©THE PROFESSIONAL MODEL'S HANDBOOK

Step	Cosmetic	Product type	Brand	Color	Tool	Procedure
	Moisturizer					
	Eyebrow					
	Concealer					
	Undertoner					
	Foundation					
	Powder					
	Contour					
	Highlight					
	Cheekcolor					
	Dark Eyeshadow					
	Medium Eyeshadow					
	Light Eyeshadow					
	Eye Pencil/Liner					
	Mascara					
	Lip Pencil/Liner					
	Lip Color					
	Gloss					
	Other					

Chapter 4 The Model's Guide to Professional Hair Care and Styling

Hair is one of the most important elements of a model's look. The way a model's hair looks has a lot to do with defining the model's image and determining the type of work for which he or she is best suited. The right hair look can make or break a model's presentation.

There are six keys to successful hair:

1. Caring for your hair.
2. Finding the right look for your hair.
3. Assembling a professional hairstyling kit.
4. Learning professional hairstyling techniques.
5. Experimenting with different hair styles.
6. Analyzing how to style hair for different situations.

CARING FOR YOUR HAIR

A model's hair must be shiny and healthy; however, there are several occupational hazards that can affect its condition. A model must overcompensate for abuses hair must endure on the job, so practicing good hair health maintenance is the best way to ensure strong, healthy attractive hair. The following points can be used as a basis for proper hair care.

Hair-Saving Tips

Maintain general good health. Your hair will look its best when you maintain healthy habits, such as adequate daily diet, exercise, rest, and relaxation. Avoid such enemies of the hair as excessive use of tobacco, alcohol, and medications.

Maintain a healthy scalp. Aim for a healthy scalp. Dandruff, alopecia (hair loss), infections, and other disorders should be treated by a trichologist. Employ brushing and scalp massage techniques to increase the blood flow to the scalp. Use proper shampooing techniques and good hairstyling tools to avoid scratching, burning, or abrading the scalp and damaging the hair.

Keep hair clean. Brush the hair to loosen dead skin cells and eliminate debris. Shampoo hair when it is dull or oily. Models often need to shampoo daily to cleanse the hair of residues from styling preparations used on the hair during assignments. Use shampoo that is specifically formulated for your hair type, whether it is oily, normal, dry, color treated, or dandruff-prone. Use correct shampooing techniques.

When shampooing use the pads of your fingers and massage gently to move the scalp and loosen debris. Don't rub or scrub vigorously when washing or drying with a towel. Using warm, soft water will aid the cleansing process.

Condition the hair. This is very important to a model whose hair is subjected to overmanipulation, heat appliances, and other hair destroyers. Select a conditioner based on the type of hair you have, and apply it according to the amount of help needed. Models should avoid overconditioning, which results in limp, dull hair. Overconditioned hair is very unmanageable for you or a hairstylist on assignment. Also, shampooing the hair on an assignment is not feasible.

Handle your hair delicately. Avoid combing and brushing roughly or excessively. Shampoo, towel dry, and comb the hair gently. Wet hair is more succeptible to breakage than dry hair, so be extra careful. Try to obtain a haircut that looks presentable with a minimum of setting, combing, and styling. Avoid pulling hair too tightly when winding around rollers or securing into braids, twists, knots, or ponytails. Don't use broken plastic combs or metal combs for combing, as they tend to break hair. Select soft natural or ball-tipped, nylon-bristled hairbrushes.

Protect your hair from harmful elements. Avoid overexposure to sun, wind, and cold air, all of which can be drying to the hair. Avoid overuse of such heat-styling appliances as blowdryers, curling irons, and electric rollers, except when you are modeling. When using such appliances, use heat styling products designed to help protect hair. Acquire good hair habits by avoiding rubber bands, tight barrettes, brush rollers, and other items that can split and break the hair. Avoid hair care and styling preparations that dry or damage the hair, such as alcohol-loaded hairsprays. Also avoid harsh permanents, bleaches, or tints.

Keep ends of hair trimmed. Regular trims will inhibit ends from splitting and breaking. A model's hair should be trimmed every four to six weeks depending on the length and cut. The average rate of hair growth is about one-half inch per month. Poor nutrition, cold weather, hormonal imbalances, and health disorders can slow hair growth. Freshly trimmed hair also looks better because the ends of the hair hold together more easily. Trimmed hair eliminates fuzziness due to split ends, and styling is made easier.

ANALYZING AND CORRECTING HAIR PROBLEMS

Consult the chart in this chapter to correct any hair problems you may have. A model's hair must be problem-free to ensure that it looks attractive and is manageable.

TABLE 1 Correction Chart for Problem Hair

Problem	Solution
Oily hair	Washing the hair daily (preferably in the morning for very oily hair) is a necessity. Using shampoo specially formulated for oily hair, or rinsing the scalp after shampooing with a fresh lemon juice rinse will help. Avoid brushing and manipulating the scalp when possible, as this stimulates oil production. Keeping hairbrushes clean is also important.
Dry hair	Wash with a mild shampoo formulated especially for dry hair. Use a conditioner or cream rinse every time you shampoo. Use an in-depth conditioner twice a month. When ends feel very dry, mix together in a spray bottle, 1 part liquid facial moisturizer or nonoily hair conditioning lotion with 1 part water. Spray lightly on dry hair, massage, and comb through. Avoid styling products that contain alcohol.

Combination hair	Many people have combination hair in which hair at the scalp is oily, whereas ends of hair are dry. To deal with this problem, concentrate shampoo on the scalp. Apply conditioner to ends only.
Dandruff	Use a specially formulated dandruff shampoo daily. Especially effective are those containing sulfur to disinfect and salicylic acid to dissolve dead skin cells. Brush hair before shampooing.
Static, flyaway hair	Use a conditioner on ends of hair after shampooing when your environment is dry. When styling the hair, spray your hairbrush, and comb with antistatic spray designed for clothes. Hairspray will also tame flyaway hair.
Tangled wet hair	Use conditioner or cream rinse after shampooing. When rinsing hair, draw a wide-toothed comb through it. Towel dry gently, then shake head, and use fingers to loosen and separate the hair. Comb through using a wide-toothed comb, starting at the ends and working your way up to the scalp. Comb through under layers of hair first.
Tangled dry hair	Use a hair pick to loosen and separate hair. Then use a regular comb or ball-tipped nylon brush to comb through ends and underneath layers of hair, working your way up to scalp and top layers of hair. For very stubborn matted tangles, massage on conditioner or cream rinse, unknot hair using fingers, then comb.
Thin hair	Consider wearing your hair in a simple, classic, sleek style. A cut that is all one length and above the shoulders is usually best. If this type of style is not flattering, consider getting a permanent wave for extra softness and fullness. Also, use protein conditioners and styling preparations to increase the size of the hair shaft.
Fine or slippery hair	After shampooing and towel drying, comb a dab of styling mousse or setting lotion through hair, then dry using a blow dryer. For more dramatic results try this retexturizing treatment once every 6 weeks: Shampoo, and towel dry hair. Mix together 1 tablespoon glycerin, 1 tablespoon shampoo, 1 tablespoon ammonia, and ¼ cup water. Massage into hair and let remain 10 minutes. Rinse with cool water. Blot dry and set in traditional rollers. For more dramatic changes, consider perming or coloring the hair. Avoid too frequent use of conditioners (more than once per month), and always opt for body-building conditioners.
Too thick hair	A body perm or chemical straightener can dramatically improve hair that is too thick. Opt for a razor cut to remove excess bulk without shortening length.
Too coarse or overcurly hair	Use a balsam conditioner after shampooing. Once a month apply a hot-oil or balsam conditioner and cover with a hot damp towel or a conditioning heat cap.
Hairspray or conditioner buildup	Overconditioning your hair can make curling and styling very difficult. To remove the buildup, use a conditioner containing salicylic acid once every week or two. Or follow a plain, detergent shampoo with a lemon (for blondes and light hair colors) or vinegar (for medium to dark hair colors) rinse. Add ½ cup lemon juice or vinegar to 1 quart water. Massage into hair and let remain a few minutes, then rinse well.
Dull hair	Chemically treated (permed, straightened, colored) hair generally has less shine than virgin hair. Avoid using more than one chemical process on your hair at a time. Hair that lacks shine can be improved by using cold water as a final rinse after shampooing. For longer lasting results, mix neutral henna (available at drug and beauty supply stores) with fresh-squeezed lemon juice to form a paste. Apply to hair and allow to remain up to 20 minutes. Rinse. Repeat every 6 weeks.

Negative environmental effects on hair	If your color-treated or virgin hair has a greenish cast, it is probably caused by chlorinated water. Use a shampoo specially formulated for swimmers, and wash hair right after swimming. Brassy hair is often caused by household water that has an overabundance of minerals. To deal with this problem, it may be necessary to obtain a water filter or to wash and rinse your hair with purified, bottled water.
Broken ends	To diminish the unattractiveness of broken ends, twist a strand of hair and clip off ends that stick out. Reexamine your brushing and combing habits and other possible negative conditions that may be causing this problem.
Incorrectly colored	Have your hair condition restored by visits to a professional cosmetologist. Before attempting color corrections, make certain that your hair is in good enough condition to accept chemicals. Don't attempt your own corrections. If your hair has been overbleached, a professional colorist will weave strands of your natural color into hair so outgrowth won't be noticeable. For hair that looks too red or brassy, a toner may be used. For too dark hair, strands of a lighter color will be bleached. Note that most of these remedies are not long-lasting. Results may fade or wash out, and correction procedures will need to be repeated.

FINDING THE RIGHT LOOK FOR YOUR HAIR

Once the condition of your hair is ideal, you must work on finding the right hair look. Establish the perfect hair look now before you spend money on photos, composites, and other investments in your career. If your hair look isn't right for modeling, it will hamper your chances for success. Prospective clients will turn you away by telling you to return when your hair is right and you have retaken your pictures. Your hair is one of the most important factors in determining your image and the types of modeling assignments for which you will be chosen.

Any individual should select a hair look that enhances his or her hair and features, but a model must be concerned with two other factors when determining an ideal hair look for modeling: marketability and versatility.

Marketability. A marketable hair look means that the model's hair cut, color, and style looks right for the types of assignments prospective clients will have. For a fashion model, the hair must be current and in keeping with the fashions that work with the model's image. For a commercial or product model, the hair must work with the types of characters the model will be asked to portray.

Versatility. A model or hairstylist should be able to quickly and easily style the hair into several different looks that will enhance a variety of different garments. A commercial or product model's hair must be able to achieve styles that will portray a range of characters. Wigs and hairpieces are usually only reserved for special effects; however, character models may employ them to create a specific character.

A popular cut for female models has been the all-one-length, blunt cut that varies in length between the shoulders and the jawline, with or without bangs. A popular male model's cut has been a traditional side-parted haircut that is neither short nor long. Both cuts afford models a wide range of possiblities, from conservative to trendy looks.

Layered cuts that display a great difference in length between the shortest and the longest layers (in excess of 4 inches), or that have a very short layer (less than 1½ inches) on the top or sides of the head, do not offer enough options in hairstyling and are usually not preferred by clients. Extremely long hair is usually not preferred because it takes a lot more time to style, covers the clothes the model wears, and obstructs important garment details. Fashion clients want to sell their fashions, not the model's hair. Very short hair is also difficult to work with because it cannot be changed by parting or curling. Many times top models may have extremely long or short styles; however, they have earned the clout to have whatever hair look they desire. Most models work their way up with more versatile hair. In general, most clients look for a hairstyle that can be worn combed back as well as parted on the side or in the middle.

Each model arrives at her ideal hairstyle in different ways. Some beginning models have the right hair look from the start. They don't need to make changes. However, most new models need to cut hair that is too long, or grow out hair that is too short or layered. Still others have hair that is incorrectly colored, permed, or straightened. Therefore, it is best to approach modeling with hair that is medium to long in length with no layering and no color or perms. This way a full range of options will be open to you and your agent for finding the perfect hair look. Having to grow out incorrectly cut, colored, or permed hair can put off the beginning of your career for several months.

Follow these steps to research the right hair look for you and your career:

1. Consider current fashion.
2. Analyze your assets and liabilities.
3. Consult with experts in the modeling field.
4. Select the right hairstylist.

Look at Current Fashion

Look at magazines to explore the variety of current hair looks. Pay attention to the images created by certain models by means of haircuts and styles. Some models choose a hairstyle that is a symbol of their own particular look. Other models maintain the same basic haircut, altering it slightly from season to season to make it look up to date. Looking current is important for any model. Sometimes just adding bangs or a certain detailing at the sides of the face can be the difference between last year's and this year's hair look.

When a model studies different haircuts, he or she must consider two basic factors: the line of the cut and the length. There are basically three types of cuts defined by the line of the cut: single- or one-line (even all around), graduated-line (for example, diagonal lines formed by hair being shorter at the face and tapering longer in back, or shorter in back and tapering longer in front), and variable-line cuts, such as layered haircuts. Second, cuts are defined by length. Short cuts have the longest layer at the earlobe and up. Medium-length cuts are from the jaw bone to just above the shoulder. Long cuts refer to those that are shoulder length and longer.

Analyze Your Assets and Liabilities

There are several factors that must be taken into consideration when selecting the right hair look. The seven basic considerations are:

Your facial features. Use the information you acquired about your facial features from Chapter 3. You can even use your diagram to draw different styles to see which ones bring out your best features and which downplay those features that are less than ideal. Use Table 1 to provide suggestions for playing down your liabilities and accentuating your assets. But remember, these are not hard and fast rules.

The shape of your head. The shape of your head has a lot to do with determining how your hair hangs. Observe your head shape from the front, side, and back before selecting a cut. For example, a head that is somewhat flat on top will look better with a cut that will give more fullness at the crown.

The size of your face. A small, delicate face usually looks best with less hair because too much hair can overpower the features. A larger face may need more hair as a frame to make it appear smaller and the features finer.

The length of your neck. A model needs a long neck to show off clothes to best advantage. The shorter your neck, the shorter your hair should be. Exposing more of your neck usually makes it appear longer.

Your figure type and body proportions. A neat, less full hairstyle looks better on a person with a petite or small-boned body type. Too much hair can be overwhelming and will make you appear shorter. A medium-to-tall or medium- to large-boned person can wear fuller hairstyles. A large person usually looks best with a neat (not too full nor too severe) hairstyle.

Hair growth patterns. The way your hair grows will affect the style you choose. You need to consider if your hair has hair streams (hair that slopes in the same direction because of follicle formation or a natural part that results from two streams sloping in opposite directions), cowlicks (a group of hairs that stand up), or whorls (a hair growth pattern forming a swirling effect).

Another important factor is absolute hair length. The length hair grows varies from one person to another and may vary on different places on the head. Hair grows to a certain length, stops growing (absolute length), lives for awhile longer, then falls out. When new hair grows in, it will also grow only to this absolute length. The growth pattern at your hairline also helps to determine your most becoming cut or style. An uneven hairline will look better with bangs or an uneven napeline may need to be concealed. It is best to try for a style that is not in opposition to your hair's growth characteristics.

Hair type. Your hair type greatly affects what you can do with your hair. There are three factors that determine your hair type: quantity, texture, and formation. Quantity refers to the number of hairs on your scalp. Hair is thin if when gathered into a ponytail it equals or is less than the diameter of your finger, or if your scalp shows through when your hair is wet. A ponytail of medium-quantity hair will be about two to three fingers in thickness, one of thick hair might be four fingers or more in thickness. A head of hair may exhibit more than one quantity, having thinner areas in the front and thicker areas at the nape of the neck, or the other way around.

So far, nothing has been devised that can change the quantity of your hair. You are born with a certain number of hair follicles just as you are born with a certain number of fingers. Aside from surgical implants to thicken the hair or plucking out hair to temporarily thin it, the only way to give it a better appearance is by way of haircuts, perms, color, and the like.

Hair texture refers to the diameter of each individual hair. Fine hair has the smallest diameter and is usually softer than other hair textures. Coarse hair has the largest diameter and sometimes feels wiry. Medium hair is in between these two extremes. Hair formation refers to whether your hair is naturally straight, wavy, or curly.

Hair texture and formation can be changed using chemical processes to curl, straighten, or add body to the hair. Temporary texturizers, such as mousse, gels, setting lotions, hair sprays, and other styling solutions, will slightly alter hair texture by adding body and by thickening the diameter of each hair shaft. These products can temporarily change the formation of the hair by altering the hydrogen bonds to form curls or to reduce curls on naturally curly and wavy hair.

Permanent Waving

A permanent wave can restructure the hair to look thicker, give body to limp hair, or give waves or curls. To add body without curl, a cold wave permanent solution used with large rollers (a body wave) is an option models sometimes choose. This is often the best choice because it still allows styling flexibility and does not strip hair of color and shine as stronger, curly permanents do. In most instances, it is preferred that models do not have permanent waves; however, if applying a perm will enhance the cut of the models hair, it is advisable. Models sometimes use spot perms that utilize a body wave only in certain areas, such as in the bangs or crown, to add volume and softness.

Chemical Hair Relaxing

Relaxers or straighteners utilize basically the same chemicals as permanent waving, but instead of reforming straight hair into curls or waves, curly or wavy hair is straightened. Many black models have their hair chemically relaxed to increase their styling options. However, the model's objective should always be to apply a minimal amount of chemicals to approach the desired effect, so as not to impair the condition of the hair.

Hair Color

In addition to playing an important part in establishing a look or image, hair color is important because of photographic considerations. Extremes in hair colors tend to be more difficult to photograph. For example, very dark hair is often difficult to photograph because it appears as a solid mass in certain lighting situations.

Artificial hair colors may also pose problems. Overly highlighted hair has too much contrast and can yield a hard look. Hair that has been bleached too blond shows outgrowth, which is very noticeable in a photograph.

Although beautiful, natural color is preferred, slightly modified hair colors are acceptable. Depending on the lighting used, all shades from medium blonde, to reddish brown, to medium brown may appear darker and duller when photographed. Hair that lacks highlights is rendered flat and dull on film. Models whose hair color is uninteresting often utilize artificial coloring techniques to enhance their appearance and combat some of the ill effects of lighting and photography. Sometimes lifting or deepening the color of the hair by one or two shades makes a dramatic difference, imparting new life and vibrancy not only to the hair but to the skin as well. Highlighting or lightening selected strands is extensively used by models because it looks natural, does not show an obvious outgrowth, is not as damaging to the hair as overall lightening processes, yet still enlivens the appearance of the hair. Mousey brown hair is often enhanced by subtly weaving in strands of blondish or reddish color. Highlighting is usually best done by hand by an artistic and experienced colorist using several gradations of color.

Consult with Experts in the Modeling Field

Before doing anything to your hair, consult with one or more agents for suggestions on the right hair look. If a good agent is very interested in you and wants you to sign a contract, follow his or her advice. You may also find it helpful to consult with photographers, hairstylists, and makeup artists.

Select the Right Hairstylist

A professional model doesn't take chances with her hair by attempting to cut, color, permanent, or straighten it herself. Instead she carefully selects a hairstylist who is trained in the latest procedures. Your most important consideration when selecting a hairstylist is that he or she is aware of your hair's requirements for occupational reasons. A hairstylist who understands what type of image you and your agent are trying to create is vital. It is also neccessary for the hairstylist to be abreast of current trends and understand the relationship of the model's hair to the fashions she will be modeling.

Even if a hairstylist can produce the style of the moment but doesn't understand the versatility needed for modeling, he or she won't be of much help. Giving you a hairstyle that looks fantastic parted only one way will wreak havoc on assignments when you or other hairstylists attempt to produce different looks. Also a good hairstylist pays attention to cutting and styling your hair to enhance your hair and facial features.

Usually you'll get best results if you act on the referrals of agents and photographers. Working with a hairstylist who is a current favorite among top models and who currently styles hair for shootings, fashion shows, and video work in your market will be advantageous. Working with hairstylists who are favored by the top models in your area will raise you to the level of your competition. You may have to spend more, but the money you put into your hair is a business investment. Entrusting your hair to only the best hairstylists is important because a bad haircut, color, or perm can destroy or limit your chances for success for several months to a year.

Realize that you may not hit on exactly the right style the first time you try. Many models have their hair cut in stages until it becomes apparent that they have achieved the optimum style. It is important to avoid a hairstylist who cuts too much of the hair or who tries to talk you into trying a new style on every visit. Allowing a hairdresser to get used to your hair and face and then maintaining regular appointments is important.

ASSEMBLING A PROFESSIONAL HAIRSTYLING KIT

A model cannot always rely on having a professional hairdresser on assignments. Like makeup artists, hairstylists are often not employed on standard catalog shootings and small jobs. They are also usually not employed for promotional and fashion show modeling, unless the bookings are very important. Sometimes the model will be able to have her hair styled professionally on her own time and at her own expense before the booking, but usually she will do her own. Also, she may be expected to change her hair throughout the assignment so that it is compatible with a number of items she may be asked to model. In addition a model must know how to style her hair when meeting prospective clients and other decision makers in order to make a good impression.

A model must acquire professional hairstyling tools that will allow her to care properly for her hair and achieve a variety of looks. The kit she will assemble should be perfectly tailored to the needs of her hair. The following are some of the items you will need.

Brushes and Combs
Hairbrushes

Standard hairbrushes are used to massage the scalp, detangle and groom the hair, and add volume. The hairbrushes you select will depend on your hair type. Thick hair often benefits from a natural boar bristle brush, whereas thin hair receives added volume when groomed with a mixture of boar and nylon bristles. A ball-tipped nylon brush with a flexible rubber base (Figure 1) works well on all hair types and is extra gentle to hair. A nylon vent brush is used when blowdrying the hair to make it dry faster and smoother.

Figure 1. A ball-tipped nylon brush.

Styling Brushes

Styling hairbrushes are used to form the hair into certain styles. They are usually used in connection with a blowdryer to reinforce the style. There are several types that yield different effects. A denman or quill brush gives a smooth straight look. It can also be used to slightly curve the ends of hair. A round brush adds curl: the smaller the diameter of the brush, the smaller the curl. A large round brush can be used to add volume to hair at the top or sides of head.

Combs

A standard comb has both large teeth for parting and detangling the hair and small teeth for styling the hair. Nylon combs offer flexibility and don't break. Plastic and metal combs can split and break hair. A wide-tooth comb is useful for combing wet hair to avoid breakage.

Styling Combs

*Figure 2.
A combination comb.*

Styling combs are available in a variety of forms. A hair pick is used to lift the hair to add height, to separate and fluff, and to add volume to teased or curly hair. It is very useful on photo shootings for arranging the hair. A teasing comb has closely spaced, alternating short and long teeth. One of the most useful combs for a model is one that combines a pick and a teasing comb (Figure 2). A rattail comb with very narrowly spaced teeth works well for achieving precise parts and for teasing the hair and creating a smooth, sleek style. It is also effective for fine hair.

**Appliances
Blow Dryer**

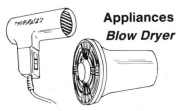

Figure 3. (a) *A blow dryer.*
(b) *A diffuser.*

A small, portable blow dryer with both drying (warm) and styling (cool) settings (Figure 3a) is a necessity for a model. The minimum wattage should be 1200. Use it to dry the hair quickly when wet or to create straight or wavy hairstyles. A diffuser attachment (Figure 3b) is useful to add body when drying the hair and to prevent pulling out curl on naturally wavy or permed hair. A conelike attachment is also useful when airstyling the hair as it will direct the stream of air to the desired area only. Male models usually find blow-drying the hair best for their needs.

Curling Iron

Each model has a preferred method for curling hair that works best to achieve the look determined by her cut and hair type. A curling iron is useful for adding firm curls or waves in specific areas. It is usually too damaging to use all over the head on a regular basis. A curling iron works best for touchups. There are several types of irons from which to choose. Your hair type will determine which type of iron you select. For example, coarse hair will need a hotter iron than thin easy-to-curl hair. Consult with a hairdresser to obtain a professional curling iron.

(a)

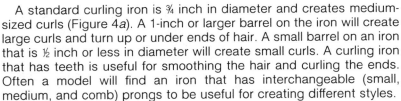

Figure 4. (a) *A curling iron with attachments.*
(b) *A straightening iron.*

A standard curling iron is ¾ inch in diameter and creates medium-sized curls (Figure 4a). A 1-inch or larger barrel on the iron will create large curls and turn up or under ends of hair. A small barrel on an iron that is ½ inch or less in diameter will create small curls. A curling iron that has teeth is useful for smoothing the hair and curling the ends. Often a model will find an iron that has interchangeable (small, medium, and comb) prongs to be useful for creating different styles.

A straightening iron has two flat parts that are pulled through the hair to straighten it (Figure 4b). Black models and other models with naturally curly hair often find a straightening iron to be very useful. A straightening iron is useful for any model who wants to quickly make a change from a curled to a straight hairstyle. There are other types of irons available for waving and crimping the hair; however, models usually won't need these unless they are specifically applicable to her particular hair look.

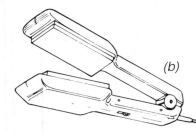

(b)

Electric Rollers

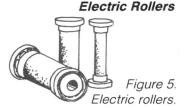

Figure 5.
Electric rollers.

Caring for Hair Implements

Hairstyling Preparations

Water

Figure 6.
A hair mister.

Setting Lotions

Thermal Styling Solutions

Hairstyling Gels

Mousse

Hairspray

Miscellaneous Supplies

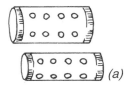

(a)

A set of electric rollers (Figure 5) is very useful for creating soft, loose waves or curls on medium to long hair. Select standard thermal rollers that do not require steam for convenience. A variety of sizes in one set is most useful. Also, select rollers having a smooth, velvety surface to prevent tangling and breaking of the hair. If your hair is very thick, you may need two sets of rollers. If your hair is hard to curl, you may need a set of rollers having only very small diameter rollers. It is a good idea to experiment with different types of electric rollers.

Clean combs and brushes work most effectively. Remove the hair from combs and brushes after each use. Clean them periodically to remove hair oils and residues from styling preparations. To clean, swish brushes and combs in warm, sudsy water (use shampoo).

To clean thermal styling appliances (blow dryer, curling iron, and electric rollers), unplug the appliance and wipe it clean using a damp cloth. Vacuum the vents of a blowdryer to clear out hair and debris.

A styling preparation is used to reform the hair into a different style, add body, and secure a style. The most useful ones for a model are the following.

Water is used to reshape the hair. Hair can be set wet on traditional rollers and air or hot-air dried, or it can be blow-dried. For faster results, misting dried hair with water (Figure 6) and then setting works well. Water is also very useful for removing curl and frizziness. A model will find a plastic bottle with an atomizer to yield a fine spray of water useful for styling the hair.

Setting lotions are designed to be used on damp hair. They add volume and help the hair to hold curl longer. Models sometimes add setting lotion to water in a spray bottle, spray it on their hair after shampooing, and then dry hair. All styling is made easier.

Thermal styling solutions are used in conjunction with electric rollers, curling irons, and blow dryers. Their purpose is twofold: first, they protect the hair against heat damage; second, they help the hair to hold curl.

Gels are usually used on wet hair to form the hair into a certain shape or curl. When the hair is dried and brushed through, the results are precise and long lasting. Gels may also be used on dry hair to slick back the sides and give a neat look to a hairstyle or to add volume to selected areas.

Mousse is setting lotion in the form of foam. It is convenient to use on wet or dry hair before or during styling. It adds volume.

Hairspray is used on dry hair to secure curl. There are different strengths of hairspray solutions. Molding sprays make the hair stiff and are useful for holding the hair firmly in position. Medium-strength hairsprays are for average use and hold the hair in place without a lot of stiffness. Mild-strength hairsprays hold the hair, yet look soft and allow the hair to move while still holding the curl. Hairspray is important for a model to have on assignments when precise styling is necessary. Hairspray is also useful while shaping and blowdrying the hair to create different hair looks. Hairspray also works well for quick sets.

Hair rollers. There are several types of hair rollers (Figure 7). Plastic rollers yield smooth, uniform curls. Velcro or self-locking rollers yield fluffy, soft, uniform curls and work particularly well for hair that is thin, fine, or lacks body. Sponge rollers are best for achieving nonuniform curls at the ends of the hair. They are also gentle to the hair and comfortable to wear. Rubber shapers yield firm, smooth curls and can be used to add curl at the scalp and/or the ends. There are other types

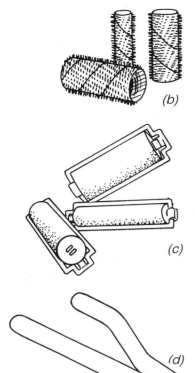

Figure 7. Hair rollers:
(a) *plastic,* (b) *velcro,*
(c) *sponge, and* (d) *rubber
shapers.*

**When to Use the
Hairstyling Kit**

of rollers such as brush and metal rollers; however, these are not recommended due to their damaging effects.

Rollers are available in a range of sizes. The smaller the diameter of the roller, the tighter the curl. Small rollers are ¾ inch or less in diameter; medium-sized rollers are 1 inch in diameter; large rollers are in excess of 1 inch in diameter. Large rollers are used to create large waves or to add volume.

Bobby pins. A collection of small and large bobby pins matched to the model's haircolor is necessary for securing the hair into rolls, twists, and knots.

Hairpins. Hairpins in large and small sizes matched to the model's haircolor are useful for securing hair into rolls, twists, and knots.

Clips. Clips of small and medium size are useful for securing regular and volume pin curls. They are also used to secure hair in rollers. Extra-long clips are used to section off the hair when blow-dry styling, curling, or cutting the hair. Clips are also useful for securing the hair out of the way during makeup application.

Elastic bands. Covered elastic bands, instead of rubber bands, are used for gathering medium to long hair into ponytails.

Hair accessories. Hair ornaments or accessories are useful for adding detail to a hairstyle or for coordinating the hair with the fashions being worn. The design, size, and color of hair accessories change with fashion. Examples of hair accessories are headwraps, headbands, ribbons, ties, cords, ornamental combs, and barrettes. Conservative hair ornaments are small and colorless or close in color to the hair (for example, pearl and gold or brown tortoise shell). Less conservative hair ornaments are available in brightly colored plastic and a variety of materials, such as rhinestones. A model should have an assortment of conservative and fun hair accessories that play up her hairstyles and enhance the fashions she wears to appointments or at assignments.

It is always important for a model to find out whether there will be a hairstylist at the booking. When a hairstylist is assigned, it usually is not necessary for a model to add her hair supplies kit to her totebag. However, she should always carry basic supplies so that her hair will look good en route to and after her assignment. If a model has difficult to manage hair, it is also wise to include her hair supplies kit, because she may find that she is more successful with her own hair than a professional hairstylist.

When a hairstylist is not employed, the model should ascertain from her booker what types of hairstyles she will be expected to produce on the booking. In these cases, the model is expected to arrive at the booking with her hair styled and only finishing touches to be made. If a model's hair is difficult to style or does not hold curl well, it is acceptable to arrive in rollers covered by a scarf or to arrive with unset hair. In either instance, the model should arrive at least 15 minutes early in order to allow her time to style her hair so that she is ready to step on the set completely made up, coifed, and dressed at the booked time.

Models who are expected to do their own hair on an assignment must include their hair supplies kit because usually they will be expected to make minor hairstyle changes throughout the booking. A model should also be aware that there are times when a hairstylist is present only at the beginning of the booking. After he has set and styled the hair and is dismissed, the model is expected to maintain the hairstyle or make minor changes as needed.

It is best if the model keeps all hair supplies in her totebag and maintains a fully stocked kit that will accompany her to assignments. A model should include all the items needed to create a variety of different hairstyles. Customize this kit to make it applicable to your hair and the type of modeling work you will be doing.

Hairstyling Kit Checklist

Tools
- ☐ Standard hairbrush
- ☐ Styling hairbrushes
- ☐ Standard combs
- ☐ Styling combs (include a teasing comb and pick)

Appliances
- ☐ Blow dryer
- ☐ Curling iron(s)
- ☐ Electric rollers

Hairstyling preparations
- ☐ Water container with spray nozzle (Obtain the type that can be closed when not in use to prevent leakage.)
- ☐ Preferred styling preparations: setting lotion, mousse, gel, thermal styling lotion
- ☐ Hairspray

Supplies
- ☐ Traditional rollers
- ☐ Bobby pins
- ☐ Hair pins
- ☐ Clips
- ☐ Accessories
- ☐ Rain scarf
- ☐ _____
- ☐ _____
- ☐ _____

LEARNING PROFESSIONAL HAIRSTYLING TECHNIQUES

Simone d'Aillencourt was a famous French model in the early 1960s who amazed clients and photographers with her magicianlike ability to change her hair into a variety of styles. She distinguished herself from her competition with this ability. Any model can improve her chances of success by being able to style her own hair effectively.

It is very important that a model know how to perform common hairstyling techniques properly; they are the basis for creating a variety of styles. Learning how to perform such procedures as effectively as a professional hairstylist will enable a model to achieve similar results. Each tool in a model's hairstyling kit can be used in various ways to create different effects.

Brushing to Massage the Scalp

The correct way of brushing the hair is done by touching the brush gently against the scalp and carrying it through to the very ends of the hair. Models use brushing to stimulate the scalp, aid in the drying of hair, brush out sets, and add volume. When using a brush to stimulate the scalp, limit brushing to 20 or 30 strokes. Too much brushing can split the hair.

Blow-drying the Hair

There are two basic reasons for using a blow dryer: drying wet hair and redirecting or styling hair.

Drying the Hair with a Blow Dryer

To dry wet hair with a blow dryer, always start with hair that has been combed. You may also want to add a heat-protective or volume styling lotion. See Figure 8 for some blow-drying tips.

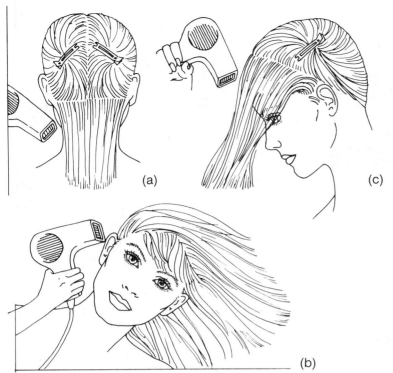

Figure 8. Professional blow-drying tips. (a) When drying or styling the hair with a blow dryer, section off underneath layers and dry hair layer by layer, finishing with the uppermost layer. If your hair is very thick and full, start by drying underneath layers at the nape of the neck and work your way toward the front. If your hair needs extra fullness at the front, dry underneath layers at the sides of your head first, working your way toward the back of your head. (b) For volume along the face, incline your head to one side and dry hair. (c) For volume in the back, bow your head to allow hair to hang forward, then dry hair. Remember to always aim the blow dryer in the direction in which the hair is flowing. Also, circulate the air of the dryer over the scalp to avoid exposing the hair to too much heat.

Straight Hair	Start with the blow dryer set at high, and brush through the hair with a vent brush while drying the hair with the blow dryer. When hair has been dried to the point that it is just slightly damp, attach a diffuser to the blow dryer, and fluff and scrunch hair with your fingers while aiming air all over hair. This technique achieves maximum volume for straight hair.
Permed or Wavy Hair	Blow-dry hair using a diffuser attachment on the dryer while scrunching hair with your fingers. Hair can be separated by using a pick. Using a blow dryer without the diffuser attachment and brushing through the hair while drying will pull out the curl.
Coarse or Frizzy Hair	Blow-dry hair using the blow dryer on high without any attachment, and brush through hair with a quill brush. When hair is just damp, switch the dryer setting to cool and finish drying.

Styling the Hair with a Blow Dryer

Curving the Ends of the Hair

Hair should be damp. For a very slight curve, use a quill brush. For a more exaggerated curl, use a large round brush. Section hair to expose just the underneath layer. Use a large clip or clamp to secure hair on top of head. Pull brush to ends of hair and rotate clockwise to achieve curled-under ends, counterclockwise to achieve flipped-up ends. When hair is dry, section another layer of hair and repeat the procedure until uppermost layers of hair have been curled. Use the blow dryer on a low setting, and attach an air director attachment to confine the flow of air to the desired area. Make certain that air is aiming in the direction you want the hair to go. This technique also works well for styling bangs and front portions of hair.

Adding Fullness in Desired Areas

To add fullness to hair at the crown, use a circular brush in a clockwise rotation to pick up hair at the top of the head. Expose roots to air. Another way to do this is to pick up the hair through your fingers and hold the strand perpendicular to (out from) the head while aiming air at the roots. For extra hold or fullness, spray hair with super-hold hairspray while blow-drying.

To add fullness to the sides, using a comb, pull hair straight out from the sides of the head. While holding comb in place, aim air at roots. For extra-holding power, spray hair with hairspray while blow-drying.

Adding Curl With the Blow Dryer

Section off a 1-inch strand of hair and curl it around a small round brush while aiming the blow dryer at it. Don't wind a strand of hair more than one and a half times onto a small brush, or the hair will get lodged in the bristles.

How to Use a Curling Iron

The correct way to use a curling iron begins by preheating the iron to the desired temperature. Test it before putting it in your hair. Follow the steps shown in Figure 9.

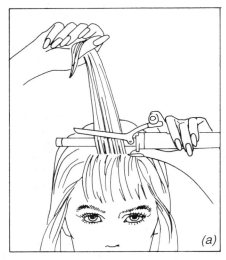

Figure 9. (a) Pick up a strand of hair that has a thickness of ½ to ¾ inch and is 1½ to 2 inches wide. First, place the iron in about ½ to 1 inch away from scalp with the clamp up. (b) Second, close the clamp and hold for a few seconds to achieve lift at the scalp. Hold the end of the strand with your left hand, pulling it gently to apply a little tension and turn the iron toward you. Open and close the clamp quickly as you rotate the iron, working more of the hair into it until the ends are wound. Make sure ends are smooth to avoid "fishtail" ends. (c) Third, hold the hair in the iron for a second to make sure it curls well. Open the clamp and slide the iron out of the curl. The curl should stand fairly well. To ensure a firm set, place a clip at the base of each curl as you complete it, and then remove clips after all curls are in place.

How to Curl Hair with Rollers

The key to a good roller set, whether you choose thermal or traditional rollers, is proper setting technique (Figure 10). To increase the life of your set, use heat styling lotion when setting hair with electric rollers and use water or setting lotion for traditional rollers. Begin by picking up a strand of hair that is a littler narrower than your roller. The base or thickness of the strand should equal the diameter of your roller. For example, if you are using a roller that is 2½ inches wide and 1 inch in diameter, the strand of hair you should part off with your comb should be 2 inches wide by 1 inch in thickness. For larger curls use larger rollers; use smaller rollers for smaller curls. Second, comb through the strand with a fine-tooth comb, then place the ends of hair around the roller, making sure they are straight and smooth, not crooked or matted. Make sure there are no strays. Neatness is vital to a good set.

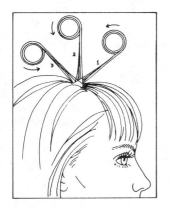

Figure 10. To achieve the desired volume, hold the strand at the proper angle to the scalp when winding the roller. For maximum volume the strand should be held at a 45-degree angle from the head. For a little volume at the scalp, hold strand straight out from the head. For no volume or flatness at the scalp, hold strand downward. When rolling hair, put a little tension on the strand by stretching it. This relaxes the hair's protein chain, making it easier for it to form itself into a new shape. Wind the roller (counterclockwise for most sets), making sure all necessary hair is included. When you wind down to the scalp, hold the roller in position, again using a little tension and secure with a bobby pin or clip at the base of roller. Repin rollers if they do not stand up firmly from the scalp, as this will yield a poor set.

Setting Patterns

There are basically three setting patterns on which all styles are based: the front-to-back, side-to-side and bricklayer sets (see Figure 11). A front-to-back set directs hair away from the face. A side-to-side set adds volume on sides. A bricklayer gives easy, free-flowing curls without ridges or partings that may result from other setting patterns.

After hair is set in traditional rollers, it must be exposed to a hood-type dryer or air until dry. A hood-type dryer will dry hair in 20 to 60 minutes, depending on the amount of hair and the type of dryer. Electric rollers should be left in hair from 30 seconds to 20 minutes or until cool, depending on how easily the hair curls and how much curl is desired.

Figure 11

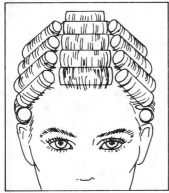

(a) *Front-to-back set.*

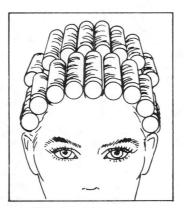

(b) *Side-to-side set.*

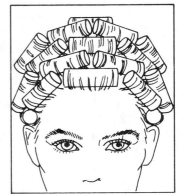

(c) *Bricklayer pattern.*

Volume Curls   Volume curls or barrel curls do not utilize rollers. After lightly misting hair with water or hairspray, hair is wound in a cylindrical form and secured at the base of the curl with a clip (see Figure 12).

The curl is air-dried or dried with a blowdryer and a diffuser attachment. Volume curls are often used by models because they work well for quickly sprucing up a style that looks tired or for creating soft volume without a lot of curl. Volume curls are often used to add fullness to bangs or hair on the sides of the head, while getting the hair out the way for makeup application.

Figure 12. A volume curl.

Pin Curls   Pin curls are used to reinforce a drooping curl or to give lots of curl without a lot of height. Pin curls work best on short hair. They are similar to volume curls except that instead of standing up horizontally from the scalp, they stand up vertically from the scalp or lay flat against it (Figure 13).

Pin curls that are made by twisting strands until they coil yield fluffy waves.

Figure 13. Three types of pin curls.

Combing or Brushing Out a Set   The combing or brushing out of a set is as important as the set. A lot of practice and skill is required to achieve a variety of styles. Always begin the combing out by removing all the rollers and allowing the hair to rest for a minute. Then brush through the curls to relax the set. Next comb the hair into place using your fingers and hands to direct the hair into waves and curls. The most commonly used comb out techniques are as follows.

Using a Brush to Add Volume   To add volume, bend over to allow your hair to hang freely from your head. Brush from the nape of the neck to the ends of the hair. Toss head back. Then use brush to lightly arrange stray hairs into place.

To add volume to the ends of hair only, move the brush to the ends and lift the hair slowly allowing it to fan out, thereby creating volume and fluffiness. Using hairspray or a blow dryer in conjuction with either of these techniques will add longer-lasting, extra volume.

To add soft volume to selected areas, use a brush to tease the hair. Rotate the brush to comb hair opposite to the way it hangs. Leave as is for a fluffy look, or lightly brush the top layer of hair over teasing for a smooth look. This technique is called *"backbrushing."*

Teasing the Hair

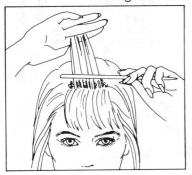

Figure 14. Teasing hair.

Teasing or backcombing to add fullness to an area or all over is used often in styling. In order to be effective it must be done properly (see Figure 14). First, use a teasing comb or one that has very narrowly spaced, fine teeth. Second, pick up a section of hair about 1 inch wide by ⅛ inch deep and hold straight out or perpendicular to the scalp. This is important. Third, while firmly holding onto the strand, put the comb in so that it goes through the entire hair strand about 1 inch away from the scalp. Push comb toward scalp. Remove comb. Repeat, starting a little further up the strand and pressing to scalp again. Use very small strokes and repeat several times until desired fullness is achieved. If hair resists teasing, try using hairspray on the strand first. After hair is teased, arrange into desired style by very lightly combing over teasing.

Styling Hair with Your Hands

Figure 15. Fingerteasing.

Fingers and hands are among the best styling tools available. There are several ways you can use your hands to style your hair.

Fingercomb. Spread your fingers and comb them through your hair. This works well to fluff hair and to tidy curly or wavy hairstyles.

Slick. When putting your hair up or back, use your palms to slick back the sides of hair. Apply a dab of setting gel, water, or hairdressing cream for added hold.

Fingertease. Tease your hair using your fingers instead of a comb (Figure 15). Hold a strand of hair straight up or out from scalp while teasing with two fingers of the opposite hand.

Scrunch. Grab a handful of hair and squeeze it in your fist (Figure 16). This adds body and will make a curly or wavy style more so. Use styling mousse, gel, or hairspray for more pronounced results.

Fingerwaving. Apply a little styling gel to wet hair. Then using a comb in one hand, create waves by pressing a finger into a section of hair to create a wedge (see Figure 17). Use clips to secure if necessary, and air or blow dry using a diffuser attachment. When combing out a set, spray dry hair to hold fingerwaves in place.

Fluffing. Toss hair with hands to create volume. Bend over from the waist and use your fingers to fluff your hair. Then flip your head back as you stand up. Use hairspray and a blow dryer while tossing for more pronounced results.

Scrubbing. To achieve volume at the roots and to make hair dry faster, place fingers in at the roots and move from side to side in a scrubbing motion.

Lifting and pulling. Place fingers or a hair pick in hair at roots and lift or pull hair away from scalp. Use spray or gel and a blow dryer when lifting for more pronounced results.

Figure 16. Scrunching.

Figure 17. Fingerwaving.

How to Create Chignons and Rolls

A model can change her hair quickly and effectively by securing it into a chignon or roll. Lots of variations can be worn when hair is styled in a roll or chignon (see Figures 18 to 20). For example, all of the hair can be slicked back, or straight, teased, or curled bangs can be worn. Hair ornaments can also be added for interest.

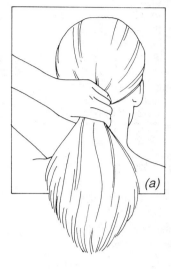

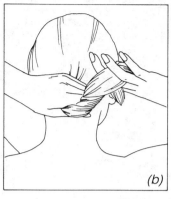

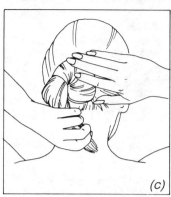

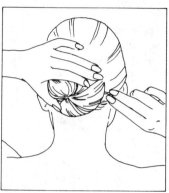

Figure 18. Creating a basic chignon. (a) Gather hair at the back of the head with one hand. Position this hand at the point where you want the chignon to be. (b) With the other hand, twist the hair until it coils. Continue coiling until all the hair is in the chignon. (c) Tuck in any strays. Secure chignon with hairpins and bobby pins.

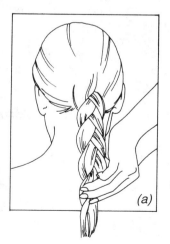

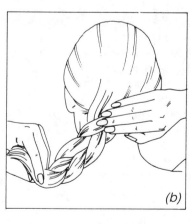

Figure 19. Creating a braided chignon. (a) Gather hair and braid. Secure end of braid with an elastic band. (b) Place braid in a circular formation by winding the braid (starting with the base) around your finger.

Tuck the end of the braid under the chignon. (c) Secure with hairpins and bobby pins. A braided chignon is an attractive, easy, quick alternative for very long or very thick hair.

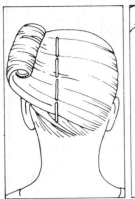  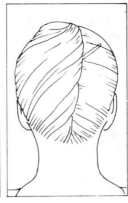

Figure 20. Creating a roll. A roll is a good alternative for hair that isn't long enough to be styled in a chignon. It also works well for layered hair. Layers at the crown can be curled or teased to create different looks. (a) Smooth hair to one side. Secure hair with a row of bobby pins. (b) Roll ends of hair toward row of pins. (c) Secure roll using hairpins to interlock with row of bobby pins.

Figure 21. The twisting technique.

How to Use a Hairpiece

A hairpiece such as a wiglet, fall, or switch will usually have a comb attached to the base. To use this type of hairpiece, make a large pin curl in your own hair at the point where you plan to attach the hairpiece. Then place the comb of the hairpiece in under the pin curl. If further securing is necessary, use bobby pins. To conceal the difference between your hair and the hairpiece, comb your own hair over the hairpiece or place a hair accessory at the joining of the hairpiece to your hair.

Hairstyling Tips for Difficult-to-Manage Hair
How to Achieve Curly or Wavy Styles on Hard-to-Curl Hair

How to Straighten Curly or Frizzy Hair

Distribute mousse or a fine spray of water or styling lotion throughout hair. For extra wavy or curly styles, form pin curls or wind the hair around small sponge rollers or rubber shapers. Wind hair around as you would a roller, or try twisting the stand before rolling for extra volume (see Figure 21). Dry hair with a hood-type hair dryer or place a conditioning heat cap over your head to heat rollers. (When thermal rubber shapers are available, use of a blow dryer or heat cap is unnecessary.) When hair has been exposed to heat for 10 to 20 minutes (depending on how easily it curls), remove heat and allow hair to cool completely in rollers. Remove rollers. Comb through hair using fingers or a pick. A brush will cause frizziness. Be creative and try setting your hair on unconventional rollers. Hairstylists sometimes use rags, wads of cotton, plastic bag twist ties, or pipecleaners.

Start with blow-dried hair that is not completely dry. Set hair on large electric rollers. When rollers have been in hair 2 to 10 minutes, begin removing one roller at a time. Each time you unwind a roller, use a quill brush and a blow dryer with a funnel attachment to further straighten hair. Repeat with each roller until whole head is done. Flip head forward, comb hair gently, then flip head back.

Another technique is to pull a curling iron straight through the hair with the prongs closed. Follow with blow-drying techniques previously mentioned if further straightening is necessary.

To straighten the hair using a thermal straightening iron, section the hair to expose the underneath layer of hair. Secure upper layers of hair on top of head. Pin the sections of hair on the sides of your head forward. Then pull the closed iron through the section of hair at the nape of your neck, then through the right and left sides. Section another layer of hair and repeat this process until the uppermost layers of hair have been straightened. Comb through hair to style. Black models often find this method effective for straightening hair.

EXPERIMENTING WITH DIFFERENT HAIRSTYLES

It is important for a model to experiment with all types of hairstyles. To better understand the different ways in which hair can be styled, see Figures 22 to 28.

Figure 22. Partings. The hair can be parted in several different ways to achieve different looks: (a) *no part*, (b) *center part*, (c) *side part*, (d) *diagonal part*, (e) *round part*, (f)) *zig zag*, (g) *half part*, and (h) *multiple parts*.

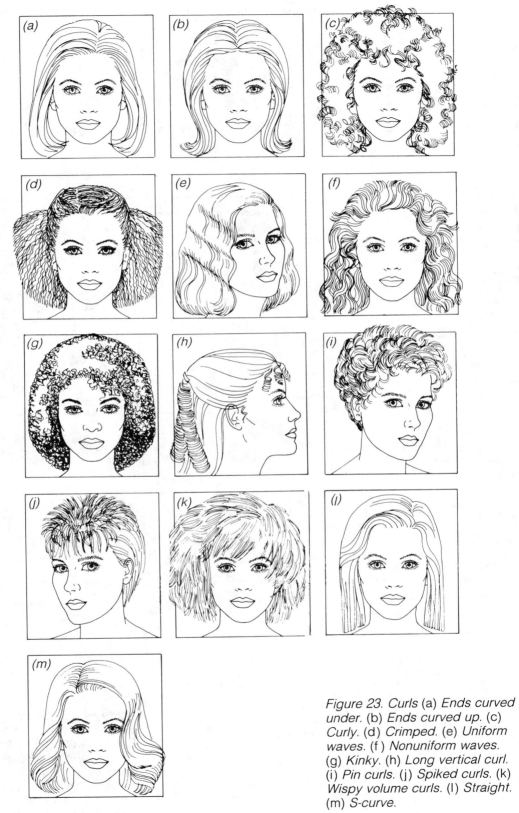

Figure 23. Curls (a) *Ends curved under.* (b) *Ends curved up.* (c) *Curly.* (d) *Crimped.* (e) *Uniform waves.* (f) *Nonuniform waves.* (g) *Kinky.* (h) *Long vertical curl.* (i) *Pin curls.* (j) *Spiked curls.* (k) *Wispy volume curls.* (l) *Straight.* (m) *S-curve.*

Figure 24. Fullness or direction. (a) *Off face.* (b) *Toward face.* (c) *Asymmetrical.* (d) *Fullness on top.* (e) *Fullness all over.* (f) *Pageboy, fullness at ends.* (g) *Symmetrical fullness.* (h) *Asymmetrical fullness.* (i) *Draped effect.* (j) *Wet hair.*

128

Figure 25. Ponytails. (a) Standard. (b) Side (low). (c) Side (high). (d) Top. (e) Pigtails. (f) Partial top. (g) Partial side. (h) Partial back. (i) Partial crown.

(a)

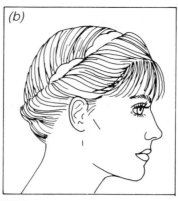

(b)

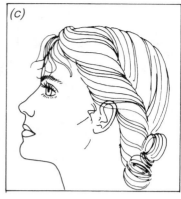

(c)

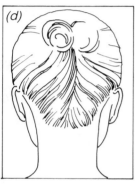

(d)

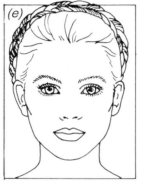

(e)

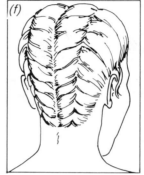

(f)

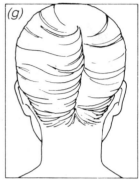

(g)

(h)

(i)

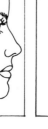

Figure 26. Rolls, twists, and braids. (a) Top swirl. (b) Tight head roll. (c) Loose roll. (d) French roll. (e) Crown braid. (f) French braid. (g) French twist. (h) Side braid. (i) Ornamental braid.

Figure 27. Knots and chignons. (a) Classic chignon. (b) Top knot. (c) Gibson girl knot.

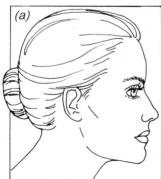

(a)

(b)

(c)

Figure 28. Accessories. (a) *Headwrap.* (b) *Cascade barrette.* (c) *Clamp.* (d) *Standard headband.* (e) *Wound cord.* (f) *Standard barrettes.* (g) *Colored gels and sprays.* (h) *Sport headband.* (i) *Fall with headband.*

ANALYZING HOW TO STYLE HAIR FOR DIFFERENT SITUATIONS

When determining how to style your hair, there are several factors a model should consider:

1. What type of assignment is this?
2. What is the concept of this ad or show?
3. Are there special circumstances?
4. Are there instructions from the client?

What Type of Assignment Is This?

Styling the Hair for Print Assignments

Different types of assignments have different requirements. Generally the following information will apply.

Hairstyling requirements for catalog shootings are dependent on the style and concept of the catalog. A conservative, straightforward, basic catalog will usually dictate simple, natural-looking hairstyles, such as straight hair or hair with curved ends or gentle waves. Such a catalog is not overly fashion conscious and avoids drawing attention away from the clothes being shown. Very complicated hairstyles are usually not feasible because of the time element and because of the fact that models must often do their own hair or have limited assistance from a hairstylist.

A trendy, specialized catalog will dictate hairstyles that depict current fashion and that work well with the clothing. Many times a hairstylist is employed for such assignments.

Whether the catalog in which the model appears is conservative or trendy, most catalog clients have two basic requirements. First, usually a hairstyle change is required with each garment change. Second, the hair must not interfere with showing the clothes or product. Catalog clients usually do not want a hairstyle that hides important garment details, such as necklines and shoulder details. If a model's hair is long, she must be able to create styles that direct the hair back or up to avoid covering important details of the clothing.

Advertisements

Advertising clients prefer a style that appeals to the type of person who would use the product they are advertising. For example, a very young-looking hairstyle would not be most effective for the model in an ad appealing to businesswomen. In most print advertising, a hairstylist is employed. An advertiser must also consider the life span of the photo for an ad or package he is creating. If the ad or package will be used over a period of years, he or she must select a hairstyle that will not look outdated in this period of time.

Editorials

Editors of fashion magazines like current hairstyles that enhance the garment's design. Most editorial clients employ hairdressers whose work sets the look in hair fashions.

Styling the Hair for Fashion Shows

Fashion show clients like anything current that expresses the designer's intentions. For fashion shows, because of timing, it is usually not required that the hairstyle be changed with each garment. This is only expected if several models are employed, allowing ample time between each model's appearances.

Since most fashion shows require quick changes, it is important for a model to have a hairstyle that works well with all of the clothing she will be modeling and that her hairstyle looks good throughout the show, withstanding rushed changes, hats, and other such circumstances. Models often wear a chignon type of hairstyle, that looks neat and doesn't detract attention from the garments being shown. Even with a chignon type of hairstyle, minor changes can be made to create different looks. For example, a model may wear straight bangs for one appearance, curled or teased bangs for another appearance, and no bangs for yet another appearance.

Some fashion show models use hairpieces to change their hairstyles. For example, a model may pull her own hair back and pin on a hairpiece such as a chignon, ponytail, braid, or fall.

Headwraps and hair ornaments can also be added to simple, basic hairstyles to create variations; however, it is always a good idea to check with the show coordinator before wearing anything that may divert attention from the clothes.

Styling the Hair for Electronic Media Assignments

Electronic media clients handle hairstyling in different ways. A professional hairstylist is usually employed to style the hair for television commercials and feature programs. Promotional videos, such as those depicting fashion shows or makeup products, also employ hairstylists. When shooting industrial or educational films, often a hairstylist is not employed because the intention is for the model to have a realistic, natural-looking hairstyle. When models are extras in television commercials, feature films, and other audio visual productions they usually style their own hair.

What Is the Concept of the Ad or Show?

Find out what type of character you are to portray, what the product is and what approach the client is using. Ask the photographer if you are to have a neatly styled hair look or one that is more casual. Look at ads and editorial pages to see how hairstyles are being combined with different fashions and products.

Are There Any Special Circumstances?

If you are modeling outdoors, your hair can be a little freer and less precisely styled than in the studio. Always bring your comb/brush and hairspray to the area where you will be shooting. If you will be working with a fan, make sure that it is blowing your hair attractively. When in any photographic situation, check to see how the lighting or the layout is set up so that you will know how to style your hair according to the angle from which you will be photographed. For example, if you plan to wear a side ponytail, you would put it on the side toward the camera to give the most appealing look. Be aware of the angle that is most attractive for the hairstyle. For example, a ponytail at the back of your head usually looks better when your head is turned in profile.

Are There Specific Instructions?

Be aware of any specific instructions from the client, photographer, director, or coordinator. Determine if the client prefers a certain style and whether he or she expects changes. Some clients will have specific ideas about the hairstyles they want you to produce, others leave it up to the model to use her own judgment.

HOW TO LEARN MORE ABOUT STYLING YOUR HAIR

A model can advance faster in her career if she can style her hair effectively. Having a knack for creating different looks is important.

- Keep an idea notebook. Assemble pages from magazines showing different hairstyles. Sketch hairstyles you see on other models or celebrities. Experiment with lots of different styles in front of a mirror.
- Don't neglect the option of hairpieces; however, always pay attention that you obtain ones that are in fashion and are a perfect match for your hair's color and texture. Black models often find hairpieces to be very useful.
- Take a few lessons. Hire a hairstylist at his or her hourly rate to style your hair and teach you some styles that will work well for photo shootings. Choose a hairstylist who does hair for fashion photographers in your area. Always be informed of new hairstyles, tools, techniques, and products.
- Pay attention at shootings to determine exactly what procedures and tools the hairstylist used. Jot notes when you get home from a shooting, and try to recreate the style yourself.

- Practice styling your hair for a few hours each week. Try out new techniques when going on appointments. It is a good idea for a model to be able to produce five fundamental types of hairstyles: a sporty look to wear with active sportswear, a casual look for casual clothes, a business look for business clothes, a fashion-oriented look for chic daytime clothes, and a glamourous look for evening wear. These five hairstyles will be suitable for nearly anything to be modeled. Minor variations can be made to create even more options. Practice styles in which your hair is up, down, and back.

- Testing provides a good way to learn how to style your hair for photographic situations. Often styling hair for photos is just a matter of placing it so that it works well with the lighting and composition of the photo. The way the back of your hair looks is often unimportant because usually you are photographed from the front or side. Models sometimes employ tricks, such as securing the back of the hair forward to create the illusion of more hair. Also being aware of how lighting affects your hair is important. For example, if you are wearing a smooth hairstyle and backlight is being used, you must be careful that there are no distracting strays to catch the light or that light is not shining through "holes" in your hairstyle.

HOW TO WORK WITH A HAIRSTYLIST ON A MODELING ASSIGNMENT

On many bookings a hairstylist is assigned to style the model's hair. Knowing how to help the hairstylist to do his or her job optimally will produce the desired results for the model, hairstylist, photographer, and client.

- Always arrive with clean, air-dried hair. Make sure your hair is not overconditioned. This will make styling difficult. Avoid putting mousse, oil, or gel in hair. The hairstylist will do this if desired.

- Always put on a button-down top before the hairstylist begins styling your hair or put on your first garment if it is the type that slips over your head. Make sure you protect the garment by covering it. This also prevents you from ruining the hairstylist's work by pulling a top on and off.

- If you have hard-to-curl, difficult-to-manage hair, it may take more effort and time to achieve the desired look. Therefore, it is often wise to set your hair prior to the booking and to arrive with hair set. The hairstylist can comb it out, or if he doesn't like the set, he can wet it down and start over. If it is a good set, usually he or she will appreciate your effort.

- Don't tell the hairstylist how to style your hair. If he asks, tell him what your hair problems are, and show him your composite so he can see what can be done with your hair. Don't insist that he use your styling tools or preparations. As a professional, he has experimented with several and has his own preferences.

- Don't limit the hairstylist by forbidding her to use electric rollers or other standard styling tools that can be damaging to the hair. As a model, you are being paid well to assume such occupational hazards. They are a normal part of a model's job. If you feel your hair can't endure such normal aspects of the job, you might consult with your agent. He or she may be able to find out what will be done with your hair, and you may be able to set it and allow it to air dry before arriving at the booking. If your hair is truly in bad condition, you should consider taking time off to give your hair a rest.

- Don't argue with the hairdresser about the hairstyle he has created. Instead, check with the client or photographer to determine if it meets their requirements. Remember, on an assignment your hair is not styled to please you; it is styled to enhance the item you will be modeling.

- Don't be childish and overreact if your hair is handled a little more roughly than you would like. Hairstyling needs to be done quickly and precisely. Keep your head straight and still. Move it only when the hairstylist indicates that you should.

- Don't fiddle with your hair or try to alter it in any way after the hairstylist has finished styling it. If a wisp has gotten loose, bring it to the hairstylist's attention so she can fix it. Always let her check your hair right before going onto the set or runway.

- There are times when a hairstylist may want to trim the ends of your hair or your bangs. If the amount is not more than ½-inch, it will probably help your hair. If he wants to do something more drastic, consult your agent. Don't be intimidated into any hairstyle or other procedure that will irreversibly change your hair.

- Be very careful about accepting a booking, the result of which promotes a hairstylist, salon, or hair-care product. Always find out very specifically what they intend to do to your hair. They may want to give you a drastic, state-of-the-art haircut that will be unmarketable for you as a model. Accept such bookings with careful forethought.

- Inform your agent immediately if you have a scalp disorder that will hinder styling or that is communicable. You may be asked to do your own hair or a replacement may be sought.

- Don't chatter while the hairstylist is working on your hair. It slows her down and makes it difficult for her to concentrate. Be ready when she is ready for you; don't keep her waiting.

Chapter 5 The Model's Guide to Wardrobe

Like cosmetics, a model uses clothing and accessories as tools to increase her chances of success in the modeling field. All models, male and female, whether their specialty is modeling fashions or products, must have an appreciation and understanding of clothing. To increase your awareness of fashion, it is necessary to understand the principles of fashion. Knowing how to use the principles of fashion to create a certain image will be important to your success as a model.

THE PRINCIPLES OF FASHION

The four principles of fashion are: line, detail, texture, and color.

Line refers to the shape or cut of a garment. For example, a skirt may have one of several different shapes, such as flared, A-line, straight, or circular. The line of a garment influences the shape and proportions of the body. Although most models are well proportioned, there are certain garment lines that may flatter your body more than others, because of your bone structure. For example, if your neck is on the short side, wearing a V-neck or open-collared shirt will be a more flattering line than a turtleneck, which tends to make the neck appear shorter. Studying the different lines of garments and determining how they affect the appearance of your body is important for successful dressing.

Detail refers to trims, buttons, decorative seams, and accessories such as jewelry, scarves, and the like that comprise a fashion look. Details attract attention to the wearer's attractive features. For example, a lace collar or an interesting necklace can draw attention to the face. An attractive belt can draw attention to the waistline. Details are also used to add interest and variety to a garment. For example, a plain black dress can be dressed up with jewels or dressed down with fun costume jewelry.

Texture refers to the feel and structure of the fabric of a garment. The four natural fibers (silk, wool, cotton, and linen) and scores of synthetic fabrics offer lots of texture options. Fabrics come in a variety of grades, weights, and types, all of which affect texture. For example, silk is found in various forms. Wild silk or tussah is made from wild silkworms in their original state and has a rough, dull, bumpy surface. Raw silk is inexpensive silk that is wound directly from several cocoons and omits several refining processes. Spun silk originates from silk waste (fibers that are tangled outside the cocoon) and has a linty, cotton-like feel. Pure cultivated silk has a delicate look and a beautiful sheen. It is very lightweight and accepts dyes magnificently. Taffeta is weighted silk, meaning that it has been treated to make it feel heavier.

In addition to the fiber from which a fabric is made, the basic yarn construction, weaving technique, and fabric finish will also affect texture. Although a model doesn't need to know the technicalities of fabric manufacturing, becoming aware of the differences and how they influence texture can add to her wardrobe creativity.

Color is important for creating different looks with clothing. A model should know which colors enhance her or his personal palette (eye, hair, and skin color), as well as paying attention to those that are currently in fashion.

Many models find that acquiring solid-colored garments is a good way to build a wardrobe. Solid colors can be easily combined and can yield effective, if not dramatic, results. They are also economical because different pieces can be interchanged and solids serve as excellent backgrounds for accessories. Updating and adding variety to your clothing using accessories allows for numerous options. Prints, plaids, stripes, and patterns are easily remembered and cannot be combined as easily with other garments.

To better understand color, a terminology has been developed. The various aspects of color can best be learned by studying a color wheel. A color wheel can be a valuable aid when selecting and combining colors of makeup, clothing and accessories.

The categories of colors are: primary colors, secondary colors, and tertiary colors. Primary colors are the three basic colors from which all additional colors are created. Primary colors or hues are red, yellow, and blue. Secondary colors are created by mixing any two of the primary colors. For example: yellow + blue = green; blue + red = violet; red + yellow = orange. Tertiary colors are colors achieved by mixing a secondary color and a primary color in equal amounts. An intermediate color is thus achieved. For example: green + yellow = yellow green; green + blue = blue-green; violet + red = red-violet.

In addition to the categories of colors there are different dimensions of color. Pure colors are the primary colors before white, black, or other colors are mixed with them. Hue refers to the name of a given color. Value refers to the lightness or darkness of a color. Intensity is the brightness or dullness of a color. Shade refers to the darkness of a color. A shade is created when black is added to a color. Tint refers to the lightness of a color. A tint is created when white is added to a color. A tone is a color to which gray or some of the complementary color has been added so that the color is neutralized or made grayer.

The way two or more colors are combined results in a color harmony. There are four types of color harmonies: monochromatic, analogous, triadic, and complementary.

Monochromatic refers to a color arrangement that is made by using one color but with variations in lightness and darkness. For example in clothing, a monochromatic scheme could be a dark blue skirt with a medium blue jacket and a light blue shirt.

Analogous refers to a color arrangment that is made by using three colors that lie adjacent to each other on the color wheel. For example, in fashion an analogous combination would be a yellow-green top with a green skirt and blue-green belt. For best results, colors in analogous combinations should vary in intensity.

A triadic combination is made by using three colors that are equidistant on the color wheel. For example, a triadic combination in clothing might be a blue skirt with a yellow top and a red belt. In makeup it might be a dark blue eyeshadow with a gold toned blush and a red lipcolor. Varying the tints, shades, and intensities of colors involved will produce attractive harmonies.

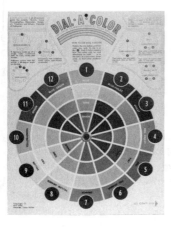

Using Color Effectively

A complementary color combination results when two colors that are directly opposite on the color wheel are combined. For example, in clothing a yellow top may be combined with a violet skirt. In makeup, a red-orange lipstick may be worn with a blue-green eyeshadow color.

Another dimension or characteristic of color is temperature. Colors are termed "cool" if they have a blue hue, whereas colors having an orange hue are termed "warm."

Black, white, and gray are called achromatic colors because they are neutrals or colorless. They can be used effectively with any color harmony or can be added to a color to make it lighter (tint), darker (shade) or neutral. Black and white mixed together yield a cool gray, whereas complementary colors mixed together produce a warm gray. When yellow or orange is added to white, the white gets warmer. When blue is added to white, the white gets cooler (See Figure 1).

Color can be used to enhance an individual's hair, eye, and skin colors. There are three color theories relating to color selection for makeup and fashion: the warm/cool or season theory, color preference theory, and makeup corrective color theory.

The warm/cool or season color theory states that everyone has either a yellow (warm) tone or a blue (cool) tone to their skin, hair, and eye coloring. People with light, warm eye, hair, and skin colors are referred to as having the coloring of spring. People who have darker, richer, more golden (warm) coloring are referred to as autumn or fall. Individuals with a blue or blue-pink undertone to the skin, dark hair, and deep-colored eyes are referred to as winter. Individuals who have fair skin with a blue undertone, medium to light ash-toned hair and softly colored blue, green, or hazel eyes are said to be summer. Individuals with spring coloring should adhere to soft, warm colors, while those with autumn coloring should select clothing and makeup in rich, warm colors. Summers should select soft, cool colors, whereas winters should opt for deep or rich cool colors.

The color preference theory states that everyone has an inner sense of color and is drawn to certain hues more than others. The colors that one is drawn to are also that individual's best colors.

The makeup corrective color theory states that any color can be worn successfully by an individual provided that foundation, eye, lip, and cheek colors are used to make the color work with the individual's personal coloring. For example, because of the ability of colors to reflect, a person with a ruddy skin should not wear red. However, in order to successfully wear red, a green undertoner can be used under foundation, and green eye colors can be worn to combat any unattractive effects. This theory often applies in modeling, where a model must look good in any color she is given to wear.

Another way color is used is to create illusion. Bright and light colors will make an area appear larger or give it more emphasis. Dull or dark colors covering an area will make the area appear smaller. For example, if an individual's figure is large, wearing dark or subtle colors will make the figure appear smaller. A small figure, on the other hand, appears larger when bright or light colors are worn.

USING THE PRINCIPLES OF FASHION

The best way to find the most flattering looks for your wardrobe is by experimenting. Take note of compliments you receive when you wear certain outfits. You may also want to consult with a wardrobe consultant or fashion stylist to help you determine your best choices. It is important to increase your awareness of fashion by reading fashion magazines. High-fashion magazines such as *Vogue, Elle,* and *Harper's Bazaar* are good sources. In addition, you should read those targeted to your age or image such as *Teen* for young juniors, *Seventeen* for juniors, *Mademoiselle* for juniors and college age, and *Glamour* for college age and young professionals. International magazines such as French and Italian *Vogue, Elegance, Elle,* Italian *Harper's Bazaar,* and *Linea Italiana* are great sources for trends and looks that have not yet come to the United States. They will keep you one step ahead. Study the pictures to see what is being shown and how it is being worn. Note the hair, makeup, and accessories shown with each fashion. Read the editorial copy for clues of trends. Other good information sources to consider are the trade publications of the fashion industry.

Always observe how clothing and accessories are used to create the image of a character, and apply these concepts to your modeling endeavors. For example, if you are a commercial model who can portray a business executive, notice how business executives in daily life and in advertisements dress to gain ideas on how to present that image. If you want to recreate a character, research the character to study the clothing he or she wore.

Another way to increase your fashion creativity is to assemble a fashion notebook. Use this book to collect magazine pages depicting clothing ideas you like. Jot down or make sketches of your ideas or ideas you may have seen on others in regard to clothing and accessory combinations and the like. Remember that it is not only what you wear, but how you wear it that can make or break your presentation.

Now that you understand the principles of fashion you will be able to apply them to dress effectively for modeling appointments. It is important to realize that the lines, colors, textures, or details of clothing that are chosen for you to model on an assignment may not always flatter your personal attributes. However, a client may have other reasons for asking you to wear certain articles. A professional model is always cooperative, knowing that he or she is being paid to wear what the client supplies. A good model knows how to alter her makeup colors to make her personal coloring look better with the color of a garment. If the line of a garment is unflattering, the model knows how to stand, walk, or pose to make the garment and her figure look ideal. If the model doesn't like the details or texture of a garment or thinks that they do not work with her image, she knows how to transcend her personal feelings and become the character that is dictated by the garment.

In addition to using the principles of fashion effectively, there are three other factors that are necessary for dressing with success: selecting the right undergarments, determining proper fit, and maintaining the condition of your clothing.

Selecting the Right Undergarments

The foundation of a successful wardrobe is well-fitting and appropriate undergarments for all items you wear. What you wear under the clothes you wear or model can enhance or detract from their appearance. Assembling a complete wardrobe of undergarments is necessary for modeling because you will be given all sorts of things to wear.

Undergarments should never show under your clothes. Select undergarments in the correct color and fit. Nude-colored undergarments that closely match the color of your skin are usually the best choice. If an undergarment is white or too light, soaking it in tea will produce the desired skin tone. Make sure your undergarments are neither too tight nor too loose. They should never create lines under your clothes. Consult an individual who is trained in fitting foundations before making purchases. Comfort and appearance do not always coincide. For modeling situations, select the undergarments that will make the clothing you wear over them look best.

A complete wardrobe of undergarments for modeling and personal wear includes the following items.

Bras

Acquire several basic bras that are flattering, comfortable, and well fitting in a nude color with no lace, trims, or bows. In addition, it is a good idea to have other bras for more options in making your body and the garments you will be modeling look great. If you have a well-developed bust (full B cup or larger), you should have bras that emphasize your shape as well as ones that will make you appear less busty. If on the other hand, you are small busted (less than a true B cup), you should have bras that show your true shape as well as ones that augment it. Bras with varying amounts of padding, such as contour or fiberfill bras, can greatly enhance what you are wearing. Bust pads are occasionally useful for modeling to help you to fit properly into a dress or to give your figure a better shape. However, when altering your bustline, check that the shape, height, and size of the bust looks natural. Maximizing or minimizing the bust more than one cup size is usually not a good idea.

A sweater bra is another necessity. A bra that has completely smooth cups with no seams, trims, or bows is necessary for wearing under clingy clothes and knits. You can often find good ones that are designed to be worn under leotards. Sweater bras in both nude and black are good to have.

A strapless bra is also an important item to have. If it will be required for an assignment, usually your agent or client will specify this prior to the assignment. Often it is a good idea to have a few strapless bras that will accommodate strapless or low-cut dresses of all kinds. A push-up bra is often a useful item. Sometimes trade show or print clients will provide you with a sexy costume that looks best when a push-up bra is worn.

Wearing a bra under some garments is impossible. If a garment is very sheer, models sometimes place round-shaped, flesh-toned bandages over the nipples so they won't show. A bandage can be cut to the proper size and shape. If support for the breasts is needed and wearing a bra will show, models usually choose one of two options, depending on what the garment will allow. One technique is to use small, crescent-shaped bust pads, which are placed under the breast to lift it. These can either be adhered to skin using mild surgical glue or sewn into the proper place on the garment. (If the garment is tight fitting, such as a bathing suit top, no glue or stitching is necessary. It will stay in place by itself.) These methods often work best for larger breasts.

The other method used for supporting the breasts is taping. Select wide surgical tape and remove excess stickiness by cutting a strip of tape and applying it to the inside of your forearm and removing it. Place tape under each breast to support it. Continue applying tape until the desired effect is achieved. Sometimes using a combination of tape and foam bust pads works best.

Hip Control

Models rarely wear girdles. A more natural look has predominated in recent decades. The emphasis should be on achieving a slender, firm figure through diet and exercise rather than on trying to hide excess pounds by corsetting them in. Plus-size models sometimes prefer girdles to give their hips a smoother line. Many models use control top pantyhose to create a smooth line under garments that show panty lines.

Body Suit

A body suit or body stocking is one of the most useful items a model can have (see Figure 2). It can be worn under most garments and gives the torso one smooth line. Select a nude-colored one with no lace, trims, and few seams. Put it on alone or over your bra and pantyhose when you get to your booking. It makes changing quicker and easier.

Slips

Half slips in the current hem length as well as a shorter one and a longer one will be useful. Select a nude-color, nonclinging type (e.g., taffeta works well). Black and white may also be useful.

Omitting Undergarments

There will be times when you will be asked to model an outfit without any undergarments to present it most effectively. Many times wearing only pantyhose or smooth, brief, snug-fitting nude-colored underpants under a garment will look best. A professional model's body should be so well toned that its smooth, firm contours make even a tight, clinging dress look ideal. Keeping ⅛ yard of a lightweight cotton knit fabric that matches your skintone in your totebag is a good idea. It can be cut to the size and shape needed and placed or tacked smoothly inside the garment using fabric adhesive or a needle and thread. Insert it in the crotch when modeling bathing suits to protect your body. It can also be used to mask areas when transparent underpants or bathing suits are being modeled.

Other Items

It is often a good idea to have a selection of shoulder pads of varying thicknesses. Adding small shoulder pads to fill out the shoulders of a garment can often give it a much better line.

Some models who have perspiration problems keep a supply of underarm shields in their totebags. These come in handy when you are under pressure and must protect the clothing supplied by the client.

THE FIT OF YOUR CLOTHING

Fit is an important consideration in any clothing selection. A garment, no matter how well designed and constructed, will not flatter you if it does not fit properly.

Selecting Your Correct Garment Size

Select your correct garment size. Use Tables 1 and 2 as a guide; however, it is important to consider that the sizing of garments made by different manufacturers and designers may vary widely. The sizes shown in these tables are those most commonly worn by models.

TABLE 1   Size Charts

Sizes for Children   Child models wear infants, toddlers', boys', and girls' sizes. In general children's ages and sizes should correspond; that is, sizes for a younger child will appear at the top of the chart. All measurements are given in inches and centimeters. Weights are given in pounds and kilos.

Infants

Size	Height	Weight	Chest	Crotch Length
NB (Newborn) or XS (up to 3 months)	Up to 24 61	Up to 14 6.4	15–17	7¾ 19.7
S (up to 6 months)	24½–28 62.2–71.1	15–20 6.8–9.1	17½–18 44.6–45.7	9½ 24.1
M (up to 18 months)	28½–32 72.4–81.3	21–26 9.6–11.8	18½–19 47–48.3	10–11⅞ 25.4–30.2
L (up to 24 months)	32½–36 82.6–91.4	27–32 12.3–14.6	19½–21½ 49.5–54.6	13½ 34.3
XL (up to 36 months)	36½–38 92.7–96.5	33–36 15–16.4	22–24 55.9–61	15 38.1

Toddlers

Size	Height	Weight	Chest	Waist	Crotch Length
1 to 1T	29½–32 74.9–81.3	25 11.4	19½–20 49.5–50.8	20–20½ 50.8–52.1	11 29.2
2 or 2T	32½–35 82.6–88.9	26–29 11.8–13.2	20½–21 52.1–53.3	20½–21 52.1–53.3	13⅛ 33.3
3 or 3T	35½–38 90.2–96.5	30–34 13.6–15.5	21½–22 54.6–55.9	21–21½ 53.3–54.6	14⅞ 37.8
4 or 4T	38½–41 97.8–104.1	35–38 15.9–17.3	22½–23 57.2–58.4	21½–22 54.6–55.9	16⅝ 42.2

Children

Children's sizes apply to boys and girls ranging in age from 3 to 6 years.

Size	Height	Weight	Chest	Waist	Hips
2	32½–35 82.6–88.9	27–29 12.3–13.2	20½–21 52.1–53.3	20–20½ 50.8–52.1	21½–22 54.6–55.9
3	35½–38 90.2–96.5	29½–35 13.4–15.9	21½–22 54.6–55.9	20½–21 52.1–53.3	22½–23 57.2–58.4
4	38½–41 97.8–104.1	35½–39 16.1–17.7	22½–23 57.2–58.4	21–21½ 53.3–54.6	23½–24 59.7–61
5	41½–44 105.4–111.8	39½–45 18–20.5	23½–24 59.7–61	21½–22 54.6–55.9	24½–25 62.2–63.5
6	44½–47 113–119.4	45½–50 20.7–22.7	24½–25 62.2–63.5	22–22½ 55.9–57.2	25½–26 64.8–66
6X	47½–49 120.7–124.5	50½–55 23–25	25½–26½ 64.8–67.3	22½–23 57.2–58.4	26½–27 67.3–68.6

Boys
Boys sizes apply to boys 7 to 17 years of age.

Size	Height	Weight	Waist	Inseam
6	46–48 116.8–121.9	47–51 21.4–23.2	21–23 53.3–58.4	20–23
8	48–51 121.9–129.5	52–26 23.6–25.5	23–24 58.4–61	21–24
10	51–54 129.5–137.2	57–75 25.7–34.1	24–25 61–63.5	23–25
12	54–58 137.2–147.3	76–89 34.6–40.5	25–26 63.5–66	24–28
14	58–60 147.3–152.4	90–103 40.9–46.8	26–27 66–68.6	28–32
16	60–64 152.4–162.6	104–118 47.3–53.6	27–28 68.6–71.1	29–33
18	64–66 162.6–167.6	119–129 54.1–58.6	28–29 71.1–73.7	30–34

Girls
Girls sizes are made for girls 7 to 11 years of age.

Size	Height	Weight	Chest/Bust	Waist	Hips	Inseam
7	49–51½ 124.5–130.8	55–60 25–27.3	26–26½ 26–26½	22–22½ 22–22½	27½–28 27½–28	23½ 23½
8	52–53½ 132.1–141	60½–68 27.5–30.9	27–27½ 68.6–69.9	23–23½ 58.4–59.7	28½–29 72.4–73.7	24½ 62.2
10	54–55½ 137.2–141	68½–76 31.1–34.6	29–29 71.1–73.7	24–24½ 61–62.2	29½–30½ 74.9–77.5	25½ 64.8
12	56–58 142.3–147.3	76½–86 34.8–39.1	29½–30½ 74.9–77.5	25–25½ 63.5–64.8	31–32½ 78.7–82.6	26½ 67.3

Sizes for Women

Juniors Junior sizes are made for young women. This figure has a more youthful look than the typical woman's figure. The shoulders are narrow, the waistline is small and defined, and the bustline is high and small. The back waist length ranges from 15 to 16 inches (approximately 38–40 cm). Junior-sized clothing also exhibits shorter sleeve and hem lengths than Misses apparel, as it is made for young women 5′0″ to 5′4″, but many junior clothing items can be worn by women up to 5′9″ tall. Junior sizes range from 3 to 15; however, the larger sizes rarely apply to models. The smaller sizes are often worn by petite models.

Size	Bust	Waist	Hips	Inseam
3	30–30½ 76.2–77.5	21–21½ 53.3–54.6	32–32½ 81.3–82.6	24½ 62.2
5	31–31½ 78.7–80	22–22½ 55.9–57.2	33–33½ 83.8–85.1	25¼ 64.1
7	32–34 81.3–86.4	23–24 58.4–61	34–34½ 86.4–87.6	26 66
9	33–34½ 83.8–87.6	24–24½ 61–62.2	35–35½ 88.9–90.2	26¾ 67.9

Misses Misses sizes are made for women at least 5'5" tall, with a fully developed, well-proportioned figure. Hip measurement is equal or approximately 2 inches larger than bust measurement. Back waist length ranges from 15½ to 17½ inches.

Size	Bust	Waist	Hips	Inseam
4	31–31½ 78.8–80	22–22½ 55.8–57.1	32–33 81.8–83.8	26¼ 67.6
6	32–34 81.8–86.4	23–24 58.4–61	33½–34 85.1–86.4	26⅜ 67
8	33–34½ 83.8–87.5	23½–24½ 59.7–62.2	34½–35 87.6–88.9	27⅛ 68.9
10	33½–35 85.1–89	24½–25½ 62.2–64.6	35½–36 90.2–91.4	27⅞ 70.8

Plus Sizes Plus- or large-sized models wear Misses sizes 12 and up. Plus models have well-proportioned, full figures. Back waist length measures from 15½ to 16½ inches.

Size	Bust	Waist	Hips	Inseam
12	34½–35 87.6–88.9	25½–26½ 64.8–67.3	36½–37½ 92.7–95.3	28 71.1
14	35½–37 90.2–94	27–28 68.6–71.1	38–39 96.5–99.1	28⅛ 71.2
16	37½–38½ 95.3–97.8	28½–29½ 72.4–74.9	39½–40½ 100.3–102.9	28¼ 71.4
18	39–40½ 99.1–102.9	30–31½ 76.2–80	41–42½ 104.1–108	28⅜ 71.5

Petites Petite sizes are made for women approximately 4'8" to 5'4" tall. Most petite size models can also wear Junior sizes 3 to 5. Petite sizes are cut with a dimunitive, well-proportioned figure as a basis. Back waist length measures 14½ to 16 inches (37–40 cm).

Size	Bust	Waist	Hips	Inseam
4P	31½–32 80–81.3	22½–23 57.2–58.4	33½–34 85.1–86.4	24⅞ 63.2
6P	32½–33½ 82.6–83.8	23½–24 59.7–61	34–34½ 87.6–88.9	25⅝ 65.1

Sizes for Men

Men's Suit Sizes

Men's suit sizes apply to men with a well-proportioned physique with broad shoulders, a tapered waist, and slim hips. Men's sizes are designated by S (short), R (regular), L (long or tall) in addition to the numerical sizes to accomodate for differences in height. Regular applies to men 5'8 to 6'0 tall. Back length applies to the neck to waist measurement. Chart A refers to suit coats, jackets, and the like. Chart B refers to jeans, pants, and trunks. Chart C refers to shirt Sizes.

Chart A: Suit Coat and Jackets

Size	Chest	Coat Length	Coat Sleeve	Back Length	Waist	Hips
38R	36½–38 92.7–96.5	30¼ 76.8	23⅞ 60.6	18 45.7	32½–33 82.6–83.8	36–38 92.7–96.5
4OR	38½–40 97.5–101.5	30½ 77.5	24⅛ 61.5	18¼ 46.7	33½–35 85–88.6	38½–40 97.5–101.5
42R	40½–42 102.9–106.7	30¾ 78.1	24⅜ 61.9	18½ 47	35½–37 90.2–94	40½–42 102.9–106.7

Chart B: Jeans, Pants, and Trunks

Size	Waist	Hips	Crotch	Inseam
30	27½–29 69.9–73.7	34–35½ 86.4–90.2	9¾ 24.8	31¾ 80.6
31	29½–32 74.9–81.3	36–37½ 91.4–85.3	10 25.4	32 81.3
32	32½–33 82.6–83.8	38–39½ 96.5–100.3	10¼ 26	32¼ 81.9
33	33½–35 85.1–88.9	40–41½ 101.6–105.4	10½ 26.7	31½ 82.6

Chart C: Men's Shirt Sizes

Men's shirt sizes are usually designated by the neck measurement and the sleeve length; for example, 15½/34. Sizes might also be designated XS, S, M, or L.

Size	Chest	Waist	Neck	Sleeve Length
XS	30–32 76.2–81.3	27–28 68.6–71.1	13–13½ 33–34.3	32 81.3
S	34–37 86.4–94	29–32 73.7–81.3	14–14½ 35.6–36.8	3 2–33 81.3–83.8
M	38–41 96.5–104.1	33–36 83.8–91.4	15–15½ 38.1–39.4	32–33/34 81.3–83.8/86.4

Big and Tall Men

Big and tall men's sizes apply to men with a large frame and over 6'2".

Size	Chest	Waist	Hips	Coat Length	Sleeve Length	Neck
42	41½–43 105.4–109.2	34½–36 87.6–91.4	39½–42 100.3–106.7	31¾ 80.6	25⅜ 64.5	16–17 41–43
44	43½–45 110.5–114.3	36½–38 92.7–96.5	42¼–44 108–111.8	32 81.3	25⅝ 65.1	17–17½ 43–44.5

TABLE 2 International Clothing Size Equivalents

Sizes are designated differently around the world. If you will be modeling in Europe or Japan, the size conversions listed here will come in handy.

Clothing Type	American Size	Continental Size	British Size
Men's suit sizes	36	46	36
	38	48	38
	40	50	40
	42	52	42
	44	54	44
Women's dress sizes (Misses)	4	34	6
	6	36	8
	8	38	10
	10	40	12
	12	42	14
	14	44	16
	16	46	18
	18	48	20
Children's sizes	4	Height 125 cm Age 7	Height 43″ Age 4–5
	6	Height 135 cm Age 9	Height 48″ Age 6–7
	8	Height 150 cm Age 12	Height 55″ Age 9–10
	10	Height 155 cm Age 13	Height 58″ Age 11
	12	Height 160 cm Age 14	Height 60″ Age 12
	14	Height 165 cm Age 15	Height 62″ Age 13
Men's shoes	8	41	7
	8½	42	7½
	9½	43	8½
	10½	44	9½
	11½	45	10½
	12	46	11
Women's shoes	6	38	4½
	6½	38	5
	7	39	5½
	7½	39	6
	8	40	6½
	8½	41	7
	9	42	7½

Checking the Fit of Your Clothing

When you put on a garment, always check that you are wearing it correctly. Check that the closure is in the right place. The following checklist will help you to determine proper or improper fit.

- Check that shoulder seams are on top of your shoulders and that the sleeve-joining seam falls at the end of each shoulder. There should be ease but no sagging. Check that the shoulder pads of a garment are in the proper position.
- Check that waistlines match your waist and that they neither dip nor hike in front or back.
- Check that waistbands do not stretch, pull, roll, or gape.
- Check that side seams hang straight and a little toward the back.
- Check that hemlines are a flattering length for your legs, are suitable for current fashion, and are even all around.
- Check sleeve length by bending your hands backward. The hem of the sleeve should just touch the bend of the wrist if the length is right.
- Check that the crotches of pants are not too long (droopy) or too short (tight).
- Check for sagging or strain in the hips and buttock area.
- Check that zippered or buttoned closures on blouses, dresses, pants, and skirts do not gap or pull.

Accessories

- Check that your shoes have a little extra length at the toe and that they do not pinch your toes or ride up and down on your heels.
- Check hats to be sure they fit properly and do not make a mark on your forehead.
- Check your gloves for proper fit at the width of the palms and the length from the base of the fingers to the tips.

MAINTAINING THE CONDITION OF YOUR CLOTHING

Just as an improper fit can detract from your fashionable appearance, so can poor condition. Your clothing and accessories should always look new. Never wear hose with runs, snags, or stains. Avoid wearing shoes that need polishing or that have scrapes or frayed, run-over heels. Never carry a purse that is torn, soiled, or frayed or has a broken strap or closure. Never wear clothing with makeup stains, soil, or odor from too many wearings. Avoid wearing clothing with broken closures, missing buttons, broken zippers, moth holes, tears, split seams, frayed collars or cuffs, falling hems, underarm perspiration stains, scorches or shiny iron areas, lint, or wrinkles.

Take good care of your clothes. They will look better and last longer. Schedule a few hours each week in which to repair, clean, and maintain your clothing and accessories.

Hang garments in the closet with ample room between them. Packing clothes too tightly in a closet can have the same effect as throwing them in a heap on the floor. Use plastic or padded, not wire hangers, especially for suits, jackets, and coats. Organize your clothes by hanging them in groups of pants, skirts, suits, dresses (separate suits into skirts and jackets as well as two-piece dresses), and so forth. This way you will get the most mileage out of your clothes by coordinating them. Store sweaters and other knit articles folded in drawers; hanging them on hangers can pull them out of shape. Keep only items you wear day to day in this closet. Discard articles you have not worn in the past two years or store them away along with opposite-season garments.

Pay strict attention to the care instructions sewn into the seams of your garments. Use a reputable dry cleaner. Handwash everything you can with a mild soap, such as castile soap. Do not wring a garment. Instead, press water out by rolling and blotting the article between two towels. Do not hang a sweater or knit garment; allow it to dry flat. Always take care that you remove stains correctly and as soon as possible.

Wash underwear by hand or in a delicate machine cycle after each wearing. Slips and bras can be laundered after every three wearings. Launder hosiery after each wearing and use either a product specially made for this purpose or beer as a final rinse to make stockings last longer and return to their original shape. Make sure your undergarments are always clean and in good repair, as other people may see them during assignments when you are changing.

Never iron a garment that is soiled. The heat will permanently set the soil into the fibers. When ironing a clean garment, use a press cloth or iron on the wrong side to preserve the look of the fabric.

To keep your footwear in excellent condition, observe the following points:

1. Use clear plastic shoeboxes for storing accessories and shoes. When storing shoes, stuff the toes with tissue paper or use shoe trees to retain their shape.

2. Always let your shoes rest a day between wearings. Avoid wearing good shoes on wet or snowy days; wear an inferior pair (carry the good ones), then change just before going into your appointment. If your shoes get wet, stuff them with crumpled newspaper and let them air dry away from any heat source. If your shoes have salt stains, remove with a solution of equal parts white vinegar and water.

3. Each time you purchase a new pair of shoes also buy the products that will be needed to maintain them. For leather shoes buy coordinating colors of paste polish. Clear is best for conditioning and adding lustre or for use on purses and other leather articles.

4. For the most effective shoe shine, use paste polish. Liquid and spray polishes are not as effective. Apply paste with a clean powder puff, allow it to absorb for a minute or two. Then buff to a shine with a clean powder puff. Use a soap eraser for stains on suede.

PLANNING YOUR WARDROBE

Planning your wardrobe will help you to get the most value for your money and effort. A model needs clothing for three basic situations:

1. A wardrobe to wear when attending auditions and appointments.

2. Clothing for test photographs (see Chapter 9).

3. A collection of clothing and other items that models may be requested to supply for assignments.

The Model's Wardrobe for Attending Modeling Auditions and Appointments

When attending appointments in search of modeling opportunities, a model should present him- or herself in a way that makes it clear that he or she has all the qualifications for modeling. He or she should always appear clean, neat, and well groomed. Nails should always be manicured; hair should be clean, shiny and freshly trimmed. Skin should be blemish-free.

Each time the model has a meeting with a prospective client she should plan carefully and make every effort to ensure a productive encounter. The model should use clothing to further herself professionally, not hinder her chances. In addition to dressing in a way that reflects his or her personality or image, the model should dress to answer the needs of the client he or she is meeting. When attending modeling appointments, models dress in one of the four ways described here.

The Natural Look

The natural look is a basic look that requires the client or photographer to use his imagination and knowledge to visualize how the model will look on the job. The model wears simple, comfortable, casual clothing that shows the contours of her figure, such as jeans and a top or other casual clothes. Her hair is freshly washed and blow-dried in a simple style, and her skin is clean and nearly makeup free. This look shows that the model has all the basic characteristics necessary for modeling: an attractive, well-toned figure, clear skin, and healthy hair. This look is often used by star models, because they do not need to impress the client with their personal appearance; they have extensive, outstanding portfolios to show. The same advice applies to male models.

This look may also be worn by fashion models who interview with photographers. Photographers are very knowledgeable about the effects of makeup, hairstyling, and lighting and are accustomed to visualizing how the model will look when she is dressed and groomed by professionals.

The natural look is not recommended for new models who don't have impressive portfolios. A new or unestablished model should do everything possible to sell the client on giving her a try. It is also not a good idea for any model to wear the natural look when meeting a client, such as a business owner, who is inexperienced at selecting models, or who does not understand or care to visualize how you'll look when your hair is styled and makeup is applied. It is also a good idea to avoid the natural look if a Polaroid or videotape will be taken of you at the appointment; you'll want to show how you look at your best.

Some clients and photographers prefer the natural look. In some markets it is the look that most models adopt for attending appointments. The model's agent should know the preferences of the clients the model will be meeting and should be able to advise the model accordingly.

The Dress-the Part Look

"Dress the part" means that the model appears in clothing, hair, and makeup similar to the styles to be used for the ad or other assignment for which she is auditioning. For example, if a model is auditioning for the part of a nurse in a television commercial or print ad, she would wear white and have conservatively styled makeup and hair. (Dressing in a nurse's uniform would be overdoing it.) If the part calls for a young executive, a business suit would be in order. For a casting order that calls for a glamourous, model type of look, fashionable clothes and more makeup would be in order.

By tailoring her look to the image the client is seeking, the model can greatly increase her chances of getting the job, because the client won't have to use his or her imagination. For a very important job, it is wise for the model to dress specifically for the audition. When a model has several auditions in one day, it is wise to change for each audition or to gear her appearance to the auditions that will result in the most lucrative jobs and those that she has the best chances of obtaining. The model should use each audition as an important opportunity for impressing a client and should therefore prepare herself as fully as possible. This can be done by using the Audition Form in Chapter 9 to record complete information when her agent informs her of an audition.

A model should also find out what she will be expected to do at the audition. If the audition involves an activity, such as dancing, pants would be preferable instead of a skirt, or wearing a leotard under a skirt would be a good idea. If a client is not casting a model with a particular look, but he needs a model with excellent legs, the model should wear a skirt or other leg-revealing outfit, rather than a long skirt or other outfit that hides her legs. Sometimes a client will ask the model to bring along a bathing suit. This is often requested at auditions for bookings involving lingerie and bathing suits.

On some occasions there will be no particular assignment for which the model is being interviewed. For example, if the model attends a general go-see to a photographer's studio, she is clever if she dresses in a style compatible with the clothing and products he frequently photographs. For example, if the photographer shoots a lot of high-fashion clothing and products, the model should dress in a high-fashion style. If the photographer can "see a potential photograph" in you, you'll stand a better chance of obtaining a booking.

Generally, dressing the part is most effective for television commercial auditions. It is also the best image to project when meeting an interviewer or client who is untrained in visualizing the effects of wardrobe, makeup, and hairstyling. Preparing for your self-promotional appointments by researching the people you will see will increase your chances of getting work. Remember that you are trying to sell your looks, talents, and skills. A successful salesman always researches his prospects and presents his product in a way that he knows will interest his prospect and result in a sale.

The Individual Look

The individual look is a strong, unique style that expresses the image and personality of the model. Although an individual look is influenced by fashion, it may not rigidly follow the dictates of current fashion. Most models who are able to carry off such a look have an innate sense of creativity in regard to fashion. Other models develop an individual look gradually. Some models use their manner of dressing as their trademark to gain recognition.

Editors of fashion magazines, fashion designers, fashion photographers, fashion coordinators, art directors, and other creative people appreciate an individual look. This type of look can inspire them to use the model in their work. On the other hand, some clients such as businessmen who are unaccustomed to seeing an individual style may not understand it. Therefore, a model should use the individual look judiciously, reserving it for clients who are most likely to respond positively to it.

Dressing in an individual look can emphasize your style and make it clear to prospective clients what types of clothing and products you will model best. For example, a model with a very exotic face and mannequin-like figure can emphasize her uniqueness by wearing memorable, creative clothing and accessories.

The All-Purpose Look

The all-purpose look strikes a balance between the three preceding looks. The natural look, dress-the-part look, and the individual look are all extremes. The all-purpose look is the one to wear when you have several appointments in one day or when you are uncertain about the needs of the prospect you'll be meeting. The all-purpose look encompasses a natural look yet gives a hint of the model's individuality. In addition, it is somewhat tailored to the needs of the model's market and potential clients. Although it isn't always possible to appeal to every client, the all-purpose look can help the model appeal to the majority of clients.

When dressing in an all-purpose look, the model wears comfortable, becoming clothes that look well throughout the day. The model does not dress in clothing as casual as jeans, nor does she dress like a fashion plate. It is usually a good idea to show up looking like one of the more basic pictures on your composite, because this is probably how the client is expecting you to look. Male models have to be sure they do not confuse people by changing their looks with different hair, beard, and mustache. All models should wear clothes that fit close enough to the body so that the client can see the figure well. Play up your assets. If you have great legs, favor skirts over pants, and shoes over boots. If you wear glasses, do not wear them to the interview, wear clear or only mildly tinted contact lenses. Wear your hair down, not up or under a hat. Clients usually want to see the length and condition of your hair. A hairstyle that doesn't require constant upkeep is also advantageous.

Wear comfortable shoes. If necessary, change shoes just before going to your appointment. Look professional. Carry a small totebag, a softsided briefcase, or an attractive oversized purse for your portfolio, extra pair of shoes or garment changes, makeup, hair supplies, and composites. Do not lug shopping bags or large items to appointments, they make you appear disorganized and unprofessional.

Some models need more makeup than others, but soft, clean makeup that lets the skin and features show through is always best. Makeup that stays throughout the day without constant touchups is what you're after. It will always be easier for your client to visualize how you'll look with more makeup, but trying to see through too much makeup is difficult. Use fashion-conscious colors and techniques, but light application and thorough blending. When in doubt, adhere to natural-looking makeup colors, such as brown, beige, and grey eyeshadows and peach or rose cheekcolors. Select natural-looking, sheer, matte (or barely frosted) colors or soft earthy tones. Such coloration is good for meeting people face to face and in a variety of lightings and situations. Bright pinks, blues, oranges, and metallics can cheapen a model's appearance and may detract from her appearance under different variables. Male and child models generally do not wear makeup for appointments.

Clothing and Other Articles Models Must Supply for Assignments

When a model is booked for an assignment she may be asked to supply accessories, shoes, and clothing. The model brings basic modeling supplies to all bookings in the model's totebag.

The Model's Totebag

A model carries his or her totebag to all modeling assignments. A totebag is a lightweight canvas bag with lots of pockets, a handle, and a shoulder strap (Figure 3). It contains items that are commonly needed on modeling assignments. All models have items that they consider necessities for a totebag. The items listed here represent those most commonly needed. Use the following checklists to customize a list for yourself by checking and adding items you find necessary for your totebag. Do not depend on the studio, client, or stylist to have these items. Even if you are told that you don't have to supply anything for the assignment, it is always best to have these items with you. Also, don't depend on borrowing these items from other models. Keep your totebag well organized so you can find what you need easily and quickly. You will not have much time to do this while on the job. Reorganize items and replenish them after each booking. Pack the totebag well ahead of the booking to be sure you have everything you need.

Totebag Checklist for Female Models

Stockings

- ☐ Three or four pairs of sheer-to-waist sandalfoot nylon pantyhose matched to your skintone.
- ☐ Two or three pairs control top sheer, sandalfoot nylon pantyhose matched to skintone.
- ☐ Two or three pairs of sheer, sandalfoot pantyhose in darker shades (taupe, sheer black), and two or three pairs in lighter shades (light beige, pearl).
- ☐ If textured or special styles or colors of stockings are fashionable, also include a few pairs. When possible, select pantyhose that are sheer to the waist.

Undergarments

- ☐ Body suit as closely matched to your skintone as possible.
- ☐ One or two regular bras that fit perfectly.
- ☐ Sweater bra (nude tone, no lace, etc.).
- ☐ Strapless bra.
- ☐ Half slips in current hem length in nude color, no lace. Black and white slips may also be useful. Taffeta is good because it does not cling

Makeup supplies

- ☐ See Chapter 3 for a checklist.

Haircare supplies

- ☐ See Chapter 4 for a checklist.

Grooming supplies

- ☐ Antiperspirant.
- ☐ All-purpose moisturizer for face, hands, and body.
- ☐ Shaver.
- ☐ Nail file, manicure kit, and five nail colors (clear, pink, red tone, orange tone, and beige) plus the one you are wearing and any fashionable colors; nail polish remover pads.

Business supplies

- ☐ Vouchers.
- ☐ Pen.
- ☐ Rate list and/or booking form.
- ☐ Appointment book.
- ☐ Promotional tools such as portfolio and composites.

Miscellaneous

- ☐ A 5 x 7 mirror, preferably with a stand.
- ☐ Something comfortable to put on between shots or shows that does not slip over the head, such as wrap-around lightweight robe or a kimono.
- ☐ Premoistened towelettes for cleaning off soles of shoes and so forth.
- ☐ Basic jewelry, Figure 4.
- ☐ _____
- ☐ _____
- ☐ _____
- ☐ _____

Totebag Checklist for
Male Models

Socks	☐ A selection of light and dark tones. Usually solid tan or beige, navy, grey, black and dark brown will serve the purpose. Also include white for combining with sportswear.
Undergarments	☐ Smooth, snug-fitting neutral toned briefs or bikini underwear.
	☐ Athletic supporter.
	☐ Elastic waistband for shirts.
	☐ Two smooth, snug-fitting white T-shirts.
Makeup supplies	☐ See Chapter 3 for checklist.
Hair supplies	☐ Blow dryer, hairspray, styling gel, and comb.
Grooming supplies	☐ Razor and shaving supplies.
	☐ Antiperspirant.
	☐ All-purpose moisturizer.
	☐ Manicure set.
Business supplies	☐ Vouchers.
	☐ Pen.
	☐ Rate list or booking form.
	☐ Promotional tools such as portfolio and composites.
Basic jewelry and accessories	☐ Wedding band.
	☐ Cuff links.
	☐ Small gold neck chain.
	☐ Sunglasses.
	☐ Eyeglasses.
	☐ Wristwatch.
	☐ Belts in brown, black, navy, and beige leather. Also include canvas or other belts for sportswear.
Miscellaneous items	☐ Comfortable shirt or robe (that doesn't slip over the head) to put on between changes and while doing makeup and hair.
	☐ A 5 x 7 mirror preferably with stand
	☐ _____
	☐ _____
	☐ _____

Totebag Checklist for Child Models

All Children
- ☐ Comb and brush.
- ☐ Scissors to trim hair if necessary.
- ☐ Wash cloth.
- ☐ Manicure set.
- ☐ Quiet toy or coloring materials to keep child occupied.
- ☐ Homework for older children.
- ☐ Messless snacks or fruit juices.
- ☐ Cheekcolor (optional)
- ☐ Powder to combat shiny noses.
- ☐ Hairspray (optional)
- ☐ Vouchers, pen, rate list or booking form, composites.

Girls
- ☐ Plain white underwear (undershirts and underpants).
- ☐ Slips.
- ☐ Hair accessories: good selection of hair ribbons in a variety of solid colors, barettes, elastic bands, headbands, etc.
- ☐ Curling iron.
- ☐ Shoes: Clean white tennis shoes, black and white Mary Janes or other dressy style, casual loafers.
- ☐ Plain stockings and socks in white, black, and other styles or colors currently in fashion.
- ☐ Miscellaneous
- ☐ _____
- ☐ _____
- ☐ _____

Boys
- ☐ Plain white underwear (T-shirts and underpants)
- ☐ T-shirts in assorted colors.
- ☐ Shoes: Oxfords or other dressy style in dark color; clean, white tennis shoes; sport shoes; casual loafers and boots.
- ☐ Socks in basic colors such as white, brown, black, and beige.

Miscellaneous
- ☐ _____
- ☐ _____
- ☐ _____
- ☐ _____

Shoes and Accessories Models May Be Expected to Provide for Assignments

Sometimes a model will be asked to supply shoes and accessories to be worn with the clothing or other items he or she will model. The client's budget and the type of booking will determine whether the model will be expected to supply shoes and accessories. Large advertising jobs, television commercials, and editorial jobs usually employ stylists who bring all the necessary items.

Shoes and accessories are most commonly needed for the following types of situations: Promotional models are often supplied with a garment imprinted with a company logo, for which they need to bring matching accessories, stockings, and shoes. Sometimes fashion show models are asked to supply shoes and accessories for the clothes they will be showing on the runway or informally. Models who are being photographed for a catalog sometimes are required to provide shoes and accessories to coordinate with the garments or other items shown. In these instances, the shoes and accessories are used to enhance the garment but do not predominate.

Pierced ears are a good idea for female models because clients will often provide only pierced (not clip type) earrings for assignments. It is not a good idea to have ears pierced in more than one place or to pierce other than the earlobe. Also, if you have pierced ears, wearing simple, small, single pearl, diamond, silver, or gold studs looks better than an empty hole.

Accessories and Shoes Checklist for Female Models

Jewelry
- ☐ Classic gold and silver earrings (studs, button style, and rings).
- ☐ Diamond or rhinestone stud earrings.
- ☐ Pearl earrings.
- ☐ Assortment of earrings currently in fashion, including styles that will combine well with dressy, business, casual, and sport fashions. Include large-, small-, and medium-sized earrings in current styles in solid colors in white, black, ivory, red, beige, navy, and other accent colors.
- ☐ Gold and silver neck chains of varying lengths and thicknesses.
- ☐ Strings of pearls (long and short).
- ☐ Bangle or chain bracelets in gold and silver.
- ☐ Matching sets of earrings and necklace or earrings and bracelet in ivory, onyx, colored plastic, wood, gold, silver, copper, or other currently fashionable materials.
- ☐ Wristwatches.
- ☐ Fashionable costume jewelry for the particular season.
- ☐ Wedding band.

Stockings
- ☐ Nylon pantyhose (see Totebag Checklist).
- ☐ Socks for sport shoes.

Scarves
- ☐ About six different colors, plain and patterned, preferably clasic, silk, designer scarves. Include long oblong and large square shapes.
- ☐ A few colorful cotton squares or western bandana-type scarves sportswear.
- ☐ Other scarves that are currently in fashion that will combine well with several outfits.

Purses
- ☐ Handbags that will blend well with several shoe and garment colors and textures. Include flat envelope and shoulder bag styles along with other styles currently in fashion. Also include a purse for dressy wear.

Belts
- ☐ Dark and light tone, all widths in leather and other fashionable materials. Blend with shoe and purse colors.
- ☐ Canvas or other styles that can be worn with jeans and sportswear.

☐ Dressy gold, silver, or lizard belt.

Shoes ☐ Classic pumps with current heel height and width for day in beige or taupe, black, brown, and navy (burgundy, gray, white and red are also useful).

☐ Black dress pumps, silver, and/or gold if in fashion.

☐ Casual loafers or walking shoes.

☐ White sport or tennis shoes.

☐ Light and dark leather boots.

☐ Two or three pairs of colorful canvas summer shoes (e.g., espadrilles if in fashion).

☐ Natural-tone strapped, low-heel summer sandals.

Miscellaneous ☐ Sunglasses, eyeglasses, berets or hats, visors, fabric flowers, hair accessories such as hair-bands, ribbons, combs, and sweatbands.

☐ _____

☐ _____

Accessories and Shoes Checklist for Male Models

Accessories ☐ Assortment of ties in current widths, patterns, and colors. Include ties that can be combined with navy, brown, grey, and beige suits. Solids and subtle prints will be most useful.

Belts ☐ Leather belts in brown, black, navy, taupe, maroon, and beige to wear with suits and dress slacks. Canvas and other belts in white, beige, tan, navy, and other colors should be included to wear with casual and sportswear.

Shoes ☐ Business shoes in brown, black, and burgundy.

☐ Dress shoes in black and brown. Light tones and white are occasionally needed.

☐ Clean white tennis shoes or sport shoes.

☐ Casual loafers.

Clothing the Model May Be Expected to Supply for Assignments

There are several instances in which a model may be asked to provide clothing for assignments. When clothing is not the product being advertised, a model may be asked to bring clothing to go with the merchandise being shown. For example, if office furniture is being photographed, the model may be asked to supply wardrobe befitting a secretary or business executive. This often occurs when items, such as food or appliances, or service-oriented businesses, such as restaurants, are being advertised.

Even when clothing is the item being featured, a model may have to provide wardrobe. For example, if sweaters are the product being shown, the model may be asked to supply a selection of skirts and pants to coordinate with the sweaters. Male models who appear with female models often supply their own clothing when it is the women's clothing being featured.

Models often have to supply clothing when used as extras in commercials and other electronic media productions. This is especially true in productions involving lots of extras, those shot on low budgets, or those in which the extras are to look like "real people." Models employed for industrial film work often provide their own clothing. In all of these cases, models are many times asked to bring the same outfit they wore at the audition.

In most cases, models are required to provide clothing when the client is working on a tight budget and can't afford to hire a stylist. Minor modeling markets more often require models to provide clothing. However, whenever the client has a very specific idea about the clothing or when the clothing is important to the success of the shot, a stylist is usually employed.

Type of Clothing Needed

The lists of clothing in this chapter should be used as basic guidelines. If supplying wardrobe is a common requirement for the work the model does, she should acquire an extensive, high-quality, appropriate wardrobe that is reserved just for modeling assignments. This will give her an advantage over other models. It is usually best if clothing supplied by the model is somewhat neutral in style, color, and detail. Classic, well-designed outfits that display excellent-quality fabric and workmanship are ideal. Clothing that is too distinctive will attract attention to you, rather than to the product being shown. In general, models should tailor their wardrobes to their images and the types of assignments for which they are best suited. For example, a model who can look like a housewife should have several outfits resembling those worn by housewives in television commercials.

A model whose potential lies in the promotional area should acquire clothing that would be suitable for promotions and trade shows. Trade show models are often required to supply their own clothing. If you are booked for a trade show and the client doesn't provide an outfit or uniform for you to wear, ask what type of outfit is preferred. The client's corporate image and his or her objectives will determine how the model is to dress. For a conservative company an attractive suit that fits close to the body or a silk dress with a defined waistline would be best. For a client who wants you to look wholesome and all-American, select an attractive, figure-flattering skirt and blouse or sweater. For a client who prefers a glamourous look, a pretty cocktail dress or body-flattering jumpsuit would be best. Generally, trade show clients like clothing that shows off a model's legs and figure. A model should always appear well dressed, avoiding outrageous, overtly sexy, or extreme high-fashion clothing.

Determine your wardrobe needs and plan carefully. The ideal opportunity for beginning to build a wardrobe is when the model takes photographs for her promotional tools (composite, portfolio).

If you are to provide wardrobe for a print or other type of assignment, be sure you know the season, color, and style that will be needed. Put together complete outfits with matching shoes and accessories for each. Remember to consider whether or not the items you supply are photogenic. For more information on selecting clothing that is appropriate for various media, consult Table 3.

When supplying wardrobe for an assignment, assemble it in a professional manner. Accessories should be kept in good order for the client to see them and to make selections. All clothing and other items must be in perfect condition, that is in good repair and freshly cleaned, pressed, and carried on hangers. To keep clothing clean and wrinkle-free, it should be transported to the assignment in a garment bag (Figure 5). Shoes should be freshly polished and in good repair when you arrive at a testing or booking.

TABLE 3   Clothing Selection for Various Media

Still Photography

Line/Shape	Detail	Texture	Color
Choose clothing with flattering lines that show the contours of your figure. Clothing with wide or bulky lines will make you appear heavier on top of the fact that the camera adds 5–10 lbs. to your appearance. Select items with lines that play up your special features and downplay your liabilities. In general, curved and diagonal lines provide interest. For headshots choose collar lines that flatter your face shape.	Details can add interest to a picture, however, avoid clothing that has too many details because they can look busy. A very busy print and lots of seams and buttons will be distracting. In general if a garment has very simple lines or very indistinctive texture, it will look better if it has more details (decorative stitching, trims, etc.).	Select clothing with interesting, attractive textures. Soft, fuzzy or rich, luxurious fabrics like satin are photogenic. Nubby knits, loose weaves, metallics, sequins, furs, suede, leather, gauze add dimension. Add textures to flat fabric with a belt, scarf, or accessories.	Usually it is a good idea to avoid white or black because the lines, details, and textures are often lost in the photographic process. Very light pastels and very dark colors often appear white or black. Most colors do not photograph as vibrant as they really are. For information on black and white photography, consult Chapter 3.

Video

Select lines that are flattering to your figure. Bulky or wide lines will make you look heavier. Also consider that most video productions are shot from the waist up so consider how the top part of your garment looks. Consider what you'll be doing on video and select clothes accordingly. For example, if you'll be walking, choose a garment that moves attractively. If you'll be sitting select one that doesn't hike up or look bulky when you sit.	Avoid prints such as small contrasting checks and stripes because they can "bloom" on camera, or look as if they are vibrating. Avoid jewelry that makes a sound such as bangle bracelets, because they will interfere with the microphone. Also note that video cameras do not capture great detail. Subtle trims or decorative stitching usually doesn't show up.	Avoid too richly textured fabrics and those devoid of texture. Be aware that subtle textures are often lost on video.	Avoid very dark or very light colors and white and black. Select well-saturated but not glaring colors or drab colors. Avoid combining too many colors. Colors that flatter you most should be near your face.

Motion Picture Film

Follow above information, but remember that film captures detail and color more accurately than videotape.

Stage

Line/Shape	Detail	Texture	Color
Wear clothing with lines that will project well from a distance. Avoid anything that enlarges one area of your figure out of proportion. Consider the length of your skirt. If you will be on an elevated stage, or will be seated while on stage, a skirt that's a little longer than normal would be best.	Details are often lost on stage due to distance and harsh lighting. Select details that will be discernible from a distance. Jewelry and accessories should be slightly larger in scale so that they are visible.	Subtle textures are often lost on a stage. Flat textures look too plain. Consider how the texture of the fabric appears from a distance.	Avoid very light or dark colors. Subtle colors can appear muddy or washed out. Black or white looks harsh. Bright, solid colored garments often look great from a distance.

In-Person Promotions

Wear clothing with flattering lines. Clothing with a well-defined waist is usually best. Avoid garments that you continually have to adjust. Comfort is also important. Wear shoes that are attractive and that make your legs look great, but also consider how long you'll be standing.	Medium to subtle details are best. Don't overwhelm yourself with too large or too many accessories. Memorable details on a garment give you an identifiable look.	Select fabrics with rich-looking textures. Avoid heavy textures or outfits that will be hot to wear. If possible, try to find out the temperature inside the place you'll be modeling.	Select skin- and hair-flattering colors. Avoid drab-colored outfits.

Quantity of Clothes   Generally clients like to have three or four outfits per shot from which they can choose. If a client asks you to bring clothing you don't have in your wardrobe, you are expected to purchase, borrow, or rent it prior to the booking. Only if an item is very unique, expensive, or important to the success of the job, will a client reimburse the model. This information will always be specified when the booking is issued. Make every effort to assemble the outfits needed for a booking, and if you cannot, make sure you inform your agent as soon as possible.

Basic Clothing Checklist for Female Models (for Modeling Assignments)

☐ Light-tone, neutral-colored (e.g., beige) suit with skirt and pants. Select either all-season fabrics or winter-weight and summer-weight fabrics. Same in dark tone (e.g., navy).

☐ Assortment of pants, jeans, and dressy slacks in neutral colors. Casual pants in solids and tweeds.

☐ Assortment of silk and cotton blouses and knit tops. Include a tube top for bare shoulders when modeling jewelry.

☐ Two or more casual shirts such as knit or lightweight wool.

☐ Assortment of sweaters in different colors (beige, navy, green, etc.) in a variety of styles (V-neck, crew neck, turtleneck).

☐ One or two silky two-piece dresses in attractive colors for business and evening wear. (Be cautious of unusual or busy prints and patterns.)

☐ Assortment of sweaters to coordinate with skirts, blouses, and pants. These should have a variety of necklines (e.g., crew neck, V-neck, etc.). Also some should be lightweight turtlenecks to be worn under blouses, sweaters, and jackets.

Basic Clothing Checklist for Male Models (for Modeling Assignments)

☐ Two conservative business suits, such as an oxford gray lightweight wool for winter and a navy lightweight blend for summer.

☐ Two sport jackets (tweed for winter, lightweight for summer).

☐ Conservatively styled wool blazer (usually navy).

☐ Dress suit or tuxedo.

☐ Navy, beige, gray, black, and brown dress slacks and several pairs of jeans in different styles.

☐ Business shirts in plain colors (white, light blue, and cream) to wear with suits. Conservative shirts in thin stripes or other current patterns.

Guidelines for Wardrobe Checks

The client or photographer often schedules an appointment prior to a booking to check if the model's wardrobe is suitable for the job. Selections are made and the model is instructed to bring those items to the booking.

When you arrive at a booking or testing for which you are to provide wardrobe, or for a wardrobe check, give the client or photographer a showing of what you have supplied. Do not expect that person to rummage through your garment bag. Show the items giving relevant comments about the types of shoes and accessories you have to go with each outfit. Remember to place jewelry in see-through cases (not boxes) to keep it in good condition and readily available. This looks more professional and saves time.

Guidelines for Fittings

When a model is booked to model clothing for catalog shootings, out-of-town location work, or fashion shows, a fitting must be done a few days or a week in advance of the booking to ensure that the clothes will be perfect for the model on the job. The model tries on different outfits in varying sizes, and the ones that fit and look best on her are the ones she models, or she tries on specified garments that are pinned to fit her and then altered before the shooting. Shoes and accessories are also decided upon at this time.

Fittings usually take place at the photo studio where the clothes will be shot or at the client's place of business; for example, for a fashion show, fittings may take place at the showroom or boutique from which the clothes will be taken.

• Treat fittings as seriously as bookings. Fittings are usually held at a time convenient for client and model. If other models are involved, fittings are conducted at times designated by the studio. Always inform the agent at the time you are booked if you will have difficulty attending a fitting prior to the booking.

• Complete a booking form and try to find out what types of items you will be trying on so you can bring appropriate shoes, undergarments, and so forth. Also find out if you are expected to supply shoes and accessories for the booking. Sometimes a client may request that you bring a particular item to a fitting. If this is the case, you may be expected to bring these items to the fitting so everything can be selected for you to bring to the booking. The purpose of a fitting is to have a preliminary check to see that everything will be in order for the booking.

- Make sure you put on the garments correctly for fittings, shootings, and shows. Check that shoulder seams are on top of shoulders, neither forward nor back, and that waistline and side seams are straight.
- Remember that you do not make the decision about what looks good on you; that is the job of the stylist, coordinator, or client. Even if a garment is not beautiful, you must make it so. That is your job as a model.
- When you try on a garment, walk a few steps. Move around. Put your hands in the pockets, or do a turn so the client can see how the garment looks on you and how you will show it. This is especially important for shows. Make it easy for the client to visualize how the garment will look in the photograph or on the ramp and to decide whether you are the right model for it.
- Always ask at the time of the fitting for information relating to the show or photo session. Reconfirm if you are to bring anything, where the booking will be held, and when. At the fitting, the client or coordinator usually completes a Fitting Sheet like the one shown here. If the model is to provide shoes, accessories, or other items for the booking, she should complete a Fitting Sheet to ensure that she will bring the right items.
- Bring along a voucher. Fittings are usually billed at a rate specified by the model's agency.

TIPS FOR THE MODEL WHO TRAVELS

Whether you are traveling or just packing your totebag and garment bag for a modeling assignment, these tips will come in handy.

When deciding what to take and what to leave behind when going to a modeling assignment, if in doubt, bring it along. Being overprepared is better than being underprepared. The photographer or client will not be interested in knowing what you left at home; all he cares about is what you can offer at the shooting.

To organize your clothing and other articles, use the Wardrobe Planner. Tack it to the back of your suitcase or by your closet when packing so that you include everything. Standard totebag items, such as hair and makeup kits, should accompany you to all assignments and when traveling. This form can also be used for wardrobe planning.

Travel Paraphernalia

- Acquire special see-through cases for transporting and organizing your jewelry, makeup, hair supplies, accessories, and shoes.
- Keep all garments you would hang in your closet on hangers in a garment bag. Press all garments prior to the shooting.
- Bring along a travel iron. Most studios have irons, and when stylists are employed, they are in charge of ironing. However, if you are not certain, pack a travel iron.
- When packing a suitcase, rolling pants and sweaters loosely will help to prevent creases. Put your shoes in plastic bags so you can pack them among your clothes. Button blouses and fold them neatly with as few creases as possible to cut down on wrinkling. Use tissue paper when folding delicate or easily wrinkled garments. Make sure there is no excess room inside your suitcase for things to move around. Fill empty spaces with a folded bath towel. You can also stuff socks and underwear into empty spots. Never pack dirty clothes because clean clothes will pick up odor and soil. Also do not forget to include a plastic laundry bag for soiled clothing and a sewing kit.

- It is always a good idea to bring your totebag to fittings. Come prepared with appropriate, well-fitting, and clean undergarments. Wear a smooth, nude bra or body suit and neutral-toned, skin tone-matching, sandalfoot, sheer-to-waist pantyhose. Bring a basic pair of neutral-toned pumps as well as flats. Beige or brown shoes that approximate the color of your skin are a good choice because they go with nearly everything and flatter your legs. Male models should be prepared with appropriate grooming tools, underwear, and the right colors of shoes and socks. All models should wear their hair and makeup to reflect a model's image.

Fitting Sheet

©THE PROFESSIONAL MODEL'S HANDBOOK

MODEL _____ DATE _____

FITTING FOR _____

Shoes	
Stockings	
Jewelry	
Accessories	
Misc.	

Shoes	
Stockings	
Jewelry	
Accessories	
Misc.	

Shoes	
Stockings	
Jewelry	
Accessories	
Misc.	

Shoes	
Stockings	
Jewelry	
Accessories	
Misc.	

Shoes	
Stockings	
Jewelry	
Accessories	
Misc.	

Wardrobe Planner

OCCASION	GARMENT	SHOES	ACCESSORIES
ALTERNATIVES			

OCCASION	GARMENT	SHOES	ACCESSORIES
ALTERNATIVES			

OCCASION	GARMENT	SHOES	ACCESSORIES
ALTERNATIVES			

OCCASION	GARMENT	SHOES	ACCESSORIES
ALTERNATIVES			

OCCASION	GARMENT	SHOES	ACCESSORIES
ALTERNATIVES			

MISCELLANEOUS _____

- When traveling, carry your makeup, hair supplies, toothbrush, soap, and other hygiene supplies, plus a fresh set of underwear and hosiery in your totebag, rather than checking it along with your luggage. This way you will be prepared even if your baggage is misplaced.

HANDLING YOUR CLIENT'S CLOTHES WITH CARE

When a client is selling clothing, he or she will provide the items models will wear. Even when the clothing is not being featured, the client may have a stylist provide clothing that ideally complements the products being shown.

A store or other concern is willing to supply clothing when they are assured that garments will be returned in their original condition. Therefore, it is the model's responsibility to take care of the client's clothing. Damaging or soiling the clothes out of carelessness will result in the model not being called back.

164

Protect Clothing You Are Modeling

• Do not smoke, eat, or drink in the clothes.

• Do not sit or make other movements that will cause the clothes to wrinkle. Avoid bending over to put on shoes and bending arms to rearrange hair. Every movement can make a wrinkle. Do not lean against anything when dressed.

• Protect clothes from perspiration stains by applying an antiperspirant frequently. Put facial tissue in underarms to absorb perspiration, but make sure you do not forget to remove it when going in front of the camera or on to the runway.

• Wear the clients shoes as briefly as possible to prevent stretching, creasing, and perspiration stains to the inside. Do not walk on uncarpeted surfaces unless the soles are masked. If the soles aren't masked and floors are uncarpeted, carry the shoes to the set or runway and put them on just before you step onto the set or runway.

• Put clothes on over your head whenever possible to prevent them from dragging on the floor. When stepping into clothes take off your shoes first.

• Protect clothes from getting harmed by cosmetics by placing a scarf, makeup mask, or other covering over your face when pulling them on or off.

• Do not force zippers or pull buttons apart, tear off tags, or handle garments in a hurried, careless way.

• Always put the dress on last, that is, after makeup, hairstyling, and jewelry.

• If something is damaged or soiled accidentally, promptly report it to the stylist, photographer, dresser, or show director. Usually you will be expected to pay for cleaning, repair, or replacement. Also, if something is missing, report it immediately because models are sometimes accused of taking items. By reporting it, you will not be held accountable. If you accidentally leave a show wearing one of the client's items, such as a pair of earrings, notify the client, stylist, or show director, and return the item as soon as possible. You will be respected for your ethical conduct.

• Many times models like to freshen up with fragrance during assignments. However, be cautious that you do not spray perfume directly on a garment. Fragrances may stain fragile fabrics or linger on fabric so that a customer will not want to purchase the garment.

HOW TO BE YOUR OWN STYLIST

Styling refers to combining clothing, accessories, and other elements to create the desired look. It also entails taking care of every detail to make a garment look perfect. Many times a photographer or client will hire a stylist to take care of these matters; however, often times the model must be her own stylist. Styling details may seem insignificant; however, they can be very important on a modeling assignment. Forgetting to wear the belt that goes with an outfit or overlooking a flaw in the garment can cost your client a lot of money because the assignment will have to be reshot or expensive retouching must be done. When a stylist is not employed, the model takes full responsibility for making the clothes look ideal. In addition to styling on assignments, anyone can benefit from this information to arrive at a model-perfect appearance.

Styling Checklist Every time you put on a garment for an assignment check the following points:

☐ Does the garment need ironing?

☐ Are there threads hanging anywhere, particularly from hemlines?

☐ Are there stains anywhere on the garment? Check especially for makeup or soil on neckline or collar. Also check for perspiration stains.

☐ Do any repairs need to be made or concealed, such as loose buttons, rips, tears, or holes?

☐ Does the garment fit perfectly? If not, where does it need to be pinned, sewn, or taped?

☐ Is the garment being worn correctly? Do you have the front, back, and fastenings in the right places? Is there a belt?

☐ Will the shoes show in the picture? If so, are they well coordinated to the garment?

☐ Are shoes in perfect condition, shined, and heeled?

☐ What accessories are needed? Check to see if jewelry, belts, scarves, hair accessories, or other items should be worn. On assignments, always check accessories with the photographer or client first. Unless otherwise instructed, always remove your personal jewelry, such as ring and wristwatches, etc.

☐ Is the garment neat or are there characteristics that make it look sloppy such as crooked or twisted seams, puckers around fastenings, unevenly spaced gathers, static cling, or uneven hemlines?

☐ Are the proper undergarments for the outfit being worn? Do undergarments show anywhere (slips, pantylines, bras through sheer fabrics, straps, etc.)?

☐ Is a slip required to prevent light from shining through the skirt?

☐ Have all garment tags been removed?

☐ Has hair and makeup been adjusted to coordinate with the garment?

☐ Are there specific instructions from the client about how the garment is to be worn? Are jackets to be worn open or closed? How many buttons on blouses and jackets are to be buttoned or left open? Are blouses or shirts to be worn tucked in or out, bloused or smooth? If there are tie belts or ties on blouses are they to be tied in a bow, square knot, or other?

The following items are necessary for a stylist or fashion show coordinator and are often useful in a photographer's studio. A model need not carry these items to assignments; however, assembling a kit such as this will come in handy when she is maintaining, repairing, and wearing her own clothing.

The Stylist's Kit Checklist Personal needs ☐ Aspirin.

☐ Basic first-aid items such as bandages, etc.

☐ Cotton.

☐ Antiperspirant/deodorant.

☐ Sanitary napkins and tampons.

☐ Facial tissues.

☐ Talcum powder. (It doubles as a dry shampoo for oily hair, underarm antiperspirant, foot powder, and body powder so clothes slip on and off easily. Use it also to cover stains on white garments.)

Clothing care

☐ Iron or steamer (Aerosol fabric relaxant to spray wrinkles is also helpful.)

☐ Clothes brush and lint remover.

☐ Antistatic spray.

☐ Dress shields.

☐ Needle and assortment of threads.

☐ Pin cushions.

☐ Straight pins, long and short.

☐ Safety pins, large and small.

☐ Hat pins.

☐ Shoe horn.

☐ Shoe fillers (tissue, plastic wrap, or cotton for putting in toes to adjust fit).

☐ Fabric spot remover.

☐ Clear spray shoe polish to shine any color of shoe quickly.

Makeup and haircare

☐ Hairspray.

☐ Clear nail enamel for stopping runs.

☐ Bobby pins and hairpins.

☐ Head masks or large scarves to shield models makeup and hair when putting on garments.

☐ Face powder.

Miscellaneous

☐ An 8 x 10 pad of paper and markers for marking racks of clothes according to model, etc. or for notetaking on choreography instructions for models. Can also be used for placing on floor of set to walk on so soles of shoes don't get soiled.

☐ Cellophane tape and sticky double-sided tape for keeping ends of belts flat or for keeping blouses and other articles with closures from gaping.

☐ Masking tape to mask soles of shoes to protect them from getting scratched or soiled on the set or runway. Masking tape can be used to remove stains such as lipstick. Just adhere it to the stained area and pull off. Masking tape can also be used to remove lint, dust, and hair that may cling to garments.

☐ Clamps for tightening belts and garments in back. Heavyweight clamps can be attached to hemlines of pants or other garments so that they hang correctly.

□ Plastic (large plastic garbage bag). This comes in handy to place on a floor in dirty areas to prevent garments or other items from getting soiled.

□ Fabric glue or fusable tape.

□ Velcro (with adhesive back).

□ Crazy Glue for repairing jewelry.

□ Soft terry cloth or like material used to wipe soles of shoes before stepping onto backdrop.

□ Small Ziploc plastic bags for odds and ends, jewelry, accessories, garment tags, etc.

□ Rubber bands of all sizes.

□ Scissors, small and large.

□ Pencils, pens.

□ Paper clips.

□ Emery boards.

□ Flashlight (may be useful during a fashion show).

□ Stapler.

□ String.

□ Tape measure.

□ Tissue paper for preventing creasing when folding garments or for inserting under skirts and in other areas of garment during photo shootings for a crisp look.

WORKING WITH A STYLIST

When a stylist is employed, the model cooperates with him or her and allows the stylist to take responsibility for the way the garment or product appears. The following points will help you to work effectively with a stylist.

• Treat the stylist as an equal. She is a skilled professional who makes a valuable contribution to the photo session, fashion show, or other endeavor. Do not expect her to pick up after you or take care of tasks that are your responsibility. When you take off a garment, hang it up. Place accessories in their proper places. A stylist is usually too busy to do this and is often absent from the dressing area because she is needed on the set.

• Do not challenge, argue, or criticize the way the stylist coordinates your outfit. Don't make suggestions about which accessories you think are better with your outfit or make other such comments. Do not protest wearing an item he assigns to you. Allow the stylist to judge what looks good on you and what doesn't look good. If you really don't like the way an outfit looks on you, consult with the photographer or client—he or she is the one who will make the decision. Remember, that as a professional model your job is not to like the item you are modeling, it is to show how great you can make any item look.

• Don't be overly sensitive in regard to less than ideal circumstances. It is not always possible for the stylist to have shoes and other articles that will fit all the models perfectly. If a pair of shoes or other articles are a size too small, make an effort to wear them. They may be very uncomfortable, but you will only have to wear them for a very short time. When on the job, a good model is always concerned with appearance first. Wearing too small shoes for a very short period of time is not damaging to the feet. This also applies to earrings that pinch, headbands, hats, and belts that are too tight, and the like. Also make sure discomfort doesn't show in your expressions or movements for the runway or the camera.

- Always bring a complete supply of undergarments to every booking to ensure that you have items that fit you perfectly. Always bring a supply of pantyhose in various shades. A stylist will usually supply these items; however, a model who takes responsibility for such matters is assured that her appearance will be ideal. Remember to always get the approval of the stylist if you will be wearing one of your own items.

- Do not rearrange something the stylist has arranged. For example, if she adjusts a hat you are modeling so that it tilts to one side, do not readjust it so it is straight or more comfortable.

- When on the set, a stylist usually prefers that you stay in position while he adjusts your garments for the camera. If he wants you to turn toward him or move, he will instruct you. After the stylist has arranged your garment, avoid movements that will cause the garment to fall out of the desired line of arrangement.

- If the stylist has pinned or tucked your garment in the back, always avoid movement that will undo the adjustments. Also check that your poses hide any pinning or tucking. When you have finished modeling the garment, if you cannot see or remove the pins easily, ask the stylist for assistance.

- If you get makeup on an article you are modeling, bring it to the stylist's attention right away and offer to cover the cost of cleaning or repair. Stylists use expense money from the client or their own money to purchase items that will accompany the garment or product being shown. (The garment or products being sold in the ad are furnished by the client.) Ideally they like to be able to return all items in perfect condition so they can get their money back. If garments are soiled or damaged in other ways, it adds unnecessary expense to the shooting or show and usually results in the model not being called back.

- Do not overreact if the stylist accidentally sticks you with a pin or some other mishap occurs. These things happen. Assume the posture you will have when in front of the camera and hold very still when a stylist is pinning your garment. Don't emphasize others' mistakes.

- Don't tell the stylist how to do her job, but if you see things that you think the stylist may have overlooked, tactfully ask her if the item in question is the way she intended it to be.

- Always check with the stylist before going on the set or runway to make sure everything is right.

Chapter 6 The Model's Guide to Personality

Although modeling is a profession that concentrates on the way an individual looks, personality also plays an important part. It is no longer possible to succeed in the field on looks alone. Today's successful models must have personality as well. In order to be successful, a model must show personality in front of a camera, on a runway, or in a live, taped, or filmed presentation. The reason clients employ models is because models add more interest or impact than the product by itself. A perfect face or a beautiful figure are not the only qualities a client seeks in a model. A model must project animation, expression, flair, or individuality so that she is interesting to look at and will draw attention to the client's product.

Not only must a model be able to project her own unique personality, she must be able to project the personalities of the characters she may be called upon to portray. This requires acting ability to create attitudes, emotions or expressions at will. A model uses her way of moving, gestures, walk, poses, facial expressions, voice, and manner of speaking to express various characters and moods. A good model distinguishes herself from her competition by contributing not only her looks but her acting abilities to a photograph or other presentation.

Although an expressive on-camera or on-stage personality is important to a model's success, a considerate, warm personality behind the scenes is also vital. A model with an attitude problem or who is unpleasant to work with is not desirable to clients or agents. There are so many attractive and qualified models already in the field, it is not necessary for a client or agent to deal with a model who is unkind, inconsiderate, conceited, or snobbish. Any client, photographer, or agent prefers to work with a model who is courteous and fun to be around. Because the modeling business has a never-ending abundance of pretty faces, clients and photographers can choose models who will be cooperative, considerate, and reliable. Any model who wants to be successful must have the combination of a pleasing personality, good manners, and a positive attitude in order to make a good impression on others.

Sometimes it is difficult for a model to retain his or her congeniality. A model must always be cheerful and eager to work, even when he or she may feel tired or unhappy. In addition, a model must be diplomatic because he or she often encounters many people in the field who are difficult to deal with. Agency employees are often rude and brusk. Photographers can be intimidating and like hairstylists, makeup artists, and other creative people often display an artist's tempermental behavior. A model may often find him- or herself working with individuals who are egotistical, artificial, self-important, or unusual. Understanding that this is how some people in fashion and related businesses are is important.

In a work situation, it is important for a model to let the clients and their assistants set the tone of behavior. Within reason, adjust to their behavior. However, avoid extreme behavior: your reputation is important, so it is good sense to avoid any behavior you might regret later, such as becoming involved with drugs, alcohol, profanity, or other unseemly behavior. A successful model is sensitive to the desires of his or her employers and knows how to adjust his or her demeanor to fit their preferences. Different clients prefer different modes of behavior. Some clients and photographers like a down-to-earth, affectionate type, whereas others prefer a more reserved, sophisticated type of demeanor. Most clients like a friendly model who is eager to enter into a team effort that will achieve the best results.

It is also important to be friendly to your co-workers such as assistants, other models, and hair and makeup artists. Avoid comparing your looks, career success, education, or financial status to that of other models: conceit and envy will not endear you to others.

In most modeling situations, talking should be kept to a minimum. Allow the people you are working for to ask the questions or conduct the conversations. Too much chatter slows down progress and makes concentration difficult for photographers, makeup and hair artists, and others with whom you are working. Offer suggestions only when asked. Telling a photographer how you want to be shot or advising a stylist on how to tie a scarf is never welcome. Experienced people (including models) do not want someone less experienced telling them how to do their jobs. Be careful not be make assumptions about people you do not know, in regard to their experience, background, and appearance.

ACQUIRING AN ATTRACTIVE VOICE AND CONVERSATIONAL SKILLS

Although some models' voices may never be heard by the public, models who seek work in live promotions and electronic media must acquire good vocal skills. These individuals should consider training to increase their chances of success. Even a print or fashion show model, whose voice is not an important key to obtaining an assignment, will want to acquire a pleasant-sounding voice and good conversational skills to add to her total professional image and individual style. Any model should try to acquire a voice that will enhance rather than hinder her advancement. No matter what line of work you pursue, your voice should show that you have self-confidence and a genuine desire to communicate effectively. Although a model's vocal image may not have a direct impact on her success, it is evident that it is an important part of her presentation and has an influence over the impression she makes on potential clients and others in a position to further her career.

Improving Your Vocal Image

There are two basic components of your vocal image: voice and speech.

Voice

It is important to be aware of the characteristics of your voice and how you can alter them to arrive at a more pleasant sound. The three basic characteristics of your voice are pitch, volume, and quality or tone.

Pitch

Pitch refers to how low or high your voice sounds. Generally, a lower tone of voice is most pleasing to the ear. Try to keep your voice pitch low, but not so low that you cannot lower it even more for selected words. You'll want to avoid a monotonous or affected sound. Be conscious of your voice pitch especially in situations in which you are nervous or excited.

Volume   Volume refers to the loudness or softness of your voice. To determine whether your volume is ideal, take cues from your listeners. For example, if people frequently ask you to speak up, you probably speak too quietly. A too quiet voice will make you seem meek, shy, and self-conscious.

Tone   Tone refers to the quality of your vocal sound. The quality of your voice is determined by the way you use your vocal cords and resonant cavities such as the nasal passages and the throat. Avoid nasal, raspy, or flat tones, and instead strive for tones that will be pleasant to your listener. Be conscious of opening and relaxing your throat to allow full-bodied, pleasant tones to emerge. Concentrate on initiating your vocal sound from your diaphragm and directing it through the throat rather than allowing it to start from your chest and travel through your nose.

Intonation is another characteristic of tone. Intonation refers to the melody of your speech patterns. A monotonous tone means that you speak in only one tone. This makes what you say seem uninteresting. A melodic speech pattern is the opposite and employs lots of variation. A too studied or put-on intonation can make you sound artificial or whiny. The ideal intonation is one which is varied so that thoughts are expressed in a meaningful, interesting way.

Speech   Speech has to do with the way you articulate and pronounce words, and the rate of your delivery.

Tempo   Tempo refers to how fast or slow you speak. Speaking too quickly makes it difficult for your listener to understand you. Speaking too slowly gives the impression that you are sluggish, lazy, or unintelligent. Be conscious of your speaking pace. Gear your pace to what you are saying. You can emphasize important words or points by speaking more slowly than you would when covering minor details or other less important information.

Articulation   Articulation refers to how clearly you sound words. Speech sounds are controlled by the placement of the tongue, the use of the teeth, and the use of the lips. Poor enunciation can make you seem uneducated, lazy, or indifferent. Overenunciating words will make you sound artificial or affected.

Pronunciation   The way you pronounce words can give an indication of your level of education, social status, and what locale you come from. An accent can be a distinguishing, endearing characteristic or it can be a hinderance. Using your accent in a way that helps rather than hinders your chances is important. Being able to turn an accent on or off at will can increase the opportunities available to you in the modeling field.

Your vocabulary, the way you phrase ideas, and your grammar are also important aspects of your vocal image. As a starting point, examine the most common mistakes listed in Tables 1 to 3 to determine if you make any of them.

There are several ways to improve your voice and speech. Using a tape recorder can help you to hear yourself as others do. Tape-record your telephone conversations with business associates, or try reading into a tape recorder to analyze where improvement is needed.

Enrolling in a class in acting or speech will also help you to become aware of how to use your voice more effectively. Individualized instruction or working with a videotape recorder will also help you to improve your vocal presentation.

Table 1 Common Grammatical Mistakes

Do you say . . .?	When you should say . . .
I'm gonna	I'm going to
I gotta	I've got to
I could care less	I could not care less
I could of	I could have
Just between you and I	Just between you and me
This is her, or it's me, or it's me Mary	This is she; this is Mary speaking (when identifying yourself on the phone)
If I was her	If I were she
I'm taller than her	I'm taller than she
She says	She said (when repeating a conversation that took place in the past)

Table 2 Words That Are Commonly Mispronounced

	Incorrect	Correct
Jewelry	Joo-le-ree, joo-ree	Jew-el-ree
Mirror	Meer	Mir-er
Pictures	Pitchers	Pik-chers

Table 3 Speech Habits to Avoid

Do you drop the ends of words and say "laughin" instead of "laughing"?
Do you say "umm," "like," "ya know," or "stuff"?
Do you say "cuz" instead of "because"?
Do you say "ya" instead of "yes"?

Polishing Your Conversational Skills

Once you have acquired an attractive speaking voice and a pleasant manner of speech, it is important to be concerned with conversation. Developing good conversational skills will help you to develop friendly relations with others. A model can benefit by observing the following guidelines:

- Be a good listener. Listen more than you speak.
- Avoid a lot of small talk. Discuss things that are relevant to the job at hand.
- Never gossip.
- Avoid dominating the conversation with news about yourself, and avoid prying into other people's private matters. In general, it is a good idea to avoid discussing the following topics: personal problems, personal financial affairs, health problems, and religion.
- Do not criticize the workmanship or personal characteristics of your agent, clients, photographers, and other business associates. Don't criticize your competition (other models). If you have valid complaints, direct them to the individual at the proper time and setting. Do not tell others how they should conduct their businesses.
- Don't be argumentative. Avoid confrontations when possible. When an issue must be settled, be willing to compromise.

- Control your emotions. Avoid losing your temper or crying in a business situation.
- Don't be negative. Center your conversations around positive ideas or solutions to problems.

TIPS FOR ACQUIRING GOOD BUSINESS RELATIONS

The following list of points for effective public relations may seem like a battery of cliches, but they are basics that can make a great deal of difference to you in your career pursuits. Modeling is a business that involves dealing with people. How you interact with others can make or break you. The circle of people involved in the modeling business is small, and your reputation will precede you. Having a good personality is important, but adding these extra touches will help you enjoy the people you work with and will make others regard you in a positive way.

Learn and remember the first and last names of everyone you meet. Some models pay no attention to the people they meet. They go on an endless round of appointments with no idea of the names or positions of people they meet. This is a mistake. You should learn everyone's name from the receptionist at the desk to the person who is in a position to offer you a job. People are flattered when you make an effort to remember their names. When you call a studio or company, it is nice to know the name of the secretary who answers and the name and title of the person you are trying to reach. Usually you will encounter the same people repeatedly, so learning names from the beginning helps you to understand how the whole business picture works.

Treat everyone with equal respect. Get to know secretaries, production assistants, and other staff members by name and treat them with respect. Do not overlook their importance. They are probably very close to the person you want to contact, and they can be of valuable influence in helping you. In a work situation, everyone from the photographer's assistant to the hairstylist to the photographer is important to the success of the job.

Be positive and cheerful. Be pleasant and cheerful, and people will always be glad to see you. Avoid unloading your disappointments, frustrations, or disillusionments on colleagues. Nobody wants to hear your problems; they have plenty of their own.

Say only good things about other people or say nothing at all. Gossip is usually traced back to the originator. Never enter into discussions regarding the quality of work, the way of working, or other negative points about other people in the business. The fastest way to gain a friend is to say something positive about the person; the fastest way to make an enemy is to say something negative. Be quick to compliment and to spread the good word about other people's talents, skills, and abilities. The people you recommend to others are apt to do the same for you when they have the opportunity.

Appreciate the help others have given you. Give credit where credit is due. Nobody is successful alone. It takes a break from an employer, advice from an agent, or help from colleagues or friends. Send thank-you notes to people who have taken the time to interview you, have given you advice, or have recommended you to an agent or client. (When doing so, include your picture, agency name, and answering service number.) Always show your agent how much you appreciate his or her efforts.

Show your enthusiasm. Always give others the impression that you have unlimited enthusiasm and energy for your job. For example, every time your booker calls with an audition, "go-see," or booking, show eagerness and enthusiasm. When you are on the job, show how much you enjoy your work. Even when things around you are discouraging, don't let your enthusiasm fade.

Do not take advantage of others. Don't try to see how many prints or rolls of film you can get out of a photographer, how many free meals or other perks you can squeeze out of a client, or how much advice you can get from others without giving anything in return. Realize that people are in business to make money. If you have nothing to offer them, they would rather not waste their time with you. Consider first how the other person will benefit from your interchange. If you cannot offer the other person anything, avoid wasting his or her time. People will regard you and your talents more highly, when you show respect for them. Always try to give more than you receive.

Always put yourself in the other person's place. You will become a good worker when you try to see things from another person's vantage point. For example, in a job situation, be fully prepared, ready to work, and efficient. If you were the client paying the model's fee, you would appreciate such a conscientious attitude. Always consider the other person's objectives, expectations, and constraints. This is especially helpful when disputes arise. Care about your clients and business associates rather than always concentrating on your own selfish needs or opinions.

Nurture your contacts. Do not let contacts you have made disappear, unless of course they lead no where for either of you. Periodically drop a note to the individuals who helped you to enter and progress in the field. Avoid the mistake of forgetting your old contacts when you move up the ladder of success. You never know when you will need their help again.

Make check-in calls to people in a position to employ you once a month to see what is going on and to ensure they they know you are still around. Keep clients updated as to your progress by dropping them a note; attach a good, new tearsheet or proof of some other recent accomplishment. Send holiday cards and postcards when you are out of town to your established clients and contacts. If you see articles of interest, tearsheets of another model, or other items that may be of interest to the person, send it to them with a short note.

Avoid ending business relationships on a negative note. If an arrangement between you and a business associate has not worked out well, do not close the door on your relationship. Express your disappointment, but leave your options open for calling on the person in the future.

HANDLING DIFFICULT SITUATIONS

As a model, you must conduct yourself in a professional manner, but unfortunately you may encounter those in the profession who do not. Increasing your awareness of questionable situations as well as having the confidence to deal with them is important.

One of the best ways to protect yourself from becoming involved in undesirable activities is to work through a reputable modeling agent. A qualified agent will know which people you should avoid. It is an agent's primary function to research business contacts for the model. The circle of people involved in the modeling business is relatively small and a good agent makes it her business to know who is who, and who is doing what.

A second primary way to avoid getting in contact with the wrong people or becoming involved in bad situations is to use common sense. Listed here are some pointers that can ensure your emotional and physical survival in the modeling field.

Sexual harrassment on the job exists in the modeling field, as it does in other types of employment. If a person with whom you work sexually harasses you, report the incident to your agency. If you feel that person might be potentially dangerous, file a written complaint with the head of the agency and keep a copy of the letter for your files. Do not take chances. Don't work for or go to see photographers or others you know to have bad reputations. No modeling opportunity is worth putting yourself in even the slightest amount of danger. In order to achieve success in the modeling business it is not necessary to be "nice" sexually to anyone, male or female. It is important to realize that decisions regarding which model is chosen for an assignment are made by several people; usually no single individual has complete power over such decisions. Avoid photographers, clients, or agents who offer you bookings in exchange for sexual favors. Even if you agree to an arrangement, there is no guarantee that the other person will come across with his part of the agreement.

Always be on your guard against suspicious people or situations. You may encounter people who use the line that they can help you in the modeling field because of some connection they have with a photographer, a magazine, or whatever. If you are already with an agency, tell such people to work through your agency. If you aren't affiliated with an agency, ask for names of their contacts so you can check it out. Always ask for a business card, and give no information about yourself. Never agree to meeting any place before checking to be sure you are being offered a legitimate job. Professional, reputable clients from out of town do not conduct interviews in hotel rooms. They either use a hotel lobby or hotel conference room or will interview you at your agency. Do not go to a private home for an interview or shooting unless you are working through an agent. Keep in mind that, generally, business is conducted during business hours, so be aware that agreeing to meet someone after business hours may give off the wrong signals.

Although a concern such as a manufacturer or advertising agency may be highly reputable, there have been instances where a representative has not exercised ethical conduct. There are people who have a very trustworthy and convincing manner who may try to take advantage of your inexperience. These are all reasons why it is important to have an ethical agent who can protect you from such potential problems.

Don't give out your home number or address to anyone but your agent. The agency will safeguard your number by not giving it to clients or others who may request it. Never indicate to anyone (photographer, client, or other) that you live alone. Use common sense.

Because of the nature of their work, models are often in many high-risk, potentially dangerous situations. They are out on the street a lot and come into contact with lots of strangers. Models travel to unfamiliar areas and cities, stay at hotels, and share apartments. Because of the large amount of space needed for their work, photographers' studios are often located in gloomy-looking buildings in unsafe areas, so taking extra precautions is necessary. Learn self-defense and read about ways you can increase your safety. Knowing how to protect yourself and being cautious will increase your confidence.

Don't allow yourself to be pressured into situations you may regret later. Posing in the nude for a few shots that the photographer tells you no one will ever see, or entering into other arrangements may come back to haunt you in the future. Think of your life and goals in the long term and decide how what you do now will affect your future. If you are confused, tell the individual you need a day or two to think about it, then talk to someone you can trust.

Don't be so overly ambitious that it distorts your priorities. If a photographer wants you to do something that could seriously jeopardize your health or safety, try to find an alternative or tell him to get a replacement. You won't score points with the people who want you to do the activity, but no amount of money is worth endangering your life or well-being.

Realize that some people you may encounter in this or any other field, may have psychological abnormalities. You may think there is a way to deal rationally with almost any person or situation you'll encounter. However, even people who may seem normal on the surface can have irrational, unhealthy, or even violent aspects to their personalities. Understanding this is difficult for most people because they have had no prior experience with such personality types. In fact, most people, especially young people, think they are immune to such dangers. They naively think that bad things won't happen to them or that they'll be able to escape when confronted. Most people avoid thinking about such unpleasant things. However, these negative aspects are facts of our current society. Models may be especially susceptible because they are appealing and attract attention. People of all kinds are drawn to them.

Getting into contact with the "wrong person" whether he or she is an agent, client, or acquaintance can often have far-reaching, unhappy consequences. Never allow convenience, money (saving it or making it), or career opportunities to distort your judgment in regard to doing business or having contact with someone whose intentions you can't read. Take full responsibility for protecting yourself by sharpening your character-judging skills. Acquiring a highly developed sensitivity to signals that may indicate potential trouble is crucial to survival. Do not invite or flirt with trouble. Always pay attention to your intuition, gut feelings, logic, and the advice of concerned friends and family in such situations. Err on the side of not trusting other people, rather than on trusting too much. Always aim to have control over any situation.

BEHAVIOR GUIDELINES FOR CHILD MODELS AND THEIR PARENTS OR GUARDIANS

- Each time the agency calls with an assignment, the parent should inform the agent of tooth loss, braces, bumps, bruises, or any other changes in the child's appearance since the last booking or time the agent called or saw the child.

- Child models should arrive at least 15 minutes before the booked time for the job. This allows time for last-minute grooming and instructions. It also allows the child to adjust to his or her surroundings.

- Only the child that has been booked and one parent or guardian should arrive at the studio. If you must bring another child or adult to the booking, you must get permission from the agency beforehand. The child should have the same parent or guardian accompany him or her to all bookings. Successful child modeling requires a partnership of child and parent or guardian. The parent or guardian must be effective in motivating and directing the child so that the booking has the desired outcome. It is the parent's responsibility to assemble the proper items and wardrobe (in excellent condition) for the job, to dress the child, and arrange the child's hair. The parent also acts as a coach, helping the child to achieve the client's goals.

- The parent or guardian must be on hand at all times during bookings; however, during shots he or she must wait in the dressing room, unless called to the set. Parents always wait in the waiting room while the child goes into auditions.

- It is the parent's responsibility to insist that the child exhibit good behavior while in the studio, on the set, or in the dressing room. Children should not handle items not belonging to them and must learn how to cooperate and be patient. The attitude of the parent has a lot to do with the child's attitude. The child should be made to feel that modeling is fun but also imparts responsibility. Children are quick to pick up on the way their parents feel toward others or toward a situation, and they tend to adopt the same behavior. It is the parent's responsibility to keep the child quiet and still before the shooting or the show begins and between shots and appearances. This is important so that the child doesn't distract others and will have enough energy and attention when called upon to perform.

- The parent should see that the child is safe at all times. Others will not watch over a child as carefully as the parent will. Don't leave a child with strangers, and always rely on an agent to set up appointments.

- It is not a good idea to reprimand the child in front of others on the set, because it will affect his or her performance. Threats should never be made against a child who is not cooperating or performing the job well. Leave family and school problems at home.

- It is also not a good idea to force the child to do a job. The best child models are those who motivate their parents to allow them to model, not the other way around. Every time the agency calls with a booking or audition, give the child the option of accepting or refusing the job. School and normal childhood activities must always take precedence over modeling. In most cities children do not make the rounds of potential clients; they attend auditions and bookings only.

- If the child is old enough, involve him or her in all aspects of the job from preparation, to filling out the voucher, to dealing with the agency. All chapters in this book apply to child models as well as adults. Modeling can be a learning experience for the child and good feelings toward work and accomplishment should be encouraged.

- Don't compete with the parents of other child models. Parents often try to out-do each other in their treatment of the agency staff in attempts to have their child promoted more vigorously. Being pleasant and professional is more important.

PART 3 MODELING AS A BUSINESS

Chapter 7 The Modeling Agency and its Functions

THE MODELING AGENCY

A modeling agency is an employment agency for models. The agency attempts to secure employment for its models from companies who need faces and figures to appear in printed materials, electronic media productions, live promotions, and fashion shows. Agencies establish contacts and arrange auditions and interviews with prospective clients. When a client wishes to employ a model, he or she contacts the model's agency, which will handle the scheduling of the model's time, negotiate the model's fee, and relay instructions to the model. After the job is completed, the agency collects the money owed to the model. For these services, the agency charges the model and the client each a commission, usually ranging from 10 to 20% of the billed time.

In most cities and states, modeling agencies must be licensed as private employment agencies and are governed by the laws of the state or municipality. Requirements vary from area to area, but usually prospective agency owners must be bonded, submit information about their financial and business backgrounds, and file affidavits from people stating that they are of good moral character. In addition, they must submit for approval copies of the model contracts, fee schedules, brochures, job order forms, and the like to be used by the agency. Many states require that anyone working in a modeling agency and acting as an employment counselor be licensed as well.

Agents who find work for models and actors in television commercials and other electronic media assignments must be franchised by SAG (Screen Actor's Guild) or AFTRA (American Federation of Radio and Television Artists) where these unions are in force. Most agencies display their license and franchise certifications clearly. Many agencies are also members of associations that set industry standards and assist in settling disputes.

There are hundreds of modeling agencies in the United States alone, and the majority of them are owned or managed by people who were initially involved in some aspect of the fashion or entertainment business. An agency may consist of one person working out of an apartment answering phones for a group of models, or it may be a bustling business maintaining over 20 full-time employees (not including models).

HOW MODELING AGENCIES DIFFER

Market

The market refers to where the agency is located and the number of clients in the area. In the United States, New York, Chicago, and Los Angeles are the major modeling markets. New York has the widest variety and greatest amount of modeling work of any city in the world. Internationally, the major markets are Paris, London, Milan, and Tokyo. The amount and type of work in a given market has to do with the products manufactured and sold in the area, the advertising agencies that are represented there, and other businesses such as stores that are located in the area.

Area of Specialization

Some agencies specialize in one type of work, promotional modeling for example, whereas others are multiservice agencies catering to clients who need print, runway, television, and promotional models. Agencies may also be specialized by the types of models they represent. Some agencies represent all types, ranging in age from infants to grandparents. Others may specialize in fashion models between the ages of 14 and 28.

Size

Size refers to the number of models the agency represents and the number of people on its staff. Some agencies represent large numbers of models and have hundreds of names and composites on file. Other agencies are small, representing fewer than 30 models.

Status, Reputation, and Popularity

Popularity runs in cycles; one agency will be the most popular until another emerges to take its place. Most cities have one or a few agencies that have remained on top for many years. An agency's status is based on the caliber of its clients, the number of star models that the agency boasts, the amount of income per model, and the size of the agency's profits.

Management Style

Agencies differ according to their styles of management. Some agencies take a somewhat dictatorial approach, tending to control their models by telling a model what he or she must do. Models consider themselves fortunate to be represented by the agency and try to fit into the mold. Other agents take a partnership-oriented approach to model–agent relations. These agents operate on a more individualized basis by entering into a business partnership with the model. The model and agent service each other. Both are equally important. Here the agency feels fortunate in having the opportunity to represent the model. Some agencies exhibit both styles of management reserving the former approach for the majority of models, the latter for the established and star models.

FUNCTIONS OF THE MODELING AGENCY

Recruiting

All agencies engage in activities to obtain new models and talent. Agencies differ as to the amount of time and energy they devote to recruiting. They also recruit using different methods. Some of the most common methods used for finding new faces are scouting, referrals, competitions, and open interviews.

Some scouting for models and talent is done in an informal, almost happenstance way. For example, an employee of a modeling agency may spot a potential model on the street or in a store and invite him or her to come to the agency for an interview. Other scouting methods are deliberate. For example, many times a representative from a modeling agency will attend beauty pageants or visit modeling schools or agencies outside of her market to look for new faces. Some agencies engage talent or model scouts whose job it is to search for young men and women with modeling qualifications. A professional scout may be an agency employee or may work on a free-lance basis and receive a discovery fee or a percentage of the model's forthcoming earnings over a period of time. Some agents and scouts conduct local seminars or lectures for groups of men and women interested in modeling and occasionally talent is found.

Many times a model will be discovered by a photographer, client, model, or other individual involved in the modeling field. He or she will refer the potential model to the agency. Usually no fee is paid to the discoverer, instead an exchange of favors may occur.

Some agencies conduct modeling contests or work jointly with a magazine, store, or other commercial sponsor to hold a model search. At any given time, there are a number of modeling contests being conducted. This is a good way for an agency to find talent because the odds of finding new models are increased when the entrants number in the thousands. It also provides lots of publicity.

Open interviews are another way in which agencies find new talent. Many agencies open their doors for a few days or hours each week for anyone to come in and apply. Applicants are expected to bring snapshots or other pictures and are seen by an agent. Well-established agencies are also beseiged through mail and telephone by hundreds up to thousands of applicants. Physical appearance, height, weight, and age are qualifications for the model's job and any agency can reject applicants who fail to meet their requirements.

Agents must be careful in selecting the models they represent. To the agency the model is an investment in staff time (bookers spend hours making calls and assisting the model) and money (costs entail sending the model's promotional materials to prospective clients, telephone bills, etc.). Like any businessperson, the agent is looking for a return on his or her investment and can only afford to put time and money into a model who will eventually bring profits.

Counseling and Training

The way in which counseling and training of the models is handled varies from one agency to the next. Some agencies are very involved on a personal basis with the models they represent; other agencies prefer to deal with models who have experience or have been previously trained. Because counseling and training can be very time-consuming, many agencies don't give much guidance to new models— they expect a model to learn on her own.

Agencies that are involved in counseling and training of models do so in basically three ways: in-house training, training by field experts, and testing board.

In-house training refers to training programs conducted in the agency. Classes may be scheduled in which a client, model, makeup artist, designer, photographer, or other authority in the field will talk to models. Such instruction may be offered at no charge or a nominal fee to models. Some agencies are affiliated with modeling schools and will have new models attend the classes. In addition, models may be given a booklet or other written material composed by the agency outlining what is expected of the models and the basic procedures they are to follow. Agencies also conduct periodic reviews of the model's progress to determine changes or improvements.

Some agencies are not equipped for or interested in conducting in-house training. Instead they refer the model to experts in the field for training. For example, a model may be sent to a designer, fashion show coordinator or experienced model to learn how to walk for fashion show modeling. To learn acting or to become more expressive, she may be sent to classes or private lessons conducted by a prominent acting coach or casting director. To learn makeup and hairstyling, the agency will refer the model to top makeup artists and hairstylists. To learn how to move for the camera, a model may be referred to a photographer or dance teacher who has worked with other models. In most instances, models are expected to pay for this type of training. If the agent is really interested in the model, costs of training may be advanced to her or him.

Many agencies have either a formally or loosely structured testing board. It is one of the best ways to train new models and to sort out the ones who have the greatest potential for success. The agency will either set up appointments with photographers or give models lists of photographers who are willing to photograph new models. Many of these photographers are inexperienced and need models to practice on. Some will charge the model or her agency a session fee, whereas others shoot at no charge or for just expenses.

The model is expected to approach testing sessions as a way to learn how to move for the camera and how to work with different photographers. In addition it provides photographs that will be used for her composite and portfolio. After each test session, the model brings her contact sheets back to the agency where the results are critiqued and selections are made for photographic prints. At intervals (for example, monthly) the model's progress is taken into consideration. One model may have acquired only a few mediocre pictures for her portfolio, whereas another may have acquired a full portfolio of excellent or promising pictures. For many models, the results of these testings may show that the model does not have enough ambition or natural ability to be successful in the modeling field. Other models may be ready to see top magazine editors and important clients.

This testing activity varies from one model to the next. Some models need up to a year and a half to develop their looks, talents, and skills. Their testing period may include a trip abroad to gain European test shots, tearsheets, and experience. Other models may prove their potential for success after just a few photo sessions. The attrition rate for new models is high, but a testing board is an effective way to sift out the most talented, dedicated, and marketable individuals. The ones who pass through these initial stages successfully and fairly rapidly are then promoted more enthusiastically by the agency.

Promotion

An agency has several ways of promoting models. Most of the following promotional materials are issued once or several times a year. The following are distributed to the agency's existing and potential clients. Distribution costs are usually covered by the agency.

Model Agency Book

This is a spiral-bound book ranging in size from 5 x 8 to 8 x 10 to 9 x 14 inches (Figure 1). It displays pictures of the models the agency has chosen to promote. The pictures are taken from the model's composite or portfolio. Usually two to five closeup and full-length shots are displayed of each model. A full page may be devoted to each of the agency's stars; beginning models may be displayed two to a page or may have just a headshot.

Model books make an impressive showing to the client, are convenient to use, and are good reference guides. In effect, they are catalogs from which clients can select models. Another advantage is that individual composites can easily get misplaced or lost. Agency books also cut down on mailing costs and inconvenience. Usually printing costs of model books are paid by each model. Depending on how many pictures of each model are displayed, whether the printing is done in black and white or color, and the number of copies to be distributed, the cost per model may range from $50 to several hundred dollars.

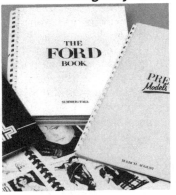

*Examples of agency
promotional books.*
(Courtesy of A-Plus Talent, Chicago; Elite,
Chicago; Ford Models, New York; Prestige
Models, New York.)

Since the agency's model book, also called a talent or promotional book, is sent to all the agency's clients, including those from out of town, the model can gain a lot of exposure, and the investment pays for itself when he or she receives bookings (particularly from out-of-town clients) that she otherwise might not have obtained.

Headsheet

A headsheet is a poster-size sheet onto which a headshot of each model represented by the agency is reproduced along with the model's name. Each model pays for the printing of his or her picture.

Poster

Posters are usually distributed in addition to a headsheet and/or model book and feature the agency's models in a group shot.

Newsletters and Brochures

Agents often send out newsletters and brochures to their clients, complete with pictures, announcing new services or talent they may have. These are usually paid for by the agency.

Composites

A composite is a 5 x 8 or 8½ x 11-inch "calling card" displaying from 2 to 10 black and white and/or color shots of the model in different moods. These are paid for by the model and assembled by the model with the help of the agent. The agency sends these to clients as an introduction or reminder of a model or in response to client requests for specific types of models. The pictures on the composite can be either the same shots as those in the model agency book or different ones, so the client can use both as a reference. The model carries a supply of composites to all modeling appointments and distributes them to clients for their files.

Agency Presentation Book

This is a 16 x 20 or larger portfolio that contains pictures, clippings, and the like of the models in the agency (see Figure 2). Usually one to two pages are devoted to each model. The agent shows this book to prospective clients of the agency, when meeting them in person.

Shown here are examples of modeling agency promotional tools. (Courtesy of the Model Team Agency, Zurich, Switzerland.)

Miniportfolios

The agency may have one or more copies of a miniature portfolio of each model, which is usually about 5 x 7 in size. These contain reduced copies of the prints and tearsheets found in the model's regular portfolio. Some miniportfolios may be 8 x 10 in size and contain exact duplicates of the items in her regular portfolio in an inexpensive, lightweight case. Miniportfolios are advantageous because they can be sent by messenger or mail conveniently and inexpensively and also do not require the model to be without his or her portfolio. Clients who are considering booking a model but who cannot see the model in person will look at a miniportfolio and return it to the agency.

In-House Portfolios

Some agencies maintain a duplicate miniportfolio or standard-size portfolio of each model that is kept in the agency. The model's pictures might instead be presented in a large wall display that the client can flip through, much the way posters are displayed in a store. Inviting the client to the agency to research models may be the procedure followed when the client wishes to do an initial survey of a large group of models—so many that it would make sending miniportfolios unreasonable.

Audition Polaroids   Most agencies are equipped with Polaroid cameras to enable them to take up-to-the-minute color pictures of talent in the agency. This may be necessary when the client needs a photo for identification purposes or to show the model's coloring. A client who auditions models in the modeling agency may want a Polaroid record to refresh his or her memory of how the model appeared on that day. Composites often make the model look very different from the way he or she appears in person. When casting electronic media and other assignments not requiring still photography, a Polaroid sometimes gives a more accurate representation of how the model will appear.

Slide Presentations   For a more impressive sales presentation, an agent might collect slides from each model in the agency to be included in a slide presentation for a meeting with a prospective client.

Videotapes   To promote the agency to prospective clients, an agency might produce a master videotape showing its best models suitable for television work. Each model appears in action sequences and is seen full face, in profile, and smiling. Each delivers a few lines telling his or her name, height, size, and other information. A more elaborate tape might also include clips from commercials in which the model has performed or pictures from her portfolio. Copies of this tape may be sent to television casting directors, clients, or advertising agencies so they can screen the models each agency represents before selecting the ones to be auditioned or as a means of making casting decisions.

Audition Videotapes   Most agencies have videotape equipment and can prepare audition tapes of their talent when necessary. For example, a client may send a script to a modeling agency and ask that several suitable models act out the script on videotape. The tape is then sent back to the individual who requested it so that initial casting decisions can be made.

Master Reels   An agency representing voice-over talent produces a master audio tape containing the voices of the talent they represent. This master reel is used by clients to select a voice for a radio spot, television commercial, industrial or educational film, or other electronic media production. If the modeling agency is franchised by the Screen Actor's Guild, it cannot charge the talent who seek electronic media work the cost of being included in a promotional book, master videotape, or master audio tape.

Promotional Events   Modeling agencies sometimes host activities to gain publicity and to allow the models and clients to get together. Such events might include an agency-organized fashion show, party, or sporting event.

Scheduling and Booking   A modeling agency employs bookers to act as the link between the clients and the models. A booker spends the day on the telephone taking down assignments for models when clients call, negotiating models' fees for individual jobs, checking with models for approval of the scheduled times and terms of the bookings, and getting feedback from clients.

Bookers have differing levels of expertise. Those just beginning are concerned mostly with scheduling appointments and performing secretarial tasks. As they progress, bookers become involved with negotiating basic contracts and bookings, which usually follow a set format of fees and conditions. Experienced bookers negotiate lucrative bookings for top models that may involve a host of contingencies.

The way in which models are booked varies. Usually the client will become interested in a model as a result of seeing his or her composite or picture in the agency promotional book. When possible, the agent will schedule a go-see so the model can go and see the client in person. Following this meeting, the client will call the agency to book the model, if he or she was impressed by her.

If the model requested by the client is unavailable, the booker will suggest other suitable models. Another instance in which the booker has the opportunity to promote other models occurs when the caller has no particular model in mind. When a client has no preference for a specific model or is in need of a "new face," he or she will request a "type," for example, an attractive career woman in her midtwenties. When this occurs, the booker will suggest models who fit the description and will send either composites or the models to the client for a "look-see." Clients rarely use models they have not seen in person—this only occurs if the model is well known or if time, location, or other circumstances do not allow for a personal interview.

Each booker is responsible for a group of models. Models may be divided into groups on the basis of their level of achievement, their type, or their place in the alphabet. The booker schedules interviews, auditions, and go-sees with prospective clients; fills job orders from clients who call; and relays all this information to the model. This information is continually being revised as clients call to book models or to make changes. Agencies use computers, large wall charts, index cards, or scheduling forms to record and update this information. Bookers have complete data about each model, such as measurements, excellent features, flaws, special talents, abilities, sports, product conflicts, experience, and the like.

Many bookings are made on short notice—that is, 1 to 3 days in advance. Some jobs are last minute, with only a 1-hour notice; others are booked 2 to 3 months in advance, for example, location trips, contract bookings, or bookings involving several consecutive days. The more in demand a model is, the further in advance his or her time must be reserved.

Agencies receive bookings requiring all types of talent, abilities, and characteristics. Depending on the model's status, the client, and other factors, a booking may not fit into the typical mold. Bookers consult with models in certain situations where the booking may involve location work, a cut rate, or certain types of products or factors that may affect the direction of the model's career. Bookings that are atypical must be carefully considered by the model before acceptance. He or she must consider how the result of the assignment might enhance or detract from her image and career in an overall view. A good agent can help the model to make the right decisions in such cases.

When a client decides on using a model, he or she makes a definite booking, stating the exact hour and the length of time the model will be needed. If the client is unsure about which model to book or hasn't finalized the particulars of the assignment (such as dates, times, and the like), he or she will make a tentative booking, also sometimes called an "option" or "hold" or a booking "on ice." This means that the client has first claim on the model for that time slot. Busy models often have tentatives and secondaries, meaning that two or more clients are waiting in line for his or her services on that particular day.

If a model has a tentative booking, and another client calls with a definite booking, the agent informs the client holding the tentative booking. At this time (or within a 2-hour period), the client must exercise his or her option to confirm or release his tentative booking. If the client doesn't give the agent notice one way or the other, the agent reserves the right to allow a confirmed booking to take precedence.

Tentative bookings can be cancelled by either the model or the client at anytime and at no charge. However, when a client cancels a definite booking, the agent requires a cancellation fee, depending on how much advance notice the client gives. Likewise, if the client shortens the time allotted for the shooting, the model must still be paid for the the original time or a portion thereof for which he or she was booked.

When a client makes a definite booking, the agent completes a job order or booking form. (See the Booking Form that follows.) This form ensures that instructions are taken down and relayed to the model accurately. It details information such as where the job will take place, directions to the location (if necessary), what the model is to bring, whether there will be a hairstylist or makeup artist, and the fee the model is to charge. Some agents fill out this form in triplicate and mail a copy each to the model and client when time allows. Some agencies supply the model with these forms to enable her to take down information efficiently as it is relayed to her over the phone by the agent. The model uses this form to help him or her to prepare for the job. He or she brings it along to the job to help him or her when filling out his or her voucher at the end of the job.

How to Use a Booking Form

A model should complete a booking form each time his or her agency calls with an assignment. This is the only way to ensure that the model will have complete instructions and be properly prepared. The form can be used at the booking to help the model complete her voucher correctly.

When you are notified of a booking, these are the questions you should ask:

1. *When is the job, what time, and how long will it last?* Write down the day and date of the booking, the time you are to arrive, and the estimated length of time of the booking.

2. *Where am I to go for the booking?* Note the booking location. This may be at the photographer's studio, a location outside of the studio where you will be shooting, or a designated meeting place. Note the address, and if necessary, get directions from your agent or client. Make sure you allow extra time if you have not been there before or if parking or public transportation might be difficult. Many agencies insist that the model arrive at all bookings 15 minutes early.

3. *Who is the client? What is the product? What is the rate?* Note the client. This means the store, company, or other entity sponsoring or paying the model's fee. Usually it will not be the photographer. Note the product you will be modeling. Note whether you will be paid your normal hourly/daily rate or if you will be charging a special rate. Always know beforehand what you are to charge.

4. *To whom do I report? Is this a "weather permitting" booking?* Note the name of the person to whom you are to report. This is necessary especially for TV jobs and jobs for large concerns. Note whether the booking is "weather permitting." If the assignment is dependent on certain weather conditions, you may be given a number to call 2 hours before the booking to ascertain its status.

5. *What type of assignment is it?* Note the type of job it is. If it is a TV spot, note whether you are an on-camera principal, an extra, an off-camera player, and so forth. For fashion shows, note what you will be doing such as fitting, looks, retail show, or floor modeling. For promotional jobs indicate whether you will be a hostess, narrator, demonstrator, or performer. For print jobs know whether the work is catalog, editorial, advertising, or other.

Booking Form

© THE PROFESSIONAL MODEL'S HANDBOOK

Job Date _____ Time (from) _____ Time (to) _____

Client _____ Product _____

Report To _____ Special Note _____

Job Location _____

Assignment Type ☐Print _____ ☐Electronic _____

Media _____ ☐Promotional_____ ☐Fashion Show _____

Fitting Date _____ Rehearsal Dates _____

Makeup _____

Hair _____

Bring: ☐Basic Totebag items _____

☐Accessories _____

☐Shoes _____

☐Jewelry _____

☐Wardrobe _____

☐Other _____

Rate or Session Fee_____

Expenses   Booking Conditions   Bonuses

_____   _____   _____

_____   _____   _____

_____   _____   _____

_____   _____   _____

NOTES:

6. *What rehearsal, fitting, or wardrobe check information do I need?* Note dates and times you are to appear for the above and what you are to bring.

7. *Will there be a makeup artist? If not, what should my makeup look like?* Note whether there will be a makeup artist or if you are expected to do your own makeup. Indicate what type of makeup look (light, heavy, high fashion, etc.) will be needed for the shooting.

8. *Will there be a hairdresser?* Note whether there will be a hairdresser, if not, how the client will want your hair to look.

9. *What am I to bring?* Know if you are to bring shoes, accessories, or wardrobe and find out the style, season, and color that are needed.

10. *Notes.* In this space note specific directions or any information that may be needed. If it is an out-of-town booking, you should note travel and hotel information.

Determining Fees

Determining the fees models are to be paid for the work they do is one of the most important functions of an agency. The fee a model is paid is dependent upon the type of assignment (print, fashion show, electronic media, or promotional) and other factors that may be involved. Basically model's fees are structured in three ways: agency-established hourly/daily rates, client-established fees, and negotiated fees.

Agency-Established Hourly/Daily Rates

The modeling agency sets an hourly and daily rate for each model they represent. The model charges this rate for the time she spends at the session. A model may be booked for a minimum of 1 hour. If she is booked for less than 8 hours, her hourly rate is multiplied by the number of hours she works. If she is booked for 8 hours, her day rate applies. For bookings that fall into the typical mold, such as catalog bookings, this is the only amount the model receives. This rate is determined by the agency by considering prevailing rates in the area, the model's level of experience, how much in demand the model or her look is, and whether she has special talents, assets, or abilities that set her apart.

On some assignments a model is paid an amount on top of the session fee when special conditions exist. These factors are called booking conditions. The most common ones are listed below.

Shopping fee. The model is paid if the client requests that the model shop for something specifically for the shooting. This occurs when a stylist is not employed and certain items, such as clothing and props, not normally found in the model's wardrobe are needed. Usually the model receives one-half his or her hourly rate, and the time does not exceed 1 hour. In addition, he or she is reimbursed for the expense of the item when the receipt is presented.

Weather permit. When the client wants to shoot outdoors he or she will specify when making the booking that it will take place if certain weather conditions permit. The type of weather permit must be specified. The client may need certain exact conditions or he may just need a day without rain. Usually the model is given a telephone number to call to check on the status of the booking 2 hours before the job begins.

If the booking is cancelled because of unsatisfactory weather conditions, the model receives half her regular fee for the booked time. If a weather permit booking is cancelled a second time, the model receives her full fee.

Cancellations. Once a client has booked a model, the client can cancel up to 2 working days prior to the booking without having to reimburse the model. If the client cancels less than 48 hours prior to the booking, the model must be paid at half fee for the amount of time he or she was booked. If the client cancels 24 hours (1 working day) or less prior to the booking, the model must be paid the full fee.

Cancellations policies differ among agencies. Some agencies, for example, those in New York, charge one-half the model's fee for the booked time if the cancellation occurs within 5 working days of the beginning of the booking; within 3 working days, the full fee is charged. If the client decides on the day of the booking to use the model for only a portion of the time originally booked, the client must pay the full fee for the original time. If the client finishes the shooting an hour or two early, the model may be paid the full fee less 30 minutes. Tentative bookings can be canceled at no charge any time prior to the booking by either the model of the client.

Overtime. A model receives an overtime rate (time and one-half) when a booking takes place before 9 AM or after 5:30 PM Overtime also applies on weekends and holidays.

Travel Time. Models are compensated for the time they spend getting to a booking if it is outside the city limits or outside of a certain area agreed upon by the client and agent. The client pays a minimum of 1 hour at the model's hourly rate. The model's normal hourly rate is charged for the time he or she spends traveling. Sometimes on long trips involving several days, a flat fee for travel in addition to expenses, is agreed upon.

Prep time. A model is paid his or her normal hourly rate during the time a professional hairdresser and makeup artist spend preparing the model for the shooting. Unless the client requires a specific makeup or hairstyle that takes an unusual amount of time or skill that the model possesses, the model is not paid for the time spent doing her own makeup and hair for a shooting. The model is expected to arrive already groomed, with only finishing touches to be added.

Polaroids. There is no charge when a client takes an ID Polaroid at an audition; if the model is required to try on wardrobe or special instructions are given for the shot, one-half the model's fee is charged.

Penalty fee. The client must pay an extra amount in addition to the model's regular rate if he or she is required to make a permanent change in appearance, which may affect the model's ability to obtain future bookings. For example, if the model's hair is cut or colored, the penalty fee is negotiated to reimburse the model for the possible loss in future earnings that may be incurred as result of the changed look.

Test jobs. When a client assigns a photographer to try out a specific concept or a particular model for a campaign, this is called a "test job." For example, a test job may be done by a cosmetic company in search of the right model to be signed for a contract or to be used in an extensive advertising campaign. Models usually receive one-half their hourly rate for test jobs, and no model releases are signed.

Undergarments. Female models receive double their hourly rate when modeling bras, foundations, panties, pantyhose, and revealing slips. When modeling nightgowns, peignoirs, slips, and body stockings, models receive one and a half times their hourly rate. Male models receive double their hourly rate for modeling briefs and undershorts.

Nudes. Nude modeling assignments always require the model's prior consent. Prior to the booking, the model must be informed as to the exact garments, situations, and types of poses that will be required. Unless negotiated otherwise, models booked through fashion modeling agencies receive triple their hourly rate for nude modeling or for modeling transparent garments. The model should also be aware that the agency has the right to request that there be a closed set for such assignments.

Rates for modeling in the nude for skin magazines are often established by the magazine. For example, a nude model doing a centerspread for a major men's magazine will receive an established fee of several thousand dollars.

Nude models working through an agency that specializes in nude modeling usually are paid substantially less than those working through fashion agencies. Most assignments are charged at a set hourly or daily rate.

Fittings. Often times for catalog shootings, fashion shows, and bookings involving several days' work or travel, the model is required to appear at a fitting so the garments can be selected or altered prior to the booking. Fittings usually do not exceed 1 hour. In New York the model usually receives full rate calculated on half-hour increments. Outside of New York, rates may vary.

Rehearsals. Rehearsals are usually billed at one-half the model's hourly rate. If a flat fee is negotiated for a fashion show, rehearsals are included.

Wardrobe check. When the photographer requests that the model provide clothing for the booking, he or she may want to check the wardrobe prior to the shooting to select items that will be needed. Wardrobe checks are billed at one-half the model's hourly rate per half hour.

Formal wear. If a model must supply formal wear such as a tuxedo, the model is paid a flat fee, for example, $25 to $50 per garment, to cover the cost of cleaning or rental.

Auditions. Clients pay for auditions when the model is required to try on garments, learn a script, or perform a specific task. Either a flat fee is negotiated or one-half the model's hourly rate per half hour is charged. Models are paid for SAG-governed television auditions when they are required to memorize a script prior to the audition, improvise during an audition, audition for the same commercial more than twice, or remain at an audition for more than 1 hour. Auditions for television commercials not governed by SAG may follow a different course of payment.

Client-Established Fees

For certain types of assignments, the model is paid a fee established by the client. This is what occurs in editorial work for magazines. The largest magazine conglomerates, Hearst (*Harper's Bazaar* and *Cosmopolitan*) and Condé Nast (*Vogue* and *Glamour*) establish the rate they will pay models appearing in their editorial pages. Because of the excellent exposure a model receives when her picture appears in the editorial pages of a fashion magazine, she receives only a small portion of her normal rate.

Sometimes a very large retailer or other concern employing lots of models will establish one rate that all models will be paid. For example, a nationwide concern that is the predominant user of models in an area may pay all models they employ one established rate.

Usually the only clients who can mandate rates are those who can offer prestigious or glamourous opportunities or career-enhancing exposure and/or those who have a great deal of work. In either case, it is usually counterproductive for the model to boycott working for such clients.

Negotiated Fees

In many bookings a model's fee is negotiated. Fees are most commonly negotiated when the client wishes to secure exclusive rights to the model's image. For example, this occurs most commonly in product advertising assignments. When a client wants to photograph a model to appear on consumer product packaging, a sales display or riser card, poster, billboard, or other display material for a product, he or she will not want the model to appear on similar items for competing products. To reimburse him or her for the loss of opportunities other clients may have offered him or her, the model's agent negotiates a bonus or usage fee in addition to the session fee he or she is paid for the time he or she spends on the set.

There are three factors that an agent takes into consideration when negotiating a model's fee for product advertising: the type of media in which the model's picture will appear, where geographically the ad or display will appear, and the term or length of time it will appear.

A model's picture may appear in several types of print media. Her image may appear on a sales display, package, package insert, hang-tag, billboard, or in a print ad in a magazine. The agent will negotiate a special price or bonus on top of the model's session fee depending on the exact type of media involved.

The more exposure the medium will have, the more the model will be paid. For example, the model is paid more for appearing on a major billboard than she would be paid if her picture appeared in a package insert of a product with limited distribution.

Where the model's picture will appear geographically is also a point of negotiation. A model receives more money if more people will be seeing her picture. For example, she would receive more money for appearing in a national ad to be run in major magazines than she would if her picture appeared in an ad seen only in one area of the country such as the Midwest.

Term or the length of time the ad will run also determines the model's fee. The longer the picture will appear, the more money the model receives. Negotiation for term or longevity follows different courses. For example, the agent may negotiate a term that lasts for a 6-month or 1-year period. Or, the agent may negotiate a model's fee in quarters, based on five quarters per year: spring, summer, fall, winter, and Christmas. The client has the right to use the model's picture for one-quarter or 13-week period and then must renegotiate if he or she wants to use the ad for another quarter. Some clients pay a "buyout," which is a flat fee that the model receives at the time of the assignment. When the client pays a buyout, he or she has unlimited use of the model's photo.

Other factors may give an agent even more leeway for negotiating a higher fee. If a popular model or celebrity model is concerned, the client will be able to negotiate a higher fee because there is no substitute for the model. If the model's name or her endorsement of the product will be a part of the advertising campaign, she receives more money.

In any negotiable situation, however, one factor must exist: recognizability. It must be apparent by her appearance in the ad who the model is. A model does not receive bonuses or print usage fees when she is not recognizable in the photograph. For example, a hand model does not receive such reimbursements. Or, if a model is photographed in a way (for example, in shadow or with her hair blowing in front of her face), she will not receive extra amounts because she is not recognizable. Recognizability is subjective to a point and when an issue falls into a gray area, the agent will negotiate a higher session fee for the model, instead of a usage fee.

Of course all usage fees are dependent on whether the photo from the session is actually used by the client. Sometimes an advertising agency will formulate a print advertisement or layout, shoot it, and then decide not to run the ad in magazines or as a billboard. If the model's picture is not used in an ad, the client does not pay any extra bonuses or usage fees. The model receives her session fee only.

Selecting an agent who is a great negotiator is to the model's advantage. A good agent is able to weigh on the model's behalf all the variables and negotiate for attractive exposure and more money. The agent's objective is to choose the most lucrative opportunities available to the model without overexposing her or cutting her out of more lucrative opportunities for competing products. Even after the client releases the model's exclusivity for his product advertising, her chances of getting bookings from similar types of companies are limited simply because the model's face becomes associated with the product, the longer a campaign has been used. Therefore, posing for one advertising campaign can yield print usage fees amounting to thousands of dollars. A skillful negotiator is able to get the highest amount possible for the model without charging an amount out of the client's range. Even though a model's face or body may be instrumental in selling a product, clients do have advertising budgets that they must not exceed.

Comparing Rates for Different Types of Modeling Assignments

Much of the preceding information applies to print bookings involving still photography. As explained, the highest paid print bookings are advertising bookings. Models receive a session fee for the time spent on the set photographing the assignment. In addition, the model receives a bonus, if for example, the picture will appear on a package, or a negotiated fee for the usage of the photo in an the ad. Catalog work is usually billed at the model's established hourly/daily rate. Modeling for an illustrator is usually the lowest paying assignment in the print area. Pictures taken during the course of an activity such as a fashion show that will later be used for publicity are usually charged at the model's hourly/daily rate.

Some print bookings, including advertising, are subject to a universal or maximum rate, which the client sets. The ability to establish a rate is dependent on a client's clout. Sometimes an advertising client will call an agency and specify the exact fee he or she will pay. If the ad agency involved is powerful, the agent may feel pressured to accept because if she refuses, the client could go to another modeling agency. Often agents will not band together, and the client can be assured that among all the agencies, he will find one that will accept his price and provide him with an adequate model. This occurs most often when any number of models would be suitable for the assignment.

Editorial rates are established by the magazines. Because of the excellent exposure a model receives when her picture appears in the editorial pages of a magazine, she receives only a small portion of her normal rate.

Fashion Show Rates

Major prestigious fashion shows (for example, designer collections showings in New York) pay the model's regular hourly/daily rate. In other shows, models may receive a lower hourly rate or a flat fee for a show. This fee is usually less than the normal hourly rate and is negotiated by the model and her agent or established by the client.

Rates vary for different types of live fashion modeling assignments. In showroom modeling, the model may be hired on a permanent, year-round basis to show the clothes and possibly perform secretarial and sales tasks. In such a case, the model is usually paid a moderate salary. If selling is a major part of the job, she may also receive commissions on what she sells.

Another way models are employed for showroom modeling is through a modeling agency by the hour or day. Basically, there are two ways in which models are booked for fitting and showroom modeling:

In the first, the showroom books all of the model's time during a given week and requires that she remain at the showroom during open hours. It is an assignment with "no outs." In the second, the showroom books the model for a given week but will be flexible if the model wishes to leave the showroom to model in a fashion show or some other type of booking, provided she gives notice as soon as she learns of the assignment. Such a booking is said to have "outs." Bookings with "outs" usually pay a lower rate.

Promotional Modeling Rates

Models booked for conventions or trade shows usually receive less than the print model's normal hourly/daily rate. These models receive a flat fee for the day, which may range from $100 up. Models are paid the least for hosting or hostessing, sampling, and platform modeling; the most for performance, narration, and demonstration jobs. If models can actually sell, explain (give technical narration), or demonstrate an involved product or service, they will receive an even higher fee.

Models booked for promotions in stores receive substantially less than convention models. Usually when a model is hired to sample fragrance or to distribute literature to customers passing through a store, he or she is booked for a 4-hour period and is paid per hour. This rate usually applies to informal fashion modeling as well.

If a model is well known or has a contract to endorse a product or service, he or she may be booked to appear at stores or trade shows where the product is sold to sign autographs or model the product. Generally fees for these promotions are specified in the model's contract, which includes a number of public appearances and print and/or television ads.

Electronic Media Bookings

Payment for commercials, industrial films, and other types of audiovisual productions not governed by the SAG or AFTRA unions will vary widely. The fee a model or actor is paid will depend on how much the model's market will bear and how good his or her agent is at negotiating. The model's client usually pays a "buyout," a flat fee that entitles him or her to unlimited usage of the model's performance. Payment for the same work falling under the jurisdiction of SAG is outlined here. Dollar amounts are set every 3 years by the unions.

Union-Scale Session Fee When a model is booked to appear in a production he or she is booked for a session that is defined as an 8-hour working day, regardless of whether the work lasts the entire 8 hours. The session can be for work on only one commercial. The fee established by the union that a model is paid for a session is called a "scale session fee." Payment of this fee is not dependent on whether the commercial is completed or is actually used. When more than one commercial is shot in a single day, a session fee for each commercial is paid. The 8 hours do not include meal periods. The session fee is highest if the model is a principal performer who appears in a closeup shot, speaks a line or lines of dialogue, or has no lines but is closely identified with the product. A slightly lower session fee applies to voiceover performers and specialty or parts models (for example, hand models). The lowest session fee is paid to extra players who are not identified or involved with the product.

Models who perform in television commercials often do not receive scale session fees. Instead a model receives her normal modeling day rate, which is usually higher than the scale session fee. However, this is not more money than an actor would be paid in the long run. If a model is not paid a scale session fee, the rate she is paid is figured into the amount the model receives from reuse payments (the amount the model is paid each time the commercial is aired). Therefore, the model receives the same amount on the day she works on a television commercial as she would for a day of modeling for print media. A special higher rate (overscale) may also be negotiated when there are special circumstances such as use of the model's name, commercials for personal products, and performances requiring special skills.

Industrial films and other types of productions all have set payment scales devised by the union. The amount charged for a session varies depending on how many people will be viewing the film or production. Talent participating in an industrial film for in-house use will receive less than talent who are used for a promotional film to sell a product or service to the public.

In addition to the session fee, a model is paid additional amounts if the following conditions apply:

Overtime. Models are paid overtime if the session exceeds 8 hours and lasts between 8 and 10 hours. Overtime is figured at one and a half times the union-established hourly rate. Time exceeding 10 hours is charged at twice the hourly rate, or double time. Work done on Saturdays, Sundays, and holidays (New Year's Day, Washington's Birthday, Memorial Day, Independence Day, Labor Day, Thanksgiving, and Christmas) is charged at double time.

Travel time. A model is paid for travel time spent getting to the location of the shooting when it is outside of "studio zones" defined by the unions. The zone may cover a radius of several miles from the center of the city or where the union office is located; this range will vary depending on the area. Information from your local union office will define the radius of a specific studio zone. Travel pay is charged at the union hourly rate.

Wardrobe fees. If a model is asked to appear to try on clothing or to test hairstyle and makeup ideas, she is paid for a minimum of 1 hour at the union hourly rate for a wardrobe call. If the model is required to supply clothing for the production, she is paid a union-established amount for each costume that is used on the day of the shooting.

Holding fees. When doing a commercial, the session fee entitles the client to use the commercial for 13-weeks following the shoot. During this time the model cannot do commercial work for competing products (see Chapter 11). If the advertisers want to continue to use the commercial after this period of time or if they want to buy the model's exclusivity, they must pay a full session fee entitling them to another 13-week period. During this time, whether or not they choose to actually air the commercial, the model cannot appear on-camera for a competitive product or sponsor. If the commercial is in use, holding fees may be applied against residual payments. If the advertiser does not pay a holding fee within 12 days of the end of the 13-week cycle, they lose the right to run the commercial.

Residuals. When a model appears in a commercial, each time it is aired, the model becomes identified with the product. Because a competitive advertiser cannot use her, this reduces her chances for employment. To compensate, the unions have arranged to pay the talent each time her performance is aired. The more people viewing the spot, the more money the talent is paid.

Residuals or reuse payments are based on several complex factors, and the unions have devised a very sophisticated payment scale based on different categories. The residuals for a commercial depend on the category under which it runs (network Class A, B, or C, wild spot, test market, dealer spot, etc.), how often it is used, how many months it is run, plus any special stipulations. The highest residuals are paid for commericals that are seen by a nationwide audience on a Class A network.

The residual payment is determined by the number of cities and the number of TV households in each city. Cities are assigned units determined by the number of households with TV sets. The major cities—New York, Los Angeles, and Chicago—are considered separately.

The majority of residuals are paid on wild spots, which are commercials that are shown by noninterconnected single stations. The size of the area where the commercial runs determines the fee the talent is paid.

Residuals are not paid in the following cases:

- If a model or actor works on a nonunion commercial. For nonunion work, a flat fee is paid for services. This can occur in nonunion towns. An advertiser and the talent and his agent agree on a lump sum of money to be paid up front for the commercial and all future residuals. This is called a "buyout."
- If the model is an extra.
- If the model is a specialty or parts model. Voice-over performers are paid residuals, but hand models are not.
- If a model works on a "demo" or nonair commercial. Not all commercials are made to be viewed by the public.

The schedule of payment for residuals is very involved. Consulting information issued by the unions and your agent is the most accurate way to learn what the payment would be in a given situation.

Collecting Fees Most agencies use the voucher system to bill a client for the work a model has done. A voucher is a form signed at the conclusion of each assignment by the model and the client or photographer, coordinator, or other authorized individual representing the client. The voucher confirms the hours worked, the fee, and the rights granted. The voucher contains a model's release, and this release takes precedence over any other release that a model may sign on the job. The voucher is used by the agency for billing the client and is usually in triplicate or quadruplicate. The model returns one or two copies to the bookkeeping department of the agency, one copy is retained by the model, and one copy is given to the client for his records. The voucher is used by the agency to write the bill to the client. All models must know how to complete a voucher before they attend a paying assignment. The layout or design of a voucher form may vary among agencies, but most require the information presented on the sample form shown here.

How to Complete a Voucher Never attend a booking without a supply of voucher forms. Always bring extra vouchers to a job in case you make a mistake when completing a voucher.

If you don't have vouchers with you on a job, and you can't borrow one from another model or the studio, call the agency and they will immediately fill out a voucher for you and mail a copy to the studio for their records. Some large studios have their own standard voucher forms that models complete. They do not use the vouchers provided by modeling agencies. Always know how to complete a voucher form. Know which copies are to be given to whom.

- Fill in all the blanks and press hard so that all copies are legible.
- Use your booking form as a guide to correctly fill out the client's name, address, and the like. If you have questions, call your agent.

Voucher

Invoice to _____ Inv. #_____

Address _____ City _____ Zip _____

Attn _____

Product _____ Client _____

Studio _____

Remarks _____

Model _____ Rate _____

Fitting date _____ Time from: _____ to:_____ Amt _____

Job date _____ Time from: _____ to:_____ Amt _____

Other _____ Amt _____

Note: Certain products, product packaging, point of purchase usage, billboards, national ads, television and similar special usage requires separate negotiations.

Agent's Commission _____ %-Fee _____ Amt _____

Subtotal _____

Expenses _____ Amt _____

Model's Release

In consideration of the sum stated heron: I hereby sell, assign and grant to above or those for whom they are acting as indicated above, the right and permission to copyright and/or use and/or publish photographs of me in which I may be included in whole or in part or composite or reproductions thereof in color or otherwise made through print media at their studios or elsewhere for art advertising, trade or any other similar lawful purpose whatsoever.

I hereby waive the right to inspect and/or approve the finished product or the advertising copy that may be used in connection with my photograph.

I hereby release and discharge the above, its successors and all persons acting under its permission or authority or those for whom it is acting, from any liability by virtue of any blurring, distortion, optical illusion or use in composite/ form that may occur or be produced in the taking of said picture or in any processing thereof through completion of the finished product.

THIS RELEASE NOT VALID UNTIL PAYMENT IN FULL RECEIVED

X Client _____

X Model _____

Terms: 30 Days

Total Amount _____
This Service

- Fill in all information on who gets invoiced, not just the company name. If necessary, ask the photographer who is to be billed (sometimes the bill goes to the photographer, sometimes to the client directly). Fill in the name of the client and product. Large studios often shoot for different clients, and if there is a billing problem, it helps to know which client employed you. Fill out the voucher completely because some agencies charge their models penalty fees for failing to be accurate and complete.

- Be sure you write in the correct date, time, and length of booking. This is absolutely necessary for the agent to double-check the amount of the voucher.

  The model's billable time starts at the time she is told is the beginning of the booked time. If the model arrives late, the booked time does not start until she is on set.

  If the photographer books the model for 2 hours and the time runs over, the model bills him for all the time she has worked. Most agencies compute charges to the half or quarter hour. This means that if the model works 1 hour and 10 minutes, she will charge the client for 1¼ or 1½ hours, depending on her agency's policy. The first hour is never broken down into quarter or half-hours. The minimum amount of time a model can be booked is 1 hour. Established models sometimes demand a 2-hour minimum.

  If the booking ends early, the model is paid either for the entire time originally specified by the client when he booked the model or some agencies have a policy in which the client is charged for the time the model was booked, less 30 minutes.

  Agencies differ as to their charge for overtime, weekends, and the like. It is the model's responsibility to know these policies. If you are unsure about the fee, ask your agency, not the client.

- Make sure you have complete information about the fee you are to charge. This should be on your booking form.

- Be certain you know of any client-approved expenses and add them to your voucher so you will be reimbursed. For more information on expenses, consult Chapter 8.

- Most agencies require you to figure and add on their percentages, so double-check your math. A quick way to figure 15% of an amount is to move the decimal point over one place to the left to find 10%. Then divide this amount in half to find 5%. Then add the two figures together to arrive at 15%. Don't figure the agency's percentage of commission on your expenses.

- Deliver your completed voucher to the agency as soon as possible to expedite the billing and payment process. Some agencies charge models a penalty fee for late vouchers.

  Credit references of new photographers and clients are always checked carefully by the agency before any bookings take place. The client usually pays the agency directly or through the advertising agency or photographer. Even with credit checks and screenings, some clients do not pay their bills. In these cases the client is taken to court. If he or she cannot be located or cannot pay the bill, the loss is absorbed by the agent and the model. The policy in such cases is specified in the model's contract with her agency. If a client has a poor paying record, the agency may offer the job to the model but tell him or her that it is at his or her risk. They will bill the client, but if the bill is not paid, the model incurs the total loss.

Payment to Models

Most agencies operate on a system whereby the models on exclusive contract with the agency are paid at designated pay periods, either weekly or biweekly, regardless of whether the client has paid the agency. Models who are not under contract and those affiliated with smaller agencies or agencies outside of major cities receive payment when the agency receives the money from the client.

How Talent Are Paid for Union-Governed Electronic Media Assignments

Residuals are usually paid by the union to the model agency. The agency receives 10% commission on work of this type and then pays the talent. Agents do not receive commissions from AFTRA minimum scale jobs; payment is made directly to the talent. Jobs paying above the AFTRA scale do go through the agent who receives 10%.

Residuals checks are often not issued by the sponsor, producer, or advertising agent but come from an independent payroll service whose sole function is to keep track of residuals and other payments. The largest such firm is T & R (Talent and Residuals, Inc.).

THE MODEL—AGENT RELATIONSHIP

The Agent's Responsibilities to the Model

- The agent counsels the model about her total professional image. This includes the model's appearance (clothing, makeup, hair) and manner of presenting herself (physical presentation, personality, and verbal presentation). After the model is established, the agency should periodically review the model's progress and recommend changes in approach, appearance, or attitude, as necessary.

- The agency trains or refers the beginning model to training in videotape, runway, promotional, and still photography modeling.

- The agency markets and promotes the model by helping her assemble effective promotional tools. This is done by arranging test photo sessions, the results of which are used for the model's portfolio, composite, and commercial headshot. The agency also includes the model's pictures in their promotional materials, such as brochures, model books, and headsheets. If the model is a voice-over artist, the agent helps the talent to assemble a professional voice tape and includes his voice on the agency master reel. The agency distributes promotional materials to introduce or remind clients of the model.

- The agent provides contacts with its clients and opens doors for opportunities in the field. The agency protects the model from being in contact with unprofessional clients.

- The agency performs the duties of an answering service and secretary, keeping appointments and records accurately. The agency schedules the model's time and relays bookings and provides information about what will be expected, particulars of the booking.

- The agency handles the billing to the client and serves as a collecting agent.

- The agency acts as a career counselor advising the model when and when not to enter into contracts with clients. They help the model in directing his career by advising him as to which opportunities will enhance or detract from his future in the modeling field.

- The agent negotiates fees for the model to achieve the optimum price for her talents, looks, and skills.

- The agency acts as a buffer between the model and the client. When disputes arise between a model and client, the agent acts as a mediator. The agent defends the model against any unfair complaints a client might make.

- The agency by its own business conduct, standards of quality in the talent it represents, and reputation, gives the model prestige and credibility.

The Model's Responsibilities to the Agent

- It is unwise for a model to lie to the agent about his qualifications. Models sometimes lie about their age, height, measurements, and experience. Lying will cause the agent to misrepresent the model to clients. This not only damages the model's reputation but the agent's as well.

The Model Must Be Honest with the Agent

- A model always consults with the agent prior to making an appearance change such as cutting or coloring the hair or getting a tan. She always informs the agent immediately of weight gain or loss, changes in sizes, skin problems, or any other abnormalities. If the agent is not informed, the agent is not responsible for cancellation of a booking, even if the model is on set. In some situations, the model may risk having to compensate all other models on set.

- If something goes wrong on a job, the model calls his agent and allows the agent to handle the problem. The model presents the occurrence accurately to the agent so the agent will be able to deal truthfully with the client. If something goes wrong that is the model's fault, the model accepts sole responsibility; he doesn't try to shift the blame onto his agent because when a model maligns the agency, it reflects badly on all the personnel and all the other models affiliated with it.

- A model must always make clear to her agent from the outset what types of jobs she will and will not accept.

- The model informs the agency about every go-see and testing in which he is involved and contacts that have been made. The model never goes behind the agent's back to arrange bookings or negotiate fees with clients.

The Model Must Maintain Close Contact

- In most agencies, a model on contract is expected to call and check in at the end of the day between 4:30 and 5:30 to obtain her schedule for the following day.

- A model must be easy to contact. This is best done by the model having his own phone and an answering machine or service. The model should check his machine or service every hour and return the agency's calls immediately.

- A model should visit the agency once a week to show agents her new portfolio pictures or the progress she has made in meeting clients or acquiring modeling skills. Models are the products the agency promotes and agents like to see what condition their models are in and how they present themselves. Personal contact is also important in establishing a good relationship with the agent. It demonstrates the model's career interest and reminds the agent of the model's availability. A model should always be in picture-perfect condition when visiting the agency in case the agent wants to send the model on an appointment or a last-minute booking. Generally, visits to the agency should not be made during the usual lunch hour (11:45 to 1:15) or at closing time. Agents need a break from models sometime. Most agencies close on weekends and holidays.

The Model Must Be Available

- Models who live more than an hour away or who maintain other jobs will be more difficult for an agent to handle. Unless a model is willing to change his situation, many agents will not bother. The majority of modeling assignments take place on weekdays from 9:00 to 6:00. Other jobs that limit a model's time will also limit opportunities to model.

- When the agency calls, a model must be available for jobs, auditions, everything, even at the last minute. While a model is trying to get established, modeling opportunities should take precedence over all other activities. If the agent knows the model is interested and can be counted on, the agent will always call her before another model who may have just as much potential, but not as much ambition.

- The agent should be notified as soon as a model knows that he will be unable to attend an assignment. If the model wishes to "book out," that is, to make himself unavailable for bookings during a period of time, he should notify the agent as far in advance as possible. A model should never leave town without first informing the agency. A model is always considerate of his clients because they are the ones who can make or break him.

The Model Must Provide the Agent with Promotional Tools

- An agent cannot offer the model to her clients if she has nothing to show them, so it is imporant to assemble an excellent composite, glossy, etc. every 6 to 9 months and keep the agent well supplied. The agent should also be supplied with pictures that can be used in the agency presentation book, model book, or headsheet. Extra tearsheets should be made available to the agent for her files.

The Model Must Help the Agent

- An ambitious model doesn't sit back and wait for his agent to do something for him. Instead he takes charge of his career. He sets goals and makes a plan for achieving them. He is ever ready to seize opportunities. The more clients and photographers a model sees, the better his chances will be for getting bookings. A model should continually make promotional visits to clients and go on all auditions the agency arranges.

- A model should frequently test and update her portfolio. A model must constantly and diligently work at tracking down pictures, slides, and tearsheets from shootings.

- The model should make an effort to motivate the agent to secure jobs and appointments. The more interest, improvement, and ambition a model shows, the more interest and confidence in the model's abilities the agent will have. Smart models exercise good public relations tactics by being enthusiastic and appreciative of an agent's efforts.

- A model continually works at improving his modeling skills. This is done by participating in television commercial acting classes, runway workshops, and other instructional events. This gives the agent the greatest possiblities for promoting the model for a variety of assignments.

The Model Must Be a Good Representative of the Agency

- An agency's reputation rests on every model it represents. Models should appear and conduct themselves in ways that favorably impress the agent's clients and reflect well on the model's agency. Models should always appear well groomed, attractive, and professional.

The Model Must Abide by Agency Rules

- Every agency has its own set of rules and regulations. A model needs to know what they are and abide by them, as they have been devised for her benefit, protection, and welfare.

The Model Must Be Considerate of the Agent

- A model should realize that an agent performs services to generate income for the agency. Agency employees have only so much time and will use it wisely by dividing it among models who show the most promise, are the most professional, or make the most money.

- A model should not waste an agent's time. When telephoning, the model knows exactly what he wants to say and if given instructions or other information, he takes notes. When the model is given constructive criticism or advice, he listens carefully and makes notes of what he needs to improve on. He doesn't force the agent to tell him the same things repeatedly. The model follows a booker's instructions to the letter. The model attends all appointments at the time the booker has designated and is properly prepared.

- The model recognizes and appreciates her agent. Most models think that they alone are responsible for their successes. But the fact is that agents spend years and a lot of money gaining the attention, respect, and business of a large base of clients—a lot more time and money than any model by herself would be capable of devoting.

- An ethical model is loyal to his agent. The model isn't easily swayed to switch agents by listening to other's opinions or when experiencing temporary downswings in his career. The model is not easily persuaded or pressured by a competing agent to change agencies.

- A model always deals in an upfront, honest manner with her agent. She does this by scheduling an appointment with the agent to express dissatisfaction or suggestions. This gives the agent a chance to change her approach. When disagreements occur or when the model thinks she is being treated unfairly, the model tries to understand the situation from all sides.

The Model Must Trust the Agent and Follow Her Advice

- A model must trust his agency and take complete advantage of its skills and knowledge. A model will find that his agent is rarely wrong. The agent is interested in increasing the model's earning power because it increases the earning power of the agency. The agent has studied the market, knows which looks sell best, and has the most effective promotional tools and techniques for his or her clientele. The agent is in touch with several clients each day and understands their needs, likes, and dislikes.

- The model attends meetings, seminars, and workshops that the agency recommends or organizes. They can only benefit the model. Any model, even an experienced one, needs help and training.

- The model should be receptive when the agent offers suggestions and realize that the agent is trying to help. The model responds in a professional manner and avoids feeling resentful, or defensive. To be successful, a model must be able to look at herself objectively.

- If there are times when the model isn't working, he doesn't harass his agent. Instead he discusses with the agent what the problem might be and keeps himself busy. The model acquires new photos, goes on rounds, and tries to make new contacts. An agent helps a model who helps himself. The model should stimulate his agent's interest by showing interest and determination. When the model experiences slow work periods, he considers putting out a new composite, changing or updating his look, or modeling in another city or country. Every model experiences plateaus. Modeling is a seasonal business and can be somewhat unpredictable.

- A model allows the agency to handle mixups and disputes with the client. She defers to the agent's decisions. If the model has a legitimate complaint or problem regarding the agency, she arranges an appointment with the head of the agency. The model avoids gossiping with other models or clients about such problems.

The Model Must Be Fair in Dealings with the Agency

- A model lives up to all contractual agreements he enters. He conscientiously honors verbal and written agreements.

- A model does not take jobs without telling the agency. If the model signs an agency contract, her agent is entitled to a percentage of the income from all jobs the model does, no matter how they are obtained.

- A model never overrides the agency or goes behind its back to work for more or less money than the fee that has been established by the agent. The model never attempts to negotiate the fee.

- A model always speaks well of her agency and the models and employees affiliated with it. If the model has complaints, he discusses them with the agent rather than with other models. Negativism and gossip will only injure a model, causing clients, agents, and others in important positions to avoid him.

The Model Always Strives for a Good Business Relationship with the Agent

- A model puts her emotions and personal feelings aside in business situations. She must deal with her colleagues in a friendly, professional way. This means also that she must know exactly what each person expects to gain from an association. A model doesn't expect her agent or other business people to pay her way or do favors without doing something in return equally valuable to the other party. A model realizes that she will always have to share her profits with others.

- The model is aware that most agents charge the model for the cost (or a portion) of the printing of her picture on the agency headsheet or in the agency model book. Composites are always paid for by the model. Reputable agents usually do not charge for general telephone and mailing costs incurred while promoting the model or for registration with the agency.

THE AGENT–CLIENT RELATIONSHIP

The Agent's Responsibilities to the Client

- The agency should know the market and the needs, likes, and dislikes of its individual clients.

- The agency should maintain a group of talent that fits the needs of its clientele and a caliber of models with the right physical requirements for various modeling assignments.

- The agency should ensure a certain level of knowledge and professionalism in the models it represents before they are sent to clients on auditions or bookings. The agency should provide training for its models and basic written guidelines of professionalism and agency policies and services.

- To best serve its clients, the agency should have complete and current information on the models it represents and be able to help the client to find the perfect model for the job. An agent should be truthful with the client about a model's availability, experience, condition, etc. The agency keeps accurate records and is able to research product conflicts for a given model.

- The agency should provide a high level of service to its clients and should give the same quality of service to every photographer or client. It should be considerate of a client's time, needs, and efforts. The agency should also try to accommodate problems that clients and photographers may encounter, for example, bookings that run overtime, misunderstandings, last-minute assignments, mistakes, and lack of responsibility on the part of the models the agency represents.

- Agents should stay in close contact with clients and keep them supplied with current composites, headsheets, and model books. Also the agency should keep clients informed of new agency policies and procedures.

- The agent should be well organized and able to acquire complete, accurate information about how the model is to appear for an assignment, what she is to bring, the time she is expected to arrive, and other particulars. The agent does everything possible to ensure that the talent is completely prepared and that the client will be pleased with the model's or talent's performance on the job.

THE MODEL'S RESPONSIBILITIES TO THE CLIENT

A model's best strategy for success is to treat the people who employ her well. An agent can expose and introduce a model to clients, photographers, and others in a position to employ her, but it is up to the model to favorably impress these individuals. Because of the high fees that models are paid, clients expect a lot. Also, because there are so many models competing for a limited number of assignments, it is not possible to succeed by performing the minimum; a model must be outstanding. Treating your clients well is also the best thing you can do for your agent. When you represent him or her well, it enhances his or her business. The following basic concepts explain a model's responsibilities to his or her clients.

- *Be punctual.* Arrive at the time designated by your agent or client. In many markets, models are expected to arrive at assignments 15 minutes prior to the booked time. Ask your agent about your arrival time if special circumstances prevail for a given assignment or if you are unsure about the policy in your market.

- *Be prepared.* Arrive at the booking with all the items you have been told to provide (use the Booking Form in this chapter). Always carry your totebag (see Chapter 5) to all assignments. If you have been given instructions for styling your own hair or applying your own makeup, arrive with all preparations made.

- *Be healthy.* Always appear at appointments and assignments in good physical condition. Get plenty of sleep. Late nights will affect your looks. You should always arrive at assignments and appointments well rested and ready to work. Always appear well groomed (manicured nails, removal of superfluous body hair), and maintain your skin and hair in excellent condition. If you come down with an illness that affects your looks or is communicable, inform your agent immediately. Minor discomforts such as headaches are usually not valid reasons for canceling obligations.

- *Have a good attitude.* Be pleasant and happy. Acquire a positive outlook—don't complain. Be enthusiastic and eager to work. Be considerate of everyone. Make an effort to enjoy working with the photographer or for the client. Be tolerant of less than ideal circumstances such as inadequate dressing rooms, too hot or too cold weather, clothes that don't fit, and tempermental co-workers. There are no excuses for putting forth less than your best effort. Be patient.

- *Be efficient.* Work quickly, but not hastily. Accomplish the client's objectives without a lot of fuss or difficulty.

- *Concentrate.* Think about how to show the item you are modeling effectively. Think about the client's objectives and his or her reasons for employing you. Closely follow all instructions you have been given by the photographer. Think about ways to employ modeling tips you have learned. Don't let your mind wander.

- *Be responsible.* Take great care with the items you are modeling. Make certain you never damage an item. If you do, offer and be prepared to replace or repair it. Be very careful around studio equipment, props, etc. Know what your responsibilities are and don't blame others for your shortcomings. Observe the job responsibilities of others involved—don't make it difficult for them to fulfill their obligations.

- *Be determined.* Go out of your way to provide the items the client requests. Go out of your way to do what the client wants you to do. Make several attempts until you succeed. Don't try once or twice and give up. Don't make half-hearted attempts. Make every effort to accomplish the desired results.

- *Be professional.* Maintain the image that is portrayed in your modeling pictures. Don't change your hair, gain weight, get a tan, or alter your look in other ways that differ from your photos. Always try to make things easier, not more difficult for your clients.
- *Be creative.* A good model is inventive. She can think of lots of ways to enhance what she is showing. Her presentation is always fresh and unique. Being full of ideas for moving, posing, expressing, and acting will assure your success.

GUIDE TO FINDING AN AGENT

The importance of agency representation in a model's career cannot be overstated. However, there may be some instances in which a model will not have an agent. For example, if the model lives in a small town with no agencies, she may approach potential clients directly. If the model wants to work part-time in local store or boutique fashion shows, usually she will make contacts on her own. Some models who work primarily in trade shows or other types of promotions approach companies directly and are able to model on a limited basis. Fitting, showroom, and house models often do not have agents. However, if you want to achieve advanced success, an agent is vital.

How to Research the Agencies in Your Market

To find out about agencies in your location, seek the advice of individuals in the fashion and advertising businesses. Consult the fashion department of your local newspaper and ask for the names of model agencies. Ask department stores or other businesses that employ models for local ads which agencies they use to obtain their models. Call the casting department of advertising agencies in your area and ask for names of local modeling agencies that they employ. If you know of photographers who use models, they may be able to refer or introduce you to agents. Write to the large agencies in New York and ask them if they have affiliated agencies in your town or can give you recommendations.

For an updated list of modeling agencies along with addresses and information, contact MPC Educational Publishers, 3839 White Plains Road, Bronx, New York 10467-5394.

Be knowledgeable about the people with whom you are dealing. Modeling abounds with charlatans who prey on the egos of people who think they have a chance for success in modeling. Although this list is not a surefire way to spot trouble, it will provide you with warning signals of the types of businesses you should avoid:

- Beware of the agent or agency who charges a registration, evaluation, or other initial fee in advance. Legitimate agents make money only on the basis of a fixed commission. In other words, they receive a percentage of the money a model makes. The evaluation of your potential for modeling success should be at no cost to you.
- Beware of the agent that has a connection with a school or other training program that has attendance (which you pay for) as a prerequisite to being represented by the agency. Several legitimate agencies do have affiliations with training programs or schools for models and talent. This most commonly occurs in smaller markets where making money strictly as an agent is difficult. However, if you are told that you must pay for a shooting with a certain photographer, attend a certain class, or the like just to be considered by the agency, be cautious. All agents have certain hair and makeup people, printers, or photographers they like and recommend, but they will not demand that the model make use of their services prior to being accepted into the agency. A legitimate agent will give you a list of his or her favorite professional people from which you can choose.

- Beware of the agent or manager who contacts you by mail or telephone without introduction or referral and wants to come to your home or arrange an appointment to conduct an evaluation of you or your children's modeling potential. Legitimate successful agents are beseiged at their places of business by hopefuls and do not need to resort to such practices. If the agent has not seen pictures of you or been referred to you by a mutual acquaintance, he or she is probably more concerned with your pocketbook than your potential.

- Beware of the newspaper help-wanted ads that state, "Models of all types wanted. No experience necessary." These are usually come-ons for businesses engaged in selling you photos and charm, modeling, or acting courses and may even be fronts for finding "talent" for illegal or questionable businesses.

- Beware of phony agents. If the agent has photos of celebrities or top models displayed in his office to make it look as if he is their agent, ask a few questions. Ask if he represents the models or talent that are pictured. Ask if you can see a list of his regular clients. If the agent acts rude or defensive in response to your request or gives ambiguous answers, continue your search for an agent elsewhere. You are there to interview the agent, just as he is interviewing you. Also, be aware that disreputable people or companies often adopt names that sound as if they are affiliated with a large, established, and reputable concern, such as a television network, a New York agency, or the like. Ask how the two businesses are affiliated. Phony agents are often hard to spot for the unitiated. You can't always judge by outward appearances. A phony's office may be plush or it may be shabby, but so may be the office facilities belonging to a reputable agent.

- If an agent pressures you to sign a contract the first time you meet, also beware. Even a legitimate agent will scramble to get you to sign a contract if you're a hot property, but she will encourage you to take the document to a lawyer or give you some time to make a decision.

Other Types of Businesses You May Encounter

When trying to obtain agency representation, you may encounter some of the businesses listed here. The following businesses are usually legitimate; however, as in other fields, there are those you will wish to avoid because they may not have your best interests in mind.

Modeling and Charm Schools and Career Centers

These schools, studios, or centers offer classes in modeling, makeup, hairstyling, wardrobe, television commercial acting, drama, fashion photography, personal development, and the like. Most are not agents; however, they may be able to put you in touch with companies that employ models.

Examine a modeling school carefully before enrolling. Ask questions about contacts they have with the industry. Many of these schools have produced pageant winners and successful performers; some have been the initial step in the careers of successful models. In addition, many ethical schools enroll people who seek only personal improvement rather than a modeling career. Even if you don't have modeling potential, a good modeling and personal development school may be the answer to overcoming a lack of confidence or posture or grooming problems. A basic modeling or personal improvement course, given by a qualified teacher, can be valuable experience for anyone. Modeling courses may also be offered within a college curriculum and are usually listed as one of the performing arts or in fashion studies.

Talent Promoters   Talent promoters are also not agents. They produce printed materials or videotapes of individuals who want to be models, commercial actors, or performers. These materials are distributed to ad agencies, modeling agencies, or anyone in a position of buying talent. The talent is charged a fee for this service.

Managers   Managers are usually employed in addition to a talent broker or agent. It is their task to consult the model or talent in regard to his or her career. Top models making the transition from modeling to acting in television or motion pictures often employ managers to advise them on the direction of their career, financial dealings, and the like. Managers can be especially effective for child models if the parents work or are inexperienced or disinterested. The manager will arrange transportation to auditions and bookings, recommend what clothing should be worn, and help in sharpening the child's skills. Child talent managers are often parents of former successful child models who have parlayed their experience into a valuable service for others.

Publicity Agents   A publicist, PR person, press agent, or public relations firm will circulate the model's name and photo in order to gain attention from the media, which in turn should further the model's career. This may be a valid service for the model making the transition to movie actress, but usually the publicity needs of a beginning model are adequately handled by a talent or model agent. Publicity agents usually charge the talent a monthly retaining fee, paid in advance. The rate is dependent upon the individual's goals, position in the industry, and the elaborateness of the publicity campaign planned for the talent.

Consultants   These are often former models who guide and assist new models who either don't have an agent or are not getting the assistance they need from an agency. The consultant charges the model an hourly consultation fee or a flat fee for seminars, workshops, or lessons.

Talent Agents   Talent agents work mainly in TV commercials, but they may also handle some print modeling assignments. Modeling agencies tend to specialize more in the print area but most have TV departments. If a modeling agency does not handle TV work (some are not franchised by the performing unions), the talent can also sign up with a talent agent. A talent agent, like a model's agent, works on a commission basis.

Casting Directors   A casting director is not an agent, rather he or she is the one who buys talent. Whereas an agent works for the talent and receives a commission for the jobs a model works, the casting director works for the client or sponsor and receives a fee for finding the talent. Casting directors contact model or talent agents when they need talent and maintain files of talent who are available for various types of jobs.

HOW TO APPLY TO A MODELING AND TALENT AGENCY   When starting out, you should try to determine whether you have potential for modeling. Remember, legitimate agencies do not require that you invest money in training or professional photographs just to get an evaluation. Initially, all you need are several current snapshots that give the agent a basic idea. Don't worry that your snapshots will hurt your chances for acceptance. If you really have potential, a qualified agent will be able to see it even in informal pictures and will be able to visualize how you would look when photographed under professional circumstances. If the agent can't determine your potential from your snapshots, he or she will send you to a photographer to have a few pictures taken (at no charge to you) on which he or she will base a decision.

Have a friend or relative take a roll of 35-mm Ektacolor or Kodacolor snapshots of you alone, outdoors with natural light or indoors with flash. Wear your hair in a comfortable style and keep your makeup simple. The agent will be most concerned with how your features photograph and whether you have camera personality. Candid, natural shots without a lot of fuss are best.

When you get your 3 x 5-inch prints back from the lab, choose four to six photos, both closeup and full length and at least one in which you are smiling. Make sure they are in sharp focus and show you at your best. Have your photo processor make five or six duplicates of each photo from the negatives. You will need several 3 x 5 to 8 x 10 copies because you will be distributing them to agents, by mail and in person. Equipped with your list of agents and your snapshots you can begin applying to agencies.

Applying to an Agency by Mail

Most agents prefer that your initial contact with them be by mail. Phone calls interrupt them, waste their time, and make it difficult for them to provide you with valuable advice. Seeing your photos will be the most productive use of their time and yours. They will be able to read your letter and look at your pictures at their convenience and give them the attention they deserve. If you live outside a major city, the mails can be a means of determining your modeling potential in the city before visiting it. Most knowledgeable agents can tell by looking at snapshots whether you have any possibilities as a model in their city. When contacting an agency by mail, you should do the following.

- Refer to the form letter that follows this list or create your own, but keep it short and simple. You may want to include a few lines about the type of modeling you are interested in doing and modeling experience you have had, including clients for whom you have worked. Also inform them of plans to visit or relocate to their city.

- Include your home address in the letter, not just on the envelope. Also don't forget to include telephone numbers (both work and residence) in the letter.

- Enclose several clear, color, sharp-focus snapshots. Write your name and telephone number (with area code) clearly on the back of each photo. The pictures should be of you alone. Don't include wedding or graduation pictures or other valuable momentos. Your pictures will not be returned unless you specifically request the agency to do so and unless extra postage is included on a self-addressed, stamped envelope. If you have a composite or glossy include them. Established models should send duplicate tearsheets and composites.

- Your letter should be typed or neatly written in pen on unlined quality paper. Don't send a business letter on personal or childish stationary.

- If you have special marketable abilities (acting, singing, etc.) or have had modeling experience, include a resume.

- If you are acting on someone's referral or recommendation, mention the person by name. If an ad agency employee, commercial producer or director, photographer, or someone who utilizes models in his or her work has recommended that you contact the agency, state the person's name, occupation, and company in your letter. If you have won a beauty pageant or other honor related to your looks and/or talents, include this information as well. This will always get attention and give you credibility.

- Don't send certified or registered letters. If your name is not recognized, they probably will not sign for your letter.

- Enclose a self-addressed, stamped envelope for the agency's reply.
- If you do not receive a reply within a month, repeat the procedure. Your pictures may have been misplaced or may not have made it through the mail.

```
Date


Name of Person at Agency
Modeling Agency Name
Modeling Agency Address
City, State, Zip

Dear Mr., Mrs., or Ms. _____:

I would like to know if I have the qualifications you seek in
the models you represent.  I have enclosed several snapshots
along with my personal statistics.  I have also enclosed a
self-addressed, stamped envelope for your reply and for the
return of my pictures.  Thank you very much for your
consideration.

Sincerely,



Your name
Your address
Your telephone number


Personal statistics:

Age and birthdate:
Height:
Size:
Bust (bra size with cup):
Waist:
Hips:
Haircolor:
Eyecolor:


(Male models should list shirt size instead of bust, and
inseam instead of hips.)
```

Applying to an Agency in Person

Agencies interview models in one of two ways, either by appointment or open interview. Some agencies request that you first send pictures of yourself. If they think your pictures show promise, they will call you and make an appointment to meet you at the agency. Many agencies have open interviews in which a few hours are set aside each week to interview applicants. You should call the agency first to find out what days and times they conduct interviews. Do not stop by without calling. Also always be prepared by bringing along snapshots of yourself to help the agency evaluate your potential for modeling.

Requesting an Appointment with an Agency by Telephone

When calling a modeling agency to request an appointment, be direct and concise. Ask when they conduct interviews for new models or talent. Do not go into explanations of who you are or why you want to be a model.

The person at the agency may ask your height and age. For fashion models, many agencies require that you are at least 5'7 or 5'8 and under 22 years old before they will grant you an interview. They may also ask if you have experience or whether you have pictures. If you want to do another type of modeling such as television or character work, which does not have specific age or height requirements, then explain this. If the agency doesn't handle the type of work you are seeking, ask if they can refer you to agencies that do. (Look up the telephone numbers of these agencies on your own.)

What to Wear to Your Appointment with a Modeling Agency

Wear your hair and makeup in a flattering, simple, natural style that lets the real you show through and makes you feel attractive. Wear an outfit that shows your legs and figure. Most agents concur that the most common appearance mistakes they see in applicants are overbleached or overprocessed (permed, etc.) or poorly cut hair, too much makeup, skin problems, and excessive weight.

Before an appointment with an agent, don't do anything, such as color, cut, or perm your hair, tweeze your eyebrows, get a suntan, or make any change that will require weeks or months to undo. If the agency likes you, they will want you to begin right away and will want the most options for changing your hair or making alterations to mold you into an image that will be marketable.

How to Conduct Yourself at the Interview

Consult Chapter 9 for information on how to conduct yourself at the interview. When you enter the modeling agency, there may be several people already there waiting to be interviewed. Give your name to the receptionist and tell her who you are there to see or that you are there for open interviews or open registration. You may be given a card such as the one shown in Figure 3 to complete. Prepare before the

REGISTRATION FORM

©THE PROFESSIONAL MODEL'S HANDBOOK

NAME ______ LAST FIRST MIDDLE MODELING NAME ______ IF APPLICABLE

ADDRESS ______ STREET APT NO. CITY STATE ZIP CODE

TELEPHONE NUMBERS: HOME ______ WORK ______ MESSAGE ______

MODEL TYPE: ☐ PRINT ☐ RUNWAY ☐ LIVE PROMOTIONAL ☐ ELECTRONIC MEDIA

☐ FASHION ☐ COMMERCIAL ☐ CHARACTER ☐ OTHER ______

SKILLS/TALENTS: ☐ MUSICIAN ☐ ACTOR ☐ DANCER ☐ SPORTS ☐ OTHER

(SPECIFY AREA OF SPECIALIZATION) ______

HEIGHT ______ WEIGHT ______ BIRTHDATE/AGE ______ SOCIAL SECURITY NO. ______

COLORING: EYES ______ HAIR ______ SKIN ______

FEMALE SIZES: BUST/BRA ______ WAIST ______ HIPS ______ DRESS SIZE ______

MALE SIZES: SHIRT NECK/SLEEVE ______ SUIT ______ WAIST ______ INSEAM ______

SPECIAL FEATURES: HANDS ______ LEGS ______ FEET ______ SKIN ______ TEETH/SMILE ______ HAIR ______

ADDITIONAL INFORMATION: SCARS, MOLES, IMPERFECTIONS ______

LINGERIE ______ TRAVEL ______ CAR ______

CONTACT LENSES ______ NUDES ______ OTHER ______

SELF PROMOTION TOOLS: GLOSSY ______ RESUME ______ COMPOSITE ______ VOICETAPE ______ OTHER ______

RATES: ______

MISCELLANEOUS: ______

Figure 3. A Sample Registration Card

interview so that you will know this information. The interviewer you will be meeting will use this for reference and the agency will retain it so that they have a record of the meeting.

If you have contacted an agency by mail, you will encounter varying degrees of interest. If an agency is very interested in the photos you have mailed, they will write or telephone to invite you to their agency for a personal interview (at your or their expense depending on how interested they are). Many agencies will arrange for one of their representatives to meet you in your city. If they are somewhat interested in you, they may ask you to send more pictures or will give you advice (tell you to get more experience in your hometown or other cities, model in Europe, etc.) and will encourage you to keep in touch or try again at a later date.

If they are not very interested in you, they will not ask you to come for an interview. They may send you a form letter stating that your pictures will be kept on file. Although they don't have a considerable amount of work for you, a specific client or job may require your looks, abilities, etc. in the future. Some agencies list large amounts of talent on a nonexclusive basis and might ask you to come for an interview or audition when a large talent hunt is conducted or when talent in numbers (extra parts for movies, etc.) is required. If an agency is not at all interested, they will send you a letter stating that they are not in need of models with your look at the present time but wish you luck in your endeavors. Some agencies send a form letter/critique. This may list several qualifications for modeling, and the agent may check off those that you do not meet.

When you apply to an agency in person, you may encounter one of four types of responses: acceptance by exclusive contract, on a trial basis, acceptance on a nonexclusive basis, or rejection.

Acceptance by an Agency on an Exclusive Basis

When an agency is very interested in a model, they will ask her to sign a contract. This means that they really believe in the model's potential and want to represent this person exclusively. The agency is confident that bookings can be secured for the model from their clients. A model should carefully consider signing a contract with an agency; it is always wise to visit other agencies before doing so. If only one agency is interested in you, the decision will be simple. If several agencies want you to sign a contract, you will have to judge which one will be the best agency for you. Use the following criteria as a guide to determine which agency to choose.

- *Does the agency handle the type of work for which you are best suited?* Agencies tend to specialize in fashion models for print or fashion shows, promotional models, or television talents. Even multiservice agencies have certain areas in which they are strongest. If you are interested in doing television commercials, make sure the agency you are considering is sanctioned by SAG/AFTRA. Look at the agency's client list to determine where you might fit in.

- *Where is the agent's place in the competition?* You should consider whether you want to be with an agent who represents many top models and who gets more calls for bookings, or a smaller agent who may have fewer models and probably fewer calls for bookings. The smaller agent will probably give you more attention and promote you more and may be more effective, particularly for a new model, than the larger agent. However, you should consider also that the large agency may have more clout and better contacts than the smaller or less established agency.

- *Does the agency have associations with other agencies or offices in more than one place?* If an agency has offices or connections with agencies in New York, Chicago, and Los Angeles, this will increase your opportunities by providing you with out-of-town work in addition to your local work. Some agencies in large cities also have connections with agencies in smaller markets and send new models to the smaller market first to train and to get established. If you aspire to model in Europe, check if the agency has connections abroad.
- *How many models of your type are currently represented by the agency? How many models are signed to exclusive contracts?* Ask to see the agency's model book, and compare. If your looks are very similar to several other models in the agency, it would probably be better to be one of a few than one of many in the agency competing for the same opportunities.
- *Has the agency been influential in promoting other models to successful careers?* Notice the signs of success or credentials the agency has on display. An agency is very proud of its successes and will display pictures or other information about its top talent. If you are a beginning model, you should ask the agency if it started or discovered the top talent it represents.
- *Do the employees of the agency appear to be professional and caring?* You will need an agent who you feel is fair, respectable, trustworthy, and caring. Make judgments about the agent beyond the surface. If he or she reflects your values, then the agent is probably right for you. The bookers and others on staff are going to be the people you will have to talk to every day. If they are rude, short, or otherwise unfriendly, you may have to consider whether you want them as a part of your business life. Notice the way the employees conduct themselves. Look around to note office organization and professionalism.
- *Does the agent seem to be very interested in having you as a model in his or her agency?* It is not only important that an agent have the knowledge, contacts, and means to help a model, it is crucial that he or she have a strong belief in your potential for success. The agent who is truly interested in you will formulate a specific plan of action for you to follow and will be able to give criticism or recommendations that will help develop your potential. This type of agent is preferable to someone who just wants to add you to the agency roster. An agent who strongly believes in you and your abilities is one of the most important criteria for selecting the best agent.

Signing the Contract

An agent who thinks you have a lot of potential will want you to sign a contract at the outset to prevent you from becoming associated with competing agents. He or she will not be willing to put a lot of effort toward training or promoting you if you are free to go to another agent who will benefit from his or her hard work. Some agents will allow you the option of working on an initial trial basis; however, most agents will not agree to this if they have a lot of hope for you.

Most modeling agency contracts outline a simple agreement between you and them, stating that you will receive all modeling work through their agency only, for the duration of the contract, which is usually 2 years. Most 1- or 2-year contracts contain a 90-day clause that is in favor of the agent. This means that if you do not work for a 90-day period, the agent can terminate the agreement.

A modeling agency franchised by the Screen Actors Guild union protects the talent or model by mandating that the agent include a standard minimum income clause that allows the talent to break the contract should he or she not have received 15 days of work within a 90-day period.

Reputable agents do not need to resort to pressuring an individual to sign a contract on the spot. It is always a good idea to consider the contract overnight or to have it explained by a lawyer.

After You Sign the Contract

After you have signed the contract, you will begin right away. As a new model you may be told not to expect much income in the first few months. You may receive help to obtain living arrangements if you are from out of town. Sometimes the agency will be able to secure living arrangements with another model or someone on the agency staff. Some agencies maintain an apartment for out-of-town models. If the agency does not provide a place for you to live, they will make recommendations of inexpensive weekly rate hotels or other suitable places. If the agency advances you money for rent and living expenses, the amount will be deducted from your checks once you start getting work. If you're invited to stay with another person, you may be expected to exchange favors, for example, babysitting, cooking, and helping around the house in addition to contributing what you can for food and rent.

At this point you will be introduced to the person who will handle all your bookings and appointments. Usually large agencies have several bookers in each division (Print, TV, Show), each specializing in a certain type of model, for example, high fashion, juniors, misses, and large sizes. The booker keeps a chart of all your appointments, from testings to go-sees to bookings. The booker and the agent will confer on what type of image you should try to acquire and how you should be marketed. They will explain basic agency procedures and may give you written guidelines to follow.

The next order of business will be working on your image and presentation. You may be sent to a hairdresser. Agencies sometimes have arrangements with hairdressers who style the model's hair at no charge or a special discount. You will also be sent to a number of photographers to see about having some test shots done. These sessions can either be free, discounted, or full fee. Even if you're an experienced model, don't be surprised if the agent tells you that your hair is all wrong and your pictures are awful. If you really want to work with the agency, you will have to trust them. After all, they should know how they can best promote you to their clients. In addition, you may be told to attend some classes to improve your skills. The costs involved in improving your appearance and presentation may be advanced to you by the agent or you may be expected to pay for them up front.

As a beginning model you will be busy gaining experience and test photos for your self-promotion tools and making business contacts. Most new models after just a few months, provided they have made a diligent effort (8 hours per day, every day) and have the proper promotion tools, are able to see whether their career is going to develop. However, it may take a year before steady bookings begin to materialize. After 2 years most models fulfill their potential and maintain it for several years. Because of this fact, many agents prefer that individuals who aspire to be fashion models begin their careers between their junior and senior years of high school.

Terminating a Modeling Agency Contract

Signing an exclusive contract is not a permanent, far-reaching, or irreversible act. A new model often thinks she is "signing her life away" when she signs a contract with a modeling agency. It is important to realize that most reasonable agents will not hold you to the contract if for some reason your partnership is unproductive. If you and the agent have made your best efforts over a reasonable length of time, and you still don't get work, the agent will probably be just as happy as you to dissolve the agreement. If you aren't getting bookings, the agent isn't making money either. Most agents don't want to have an agency full of nonworking models.

It is important to realize that there will be times when you and your agent will disagree about the direction of your career, promotion, and the like, but these differences must be balanced by looking at the entire picture. Discuss dissatisfaction with the agent before it escalates into a problem. Realize that he or she wants you to achieve as much success as possible, and if you are successful, it will be because the two of you accomplished it together.

It may be necessary to change agents at sometime in your career. The following are some of the reasons you should contemplate a change.

- If your agent consistently fails to honor agreements regarding payment for the work you have done, you should consider acquiring an agent who has a better reputation for payment.
- If your agent consistently lies, omits information, or misrepresents assignments you should look for a more ethical agent.
- If your agent is very disorganized, which repeatedly causes you inconvenience or makes you look incompetent to your clients, you should look for a more efficient, professional agent.

If you are considering changing agents, always have a discussion with the agent so that he or she is aware of your dissatisfaction and will have a chance to correct problems. If the agent is still unsatisfactory and you decide to terminate your arrangement, schedule an appointment with the agent to tell him or her that you are leaving and why. Always end a liason in an amicable and honest manner.

Acceptance by a Modeling Agency on a Trial Basis

In some agencies "trial basis" is the only way that new models are accepted. The agency usually sends the model to a hairdresser and makeup artist and puts her on the agency testing board. Then, after noting her progress in getting good shots for her portfolio and getting feedback from photographers regarding how the model works and what her potential assets or problems may be, the agent will decide whether to sign a contract with her or let her go. This arrangement will usually last from 1 to 3 months but can go on indefinitely. The model may be advised to go to Europe to gain tearsheets for her portfolio or to get experience in cities outside New York. In such arrangements usually no written contract is made and no money is advanced to the model. However, the agency may make a verbal agreement that should things go well, the model will sign a contract.

Because of the great number of potentially qualified people entering the modeling field, many agencies have adopted the following practice: An agent who is interested in a model, before signing her, will help her to assemble a professional-looking composite. The agent may do this just by referring the model to composite photographers. When the model returns with the finished composite, the agent will distribute it to clients. When the model receives a positive response or actual bookings, the agent will ask the model to sign a contract.

The agent's objective is to expose numbers of potentially qualified faces to clients without making a sizeable investment of time or money. The models who excel in this manner move up the in ranks of the agency.

If You Are Told to Come Back

One of the possible outcomes of an interview with an agency is that you may be asked to come back or reapply:

- At a later date when the agency will be looking for new talent.
- At another time when several other new models will be starting, for example, during summer vacations, or when the agency doesn't have so many newly acquired models.
- When you have moved to the city and are settled. If you are from out of town, the agent may see potential in you but may not be sure about how well you will do. If she uproots you or encourages you to move from your hometown to her city, she will feel partially responsible for you. Unless you are a sure bet, most agents will not take the risk.
- When you have gained experience, more specifically, have more photographs or tearsheets in your portfolio, have a composite, or have modeled in Europe.
- When you have made some change in your appearance, such as losing weight, growing your hair, growing out a perm or artificial hair color, or have cleared up your skin.

After interviewing with other agencies you would like to join (never interview with just one) and if they all say the same thing or reject you, take the suggestions of the agent who asked you to come back and act on them. It will probably take you at least a month or two, and the agency probably will not be anxiously awaiting your return. In fact, they may not even remember you when you come back with your problem corrected. Remind them of what they said. When you return, one of three things will happen: you will be accepted on either a contractual or trial basis, you will be rejected, or you will be told to improve some other aspect before the agency will give you a decision. If they tell you to improve on something and return again, they are not breaking any records to sign you, so you can assume they don't have much hope for you. If you have the energy and money to act on the new suggestions, you might try once more. Otherwise, it is probably a good idea to forget that agency.

Acceptance on a Nonexclusive Basis

Representation on a nonexclusive basis does not exist in all markets, nor is it a practice held by all the agencies in a given market where it does exist. Modeling on a nonexclusive basis is also referred to as free-lancing or multilisting. As a nonexclusive or free-lance talent, an individual can register or list with and obtain auditions and bookings through several different agencies in a given market. This practice has its advantages and disadvantages. Even though the talent can potentially get more opportunities with more agents representing her, difficulties do arise.

Most agents prefer to represent talent on an exclusive basis because they can devote more time and energy to promoting the talent who have a committment to them. Clients often prefer this same type of arrangement because it eliminates the problem of keeping track of which model was sent by which agency. Scheduling conflicts between the agencies that may be booking one model at the same time period for three different clients are also a common problem that exists with multilisting.

Free-lancing does have definite advantages for the following models: the model who has not been asked to sign exclusively with an agent and the model who works in several different areas of modeling and cannot get adequate representation in all areas by one agent. For example, the model may have an exclusive contract with one agent for fashion show work, but she may work through several agents to obtain electronic media, print, and/or promotional modeling assignments. Free-lancing may be advantageous for the child, specialty, or character model whose market may not provide an abundance of work and who will need all the opportunities possible.

If You Are Rejected by a Modeling Agency

An agent will reject an applicant if he or she does not think the individual will be able to make money for the agency. Some agents operate on quantity, taking on any model who may have the potential of getting a few bookings. Other agents are very selective and will only sign a model who they are quite certain will be able to earn a certain minimum sum, for example, $40,000 per year, once he or she is established. An agent will take on more models of the types his clients most frequently demand and fewer models representing types that are less in demand. Agents rarely take on two models who have a strong resemblance (unless they are twins) or several models with the same look because it may not be possible to provide work for all of them.

It is important to realize that agents have different ways of rejecting applicants. Face-to-face rejection of an applicant is an unpleasant but necessary part of an agent's job. Some agents will be painfully direct and say things that may hurt your feelings. Other agents will tell you why they can't use you in a very matter-of-fact, business-like way. Still others may be so indirect that the model doesn't even know she is being rejected. For example, in order to avoid hurting your feelings, an agent may tell you one thing, but mean another. The agent may say "I think you have a great look, but you need more pictures, a composite, or more experience before I can accept you." If an agent is really interested in you, he or she will arrange appointments or refer you to test photographers, hairstylists, and makeup artists or establish a specific plan of action.

Sometimes if an agent isn't interested in you but wants to avoid giving you an absolute "no," he or she may tell you to keep trying, knowing that most people won't make the effort and won't come back. If you correct the characteristics that were the agent's reasons for rejecting you and return, the agent will be impressed by your ambition and determination. However, if you don't have the qualifications, it won't matter what you do or how often you return, you still won't be accepted. In other words, you have to be perceptive enough to hear "no," even when the agent isn't professional enough to say "no."

If you are rejected by an agent, don't react in an emotional way. The agent is making a business decision and is not out to hurt you personally. Being rejected doesn't mean you are unattractive; it simply means that you don't have a particular "look" that the agent thinks his or her clients will want at that particular time. Being turned down should not discourage you; some models who later became very famous were rejected on their first rounds of the agencies.

If possible, the interview should be used to gain information or contacts. Most agents are willing to give a bit of advice, provide information, or steer an applicant in the right direction. Be professional and pleasant, regardless of how the agent treats you. A smart agent knows that it is good public relations to treat rejected applicants in a friendly, considerate manner. An intelligent applicant willingly accepts whatever the agent says even though it may not be what the applicant wants to hear. Don't show your disappointment or argue or challenge the agent's decision. Take up no more than 5 to 10 minutes of the agent's time. Accept whatever he or she says. Leave with a smile and a thank you and you'll be remembered in a positive way.

There are several courses of action you should consider if you are rejected by an agency.

- Interview with other agencies. Don't give up after trying one agency. Ask each agent which agency she would recommend you try next. Another option worth trying is to interview with different departments within the agency. For example, if you are 5'6, and look like a "girl next door," the agent from the fashion department will probably reject you. However, an agent in the TV or promotional modeling department might think you're just right.

- Try another market. If you're a high-fashion type and there's not much call for that type of work in your hometown, you should consider other markets, such as New York. Send your picture for an evaluation before you go, and if you are encouraged, make the trip for an interview. Europe might also merit a try.

- Reanalyze your assets and liabilities. Take an objective look at yourself. Do you really meet the requirements? Maybe a weight loss or gain would be helpful. If a modeling career is important to you, you might be willing to consider making minor improvements via cosmetic dentistry or cosmetic surgery.

- Change your look. Get opinions from hairdressers on new looks. Try new cuts and styles. Have different makeup artists do your makeup. Try changing your style of dress. Repackage and remarket yourself. Retake your pictures to present your new look.

- Consider becoming a different type of model. You may want to be a glamourous fashion model, but it might be that you'll be more successful as a character model. If you really want to earn money in modeling, you will have to become the type of model clients want you to be.

- Try again at a later date. Maybe you're attractive but don't have the "look of the moment." Having the right look at the right time is important. It may be necessary to try again in 6 months or a year. If you are already modeling, collect more pictures, make a better composite, try modeling in Europe, then interview again.

- Attend classes to increase your marketability. Although training doesn't guarantee success, it can qualify you for more opportunities. Take acting classes, modeling classes, or other types of instruction. Find out from agents which ones they recommend. When considering schools, ask what percentage of their graduates have had career success. Ask about the qualifications of their instructors.

- Consider a different approach. Black superstar model Naomi Sims had done an ad and appeared on the cover of the *New York Times* fashion magazine when she first made the rounds of the New York modeling agencies. She was rejected by all of them so she tried a different approach. She bought 100 copies of her *Times* cover and mailed one to every advertising agency in the *Madison Avenue Handbook*. Attached to it was a card saying that she could be contacted through the Wilhelmina Agency. Naomi had made an agreement with Wilhelmina, who had also rejected her, that she would use the Wilhelmina Agency as an answering service. Naomi would pay full agency commission if she got any bookings. All the agency had to do was to relay the messages. Days after her promotional piece was sent, the Wilhelmina agency received a deluge of phone calls from clients requesting to see and to book Naomi Sims.

- Obtain a portfolio and composite of impressive, professional pictures. This will make your modeling potential more obvious to agents, show what you are capable of, that you have experience in front of the camera, and are serious about a modeling career.

- Enter modeling and beauty contests. Modeling and beauty contests are a good way for an aspiring model to gain exposure to important people in the modeling business, gain publicity, and sharpen modeling skills. Enter as many as you can, you'll gain valuable experience and have fun.

- Try to get into modeling through a different line of work or area of interest. It may be wise to try a different avenue. If you have styling, makeup artistry, hairstyling, photography, fashion merchandising, or public relations ability, use those skills to gain contacts with those who might also consider using you for your modeling skills. If you can dance and do some acrobatics, consider trying out for a professional cheerleading squad (contact the offices of professional football, basketball, soccer, or other teams in your city for information). This is a great way to gain exposure and modeling opportunities. Or, consider some other type of public relations or entertainment group. When pursuing your modeling career, always keep an open mind.

- Try a promotional gimmick. Many models have succeeded with a gimmick. Candy Jones, a prominent spokesmodel for Procter and Gamble in the 1950s and 1960s changed her name from Jessica Wilcox and had just about everything she owned done up in candy stripes. She left matchbooks everywhere, with the inevitable stripes and the legend "Candy Jones Was Here," carried a candy-striped bag, and so on. Her gimmick got her name known in agency circles. Jean Patchett, a top model in the 1950s, became known by her trademark beauty spot. In the 1960s Twiggy's super thin figure and painted-on lower lashes got the attention she needed to become a superstar. Brooke Shields' full eyebrows got her noticed. Of course, each of these models had great merit beyond their natural or manufactured gimmick. But in each case it was that characteristic that distinguished the model from her competition. Your gimmick might be a natural asset or a trademark hair look, clothing color, or name.

- Invite agents to a showcase of your talents. Usually the reason you've been overlooked is that your assets have not been emphasized for the agent. If you'll be appearing in a fashion show, dance, or theatre performance, send the agent, an invitation with a personal note encouraging her to attend. Include your photo in your invitation.

- Model without an agent. Modeling without an agent is difficult, but not impossible. Follow the advice on the following pages and keep tabs on your progress. It will take you longer to get established, but once you have made a name for yourself, agents will sign you.

- Consider another career. If you have tried everything and have been trying to model for a year or more and still see no valid signs of hope, quit before you drain your financial and psychological resources unnecessarily. If you truly enjoy the pursuit and have no illusions, treat modeling as a hobby and nothing more. You should consider, though, that your time, energy, and talents could be spent more wisely. Stop and make objective evaluations from time to time and rethink your reasons for wanting a modeling career.

Whether you want to gain a little modeling experience before meeting agents or are currently registered or signed with an agent and want to know how to increase your opportunities, the information here will be helpful. Anyone entering into modeling should understand the importance of self-promotion, stirring up contacts, and being in the right place at the right time.

Even if a model is represented by an agent, she or he should realize that contacts are not limited to those received through the agency. If a neighbor, relative, friend, or friend of a friend has a job that employs models, the model should try to use the contact to advantage. Being overly aggressive is not right, but letting people know what you can do and that you are available is. Of course, if you are under contract to an agent, the booking, fee negotiation, and collection must be handled through the agent, and they will receive their normal commission.

Getting work in all areas of modeling, especially without an agent, is difficult. You should be as diversified as possible by continually working on increasing your skills to enhance your marketability. Being able to work in one area may lead to work in another. For example, having a great personality will secure you work in trade shows, and the companies you work for may also be impressed by your appearance and ask you to appear in their print and electronic media promotions. Do everything you can to get exposure—join a performing troupe; enter relevant contests such as talent searches, modeling, and beauty pageants; participate in events for charity, education, and other social organizations that utilize models and talent. Sign up for classes. Being among other models or actors often provides you with word-of-mouth information about who needs a model or actor. Many of these classes are conducted by people actually involved in the business, for example, casting directors or models' agents.

Conduct yourself in a professional, business-like manner. Acquire basic business tools, such as a typewriter and letterhead stationary to use for correspondence and billing. Your own phone and an answering machine or service are also musts. Use the forms in this book (voucher, form letters, etc.) as a guide to what you need.

Of course, most important are effective promotional tools. Assemble a TV glossy and resume to secure TV, film, and other types of audiovisual work. Produce a voice tape to secure work in radio, TV voice-overs, and the like. Assemble a composite and portfolio to obtain print, fashion show, and promotional modeling jobs. Think of creative ways to promote yourself.

Be Self-Motivated

Be aware that you will have to be highly self-motivated. Although it is certainly not impossible to model without an agent, nearly all successful models are or at sometime were, signed by agents, particularly in the beginning of their careers. If you embark on a career on your own you should be prepared to spend quite a long time establishing contacts. One of the most important functions of an agency is to give the model prestige and credibility. Some clients will not deal with a model unless she has agency representation.

A few successful models in the United States, particularly in cities outside of New York, Chicago, and Los Angeles, and in Europe do handle their own bookings, manage their accounts, and use an answering service. If a model can eventually collect a group of steady clients to depend on for regular work, she will be able to make it on her own. Many such models are successful by attaining exclusive or semiexclusive contracts with a major manufacturer, distributor, or retailer in their area. They may perform a variety of functions ranging from runway modeling and informal modeling in the store, to photo shootings and special promotions.

Investment money is a necessity for a self-represented or independent free-lance model. When you model without an agent, you are in effect starting your own small business. You won't get very far if you have no money to invest in testings, composites, and other things that will further your career. Also, not having to rely on modeling for income will improve your attitude toward the job. You won't get discouraged when your modeling career isn't progressing as well or as fast as you thought it would. If possible, try to obtain a job where you'll interface with individuals who may be in a position to employ you as a model. Working as a makeup artist, stylist, photographer's assistant, or secretary or in fashion merchandising might increase your chances.

Establishing and Collecting Your Fees

A rate that is slightly under the standard established by the modeling agencies in your market is usually best, because clients and photographers not going through an agency are usually trying to save money. If you get a job that involves a lot of exposure, enlist an agent or someone else with experience to negotiate the fee for you, and give him or her a commission.

Your other major problem will be collecting fees for the work you do. Agencies have collection departments and lawyers who handle these problems; you won't have the leverage they do. The best way to handle payment is to tell the client at the time he or she books you that you expect to be paid in cash at the assignment. If it is a photography assignment, do not sign a model's release until you are paid. Upon receiving your payment, write out a receipt or voucher and sign a release. Give a copy to your client. Retain a copy for your files.

Where to Look for Work

The following are suggestions on where and how to look for modeling and related work. In addition, be alert to names and events in the news that may affect you and your career. Read the newspaper and pay attention to articles on prominent designers, photographers, producers, directors, and others in your area. Look for open casting calls listed in the features page by the movie listings. Look at the classified ads. Be aware, however, that a lot of these aren't legitimate especially if they ask a high price for the opportunity. Read the advertising column in the paper to see which ad agencies are doing what. Becoming familiar with the names of top ad agencies and other individuals prominent in your field locally and nationally is helpful for any model. Become aware of who's shooting what by noticing the fine print along the side of photos indicating the name of the photographer who shot the photo.

Read the trade publications for the fashion, motion picture, television, and advertising industries. Buy creative directories that list the names of individuals who use models for advertising. *The Creative Black Book*, *Madison Avenue Handbook*, and *Ross Reports* list names of advertising agencies, casting directors, film production companies, photographers, and other potential clients nationally. Go to the library and look up *The Red Book* or *The Standard Directory of Advertising Agencies* to find all the products advertised on television, their manufacturers, and their advertising agencies. This will give you insight into which manufacturers and ad agencies are active in your local area. Check *The Wall Street Journal* to see which companies are coming out with new products, where they will be test marketed, or whether the company has switched ad agencies. Look at national publications, such as *Advertising Age* or *Adweek*, to familiarize yourself with current advertising trends and events.

To contact the entities explained on the following pages, use written correspondence. Always send a cover letter following the style of the form letter shown under the section "Applying to an Agency by Mail". A neatly typed letter on professional-looking stationery that clearly states the reason for your correspondence is important. Inquire as to whether the company employs models with your looks and qualifications. Send your promotional materials in a neat, professional-looking packet. Follow up with a phone call after a few weeks.

It is important to keep a notebook or card file in which to make notes about people to contact, those contacted, and other information. Use the Contact Record and forms found in Chapters 8 and 9.

Opportunities in Print Modeling Contact art directors, talent coordinators, or casting directors in advertising agencies to appear in print ads, catalogs, and brochures they produce for their clients.

To appear in the fashion section of your local newspaper, contact the editorial or fashion department. Contact the advertising office to appear in ads promoting the newspaper or functions the newspaper may conduct.

Contact retailers in your area, such as department stores and boutiques, to be used in their advertising campaigns. Send your composite to the fashion director or coordinator, store owner, manager, fashion office, or the public relations or advertising departments.

Send your picture to national magazines to be featured as one of their makeovers or in hopes that you'll be discovered for a special editorial assignment. Contact the model editor, fashion editor, or beauty editor.

Local publications often devote an issue or a few pages in each issue to fashion or feature layouts. Contact the editor-in-chief, managing editor, or features editor to determine which person handles fashion issues. Enter cover model contests conducted by national and local magazines.

Contact the catalog production department of large stores and mail-order concerns. Sometimes large stores and other concerns that produce catalogs will test the garments and accessories on stand-in, less expensive free-lance models when deciding which garments will be featured and how they will be shown in the catalog. They will be determining which are most photogenic, which accessories look best, and what poses should be used. You may even be called to participate in the final shoot for the catalog. This stand-in type of modeling is also done by ad agencies when drawing up the concept and layout for an ad.

Find out from advertising departments of local stores the names of illustrators they employ and then send your picture to these artists in hopes of being used as the model for a fashion illustration.

Find a photographer with whom you have a good working relationship and do lots of testing together. Eventually you may be able to collaborate your skills and efforts by doing photos on a free-lance, speculative basis for small stores, hair salons, and other local concerns that can be used for brochures, flyers, or posters.

Increase your chances of meeting photographers by connecting with national and local photographer's associations and clubs where you'll meet people who need models for practice and assignments.

Send your composite to people and organizations who may need models. If possible, send documentation, that is, a tearsheet, ad, brochure, and other published pictures that show you've worked. People will be much more receptive to you when they see that your pictures have been published and you have experience.

Opportunities in Fashion Show Modeling Showroom models often do not have agents. Because these jobs may entail other duties, such as secretarial, administrative, or sales tasks, a model should apply for these as she would any other job. Send a resume, making sure you play up applicable skills. Include a composite. Most of this work is done on Seventh Avenue in New York, but all major cities have apparel marts where you can scout for potential employers.

House modeling is similar to showroom modeling, and often exclusive stores and hair salons have full- or part-time positions. Fitting modeling often goes hand in hand with showroom modeling. Consult *The Yellow Pages* to find clothing manufacturers in your area that need models to show or fit new lines. There are over 5000 apparel manufacturers represented in New York alone; other states also prevailing in clothing manufacture are California, Texas, and New Jersey. The classified ads in the newspaper and in trade publications such as *Women's Wear Daily* also tell of job openings. Fashion design classes in colleges and art schools often need models on which to design, fit, and show students' works.

Many runway models do not have agents. You may be able to obtain runway work by going to the fashion offices of local department stores. Contact owners or managers of boutiques directly to obtain fashion show work. Modeling of this nature is available in suburbs, smaller towns, and larger cities. Local designers, furriers, and others also need models. Contact free-lance fashion show producers or those in apparel marts because many companies contract out fashion shows to these individuals who handle all the arrangements. You might even consider putting together your own fashion show troupe of four or five models. Avail your services to smaller stores by offering a package. Arrange to receive a flat fee, which can be divided among the models.

Attend fashion shows and afterward give your composite to the commentator or coordinator and express an interest in participating in upcoming shows. Also you might consider applying to be one of the models in a traveling fashion show troupe. *Essence* conducts auditions for models all over the country for their traveling fashion showcase.

Opportunities abound for informal modeling. The information above also applies in this area. Obtain the names of sales representatives for different cosmetic and clothing lines, and contact them for informal modeling jobs. You may be selected to sample fragrance or show garments. Contact the advertising office for appliance demonstration or other part-time sales promotion jobs. Or consider becoming involved in high school, college, or career fashion boards organized within department stores.

Opportunities in Promotional Modeling There are quite a few opportunities for promotional models, especially for the lower-paying booth assistant or hostess jobs. Write to the convention center office or to your city's Bureau of Conventions and Tourism for a schedule of their upcoming exhibitions. Another source, *The Trade Show Convention Guide* published in New York, gives a comprehensive listing of local and national shows and exhibitions held in the United States. Sometimes it is a good idea to go to the convention hall in the morning of the opening day of the trade show to see if extra help or replacements are needed. Often when the show is successful, more models are needed to register the people attending.

Contact the companies directly for which you would like to work. Address your letter to the public relations director and enclose a glossy and resume along with Xerox copies of two or three letters of praise or recommendation from companies for whom you have previously worked. It is a good practice to encourage former clients to write letters commending your work.

The classified ads often list opportunities for promotional models. Cosmetic companies often advertise for models to do in-store promotions on a regular basis. The ability to instruct customers on how to apply makeup is sometimes a requirement. However, a company will often train the model to do this. Contests and sporting events often lend opportunities for the promotional model to participate in awards presentation ceremonies and the like.

Opportunities in Electronic Media There are probaby the greatest number of opportunities in the electronic media field. Increase your acting skills and perfect your voice for voice work. For TV commercial work, approach casting directors and producers from advertising agencies, production houses, and audiovisual departments of firms who may do their advertising in-house.

Consult *The Red Book* or *The Standard Directory of Advertising Agencies* to find which advertising agencies handle which accounts. Send your photo and resume to the agencies handling products that you think you are right for, along with a note to the attention of the casting director. You can also send this note to the advertising department of the manufacturer to be forwarded to the ad agency.

Another approach you might like to try is to write a "satisfied customer" letter. Write letters to the manufacturers praising those products you have tried and like. Describe your experience with the product, uses you have found for it, things you like about it, in general, how great it is. You can put a tag line saying that you'd love to have the opportunity to tell others about it. When the manufacturer does a testimonial type of commercial, the files will be searched for possible candidates to appear. Because of truth-in-advertising laws, people appearing in such commercials must have actually tried and had a positive encounter with the product or service.

When watching TV, note which local businesses advertise (automobile dealers, grocers, druggists, etc.) and send a glossy, composite, and resume to the company's advertising or public relations department along with a cover letter stating that you'd like to audition for their next television commercial.

Watch local TV and cable stations and note the shows that are produced in your area. Look at the credits after the show and take down the names of the producer, casting director, and director, and send them a glossy and resume along with a short note, stating what you would like to do for the show. Send your picture and resume to the advertising and program department of local stations in case models are needed for station promotions, features, or other types of programs.

Contact independent directors and film production companies directly, especially those in the suburbs, to appear in industrial films. Send a glossy and resume. Send a voice tape to these same concerns and local radio stations to obtain announcing jobs or for program work.

To obtain extra work in films, contact your State Film Board and City Film Office to learn which productions are going on in your town and which people are casting. Regularly visit your entertainment or performer's union office in your city to look at bulletin boards displaying information about upcoming opportunities. Send your glossy and resume to film companies, to the attention of the casting or production departments, and ad agencies. Extras are sometimes needed in the background of television commercials. Extra work is a great way to make contacts and get on-the-job training. Put "Available for Extra Work" in a prominent place on your resume such as under your telephone number.

Chapter 8 The Model's Side of the Business

When an individual becomes a model, he or she is in effect starting his or her own small business. The prospective model follows the same course as any individual who produces and sells a product. The model's product is herself—her looks, talents, and skills. The model begins by researching the field to see where opportunities lie and how he might fit the needs of those who utilize models' services. These aspects are covered in Chapter 1. The second stage involves developing the prospective model in ways that will make his looks and abilities marketable. The model concentrates on the basics of grooming and physical presentation covered in Chapter 2. He then works at acquiring knowledge in hairstyling, makeup artistry, and wardrobe so that he can present an image that potential clients will respond to. These aspects are covered in Chapters 3, 4, and 5. To complete his product development, he polishes his personality so that it works well in the businessplace. This is the topic of Chapter 6.

After the model has worked on his appearance and personal skills, he tries to secure an agent who will guide his further development, put him in touch with clients, and negotiate deals on his behalf. However, an agent can only do so much. The model himself is always ultimately responsible for his own success or failure. Many models fail because they don't approach modeling as a business. They wait for others to do things for them, rather than investing their own money, time, and energy to make things happen that will lead to their success. Understanding basic business principles and how to apply them to modeling will motivate you and help you to succeed. The basic areas with which a model should be concerned are

1. Preliminary business considerations.
2. Making career plans.
3. Investing in your career.
4. Acquiring business tools and using them effectively.
5. Keeping written records for your business.
6. Managing the money you earn.
7. Dealing with legal matters and other concerns that affect your business.

PRELIMINARY BUSINESS CONSIDERATIONS

An individual doesn't need a license or any type of diploma or certification in order to obtain modeling work. However, he or she must have a Social Security number. If you have never been employed, you may not have a Social Security number. Everyone seeking work in the modeling field must have a Social Security card on which the number is printed. This includes babies and children. Before approaching a modeling agency, apply for your Social Security number.

To apply for a Social Security number, you must provide identification, such as your birth certificate or baptism record. If these are not available, other identification, such as a receipt from a doctor's office, may be acceptable. Parents of children must also present identification. Take this documentation to the nearest Social Security office (see your telephone book) where an application is completed. You may be able to do this by mail, but it is safer to go in person to ensure against loss of personal documents.

After the information is processed, your Social Security card will be sent to you within 4 to 12 weeks. In the meantime you will be issued a receipt that will enable you to obtain work.

In some states or countries where you may want to model, it is necessary for minors and/or adults to obtain specific work permits. Consult with an agent through whom you will be obtaining work to determine if this applies to you.

MAKING CAREER PLANS

The saying, "Plan your work and work your plan," really applies to models. Planning will help you to establish realistic goals, give you a time frame in which to accomplish them, and help you to measure your progress. It is unwise to begin a new career with no direction or goals. You will encounter more disappointments and waste time, money, and energy when you have no specific aims.

Models often leave their careers up to fate, thinking that somehow opportunity will arise without their participation and preparation. Any worthwhile endeavor requires planning, preparation, and performance. Also, relying on others to plan your career is unwise. Take responsibility for your own career. Acquiring good planning habits and conducting yourself like a mature, professional businessperson is essential for anyone who wants to succeed.

Plan Ahead

A smart businessperson makes plans for large segments of time and then details his or her activities to achieve his or her goals within smaller increments of time. A model can plan effectively by considering what he or she wants to accomplish within the framework of a year. Use the Planning Form shown here along with the information that follows and advice from your agent to help in making your career plans.

Modeling work revolves around the selling of consumer goods. The early months of fall and the early months of spring are when clothing designers and manufacturers show their collections for the buyers who are making purchases for their stores. After orders are placed by the buyers, photo sessions take place, the results of which are used in advertisements, catalogs, and editorial layouts for magazines. In general, models model fall and winter fashions in the summer, and spring and summer fashions in the winter.

Retail fashion shows, that is, fashion shows conducted by the stores for their customers, are usually held closer to the actual season of the clothing being shown. These shows are conducted to promote interest at the beginning of the consumer selling season when stocks are new and in full supply.

Items other than fashion are geared to peak purchasing times, depending on the nature of the product. For example, goods sold as Christmas items are photographed 4 to 6 months in advance for print advertising and television commercials. Photographs advertising products such as soft drinks are taken in advance of the summer so they will be ready for use during the summer months.

Planning Form

	Sept.	Oct.	Nov.	Dec.	Jan.	Feb.
FALL/WINTER						
	March	April	May	June	July	Aug.
SPRING/SUMMER						

In general, slow periods for modeling work occur in December and January because of the holidays and in June and July when clients and others are on vacation. However, there may be exceptions. It is a good idea to check with your agent to determine when major clients and retailers in your area produce their catalogs and advertisements.

Promotional modeling work follows a different course. It is possible to obtain a schedule of all the trade shows and conventions that are held in your town each year by contacting the Bureau of Tourism and Conventions in your area. Your agent will also have this information.

In order to obtain the greatest amount of work, the model should gear her self-promotional efforts around these facts. For example, working on your composite in the early months of summer will allow you to take advantage of good outdoor light for photographs, and it will also allow you the necessary time to assemble and print the composite. This way it will be ready to send out in advance of the fall months when clients are making booking decisions.

You will also want to consider when your agency will be assembling their yearly or quarterly promotional books and headsheets so you will have good, new photos to submit. Many agencies send their new books out in January, so in order to be included you would have to submit your photos in October or November.

Determine Your Priorities

Always think in terms of more than a day or a few hours. Don't operate on anxiousness, instead operate on your plan. To help you to adhere to your long range plans, at the beginning of each day, write down the six most important things you have to do that day and then do them.

Avoid Procrastination

Don't put off anything you can do at the present time. Don't expect other people to make up for time you could have used more wisely. Avoid procrastinating until time is critical and you must do everything in a rush. Mentally set your calendar a day or week ahead. You will often find that tasks that involve the most difficulty or that tend to upset your nerves are the easiest to postpone.

Concentrate on Quality First, Timing Second

It is usually wise to spend the time to get something right. Planning ahead and scheduling your activities will help you to obtain quality in your work. Everyone does a better job when there is time. For example, it is a mistake to assemble your composite hurriedly when you know it takes time to do it well. Making a composite is something you do only once or twice a year and it is your most important sales tool. Taking an extra week or a few weeks to get it right will have a much more positive effect on your career than issuing a composite that is not up to standards.

Never put pressure on others to do something in a rush unless you yourself are prepared to sacrifice quality or pay a higher price. For instance, don't tell a photographer that you must have your prints the day after the shooting because he or she also has his or her own schedule. Always consider other people's time limitations and scheduling activities. Realize that other people's activities do not revolve around you and your needs. They have other people putting demands on them, just as you are.

Be Flexible

Always allow extra time in your planning and schedules. Allow extra time when going to appointments for transportation delays or any mishaps that might occur. Allow grace periods for people doing work for you. For example, planning to leave town on the same day the printer has promised your new composites is not very smart. If they are not completed on time or are not satisfactory, you will have complications. Instead, leave a grace period to allow for possible problems. This lessens the pressure on everyone involved.

Think Ahead

Stock up on items you know you will need in the future. For example, when at the lab, get two prints of your favorite shot instead of one. You might save money this way, and you will have an extra you can always use. Remember to order another printing of your composite when you are down to your last 100 copies; do not wait until you have only one left.

Always Have a "Plan B"

A "Plan B" is an alternative plan to follow if things don't go the way you had initially planned them. You will find that events often don't occur as you thought, hoped, or planned that they would. Having alternative courses of action is always a good idea.

INVESTING IN YOUR CAREER

Any business requires capital to get started, and modeling is no exception. The amount of money you must invest in a modeling career is actually quite small compared to the amount you must invest in other businesses that yield comparable benefits. It will cost you time, money, and energy to present a marketable, professional image. Don't expect others to pay your way; no one owes you a chance in the modeling business. Being a model is a decision you make out of choice. Obtain a job in a related or unrelated area, and start saving money before you actually embark on a modeling career. Continue to work part-time and on weekends or nights to provide yourself with a cushion for security and extra investment money for modeling. It is important to realize that the greatest investment will be in the beginning of your career, before you actually know whether you will be successful in the modeling field. It is important to realize that taking risks is essential to building any business. It is impossible to predict with absolute certainty which prospective models will be successful; however, it is absolutely certain that models who invest nothing and take no risks also have no chance of success.

It is helpful to examine the expenses you will incur to establish and maintain your career as a model. To understand what is involved use the Investment Planner (Table 1). Complete this form at the beginning of your career. Arrange a meeting with your agent so she or he can discuss these areas of investment with you. Find out how much you'll need to invest and what your options are. Looking at the entire investment picture will help you to acquire the money you'll need and to spend it wisely. Using the Investment Planner throughout your career will help you to project your on going expenses.

Table 1 **Investment Planner**

Area		Total Amount
Hair	Hairstylists fees; hair supplies; miscellaneous	$_____
Makeup	Makeup artists fees, cosmetics	$_____
Grooming and skincare	Manicures, pedicures, facials, waxing, grooming and skincare supplies; dermatologists', dentists', and doctors' fees and medication	$_____
Wardrobe	Wardrobe to wear to modeling-related appointments; wardrobe for testings; wardrobe for assignments; totebag, garment bag, and totebag supplies	$_____
Instruction	Classes in modeling, acting, dancing, and exercise; makeup/hair lessons; seminars; workshops; conventions; competitions; books; magazines; etc.	$_____
Business tools	Telephone, telephone-answering machine or service, appointment book; postage, envelopes, and stationery for correspondence; business forms, etc.	$_____
Transportation	Airline tickets, buses, taxis, trains, car, etc.	$_____
Self-promotional tools	Photographers' fees for test photos; photographic prints; composite printing costs; portfolio case; photo duplication for glossies; set-up and printing costs for resumes; modeling agency costs for printing pictures in the agency model book and other agency promotional materials	$_____
Miscellaneous		$_____

ACQUIRING BUSINESS TOOLS

Acquiring good business and organizational skills will serve you well, regardless of the career or life-style you choose. The following explains business tools that a model needs.

The Appointment Book

An appointment book is one of a model's basic business tools. Your appointment book is used to help you to schedule your time and tasks and to ensure that you fulfill your appointments. Your appointment book will also be a valuable source of information for future reference. Write everything in it including information regarding appointments, interviews, and auditions, the names of co-workers, and expenses incurred while modeling (for example, taxi and bus fares, car mileage, and pay telephone calls). Record information in your appointment book daily. Update it by making notes when enroute to engagements or when waiting at auditions. Your appointment book should be carried with you at all times and should have the following characteristics.

- A handy size so that it can be carried in your purse, totebag, or portfolio. There should be one page allotted for each day to allow enough space for notations.
- An index for telephone numbers such as those of your agency, hairdressers, salons, makeup artists, stylists, photographers, printers, photo labs, models, airlines, and travel agencies.
- One or two pockets to store receipts for taxis, hotels, hairdressers, Polaroids from shootings, vouchers, business cards, etc.
- A page for important information, such as the person to contact in case of emergency, etc.
- Ample room at the bottom of each page or a special place to record expenses.
- A place to keep two or three composites. A larger supply will be in your portfolio.

Suggestions for Using the Appointment Book

- Always have your appointment book open to the current date when making modeling-related phone calls.
- Write down all kinds of pertinent information in this book, for example, the names of people you meet, makeup tips or other things you've learned, the amount of money you spend on parking fees, tolls, and other expenses. Write down workshops, seminars, agency functions, meetings with your booker, and any other information you receive from other models or your agency. Record everything, even if you are not sure whether it is important. The information may be useful in the future.
- At the end of each week, study what you accomplished by looking at your appointment book. Establish a plan for the upcoming week by making notes of what you want to accomplish on the Sunday page.
- Some of the appointments you will have will involve receiving services from experts such as hairstylists, makeup artists, and the like. Attach the Tipping Guide to the inside of your appointment book to ensure that you will reward others properly.

Tipping Guide

A model often needs services where tipping is expected. A model need not overtip, but neither should he or she be stingy. Tipping depends on the amount and quality of the service received. See Table 2 for guidelines.

Table 2   A Tipping Guide

Where	Who	How Much to Tip
Salon[a]	Hairstylist	10–15%
	Shampoo person (shampoo only)	$1.00 and up
	Hairstylist's assistant	5–10%
	Colorist	10–15%
	Go-for	$0.50–$1.00
	Manicurist/pedicurist	15% and up
	Coat check	$0.50–$1.00 and up
Restaurant	Waiter	15–20%
	Coat check	$0.50–$1.00 and up
	Parking valet	$0.50–$1.00
When traveling	Taxi driver	10–15%
	Bellperson	$0.50 per small item; $1.00 for each suitcase and large item
	Porter	$0.50 to $1.00 per item
	Delivery person	$0.50 to $1.00
	Hotel room attendant (maid)	$1.00 per night
	Restroom attendant	0.25 and up

[a]*In many salons there are specialists for different services (hairstyling, perming/coloring, nails, makeup, etc.), and each person is tipped according to the amount of each service itemized on your bill. In a general-service salon where one individual provides a variety of services, you tip according to the amount of the total bill. The information here is a basic guide, so use your own judgment.*

The Telephone as a Business Tool

The model uses the telephone for many reasons: to call his or her agency, to set up appointments, to take down booking and audition instructions, to follow up on contacts or leads, and much more. Because the telephone is often the first contact a model may have with an agent, client, or photographer, it is important to know how to use it as an effective business tool.

Telephone Technique

Observe the following points when using the telephone:

- Always identify yourself (first and last name) immediately. Even though you think the person you are calling should know you on a first-name basis, you may not be the only Kim, Sue, or John he or she knows. Recognizing a voice over a telephone is often difficult. It is rude to keep your listener guessing. To give only your first name when making business calls sounds childish and unprofessional.
- Speak slowly, clearly, and audibly.
- Use a cheerful tone of voice and be as courteous over the phone as you would be face to face. Smiling while you speak helps. Don't begin a conversation on a negative note.
- Don't try to solve complicated problems or complaints on the telephone. Whenever possible, call for an appointment to discuss the matter in person.
- Speak in a clear, affirmative tone that indicates that you have a definite purpose and that you are professional, mature, and confident.
- If you are calling someone, briefly state the purpose of your call right away. Don't assume that the other person knows who you are or why you are calling. Avoid beginning with excuses, apologies, or long introductory remarks.
- Listen attentively to the other person to avoid asking for information to be repeated. It is often a good idea to take notes. If directions or detailed information are given during the course of the call, repeat back the key points, such as date, time, location, and so forth, to

make sure you have taken them down correctly. Make use of booking, audition, and contact record forms found throughout the book.

- Always keep business calls as short as possible. An extended conversation is best conducted after business hours or in person. Plan your conversation before you make your call. Jot down key points you wish to discuss.
- Always keep a pen and paper by your phone.
- Don't make your caller wait.
- Don't eat, snap gum, or carry on other conversations while on the phone.
- Don't leave the line without excusing yourself first or for more than a few seconds.
- Always leave a pleasant feeling when you close a conversation.

How to Make Appointments by Telephone

In New York, nearly all models' appointments are made by the agency. However, after the initial contact is made, the model may be responsible for making follow-up calls. In most other cities, the model is given a rounds list (an alphabetical or geographical list of photographers, ad agencies, and other potential clients) and is responsible for arranging appointments on her own. In Europe, initial appointments are made by the agency. Follow-up calls are also made by the agency if there is a language barrier.

Requesting an Appointment with a Potential client

Right: "Hello, my name is _____. (Always give your first and last name.) I am a model with the _____ (agency name) and I'd like to stop by to _____. (Examine the list of good reasons for calling or requesting an appointment and then tell why you want to see the person.)

Wrong: "Hi, do you see models?"

"Hi, um, I am interested in getting into modeling. . . ."

"Hi, what kind of work do you do?"

"Hi, um, I'm just starting out and I don't have a composite or a portfolio or anything, but. . . ."

"Hi, do you do testing?"

"I'm going to be in town for the next two days and was hoping to get some jobs. . . ."

"Hi, I'm in the city and will have time to see you at 11:00." (This shows lack of respect for that person's time.)

Photographers and clients tend to put interviewing models at the bottom of their priorities. They tend to put off looking for new faces until they actually need one for a specific job. Interviewing models is time-consuming, nonincome generating, and often unproductive. When the model calls, these people will often say that they are too busy, are not in need of models at the present time, or have some other excuse. The key is being persistent without becoming a pest. You will often have to see a client or photographer several times before he or she decides to book you.

Reasons to Call or See a Client

Clients are busy people and should not be bothered with nonessentials. The following are good opportunities for calling or seeing a client.

- You are new to the business or have just arrived in town.
- The photographer has not seen you in person.
- You have a new composite.
- You have new pictures in your portfolio.

- You sent the client a composite and would like to meet him or her in person to show your portfolio.
- You have gained experience since you last saw the client.
- You have had special training you want the client to know about.
- There has been an important milestone in your career, such as a magazine cover, a national commercial, a print advertising campaign, a fashion layout, etc.
- Your agent wants you to see the client.
- You have been referred to the client by another person.
- You have acted on some advice the client gave you the last time you met.
- You have a new look, such as a new haircut or color, or you have lost weight or otherwise improved your appearance.
- You have just returned from modeling in another country or city.
- You have not seen the client for 3 months or longer.
- You have returned from a leave of absence due to vacation, illness, etc., and are ready to work again.
- You have changed agencies.
- You need to test and have some ideas for shots.
- You have read or heard that the client is working on a project or has an account for which you would be suitable.
- You read an article written by the client, saw him on television, etc. or saw his or her work in a recent publication and would like an opportunity to introduce yourself.
- You are appearing in an important fashion show, theatre production, etc., and would like to invite the client to see the performance.
- You need advice, direction, or help regarding your career.
- You have a booking or audition in the client's area and would like to stop by. A booking is a better excuse, but don't make up a false story.
- You saw in *The Red Book* that the client's agency handles accounts for products that are suited to your type. (This is a good reason to see casting directors and advertising agencies.)
- You have a 2- or 3-minute scene you would like to audition, or you would like to come in to play your voice tape. (This is also for casting directors of TV commercials.)
- The client told you to call or come back at a later date.
- You've heard the client is testing or you have seen test shots of other models and would like to be considered for testing.

After you have found a good system for making appointments, it is important to keep them. Keep promises you made during your calls. If you said you would stop by at 2:00 PM, be sure to arrive on time. Once you make an appointment, keep it. Cancel an appointment only when a booking or emergency arises, and never call and postpone appointments two or three times. Learn to stick to your schedule. If a booking or important appointment has detained you, call your next appointment and tell them the time you will arrive. Apologize for the inconvenience, but don't go into excuses. Always call and cancel as soon as you find you will not be able to make an appointment. When you make an appointment far in advance (one week or more), call to confirm it a couple of days in advance. If at all possible, do not cancel an appointment less than a day in advance.

**The Telephone as a
Time and Money Saver**

Making telephone calls can save you both time and money. If you are effective on the phone, you will be able to gain entry into numerous places to which you would not otherwise have access. There are so many models competing for assignments that the amount of time photographers and clients have available for interviewing is severely limited. With rare exceptions, sending a composite before telephoning is the best way to get a foot in the door.

To organize and save time, do the following.

- Set a definite number of telephone calls to make each day.
- Set aside 30 minutes to an hour per day to make calls.
- Try to complete all calls on your list during each telephoning session.
- Realize that it may take several hours or even days to reach the person you are calling.
- Call at times when you are most likely to reach clients. In the morning around 9:00 or 10:00 early in the week is a good time. Most clients, agents, etc. do not like to be bothered during lunch hour or at the end of the business day (4:30 or 5:00). Also Fridays are not good days for calling because most people are trying to wrap up their week's work.
- Have lists and telephone numbers ready before calling. Have paper, pen, and your appointment book open to the current date. Know your schedule before calling. Keep a supply of Contact Record forms (see Chapter 9) or 3 x 5 cards on your desk for recording names and important information and keep this in an alphabetical or chronological index file or ring binder.
- Arrange interviews in the same geographic area on one day, schedule other interviews on another day to avoid wasting time and money.
- Schedule appointments 30 minutes apart. Auditions may take longer because there may be other models waiting ahead of you.
- Put on makeup, do your hair, and dress as if you were going on appointments before you sit down to make your calls. This way you'll feel more attractive and professionally motivated; you will also be ready for spur of the moment opportunities.
- Whenever you reach an answering machine or service, always leave a message. Give your first and last names, telephone number, and your reason for calling. Even if you think the person has your number, leaving it will save him or her from having to look it up.

**Telephone-Answering
Machines and Services**

An answering service or machine is one of the most important tools a model can have because accessibility and availability are crucial to success. An agent who can reach you easily will always think of calling you first. Don't leave opportunities to chance by depending on a friend or relative who may not be at home or who may not be courteous on the phone. Also, it is important that you get accurate messages and that they are relayed to you promptly. Consider acquiring an answering machine or service.

The Answering Machine

This is a small machine ranging in price from about $75 to $300 that is attached to your home phone. It gives an outgoing message telling callers to reach you at a certain number or to leave their name and number so you can return the call as soon as possible. Incoming messages are recorded for a certain length of time, usually a minute or so. There are two types of answering machines: one type requires you to be where the machine is to retrieve the messages and the other enables you to obtain your messages by use of a remote device that you carry in a pocket or your purse.

The Answering Service

With an answering service, an operator at a switchboard answers and takes messages. The pickup service is the type that intercepts calls that come in on your home phone. The other type is a central message exchange, which is a separate phone number where callers can leave messages. You pay a monthly fee for these services. Some services also have an additional per-call charge. When considering live answering services, it is important that operators are courteous, competent, and helpful. Many times a good live answering service is preferred because callers will be more likely to talk to a person than to a machine.

The most important consideration with either type of service is that you check for calls frequently, at least a few times a day. A good time to check is just before lunch hour, in midafternoon, just before the close of the business day, or whenever more than 3 hours have elapsed. Even when it seems that you never get messages, the one time you fail to check is the time an important message will have been left. Be sure to return all calls promptly.

Business Supplies

It is a good idea to have professional-looking stationery on which your name and address are imprinted along with envelopes to accommodate photographs and other items you may be sending through the mail. You will also want organizational tools such as notebooks or three-ring binders to collect posing, makeup and hair ideas, magazine and newspaper articles of modeling interest, price lists and information on various services, and the like. In addition you will want to have on hand file folders or a drawer for storing important modeling papers, such as contracts, vouchers from jobs, agency rules of conduct, rounds lists, and so on.

KEEPING WRITTEN RECORDS OF YOUR BUSINESS

Keeping written business records will help you in many ways. They will help you to make plans, determine your progress, and decide where changes or improvements need to be made. There are several forms appearing throughout this book that can be useful to the model.

Keeping Track of Your Progress

The only way to tell how successful you are is to study the records you have been keeping and to compare them to the goals you have set. At the end of every week, complete a Progress Report form. It will also help you plan. Share this information with your booker and provide him or her with a copy along with Polaroids or contact sheets from testings or bookings you completed. Whether the progress report is negative or positive, it will motivate you to keep up the good work or improve, as the case may be.

MANAGING THE MONEY YOU EARN

Most of this book is devoted to how to perform on the job; however, advice will be scant once you start receiving checks for the work you have done. Agencies usually do not have classes to help you with financial matters and it is unwise to ignore this issue or to totally rely on someone else to handle it for you. Mastering money matters can be quite simple once you set an effective system into place.

Open a Checking Account

The day you begin planning a modeling career open a checking account that will be reserved for writing checks related to modeling expenses. These checks will help you to keep track of your business-related spending habits. If you are financially secure enough to maintain a minimum balance at all times, choose a NOW account or one that pays a small amount of interest monthly. Write checks for as many bills and purchases as possible. Keep your checkbook balanced to the penny, and save all canceled checks and statements from the bank for up to 3 years. When checks are not accepted, use money orders or charge accounts so you have a written record of payment. Obtain a separate checking account for your personal use.

Save All Receipts Get in the habit of saving all receipts, especially for items for which you pay cash. Save all receipts for parking garages, gas stations, and the like. Keep these in an envelope at the back of your appointment book; empty it and record the amounts daily. File these receipts in a large index card file box divided into months of the year.

Progress Report

©THE PROFESSIONAL MODEL'S HANDBOOK

MODEL _____ WEEK OF _____

Go-Sees	Auditions	Bookings	Testings
		Correspondence	Training

Money spent on modeling $ _____ Money earned modeling $ _____

Next Week: _____
_____
_____
_____
_____

(Use back of form if necessary)

238

Open a Passbook Savings Account, and Save a Portion of What You Earn

There are two reasons why this is important for models. First, modeling agencies do not take out taxes from models' checks, and you must save a portion of your earnings for income taxes, which are due on April 15 for the income earned during the previous year. The IRS recommends that you retain 20% of all income for this purpose. Another option is to pay taxes quarterly based on estimated income for the year. You will also have to pay Social Security for a self-employed person. Generally this is one and a half times higher than the average rate. Usually it is around 7%. Therefore, save about 30% of what you make. Missing deadlines at tax time or evading payment can cause you to incur severe penalties.

Second, you should retain at least an additional 10 to 20% for savings and investment. Modeling is a seasonal business, and all models experience plateaus throughout their careers. If you plan to make a career of modeling, you should continually save so that when your career is over (it will happen eventually), you will be able to invest in a new venture or at least have some flexibility regarding your future.

Obtain a Major Credit Card

This may not be easy if you are a beginner, because you won't be able to prove that you make a substantial steady income. Try to get a credit card from a local store and make payments on it conscientiously so you can prove to major credit card companies that you are not a risk. Credit cards are valuable for several reasons. They help you to establish credit, are convenient for making large purchases related to business, such as airline tickets, and in many instances are a necessary form of identification for cashing checks.

Keep Records of Money You Spend and Earn

Use The Model's Bookkeeping System shown here to keep track of your finances related to modeling. The best bookkeeping system is one that is easy to use and as undetailed as possible. Any system must be used daily to be effective and accurate. The simplest and most complete system involves three areas: expenses (money you spend), income (money you make), and billing (money you expect to be paid for the work you have completed). Be very conscientious about keeping accurate records. They will save you money and help you to make more money by teaching you how to be more productive and profit oriented.

Recording Your Expenses

The Expenses form is where you record money you've spent related to modeling. It's a good idea to mark in your appointment book every time you spend money on anything. List the item and the amount. This is the best way to keep track of your spending habits and to keep a record of your profit. Collect all receipts, and at the end of each day copy all amounts onto your Expenses form.

The following is a description of the information needed to complete each column on the form.

Column	Information
1	The date of payment.
2	To whom you paid the money.
3	A description or name of the product or service.
4	The total cost of the product or service.
5	The amount you paid.
6	The amount still owed.
7	The form of payment, check, cash, or money order.
8	In the comments column, note the date you received the bill to help remind yourself to pay it or any other special information.

239

Expenses

The Model's Bookkeeping System

Date	Paid to	Description	Total Cost	Amt. Paid	Amt. Still Owed	Payment Type	Tax Ded.	Comments

Recording Your Billings

The Billing form records information about money you expect to be paid from work you have done. After each booking, record the following.

Column	Information
1	Date of job.
2	The name of the photographer and name of company.
3	What you modeled, where the photos will appear.
4	The number of hours you worked. This should correspond to the hours on your voucher.
5	Your hourly/daily rate or the fee you are to be paid.
6	Multiply hours by rate and record the total.
7	If you had to pay for transportation or had to supply an item for the job, list the total amount. List client-approved expenses that were listed on your voucher. If the client paid cash for your expenses at the time of the booking, note the amount and write "paid cash" beside this information. Don't list expenses that were not client-approved; these will appear on your expense form.
8	Note the total amount of the voucher. If the client paid expenses at the time of the booking, eliminate the amount.
9	Subtract the amount of commission the agent will take.
10	When you receive your check, note the date of the check.
11	Note the amount of the check.
12	In the comments column, note any special information.

Billing	Date	Client	Description	Hours	Rate	Expenses	Total Amt.	Less Comm.	Date Paid	Amt. Paid	Comments
©THE PROFESSIONAL MODEL'S HANDBOOK											
The Model's Bookkeeping System											

Recording Your Income   The Income form is used to record money you have been paid minus expenses. Fill in the columns with the following information.

Column	Information
1	Date of the job.
2	The name of the client.
3	A description of the kind of modeling you did.
4	The amount of money you made minus expenses. Don't forget to subtract commissions.
5	Use the comments column to note miscellaneous information.

Income	Date	Source	Description	Amount	Comments
©THE PROFESSIONAL MODEL'S HANDBOOK					
The Model's Bookkeeping System					

Financial Summary   At the end of each month, it is a good idea to sum up all the entries on your Expenses form, all the entries on your Billing form, and all the entries on your Income form. This will help you to determine your financial progress in modeling.

Understand Your Tax Obligations   Just as everyone has to have a Social Security number to work, everyone must pay taxes on what they earn. If you make a minimum annual income as specified by the Internal Revenue Service (IRS), you must pay taxes. Your agent can tell you what the current minimum is, or you can find this information on the 1040 form issued by the IRS.

In the eyes of the government there is no valid excuse for not paying income tax. This includes ignorance of the law. No matter how young or how uninformed you are, if you have earned the minimum annual income, you must pay your taxes. If you try to avoid paying taxes, you will eventually incur severe penalities, which could include anything from penalty fees to imprisonment. You don't have to earn a high income to be investigated or audited. It is your responsibility to learn and obey the law.

You may want to hire an accountant to help you keep track of the taxes you owe as well as business expenses that are tax exempt. An accountant can save you money, time, and assure your peace of mind. However, you must realize that an accountant can make errors in figuring your taxes so that you pay less than you owe. Although the accountant is operating on your behalf, it is you who must accept responsibility and incur possible penalties. If you overpay, you will be issued a refund for the amount in excess of the amount that was due.

Tax Deductions   There are many legitimate business expenses that a model can claim as tax deductions. Some are clear-cut, whereas others fall into gray areas. For any single expense over $25 you must present a receipt or cancelled check. For items under $25, your notation in your diary is adequate for the IRS's purposes. If your deductions exceed your earnings, you will not have to pay taxes; however, you will still have to fill out a tax form showing your earnings and deductions to prove how you arrived at your conclusion. You must be able to explain the expenses and why they are reasonable and necessary to your business. It is important that you keep abreast of tax laws. Allowable deductions may change with each new presidential administration. The following is a list of common tax-deductible items for modeling.

- Business supplies such as stationary, ledgers, filing systems, appointment books, briefcases, and postage.
- Telephone, if it is in your name.
- Telephone-answering machine or service.
- Modeling promotional tools such as composites (photography, printing, etc.), glossies, resumes, demo tapes, portfolio case and prints, talent and agency promotional books, and directories.
- Business entertainment and gifts. If you attend a play (if you are an actor) or a fashion show (if you are a model), you can use this as a legitimate business expense by proving that it furthers your knowledge of your career. Note the time, place, date, amount of expense (tickets, transportation, etc.), people you entertained, their business relationship to you, and the business purpose of the entertainment.
- Transportation: Parking, airline tickets, tolls, taxi fare and tips, bus and subway fares, and mileage (your car) are all deductible if necessary for the job. Your trips to and from the agency are not deductible.

242

- Clothing: Certain items of clothing are tax deductible if reserved only for assignments and auditions and not for personal use, for example, when you have to furnish wardrobe, such as an evening gown or specific costume, that you would not ordinarily need to purchase.
- Business clothing upkeep such as laundry and repair.
- Education: This includes lessons and classes for modeling and related skills such as acting, singing, and dancing. Because these activities further your career, they are deductible. Health club memberships are usually not deductible because they are considered personal rather than a business expense.
- Hair: Haircuts and hair products, as long as you can prove they are essential to enhance your career success.
- Makeup: Makeup artist's fees, products, etc.
- Commissions: Commissions paid to agents managers, etc.
- Union dues: SAG, AFTRA, etc.
- Trade association memberships: Membership dues in organizations for fashion businesspeople, models, actors, etc.
- Professional fees: Fees to lawyers, accountants, bookkeeper (tax preparation), dermatologist, cosmetic surgeons, and dentists.
- Trade publications: Fashion magazines and books related to modeling, acting, or advertising.

When in doubt about other tax deductions, check with your tax accountant.

Obtain Insurance

Everyone should have a health and accident insurance plan. An illness or injury could present a major setback not only because of lost work but because of hospital and doctor bills. Insurance takes care of some or all of these expenses. Without adequate insurance the money you will need to get started again will have been used to pay bills. You should also have personal property insurance. This is insurance on valuable property, such as jewelry, expensive clothing, and your car. A model can even insure his or her portfolio for the cost of replacing the prints and other items it contains.

For more information on insurance, refer to "On-the-Job Insurance" in this chapter.

Maintain Ethical Financial Dealings with Others

Always maintain ethical financial dealings with others. Assume there is a charge for every service and product you receive and always spell out clearly at the outset of an arrangement what amount you will be expected to pay, how, and when. Always get written receipts for money you've paid so there is no confusion on your or the other person's part. Never give a bad check to a printer, photographer, or other individual or firm. Not only is this unethical, it is illegal.

Never try to avoid paying a bill. If a person has completed a task for which you agreed to pay a certain amount, and you avoid payment, this proves that you are a dishonest person. Be aware that news of such dishonesty will be circulated among your agent, competitors, and prospective clients and will affect their attitude toward you. In addition more serious consequences may befall you. The unpaid firm or individual may enlist a bill collection firm to hound you until the money is paid or begin with legal proceedings.

In most situations, payment in full is required when a product or service is delivered to you. If someone doesn't have this type of arrangement, but bills you, pay the full amount as soon as possible. Most companies will give you up to 30 days to pay before beginning legal or collections procedures.

Be forewarned that because models tend to be financially undesirable to deal with, that many of the printers, photographers or other businesses whose services or products you require will accept only cash or money orders.

Managing the Money You Earn

When you begin modeling, the biggest challenge is to figure out how you can make money. After the checks begin to come in the next biggest challenge will be managing your money. After you take care of the basics, such as expenses and taxes, you will be able to make your money work for you. A model's career is similar to that of a professional athlete's; the money is excellent but the career is short. A model's good earning years will last anywhere from 2 to 10 years, with exceptions. The model's objective should be to earn the greatest amount of money in a limited amount of time. During this time he or she should save and invest money wisely. Investing and saving ensure options for beginning a new career or business once modeling opportunities dwindle.

Because of overspending, poor investments, or entrusting their money to the wrong individuals, some models are penniless even after lucrative modeling careers. Even a model who is cautious will find that inflation, taxes, and the cost of living can deplete spending power and depreciate assets. Making money is not the only key to financial success; holding onto money and making it grow is equally important.

Even if you don't earn a lot of money after you have covered expenses and paid taxes, you should save and invest as much as you can. Good financial planning will help you to endure slow periods, which are a part of the modeling business. There are many good investment opportunities that can be obtained for as little as $500. Good money management requires constant study of current economic trends and information on investments. It can even develop into a challenging hobby or second career.

The model earning $10,000 a year and the one earning $1,000,000 a year have one thing in common: they both make the ultimate decision on how their financial matters will be handled. It is the model's responsibility to decide who will handle or manage his or her money. The model must also decide where to seek counsel on money matters. To get started on a sound plan, observe the following points:

- Never rely totally on another person to handle your financial matters. Accept the challenge and responsibility of spending, saving, and investing your money. Rely on several information sources to formulate your final judgments. Models sometimes rely on friends or family members to act as their financial advisors or turn their money over to an accountant to manage. They dismiss this with the attitude that their advisors will take care of everything. Although you do not need to be totally distrustful of everyone, you should realize that the lure of money often alters peoples' behavior.

- Learn as much as you can about money management by gathering information and asking questions. There are many ways to increase your knowledge of finance. You can study books and magazines devoted to money, some of which are geared to beginners. There are newsletters and television programs that specialize in investment information. It is also helpful to talk to bankers, investment counselors, accountants, stock brokers, and tax attorneys.

- When working with your money, consider that it should be invested in ways that reflect your values. If you are the conservative type, stick to more conservative kinds of investments with which you will feel comfortable. It is best to start small. Once you have done a few low-risk investments and have gained some confidence, you can gradually move up to higher-risk and greater-return ventures.

- Make sure your investments are diversified. In other words, avoid investing in only one area, such as the stock market or real estate. You reduce the risk of losing money if you invest in several different ventures. Consider all options including Individual Retirement Accounts (IRA), stocks, bonds, limited partnerships, certificates of deposit, and money market funds. Some models incorporate themselves,and the corporation then receives their earnings and pays them a salary. The rest of the money held by the corporation is not taxable until used. Insurance benefits are tax deductible for the corporation. There are many other ways to manage your money that can be suggested by a lawyer, accountant, or other qualified individual. Avoid "get rich quick" schemes as they rarely live up to their labels.
- Be careful in selecting people who will invest or keep track of your money. Don't rely unconditionally on contacts that other models, your colleagues, or friends may recommend to you. Check them out on your own. It is unwise to try to imitate the way other people handle their money, especially if they seem to have financial savvy that you may lack. Before entrusting your money to any individual or firm, ask for a reference from a bank and a major law firm. It is also helpful to ask for client references and to talk to a few who have had dealings with the individual or firm over a period of years.

LEGAL MATTERS AND OTHER CONCERNS

The modeling business, like any other business, has aspects that deal with the law. The most common legal documents that a model will encounter are model's releases and contracts.

The Model's Release

The model's release is a form signed by the model that allows a photographer or client the right to sell or use pictures that were taken of him or her for commercial purposes. Some studios and advertising agencies have their own releases drawn up by a lawyer, whereas others use standard forms. The wording of model's releases may vary but most cover the points of the one shown in Figures 1–3. In addition to the model's signature on the release, another factor must exist to make a release valid: there must be some exchange of consideration. Consideration means a dollar amount (the minimum is $1.00) or something of value that amounts to $1.00 or more, such as a photographic print. Of course, the rate or fee a model is paid for a booking is valid consideration to make a release legal.

It is important to realize that when a model accepts a booking, it is with the understanding that she will sign a release at the conclusion of the session. It is important that the agent obtain complete, accurate information from the client about what will be involved and that the agent inform and advise the model accordingly. It is at this point that the model decides whether to accept the job, not after the shooting when she is to sign the release. Releases are never signed before a photo session; however, occasionally a client may ask the model to sign an agreement prior to the session that outlines what will be expected of her. For example, if the client books a model for an assignment involving special circumstances such as partial nudity, he or she will not want to encounter any surprises when the model appears at the shooting claiming that she knows nothing about such circumstances.

MINOR RELEASE

In consideration of the engagement as a model of the minor named below, and for other good and valuable consideration herein acknowledged as received, upon the terms hereinafter stated, I hereby grant to [PHOTOGRAPHER], his/her legal representatives and assigns, those for whom [PHOTOGRAPHER] is acting, and those acting with his/her authority and permission, the absolute right and permission to copyright and use, re-use, publish, and re-publish photographic portraits or pictures of the minor or in which the minor may be included, in whole or in part, or composite or distorted in character or form, without restriction as to changes or alterations from time to time. in conjunction with the minor's own or a fictitious name, or reproductions thereof in color or otherwise, made through any medium at his/her studios or elsewhere, and in any and all media now or hereafter known, for art, advertising, trade, or any other purpose whatsoever. I also consent to the use of any printed matter in conjuction therewith.

I hereby waive any right that I or the minor may have to inspect or approve the finished product or products or the advertising copy or printed matter that may be used in connection therewith or the use to which it may be applied.

I hereby release, discharge, and agree to save harmless [PHOTOGRAPHER], his/her legal representatives or assigns, and all persons acting under his/her permission or authority or those for whom he/she is acting, from any liability by virtue of any blurring. distortion, alteration, optical illusion, or use in composite form, whether intentional or otherwise, that may occur or be produced in the taking of said picture or in any subsequent processing thereof, as well as any publication thereof, including without limitation any claims for libel or invasion of privacy.

I hereby warrant that I am of full age and have every right to contract for the minor in the above regard. I state further that I have read the above authorization, release. and agreement, prior to its execution, and that I am fully familiar with the contents thereof. This release shall be binding upon me and my heirs, legal representatives. and assigns.

DATE: _____

_____   _____
(MINOR'S NAME)   (FATHER) (MOTHER) (GUARDIAN)

_____   _____
(MINOR'S ADDRESS)   (ADDRESS)

_____
(WITNESS)

ADULT RELEASE

In consideration of my engagement as a model, and for other good and valuable consideration herein acknowledged as received, I hereby grant to [PHOTOGRAPHER]. his/her heirs, legal representatives and assigns, those for whom [PHOTOGRAPHER] is acting, and those acting with his/her authority and permission, the absolute right and permission to copyright and use. in his/her own name or otherwise, and use. re-use. publish. and re-publish photographic portraits or pictures of me or in which I may be included. in whole or in part, or composite or distorted in character or form, without restriction as to changes or alterations, in conjuction with my own or a fictitious name, or reproductions thereof in color or otherwise, made through any medium at his/her studios or elsewhere, and in any and all media now or hereafter known for illustration, promotion, art. advertising, trade, or any other purpose whatsoever. I also consent to the use of any printed matter in conjunction therewith.

I hereby waive any right that I may have to inspect or approve the finished product or products and the advertising copy or other matter that may be used in connection therewith or the use to which it may be applied.

I hereby release, discharge and agree to save harmless [PHOTOGRAPHER], his/her heirs, legal representatives and assigns, and all persons acting under his/her permission or authority or those for whom he/she is acting, from any liability by virtue of any blurring, distortion, alteration, optical illusion, or use in composite form, whether intentional or otherwise, that may occur or be produced in the taking of said picture or in any subsequent processing thereof, as well as any publication thereof, including without limitation any claims for libel or invasion of privacy.

I hereby warrant that I am of full age and have the right to contract in my own name. I have read the above authorization, release, and agreement, prior to its execution, and I am fully familiar with the contents thereof. This release shall be binding upon me and my heirs. legal representatives, and assigns.

DATE: _____   _____
                                      (NAME)

_____   _____
(WITNESS)   (ADDRESS)

SIMPLIFIED ADULT RELEASE

For valuable consideration received, I hereby grant to [PHOTOGRAPHER] the absolute and irrevocable right and permission, in respect of the photographs that he/she had taken of me or in which I may be included with others, to copyright the same, in his/her own name or otherwise; to use, re-use, publish, and re-publish the same in whole or in part, individually or in conjunction with other photographs, and in conjunction with any printed matter, in any and all media now or hereafter known, and for any purpose whatsoever, for illustration, promotion, art, advertising and trade, or any other purpose whatsoever; and to use my name in connection therewith if he she so chooses.

I hereby release and discharge [PHOTOGRAPHER] from any and all claims and demands arising out of or in connection with the use of the photographs, including without limitation any and all claims for libel or invasion of privacy.

This authorization and release shall also inure to the benefit of the heirs, legal representatives, licensees, and assigns of [PHOTOGRAPHER], as well as the person(s) for whom he/she took the photographs.

I am of full age and have the right to contract in my own name. I have read the foregoing and fully understand the contents thereof. This release shall be binding upon me and my heirs, legal representatives, and assigns.

DATE: _____   _____
                                            (NAME)

                                    _____
_____
        (WITNESS)   (ADDRESS)

Releases are never signed for test jobs. In a test job a model is paid for testing out an idea with the photographer for the client. If a model signs a release, the client could theoretically use the pictures taken at the test job for the intended advertisement, thereby saving money on the actual shooting, bonuses, and other sums that would be due the model depending on the use of the photo.

Model's releases are also usually not signed at the conclusion of a test session. Test pictures are not intended for publication. The model's agent will always advise against signing a release; however, a model may agree to do so if she chooses. When a release is signed at the end of a test shooting and the photographer gives the model consideration, he or she forfeits any money that is made from the photograph. Photographers often sell slides they have taken to stock photo agencies who in turn sell the photo to ad agencies and other concerns needing a photo for an ad or for other reasons. The photographer receives a royalty or other fee each time the photo is sold.

Sometimes a model may choose to sign a modified release. For example, she may cross out certain statements on the release or she may add a provision of her own. If she intends to do this, the matter must be discussed with her agent and the client prior to the shooting. Also, any statements that are altered or added to the release must be initialed by the model.

Minor Release

Sometimes a minor release is used instead of the normal adult release. Any model under the age of 18 must have the signature of a parent or guardian on the model release. Models' releases may vary in wording, so it is wise to read them over before signing.

Contracts

A model who achieves any level of success at one time or another will encounter contracts. The most common types of contracts he or she will encounter are listed here.

The Modeling Agency Contract

Modeling agency contracts describe what the agency will do for the model and what the model is supposed to do (see Figure 4). They state the amount of commission the agent will be paid, how the model's money for assignments will be collected, and how the model will be paid. Most modeling agency contracts state that the model will receive all modeling assignments and related engagements through the modeling agency only and that the agent will negotiate the model's fee and terms. The jurisdiction of a modeling contract usually covers only a single major market. For example, this means that a model can legally sign a contract with one agency in Los Angeles and another agency in New York. In addition to geographic jurisdiction these contracts also contain a clause stating the length of the contract (usually 2 years).

Figure 4. Sample modeling agency contract.

CONTRACT

Agency Agreement entered into this _____ day of _____, 19 ____, by and between

_____(Agency Name), a _____

(incorporation details) hereinafter called the "Agency", having its principal place of

business at _____ (agency address) and _____

_____(Model's Name), hereinafter called "Model", residing at

_____ (Model's address).

1. The Model hereby employs the Agency to obtain modeling and acting capacities in live fashion shows, print media, electronic media and live promotions and related engagements for her or him, and the Agency accepts such employment and agrees to use its best efforts to procure such engagements for the Model.

2. In consideration for your agreement to manage my career, I the undersigned, hereby employ you to act as my exclusive manager to direct my career as a model and actress or actor only and agree to accept from you for my services a gross sum equal to 85% of all monies you receive in connection with my modeling assignments, or monies received as a result of contracts made that I do during the term of this contract.

3. The terms of this contract are for two (2) years from the date executed below. The contract is automatically renewed each year thereafter unless written notice is given to you from me terminating this agreement. The contract will then be terminated ten (10) days after your receipt of my notification.

4. You are hereby appointed by lawful attorney in fact with full authority to demand, collect and receive in my name any and all payments, whether by cash, check or otherwise, to which I may become entitled; to make, execute and deliver receipts; and endorse, deposit and collect any check, note, draft or other instrument for the payment of monies that may be payable to my order; and to sign photographic releases and to do and perform any matter or thing whatsoever for and on behalf and in my name, all in connection with my services in the field covered by this agreement.

5. It is agreed that you will pay me a gross amount of 85% of the face amount of my signed vouchers, and in the event you are unable to collect said amount from the client, I agree that I will suffer the loss. This guarantees against loss of course, and does not cover legitimate client disputes or adjustments.

6. It is agreed that on all AFTRA, SAG and EQUITY employment the commission of 10% will be paid to the Agency.

7. In consideration of payments to be made by you to me, I hereby agree that you own the proceeds of the modeling assignments against which the payments are made.

8. You are hereby authorized to use my name, portrait and pictures to advertise and publicize me in connection with your representation of me.

9. The _____(Agency Name) is an _____ (incorporation detail)

licensed by the _____ (Government Department) and franchised by

_____ (Performer's Unions).

The parties hereto have executed this agreement the _____ day of

_____, 19 ____.

Signature_____ Model

Signature _____ Agent

When a model signs a contract with the television department of a modeling agency, he or she signs a modeling agency contract that is approved by SAG or AFTRA if the agency is franchised by one of these unions. This type of modeling agency contract must adhere to certain union provisions. Some of these provisions are the following.

- Talent can sign only for 1 year the first time with a particular agent. If the model is pleased and would like to sign again, he or she can do so for up to 1 year at a time.
- Talent has a 91-day out clause that allows the talent to get out within that period of time if it is felt that the agent is not working hard enough on behalf of the talent.
- Talent must earn $2000 or more within the 91 days or the agent may terminate the contract.

SAG Union Standard Contracts

When a model makes a television commercial under the jurisdiction of the Screen Actors Guild, he or she must sign a standard employment contract for television commercials. This contract gives the commercial maker the right to use the commercial and ensures the exclusivity of the talent. The talent cannot make a commercial for a competing or conflicting product after this contract has been signed. For more information, see Chapter 11.

Exclusivity Contracts

These contracts are signed for print and promotional assignments when a model agrees to lend her face, name, and talents to a client exclusively. He or she agrees to refuse assignments from clients producing a competing product for the length of time stated on the contract.

Other Contracts

There may be other instances in which a model must sign a contract. For example, whenever the amount of a single job exceeds $5000, in accordance with the U.S. Commercial Code, a contract must be signed.

Recommendations for Dealing with Contracts

There are several points to keep in mind.

- Don't sign a contract without first reading and understanding it.
- Don't sign unless you are given 24 hours to think about it. (This would not apply to SAG Television Commercial Contracts. Your agent or producer will tell you beforehand what you will be expected to sign.)
- Live up to all contractual agreements you enter. Models who fail to fulfill contractual obligations are not only operating unethically but are in violation of the law. You have only one reputation to protect.
- Keep records of all legal documents you have signed.

Reading and Understanding Contracts

Look for the following points in a contract. If you do not understand any part of a contract, ask the person giving you the contract for clarification. If you are still uncertain, take the contract to a lawyer, your agent, or other individual who may be able to help you check out its provisions.

- Find out the geographic jurisdiction of the contract.
- Find out the duration of the contract. Note how long the contract lasts.
- Find out the fees, commissions, or other monies to which the agent, photographer, or other individual with whom you are signing the contract is entitled.
- Find out what skills, abilities, and the like are required by the contract. Find out what your obligations are.

- Determine how the contract is renewed. Your will want to know if it is automatically renewed unless you have given written notice prior to its expiration or if there is some other provision for renewal.
- Find out on what grounds the contractor can terminate his or her arrangement with you.
- Find out on what grounds you can terminate the agreement made with the contractor.

Dealing with Legal Disputes

With hope you will never be involved in legal disputes in connection with your modeling career. There are several ways you can protect yourself and avoid legal problems. The first, most obvious way is to be fully informed about the laws that affect your business.Obtaining a qualified model's agent who can advise you about such matters will be the best way to take care of this aspect. Second, conduct yourself in an honest manner. For example, if you have signed a contract, abide by its provisions. Third, carefully research every person and situation you may encounter before any business transactions take place.

Even though you may conduct yourself in a legal and ethical manner, there may be times when other people infringe on your rights. If someone does something which infringes on your legal rights, you must always consider the seriousness and actual damage such infringement causes to your reputation or career. It is always best to try to solve problems in a simple, humane, and equitable manner. Talking directly and in a mature, open-minded, honest way to try and reach an agreement that is suitable for you and the other person is always a good way to settle a dispute. You should always try this course before enlisting a lawyer. Unless an infringement seriously jeopardizes your stature or career, you may find that calling in lawyers will make you the biggest loser and the lawyers the biggest winners. You may win your case, but there are other things you must consider. If you choose to involve lawyers or even threaten legal action against another individual, you may find your career to be over suddenly. News of how you deal with others will travel quickly through the modeling and photographic communities and will cause people to avoid you. Rather than risking possible legal problems, they will opt to not deal with you at all.

ON-THE-JOB INSURANCE

On-the-job insurance as it applies to models often is the responsibility of someone else. This is usually the photographer, producer, or other individual for whom you are working. One large expense that photographers have is insurance, not only on their valuable equipment, but also to protect themselves and others from mishaps in the workplace.

Many photographers and electronic media producers and directors belong to professional associations that offer insurance packages. However, when an accident occurs that is clearly your fault, you should make every effort to offer a solution or monetary reimbursement. For example, if you trip on a cord causing the photographer's camera to fall and break, even though his or her insurance probably covers that type of incident, you should offer (and be prepared) to reimburse him. Your client and the photographer will respect you for being responsible.

If an accident on the job causes you injury, the photographer's insurance probably will have a liability clause. This means that his or her insurance will cover a specified amount of your medical bills. On the other hand, a photographer may not have proper insurance coverage. He or she may not be able to afford it or may have failed to obtain or renew his or her policy. Therefore, it is always important to have your own adequate medical insurance coverage.

If you damage or lose an item furnished by the client, most photographers' insurance will cover it; however, there is usually a deductible amount. For example, if the deductible amount is $200 and the item cost less than that amount, the insurance will not cover it. In such cases, you should be prepared to pay for a replacement. If the item is worth more than $200, you should offer to pay the $200. The insurance will cover the amount over $200.

Many people don't place importance on insurance until an accident or other mishap occurs. They may have the misconception that other people will take responsibility for them, but this is not the case. It is wise to protect yourself as fully as you can.

Chapter 9 The Model's Guide to Self-Promotion

No matter what career you pursue, you will need to promote yourself. Selling others on your qualifications for an opportunity is something you will do all your life. In modeling, self-promotion is very important. You may be extremely attractive and talented, but if people in influential positions don't know about you, you won't progress far.

HOW MODELS PROMOTE THEMSELVES

There are several ways in which models promote themselves. The most common ways are by distributing self-promotion tools and by the model attending self-promotional appointments.

Self-Promotion Tools

The most common self-promotion tools used by models are the composite, glossy, portfolio, resume, and voice tape. These self-promotion tools are distributed or shown to potential clients. Clients utilize these tools to help determine which models might be suitable for a proposed assignment. The type of promotion tool used is determined by the type of work the model or talent is seeking.

Composite

A composite is a printed promotional brochure or calling card onto which the model's best black and white or color photos are reproduced (Figure 1). The model will usually have a quantity of 500 to 2000 composites, depending on the market(s) in which she intends to seek work. The model and her agency distribute a composite to every photographer, client, or other concern who might consider using his or her services. In addition to the pictures, the composite lists his or her name and relevant measurements, and the name and telephone number of his or her agency.

Figure 1a. Example of a model's composite (four-sided). Courtesy Click Model Management, New York.

LISA KAUFFMANN

Height 5'10 Dress Size 8 Bust 34B Waist 24 Hips 35½ Shoes 8½ Hair Blonde Eyes Blue SAG

Hauteur 1.78 Confection 36 Poitrine 86 Taille 61 Hanches 90 Chaussures 41 Cheveux Blonds Yeux Bleus

Figure 1b. Example of a model's composite. Courtesy, Pauline's Model Management, New York/Paris.

The most common type of composite is the 5 x 8-inch (15 x 21 cm) card type, which is also called a "card" or "Zed card." A basic composite is in black and white and has one photo on the front and three photos on the back. Minicomps or one-sided composites have one or two photos printed on one side only. They are cheaper than regular composites and are an excellent alternative for the beginning model who doesn't have several good photos or who doesn't want to make a large initial investment. One-sided composites are also useful for the model who is between composites. The most elaborate cards are printed in color on very high gloss or laminated heavy card stock and may fold out to have as many as six sides.

Another form of composite measures 8½ x 11 inches and is printed on paper stock. Like the smaller card-type composite it may have one, two, or three pages of color or black and white photos printed on both sides.

Composites are used by all models seeking print modeling work. Models in search of work in live promotions and fashion shows also use composites. Sometimes actors seeking work in television commercials also have composites. Hairstylists, makeup artists, and stylists attempting to style models' hair, makeup, and clothing for fashion shows, print, electronic media, and live promotional assignments also use composites to display pictures of models on which they have styled the hair, makeup, and clothing.

In most markets, the 5 x 8 European card-type composite described above is preferred; however, in some markets the larger paper-type composite is still used by commercial, character, and promotional models. The selection of photos to be displayed on the card is dependent on the model's look and the types of assignments he or she is seeking. For specific information on required shots for various types of models or talent, consult the section "A Step-by Step Guide to Making a Composite" in this chapter.

Commercial Headshot   A commercial headshot or glossy is a black and white 8 x 10 mass-produced photograph of a headshot of a model or talent (Figure 2). The individual's name also appears on the glossy. Glossies are the standard self-promotion tool used by models and actors who seek work in electronic media productions, such as television commercials. The talent or her agent distribute a glossy to every casting director, electronic media producer, or other concern who might require her services. The type of headshot displayed will depend on the talent's "type." For more specific information, consult "The Commercial Headshot" in this chapter.

CYNDI WYATT

Figure 2. A commercial headshot.

Resume   A resume is an 8 x 10 or 8½ x 11 sheet of paper containing an organized typewritten or typeset list of information about the model's experience, training, and other qualifications relevant to the assignments she is seeking (Figure 3). There are basically two types of resumes used by models: a resume that is designed to secure work in electronic media productions and is attached to the back of a glossy and a resume that is designed to secure work in live promotions. For more information on assembling a resume, consult the section "The Resume" in this chapter.

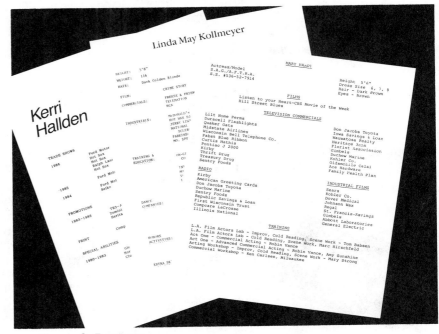

Figure 3. Resumes.

Portfolio   A portfolio is a 8 x 10, 9 x 12, or 11 x 14 scrapbook containing 10 to 20 black and white and color prints and slides from testing the model has done as well as clippings from published materials in which she has been featured (Figure 4). Models seeking print work must have portfolios. Those seeking work in live promotions and fashion shows also commonly need portfolios; however, portfolios are rarely needed by those in search of electronic media assignments. The portfolio is shown to a potential client when the model appears for an appointment, or it is sent to the client. The portfolio affords the client a very complete look at the model's experience and abilities. The content of the portfolio is dependent on the type of work the model or talent is seeking. For more information, consult "The Model's Portfolio" in this chapter.

Figure 4. A standard-size portfolio and miniportfolio.

Figure 5. A voice tape.

Voice Tape   A voice tape is a professionally produced cassette or reel-to-reel audio tape that exhibits samples of the talent's recorded voice expressing a variety of styles and moods (Figure 5). Voice tapes are used by individuals seeking voice-over work. The content of the voice tape is dependent on the type of voice the talent has and the type of work he is seeking. For more information, consult the section "The Voice Tape" in this chapter.

Optional Self-Promotion Tools   The self-promotion tools described below are not required tools for obtaining assignments. A model or actor will use them in addition to the items previously described.

Audition Tape   An audition tape is a videotape containing clips from electronic media productions, such as television commercials and programs in which the model has appeared (Figure 6). It may also or instead include a reading of a script that the individual has selected to demonstrate his or her acting ability or performing talents (for example, an ability to sing or dance). This tape is shown or copies are distributed to clients casting models and talent for electronic media productions and live promotions.

Figure 6. An audition tape.

Composite-Glossy

A composite-glossy is a mass-produced 8 x 10 sheet of photographic paper displaying two to four color or black and white shots of a model (Figure 7). Composite-glossies are cheaper, available in smaller quantities, and take less time to produce than printed promotional pieces. They are often used by beginning models, models who are between composites, and specialty models. They are also sometimes employed by promotional models, electronic media models, makeup artists, hairstylists, and stylists. They are most commonly used by child models.

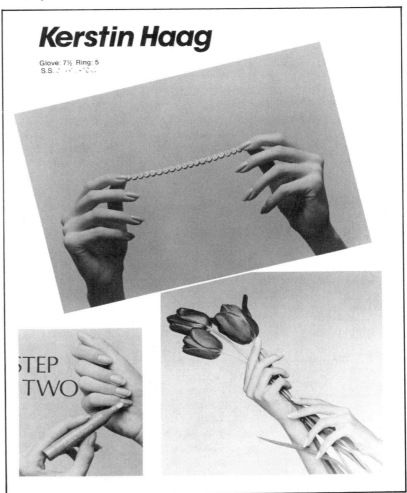

Figure 7. A composite-glossy of a hand model.

Postcards, Talent Cards, and Greeting Cards

Some models use 3 x 5 postcards displaying one of their newest, best color, or black and white photos printed on one side. On the back a message can be written and the card can be mailed to a client. For example, a model who has worked successfully for a client is clever if she sends one of these postcards in advance of a trade show for which she was booked the previous year. This is a timely reminder for the client and will increase the model's chances of being booked again. A model might also use postcards to keep his clients posted on his whereabouts and progress when he is out of town. For example, if he is modeling in Europe, he might have one of his outstanding recent European pictures printed on postcards and sent to his valued clients at home, indicating his planned date of return.

Some models and modeling-related talents (for example, stylists) send holiday greeting cards displaying a recent or holiday-oriented photo of themselves or their work to clients and other business contacts (Figure 8). The model might include a 3 x 5 mass-produced color glossy print placed inside a standard greeting card, or she may have a special photo card made. Art supply stores sell blank cards with matching envelopes to which a color photograph can be adhered.

Figure 8. Greeting cards.

Self-Promotional Appointments

Once the model has acquired some photographs and knowledge, he will be sent on promotional appointments. Promotional appointments are in-person meetings with potential clients so that the model can present his skills and assets to the client. These are sales calls that afford the model the opportunity to impress the client with his looks, abilities, and personality. For more information, see "Self-Promotional Appointments" in this chapter.

HOW MODELS ASSEMBLE SELF-PROMOTION TOOLS

The process of acquiring your self-promotion tools will help you to fine tune your best looks and increase your modeling skills. However, before you begin working toward these tools, you should have a basic idea of your "type" and the kinds of modeling assignments for which you are best suited. To be most effective, the model must gear her self-promotion tools to specified types of clients. Understanding your competitive advantages and then capitalizing on them is also important. Consult the information in Chapter 1 and confer with agents to determine what your objectives should be. It is always best to have an interested agent to guide you through the process of acquiring your self-promotion tools.

Formalizing Your Approach

Achieve your best, most marketable image before you begin promoting yourself. If suggestions have been made, follow them now, before you begin spending money, time, and effort on photographs. Lose excess weight, get a better haircut, or clear up your skin. You'll want your pictures to show you at your best. Clients will not try to visualize how you would look after certain improvements have been made.

Your approach or "package" includes your hair, makeup, wardrobe, physical presentation, and personality as well as the professional name you will use. Although many models do not have modeling names, some do find it advantageous to adopt a professional name. Now is the time to make a decision about the modeling name you will use. If your name is long and complicated, consider shortening it or changing it to something that clients will be able to pronounce and remember easily. If your name is very plain or common or doesn't work with the image you are trying to project, you might also want to change it.

There are other considerations involved when adopting a professional name. If your given or proposed professional name is the same or very similar to that of another model or actor currently working in your market, you will want to change your name. Two people with the same or similar names will confuse agents and clients. Also, if you plan to become a member of the Screen Actors Guild, you cannot use the same name as someone else already in the union.

You may wish to use your middle name as a last name if it is unique or sounds like a last name. You might use your mother's maiden name or other family names. If these ideas yield no possibilities, select a name from the telephone book that works well with your first name. When changing your name, avoid names that sound fabricated.

Sometimes a model will choose to use just one name. Many top models have chosen to use just their first names. Wilhelmina, Paulina, and Iman are examples. If you are considering this, do so only if your name is one-of-a-kind or very uncommon, otherwise it will confuse agents and clients. Another practice you might consider is to create one unique name. Top model Verushka was born Vera von Lehndorf. Twiggy's birth name was Leslie Hornby.

Planning Your Self-Promotion Tools

After formalizing your image or approach, you can begin making a plan for assembling effective, professional self-promotion tools. Understanding the types of tools you will need as well as their specific content and establishing a plan for acquiring them is important. Rely on agents and other experts in the field to give you suggestions. All models and talent need photographs for their self-promotion tools. The following information explains the methods used in acquiring the right kinds of photos.

How to Acquire Photos for Your Self-Promotion Tools

Testing is the most common way models acquire photos for their self promotion tools. Testings are practice photo sessions that help the model to gain experience in front of the camera. The model uses testing to experiment with ideas for posing, expression, makeup, and hair and for learning how to work with different photographers. The resulting photos from these sessions are used for the model's composite, glossy, and portfolio. A test differs from an actual assignment in that the results are not intended for publication and no payment to the model is involved. However, there are exceptions. Clients, photographers, and models engage in testing for different reasons. Basically four types of situations exist in regard to testing.

1. *Model or talent tests.* Photographer's fee and expenses paid by the model.
2. *Mutual tests.* Expenses paid jointly by the model and photographer.
3. *Photographer tests.* Expenses paid by the photographer.
4. *Client tests.* Expenses and partial fees for the model and photographer are paid by the client.

Model or Talent Tests

This type of arrangement commonly exists when a model is just beginning her career. The model needs photos for a portfolio or composite to convince other photographers and clients to photograph or book her. In this instance, the model needs very specific types of shots to prove her potential as a model, for example, basic headshots showing different facial angles, expressions, makeup, and hairstyles and body shots showing her legs and figure. Experienced models use photos from bookings (for example, magazine pages in which they are featured) for their self-promotion tools. However, even an experienced model may need to test when a specific shot is needed to round out a portfolio or composite. An actor, actress, or model seeking a good headshot to be used for a glossy nearly always consults a model or talent test photographer to obtain the formula-type of shot necessary for securing electronic media work.

In some instances, the model's agency will pay for testing. In such cases, the agency will advance money for model tests and subtract the sum from the model's forthcoming checks.

Model tests are the fastest, most efficient way for a model to obtain the pictures she or he needs. Because there is an exchange of money for services, the model and agent can dictate what types of shots will be taken and require the results within a specified time frame.

When an individual wishes to begin a modeling career, the first step he should take is to set up appointments with several modeling agencies so that they can evaluate his potential for success in modeling. This can also be done by mail (see Chapter 7). At this stage, all that is necessary, are informal, straightforward, personal snapshots. If the agency encourages you, they will give you the names of professional photographers of varying price range, expertise, and style. They will often want you to go to a photographer who specializes in model or talent tests because this type of photographer knows exactly what shots a new model needs. He or she is geared to selling the model's look and attributes, rather than what he is wearing or holding. It is always a good idea to work with the photographers the agency recommends as you can be assured that they are legitimate and will produce results that the agency will accept. The model should interview several and judge each according to the following considerations: area of specialization and style, services offered, competency, rapport, and cost.

Mutual Tests   In this type of testing, the expenses for shooting are shared by the model and the photographer. Photographers who enter into such arrangements are usually either beginners who need practice and pictures to build up their portfolios or established photographers who want to cut down on testing costs, while experimenting with new models, techniques, equipment, etc. Usually the cost of film and processing is split or a flat fee per roll is agreed upon; prints are paid for by each. The model and the photographer decide together on the type of photo they both need.

Traditionally testing was done by the model volunteering her services and the photographer giving her or him prints in exchange. The model and the photographer benefitted equally. However, today a photographer's costs are too high to allow him or her to enter into such arrangements frequently. Therefore, splitting the expenses helps to make the costs reasonable for both the model and the photographer.

Mutual tests are often a difficult way to acquire the pictures that a beginning model needs. This is because a photographer who is really good at taking pictures for models won't have the time or energy to shoot all the models who approach him or her. The not-so-good or inexperienced photographers may be ready and willing but aren't able to produce photos good enough to be used for a model's portfolio or composite. However, just because a photographer is a beginner doesn't mean he or she isn't talented. Neither are a nice studio and expensive equipment guarantees of good work—more important is how the photographer makes use of what he or she has. Make some discoveries of your own. Check your agency bulletin board. Investigate art schools, college photography departments, local camera stores, and camera clubs for photographers who are willing to do mutual tests.

Many good photographers are willing to do mutual tests. All they may need is some inspiration from you. Most photographers are inspired by great ideas and great models. If you have a unique idea for a shot, can organize interesting, unusual, or expensive or high quality clothing or jewelry, have access to an otherwise inaccessible

260

location, or can produce a beautiful or unconventional makeup or hairstyle, you stand a better chance of motivating photographers to test you. In other words, you will have to "sell" the photographer on doing the test.

Mutual tests are a good way to practice modeling, gain new ideas, try out new makeup and hair looks, as well as supplement, round out, or update portfolios and composites.

Photographer Tests   In this type of testing situation, a photographer pays for the cost of the shooting. He or she may do this for several reasons:

- To try out a model before booking him or her.
- To experiment with a lighting set up, equipment, film, location, or photographic technique.
- To use a model as a stand-in for the model who will actually be used for the assignment so as to judge concept and setting or to gain ideas for shooting a garment or item belonging to one of his clients.
- To acquire samples to show to a potential client or to include in his portfolio.

Photographers who are usually most willing to test at no charge are those who are very successful and well established. Staff photographers and their assistants at large studios often receive free film allowances and also frequently test to build their own portfolios. Individuals who dabble in photography or who have another source of income are also good contacts. These will be the types of people for the model to approach if he or she does not want to pay for photos. However, he or she should realize a few things about such arrangements.

- If the model does not intend to pay for the shooting, she or he can't expect to dictate what will be done. The person paying for it is the one who decides.
- Because there is no clear-cut agreement or exchange of money for services, the model has no recourse if the session is unproductive. Be forewarned that such arrangements often involve a lot of time and frustration. If you are not paying for it, the other person really doesn't have any clear-cut obligation to give you prints. Getting prints or slides from the shooting may be next to impossible, as photographers tend to put nonincome-generating tasks at the bottom of their "to-do" lists.
- Most people don't enter into arrangements expecting nothing in return. Occasionally you may meet individuals of both sexes who use photography as a way of meeting attractive young people. Sometimes a photographer is willing to photograph you at no cost because he or she would later like to shoot pictures of you in the nude or elicit sexual favors.

Photographer tests are the most difficult arrangement for the model's purposes. Usually when the photographer is paying for the shooting, she will select a model who is experienced and whose looks interest her. This is especially true if she is trying to do sample photographs for her own portfolio. Keep in mind that some photographers have no interest in shooting inexperienced models, whereas others enjoy making discoveries. In other words, you will have to wait for her to ask you to test. If she is interested, she will ask, with little or no prompting from you. (It is all right to mention that you admire her work and are interested in testing.)

If a photographer agrees to test at no charge, you may find it very difficult to set a definite date and time for a session; it may be even more difficult to obtain the results of your shooting. Such photographers are very busy and have little time. A gesture that might make the photographer remember you in a positive way and motivate her to follow up is to give her a small gift after the shooting, such as a nice bottle of wine or fragrance, expensive candy, a book, or something you made yourself.

The model should approach photographer tests as a means of gaining experience in front of the camera and of proving herself to the photographer for future paid assignments. These arrangements work out best for the model if she already has a composite and basic portfolio pictures and doesn't really need any particular type of photo. Unless you question a photographer's motives or ability, you should always take advantage of the opportunity to test. You will gain experience, establish contacts, and you might even get some great add-ons for your portfolio and composite. Treat the testing as if it is your money being spent and do everything you can to ensure that both you and the photographer get great results.

Client Tests

In this situation a client pays the costs of the test session. In addition, the model and photographer are often paid. There are several ways in which this works.

Shooting on speculation. When a model and photographer do a shooting on speculation, they use the client's clothes or product and shoot according to the client's specifications. Only upon the client's acceptance of the photos are the model and photographer paid. Sometimes the specifications are very exacting; other times a general concept or idea is needed.

Shooting for stock. Some photographers shoot generic photos that are sold through stock photo agencies to advertising agencies or other concerns needing a photograph for publication. Many photographers shoot stock photos that are purchased by greeting card companies. The photographer sells the photo for a flat fee or she receives a royalty every time the photo is used by these concerns. The model also receives a royalty provided he has included such a stipulation on the model's release he signed. If he has not signed a model's release, the photographer does not have the right to sell the photo of him. If he signed a release with no such stipulation and the photographer gave him consideration such as a dollar amount or a print or transparency as compensation for the shooting, the release is validated and he receives no further payment.

Test jobs. When a test job is booked through the model's agency, the model is paid one-half her hourly rate or a fee specified by the agent for the session. No model's releases are signed.

Planning for Testings

Testing with no goals in mind is usually unwise. You may end up with some nice pictures, but many won't be what you need to define your image or further your career. Although you should always be flexible and open to new ideas, you should also have a basic strategy. Having a direction for your career will save you money, time, and effort. Discuss ideas for testing sessions with your agent and other experts in the field, then plan the photos you will need. There are several steps involved in producing great results from test sessions. The basic steps involved are the following.

1. Determine the look you will trying to achieve in the photo.
2. Decide on what the photo will be used for.
3. Determine what type of photo will be needed.

4. Research the photographers who are available and will be able to produce the look you need.
5. Determine your clothing needs for the shot.
6. Decide on makeup.
7. Plan for hair.
8. Prepare for the photo session.
9. Attend the photo session.
10. Follow up on the photo session.
11. Select the best photos for enlargement.
12. Order prints from your selections.
13. Consider techniques for improving your photographs.

Use a Testing Worksheet to help you to plan every aspect of a test shooting. Use one worksheet for each photo you will need. These worksheets can also be used as a record of what was done at a testing to help you to learn and remember.

Testing Worksheet

c THE PROFESSIONAL MODEL'S HANDBOOK

Model _____ Session Date _____

Type of Look _____ Photo for _____

Type of Photo needed: ☐ Color ☐ Black and White

☐ Head Shot ☐ ¾ Length ☐ Full Length ☐ Other _____

Setting: ☐ Studio ☐ Location _____

Photographer _____

STYLING

Stylist/Source _____

Clothing Ideas: Outfit _____

_____

Shoes _____

Accessories _____

Props, etc. _____

MAKEUP

Makeup Artist _____

Notes:

HAIR

Hair Stylist _____

Hair Notes:

MISCELLANEOUS

263

Determining What Types of Photos You Will Need

Know your "type" and discuss with your agent(s) or other experts in the field to determine the looks you should display in your photos. Determine what types of clients you will be approaching and the kinds of assignments you want to obtain. Observe television commercials and look through magazines for ideas. Determine whether your photos will be used for a composite, glossy, portfolio, or other purpose. You will also need to know whether you need headshots (head and shoulders), close-ups (neck up), full-length shots (feet and top of head included), or three-quarter-length shots (cropped at the knees or thighs). Planning the setting of the photo, whether it will be shot in a studio, out-of-doors, or at another location will also be necessary.

Photos Needed by Female Fashion Print Models

You will need photos for a composite and portfolio showing that your face, figure, expressions, and movements are photogenic and can attractively display a variety of current fashions. For specific information on recommended shots, consult "The Model's Composite" and "The Model's Portfolio" in this chapter.

Photos Needed by Male Fashion Print Models

Generally the preceding information applies to male models also. For specific information on recommended shots, consult "The Model's Composite" and "The Model's Portfolio."

Photos Needed by Child Models

If your child is younger than 3 to 4 years of age, he or she will be changing every few months, so test photos are usually not feasible. The best alternative is to have photos taken by one of the reasonably priced portrait studios in major department store chains. The session is inexpensive, and you can get several copies (3 x 5 color prints are acceptable) for distributing to agents and potential clients. Children under 4 should have new pictures taken every 4-6 months.

For children older than 4 years of age, basic headshots from varying angles showing the child's features and hair and two or three full- and three-quarter-length shots showing him or her in different moods, settings, and clothing are necessary. At least one shot should be smiling and others should be slice-of-life, showing the child in school, play, and dressed-up clothing and situations. A natural, uncontrived look should be sought. To gain ideas, look at ads, catalogs, and magazines depicting children similar to the type of look your child has. These photos will be used on a composite-glossy, which can be updated frequently and inexpensively, or a standard printed composite. The type of tool used will depend on your market and your agent's preferences. In general children should have new test shots taken every year to depict growth and maturity changes.

Photos Needed by Straight Product/Commercial Models

Most straight product/commercial models need photos for a composite and portfolio to obtain print assignments and a glossy to obtain electronic media assignments. For specific information on the types of shots needed, consult the sections on each type of self-promotion tool. You will need to have basic headshots showing different expressions and facial angles as well as three-quarter- and full-length shots showing you in a variety of commercial roles such as parent, spouse, executive, etc. The roles you select to portray will be dependent on your look. You should also include photos in which you are interacting with products that work well with your "type." Study TV commercials, print advertisements, and product catalogs to gain ideas for shots.

Photos Needed by Character Models

A character model needs photos of the characters he or she does best, complete with makeup, hair, clothing, movement, and expression. These will be used for a composite and portfolio to obtain print assignments. A separate glossy for each character is often necessary to adequately position the talent for the greatest number of electronic media opportunities. Headshots are usually needed; however, three-quarter- or full-length shots may also be useful if they help to express a particular character.

Photos Needed by Promotional Models

Although some promotional models are able to secure work with just a glossy and a resume, most have more success with a composite and resume. Consult "The Model's Composite" and "The Commercial Headshot" for information on the photos you will need.

Photos Needed by Models and Actors for Electronic Media Work

Models seeking work in television commercials and other audiovisual productions need a headshot to be used on a glossy. Most models or actors aim for a picture that shows they can portray one of the commonly requested types found in commercials. For more information on the most commonly used types in television commercials and the type of photograph needed, consult "The Commercial Headshot" in this chapter. Some talent in search of electronic media work also have acting composites, which display pictures in which they are shown in a variety of roles or characters and interacting with products. These pictures should look like freeze frames from a television commercial rather than stiff, posed photos.

A voice-over artist may want to put a photo of himself or herself on the case containing his or her voice tape.

Photos Needed by Fashion Show Models

To provide proof of their experience and their photogenic qualities (fashion show models are often photographed on the runway), show models need composites and portfolios. The types of shots included will differ slightly from those required by print models. For more information, see "The Model's Composite" and "The Model's Portfolio."

Photos Needed by Special Types

Hand models. If you are a hand model, you should have pictures of your hands alone. Concentrate on showing the texture of the skin as well as the shape of the hands. It is also important to show that you are dextrous and can move both hands attractively. If you have an attractive face, take a few pictures of your hands and face together.

It is also a good idea to have pictures of your hands holding objects that advertisers may need to photograph. Select the products according to the look of your hands. For example, if you have beautiful, glamourous hands with long tapering fingers and nails, add jewelry and beauty products. If you have noncosmetic hands, for example, your hands look like homemaker hands, combine them with household products. The shape of your hands and fingers, skin texture, and contours, as well as the length of your nails will determine the personality of your hands.

Male hands can benefit from the same information. A typical male hand looks masculine and is average in size. A cosmetic male hand is smooth with long fingers and little hair, whereas a character hand, such as a blue-collar hand, is strong and broad without being too large.

Both male and female models should take care when shooting that their hands don't appear large in photographs. Most clients do not want a hand model whose hands overpower the product. These photos can be used for a composite or composite-glossy and portfolio so that clients will consider the model for all kinds of assignments.

Beauty or cosmetic models. If you are qualified to do beauty modeling, you should have a few excellent-quality, tight close-ups taken with minimal makeup to show off your skin and facial features plus shots showing a variety of makeup styles. If you have excellent hands and/or hair, be sure to play up these assets, as they are often shown in conjunction with beauty products. Study cosmetic and jewelry ads and editorial beauty pages in magazines for ideas. These shots should be included in a portfolio and composite. If you have some acting ability, have a glossy made in which you are depicted as a cosmetic model. For more information see the section on assembling a glossy.

Leg models. If leg modeling is your aim, consider acquiring photos in which you are modeling pantyhose, lingerie, shorts, short skirts, and bathing suits. A few photos taken from the waist or hips down will focus on your legs. Take care that your feet do not appear large. These shots can be included in a portfolio and composite.

Foot models. Acquire photos of your feet bare and perfectly manicured as well as shots in which you are wearing different styles of shoes. Select open, strappy shoes to show off your feet attractively. Look at ads to gain ideas for shooting articles related to the feet. Assemble a composite or composite-glossy that shows your feet and ankles.

Nude or figure models. To find out if you have the qualifications to appear in a nude layout of a men's magazine, enlist a photographer to shoot two rolls of Kodachrome or color slides in studio of your body. The shots should include nude and seminude (for example, bikini) body shots and face shots from different angles. Avoid extreme soft focus and intense shadowing, which will hide the shape of your body. After the session, discard any obvious rejects and have duplicates made that can be sent directly to the photography department of the magazines in which you are interested.

Lingerie and bathing suit models. Aim for photos in bathing suits (one and two piece), leotards and tights, shorts, lingerie, and other articles of clothing that show off your figure. A waist-up bra shot is a good marketable picture to have for your portfolio.

Celebrities, experts, business owners, etc. These individuals often have a publicity headshot taken for a glossy that shows the individual in a commercial, yet true-to-life, manner. This will show that the individual can promote products and services in print ads, electronic media, and live promotions.

Photos Needed by Modeling-Related Talents

Makeup artists and hairstylists. Makeup artists and hairstylists usually specialize in one of three areas: fashion, straight, or character makeup. Some are versatile enough to work in more than one area. Fashion-oriented hairstylists and makeup artists focus on current trends in hairstyling and makeup. They are employed to apply makeup and style hair for models seen in fashion and beauty-related product advertisements and television commercials as well as for fashion shows and fashion editorials in magazines.

Makeup and hair experts specializing in straight makeup and hairstyling are often employed to apply makeup and style hair for the people appearing in print ads and television commercials. They concentrate on making an individual look natural, attractive, and photogenic.

Makeup artists specializing in character makeup are often employed to apply makeup for theatrical productions, television and film productions, and print advertisements. These makeup artists are proficient in creating historical, fictional, and other types of characters. This may involve applying latex rubber face pieces to reshape features, hairpieces, special makeup bases, and colorings to create a realistic effect. Hairstylists specializing in this area are knowledgeable in regard to researching and recreating period hairstyles.

A makeup artist's or hairstylist's area of specialization will determine the types of photos he or she will aim for. Makeup artists and hairstylists should acquire both black and white and color photos (the majority should be in color) of models or other individuals on whom they have applied makeup or styled hair. These are then displayed in a portfolio. Makeup artists and hairstylists also need color composites or glossies or other promotional materials that show sample photographs of their best work.

Stylists. Stylists specialize in one or more areas such as food, still life, fashion, illustration, catalog, interiors, costumes, and sets. Stylists should have photos in both black and white and color (the majority should be in color) that capitalize on the individual's area of specialization and his or her style. A fashion stylist, for example, should test for photos that show she or he is knowledgeable and creative at combining current clothing, accessories, props, and other elements. These pictures are used for a portfolio and a color composite. Assessing your natural abilities and targeting potential clients is primary. Working toward photos that will catch the attention and satisfy the needs of your market is important.

Researching Photographers for Testing

Relying on mutual, photographer, or client tests to produce the photos you'll need when starting a modeling career is usually not the best course. Because you won't have total control over the photos being shot, it may take a year or more to assemble the quality, type, and variety of photos needed for your self-promotion tools. Instead, it may be wiser to enlist a model or talent test photographer to shoot exactly what you and your agent need. You'll receive results in a specified amount of time that you know you will be able to use. Consider model or talent test photographers based on area of specialization and style, services offered, competency, rapport, and cost.

The Photographer's Area of Specialization and Style

Photographers specialize in different areas of photography. The main areas of specialization that a model may encounter are listed in Table 1. To achieve best results it is important to match the photographer's area of specialization to your needs. Many photographers think they can shoot anything skillfully; very few actually can. The best way for you to judge is to look at the photographer's portfolio or ask to see samples of composites or glossies he or she has shot.

It is also important to realize that within each area of specialization, photographers' styles differ. For example, one fashion photographer may exhibit a very high-fashion, editorial style, whereas another fashion photographer may have a more straightforward catalog or commercial style. It is wise to take your looks and career objectives into consideration when enlisting a photographer.

Matching the Photographer's Area of Specialization and Style to Your Needs

If You Are a Female Fashion Model Consult fashion photographers who specialize in photographing women's fashions. If you are a junior type, you will need young, smiling, animated shots, such as those seen in *Seventeen, Teen,* and *Mademoiselle.* If you are a high-fashion type, you will search for photographers who can produce photos that resemble those in *Vogue, Harpers Bazaar,* or high-fashion European magazines. If you are a general-fashion type hoping to find work in print ads and catalogs, search for a photographer with a clean, commercial, or catalog style. A contemporary woman type of fashion model should avoid a photographer with a very high fashion style and opt for one who can produce shots such as those in *Redbook* or *Good*

TABLE 1 The Photographer's Area of Specialization and Style

Specialization	Activities
Fashion photography	Focuses on shooting fashions. Some photographers specialize in shooting menswear, womenswear, or children's clothing. Some photographers also specialize in beauty shots, which are headshots that focus on the makeup and hair.
Glamour photography	Concentrates on making the subject look glamourous and beautiful. Examples are pictures of glamourous Hollywood movie stars used to promote the star. Currently many glamour photographers are also figure photographers.
Figure photography	Specializes in shooting nudes and seminudes.
Composite and portfolio photography	Specializes in shooting photos for models' composites and portfolios. Some of these photographers have a fashion-oriented style, whereas others have a product/commercial style. These photos are geared to promoting the model, not the articles she is wearing or holding.
Portrait photography	Specializes in shooting portraits in which the objective is to capture the subject's personality. Traditional portrait photos don't have the fashion-oriented or commercial look that is usually needed in the modeling field.
Still life photography	Specializes in inanimate objects.
Product photography	Specializes in shooting products such as food, household products, and the like. Occasionally hand and straight commercial models appear in photos.
Advertising photography	Specializes in photography of products and people (especially straight and character commercial models) for advertising. Sometimes also called people photography.
Illustration photography	Specializes in photos of people involved in situations or photographs that tell a story. Usually associated with advertising photography.
Corporate photography	Specializes in creating photos for a company's annual report and executive portraiture.
News photography	Documents current events usually for newspapers. Also referred to as editorial photography.
Art photography	Specializes in photos to be sold as artworks. These photos often depict faces, nudes, scenes, or inanimate objects and have a timeless quality.
Publicity headshot photography	Specializes in publicity headshots for actors, actresses, and other performers. You can research such photographers by looking at the ads in newspapers geared to theater people (e.g., *Variety, Audition News*), by contacting local television stations to find out who does the publicity headshots for the on-camera newspeople, or by consulting with television talent agents and casting directors.

Housekeeping. You may want the photographer to shoot you in an outdoor or office setting. If you are a classic woman, you will want to make sure that the photographer is adept at shooting mature women. Petite and large-size models should check that the photographer under consideration has had experience shooting petites and large sizes.

For all fashion models it is important that the photographer you select have an awareness of current fashion, makeup, and hair and that he or she is able to give you good ideas for posing the way models are currently posing. Select a photographer who can produce great beauty shots that focus on hair and makeup and figure-flattering yet fashion-conscious body shots.

If You Are a Male Fashion Model Aspiring male models should contact fashion photographers who specialize in shooting men and menswear. Not all fashion photographers are equally adept at shooting men and women. Male models should also consider asking female models to include them in their tests. When doing this it may be possible to split the photographer's fee.

If You Are a Child Model Select a photographer who knows how to work with kids. For children older than 3 or 4, working with photographers who are experts at shooting commercial kids and child fashion models is advisable. Your agent should be able to recommend several. You can also obtain names by asking the parents of successful child models. Look at ads depicting children for ideas. Portrait photographers aren't usually able to produce the commercial look a child must present for modeling. If your child is younger than 3 to 4 years of age, photos taken by one of the reasonably priced potrait studios in major retail department store chains are usually sufficient. sufficient.

If You Are a Character Model Select a photographer whose work shows that he or she has had experience shooting character models. Advertising, illustration, and publicity headshot photographers would probably be the best choices. If you are impersonating a character who is glamourous, you'll often get best results by consulting a glamour or fashion photographer. If your character is a famous politician or business tycoon, you might achieve unique results by contacting a news or corporate photographer. All types of character models might also benefit by contacting photographers who shoot publicity stills for theatrical productions.

If You Are a Promotional Model Many fashion photographers have a style that is too fashion oriented or extreme for a promotional model's needs. If you are considering a fashion photographer, choose one who can produce clean, commercial-looking photos. Glamour and advertising photographers also merit a try.

If You Are a Modeling-Related Talent If you are seeking work as a makeup artist, hairstylist, or stylist you should search for fashion, advertising, illustration, and product photographers, depending on your area of specialization. It is usually easiest for a makeup artist, hairstylist, or stylist to do testing by posting small ads or business cards in several modeling agencies. Services could be offered at a minimal charge to models who are testing. It is also helpful for makeup artists, hairstylists, and stylists to make their services available to photographers for testing. This might be done by contacting photographers in your area or by placing ads in publications geared to professional photographers such as creative directories and journals.

If You Are a Special Type Hand, leg, and foot models should contact fashion and product photographers. Lingerie, bathing suit, nude, or figure models should contact fashion, glamour, and figure photographers. It is best if the photographer has had a lot of experience shooting nudes, so you will both feel at ease. Beauty models should approach fashion photographers who specialize in beauty shots.

If You Are an Electronic Media Model or Talent When testing, you are trying for a photo that will be suitable for a mass-produced headshot glossy that can be sent to advertising agencies, casting directors, and video and film producers. You should contact photographers who do publicity headshots for actors and actresses. Fashion photographers might make you look too glamourous. If you are also working toward an acting composite, have shots done by an advertising, illustration, or product photographer. Voice-over artists should contact photographers who shoot publicity headshots for actors and actresses to acquire a photo to accompany a voice tape.

Services Offered by Model or Talent Test Photographers

After obtaining a list of model or talent test photographers, you should telephone each one to obtain basic information. For fuller explanations of what is offered by different photographers, the model should arrange appointments with each. If the photographer doesn't provide a brochure or price list, bring along paper and pencil to take notes and prices. Ask the following questions.

- How many outfits/concepts does the session include?
- How many exposures will be taken (color or black and white)?
- Is hair, makeup, and styling included? Do I have to arrange for the stylist, makeup artist, or hairstylist or does the photographer make recommendations?
- Does this fee include expenses for film and processing? Will I receive contact sheets and/or slides as a result of the shooting?
- Are prints (enlargements) included? If not, how much extra are they?
- Can additional prints be ordered at a later date? How long does the photographer retain the negatives? Will the photographer release the negatives?
- Will I be able to make my own selections from the contact sheet? Does the photographer offer advice on photo selection?
- How long will the shooting take?
- When will I get the results?
- Will the photos be shot in studio or outdoors? Is there an extra charge for location shots?
- Does the fee include retouching of the prints, photo duplicating for glossies, and printing of composites?
- What if I am unhappy with the results? Will the photos be reshot? Is there an additional charge for reshoots?
- Can the photographer give advice on image, posing, wardrobe, hair and makeup, or can he or she refer you to people who can? Does the photographer have contacts with agents or other influential people in the field who can provide you with modeling opportunities?

Each photographer has different offerings in expertise and services. Most model or talent test photographers include the cost of film, processing, contact sheets, and their fee for shooting. Some of the services a photographer may also include in the testing fee are:

- Makeup.
- Hairstyling.
- Styling.
- Clothing and accessories for the shooting.
- Printing of composites or photo duplicating of glossies.
- Enlargements (prints).
- Referrals to agents, clients, and others in the business.
- Training (private lessons) in modeling.
- Image making, makeovers.
- Counseling.
- Portfolio.

Judging the
Photographer's
Competency

In addition to considering the photographer's area of specialization and style, you will have to judge his or her competency. One of the best ways to find a good photographer is to look at other models' composites and pictures to determine which photographer's names predominate. Word-of-mouth (from agents, other models, etc.) is usually the best way to determine a photographer's competency. Arrange a meeting with the photographer so you can see his or her portfolio. Realize that with a basic amount of talent and skill it is no great feat to take a good picture of an excellent model. If you are a beginner, ask to see pictures of other new models that the photographer has taken. As a beginner, you will need a photographer who is aware of current modeling techniques and is able to teach you how to move for the camera.

To judge the quality of a photographer's work, consider the following.

- Is the photographer creative? Does her photography have an attractive style? Do the pictures display attractive composition, backgrounds, and lighting? Does the photographer have a good eye for color or black and white?

- Is the photographer's work consistent? Do all of the pictures he shows you look equally good? Does he have a lot to show indicating a lot of experience?

- Does the photographer's work have a current look? Do her photos look like the photos you might see in a current issue of *Vogue, Glamour,* or *Seventeen*? Or, do the clothes look outdated, the poses old fashioned, or the photographic style (lighting, color, etc.) out-of-date?

- Does the photographer pay strict attention to details? Do the model's clothes look unattractive? Are there mistakes that the photographer has overlooked in hair and makeup?

- Is the photographer able to capitalize on the subject's assets? Do the models in his photographs look beautiful? Are their expressions good? Would you like to look the way they look? Or do the models appear unattractive with false, uncomfortable-looking expressions and stiff poses.

- Does the photographer's work exhibit good technical skills? Do his pictures exhibit good lighting that enhances the model's features? Does the skin look smooth and healthy? Are the pictures focused and exposed well? Are the prints he shows you of good quality with no blemishes? Are colors true and rich? Does the photographer's work have a professional look?

Consider Your Rapport
with the Photographer

On a paid assignment, you must be able to get along well with any photographer. However, when you have a choice, it is wise to select a photographer with whom you'll enjoy shooting. It is important that you feel comfortable and uninhibited with the photographer and that both of you are interested in arriving at a great result. Also a photographer who is accustomed to working with beginning models will make you feel more relaxed. Ask other models about the photographer. Find out what he's like to work with, if they recommend him, and what faults they may have found. Check his reputation. Shady stories abound about some photographers. Don't test with a photographer who may have questionable intentions.

It is also a plus if the photographer has a genuine interest in photographing you. If the photographer just wants your money and doesn't care about providing you with the right types of photos, you probably won't get satisfactory results. On the other hand, a photographer who has ideas about how you should look, or who can give good suggestions on posing and wardrobe will be a great asset. It is a good idea to ask the photographer how much success has been attained by beginning models he has previously photographed.

Always try to meet with the photographer prior to the shooting. Discuss what types of shots you would like, what your agent wants to see, and ask her for her suggestions. Bring along a Testing Worksheet for notetaking. You might bring along magazine photos that appeal to you. Tell her specifically what it is about the photos that you like—the lighting, the colors, the styling, and so on. Don't present her with a page from a magazine on the day of the shooting and instruct her that you want a direct copy. To meet such a request, she may have to make special arrangements for equipment or background. Also take advantage of her talent, experience, and knowledge and allow her to exercise her own creativity. Most important, rely on your own resources to obtain great test shots. Make every effort to organize the best clothes, accessories, and props for the shooting and to extend your own creativity.

The Cost of Model or Talent Test Photography

While you may be lucky enough to work with a photographer who tests without charge, others will charge. Don't judge photographers by price. Consider quality and offerings first, then consider the cost. In general you get what you pay for. It makes sense that the best photographers will charge more than mediocre or beginning photographers. Your pictures are one of the few ways you have to promote yourself. Therefore, make certain that your pictures are as good as they can possibly be and as good or better than your competition. This is an investment in your career, and if you have potential for success in the field, you will be able to recover what you have spent.

Testing with a photographer who has lots of good contacts with clients, agents, and others in the business may be very valuable. He or she may be able to help you to obtain interviews, special attention, or other opportunities. A photographer who knows a lot about modeling and has helped other models to get started or to advance to successful careers can be very valuable for advice and career counseling.

Determining What to Wear for Test Photos

When testing usually you will have to provide the garments you will wear. If you are a beginner, it is often a good idea to enlist a stylist to select clothing that is perfect for you and the look you want to create. The stylist may also attend the shooting to accessorize and arrange the outfits in the most creative manner. To find a stylist, try to obtain recommendations from your agent, your photographer, or other models. Ask to see the stylist's portfolio and judge him or her according to the same specifications you used to judge the photographer. Most stylists charge an hourly rate but a beginning stylist may be willing to work for a discounted fee, if he or she can get portfolio prints.

If you can't afford a stylist, make sure your photographer has a good eye for fashion and styling. Some photographers have great fashion sense and unique ideas. They may even have connections that will provide clothing for the shooting. If you will be handling your own clothing arrangements, list ideas for outfits and coordinating shoes, accessories, and props. If you can't arrange a wardrobe check with the photographer before the shooting, bring lots of different outfits so you and the photographer have plenty of options. The most important qualifications for choosing clothes for a test shot are the following.

Clothing That Expresses Your "Type" or Look

Decide on what types of clients you want the test to appeal to—high-fashion editorial, catalog, advertising, promotional, or electronic media. Decide on what look you want to project, then determine which outfits might work with that look. If you are a new model, you are still finding your best looks and figuring out which clients might potentially book you, so it is a good idea to experiment with different styles in hair, makeup, and clothing. Agents and photographers will be able to guide you with ideas and suggestions. For clothing ideas according to the image you want to project, consult Tables 2 and 3.

TABLE 2   Clothing, Hair, and Makeup Suggestions for Model Tests

Model Type	Clothing, Hair, and Makeup Suggestions
Male fashion models	Include suits and a selection of shirts and ties, both patterned and plain, for a business or dressy shot. Also include sports jackets (e.g., tweedy) that can be worn with sweaters or a sweater vest and shirt. Add corduroy or other casual slacks or substitute a richly textured sweater for the sport jacket. For a dressed-down look, consider jeans and a jean or leather jacket or sportswear. Outerwear such as a trenchcoat often looks good for a different type of shot. For shots that will show your body, select swimwear or workout wear. Look at men's fashion magazines and catalogs that display your image and copy the clothing and styling in photos that you like.
Female fashion models	For ideas for headshots, look at magazine covers. Select necklines to complement your face shape. Add jewelry, scarves, or other accessories for interest. Select colors that flatter your skin tone and hair color and fabrics that have visual interest. Make sure you include a bathing suit or workout wear (leotard, tights) to show off your figure and legs. Also include a basic fashion shot in a dress or skirt that shows your legs. For other shots, select dressy, work, and casual clothing according to your look or type whether high fashion or general fashion. Look at editorial pages in magazines, catalogs, and ads that fit your image, and copy the clothing and accessories. Avoid very bulky clothes or lots of layering because your figure will look heavy or out of proportion.
Large-size models	Select the same types of clothing as for fashion models. Because you will often be called upon to model sophisticated clothing, favor these types of outfits. Also many large-size models omit a body shot in lingerie or workout wear. Instead they aim for a shot in casual clothes or sportswear such as a golf skirt and top.
Fashion show models	Fashion show models need the same types of clothing as female and male fashion models. Clothing might be a little more dramatic, and it is also a good idea to feature one outfit that moves attractively (for example, a full skirt) to show a creative movement you might implement on the runway. Clothing that shows your body and legs is helpful for potential clients trying to judge how you'll appear on the runway.
Petite models	Petite models require the same types of clothing as female fashion models. Select clothing that is neither bulky nor too detailed. Clothing that makes you appear taller will compensate for the shortening effect of the camera. Look at magazines and catalogs in which petite models are featured to gain clothing ideas.
Junior fashion models	Select a few conservative school outfits, such as skirts and blouses or shirts and pants. Select stripes, plaids, or other patterns, but avoid anything too busy. Be careful not to combine too many styles.

Bring props, such as school books, sporting goods, hair ribbons, neck ties, socks, jewelry, purses, and the like. In addition to school clothes, select a few trendy outfits that are for play or school. Consult current teenage magazines, such as *Teen, Seventeen, Young Miss,* and *Mademoiselle,* for ideas. Sports outfits, such as bathing suits, shorts, and tops, are also good because they show the body. Adding a dressy outfit such as a prom dress is fun. Include jewelry and the right shoes, and combine it with a curlier or dressier hairstyle. The important thing is to keep the teenage model young looking. Use only scant makeup. Boys should use just a trace of powder to combat shine. Girls should have powder plus a touch of cheekcolor, a dot of gloss on lips, and a little mascara. Select unfussy hairstyles. A smiling shot is important.

Child fashion models
Clothes that have a cute design and are flattering to the child are most important. For children 6 to 12 years old, select a few dressy outfits, play clothes, and school clothes. Also include as props some of the child's favorite toys, but coordinate them with the outfit. For example, an elegant baby doll with a little girl in a dress, and a baseball cap and mit for a boy in play clothes would be appropriate ideas. Select stuffed animals and clothes that are in good condition.

Straight commercial/ product model
A wholesome, smiling headshot with simply styled hair and makeup is important. Also include headshots that show a variety of animated moods. Clothes should be similar to those worn by average people and should be chosen to portray a range of commercial roles. For example, select one outfit to portray a housewife, another to show you as a mother interacting with a child. In another you might adopt a work role and appear in a nurse's uniform. Props to go with your outfit are important. Also include pictures in which you are holding or using various products. Look at ads and commercials for clothing ideas.

Promotional model
Select clothing that is flattering to your figure and that will appeal to a variety of potential clients. Select a figure-flattering business suit, dress, or skirt and blouse for a basic, spokesperson look. A dressy, glamourous outfit for another shot is often a good idea. A bathing suit or leotard and tights is often a good idea to show your figure. Sportswear and casual clothes are good for a girl-next-door look. Avoid extreme, high-fashion clothes. Keep hair simple but well styled. Makeup should be visible, but not overdone or too fashion conscious.

Courtesy of Elite, New York.

**TABLE 3   Clothing, Hair, and Makeup Suggestions for a
Commercial Headshot**

Image or Look	Clothing, Hair, and Makeup Suggestions
Housewife	Select plain or subtly striped oxford shirts to wear under crewneck sweaters. A subtle plaid shirt alone or combined with a sweater vest also works well for a headshot. Makeup that is subtly applied using colors that simulate the natural color of your cheeks and lips is important. Avoid contour, highlighting, and frosted makeups. Wear eye makeup that subtly defines your eyes rather than exaggerates their size, shape, or color. Wear hair in simple, soft natural styles that are neither straight nor curly and not cut below the shoulders or above the ears.
Young mother	For a headshot select a subtle floral print or soft pastel cotton blouse (possibly with a small ruffle at the neck) or a soft-fabric, pastel-colored sweater with a round neck. Avoid jewelry. For makeup use a very soft touch with young-looking, slightly pinkish cheeks, and natural-looking lips (use just a touch of gloss—no dark, light, or frosted colors). Define eyecrease with soft brown eyeshadow and use a touch of mascara. Soft shiny hair that waves attractively around the face is usually best. Avoid fashion-conscious hairstyles, teasing, hairspray molded, or overly short or long styles.
Young husband or father	A plaid shirt, plain sweater, or conservative sports jacket worn with an open-collar oxford shirt can work well for a headshot. Use only powder to combat shine. Hair should be conservative, for example, side parted and average length with a slight wave.
Young woman-next-door	Select a subtle, light-colored plaid, striped, or plain oxford shirt or plain blouse and combine it with a crew neck sweater or a slightly fuzzy, soft V-neck sweater or sweater vest. Makeup should look natural with radiant-looking skin showing through. Lip and cheek colors should match natural coloring. Add a touch of gloss to lips and use mascara. Avoid heavy eyeliners and lip liners. Hair should be soft, fluffy, natural, and shiny ranging in length from chin length to long. You should look pretty, but not fashiony or glamourous. A wholesome, natural smile is usually best. Effervescence and a glowing enthusiasm are the objective. Wholesome sexiness, friendliness, and an open expression are best. You should appear to be 18–25. A headshot displaying this look is best for most fashion models who seek work in television commercials.
Glamour girl	Select clothing that has a glamourous look such as a satin blouse. Add diamond-like or jewel earrings that aren't too large or shiny. Don't allow what you wear to overpower you. Hair should be full and shiny. Adding a soft, shimmering hair light is a good idea and employing "movie star" or butterfly-type lighting is also advisable. Makeup should look glamourous but not overdone. Lips should be full, shiny, and sexy. Cheeks should be defined. Avoid heavy eye makeup.
Cosmetic model (female)	Select clothing that is fashion conscious but not too extreme. Choose a flattering color or tone and neckline, for example, an attractive silk blouse or shirt. Pearl studs or small diamond, gold, or silver earrings are best. Use a style of makeup that best expresses your looks. For example, think of the cosmetic companies you would like to work for—do you have a young Bonne Bell look, a fresh all-American Cover Girl look, or a sophisticated Marcella Borghese look? Look at the models representing these companies and copy their clothing and makeup styles. Beware of using a lot of makeup. You want your flawless skin texture, beautiful features, and thick, shiny hair to show through.

Handsome man	This model is often selected from the fashion model category and can be found in a variety of television commercials and print ads. There are basically two variations of "handsome men" types: one is the rugged, athletic type and the other is the male equivalent of the cosmetic model, who is good-looking, masculine, sexy, and romantic. Select clothing that suits the type you are. If you are the rugged, macho type, select a sports jacket and open-collared shirt. An attractive smile, slightly ruffled hair, and a sexy expression in the eyes are most important. If you are the cosmetic type, select an elegant-looking suit, shirt, and tie. Glamourous lighting with a soft hair light will give an attractive look. Look for clothing, hair, and makeup ideas by studying the male models in ads for grooming supplies manufactured by cosmetic companies.
Businesswoman	Select a business suit, an attractive blouse, and subdued jewelry. Opt for a conservative but contemporary hairstyle. Natural tones are best for makeup. Avoid anything overly sexy or glamourous. You'll want to look professional and successful.
Businessman	Select a gray or dark business suit and a light blue shirt and subtle print tie. A conservative, side-parted hairstyle with a clean-shaven face is preferred.
Spokesperson	This is a look similar to the businessperson; however, it may have a more friendly or personal tone. Select a business suit or an attractive conservative blouse (for women). To obtain ideas look at the clothing worn by anchorpersons on news programs. Clothing is usually conservative and well coordinated. Subtle jewelry and middle-of-the-road hair and makeup looks are best.
Real person	Aim for a look that is not studied. Comfortable, nondescript clothes are best. Very little or no makeup (except for powder) and average hairstyles are important. You do not want to appear to be a professional model or actor. You want to look average with an appealing personality.
Character model	Clothes will be dictated by the characters you are portraying. Also keep in mind the aspects of clothing that may not be photogenic. Body shots showing the legs and figure are not important unless germaine to the character being depicted. There are several character model and actor types: celebrity look-alikes, fictional characters, historical figures, comedians, and off-beat versions of straight models. For every type of straight model there are character versions. For example, a character housewife might have a zany or harried look. What is important is that your acting ability to draw realism and attention to the character you are portraying shows through.
Actor/Actress	If you want to position yourself as an actress or actor for theatre work or for dramatic roles in television productions, opt for a simple, classic look. A plain black or grey turtleneck will give you a strong presence. (Choose a turtleneck based on the length of your neck. A high turtleneck will shorten a too-long neck; a short or floppy cowl-type turtleneck will look best on a shorter neck.) A black or grey T-shirt, tank top, round or scoop necked sweater or a collarless blouse or shirt might also be good ideas. Some actors and actresses even opt for a bare shoulders look. Avoid jewelry except for perhaps small pearl, gold or diamond earrings. Avoid trendy or overdone makeup and hair. An intriguing, earnest, serious or sensuous expression should be your aim. This look also works well for the cosmetic model.

Clothing That Is Flattering to You

On a booking you have no choice. A client may ask you to model an outfit that is an unbecoming color or style for you, and you must do as directed. On a testing, it is your choice. For your first general testings, bring outfits that make you look and feel attractive. For head-shots, choose clothing with interesting necklines that flatter your face shape. Bring clothes in flattering colors (or tones for black and white) that compliment your skintone and hair color. For full-length shots, choose clothing that shows your body clearly, attracts attention to your best features, and gives your figure ideal proportions.

Clothing That Is Photogenic

Clothing that is to be photographed must be interesting. It must work perfectly within the confines of your look, the setting, and the objective of the shot. Clothing need not be new and outrageously expensive. Frayed jeans and a beat-up leather jacket can look great with the right concept in lighting, styling, background, and expression. Unless you are after this kind of rough, rustic look, clothing to be photographed must be in perfect condition. Unless you are after a special effect, avoid outrageous outifts, T-shirts with messages, and cheap-looking fads. Well-designed and beautifully constructed garments are always photogenic.

Concentrate also on bringing complete outfits. Garments that are well styled, complete with coordinated jewelry, shoes, belts, and other accessories will make the difference between a shot that looks like a test and a shot that looks like it was a booking.

When choosing articles in light of how well they will record on film, keep in mind that some photographers do not like to shoot all black or all white garments. Select garments that have visual interest and ideal proportion. For specific information on photogenic clothing, consult facts on wardrobe selection for various media in Chapter 5.

Ideas for Organizing Great Clothes Put a lot of energy and creativity into organizing wardrobe for your test shots. You'll inspire the photographer and get better results. The ideal outfits may not be hanging in your closet so you may have to consider other sources. Borrowing items from friends is a good place to start. Some stores rent clothes for a specified fee depending on the outfit. Fashion or accessory design students often want photographs of their work and will allow you to use articles they have designed if they can obtain prints from the shooting in exchange. Think of unique, interesting ideas—an antique dress, a mechanic's overalls, an equestrian habit, or an unusual one-piece bathing suit. Comb sporting goods stores, Army/Navy surplus stores, and dance- and theatrical-wear stores for clothing and accessories. Scouring the family attic may often yield ideas such as a military uniform, an old prom dress, or a wedding gown. Consider also that your pictures need not even depend on getting clothing. A great hat, hair ornament, or matching set of jewelry (necklace, earrings, and bracelet) can create an eye-catching beauty shot. Look through magazines and if you find a photograph you really like, duplicate it by shopping for the same or similar clothes, accessories, and props that are displayed.

When assembling your clothes for the session, think of ways to make your shots complete. If you are creating a business look, bring along a briefcase, a purse, a pair of eyeglasses, and a copy of *The Wall Street Journal.* For a bathing suit, a coordinating towel, bathing cap, beach bag, skin diving gear, or inflatable water toys can add interest. For a sporty, outdoors shot, bring sporting equipment that goes with your outfit. For an indoor workout leotard shot, bring a sweatband, wristbands, sport socks, or leg warmers plus things you might use when working out such as attractive weights or a jump rope. Choose medium-tone tights (red, blue, green), because they will flatter your legs and photograph well. Avoid black, white, textured, or shiny tights as they tend to make legs look heavier. Don't wear nylons for your bathing suit shots because your legs will look much darker and shinier than the rest of you.

Bring a selection of two to three outfits for each shot so the photographer can choose what will photograph best. Use the Wardrobe/ Planner Chart in Chapter 5 to ensure that the outfits you supply are complete with matching shoes, accessories, blouses, etc.

Arrange for Makeup

It is always a good idea for a beginning model to enlist a makeup artist for test sessions. Ask your photographer, agent, or other models to recommend makeup artists. A beginning makeup artist will often donate his or her time if he or she can also get prints from the shooting, but make certain that you examine the artist's portfolio carefully. If you are willing to pay, it is worthwhile to book a makeup artist who is well known for working with fashion photographers. Pay attention to the cosmetics and techniques the makeup artist uses so you can duplicate them yourself for future assignments.

If you are going to do your own makeup, plan and practice beforehand. Look at fashion magazines to ensure that you use current products and techniques. Refer back to Chapter 3 to sketch out ideas and arrive at attractive color schemes. Remember to keep makeup well blended, clean, and simple.

Plan for Hair

It is also a good idea for a beginning model to employ a professional hairdresser for the shooting. The hairdresser you normally use may not be familiar with hairstyling techniques for photography. Ask if he or she has had experience in this area and if you can see photo samples.

If you're going to do your own hair, plan and practice beforehand. Look at fashion magazines for ideas. Remember, simple, well-cut, healthy hair always looks good.

Prepare for the Photo Session

The day before your photo session, go through a final dress rehearsal, complete with hairstyling, makeup, and clothes. Practice moving in front of a mirror. Look at ads, editorial pages of magazines, and other sources for ideas. Practice poses and expressions so that when you go, you'll be flexible rather than stiff or unexpressive.

Call the day before and confirm your appointment with the photographer. Also call the hairstylist and makeup artist, if you plan to use them.

Pack everything you will need—extra pantyhose, correct undergarments, loads of accessories, and an iron. Take full responsibility for all the details. Don't expect others to cover for you. Make sure your shoes and accessories are perfect for your garments (not just what you have available). Check that your fingernails are polished and coordinated to your garments and makeup. If toes will show, they should be well groomed, and nails should be polished. Make sure that underarms and legs are clean shaven and that superfluous facial hair has been removed above upper lip. All these little things will have a big impact on the final result.

If you will be shooting outdoors, call the morning of the shooting if the weather looks questionable. Be sure to get plenty of sleep the night before.

Attend the Photo Session

Treat the testing as seriously and professionally as you would a booking. Be on time and well prepared. Be attentive, cooperative, and pleasant. Photographers, hairstylists, and makeup artists will start forming opinions about you, and this is where your reputation starts. The modeling business is a small industry and word travels fast. Don't bring other people along to a test session. Many beginners do this to give them moral support. However, most photographers do not like strangers milling around their studios. For the model, an onlooker can be a distraction because a beginner is more apt to feel inhibited and self-conscious in front of the photographer when a friend or relative is present.

Don't cancel a test shooting unless you have an emergency or have gotten a booking. If you must cancel, do so at least a day in advance, not an hour before the shooting. Remember, every photographer with whom you shoot is a potential client.

Avoid planning anything else on the day of your photo session. It is senseless to be preoccupied about getting somewhere on time or having to do something afterward. Testings often run longer than expected. If you are under other pressures, your anxiety might show in your photographs. When you become a professional model you may have two or three bookings and a few auditions in the course of a day, but when you're just beginning and when you have a choice, reserve ample time or a full day for your first shooting.

Don't be nervous. Concentrate on your contact with the photographer, and put all your energy into posing well and expressing the desired moods. By focusing all your attention on what you're supposed to be doing, your nervousness will subside and you'll achieve better results.

Don't forget to change your hair and makeup throughout the shooting (preferably every time you change outfits). Start with light makeup and build up to more dramatic makeup by using stronger colors. Begin with simple hairstyles and work into more complicated styles. For example, start with your hair down and end with it up or pulled back. Because at this point you really don't know what works best for you in photos, it is a good idea to vary your looks so that you'll have lots to choose from and will learn more in the process.

Test Session Followup

Follow up on your testing sessions. Often, you will never see the results unless you are very persistent. Don't expect photographers to call you; you'll have to call them. Find out at the time of the shooting when the pictures you shot will be ready. Processing can take as little time as 1 hour or up to 10 days. Even if the photographer promises your pictures on a certain day, when the day arrives, always call first to make sure they are ready before you make the trip to his or her studio.

As a result of your photo session the photographer will give you contact sheets, slides, or transparencies (see Figure 9). This will depend on the type of film used.

Figure 9a. Examples of contact sheets, 35mm and 120 2¼'' film. (Actual contact sheet size is 8'' x 10''.)

Figure 9b. Negatives.

Figure 9c. Color slides, color transparencies, color negatives and Polaroids.

Contact Sheets

As a result of a black and white shooting, the photographer will give you a contact or proof sheet that displays all the exposures from a single roll of film. These images are the same size as the negatives. Because everything in the negative is reversed, blacks are whites and visa versa, a contact sheet must be made so the images can be viewed. There are usually 12 to 36 exposures on a single contact sheet, depending on the type of film and camera that was used.

As a result of a color shooting, a photographer may give you a color contact sheet, if color negative film was used. In color negative film all the colors are reversed (reds are greens, blues are oranges, etc.), so a contact sheet must be made so the image can be viewed.

Some photographers produce 3 x 5 color proofs or machine prints as a result of a color negative shooting. Although these are larger and easier to see, these prints do not represent the colors found in the film as accurately as contact sheets will.

Slides or Transparencies

Slides or transparencies are the actual film the photographer shot that has been processed. No print or other process is needed to view the image. The colors and exposure found in the subject are recorded on the slide or transparency. These are best viewed when held up to the light, put on a light box, or seen through a slide projector.

When slides or transparencies are the result of the shooting, and it was a photographer or client test, you probably won't be given the slides. The photographer will have duplicate slides made of your choices or give you the rejects. If it was a mutual test, you will divide up the best slides with the photographer.

If he or she has the time, ask the photographer to evaluate the shooting. He or she will be able to teach you valuable lessons to help you to better present yourself for the camera. Accept the criticism he or she offers. Don't take up a lot of the photographer's time. Take your contact sheets or transparencies home and study them.

Select the Best Photos for Enlargement

The best way to select photos for enlargement is to consult a variety of people. Ask the photographer to mark the photos that he or she thinks are best and will make great prints. Ask your agent which pictures are most marketable. Obtain the opinions of hair, makeup, and styling people you may have worked with. Each individual will judge according to his or her area of expertise. You will find that in most cases, experienced people all tend to make the same selections. Your friends and family are usually not good judges because they will look for pictures that represent the way you look to them, not the way people in the modeling business will want you to look. The contact sheet photos or slides that end up with the most marks are the ones you

280

should choose for enlargements. Remember, it is not necessary that all the photos on the contact sheet are perfect. All you are looking for is one ideal photo from each change of clothing or concept.

Photo Supplies for Models

To aid in the process of selecting your photos for enlargement, a model needs certain tools. These three items will come in handy during the course of your career. They are inexpensive and can save you time and money. Acquire them now and use them when looking at the results of your shootings.

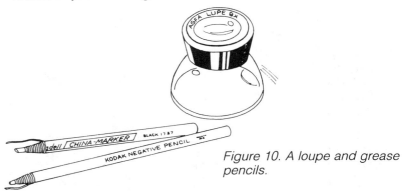

Figure 10. A loupe and grease pencils.

Loupe A loupe, or magnifier, which is available at camera shops, is an indispensable, inexpensive tool that will give you the best possible indication of how your contact sheet photos, slides, and transparencies will look when enlarged (see Figure 10). A loupe will magnify your contact photos from 2 to 10 times, depending on which type you select. (The greater the magnification, the better.) Loupes are smaller, handier, and more accurate than magnifying glasses. Never order prints without first looking at your photos through a loupe; the loupe will make flaws in your photos more apparent. When a flaw is visible through the loupe, you can be assured that it will stand out even more in the final print or enlargement.

To use a loupe, place it (widest part down) on the surface of your contact sheet, directly over the photo you want to examine and bring your eye right up to it. If a contact sheet is dark or details are hard to see, hold it up to the light when looking through the loupe.

Grease Pencil or China Marker These pencils, which are available at art supply stores, will allow you to mark freely on your contact sheets to indicate your favorite shots (see Figure 10). You can also draw in cropping lines so that your photographer or photo lab can enlarge the photo to your specifications. Unlike a pen, a grease pencil mark can be rubbed off with your fingers if you change your mind during photo selection. Grease pencils are available in several different colors so you can color code choices according to the people who made them. Never mark on transparencies, slides, or negatives unless they are encased in acetate protectors. When marking on acetate encasements, press very lightly.

Photo Templates A photo template allows you to look at each photo individually, with no extraneous matter blocking your concentration. It is also a valuable tool, because it allows you to crop your photos so proportions will coincide from negative or contact sheet photo to print. By using the templates in Figure 11 you will see what sizes and proportions are possible.

Figure 11. A photo template.

The template will show exactly how your 35-mm or 2¼-inch photos will be composed when enlarged to an 8 x 10. (It is important to realize that neither film size corresponds exactly to an 8 x 10. Some cropping or bordering must be done.) To use the photo template in Figure 11, trace the boxes then cut along the lines so that you have a stencil. Place the template over your contact sheet photo, slide, or transparency to arrive at the desired cropping and proportion. You will be able to preview any cropping or bordering adjustments on an 8 x 10 print.

The Selection Process

Using a loupe, look at all your slides or contact sheet photos and set aside or mark with a grease pencil the ones that catch your attention. You are looking for a picture that makes an overall positive impression.

Once you have made a preliminary selection, go back and look at your choices more closely. Decide on your priorities and critically appraise each picture according to your needs, standards, and the image you are trying to create. Judge your photos using the following criteria.

Modeling Criteria Modeling criteria refers to poses, movements, and expressions. Expressions that show you have acting ability are important. Expressions that are devoid of mood or feeling are usually not desired. Movements that show your body and what you are wearing to advantage are also necessary. Posing in the way models are currently posing is also important.

Fashion and Beauty Criteria Check your makeup, hair, and clothing very carefully for technical problems. Analyze the fabric, fit, design, draping, and details of your clothing and whether it is attractively presented. Clothing must flatter your figure and give it ideal proportions. Judge your hair according to how well it works with current fashion or the character or look you are portraying. Look for technical problems. Look for makeup mistakes such as uneven lip liner, poorly blended cheekcolor or eyeshadow, and unflattering application. Determine whether your makeup accomplishes the look you are trying to achieve.

Photographic Criteria This refers to lighting, focus, composition, color, technical flaws, and the like. Often an enlarged image will not look as ideal as it did when it was small. Flaws that are small and barely noticeable will become much more prominent in the enlargement. For these reasons, study your contact sheets closely for flaws and consult with the photographer. Photographers are experts at looking at contact sheets and knowing which image will yield the best enlargement, so rely on their expertise.

When selecting images for enlargement it is also important to choose a slide that meets technical requirements. The best way to ensure that you get a good print is to choose a good negative, slide, or transparency from which to make the print. Always choose an image that is perfectly exposed to ensure optimum results. Also examine the image to detect any lack of sharpness or detail or excess graininess that may detract from the subject. When selecting color slides, make sure the image has good color saturation. If the colors in the slide seem faded or dull, they will be even more so in the print. Make sure that skin tones in the slide are true and flattering. Because you will be using the picture to promote your appearance, the attractiveness in the negative or slide of your skin, hair, and eyes should be your most important priority.

Go back the next day and repeat the selection process. See if you arrive at the same selections. Mark your final selections for enlargement with an X.

If you can't decide between two images, order both. This is the only way to eliminate any doubt about which image is best. Spare prints can always be used. If you are selecting images for color enlargements, because good color prints are expensive have 8 ½ x 11 color Xeroxes made of your choices. Use these to decide which slide or transparency merits the investment of a color print.

Ordering Photographic Prints

Many times making enlargements is a service that a model or talent test photographer will offer. Many photographers who shoot black and white make prints in their own darkrooms. It is almost always preferable to have a print made by the photographer who shot the photograph. Because of the amount of time and inconvenience involved, many photographers do not do their own darkroom work and will instead have prints made by a professional photo processor.

Most photographers who don't charge for testing will not give you color prints because of the expense. Instead they will divide up the slides with the model so that she can have prints made on her own.

If a photographer gives you the slides or negatives, follow his or her recommendations on labs and techniques for having your prints made. Your local photo finisher (quick photo service, local camera, grocery, or drug store) is less costly because the prints are done by machine. However, the quality is usually not good enough to be displayed in a portfolio. It is better to take your slides to a professional or custom lab for "custom printing."

In most cases, you get what you pay for. A cheap print usually won't bring out the refinements in your slide or negative as well as an excellent, professional custom print. Cheap prints will also distort the colors found in a slide or negative. Such prints may make your skin appear sallow or reddish and blotchy even though it looks beautiful in the slide. You may save money, but if a picture doesn't show you as attractive as you really are, it certainly won't promote you.

You will also get better service because top professional labs will assist you when ordering your print. They will tell you if problems exist in your slide or negative and can forewarn you about the results. When a high-quality custom lab produces a print that is not as good as it should be, they will redo it without protest. Of course, if the error is due to something beyond their control that they informed you about when ordering, they are not responsible for the outcome.

It is important to know the options available to you in order to achieve the best results when ordering photographic prints. Being specific will also ensure that you get optimum results. When you order a print or enlargement from a professional photo lab, these are the decisions you will have to make and the information you will have to provide.

1. Print size.
2. Number of prints.
3. Type of photographic paper.
4. Identification of the slide or negative to be printed.
5. Cropping instructions.
6. Image presentation.
7. Type of photographic printing process to be used.
8. Special instructions to enhance the printed image.

Specify the Size of Print You Want

Prints are available in several sizes. Although there are no rigid size requirements for photographic prints to be used in the portfolio, models most commonly use 8 x 10 (American) or 9 x 12-inch (24 x 30-cm European) print sizes. These measurements refer to the size of the paper on which the image appears. The image either bleeds off the edges of the paper or is surrounded by a white border. Whether your print is borderless, bordered, or bordered and framed will depend on the size of the negative, the cropping adjustments made, and the way your photo is best presented. Prints are also available in 3 x 5, 4 x 5, 5 x 7, and 11 x 14 inches.

Tell How Many Prints You Want to Have Made

Usually you will order one print. However, some labs have special arrangements in which you can get two prints for the price of one if you allow 1 week for processing or the second print will be available at a discount. Having an extra print is always a good idea.

Specify the Print Finish or Type of Photographic Paper You Prefer

In addition to different sizes, photographic paper is available in three types of surfaces. The surface you choose will depend on what your photo will be used for and how it will best be presented.

Glossy. This paper has a high-gloss, shiny surface that looks bright and crisp. An alive, sparkling, slick type of image often looks best when printed on glossy paper. On the contrary, a soft color or black and white photo often looks harsh when printed on glossy paper. When reproduction is involved, printers prefer to shoot halftones from black and white glossy prints.

Matte. This paper is the opposite of glossy paper. It has a dull, no-shine surface that looks subtle and refined. A quiet, soft, or subdued subject often looks better when printed on matte photographic paper. Other types of images may look dull and lifeless on this same paper.

Semimatte. This photographic paper has a surface finish that is in between glossy and matte. It has a smooth, rich look and is usually the best choice for most images. Color photos look well when enlarged on semimatte or pearl surface paper, as it is sometimes called. Semimatte paper tends to have the most natural look of all photographic papers.

There are other paper surfaces available, such as silk finish and textured papers; however, these are usually not used by models and are not suitable for reproduction.

Identify the Negative or Slide to Be Printed

To order a black and white print from black and white film, you will need to provide the negative and the contact sheet. Each negative is assigned a number on the film. This number will appear on your contact sheet along the right side of the image. Indicate which photo you want enlarged by marking it on the contact sheet and listing the number of the frame on your order form. If two numbers appear on one frame, note both numbers, for example, 2/2A. Make sure your markings are clear. Erase any irrelevant markings on the contact sheets to avoid confusion.

To order a color print from color negative film, follow the same procedure as above.

To order a color print from a slide, set aside the desired slide. Indicate on the order form the number found on the cardboard encasement of the slide.

To order a color print from a color transparency, mark an X on the acetate sleeve over the desired image using a grease pencil. On your order form, indicate the frame number that appears on the film.

Do not cut apart a single negative or transparency or remove a slide from its plastic or cardboard mount. If this is necessary, the lab will do it. Also, if you are ordering prints from several different negatives and slides along with individual instructions for each, enclose each strip of film in a separate envelope and write the instructions on the outside.

Treat negatives or transparencies with care. It is best not to handle them to avoid scratches and fingerprints. Often fingerprints cannot be removed without damaging the film. Scratches can rarely be repaired and when enlarged on a print are very obvious and nearly impossible to camouflage by retouching. Processed film is very delicate and should always be encased in acetate sleeves. Always keep negatives and slides at room temperature in a dry place. Extreme heat and moisture will damage them.

Indicate How You Want the Image Cropped and Presented

In most cases no cropping will be necessary. You will inform the lab that you want the image printed "full frame" (see Figure 12). If you want to crop the photo, consult with the photographer to get his or her opinion and suggestions. Use a photo template to help you to envision cropping adjustments.

Figure 12. Shown here are the different options for image presentation. (a) borderless 8 x 10 print (b) full frame bordered 8 x 10 print.

Sometimes cropping is necessary. Remember, neither a 35-mm nor 2¼ negative or transparency size corresponds to an 8 x 10 print. If your slide or negative is 2¼ and you want a full 8 x 10 print, the sides of the image will have to be cropped out. If you have a 35-mm negative or slide that you want to have made into a full 8 x 10 print, you will have to crop out the top and/or bottom edges. Either of these methods will allow you to have a borderless print.

If your negative or slide is to be printed full frame on an 8 x 10 print, there will be a white margin surrounding it. Usually the lab will leave ¼-inch margins at the top and bottom and ¾-inch margins along the sides of a 35-mm image. When printing a 2¼ image full frame, the image size will usually be 7½ x 7½ due to the square format. This means that there will be ¼-inch margins along the sides of the image, with wider margins at the top and bottom.

Indicate the Photographic Printing Process to Be Used

There are different processes used to make prints depending on the type of film that was used and the individual slide or transparency. Your photographer and photo processor should be able to guide you to the best result. The following information explains the four basic processes used.

Black and white prints. A black and white print is made directly from a negative; however, a negative can be printed to appear several different ways. There are approximately 12 degrees of contrast in which your image can be printed ranging from low to high contrast. Your image can be underexposed to appear lighter or overexposed to appear darker. In addition, selected areas of the image can be lightened or darkened.

Color prints from color negatives. Color negative film records colors exactly opposite of those found in the subject, for example, reds are greens. These can only be viewed by having a color contact sheet or color machine prints or proofs made. Examples of this type of film are Ektacolor, Vericolor III, or any type of film with the suffix "color." Color negative film has the advantage of having great exposure latitude. This means that there are more options for correcting or changing colors when a print is made. Prints made from color negative film are called C-prints.

Color prints from color slides or transparencies. Film yielding color slides or transparencies is called color-positive film. It is the most commonly used type of film and is often used when shooting ads, catalogs, and other print assignments. Examples of this type of film are Ektachrome, Kodachrome, or any type of film with the suffix "chrome." These films yield rich, vibrant, and true colors.

The important thing to remember when selecting shots from contact sheets and slides is to not discount a picture because it isn't perfect. The defect might easily be corrected. The only thing that cannot be changed is your facial expression and body movement. A stray hair, caked makeup, a pimple, a hanging thread or a wrinkle in your clothing can all be eliminated. Rely on the skills of your photographer, photo lab, and retoucher to achieve the best results.

Direct prints. Direct prints are made directly from the slide. These are often referred to as Cibachromes (an Ilford brand name) or R-prints and yield a sharp, colorful result. They are also usually quicker and cheaper than internegative prints. This direct method is recommended for printing Kodachrome slides and other slides that have vibrant, true colors and perfect exposure. A good range of tones is important as direct prints tend to have greater contrast than internegative prints.

Internegative prints. Internegative prints mean that your slide or transparency is converted into a color negative, and then a C-print is made. This may take longer and will cost more than an R-print, but it is often the best choice because there is greater control over the colors found in the slide. Internegative prints have the advantage of yielding more pleasing contrast and subtler colors than direct printing. More adjustments can be made in exposure and color balance.

Indicate Any Special Instructions for Making the Print

If the contact sheet image looks ideal, you will inform the lab to match the print to the contact sheet. Consult with your photographer to determine what procedures should be followed by the lab to make the best print from your slide or negative.

Some of the options you will have are: increasing or decreasing contrast, overexposing or underexposing (lightening or darkening overall), and darkening (burning in) or lightening (dodging) certain areas. Softening the image is another option you might consider. Color corrections are important to consider when a color print is being made. For example, if your skin appears sallow in a slide, the lab can change the color filtration so that in the print your skin will look less yellow. For more complete information on these procedures, consult "Techniques for Improving your Photographs" in this chapter.

Checking the Finished Print

Usually making photographic prints requires from two days to one week. When picking up your prints, always examine them carefully. Check your print against your slide or contact sheet photo using the following checkpoints (see also Figure 13).

- Check for correct exposure (overall lightness or darkness).
- Check for detail in highlights and shadows.
- Check for correct colors.
- Check for contrast.   • Check for blemishes
- Check for cropping.   • Check for sharpness.

Figure 13. How to tell a good print. These photographs show how one negative can yield different results in a photographic print. (a) This photo shows how a negative looks when printed in very high contrast. (b) This photo shows the opposite—very low contrast. (c) This photo shows neither too high nor too low contrast, but the wrong exposure, yielding a print that's too dark. (d) This photo shows another extreme of the wrong exposure. This one is too light. (e) This photo has good contrast and exposure, but it is out of focus. (f) This photo displays good contrast, ideal exposure, and sharp focus, but it exhibits blemishes such as dust specks, scratches, and stains. (g) Shown here is an example of a perfect photographic print.

(a)

(b)

(c)

(d)

(e)

(f)

(g)

Use Tables 4 and 5 to evaluate the quality of your print. If there are problems with the print, discuss them with the lab technicians. If problems are not resolved, consult your photographer to determine if and where problems exist or corrections can be made.

TABLE 4   Evaluating a Black and White Print

Good Print	Bad Print
Print displays perfect contrast. It exhibits deep, rich blacks, true, stark whites, and lots of shades of gray in between.	Image is too contrasty, yielding only black and white, no grays. Or, image lacks contrast, meaning there are no crisp blacks or whites, only varying shades of gray.
Print exhibits perfect exposure.	Print is too light, appearing washed out. It needs to be darker. Or print is too dark or murky. It needs to be lighter.
Image is sharp and clear.	Image is blurred, soft, or out of focus. (If it's in sharp focus on the contact sheet, it should be in sharp focus on the print.)
Print displays every detail that appeared in the image on the contact sheet.	Details in highlight or shadow areas are lost yielding instead empty white highlight areas or solid black shadow areas.
Print is of professional quality.	Print has scratches or black or white specks.

TABLE 5   Evaluating a Color Print

The above criteria also apply for color prints. In addition the following should be taken into consideration when judging color prints.

Good Print	Bad Print
Colors in the print are accurate.	Colors in the print do not match those in the slide or negative, for example, print appears too blue with warm tones absent or vice versa.
Colors in the print are vivid and vibrant (there will be a slight loss in this area).	Colors are dull, flat, muddy, or washed out.
Flesh tones are rich and natural.	Flesh tones are yellowish, greenish, purplish, bluish, or whitish.
Whites are white.	Whites are pastel blue, off white, gray, or any color but white.

Copy Negatives If you want to have an additional print made of one of your photos, you will always achieve optimum results by having it made from the negative or transparency. However, if the negative or transparency is not available, you will need to have a copy negative of your print made, and then a new print will be made from this negative. This same process is used when you want to convert a color photo or tearsheet to black and white so it can be printed on a black and white composite.

Copy negatives are available in 35-mm, 2¼, 4 x 5, and 8 x 10 sizes. If you are going to have an 8 x 10 print made, request a 4 x 5 or 8 x 10 copy negative and one 8 x 10 print. You will always achieve best results with this process if the photo to be copied exhibits a full range of tones, lots of detail, and sharpness. It is important to realize that even with a good original print, contrast will increase and sharpness may decrease slightly in the copy. If you are having a photo from a magazine page or other reproduced material copied, it is important to realize that a screen or dot pattern resulting from the halftone or color separation process may be visible in your copy.

Dupes Dupes or duplicates are copies of a slide. Sometimes a photographer will have duplicate slides or transparencies made of the best images from the shooting and give them to the model. A dupe will have a very slight loss of quality from the original slide, but it is fine for a model's purposes. The better the quality of the slide or negative that is being copied, the better the dupe will be. Dupes are inexpensive and are often exhibited on a slide sheet in the model's portfolio. When making a color print, you will usually achieve better results when a print is made from the original slide rather than from a dupe.

Polaroids Occasionally a photographer will give a model Polaroids from a test shooting. Polaroid film differs from regular film in ways other than instantaneous development. It does not record as much detail, color, and contrast as regular film. It makes objects appear softer and slightly diffused. Photographers shoot Polaroids before the regular film to check on composition, lighting arrangement, and details. Examining a Polaroid is helpful for the model to check on hair, makeup, styling (when makeup, hair, and styling people are not employed), expression, and movement.

It is possible to obtain enlargements from Polaroids. The lab will make a copy negative and the color print will be made from this. Because Polaroids are inherently soft, the print will not be very sharp and clear, however, this soft effect might be attractive. The larger, sharper, and more colorful your Polaroid is, the better your result.

Polaroid Slides Polaroid slide film is shot using a 35-mm camera. The photographer can develop the film into slides instantaneously using a special device he or she owns. This type of film has a grainy, soft look. To make prints from either color or black and white Polaroid slide film, a lab will make an R-print.

*Consider Techniques for
Improving Your
Photographs*

The information here is given because as a beginning model you may frequently test with fairly inexperienced photographers. Very few models have their initial test shots done by the best photographers. Photographs taken by an excellent, experienced photographer are nearly perfect and require no or only very slight improvements. No cropping needs to be done to improve the image because the photographer has composed the image in the camera optimally. No exposure correction is needed, and no retouching is necessary. However, because your beginning photos usually will not be done by such photographers, it is helpful to understand ways in which you can improve the appearance of your photos to make them look more professional.

Minor flaws in your photos can be improved by means of various techniques. Remember, subtle changes are more powerful than heavy-handed adjustments. If major changes are needed, not enough care was taken at the shooting or in the darkroom. Photographic enhancement techniques can be used to do the following.

- To eliminate flaws in makeup, hairstyling, and clothing that were unnoticed at the time of the shooting, not to change the model's features or to hide permanent imperfections.
- To cover a photographer's mistake or a problem resulting from composition, lighting, exposure, film processing, or print making.
- To improve a photograph for reproduction. Photo enhancement techniques can enrich and enliven skin tones, reduce grain, whiten whites, and crispen linear elements, all of which can dramatically enhance a photo for reproduction. Because the reproduction process tends to dull colors and decrease sharpness, intensifying these aspects prior to printing will compensate for potential loss.

The important thing to remember when selecting shots from contact sheets and slides is not to discount a picture because it isn't perfect. The defect might easily be corrected. The only thing that cannot be changed is your facial expression and body movement. A stray hair, caked makeup, a pimple, a hanging thread or a wrinkle in your clothing can all be eliminated. Rely on the skills of your photographer, photo lab, and retoucher to achieve the best results.

Don't overdo photo enhancement techniques. Don't dismiss physical flaws by thinking clients will always retouch your pictures before publication. Depending on the client and the job, retouching may not be in the budget. And besides, if it is, retouching will more likely be done to enhance the product or garment, not the model. Extensive retouching can only hurt your chances. For example, a client issues a casting call for a young woman 18 to 25 years old with perfect skin to advertise a new complexion lotion. If you are 40 and look it but have had a retoucher take out your wrinkles so you look 25, when the client sees you, you may not even be auditioned because you will not fit the part. On the other hand, if a casting call is put out for a 40-year-old businesswoman, you will be overlooked and not invited to audition because in your photos you look too young. Retouching must be used with discretion and common sense and should not be used to misrepresent your looks to potential clients. Camera lenses often pick up or exaggerate characteristics that are barely noticeable in person, so toning down or eliminating these flaws is acceptable.

For perfect shots, concentrate on trouble-shooting before and during the photo session. Pay strict attention to details to avoid having to retouch. A photo that needs no correction or enhancement is always best. The techniques listed here are the most common ones used by retouchers, photographers and custom photo labs.

Spotting. While a print is being made in the darkroom, dust, lint and other debris often occur on the negative or photographic paper, resulting in tiny white specks or scratch marks on the finished print. Because it is impossible to have a completely dust-free darkroom, most prints need some spotting. Spotting is done directly on the print by using a retouching dye and a very fine paint brush to paint tiny dots simulating photographic grain where there is none. Sometimes the same technique is used to paint in or augment eyelashes or to define a seam or other detail of a garment.

A photographer or professional lab should always spot your prints before giving them to you.

Cropping. Cropping is one of the easiest ways to enhance a photo. Cropping can be used to improve composition or to eliminate a distracting aspect of a photo. Use cropping to improve composition by framing the part of your picture that is most attractive or important. You can be creative because there are no set rules that necessitate displaying the whole head, entire face, or body. Look at fashion magazines for ideas on cropping. You can do the same with your photos by using the photo template in Figure 11 to visualize different effects. Avoid using the smallest row of template windows because enlarging your photo to the size of these boxes will usually not yield a good result. The more you enlarge a negative or slide or a portion of it, the more grain and contrast, and less sharpness and refinement in your final print. Cropping is most commonly used to cut out distracting or unimportant backgrounds. Also, ask your photographer for his or her opinion when cropping. Many photographers prefer that their work be left intact.

Burning in. Burning in refers to a technique used in the darkroom while the print is being made. It involves exposing a portion of your print to more light to make it appear darker in that area. For example, a white sweater you may have worn in the photo might look washed out and will benefit by burning in the area to reveal textures that were in the sweater.

Dodging. Dodging is also done in the darkroom at the time your print is made. It involves covering an area so that it receives less light so that the area will appear lighter in the finished print. This is a technique commonly employed for models to lighten hair that photographs too dark in black and white or to subdue a shadow on the face or body.

Softening. Softening is done in the darkroom during the print-making process. It is often used on sharp-focus color portraits to flatter the subject. A special filter is used to soften the image slightly. Although the eyelashes will be sharp, the pores of the skin will be less apparent, giving the skin a smoother, more refined appearance.

Color correction. Color correcting is a technique used to ensure that the colors found in a color slide or negative are correctly or attractively translated in the color print. To determine whether an image you select would look better with a little red, yellow, or blue added or subtracted, you can view it through special color correction filters. These filters are referred to as a color viewing kit and are furnished by a custom color lab. After determining what corrections should be made, the lab will make adjustments when your print is made. For example, if your skin looks too yellow or pink, adjustments can be made to subdue or eliminate the unwanted tones. When using this technique, employ it to correct or enhance your personal coloring (hair, skin, and eyes), rather than the background or what you are wearing.

Toning. Toning is done by a retoucher directly on the surface of the print or on the negative or slide. It is the process of using chemicals to change the colors or to darken specific areas in a print or an entire print. For example, toning is used to fill in tan lines or make eyes or clothing appear more colorful. It can even be used to add color to a black and white print. For example, a black and white photo can be given a sepia tone to make it look rustic or old-fashioned.

Bleaching. Bleaching is done directly on the surface of a photographic print or on the negative or slide. Bleaching is performed by a professional retoucher to lighten a specific area or an entire print. The retoucher applies chemicals to the desired area or to an entire print to lighten. When major alterations need to be made, the retoucher erases the area with bleach and then reconstructs it using toning dyes or an airbrush. Bleaching can be used to lighten a blemish, to highlight hair, eyes, and skin for a more luminous effect, to lighten teeth and whites of eyes so they appear clean, white, and bright, and to erase or subdue unflattering shadows or dark-toned imperfections.

Airbrushing. Airbrushing is usually done on the surface of a photographic print. It must be done by a skilled retoucher who uses a fountain pen-like instrument that distributes a very fine spray of retouching dye or paint. Best results are often achieved if it is used in conjunction with other methods (e.g. bleaching). When done poorly or when overdone, it can yield an artifical, retouched look. When done skillfully, it can smooth and refine skin, fabrics, backgrounds, and the like.

THE MODEL'S COMPOSITE

For a model, great pictures are important. However, the best photographs imaginable are worthless if nobody sees them. A composite is a model's most important promotional tool. It serves several functions.

- The composite is an excellent way to introduce a model or a model's new look. Often the composite is the first exposure a model has to a client. It can expose her to out-of-town clients and to many more people than she would be able to meet in person.

- The composite is a good reminder. Even though a client may have interviewed or worked with a model, a new composite can be a reminder that the model is available. It keeps the client posted as to the model's progress, appearance changes, and so on.

- The composite is an effective reference tool. It can be kept in the client's files for future reference. After interviewing scores of models, the only reminder of the meeting is the composite.

- The composite sells the model. The composite is documentation of the best testing and work the model has done. It provides proof of the extent and variety of her capabilities. It displays the highlights of her tests and portfolio and acts as a brochure that can be left behind. It can be the instrument that persuades a client to book, audition, or see the model.

A STEP-BY-STEP GUIDE TO MAKING A COMPOSITE
Step 1: Select Photos for Your Composite

Select Photos According to Your Look or Type

Go through your portfolio and contact sheets with your agent, and select your best pictures. Have prints made, which may include converting color slides or prints into black and white. Edit this group of photos by taking your priorities and the following factors into consideration.

Know exactly what types of work you are qualified to do and which clients you should be approaching. Select photos geared toward specific types of clients and assignments. The type of modeling you are best qualified for should be evident by looking at your composite. Formalizing your approach and then creating a composite to promote your look to clients who utilize models of your type is your objective. Trying to show that you can do all types of modeling (for example, fashion, product, character) in one composite is not a good idea because it confuses clients. Instead, you should concentrate on assembling one of the following types of composites. Basically there are eight different types of composites.

Female print fashion model composite. A composite that will promote you as a print fashion model usually includes a headshot that clearly shows the skin and facial features. It should also include a body shot showing the figure (for example, a bathing suit, leotard, etc.) and a full-length fashion shot that shows the legs (for example, a dress or skirt and blouse). One shot, preferably the headshot should clearly show the cut and length of the hair. Also, if the model can do specialities (for example, she has excellent hands, legs, etc.), one shot should prominently display this asset. Showing a variety of moods or expressions is important: it is always a good idea to have one smiling shot showing teeth. It is also necessary to show a variety of clothing, makeup, and hairstyles as well as different movements that display the model's look and the type of fashion model she is. For example, a high-fashion model would show trendy yet sophisticated clothing, makeup, hair, and movements, whereas a junior model would show trendy yet youthful concepts in these areas.

Male print fashion model composite. A male fashion model should have a composite that includes a headshot clearly showing the facial features, skin, and cut and style of his hair. A body shot that shows the physique (for example, active sportswear, bathing suit, or workout wear) is a good idea. It is also a good idea to display one shot taken with a female model. Showing that the model looks good in a variety of clothing styles (businesswear, formal wear, casual clothes, sportswear, outerwear, leisure clothes) that are suited to his look is the objective. Showing that the hair can be styled in more than one way is also a good idea. A range of expressions with one smiling shot is also necessary. The clothing, makeup, hair, movements, and moods depicted will depend on whether the model is a high-fashion or general-fashion model.

Child model composite. A child model's composite should include a headshot that shows the cut and style of the hair, the quality of the skin, and the facial features. Pictures that show the child in play clothes, school clothes, and dress wear are important. A range of expressions, with at least one smiling shot, should be the objective.

Fashion show model composite. The fashion show model uses a composite similar to the print fashion model, but it is often a good idea to include a shot taken on the runway. Photos that show the model head-to-toe, highlighting the quality of her figure and her ability to move, are more important than those that capitalize on the face.

Straight product/commercial model composite. This type of composite is used by male or female straight product/commercial models seeking work in print ads and television commercials. A good basic headshot that shows the cut and style of the hair, skin texture, and facial features is important. The model should look expressive yet sincere, with an average or attractive look. He or she should not look like a fashion model. Candid, slice-of-life, three-quarter-length, and full-length shots showing the model in a variety of roles (for example, executive, doctor, parent, or next-door neighbor) should be included. It is a good idea to have one smiling shot and one shot in which you are holding, using, or accompanying a product. Acting ability should be apparent by looking at these pictures. They should look like freeze frames from a television commercial, not like stiff, posed pictures.

Character model composite. A character model's composite is used to secure print and television assignments. A variety of headshots showing the characters the model portrays most convincingly is necessary. Three-quarter- and full-length shots can also be used, if they are important for depicting a character. One shot in which the model is out of character as her-or himself is also a good idea. Complete props, outfits, and other details are an absolute must to make the composite look professional.

Promotional model composite. A promotional model's composite usually has one picture on the front such as an attractive, friendly head-shot, preferably smiling, that shows the model's features, hair, and personality. A body shot or shot that shows the figure and legs is a good idea as are full length and three-quarter-length shots showing the model in a variety of settings. A promotional model should portray looks such as an authoritative spokesperson, a glamourous beauty (for example, an all-American beauty pageant winner), and a wholesome, girl-next-door, because these types are most often requested by trade show clients. It is also a good idea to include a shot that shows the model demonstrating a product or at an exhibition. In all of these shots the model's aim should be to appear attractive or pretty, but not like a high-fashion model.

Specialty model composite. An individual who is qualified to model only her hands, legs, and/or feet should aim for a composite that shows her excellent feature(s) alone and accompanying a variety of products. The products selected should combine well with her special feature.

Select Pictures That Represent You Accurately

The pictures should be an accurate representation of you and the looks you can easily recreate. The pictures should also be current. Avoid using photos that are over 6 months old.

Select Pictures That Display Variety

Each picture on the composite should display a different facial expression or mood, clothing, hairstyle, makeup, and movement. Use photos from more than one photographer. Clients will be interested in how you look in all sorts of lighting situations and photographic styles. If all the photos on your composite are done by one photographer, make sure there is a mixture of different backgrounds, lighting techniques, and moods. Aim for a variety of settings by having one shot taken outdoors.

Select Pictures That Will Appeal to Your Market

Assembling a composite that has beautiful pictures but that does not fit the needs of the clients in your market won't help to promote you as a model. The best way to ensure that the photos you select are right for the market is to have an agent assist you in the selection process. Consult your agent as to how she or he thinks your card should look. A composite is one of the tools the agent uses to market you so it is important that he or she likes it. If it is not up to the agency's standards, they might not distribute it. Follow the agency's recommendations on which photographers shoot good composite photos.

Pay strict attention to the type of work that is best suited to your look and the availability of that type of work in your market. It is senseless to put all high-fashion, editorial-type photos on a card that you will be using in a town where only very ordinary catalogs are shot. You may want to include one fun or unusual shot to draw attention, but the majority of the card should be aimed at the clients in your particular market. In general, select photos in a similar style to those of the clients and photographers with whom you would like to work.

Aim for visibility. Make your assets and versatility obvious to clients. Keep in mind that clients don't use their imaginations when looking at cards. If you have curled hair in every picture, they will assume that your hair is naturally curly and that you can't do it in any other style. If you have no smiling pictures, clients will assume you have bad teeth or an unattractive smile; if you don't show legs, they'll assume you have problem legs.

Play up the abilities and features that set you apart from other models. If you are a fashion model, select photos in which you are wearing clothing that will help potential clients to envision how you will look in the items they are selling. For example, if a male model is the right type for formal wear, including a picture on the composite in which he is wearing a tuxedo will more likely secure him work from tuxedo rental companies than the model who doesn't have this type of picture. A female model who wears a 34B bra and has all the other qualifications necessary for modeling lingerie will gain the attention of lingerie companies with a beautiful lingerie shot that shows her figure to advantage. Even a model who is too small to model fashions can turn her size into a marketable asset by including a picture of herself standing by an attractive piece of office furniture. Furniture manufacturers usually select a smaller model because she will make the furniture appear larger and more outstanding.

It is important to realize that one composite will not appeal to all types of clients. Versatility is a valuable asset for a model but printing 10 pictures on a card in which you're barely recognizable as the same model in each only confuses clients and makes it more difficult for them to categorize and remember you. Determine your potential clients and create a composite for them. For example, if you can do fashion modeling in addition to product/commercial modeling, it is wiser to have two composites. One composite will show you in fashion-oriented clothing and settings, whereas the other composite will show you adopting a variety of moods and commercial roles, holding products, and in a nonglamourous way. When distributing your composites, you'll give the fashion composite to fashion clients, the product/commercial composite to advertising, product, and illustration photographers. You'll increase your opportunities in both areas.

Your composite is an important reference tool for a client and will be retained by him or her for several months or longer. Therefore, it is wise to spend an extra week or two to obtain an important shot or to replace one of your shots that isn't quite up to standard. Test until you achieve results worthy of a potential client's attention. Review the necessary photos for different types of composites and make sure your composite includes them. A fashion model who assembles a composite that doesn't clearly show her legs or figure makes it difficult for clients to judge whether she might be right for their assignments. The average photographer has hundreds, even thousands of cards in his or her files, so it is important that your composite really "sells" your attributes.

Plan your card carefully. Assembling an excellent composite takes time. Do not try to put a composite together in a rushed manner because you'll spend more and sacrifice quality. On the other hand, taking months to acquire a composite is not advisable. Being without a composite will keep your career at a standstill. If you are a beginner it is important to realize that your first card probably won't be your best. You should aim for basic, straightforward shots that will allow clients and photographers to make comparisons between you and other new models. Waiting until you have a collection of several great shots can take a long time. Instead, concentrate on getting a good headshot and full-length shot and have a simple card made. Don't delay making your composite because you are afraid of rejection. Choose only photos that meet the previously listed requirements and the standards you and your agent have set.

Make certain that you have an interested agent's input, but realize that one composite may not work equally well for all agents. Agents differ as to their preferences in composites. Each agency has a different approach—each one must offer something that will distinguish the agency from their competition. Select the agent or agents you want to work with before you begin making your composite. This is the only way to guarantee that your composite will be usable.

It is also important to be aware that one composite may not work equally well in all markets. If you want to model in Europe it may be necessary to obtain new pictures and remake your composite when you get there. European markets tend to be ahead of American markets, especially in fashion trends. Also, your card for use in Europe must include metric measurements.

Select Professional-Looking Photographs

Select pictures from actual bookings (prestigious advertisements and fashion editorials are found on the best models' cards) or ones that look as if they were taken under professional circumstances. Avoid those resembling beginner's test shots. Choose pictures that exhibit good lighting, well-styled clothing, and attractive makeup and hairstyling. Excellent, professional quality photographs always catch a photographer's or client's eye.

Select Photographs That Will Reproduce Well

Though virtually any photograph can be reproduced, some photographs will reproduce better than others. The printing process is not capable of improving the quality of a photograph. Rarely does a reproduced photograph look identical to its original; there is always a slight loss in quality. The quality of the photos you select has a lot to do with the quality you obtain in your finished composite. You will be more likely to obtain good results by relying on your printer's advice and by following the guidelines in Table 6.

Example of a contemporary woman's composite. Courtesy Elite Models, New York.

TABLE 6 Guide to Selecting Photographs for Reproduction

The most difficult types of photos to reproduce are . . .	Instead choose . . .
Photos with high or low contrast. Be aware that many times color photos are shot with low contrast, soft lighting that will not look well when converted into black and white or printed on a color card. The opposite, too high contrast photos, are also difficult to reproduce. If the contours of the face (especially the outline of the nose and jaw) and the texture of the skin barely show in the photo, they will not be visible in the printed composite.	Images that display a full scale of tones and photographic prints of medium contrast.
Photos shot with a very grainy effect or photos with a fuzzy, mottley appearance.	Fine- or medium-grain photos.
Photos that are out of focus or extreme soft focus.	Sharp focus shots that show detail well.
Sloppy prints with specks, scratches, fingerprints, dents, stains, etc.	Flawless glossy photographic prints.
Photos shot, developed, or printed with the wrong exposure. In color, photos with off-color skin tones.	Photos that are ideal—neither washed out nor too dark. In color, strong, beautiful colors that are neither muddy, dull, nor washed out.
Photos with large, murky, or shadowy areas that hide important details. Photos with large, washed-out highlight areas that obliterate details.	Photos shot with medium- to high-contrast lighting or even light, soft shadows or well-defined shadows.
Poorly, extensively, or obviously retouched photos.	Photos on which slight, expert retouching has been done can enhance it for reproduction but inform the retoucher beforehand that you plan to use the photo for reproduction.
Photos displaying a similar color or tone of background as the subject (for example, dark hair against a dark background). The two will blend into one another.	Photos with different colors in background and subject.
Photos from newspapers and other low-quality reproduction processes.	Composites printed from original photographic prints are highest in quality. However, pages from many high-quality magazines also print well.

Step 2: Decide How Much You Want to Spend on the Composite

Decide how much money you want to invest in the composite. Although the majority of your energy and money should be devoted to getting the right photos, using them effectively is also important. Aim for the best-quality composite you can afford. You will want your composite to look professional and equal to or better than the models with whom you will be competing. Don't scrimp as the composite is an investment in your career. Consider all the things that go into making a composite and research prices and offerings of several printing companies. Then set a budget and adhere to it. Some of the options are the following.

Color or Black and White

Color composites are about three to four times more expensive than black and white composites. Your composite can exhibit both black and white and color shots. Many models choose a color front and a black and white back, or on a four-sided composite, a color front and back with black and white inside. In recent years, color has become much more popular and several models have color cards. Clients do not insist on color composites; however, those who shoot the majority of their work in color often prefer them. Because color or black and white composites can misrepresent a model's actual coloring, a model is usually asked to appear for a personal interview before she or he is booked for an assignment. The purpose of the composite, whether you choose black and white or color, is to spark the client's interest and persuade him or her to interview or book you.

There are several good reasons why you might consider choosing a color composite over a black and white one. If you have very distinctive, photogenic coloring and consider it to be a very marketable asset, such assets will be overlooked in black and white. If you have very impressive color photographs and tearsheets that lose their impact when converted into black and white, you should opt for a color composite. If you are an experienced model and the investment is justified, you will be drawing income that will allow you to recover the money you spend on the card in just a few bookings.

As a beginning model you will be improving rapidly. You'll want to update your cards often to show your progress and improvement. Most models start with a a simple one or two-sided black and white card and then, if justified, print a color composite or a more extensive black and white one in 3 to 6 months. Limit your investment in the beginning. When you begin to obtain opportunities and assignments, reinvest your money in a more expensive composite.

Don't be fooled by printers who offer very low cost color cards. Ask to see samples. Color printing is best done by experts who have a lot of experience working on model's composites. It is better to be safe with a black and white card than to take a chance with cheap color printing that may render unflattering skin tones and off-color hair colors.

The Form of Composite.

There are basically two different forms of composites: card type and paper type. The form you choose should depend on what is most popular in your market. The number of sides depends on how many looks and high-quality photos you have to display.

Standard sizes for card-type composites are

- 5½ x 8½ format (also 6 x 8, 6 x 9) printed on one side or both sides. It can depict from two to five photos. (Depending on the proportions of the photos involved, it may be possible to fit up to 10 photos on a two-sided card.)
- A double card measures 5½ x 17, is folded in half and is printed on four sides. It can display 4 to 10 photos.

This form is printed on card stock and is currently the most popular among models. Nearly all fashion models in the United States and Europe use card-type composites. The most common is the two-sided composite or flip card. There may be slight deviations in sizes depending on the printer or the country where the composite was printed.

Paper-type composites are available in standard sizes:
- 8½ x 11 format printed on one side or both sides.
- 8½ x 17 folded in half and printed on four sides.

This form is sometimes used by character, promotional, and product models. In general, card-type composites are more expensive than paper-type composites.

Printing Considerations

There are several factors relating to the printing of a composite that will increase or decrease the quality and the cost. The printing company you select will affect the cost. Printers differ in price depending on where they are located, their experience, offerings, and the quality of the equipment they use. Printers who offer the model a lot of guidance when putting the composite together are also higher priced.

The quantity will also influence the cost. Most printers establish minimum quantities of 250 or 500 composites. The minimum quantity for a color composite may be 1000. The larger the quantity, the lower the cost per composite.

Considerations such as the quality of paper you select on which to have the composite printed will raise or lower the price. Most card-type composites are printed on 100-pound card stock. If you want a glossy or matte enameled paper to give your composite a slick or smooth look, the price will be higher.

A host of other factors will also determine the price of the composite. For example, the design you select may affect the price. Printers usually charge extra for the set-up costs involved if you want a special layout, rules framing the edges of your pictures, a special typeface, or other design details.

Selecting special features will increase the cost. For example, if you order a double or four-sided composite, it will be necessary to "score" the composite so it can be folded. Laminating is a feature you may want for a color composite because it provides a protective plastic coating and a slick, professional appearance.

In addition to these considerations, the process used to print your composite can increase or decrease the cost. Gang printing, or printing your composite together with other models' composites, will decrease the cost. However, in most cases, individualized printing processes will yield the best results.

Design Your Composite

The design of your composite contributes to its effectiveness. Agencies sometimes have a custom design established for the composites used by all the models in the agency. Adhere to the agency's style and use the printers they recommend. If this doesn't apply in your case and you would like to design your own card, be sure that it matches the standards of the agencies through which you will be working and obtain their approval for the design.

Arranging the Pictures on Your Composite

Various composite styles can be effective. The format selected will depend on the strength of the individual photos involved, what the model's objectives are, what the preferences of his or her market are, and advice from his or her agent.

A standard composite has a headshot on the front and three full- and three-quarter-length shots on the back. If you will be using this format, aim for a good headshot. This photo will be the most important one of all because it will catch the viewer's attention and encourage a closer look. It is usually best to use an attractive yet basic headshot, one that will not only convince viewers of your good looks but also give the appearance that you are able to fit into several different categories and work for several different clients. It is also preferable, particularly for a beginning model, to select a shot that exhibits your predominant look. It is ideal to show up for appointments looking like the photo on the front of your composite.

Another format that is commonly used is to have two headshots on the front of the composite. A model might do this to highlight her versatility. For example, she might display one photo such as the one described above, and next to it show a more glamourous or unusual type of photo.

Some models chose a third type of format for setting up their composites. This type of format makes it indistinguishable which is the front and which is the back of the composite. For example, both sides display her name and agency logo. On each side a headshot and two full-length shots are displayed. The model's statistics usually appear on one side only.

There are several other ways in which a model might arrange the photos on her composite. For example, a model who wants to highlight her face might include several beauty shots on the front of her composite. There are no specific rules. What is most important is that your composite highlights your competitive advantages.

Composite Design Tips

- For easy viewing, keep photos as large as possible. Full-length shots that are reduced too much make the model's face and other details difficult to see. Keep in mind that the most important or attractive shot should command the most space. Determine priorities. The model should be the focal point. The model's face and figure are the most important elements and should be kept as large as possible. Crop out unnecessary or unimportant backgrounds that take up valuable space. If you can't crop out empty backgrounds, consider putting an inset photo in the available space.

- Obtain photographs from your photographer that have been printed full frame. An image that is composed so that there is some background space around the model rather than one that is tightly cropped will also give your printer more options for fitting the photo onto your composite.

- If certain parts must be cropped out of your photograph so that it will fit into a specified space on the composite, avoid cutting out parts of you that a client will want to see. For example, don't crop out your legs. On the other hand, elbows are usually not a factor that clients often consider, so cropping out the edge of an elbow that sticks a little too far out of the picture is acceptable.

- The layout should encourage the viewer to look at the pictures. Always choose a simple, uncluttered layout (see Figure 14). Leaving some blank space somewhere on the card will allow clients to make notations. Be consistent on the front and back of your composite. If pictures are framed on one side, the pictures appearing on the reverse side should also be framed. Also, it is ideal to have pictures appearing either horizontally or vertically on both sides of the card.

- Make certain the design of your composite looks current. Notice layouts in your favorite magazines and on cards used by other models. Collect samples from your agent of composites he or she thinks are well designed.

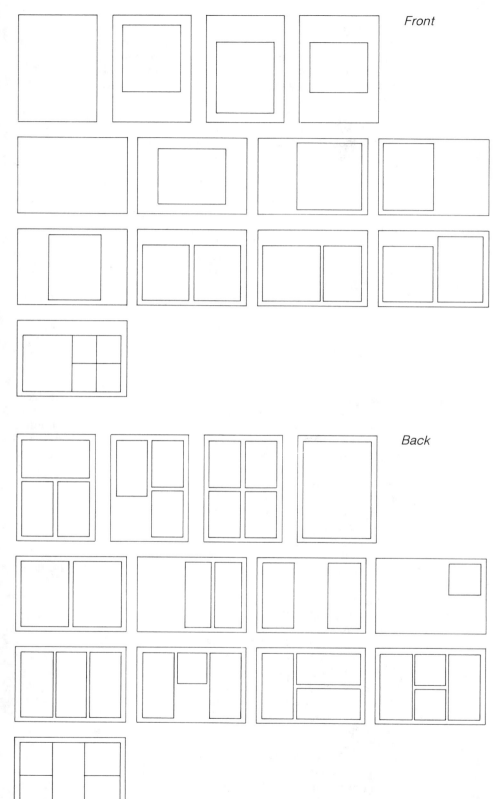

Back

Figure 14. Composite layouts.

- Rely on the expertise of your lithographer and printer. They will use a proportional scale to find what reductions are possible with your photos. You will not always be able to reduce pictures to the sizes you would like because of the ratio of proportions involved. You will have to make decisions. Either you will have to eliminate one of your photos to allow enough room or you will have to crop out parts of your photos in order to make them fit on the composite. For example, a full-length shot with your arms outstretched will not fit into a long narrow space on the composite without some cropping. Horizontally composed photos (for example, when the model is lying down and the body is shot as a landscape) are the most difficult to fit onto the composite along with several other photos. Don't try to put every picture you have on the composite. Include only the very best, essential photos.

- If you are including a picture from a magazine cover or tearsheet, try to include a portion of the type and graphics found on the page so that the client can see it was a job and appeared in a publication. After your first card, you should include at least one picture from a job to lend prestige and professionalism to your composite.

- Aim for a layout that flows, that catches the viewer's attention, and that leads the viewer from one shot to another. Photos that have a similar expression or setting should not be placed side by side. Also, don't put pictures side by side in which you are facing in the same direction. Your printer can "flip" your picture so that it has the desired orientation. In most cases, photos are placed so that the model faces in toward the center of the composite.

- If one of the pictures you want to put on your composite includes another model, crop him or her out of the picture. It is not a good idea to include the other model, especially if you are the same sex and age. This is because attention will be drawn away from you and it will confuse the viewer.

- When designing your composite you will need to decide where on the composite your name and statistics will appear and whether your pictures will be bled (picture extends to the edges of the paper, no border), bordered (a white, gray, or black border around the pictures), or framed (a white or black narrow line around the edges of each picture with a wider contrasting black, gray, or white border around all pictures).

- Study different composite layouts included in this chapter. Often fitting all the pictures onto a composite is a little like assembling a jigsaw puzzle. With knowledge, creativity, and a realistic approach you can usually arrive at the desired result.

Information to Include on a Composite

In addition to your photos there are other elements that must be included on a composite. The following explains the nonpictorial elements that should be included.

Your Name Your name should stand out on the composite above everything else. Always list it on the front, and if the statistics appear on another side, list the name again beside the statistics.

Select a good typeface in which to print your name and statistics. Make sure it is easy to read and stands out. Stick to classic, simple styles that lend importance to the information. Avoid outdated styles or frilly styles that lack credibility. Obtain samples of typefaces from other models' composites or magazines and ask your printer if he or she can supply them for your card. Generally it is a good idea to use the same typeface for all information on the card.

Never put just your first name on the composite unless it is one-of-a-kind. This is very confusing for agents and clients. If you are considering using a different name on your composite, check it with your agent first.

Agency Logo Having an agency logo imprinted on your composite gives you credibility and ensures that clients will know how to contact you. In order to use an agency logo, you must have signed a contract with an agency or you must obtain their permission. Don't forget logos of agencies in other cities if you will be using the card there or if they are well known. Association with a well-known agency adds prestige and draws attention.

Your Measurements and Information The personal information you include on your composite will depend on what type of model you are. Consult Table 7.

TABLE 7   Statistics to Include on a Composite

Fashion and promotional models[a]

Female Models	Male Models
Height (in feet and inches) in stocking feet	Height
Size (misses and/or junior) (Most models can wear a range of sizes, 7–8–9.)[b]	Suit size (40 R)
Bust (in inches) taken at the fullest part (Also indicate cup size if B because it will make you eligible for modeling bathing suits and lingerie.)	Shirt size (collar and sleeve length in inches)
Waist (in inches) taken at slimmest point	Waist
Hips (in inches) taken at the fullest point (usually 7 inches below waistline)	Inseam (from crotch)
Shoes (length)	Shoes
Hair color (specify color whether it is dark, medium, or light. See list of commonly listed shades.)	Hair color
Eye color	Eye color

[a]Large-size fashion models often omit measurements of bust, waist and hips. Instead they give blouse and pant sizes.
[b]Petite models should give the Petite dress size they can wear.

Product/commercial models or actors and actresses

Height	Height
Size (dress)	Size (suit)
Hair color	Hair color
Eye color	Eye color
Union affiliations	Union affiliations
Special abilities, skills, or talents (for example, voiceover)	Special abilities, skills, or talents

Child models

Height (in inches if under 5 feet)	Height
Weight	Weight
Size	Size
Date of birth	Date of birth
Hair color	Hair color
Eye color	Eye color
Shoe size	Shoe size
Waist and inseam (optional) for boys	

Be truthful about your statistics because if you are booked for a job, clients will use the sizes on your composite for the clothes they will bring to the booking. If you will be using your composite in Europe, your measurements must also be noted in metrics. Consult Table 8 for conversions.

TABLE 8   Conversion Chart for Composites to be Used Internationally

American	French/Continental	American	French/Continental
Height	**Hauteur (cm)**	Size	Confection
5′6″	1.68	Collar	Cou
5′6½″	1.69	Inseam	Pantalon Int.
5′7″	1.71	See all size conversions in Table	
5′7½″	1.72	2 in Chapter 5. Composites used	
5′8″	1.73	in Europe and Japan list French	
5′8½″	1.74	terminology and metric	
5′9″	1.75	measurements.	
5′9½″	1.77	**Shoes**	**Chasseures**
5′10″	1.78	See shoe size conversions in	
5′10½″	1.79	Table 2 in Chapter 5.	
		Bust	**Poitrine**
5′11″	1.80	32″	81 cm
5′11½″	1.81	33	84
6′0″	1.83	34	86
6′½″	1.84	35	89
6′1″	1.85	36	91
6′1½″	1.86	37	93
6′2″	1.88	**Waist**	**Taille**
		21	53
		22	56
		23	58
		24	61
		25	64
		26	66
		Hips	**Hanches**
		Refer to Bust/Poitrine above.	

English	French	English	French
Hair	**Cheveux**	**Eyes**	**Yeux**
Light blonde	Blond clairs	Blue	Bleus
Blonde	Blonds	Light blue	Bleus clairs
Honey blonde	Blonds miel	Blue-green	Bleus-verts
Strawberry blond	Blonds roux	Blue-grey	Bleus-gris
Ash blonde	Blonds cendres	Green	Verts
Dark blonde	Blonds fonces	Hazel-green	Noisettes verts
Light brown	Chatains clairs	Grey	Gris
Medium brown	Chatains	Hazel	Noisettes
Brunette/brown	Bruns	Light brown	Bruns clairs
Chestnut	Marrons	Brown	Bruns
Dark brown	Bruns fonces	Red-brown	Marrons
Brown-black	Bruns noir	Black	Noir
Auburn	Chatains roux		
Black	Noir		
Salt and pepper	Blanc et marrons		
Grey	Gris		
Red	Roux		

Other useful conversions

2.2 pounds = 1 kilo

1 inch = 2.5 centimeters

Don't lie about your measurements even if you plan to lose weight or begin an exercise program. Don't misrepresent your height. Your card indicates your actual sizes, hair length, hair color, etc. Obtain your ideal measurements, then have your pictures taken and your composite made. If you do make changes after your composite has been assembled, you will have to update your photos and make a new card or notify and visit your clients so they can see the change. Models often fudge on the truth about measurements by about ½ inch and most clients allow for this, but greater exaggerations are inexcusable.

Other Information to Include

Your specialities. If you have features that are outstanding, they should be marketed as well. The most commonly listed specialties are excellent hands and excellent legs. Excellent skin and excellent feet are also sometimes noted. Some models also note "actress," "singer," "dancer," or "sports" when they have talent and training in these areas. If you have a voice tape, note "Voice-over." If you are a member of a performer's union, list the initials of the union, for example SAG (Screen Actor's Guild) and AFTRA (American Federation of Television and Radio Artists).

Credits. The photographer's name should appear in fine print alongside each photo. You should include a photo credit unless the photographer asks you not to include it. If makeup artists, hairstylists, and fashion stylists did your makeup, hair, and styling, you may also want to credit them. Anyone who donated his or her items or services for the shooting (for example, a design student who allowed you to use one of his or her garments) should always receive credit. This will help these individuals to further their careers. Always make sure you spell the person's name correctly.

Social Security number. Listing an "S.S.#" is optional, but it is a common practice in certain cities and it is a good idea for models without agents.

Answering service number. List your answering service number if you are not working through an agent. Don't list your home telephone number or address.

Season and year the composite was printed. Listing this information helps photographers and clients when updating their files; however, agents often prefer no date.

Printing Your Composite

Aim for the best-quality printing you can afford. A composite is one of the few self-promotion tools a model can use to secure bookings, auditions, testings, and other opportunities. It should show the model at his or her absolute best and make a professional presentation. Your agency should be able to recommend printers of differing quality and price. Examine samples of the printers you are considering. Ask to see models' composites they have previously printed. Bring along samples of composites that you think are well done so the printer has an idea of the quality you expect. Generally, it is not a good idea to engage a printer who has had no experience with composites.

Keep in mind that you'll have to pay more for higher quality. Often models spend a lot of time and money assembling good pictures, thinking they'll be able to save money by having the card done by a fast, inexpensive print shop. Good photographs can be ruined, and their effectiveness diminished by poor reproduction. A poorly printed composite makes an unprofessional appearance.

A model's composite is printed using offset lithography. For a black and white composite, black and white tearsheets or prints are selected by the model and converted into halftones for printing. The standard printing process requires only two tones, black and white; however, a photo of a model must display a variety of tones ranging from black to grays to white. By placing a special screen with dots or fine lines over the material to be reproduced, the halftone is produced. Generally for composites, a 133- or 150-line/inch screen is used. The greater the number of lines, the finer the detail and quality.

For a color composite, color separations are required. Four separate negatives from the model's transparency or color print are made, isolating in each the yellow, black, red, and blue present. These films are then printed together to arrive at a four- or full-color composite. The color photographs are screened the same as for black and white; the colors and gradations are broken down into dots so that the photo can be reproduced using ink, the press, and paper.

When halftones or color separations are completed, the linework (graphics, type, etc) is shot, and all the elements of the composite are assembled on a piece of film from which the plates for the printing press will be produced. At this stage, a proof is made. After the proof has been corrected and approved, the composite goes to press. The pressman does several "make readies" or test prints to make sure that the finished printed piece closely matches the proof. During the printing he or she monitors the press so that all composites from the first to the last are consistent in quality. When the composites come off the press, the ink must be allowed to dry for several hours. When dry, the composites are trimmed to the correct size and the job is complete.

Preparing Your Materials to Submit to the Printer

The following is a list of the items you will need to submit for printing a composite. Always give clear, written instructions.

- Black and white prints (for a black and white composite), color slides, transparencies, or prints for a color composite. Printers do not use the negatives. Check that prints are in perfect condition. Printers usually prefer 8 x 10 glossy prints. Write your name lightly in grease pencil on the back of each print.

- A sketch of the layout indicating where each picture is to go. Note positions 1, 2, 3, 4, 5, etc. on the layout and write the corresponding numbers on the backs of your photos.

- The typeface or a sample of the lettering you would like used for your name and statistics.

- A typewritten or clearly printed list giving your name as you want it on the composite, measurements, and specialties. Include a list of photo credits and also indicate the name of the photographer on the backs of pictures taken by each (Note "Photographer:" to avoid the printer confusing your name with the photographer's name)

- Copies of the agency logos you wish to have printed on the card.

- The type of paper on which you wish the composite to be printed. Many printers will not offer this option. If given the option, select a matte or glossy stock depending on which enhances your photos. Matte enamel card or paper stocks are often chosen for black and white, whereas glossy stocks are usually preferred for color printing.

Always choose a paper with a smooth rather than textured surface. Also, select the whitest paper available. Inexpensive papers often have a slight grey or yellow tinge, which detracts from your photos.

- The quantity (number of composites, for example 500 or 1,000)
- A telephone number where you can be reached.
- A deposit for printing. Most printers require a 50% deposit.

Find out at this time when the proof will be ready. Always call first before making the trip to the printer to confirm that it is ready.

Proofing Your Composite After you have submitted the necessary materials, the printer will produce a proof. This is the only way to preview what your finished composite will look like and to make changes before it goes to press. The proof is your insurance. If you have made corrections or alterations on your proof, but the composite comes out looking totally different, your proof will be your evidence and will entitle you to have your composite reprinted at no extra charge. It is always a good idea to insist on seeing a proof. This prevents misunderstanding and serves as a protection for you and the printer.

There are basically two types of proofs that printers use for black and white printing: Dylux or "blue line" and Kodaline or "silverprint." The blue line type of proof is usually included in the printing price. It is blue and yellow and printed on thin paper. It does not indicate contrast or gradation in your photographs, nor do flaws show up as plainly. A blue line will allow you to check that the typesetting and layout are correct.

A Kodaline or silver print is a high-quality proof and you must specify that you want this type. There may be an extra charge, but it is worth the money because it is far more accurate in rendering the final result. Kodaline proofs are black and white and are printed on a high-quality photographic type of paper. These proofs look the way your finished composite will look. They allow you to preview how your picture will look and how the typesetting and layout appears. It is always best to look at a Kodaline proof, especially if you are unaccustomed to dealing with printing.

The Proofing Checklist Consult this checklist to determine what to look for when checking a printer's proof.

☐ Check that photos are in the correct positions, properly oriented (top of photo appears top), and in the specified order.

☐ Check that photos have been cropped to specifications.

☐ Check that your name, measurements, and the agency logo have been correctly typeset and placed.

☐ If you have included photographer's credits, make sure the photos and names match up correctly.

☐ Check for blemishes, such as lint marks, scratches, and specks, that were not on the photos that you submitted. Try wiping away anything you see on the proof with your fingers first, then circle anything that remains.

☐ Check for contrast. Compare the contrast of the proof photos against the contrast of the original photos. Make sure that the outline and contours of your face and features (particularly the nose and jaw) are as apparent in the proof as they are in your photos.

☐ Check for sharpness. If the photos in the proof appear fuzzy or slightly out of focus, yet were sharp in your prints, bring it to the printer's attention. The cameraman may not have focused correctly on your photos when shooting the halftones.

☐ Check for density. Hair and skin tones in the proof should match your photos in overall lightness and darkness.

In color printing, your printer will supply you with either a color key and/or a Chromalin proof. Each has its advantages. A color key proof is good for the pressman because it makes it easy for him or her to check the density of each color that is printed. A Chromalin is usually the model's preferred proof because it looks like the actual printed composite (see Table 9). When looking at your color proof, take all of the above factors into consideration plus the following.

☐ Check that colors found in the Chromalin closely match those found in the photos you submitted. Look for unwanted reds, yellows, blues, and greens in the color of your hair and skin. Since the composite is supposed to sell you rather than the garments you are wearing, accurate hair colors and flesh tones take priority.

Whether you are proofing a black and white or color composite, discuss anything you are in doubt about with the printer and don't take anything for granted. Be sure to clarify each item that needs to be changed at the close of your meeting with the printer. Note any changes that are to be made by writing directly on the proof. If extensive or complicated alterations need to be made, have a second proof made to ensure that changes have been made correctly.

Once you okay the proof, you are agreeing that everything in the proof is exactly as you want it to be in the finished composite. If you overlooked something at the proofing stage, your printer is not responsible for reprinting, providing the finished product matches the proof.

TABLE 9   Evaluating Printing Quality

Good	Poor
Photographs on the composite are of the same contrast as the original photos given to the printer. The composite photos may be slightly higher in contrast but exhibit a good balance of black, white, and a multitude of grays.	Photographs on the composite are much higher in contrast than the original, so much so that they look washed out, too light so that the nose or jawline disappears, or the opposite, too dark with some areas showing only darkness with no detail, for example, the eyes or the hair.
Photos show good flesh tones. They should fall into the soft, very light to medium gray range. On a color composite, photos should have true, slightly pinkish or peachy flesh tones. Skin should look smooth and even.	Flesh tones are washed out white or muddy gray. In color, flesh tones are washed out or a color cast not found in the original photo, for example, reddish, orangey, yellowish, or bluish skin tones are present. Skin may look blotchy.
Pictures on the composite are perfectly clean copies of the original photos.	Photos on the composite exhibit black or white specks or have a mottled or uneven look.
The pictures on the composite show only a slight increase in grain from the original photos.	Photos on the composite appear grainy, wooly, snowy, unsharp, or blurred.
All the composites are of the same quality. Except for some rejects, all are uniform.	Many of the composites (more than 5%) are too light or dark or have white spots or areas that didn't print.
Ink coverage and quality is acceptable.	Too much ink was used, yielding overall darkness, increased contrast, no pure whites, and solid, no-detail blacks. Too little ink was used yielding sketchy or grainy coverage; dark grays exist where there should be true, rich blacks. Composites smudge when handled.
Paper is heavy and sturdy. Paper is white and its matte or glossy surface enhances your photos.	Uneven or splotchy ink coverage can be the result of defective paper. Papers under 80-pound weights are usually not the best selection. Cheap papers are yellowish, not bright white.

After your approval at the proofing stage, the composites are ready to go to press. Make sure your printer knows the type of paper to be used and the quantity.

Evaluating the Finished Product

When your composites are ready you will want to check them carefully to make sure everything looks good. Although everything was okay at the proofing stage, things can go wrong when your composite goes to press. For example, too much ink can make photos appear dark, or too little ink can cause composites to appear sketchy or washed out. If you did not proof your composite, consult the checklist for proofing composites in addition to the items listed in Table 9.

Composite Checklist

☐ Quickly flip through all of your composites to make sure they are uniform.

☐ Reclaim your artwork (original photos) for your personal file.

☐ Pay the balance of your bill.

☐ If there is something wrong with the composites, check them against your proof. Don't be overly critical; the composite will not look quite as good as the originals or the proof. However, if your hair was blond in the proof and in the composite it came out dark brown, you do have a right to appeal to your printer for a reprint. Do not sign for, pay for, or take your composites. Ask for one or two copies and your proof to take to your agent and perhaps another printer to find exactly where the problem lies and how you should present your case. Reputable printers will reprint without an argument if your complaints are justified. When selecting a printer you must realize that with a lower price you will have to make sacrifices in quality and service.

Distributing Your Composites

Your agent will probably want at least half of your composites to have on file for mailing to clients. You should also keep a supply of composites in your portfolio to distribute to clients at appointments. Always have a supply of composites with you.

Using Your Composite Effectively

• Don't make dramatic, irreversible changes in your appearance right after getting your new composite. For example, don't cut or color your hair. This is a common error that many neophytes make. Your composite is supposed to be an accurate representation of the way you currently look. When clients are considering you for an assignment on the basis of your composite, they expect you to appear looking just like the photos. If you appear with a totally different haircut, it is unprofessional on your part and extremely frustrating to your client. Therefore, be thorough in your preparation before assembling your composite. Lose the weight, style your hair, and make other changes before you have your pictures taken and your composite assembled. Plan your look carefully and then promote it. Once your composite is assembled, you should retain the looks it depicts until you have a new composite made. Making minor changes or improvements are the only exceptions. If you do change, always see clients in person when you are being considered for a job so they know what to expect. Too frequent changes in your appearance will confuse clients and cause them to avoid you.

• Don't leave town or decrease your availability in any other way right after distributing your composites. When you or your agency send out your composites, interested clients will begin calling right away and in the next month or two. If your composite sparks their interest, you must take advantage of the opportunities while they are fresh.

- "Work" your composite. Ask your agent when he or she will be conducting a mailing. Agents usually send a group of models' composites in an envelope to potential clients. If you are sending out your own, assemble a card file or use Contact Record forms (see "Self-Promotion Appointments" in this chapter) to keep track of each client, agent, or photographer you sent your composite to along with the date it was mailed. Make follow-up calls by asking the people whether they received the composite and try to arrange a personal interview to show your portfolio. Don't expect to get an avalanche of responses just by sending out a few composites and then sitting by the phone.

- Don't try to conserve your composites. The purpose of the composite is to expose your looks to as many prospective clients or other influential people as possible. The minimum number of composites you should have printed is 500. Your agency may require as many as 2000 to do a complete mailing to their contacts. It is always better to err on the side of distributing too many than too few. You'll increase your chances of obtaining job opportunities by making certain that your composite is representing you in the greatest number of places as is possible. Send it to every contact you would like to make. If you'd like to work in New York or Europe, send your composite to agencies in those locations. It is always a good idea to include a brief cover letter explaining who you are and why you are sending the composite. If you did not have an agency logo imprinted on your composite, make sure that each composite you send displays an agency logo stamp or information so that a contact can reach you if he or she is interested.

- Be prepared to receive a variety of opinions about your composite. It is unrealistic to expect that every prospective client and agent you send or show it to will like it equally well. Each judges according to his or her own business needs and preferences. Listen to and write down their comments. When you make the next composite, employ the opinions that were in the majority. Although a composite with poor photos or a composite that promotes you in the wrong way (for example, as a fashion model instead of a promotional model) will not help your chances, it will also not destroy your career future. If you truly have what it takes to succeed in modeling, perceptive agents, clients, or photographers will be able to spot it when seeing you in person. They will be able to give you advice and encourage you toward a more effective composite.

- Begin working on your next composite now. Don't wait until your supply of composites dwindles to begin thinking about your next composite. Begin working on it right away—this way you'll have more photos to choose from and the quality of your photos will be higher. Plan on making a new composite every time you change your look and every 6 to 9 months. If your supply is exhausted before this time, order 500 more composites from your printer. He or she will retain the printing negatives from your composite and will be able to reprint it at a lesser charge than your initial printing. Figures 15–22 are examples of composites.

JAN LEIGHTON

THIS IS JAN LEIGHTON. And Jan Leighton. And so on. It's the face that has launched absolutely no ships, but a lot of great photographs, T.V. commercials and shows. If you don't like the way he looks, he'll look some other way. Just about any other way.

By the way, Jan is in the Guinness Book of World Records having professionally performed 3372 historical notables which have garnered a modest number of awards.

What goosebumped Jan's goosebumps was filming as: George Washington opening the General's own camp chest in Mt. Vernon, Va... Abe Lincoln in Springfield, Ill... Mark Twain shooting pool at his home in Hartford....Edison sitting in his Menlo Park workshop....Andy Jackson in his Nashville Hermitage....Christopher Columbus in Puerto Rico... Kit Carson in Bents Old Fort, Colorado....both Ben Franklin and Thomas Jefferson inside Independence Hall, Philadelphia.

Figure 15. An example of a character model's composite. Courtesy Jan Leighton, New York.

Figure 16. An example of a female fashion model's composite. A model who is qualified for runway modeling should include head-to-toe shots and photos that highlight her ability to move creatively and gracefully. Courtesy Elite, New York.

Cindy Crawford

Height 5'9½ Dress Size 6-7 Bust 34B Waist 23 Hips 33 Shoes 9 Hair Light Brown Eyes Dark Brown
Hauteur 1.77 Confection 36-37 Poitrine 86 Taille 58 Hanches 84 Chaussures 40 Cheveux Chatains Clairs Yeux Bruns Fonces
SAG

elite

John Casablancas
111 East 22nd Street, New York, New York 10010 Tel: 529-9800 Telex: 428546 Book

Figure 17. Example of a fashion model's composite (two-sided). Courtesy Elite, New York.

Figure 18. Example of a male fashion model's composite. Courtesy Elite, New York.

size 12   height 5'9"   bust 38   waist 30   hips 39   hair strawberry blonde   eyes green   shoes 9

wanda

CUINGTON MODEL MANAGEMENT
38 East 19th Street, New York 10003 New York   Tel: 212-228-9842

CUINGTON

models

wanda

A NEW **SHOP FOR WOMEN**

The beautiful balance of style with sizes 14 to 22

bloomingdale's

COVER MAKEUP HAIR ALLAN FORBES

Figure 19. Example of plus-sized model's composite. Courtesy Cuington Model Management, New York.

Figure 20. An example of a straight commercial model's composite showing the model in a variety of roles such as working woman, young mother, and woman-next-door.

(a)

(b)

Figure 21. The purpose and true test of a composite is to secure the model daily bookings, auditions, and other opportunities. (a) A junior model's composite. (b) A trade show model's composite. Courtesy A-Plus Talent Agency, Chicago.

Christina Sylvester

Eyes — Brown   Hair — Dark Brown

Photography by Kendra Dew   A Picture Company Composite ©1988   (313) 545-0973

DEVON FALVEY

RASCALS unLimited

Talent Agency
135 East 55th
NYC NY 10021
212-517-6500

Figure 22a. Example of a child model's composite-glossy. (b) Example of a child model's composite (one-sided). Composites courtesy of Rascals Unlimited Talent Agency, New York.

THE MODEL'S PORTFOLIO

The model's portfolio is one of her most important sales tools. It serves several functions.

- It shows how the model looks in a variety of situations, different lighting, moods, angles, and so on. It gives prospective clients and photographers an idea of how photogenic she is, how well she moves in front of the camera, and how she looks in a variety of clothing, makeup, and hair styles.

- It is documentation for the prospective client of the work the model has done and the clients by whom she has been employed (tearsheets, covers, and other published materials). Most clients prefer to book a model only when they know that other clients have employed her successfully.

- It depicts the model in clothes and products similar to those of the client and enables the client to visualize how the model will look in a particular advertisement or catalog.

The model's portfolio or "book," as it is referred to in the business, is an absolute necessity for print models. For some models, particularly those seeking work in television, fashion shows, and trade shows, the portfolio may not always be needed; however, for most clients it is proof of the model's experience.

Your book will accompany you on every interview, whether it is for an audition or a testing. It is also a good idea to pack it in your totebag when attending a booking because some of the people there may have only seen your composite. Showing them your book may give them ideas about how to utilize you for their upcoming assignments.

Types of Portfolios

There are different types of portfolios depending on the type of work the model is seeking. It is important for a model to assemble a portfolio that is tailored to his or her type and look and the kind of work he or she is seeking.

Fashion Portfolio

This concentrates on showing the model in a variety of current fashions that work best with her looks and special features. Her figure and movement are highlighted. It also contains beauty shots that focus on the model's hair and makeup in current styles. Her facial structure, skin and hair quality, and expression are highlighted.

Product/Commercial Portfolio

The pictures in a commercial portfolio are aimed at securing non-fashion related print ads for the model. Some of the pictures may show her holding, standing next to, or using products unrelated to fashion and beauty and in a variety of roles such as homemaker, young mother, businesswoman, and so on. Specialty or parts models carry commercial portfolios that, for example, show their hands modeling a variety of products. Character models also carry commercial portfolios that show them portraying various characters that they have developed by means of acting ability, makeup applications, and hairstyles.

Forms of Portfolios

In addition to different types of portfolios, there are different forms (see Figure 23).

Standard Portfolio

A standard portfolio measures $9\frac{1}{2}$ x 12 inches and contains 10 to 24 color and black and white tearsheets, photos, and other items, that depict the model in a variety of moods, items and the like. For an experienced model, the portfolio acts as a pictorial resume.

Miniportfolio

A miniportfolio or minibook is a 5 x 7 or 8 x 10 lightweight portfolio that contains duplicate color and black and white pictures found in a fashion or commercial model's regular portfolio. The model may have

Figure 23. Shown here is a model's standard portfolio (top) with portfolio accessories such as slide sheets (bottom), which are stored in the pocket of her portfolio along with her composites. Shown in the center is the model's mini-book.

several minibooks, which, because of their size, can be conveniently sent by mail or messenger to an interested client who needs to see more than the composite to make a decision about booking the model.

The Portfolio Case

The right pictures on the inside are the most important part of a model's portfolio. However, the way you display your pictures has an impact on their effectiveness. You will want the outside and the inside of your portfolio to have a neat professional appearance.

Don't carry your pictures around in a box, envelope, or family album. It looks as if you are not really serious about a modeling career. Also, pictures stored like this are easily damaged. Some agencies provide their models with portfolio cases that are imprinted with the agency name and information. If you must find your own, look for an attractive binder that holds transparent page protectors. Be aware that styles and sizes of model's portfolios go in and out of popularity. Currently, the most popular size is the European size 24 x 30 cm or 9½ x 12 inches (Figure 24). This size is more in keeping with most magazine sizes and is more convenient because it fits into a totebag. Look for a portfolio case that is sturdy (it will get a lot of use and abuse) and preferably one having inside pockets to store composites, slide sheets, or an appointment book. A handle makes for easier carrying. Portfolio cases are available in vinyl, canvas, or leather and range in price from $20 to a few hundred dollars, depending on the material and style. Good sources for purchasing them are art supply, luggage, and stationery stores.

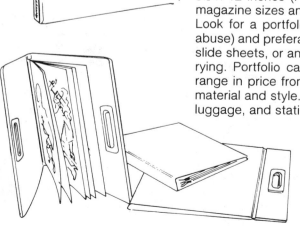

Figure 24. Examples of portfolio cases. On the left is a 11 x 14-inch leather portfolio with handles and a zipper. In the center is a French press book that is 9½ x 12 inches with an attached handle section (also shown flat at the extreme right). The simplest and most inexpensive portfolio is a pig grain leather or vinyl binder in sizes 8-½ x 11 or 9 x 12 inches shown on the right.

The Portfolio Pages

The portfolio should contain 10 to 12 large sheet protectors or sleeves that will encase and protect your photographs and cuttings. Choose nonglare, vinyl sheets, since they don't scratch as the acetate ones do. They give your photos a more attractive appearance and make them easier to see.

When storing the book, always place it on one of its edges, not flat or on the binding. If stored on the binding, the pages will curl and be difficult to turn. If stored flat, the pages will wrinkle. To clean plastic or vinyl pages use a cotton ball saturated with ammonia and water. To clean the inside of the page, use a photographer's antistatic cloth. Replace the sleeves when they begin to lose their transparency because of scratching or yellowing. Also, avoid storing your portfolio in a hot place because this will cause vinyl pages to ripple. Always select a portfolio that has replaceable sleeves or sleeve cartridges.

Instead of using page protectors and a ring binder, some models choose to have their tearsheets and prints laminated with a hard, durable plastic. A collection of these one-sided sheets is assembled loose in a flat case that resembles a portfolio lacking a ring binding. This method allows the model to easily customize her portfolio for each interview. Although laminated pages are more expensive than vinyl page protectors, they give permanence to the tearsheets or prints and make a very attractive presentation. Unbound portfolios containing laminated pages are very useful for stylists, makeup artists, and hairstylists.

Materials to Include in the Portfolio

Photographic Prints

Most models use 8 x 10 prints for the portfolio; however, there are no rigid rules on uniform or standard print sizes. A print might be any size from 5 x 7 to 11 x 14. Semimatte surface prints are usually easier for viewing than glossy prints.

Remember that all prints displayed in the portfolio should be technically perfect. Ideal exposure and printing are important. Sloppy-looking prints make an unprofessional appearance and will distract a viewer's attention.

Black and White Prints

Because some of your clients will be shooting in black and white (newspapers and magazines), it is a good idea to display several good black and white prints. Black and white is good for beginning models because film and prints are much cheaper than for color. It is best to practice and start a portfolio with a majority of and black and white prints and then add more color shots as you improve.

Color Prints

The majority of your prospective clients will be shooting color, so it is important to include color prints. Before displaying any color print in your portfolio, always make sure that it shows you hair, eye, and skin colors as vibrant and attractive as they really are.

Tearsheets

Tearsheets are cuttings from magazines, catalogs, newspapers, brochures, posters, calendars, or other printed materials in which your pictures appear. Tearsheets are an important component of a portfolio. They are proof for a prospective client of what you are capable of doing on the job, who you've worked for, and what publications you have appeared in.

The successful model's book consists entirely of tearsheets. However, good tearsheets are the most difficult to obtain for a beginning model. It takes a lot of bookings to assemble several good tearsheets because some will not be usable because of poor reproduction quality or other reasons. Newspaper tearsheets should be included only if newspaper ads make up a prominent part of the modeling business in your area. When possible try to obtain a galley or proof from a newspaper photo.

In order to obtain your tearsheets you will have to put a lot of effort into tracking them down. Don't count on clients or agents to send tearsheets, even when they say they will send them. You have to collect them yourself. Always express an interest in seeing the results of your work. Ask the client when and where the photo will appear and make a note of it in your appointment book. Call the client or photographer on or after the date and ask if you can stop by to pick up a copy. If a photo will appear in an out-of-town publication or one not usually available to you, mail your client a self-addressed, stamped envelope that will accommodate the tearsheet and include a friendly note requesting a few copies. Also send your composite and a few details, such as the items modeled, the location, the date of the shooting, the proposed date of publication, the photographer, etc. to refresh the person's memory.

If a photo will appear in a catalog, magazine, or newspaper that is available to you, purchase several copies. If you missed your pictures when they appeared, contact the back issues office of the publication and order issues published during the time your pictures were to appear. Always get as many copies of your tearsheets as possible. You will find that they disappear quickly. Your agent may want copies, prospective clients may request them, and you may need backups in case the ones in your portfolio are lost or damaged.

Always keep in mind that only your best work is displayed in a portfolio. Don't display an unflattering picture just because it is a tearsheet. Avoid using tearsheets containing small-sized, poor-quality photos or ones in which there are too many other models.

To determine when your pictures from a booking will appear, use the following table. It shows the amount of time between the time the photo is shot and the time it appears in a publication or other media. These are general estimates.

Editorial pictures in a fashion magazine	3–4 months
Catalog pictures for a major catalog	4–6 months
Catalog pictures for an in-between season or minor catalog	1–3 months
Newspaper ad (local advertising)	2–4 weeks
National ad	6 weeks–4 months
Brochures, etc.	2 weeks–2 months

Slides
Slides are good additions to a portfolio. You can often get photographers to give you reject slides or duplicate slides from your shootings. Display only the best and, at most, two to four from each concept (clothes change).

Photocopies (Black and White and Color)
Although the technology for black and white and color photocopies has greatly improved in recent years, the quality is not as good as a photographic print or tearsheet. A photocopy does not have the range of tones, refinement, or subtlety that a print does, and in nearly all cases a print is preferred.

Color Xeroxes can be made from your slides and often resemble tearsheets. However, they do not contain the true colors, gradations, and fine grain that a color print or transparency does. Color Xeroxes are much cheaper (around $2 to $5 each) and faster, often made while you wait, than print processing. They may be a good option for a beginning model to have in a portfolio in addition to a few color prints.

The best way for a model to use color Xeroxes is in determining the best slide from which to have a photographic print made. Have several slides that you like Xeroxed, then decide which one merits the investment of a color print. Also you will be able to visualize cropping or other adjustments that might improve your photo. Color Xeroxes are also good for distributing to clients when you are between cards or when more than the composite is requested.

Miscellaneous

In general, Polaroids and contact sheets from shootings are not included in the portfolio; however, you might put a few good ones in the pockets of your portfolio. Don't put anything in the pockets of your portfolio that you don't want a client to see or that does not show you at your best. Clients are curious and will often rummage through the pockets if they see something of interest. Your portfolio should be a showcase of your best work. Along with your composite it is your most valuable sales tool, and you should consider any money you put into it as an investment in your career. Establish a realistic budget for your portfolio and work within it.

A Step-by-Step Guide to Assembling a Portfolio
Step 1: Obtaining Basic Shots for a Foundation

Before meeting clients, it is important for the model to have a collection of photos to show. Having only a few photos or only duplicates of those on the model's composite will usually cause a photographer to tell the model to return when he or she has more to show. Therefore, the model should try to assemble a core of basic shots on which to build his or her portfolio. The ones clients most commonly like to see are listed below.

Fashion Portfolio

- Headshot: face from front.
- Headshot: face from three-quarter angle.
- Two basic full-length fashion shots that show your legs and figure.
- Full-length or three-quarter length (from knees up) body shot. Choose swimwear, dancewear, lingerie, a leotard, or colorful exercise togs.
- One shot (full length, three-quarter, or headshot) showing the face in profile.
- One smiling shot.
- One action shot.
- One or two pictures focusing on any special features (skin, hands, hair, legs, feet).
- At least one color shot each, full length and headshot.

Tips for Basic Fashion Portfolio Shots

Headshots. Your headshots should display two different current hairstyles (for example, one curled and one straight) and makeups (one with very little makeup, another a more glamourous or trendy look). One shot should show you smiling. If you have freckles or beauty spots, let them show in one photo and camouflage them for the second photo so clients can see how you look both ways. Keep your hair simple and your makeup clean and simple. Concentrate on good expressions.

Body shots. Your body should be in top shape before attempting a body shot. Simple, natural, or action poses are usually best. Experiment with different poses that elongate and flatter your body. Keep the style of your clothing in mind when choosing your settings.

Full-length shots. Choose clothing according to your look. Select clothing that shows your body well. Often summer fashions are best. Avoid coats, capes, and heavy winter fashions that are bulky and do not show your figure. Male models might choose close-fitting casual shirts, sweaters, and pants.

For all beginning shots, gear your movements to the mood, style, and construction of the fashions you are modeling. Clients will be looking at your ability to show clothing effectively and express various moods. Avoid stiff, posed, expressionless shots and extreme, "artistic" poses.

Commercial Portfolio

- Headshots showing full face, three-quarter angle, and profile. At least one shot should be smiling.
- One shot in which the model is interacting with another person (for example, parent and child).
- One shot in which the model is holding a product.
- One or two shots showing any specialties, such as hands.
- Shots showing the model in a variety of roles for which he or she is best suited. Roles should involve work (for example, secretary, homemaker, flight attendant, or doctor), leisure activities (engaged in sports or playing with a child or pet), and special occasions.
- Full-length and three-quarter-length shots. A body shot is not necessary unless it will help in promoting the model for a certain role (for example, lifeguard).

Tips for Basic Commercial Portfolio Shots For headshots and full-length shots, concentrate on showing a variety of moods according to the roles you are portraying. Aim for natural, simple, animated movements and expressions. Photos should be taken in different settings such as the home, office, or outdoors. Clients will be looking at your ability to express a wide range of emotions and to represent or appeal to targeted consumers.

The quickest and easiest way to obtain the foundation of a portfolio is to enlist model or talent test photographers to shoot exactly what you need. Many composite and portfolio photographers offer a package that includes these basic portfolio prints; however, it is best to enlist several different photographers to produce these photos so that they will depict more variety.

These first basic shots must show your best features and personality in a straightforward and persuasive way, so that other photographers, clients, and agents will be able to visualize how you might look in their work. Gimmicky shots or those with interesting or imaginative lighting, clothing, props, makeups, and hairstyles will be great to add to your basic shots, but these will come later. What you are trying to accomplish in these first shots is to show that you are photogenic, expressive, and have the necessary qualifications for the type of modeling you want to do.

Step 2: Adding to the Foundation

To these basic shots, add any pictures that were taken but not used when assembling your composite or glossy. With this collection of pictures, you should be able to persuade other photographers to test. Begin making the rounds of photographers, trying to arrange as many mutual and photographer tests as possible. A beginning model should test at least twice a week. The more tests you are able to arrange, the faster you and your portfolio will improve. At this point you should be concentrating on gaining experience in front of the camera, trying out new hair and makeup looks, and adding to the essential shots you have. Try to attain the collection of photos in the list in the Portfolio Contents Checklist.

It is helpful to establish a portfolio plan so that you won't acquire lots of pictures that aren't marketable or usable in your portfolio. To do this, study magazines, television, catalogs, and other media for which you would like to model. Then sit down and make a list of the types of fashion or commercial types you could portray. For example, a pretty, 19-year-old model might list college girl, bride, trendy teenager, beach bum, outdoor girl in jeans, freshly scrubbed, no-makeup girl-next-door, and so on. Using a Test Photo Worksheet, you can plan each type of picture you would like your portfolio to contain. List photographers whose style you think would lend well to the shot and who would be interested in doing it. List makeup artists or makeup ideas to accomplish the look. Do the same for hairstyling. Then list stylists or clothing sources and ideas to provide the fashion for the shot. Also estimate costs such as photographers' and stylists' fees and lab charges for having prints made. This will help you to establish a realistic budget for building your portfolio.

Assembling a portfolio is a long, sometimes frustrating task and most models find that it takes at least 3 months before they have acquired several excellent shots. Just because you don't have a portfolio filled with magazine covers displaying your picture does not mean you won't be able to put together a good portfolio or get jobs. A few good, basic shots is all it takes to persuade agents, photographers, and clients to try you.

Building Your Portfolio

The pictures in your portfolio should work within the framework of your look. Finding your best looks and knowing the types of work for which you are best suited will give direction to your portfolio. Rather than trying to be all things to all clients, focus on styles and looks that you do best and alter them for variety. Emphasize your strongest features. If you have a great figure, you should have several good shots showing it off. If your face or hair is where your fortune lies, you should have lots of headshots showing different angles, makeup applications, hairstyles, and expressions.

Commercial and character models should include shots showing a variety of expressions, moods, props, products, and accessories to show off the commercial types and characters they can portray best.

Portfolio Contents Checklist

The ideal portfolio consists of 16 to 24 photos and contains a collection that exhibits the following variables. All these variables apply to fashion portfolios, most apply to commercial portfolios. Character and specialty models' portfolios do not have any set requirements.

Female Models

☐ Headshots: head and shoulders.

☐ Full-length shots: include dressy, business, casual, and sporty looks.

☐ Three-quarter-length shots: in between full-length shots and headshots, good for showing off detailed fashions.

☐ Body shots: full-length bathing suit, clinging sportswear, leotard, and lingerie.

☐ Pictures showing any specialties: extreme close-ups for skin/beauty, hair, hands, feet, teeth, hats, shows (on runway), product shots, situational shots (e.g., mother and child shots). Promotional models may include candid shots taken at exhibitions showing the model on the job demonstrating a product, giving a narration, etc.

☐ Black and white and color photos.

☐ Action shots.

☐ Pictures shot in a variety of locations: include studio shots with artificial light and location shots with natural light.

☐ Pictures shot by a variety of photographers, in many different kinds of lighting arrangements.

☐ A shot of each type that appeals to catalog clients, magazine editors, and advertising clients.

☐ A double shot or shot with a male model.

☐ Pictures in which you have styled your own hair and makeup and pictures in which different makeup and hair artists have been employed.

☐ Pictures displaying at least three different hairstyles.

☐ Pictures displaying at least three different makeup looks.

☐ Pictures displaying at least three different moods. One should be a smiling picture.

☐ Pictures displaying at least three different facial angles.

☐ Pictures in which you are modeling at least three different styles of clothing, for example, sportswear, dress wear, and business or school wear.

Male Models   Follow the above list, but also include the following.

☐ Pictures with female models.

☐ Picture in a business suit.

☐ Picture in active sportswear, bathing suit, shorts, etc. to show build and legs.

☐ Picture in dressy or formal wear.

☐ Picture in casual wear, sport jacket, or college-prep look for younger men.

☐ Pictures of specialties, such as hands, hair, skin, teeth, underwear, situational shots, and shots of sports or other activities in which you excel.

Step 3: Editing and Updating

The most important thing to do after you have assembled a portfolio of several pictures is to consistently edit and update it. Assembling an excellent portfolio, one that really helps you to secure bookings is an on-going process. You should always try to improve on what you have by replacing the weaker pictures with stronger ones and the older pictures with newer ones. Generally pictures in your portfolio should not be older than 1 year. The only exceptions are magazine covers or very prestigious jobs. Any photos that show outdated, out-of-fashion clothing, hair, and makeup or that fail to show you as good as you really are should be eliminated.

Arranging Pictures in the Portfolio

• Include only your best shots in the portfolio. Quality counts, not quantity. It is better to show 4 or 5 five great pictures alone than 10 or 12 mediocre ones or 10 mediocre ones with 4 or 5 excellent shots mixed in. It is important to exhibit only prints that are of high technical quality because they will be viewed by the discerning and experienced eyes of photographers, editors, and other professionals. Always make sure prints are clean with no specks, scratches, or fingerprints. Also don't display photos on which obvious retouching has been done.

• The best shot should be on the first page, the second best on the last page.

• Include tearsheets (pages from magazines, newspapers, or advertisements featuring the model) along with test shots. When your book improves, include only the highest-quality tearsheets and covers. Include tearsheets that represent the types of work available in your market. For example, if a lot of catalogs and newspaper ads make up the majority of the modeling work in your area, include a few to help clients visualize how you'll appear in a catalog or ad similar to the ones they produce. Don't include an unflattering picture in your portfolio just because it was a booking. In the beginning your tearsheets may not be as good as your test shots; however, if they detract from your appearance, eliminate them.

- The newest shots should always be in the front of the book.
- The better shot should be on the right-hand page because the observer looks first at this page, then at the left page and then back to the right-hand page.
- If you have three or four very strong shots, put them in the front of the book on the right-hand pages and leave the left-hand pages blank. This way nothing will take attention away from your best shots. Arrange the rest of your book normally. This is also a good idea if you have very few shots.
- Trim your pictures if the white margins around the edges of the image are overpowering, uneven, or unattractive. If your photo displays an image with a black background, it will usually look best if surrounded by a margin of white in order to set it apart from the black paper in your portfolio. Trim the edges of tearsheets to eliminate jagged, worn, or torn edges. Always use a paper cutter or a single-edged razor blade and a metal ruler to achieve a clean, smooth trim. Your portfolio pictures should look neat and professional.
- Use a piece of double stick cellophane tape to keep your pictures from moving around inside the page protectors.
- Arrange your pictures so that they flow, encouraging the viewer to turn the page. Avoid putting pictures side by side that clash in colors or styles.
- Limit your portfolio to 10 to 12 pages (20 to 24 pictures). More than this will lose your viewer's attention. Avoid repetition. Don't display more than two prints from a single photographic series (same clothes change) or more than three or four slides from the same series.
- If you have good horizontal pictures, it is always a good idea to have them printed so that they can be viewed vertically. This way the viewer will not have to keep turning the porfolio around to get a better look.
- Always aim for quality in your portfolio. Consult your agent about which pictures to include. Listen carefully to responses you receive from prospective employers regarding each picture in your portfolio and take them into careful consideration when editing.

Step 4: Using Your Portfolio Effectively

Two Portfolios or One

Some models who are very versatile can work equally well in the fashion and commercial/product areas. For these models, it is wise to assemble two separate portfolios or to separate the fashion and commercial photos in one portfolio. The fashion portion should include glamourous pictures and those in which the objective is to show fashion and beauty-related items. The commercial portion would show you holding products not related to fashion and beauty and in a variety of roles. The fashion portion or portfolio should be shown only to fashion clients, whereas the commercial portfolio should be shown only to nonfashion-oriented commercial photographers and clients. This way clients will be less apt to be confused as to how to type or categorize the model.

Tailoring Your Portfolio to the Audition

When you appear at an audition, your portfolio is used as a sales presentation tool. You can increase your chances of landing the job by editing your portfolio so it contains pictures that will suit the client's needs. For example, if the model is going on an important fashion casting for blue jeans, she will pad her book with pictures in which she is modeling jeans along with looks that she thinks the client is after. Often a model will be booked simply because in one of her pictures she is wearing an outfit similar to the one being photographed for the client or because the shot looks similar to the one the client wants to produce. Pay attention to which portfolio photos get favorable comments from clients and note which photos convinced clients to audition or book you.

Safeguarding Your Portfolio · The amount of effort and money required to assemble an excellent portfolio is substantial. Along with your composite, a portfolio is your most important sales tool. Therefore, you should take protective measures in the event that it is lost or stolen. Always have duplicates (or the negatives or transparencies) of all prints and tearsheets in your portfolio. Have duplicate slides and copy negatives made. To safeguard against losing a portfolio, copy the following label and add your agency's logo, name, and address to it. Never list your name and home address. Attach the label to the front inside cover of your portfolio.

Please do not remove any materials from this book. If you would like a copy of one of the items, please contact the agency.

Anyone finding this book will receive a generous reward upon its return to:

Agency _____

Address _____

Telephone No. _____

Never send your standard portfolio to an out-of-town agent or client. Instead assemble a duplicate or miniportfolio made for this purpose. You will not want to be without a portfolio for the days or weeks an agent or client may retain your portfolio. Also, when sending your portfolio, always insure it for the cost of replacing the case and contents.

THE COMMERCIAL HEADSHOT

A commercial headshot is a mass-produced 8 x 10 black and white photograph used by individuals seeking work in television commercials and other audiovisual productions. A commercial headshot is often referred to by other names such as an actor's headshot, a commercial glossy, or a glossy. The model's composite alone may be sufficient to secure him or her work in electronic media productions, however, a glossy is another tool that will help to promote him or her. Because the glossy is the standard tool used by casting directors and other television decision makers, the glossy has the advantage of making the model appear as if he or she has the qualifications for this type of work and is specifically seeking it. Most product and character models use glossies, as do specialty models, in securing TV bookings. Actors, actresses, singers, and other performers have glossies.

Figure 25. Example of a character actor's headshot. Shown here actor Jan Leighton portraying Franklin D. Roosevelt. Courtesy Jan Leighton, New York.

The purpose of the glossy is to secure the talent an audition. When a client produces a television commercial for a product, he or she consults with the ad agency to decide on the characters and the script. When a call is put out for casting the parts, the ad agency or independent casting director searches his or her files of glossies for individuals who fit the type required. These individuals are then invited to audition. The glossy is often the only introduction a talent has, so its importance cannot be overemphasized. When the model or talent is called to audition, he or she is expected to show up looking like the glossy.

The Two Basic Types of Commercial Headshots

A commercial glossy should be a basic shot that shows personality. A captivating expression in the eyes and animation in the face is a must. The parts or roles the talent is best suited for should be apparent from the photograph. Basically two types of models or actors are found in television commercials: straight and character. Straight models or actors have average or attractive looks and can realistically portray a variety of roles commonly found in society. Character models or actors have unique looks or talents and can portray fictitious characters or characters who are exaggerated or comedic versions of reality. Character models might also impersonate celebrities or historical figures.

Preparations for Assembling a Commercial Headshot

The first task for a model or actor assembling a glossy is to decide whether his or her looks, talents, and skills are those of a straight or character model or actor. The best way to start is to look at the images prevalent in commercials, and to determine which one(s) you could portray. Note the clothing, hair, and makeup that is worn in different situations and plan your appearance for your glossy accordingly. Consult with agents and others to help you determine your most attainable and marketable images.

Plan your photo session by considering which photographer to use. There are many photographers who specialize in shooting glossies for television and acting talents. Consult the information in Tables 1 and 3. Complete a Testing Worksheet so that you will be prepared. If you can portray two opposite looks, you should consider making two glossies, rather than trying to accomplish everything with one.

The important thing to remember is that the key ingredient of a successful commercial headshot is personality. Expressiveness and spontaneity that command attention are what most casting people want to see.

The Character Commercial Glossy

When a character role is being cast, the casting director looks for photos in which a model or talent shows acting ability that realistically portrays a certain character. The photo must also demonstrate that the talent has an understanding of the makeup, hairstyle, and clothing necessary to duplicate the character completely and accurately. Usually a character model will have a separate glossy made to depict each character he or she is capable of recreating.

The Straight Commercial Glossy

When a model or actor is being sought for a straight commercial role, a casting director will want to see a straightforward, no-nonsense picture that gives the talent the appearance of being able to fit into several different roles. The casting director is able to visualize the effects of hair, makeup, and clothes for a particular job and how he or she might want to change you, so a basic photo will make his or her job easier. In order to position yourself for the greatest number of roles, it is wise to pattern your photo after one of the most common commercial roles. These are listed in Table 10. Specific clothing, makeup, and hair suggestions can be found in Table 3.

TABLE 10   Common Commercial Roles

Role	Image
Housewife	Your photo should make you appear between 21 and 40 with average or slightly above-average looks (but not too glamourous or sexy). Your personality should express pleasantness, warmth, and natural wholesomeness. Study commercials in which housewives appear selling household, family, and food products.
Young mother	You should look 21 to 34 years of age. A soft, fresh, radiant, wholesome look is the ideal. A lovely smile that projects either sweetness and inner contentment or a soft, glowing look is usually desired. Expressions must look natural, not artificial or contrived. For ideas, look at commercials in which young mothers sell diapers, toys, and other items for children.
Young husband or father	A young husband or father usually appears 25 to 35 years old and has a lovable, warm, vulnerable look. He has good looks but is not too handsome or sexy. He looks like a family man. A smile is usually the best expression. Study commercials in which husbands appear with wives or fathers appear with families to pitch a variety of products ranging from automobiles and insurance to family and household products.
Young woman-next-door	You should appear to be 18 to 25 years old. You should look pretty, but not fashiony, sophisticated, or glamourous. A wholesome, natural look and a friendly smile is the ideal. Effervescence and a glowing enthusiasm are the objective. An open expression is important. Examples can be found in commercials for fast food, soft drinks, and basic grooming products, such as soap and toothpaste. A headshot displaying this look is best for most fashion models who seek work in television.
Glamour girl	A model who has a glamourous, sexy, mysterious, or charismatic quality or a model who is an attractive, talented performer will often have this type of photo. Examples of this look can be found among glamourous television soap opera stars and models who appear in commercials for glamourized items, such as automobiles, travel, and the like. Glamour girls usually appear to be 20 to 28 years of age and have a "movie star" look.
Cosmetic model (female)	Usually cosmetic models are selected from the fashion model group, but if a model with a beautiful face is too short to model fashions, or if a fashion model wants to compete specifically for cosmetic ads, she should acquire photographs that show her as a cosmetic model. A glossy that shows that the model has acting ability in addition to beautiful hair and facial features is important. For television, casting people usually need cosmetic models with large eyes that are medium to light in color with a well-defined iris and pupil. Thick lashes and ample brows are also assets. A beautiful smile with even, white teeth is important. Hair in a medium to dark blonde color is often preferred. Very dark or very light hair colors are usually not requested. Flawless skin is a must.
Handsome man	This model is often selected from the fashion model category and can be found in a variety of television commercials for shaving products and other grooming supplies. There are basically two variations of the "handsome man" type: one is the rugged, athletic type; the other is the male equivalent of the cosmetic model who is good-looking, masculine, sexy, and romantic. With either look, your glossy must depict good bone structure (especially a strong jaw), a good complexion and a head of thick, shiny hair (with an even hairline). Most handsome men types are 6' to 6'3", wear a 40 R suit,

and appear to be 25 to 45 years of age. A sexy smile is often the best expression.

Businesswoman Your expression should make you look authoritative, sincere, and ambitious. You should have a "dressed for success" look. A businesslike, sincere, yet open expression is important. You should appear between 28 and 55. You will want to appear attractive but not cute or soft. Examples can be found in commercials for business publications, computers, and the like.

Businessman Businessmen are found in commercials for banks, stock brokerages, legal firms, office equipment, and the like. Your expression should show authority, credibility, warmth, success, and energy. Businessmen in television commercials are usually 30 to 60 years of age.

Spokesperson A spokesperson often encompasses two different types such as a businessman/father or a working mother. A spokesperson must appear friendly, trustworthy, and knowledgeable. An honest, sincere expression is usually best.

Real person A real person looks average. You do not want to appear to be a professional model or actor. An average look with an appealing personality is the ideal.

Shooting Guidelines for the Commercial Headshot

- A good commercial glossy shows "the pores and the personality" of a talent, yet makes the talent look perfect for the parts he or she is trying to obtain. Avoid fancy lighting. Favor simple lighting set-ups such as reflected light or single source lighting. Avoid harsh shadows or highlights and complicated backgrounds. Avoid contrasty photos where there are no midtones to show the details and texture of your skin and features. Avoid soft-focus or out-of-focus shots. Select a photo with single highlights in each eye. Too many highlights are distracting and will add too much excitement to the basic type of shot. The lens should be positioned in line with the face—high- or low-camera angles are not suitable for these basic shots.

- Avoid stiff poses. Hands-to-the-face shots, the head cocked, or shots in which you're holding a prop or a product or other unnatural position are usually not advisable.

- Avoid false expressions. Expressions that look unspontaneous or too posed won't say much for your ability to act. Choose a candid, open expression. A smile is often preferred. Look right into the lens of the camera.

- Generally straight-on shots are best. Use a slight three-quarter angle if you prefer.

- Crop carefully. Generally your photo should be cropped so that all of your hair is included with a little extra space around your head and the points of your collar showing. Extreme close-ups and waist-up shots are best reserved for the composite or portfolio.

- Be sure your makeup has been done appropriately for photography. The makeup (except in character glossies) should not be overdone and should show your skin and features for the camera. Hair should be simple, healthy-looking, and shiny. Avoid overuse of hairspray and oils. Avoid windblown hair or strong backlight. It is often a good idea to do your own hair and makeup for this shot to achieve the most natural look. It is ideal if you can appear at auditions looking just like your headshot. Avoid obvious contouring, heavy foundations, and other makeup tricks that don't show you the way you really are. Make sure you have used powder adequately to delete excess shine on nose, forehead, and chin.

Selecting the Right Photo for Your Glossy

- When you obtain the contact sheets from your shooting, bring them to your agent so he or she can help you to decide which photos would be best to have enlarged. Photos that look good on the contact sheet may not look equally well when enlarged, so selecting 2 to 4 for enlargement is a good idea. When you receive the prints, take these to your agent and ask him or her to help you to select the one to have mass produced. If you don't have an agent, ask the opinion of agents with whom you hope to work or ask your photographer.

- Spend the extra money to have any minor retouching done to make your photo appear ideal, but use it sparingly. You don't want to obliterate skin texture in this type of shot, so don't cover up pores, wrinkles, and the like. If you show up looking very unlike your glossy, you probably will not be auditioned.

- If you can't decide between two photos, have 50 glossies made of each. When you begin to distribute the glossy to prospective clients, you will see which one they favor and can have additional copies made accordingly. You may find it to your advantage to have two different glossies; for example, one glossy may show you more glamourous, another may show you slightly plainer. This way you can satisfy clients with opposing preferences.

Mass Producing Your Glossy

- To have your photo mass produced, you will need to consult a company that specializes in this service. (This is not the same process used for composite printing.) Your agent or photographer can recommend ones of differing quality and price. Photo labs often offer quantity runs, as this service is called; however, many require that you provide any typesetting that is to be included. Always find out what the set-up costs are such as making the copy negative, typesetting, and stripping, as these are usually in addition to the copies. Don't scrimp on quality at this point, or the energy and money you put into your photo session will be wasted.

- When you have your photo copied, you will need to provide several items:

  1. One clean, flawless 8 x 10 glossy black and white print. The negatives are not used. The duplicator will make a copy negative of your print and then prints will be mass produced using a special machine.

  2. Your name and any other information.

  3. Design instructions. You will need to instruct the photo duplicator what type style you prefer for your name and where you want it imprinted on the glossy. You will have to give other instructions for the layout. There are different styles of glossies from which to choose. Your photo can either have a thin white border around the edge of the paper or it can be bled off the edges. Your name can either be superimposed over your photograph or printed in a white margin below your photo. Although it is highly unlikely that a casting director or other decision maker would pass you over for an audition or assignment due to the style of your glossy, it is important to follow the style that is currently preferred.

- The type of paper you prefer. Another option that may be available is glossy, matte, or semimatte surface paper.

- Deposit of one-half the amount.

- When ordering your glossy, always ask to see a proof before copies are made. Check the proof for unwanted specks, scratches, or lint marks. Check that your picture is centered and cropped correctly. Check that your photo is not too light or too dark.
- When your glossy is ready (the process usually requires 3 to 7 days) check over everything carefully. Check that the mass-produced copies closely match the original. There may be a slight loss in quality; however, there should be no flaws or obvious increases or decreases in tonality (contrast, overall lightness or darkness, etc.). If there are problems, point them out right away. If there is a dispute, ask to have one representative photo print and your original and take them to your agent or photographer for his or her opinion. They will be able to judge the quality and tell you where corrections need to be made.

Using Your Glossy Effectively

- Because you will be pursuing assignments that will require you to act, you will need to assemble a resume and staple it to the back of each glossy.
- Mail your glossy to agents, independent casting directors, advertising agency casting directors, production houses, and other potential clients. Make certain that the resume attached to your glossy has a telephone number where you can be reached.
- Follow up on your glossy. When you send your glossy to a casting director, make a follow up call after a week or two to request an appointment to meet her or him in person or to give a reading of a scene.
- Follow the same procedure above after you have sent your glossy to an agent. After you have met the agent, periodically visit the agency to make sure they have an adequate supply of your glossies.
- Listen carefully to reactions of clients and agents in regard to your glossy. Implement their opinions when making your next glossy.
- If you are getting negative reactions or no response from your glossy, retake your picture and have a new glossy made.
- Do not make changes in your appearance right after your glossy is made. Every time you change your haircut or color, you must have a new glossy made.

THE RESUME

For most of the work a model does, his or her picture is the most important marketing tool. Either a model has or does not have the look the client needs. However, when a job requires special abilities, or when an agent, casting director or client needs more information about the model, the resume is very valuable. Fashion models rarely have resumes because their portfolios provide proof of their experience. However, electronic media and promotional models must have resumes.

The Two Types of Resumes

There are two basic types of resumes. A resume geared to secure a model work in live promotions highlights his or her ability to welcome people or to act as a host, demonstrator of a variety of products, and narrator or speaker. This resume also emphasizes his or her talents for performing (for example, singing, dancing, and acting) and other skills that may apply to live promotions (for example, knowing how to use a computer to input data such as leads for salespeople to follow up on).

A resume geared to securing assignments in electronic media such as television commercials and industrial films will highlight an individual's acting ability. This resume lists live, filmed, and videotaped assignments in which the individual has been featured as well as skills and assets relevant to a prospective client's needs.

A resume should contain the following:

- Your name.
- The capacities in which you work. On a promotional model's resume, for example, Model/Actress/Dancer might be listed, depending on her abilities. On a resume for electronic media work an actor might choose to list his type, for example, father, businessman, office employee, or blue-collar worker.
- Contact telephone numbers.
- Your Social Security number.
- Exclusivity with an agent.
- Performers' union membership (SAG, AEA, AFTRA).
- Vital statistics: Height, weight, eye color, hair color. Age range is optional.
- Experience.
- Special talents and skills.
- Training.

How to Assemble a Resume

Determining your type and abilities and deciding which clients and assignments would most likely utilize your looks, skills, and talents is the most important base from which to start. Do not try to accomplish everything in one resume. If you want to do both promotional and electronic media work, assemble a specialized resume for each.

It is not important that your resume follow one specific style or be confined to one page. What is most important is that it contain information that will persuade a potential client to use you. Simply listing trade shows or electronic media productions in which you've participated won't give a potential client an indication of the depth and scope of your experience. However, pinpointing the special qualities you possess and have implemented in other situations will sell your unique qualifications.

Gathering information about yourself that a client may need when deciding whether to audition or book you can be done in a variety of ways. One of the most efficient ways is to use 3 x 5 index cards. On one card list your name. Under your name you may want to list the capacities in which you work or your type. On a second card list your telephone numbers, for example your agent's number and/or your answering service number. List exclusivity with an agent and any performers' union memberships. On a third card list your vital statistics, that is, height, weight, eye color, and hair color. List your Social Security number. Electronic media talent may also want to list an age range. This is a 5- to 7-year span of the ages you can portray.

Next, use one card to make notes on each major or relevant assignment you have had. Note complete information by answering the questions, what, when, where, and how. The important concept behind writing an effective resume is that it should list your experience and qualifications in a colorful, attention grabbing way. Listing the plays you were in and the characters you played, unless they are very well known, is meaningless. Instead, list a credit in an interesting way by describing the role. Also note any details that enhance the information such as the names of the director or other actors, if recognizable. If your performance obtained a positive review by the press, excerpt a succinct or abbreviated quote. You may also want to note where the play took place, if it enhances the information. For example, at the top of your index card, you would write: "The Second Trial" (play name). Played Laura Briggs, a young, ambitious, yet caring lawyer (role name and description), directed by John Q. Famous (enhancement).

If you are assembling a promotional modeling resume, you can follow the same procedure. List the trade show, the company you worked for, and your duties. For example, National Housewares Show, Sunset Greetings, Narrator for "Creative Displays" Slide Presentation. List print jobs indicating the client and what the job was for (poster, pamphlet, catalog, etc.). Note "Portfolio available upon request." List fashion shows you have been in by naming the client.

Use these cards to position the information in the way you will want it to appear on your resume. Compile the cards according to the type of assignment. For example, for a promotional modeling resume, separate the cards into groups of trade shows, promotions, and special events. Print, fashion show, film, television, acting, or performances should also be in separate groups. Then determine the order of the information within each group by putting the most recent, impressive, and extensive experience first.

For an actor's resume, group cards according to industrial films, films, television, voice-over, and theatre. Order cards within each group putting most recent and impressive experience first.

After you have arranged all your cards, make a rough draft of your resume. Put your name, contact numbers, "type," and statistics first and experience next. List training and special abilities last.

Both electronic media and promotional models should list special abilities and training. Following are suggestions on what to include:

Special abilities. List talents you possess that you feel confident you could perform for an audience. List talents such as dance (the type, i.e., modern, jazz, and ballet), sports (the type, i.e., tennis, karate, and scuba diving), singing (the type, i.e., country and rock), impersonations, musical instruments you can play, magic, etc. List skills or characteristics that a client may need, such as knowledge of foreign languages, extensive experience working with children, gourmet cooking skills, accents, dialects. Also include mechanical skills such as operating specialized machinery and typing. List licenses or certifications you have. List only activities you feel you could perform well enough should you be asked to do so in a commercial or exhibition.

Professional training. List courses by subject matter and school or teacher for acting, singing, speech, dancing, mime, acrobatics, television technique, modeling, and music. Also list college degrees.

Resume Design and Production

After you have determined what you are going to include on your resume, you'll have to consider how you'll present the information. Your name should be placed conspicuously and in bold, readable type. Sometimes a model will use the same type style for her name on her resume, glossy, or composite to give a consistent look.

Your contact number is the second most important piece of information. List it near your name. It is helpful if you can list an answering machine or 24-hour answering service telephone number, in addition to your agent's.

To determine which kinds of experience to include, use the following suggestions.

Electronic Media Models and Talent

Theatre experience. Professional theatre, community workshops, local playhouses, summer stock, readings, etc.

Work in films. List extra work in feature films, college films, and industrial films.

Announcing. List emcee, voicework, etc.

Television. List program work, soaps, cable, local shows, specials, series, fund-raising for public TV, etc.

Television commercials. There are two ways to handle this subject. One type of resume gives television commercial credits by listing each company the model has made a commercial for; the other type of resume does not list this information. Instead the phrase "TV Commercials: Upon request" is noted. The reason for not listing specific TV commercial experience is that a casting director or potential client might see something that he or she erroneously will regard as a conflict, thereby eliminating you from the running for a specific type of product.

Promotional Models

Trade shows. List the company you worked for. It is also a good idea to note any capacities in which you worked other than hostessing, for example, product demonstration, narration, or performance.

Promotions. List in-store promotions by client and/or product name; exhibitions, awards ceremonies, and publicity assignments.

Special events. List parades, charities, and appearances,

Television. List any television commercial or program experience you have had.

Other important information to list near your name are union affiliations, vital statistics, and your type. Some models and talent seeking extra work in television and films note "Available for Extra Work."

Your experience is the next grouping of information. You should list your experience under subheadings. The subheadings should be ordered according to your credits and the type of work you are pursuing. For example, a promotional model should list trade shows/conventions first, followed by special events and promotions (see Figure 27). Print, electronic media, and fashion show assignments might be other subheads. An electronic media talent might list industrial films/videos first, followed by films, television programs, commercials, and theatre, according to his or her own experience.

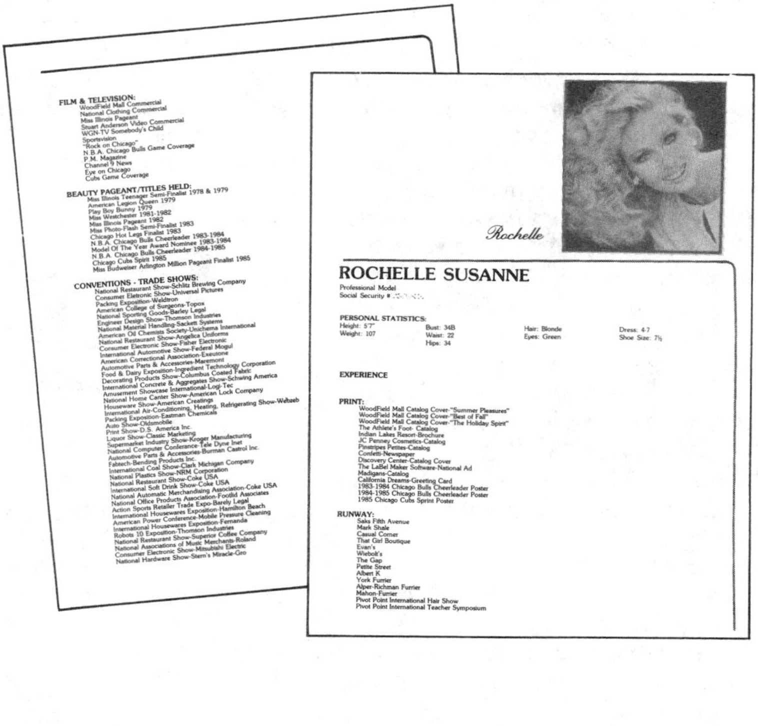

Rochelle

ROCHELLE SUSANNE

Professional Model
Social Security #

PERSONAL STATISTICS:

Height: 5'7"	Bust: 34B	Hair: Blonde	Dress: 4-7
Weight: 107	Waist: 22	Eyes: Green	Shoe Size: 7½
	Hips: 34		

EXPERIENCE

PRINT:
WoodField Mall Catalog Cover-"Summer Pleasures"
WoodField Mall Catalog Cover-"Best of Fall"
WoodField Mall Catalog Cover-"The Holiday Spirit"
The Athlete's Foot- Catalog
Indian Lakes Resort-Brochure
JC Penney Cosmetics-Catalog
Pinstripes Petites-Catalog
Confetti-Newspaper
Discovery Center-Catalog Cover
The LaBel Maker Software-National Ad
Madigans-Catalog
California Dreams-Greeting Card
1983-1984 Chicago Bulls Cheerleader Poster
1984-1985 Chicago Bulls Cheerleader Poster
1985 Chicago Cubs Sprint Poster

RUNWAY:
Saks Fifth Avenue
Mark Shale
Casual Corner
That Girl Boutique
Evan's
Wiebolt's
The Gap
Petite Street
Albert K
York Furrier
Alper-Richman Furrier
Mahon-Furrier
Pivot Point International Hair Show
Pivot Point International Teacher Symposium

FILM & TELEVISION:
WoodField Mall Commercial
National Clothing Commercial
Miss Illinois Pageant
Stuart Anderson Video Commercial
WGN-TV Somebody's Child
Sportsvision
"Rock on Chicago"
N.B.A. Chicago Bulls Game Coverage
P.M. Magazine
Channel 9 News
Eye on Chicago
Cubs Game Coverage

BEAUTY PAGEANT/TITLES HELD:
Miss Illinois Teenager Semi-Finalist 1978 & 1979
American Legion Queen 1979
Play Boy Bunny 1979
Miss Westchester 1981-1982
Miss Illinois Pageant 1982
Miss Photo-Flash Semi-Finalist 1983
Chicago Hot Legs Finalist 1983
N.B.A. Chicago Bulls Cheerleader 1983-1984
Model Of The Year Award Nominee 1983-1984
N.B.A. Chicago Bulls Cheerleader 1984-1985
Chicago Cubs Spirit 1985
Miss Budweiser Arlington Million Pageant Finalist 1985

CONVENTIONS - TRADE SHOWS:
National Restaurant Show-Schlitz Brewing Company
Consumer Eletronic Show-Universal Pictures
Packing Exposition-Weldtron
American College of Surgeons-Topox
National Sporting Goods-Barley Legal
Engineer Design Show-Thomson Industries
National Material Handling-Sackett Systems
American Oil Chemists Society-Unichema International
National Restaurant Show-Angelica Uniforms
Consumer Electronic Show-Fisher Electronic
International Automotive Show-Federal Mogul
American Correctional Association-Exeutone
Automotive Parts & Accessories-Maremont
Food & Dairy Exposition-Ingredient Technology Corporation
Decorating Products Show-Columbus Coated Fabric
International Concrete & Aggregates Show-Schwing America
Amusement Showcase International-Logi-Tec
National Home Canter Show-American Lock Company
Houseware Show-American Creatings
International Air-Conditioning, Heating, Refrigerating Show-Webzeb
Packing Exposition-Eastman Chemicals
Auto Show-Oldsmobile
Print Show-D.S. America Inc.
Liquor Show-Classic Marketing
Supermarket Industry Show-Kroger Manufacturing
National Computer Conferance-Tele Dyne Inet
Automotive Parts & Accessories-Burman Castrol Inc.
Fabtech-Bending Products Inc.
International Coal Show-Clark Michigan Company
National Plastics Show-NRM Corporation
National Restaurant Show-Coke USA
International Soft Drink Show-Coke USA
National Automatic Merchandising Association-Coke USA
National Office Products Association-Footlid Associates
Action Sports Retailer Trade Expo-Barely Legal
International Housewares Exposition-Hamilton Beach
American Power Conference-Mobile Pressure Cleaning
International Housewares Exposition-Fernanda
Robots 10 Exposition-Thomson Industries
National Restaurant Show-Superior Coffee Company
National Associations of Music Merchants-Roland
Consumer Electronic Show-Mitsubishi Electric
National Hardware Show-Stern's Miracle-Gro

Figure 26. Example of a trade show model's resume. Promotional models' resumes often display more creative designs than actors' resumes. Notice the type style and graphics on the one shown here. Also, because a promotional model's resume is usually not attached to her composite, including a picture is often a good idea.

After experience the next heading should be "Training." The last heading should be "Special Abilities."

The appearance of the resume reflects on you. If it is neat and professional, it will make a good impression. If it is filled with spelling errors, erasures, strikeovers, globs of ink, or correction fluid, it makes an unprofessional and unfavorable impression. Use good-quality bond paper in standard letter size.

- Leave ample margins at the sides, top, and bottom of the page. Clients often like to make notes in the margins, and such a layout is more pleasing to the eye and will draw attention to important points.

- Try to confine your resume to one or two pages. It should be clear and to the point. Include only the most outstanding and relevant things you have done.

- Make a rough draft and when you are typing, position everything in an attractive, simple layout. Make sure margins, indentations, and listings all line up vertically.

- It is always a good idea to have your resume typed on word-processing equipment to ensure perfection. Some models and talent have their resumes typeset. This is attractive but increases the cost. When typesetting is done, the cost and inconvenience of updating should also be considered. Usually a typeset resume is best for established talent.

- Always have an agent or other knowledgeable individual check your rough draft. You may even want to work up several variations containing different information and have the agent select the resume that is most effective. She or he will be able to give valuable suggestions.

- Have your perfect, final draft quick printed by a good printer in the same quantity as your glossy (usually 100). Be sure that your resume corresponds to the size of your glossy (8 x 10 or 8½ x 11). Printing usually takes 3 to 5 days. When you pick them up, check through them. Staple one to the back of each glossy.

Editing and Updating Your Resume

Your first resume will be the most difficult one to assemble. As you continually acquire experience, it will be important to frequently update your resume. Eliminate assignments that took place more than 2 years ago or that are not as impressive as ones you may have had subsequently.

THE VOICE TAPE

An individual who wishes to promote himself or herself for voice-over work in television commericals and other audio visual presentations will need a voice tape. A voice tape is a 3-minute-maximum reel-to-reel or cassette audiotape that gives samples of a voice-over artist's voice. It usually contains several 5- to 30-second segments taken from commercials or copy the artist has written him-or herself. The lines of the copy that are chosen are perfectly tailored to the artist's voice, and the way his or her voice can best be marketed. For example, if the voice-over artist can put on a voice that sounds very appetizing, he or she would read a segment from a food commercial.

Types of Voice Tapes

Voice tapes are categorized by clients according to the four types of voices: straight announcers, character voices, industrial/educational voices, and jingle singers. If the voice-over artist can specialize in more than one area, he or she should have two voice tapes, rather than trying to sell all his or her talents on one tape. For example, one tape could be for character voices and one for jingle singing. Although this is more expensive, it is better for filing purposes and will ensure that the talent's tape will be in the right place at the right time.

Producing a Voice Tape

When done well, a voice tape can be very expensive to produce. Recording studio time, an engineer, mixing in stock music or sound effects, editing, duplicating of the reel-to-reel and cassette tapes, and other costs, such as a package for the tape, are involved. Recording studios do exist that will help the talent to select the material to read, coach the talent on the reading and recording, duplicate, and package the tape. However, many times all these tapes end up sounding alike. Therefore, it is wise to have an interested agent to guide you through the process. Although an agent will make no solid guarantees of success, it is also obvious that he or she would not waste time if the talent doesn't have money-making potential. Before attempting to make a voice tape, it is important that the voice be trained to its highest potential.

An agent will also be able to counsel you as to your best voices (for example, cosmetic, corporate, food, character female, etc.) as well as the specifics necessary for recording your tape. In most markets it is required that reel-to-reel tapes be on 4- to 5-inch diameter reels and recorded at 7½ rpm. Your name and number (or agent's logo) should be on the box and the reel and a listing of the commercials by product contained on the tape should appear on the inside of the box.

Distributing Your Voice Tape

After the voice tape has been produced, duplicates will be made for distribution. A voice tape is distributed to producers and casting directors in need of voices. Although most of these individuals will listen to unsolicited tapes, it is better if your tape is sent by an agent. An agent will know of all the clients who use voices of your type and will give you credibility. Also when a call comes into the agent requesting a voice of your type, your tape will be sent out. In addition, the agent will make an Agency Master Reel or Tape containing short samples of all the voice talents he or she represents in each category. This is sent to clients for reference purposes. A union-franchised agent must pay the cost of producing the agency master reel.

Casting for voice talent is usually done in one of two ways: by auditions or by listening to voicetapes. Usually when a talent is booked directly from his or her voicetape rather than an audition, the talent is well known or the casting director has a lot of trust in the voice talent's agent. In these cases it is very important that an agent know exactly what the talent is capable of doing. This is the reason why even if you approach an agent with a professionally recorded tape, he or she will ascertain whether any local producers have worked with you. Also, the agent will ask you to come in for a taping to see if you can easily duplicate what was done on your voice tape.

Using Your Voice Tape Effectively

In most cases, a casting director will want to hear how the talent applies his or her voice to the script that will be used for a proposed commercial or other production. Therefore, the casting director will select several individuals to appear for an audition based on voice tapes or agency master reels. At an audition, a voice talent may be asked to give a reading of a script in an advertising agency sound room complete with professional recording equipment, or he or she may have to read the script into a portable tape recorder in a casting director's office. The voice talent must be prepared and realize that his or her ability to interpret the particular script is what is being evaluated. Being able to accept and expand on direction the talent is given is also vital. The casting director usually relies on the voice tape to determine whether a talent has the necessary qualities.

338

SELF-PROMOTIONAL APPOINTMENTS

A self-promotional appointment occurs when a model appears in person to meet a prospective client, coordinator, editor, photographer, or other individual who might be interested in utilizing his or her looks and abilities. After the model has obtained professional self-promotional tools, his or her next step will be meeting prospective clients. A model uses self-promotional appointments to impress clients with his or her personal appearance and presentation. The model displays his or her capabilities by showing a portfolio or by performing a specific task that is relevant to the job. At the close of the appointment, the model leaves a composite or other type of reminder of the meeting that the client can retain for future reference. A successful self-promotional appointment leads to a booking.

Selecting models for assignments is done in a variety of ways. Clients usually rely on photographers, coordinators, and casting directors to screen all the potential models for a particular job and ask them to submit composites or glossies of the preferred candidates. The client then makes the final decision about which models will be employed. At other times the client will attend the audition to see all the candidates for the job in person.

Every model at some point meets clients, photographers, coordinators, and other casting decision makers in person and must therefore know how to make a good impression. When a model meets with a prospective employer, he or she is judged according to how well he or she fits the image needed. This image is usually defined by age, size and figure type, look or type, special features, and skills or talents. Not only are the model's physical features a factor, his or her projection, personality, intelligence, and professionalism are considered.

Types of Self-Promotional Appointments

There are different ways in which clients, photographers, and other decision makers look for models. The following methods are also opportunities for the model to promote him-or herself.

Auditions

Auditioning is a method used to select models and actors for a specific assignment, such as a television commercial, an advertising campaign, a fashion show, or a print booking. Models appearing at auditions have often been preselected by the client, casting director, or other individual on the basis of their composites or their pictures in modeling agency promotional books or headsheets. If the client or casting director does not prescreen models by their pictures, usually he or she will place a call to several modeling agencies requesting each to send the models they represent who possess a certain image or set of characteristics.

Cattle Calls

A mass interview or audition where tens or even hundreds of models and actors report at the appointment at the same time is often referred to as a "cattle call." These are usually for advertising bookings and most often occur when the client is in search of a new face.

Go-Sees

A go-see is an appointment with a photographer or client so that he or she will know what the model looks like.

Rounds

"Making the rounds" is a general term for calling on people who may require a model's services at some time in the future. Beginning models go on rounds to see photographers in order to arrange testings, the results of which can be used for his or her portfolio and composite. In many cities the modeling agency gives each new model a "rounds list" that gives the names, addresses, and telephone numbers of all the clients the agency has. The list may contain hundreds of names of photographers, catalog studios, retail stores, and other entities in need of models. The model is expected to call on the people on the list to meet them in person, to show his or her portfolio, and to drop off a composite. Some may have designations alongside the names, such as "call first," which means the model must telephone for an appointment prior to coming, or "agency appointment only," which means an appointment must be arranged by the model's agency.

Casting

Casting is a general term referring to the act of selecting a suitable model to represent the image or character in a proposed ad, television commercial, etc.

Call Back

Call back is a term most commonly used in connection with television assignments and refers to a second audition for the same product. A call back is an indication that the model or actor is seriously being considered for the job. Advertising agencies will often call back a model to perform his or her audition again to take a closer look, to double-check on the model's performance, to compare him or her with other serious contenders for the job, or to experiment with different approaches for the job at hand.

How to Prepare for Self-Promotional Appointments

When attending modeling appointments your best strategy to get clients, photographers, and other decision makers interested in you is to be prepared. It is not easy for a client to ascertain in a 5- to 10-minute interview whether a model will be right for a particular assignment. Therefore, presenting yourself in such a way that the client doesn't have to rely heavily on his or her imagination is wise. Your aim is to make it easy for the client to see that you are the best model for the job. There are basically four rules of preparation a model should observe.

1. Present the right image.
2. Provide the necessary items.
3. Act professionally.
4. Approach appointments with the right mental attitude.

Present the Right Image

The way you must present yourself will depend on the types of clients you will be seeing. Always have a clear concept of your type and make your assets visible to your interviewer. When attending appointments, keep your hair and makeup simple, clean, and natural looking. Don't pin up or obscure your hair because the client will want to see it. If you wear glasses, don't wear them to interviews. Wear clothing that flatters your figure and that fits close enough so your body can be seen. Be sure your weight is ideal. Go on appointments only if your health, skin, and hair are in good condition. Express your image through your clothing, hair, and makeup. Consult Chapter 5 for more detailed information on what to wear to appointments.

The appearance of your hair, skin, and figure are not the only means by which photographers and clients will be judging you. They will also be trying to ascertain how well you project. If you're self-conscious, meek, awkward, or disinterested, they will probably avoid you. Your personality and physical presentation should project an image that the client thinks he or she can use. The photographer and client are looking not only for someone who looks like a model, but who thinks like a professional model. They don't want to spend a lot of time and energy to elicit a performance from a model. They want a model who can convincingly portray the images they need.

When called for an audition, always try to obtain as much information as possible from your agent. Use an Audition Form to help you to cover important details. Always try to find out what type of look the client is in search of. You'll increase your chances of getting the job if you are prepared and present the image your client is looking for. For example, if the client is looking for a businesswoman, the model should wear a business suit, a fairly conservative hairstyle, and toned-down makeup.

Audition Form

©THE PROFESSIONAL MODEL'S HANDBOOK

Audition Date _____ Time _____

Job Date _____

Type of Assignment:

☐Print   ☐TV   ☐Show   ☐Promo   ☐Other _____

Product _____

Client _____ Report to _____

Where _____

Look _____

Bring/Wear _____

☐Videotape   ☐Polaroid   ☐Fitting   ☐Other _____

Rate, if applicable _____

Notes: _____

_____

_____

_____

_____

_____

_____

_____

When a client, agent, or other person invites you to audition for an upcoming job, use the Audition Form to record information. Here are the questions you should ask.

1. *What is the date and time of the audition?* Sometimes you will be given an exact time, other times you may be told to stop by within a given span of hours.

2. *When is the job to take place?* Find out the date of the job right away. There is no sense in attending the audition if you know you won't be able to make it to the booking if you land the job. This is sometimes referred to as the "avail date."

3. *What type of assignment is it?* Is the booking for a live promotion, TV spot, etc?

4. *What is the product?* Knowing the product gives you an indication of the type of look the client is seeking. When a print ad or television commercial is being produced, you will have to know the product in order to check if you have a product conflict. If the interview is with a large concern such as an advertising agency, there may be several auditions for different products going on simultaneously. Therefore, knowing which product you are auditioning for is helpful.

5. *Who is the client and who am I to see?* The person you are to see may be the client (an individual who works at the concern that makes the product or service) or an individual enlisted to conduct the audition, such as a photographer, advertising agency, casting director, producer, or editor. Knowing to whom you are to report is important when auditioning at a large concern such as a magazine where there are several editors casting models for various reasons.

6. *Where is the audition?* Write down the name of the place where the audition will be held. An audition is not necessarily held at a client's place of business. It may be held at a showroom, photographer's studio, your modeling agency, or a casting director's office. Jot down the address and if it is unfamiliar to you, look it up on a map or ask your agency.

7. *What type of look should I have?* Your agent will tell you what kind of look they are after. When the client calls the agency to find a model, he or she will usually specify a certain type or look. For example, the client may request a girl-next-door, a high-fashion European look, or a young mother. Your agent should relay this information to you so you can do your hair and makeup accordingly. If the agent does not specify a particular look, and you are familiar with the client's work, try to look the part of the models he or she uses. When auditioning for live promotions and television commercials, you may be meeting businesspeople who cannot visualize the effects of makeup and hair, so you'll have to present a polished image. On the other hand, photographers are experienced in visualizing these effects. Still, with either type of interviewer, you'll increase your chances by looking perfect for the job.

8. *Do I need to wear or bring anything specific?* Occasionally clients may request that you wear a skirt so they can see your legs, or they may reqest that you wear jeans so they can see how you look in pants. Clients who are shooting pictures for makeup or jewelry may ask you to bring a tube top so they can see your neck and shoulders. Bring your portfolio, glossy, resume, etc. to all appointments.

9. *What will I have to do? Is this a paid audition?* Your agent should inform you beforehand if you will have to read a script, have a Polaroid or videotape taken, or try on clothing or other items. Depending on what you have to do, you may be paid a fee. Know the amount of the fee and bring along a voucher.

10. *Write down any other useful information you may be able to obtain.*

Provide the Necessary Items

In most instances, going on rounds, go-sees, and auditions is a waste of time if you have nothing to leave with the client or photographer. A photographer sees many models who won't be remembered if he or she cannot later refer to a picture. This is why you should always have a composite to leave behind. For television commercial auditions, you will need to leave a glossy and resume. If you do voice-over work, leaving a copy of your voice tape for electronic media clients will be necessary.

If your agency's logo isn't imprinted on your promotional materials, stamp them or affix labels indicating how you can be reached. If your composite is being prepared, leave a Polaroid, photocopy, or duplicate portfolio print or tearsheet with your name and agency noted on the back. Generally, giving prints from your portfolio is not a good idea because you may never get them back, and if you do, they probably won't be in good condition. Casting directors sometimes refuse to allow talent without glossies or composites into auditions. At some appointments, you may be asked to leave two or three composties, one for the photographer and others for the client and art director.

A model always carries his or her portfolio to appointments and auditions. It should be in top form, look neat, and contain at least 8 or 10 black and white and color photos following the guidelines in this chapter.

It will be necessary to take a voucher with you to some auditions. You may be paid if you are required to try on items or to have a test photograph taken. Consult your agent beforehand.

Among the personal items you should have at appointments are your appointment book, money (especially change for telephone calls, parking meters, public transportation, etc.), comb, mirror, and cosmetics.

Be prepared to give information about yourself and your experience. By anticipating what they may ask, your responses will be immediate and precise. Clients often ask the following questions:

How old are you? Clients often ask a model's age when the model they are seeking must appear a certain age. Or if the model's age is a part of a commercial, because of truth-in-advertising laws, the model must be the age she purports to be. Or there may be an age requirement, depending on the product that is to be modeled. In the case of cigarettes, the model must be 25 and over; for beer and liquor advertising, the model must be 21 or over.

What is your availability? If a definite date for the booking has not been set, the client may want to know if you will be booked or out of town on the dates being considered. Or if the photographer is available only on certain dates, the client may ask if you are also free. Know your availability, and don't go to audition if you will be unavailable on the date of the job.

What is your modeling experience? Potential clients like to know you have been tried by other clients. This is a chance to sell yourself. It is not the time to be self-conscious or downplay your accomplishments and abilities. On the other hand, don't boast. Be specific. Give the names of clients, photographers, studios, and ad agencies for whom you have worked. Begin with the most recent assignments and make sure you describe any prestigious jobs you have had. Describe jobs that are relevant to the client's needs. It is never a good idea to fabricate bookings. The circle of people involved in the modeling business is small, and you are likely to be caught in a lie. If you have had no bookings, mention testings and nonpaying assignments; there is no need to indicate they were done at no charge. Don't tell the client what a rough time you have had trying to get work. The sympathy ploy rarely works.

In print modeling, the model's portfolio is proof of his or her experience. However, clients often ask how old certain pictures are, which photographer shot them, or whether the model did her own hair and makeup. Make a point of remembering the first and last names of people with whom you have worked. Some photographers will ask the model if he or she has worked for the client previously.

Runway clients may ask which shows you have modeled in or for which stores or designers you have done fashion shows.

Electronic media clients will want to know if you have product conflicts with the item for which they are auditioning you. They will want to know what commercials you have currently on the air and past commercials you have done. You should remember where and when the commercials were shot, and for which client and ad agency you worked. You may be asked if you do extra work or if you have had experience in industrial or educational films.

Clients casting models for live promotions may engage in small talk to see how personable you are. They may also ask you about facts that appear on your resume such as which trade shows and clients you worked for and what your duties included. It is important to realize that many times promotional modeling clients rely heavily on modeling agents to determine which models are right for an assignment. Therefore, make sure that your agent is fully informed about your qualifications, experience, and professionalism. Also continually work on establishing a good relationship with the agent.

Clients of all types commonly ask your hourly and daily rate. They may also ask you if you possess a certain skill required for the job. Never lie to a client about a product conflict, your availability, your experience, or your qualifications.

Act Professionally   Your looks and qualifications are ultimately going to determine whether or not you get the job, but observing the following points of etiquette will also be helpful.

- Be punctual. If you are running late, call your agent so he or she can inform the client. If you arrive more than 15 minutes early for an appointment, use this valuable time to go on a quick errand or check with your agent or study your appointment book.

- Don't arrive in a condition requiring apologies. Never apologize for your portfolio, appearance, or composite, because this shows a lack of self-confidence and professionalism.

- Treat everyone at the studio with equal respect. Often models will ignore the secretary at the front desk and demand to see the photographer. The person you ignore may be the one who is in charge of bookings. Photographers often designate the task of model selection or screening to receptionists, secretaries, or assistants. Make a point of remembering the names of all the people you meet.

Casting Sheet

©THE PROFESSIONAL MODEL'S HANDBOOK

INFORMATION

Name _____ Date _____

Agency _____ Rate (hour/day) _____

Home Address _____

Telephone Nos. (home) _____ (Answering Service) _____

Soc. Sec. No. _____

Age _____ Birthdate _____ Height _____

Weight _____ Haircolor _____ Eyecolor _____

SIZES

Suit _____ Dress _____ Shoe _____

Shirt _____ Pants _____ Waist _____

Bra _____ Glove _____ Hat _____

PHOTO

FOR INTERVIEWER'S USE – DO NOT WRITE IN SPACE BELOW

REMARKS

Client/Job _____ Agency _____

- Don't bring anyone (girlfriend, boyfriend, mother, etc.) with you to a go-see or audition. Only child models should be accompanied to appointments. If you need to bring someone along, have the person wait outside for you.

- Do not go to a studio or office without an appointment. Always call to give prior notice before stopping by a studio or office. This shows basic consideration and will also prevent you from interrupting an important shooting or other event that may be transpiring there.

- When you arrive, always introduce yourself. Smile and state your first and last name clearly, and tell the name of the agency or individual that sent you. Don't appear at the interview expecting the person to know who you are and why you are there. Greet your interviewer by name when possible (make a point of calling people by name) and look the person in the eyes. Hand your portfolio to the interviewer unzipped, right side up. Have a composite, glossy, or resume ready to hand over.

- Be courteous. Common courtesy applies as in any interview situation. Don't eat, smoke, or drink unless you are invited to do so. Don't chew gum, fidget, pick your nails, or play with your hair, keys, or jewelry. Don't handle or read items on an interviewer's desk or hover over the client's shoulder when he or she is looking at your book. Don't chatter. Let the client concentrate and ask the questions.

- Be efficient. Find out from your agent beforehand how much the job will pay. It is not your job to negotiate fees with the client; this is your agent's job. If you are asked, give your hourly and daily rate.

- Do not arrange bookings directly with a client. It is fine to arrange testings and other nonpaying assignments; however, keep your agent informed of such matters. Always tell the individual you can be contacted through your agency. If you don't have an agent, give the number of your answering service. Avoid giving your private telephone number to clients and photographers.

- Don't ask to use the client's telephone. Make your calls from a public phone when you leave the studio or office.

- Don't invite yourself to auditions. The only time you are to go for an audition is when your agent has informed you or the client has asked you. Just because a model friend of yours has been sent to a particular studio, does not mean you can go too. The client may not even have requested your type. It is up to your agent and client to make a judgment about which auditions you should attend.

- Don't be a no-show. If a problem arises that makes it impossible for you to attend an audition, call your agent as soon as possible.

- Don't take up more than 5 or 10 minutes of an interviewer's time unless you are specifically asked to stay. Avoid gossiping or discussing matters unrelated to the assignment. Don't make derogatory comments about other models, agencies, or photographers. Do not act shy or unsociable at appointments or give short answers that show you can't converse. Don't mumble and act indifferent. This may show that you don't care if you get the job. Maintain eye contact so the client can see your face to determine if you meet her requirements. Be enthusiastic. This is your time to shine so use it wisely for you may not have a second chance.

- Act as if you want to work for the client. Show him or her what you can do if you're given the opportunity. If you have been given a script or an outfit to try on, try to generate ideas. For the script, think about how you are going to execute it; for the outfit, do a few turns or movements.

- Be concerned with the client's needs. Listen to directions carefully as the client will be determining how well you take instruction.
- Notes for child models and their parents: Although you will accompany your child to an appointment, you should not accompany him or her into the actual audition. Usually there will be a nearby waiting room for parents. Talent buyers generally want to see your child's ability on his or her own without your prompting.

Approach Appointments with the Right Attitude

Realize that every time you meet another person, you may be in line for another opinion. Everyone will have a different opinion about your looks, your abilities, and your potential. One agent may tell you to lose five pounds, the next may tell you to gain five. Your photographs may generate even more comments and opinions. One photographer may praise them, whereas another will criticize them. Don't let negative comments get you down. It helps to understand that the people you meet will be evaluating you and your photos according to their specific needs. Also, always consider the source; a photographer, agent, or other individual who stands to make money by making new photos for you won't usually give you an unbiased opinion. Be open and receptive to advice and go with the majority opinion. If clients, photographers, and agents tell you certain photos in your portfolio are unsuitable, you should replace or eliminate those that generate the most unfavorable comments. Don't be defensive or disappointed when comments or opinions are offered. Not every client will like your look, and if one does, he or she won't necessarily like everything in your book.

Don't let nerves get the better of you. Even a top model experiences the jitters when vying for an important job. Realize that all the other models are nervous too and that even the person interviewing you may be nervous because he or she has to choose the right model. A lack of composure not only affects your personality, but also your looks. Letting your nervousness show will not inspire a client's confidence in you. You may have only one chance to meet and impress a client, so putting your best foot forward is important.

Don't ask the client whether you got the assignment. It is very rare that you will leave an audition knowing whether or not you have gotten the job. The client needs to see all the candidates for the job and may need to secure approval from others in the company before making a final decision. Don't try to talk a client into promising to use you. It reveals a desperate feeling. Even if a client says she will use you, you should still not count on getting the job. The job is only for certain after the client has called your agency to confirm the date, rate, and other particulars. An aggressive, hard-sell approach rarely works and will cause clients to avoid you.

Think of your appointments as a way of doing research. At an appointment you can find out the types of work the client or photographer does, how often he or she needs models, and whether he or she is interested in doing test shots, etc. If the client or photographer is not interested in booking you but seems helpful, you might ask him or her if he or she knows of photographers who might be interested in your look. Photographers and clients can also be valuable sources of other information. They may know of events in the business that affect you, or they may give you advice for changing your look, composite, or approach. Use the Contact Record form to make notes of what everyone tells you. Analyze what they say, and act on your findings. Study your records, and learn from your experiences on rounds.

If the client or photographer is someone you could work with, try to leave with a tip or recommendation, such as a testing, an upcoming booking he or she may have mentioned, or a client he or she suggests you see. Then make certain you follow up on the suggestion.

Each client or photographer handles appointments differently. One may flip through your book in a matter of seconds and end the meeting, the next might converse with you over a cup of coffee. A lot will depend on the time restraints he or she has that day. Don't take such things personally; they usually have nothing to do with his or her actual regard for you.

Don't take turndowns or setbacks negatively. Maintain your strength and confidence no matter what. Accept such situations as challenges. Realize that, especially in the beginning, the rejections will outnumber the acceptances.

When meeting clients in person, be aware that most clients will be very hesitant to tell you whether or not they intend to use your services. If they are not interested in you, some will not frankly say so. If they don't think you are model material or if they cannot use you, they will give you excuses.

In general, rather than just accepting excuses on the surface, consider their validity or actual meaning. Try to ascertain what the person is really saying. Is he or she truly interested in you as a model or is he or she just giving you ''put-offs'' to avoid flatly rejecting you? A photographer or client who's genuinely interested will give you concrete suggestions or refer you to people or places who may be able to help you. He may be willing to test or he may take a Polaroid so that he won't forget you.

When going on appointments, you will encounter three basic types of responses from the people you meet. The first type of response is one that indicates that the client is definitely interested in you as a model. He or she usually has a specific job or client in mind for you. She might send you to her client for approval, ask you to do a test session, or ask you about your availability.

The second type of response indicates that the client or photographer will probably not use your services. He or she may not handle assignments utilizing models of your looks, type, or skills. He or she may use models of your type but may not like your look or may think your skills are lacking.

The third type of response falls between these two extremes. Such a client may be interested in you for the future but doesn't have a specific assignment presently for which he or she can book you. Or the client may think you have potential but doesn't want to make a commitment or take a chance on you now because you don't have enough experience or your look is not quite right.

Obviously you should direct your efforts toward the clients who respond favorably and those who are undecided. Following up on possible opportunities is vital to success.

Keeping Records of the Contacts You Make

The only way to keep track of the people you have met is to keep written records. The Contact Record form is used to note every client, photographer, or other individual that you have met through self-promotional appointments. It is used to keep track of any business correspondence such as phone calls or mailings of your self-promotion tools. The Contact Record form can be a valuable tool for a model. By keeping records of appointments, auditions, and go-sees you attend, you can judge your progress, note any patterns that are emerging, and then decide on changes of approach. It is also a good reminder for following up on your self-promotional appointments.

Contact Record

©THE PROFESSIONAL MODEL'S HANDBOOK

Company _____ Phone _____

Address _____

Contact Name _____ Position _____

Type of Work _____

Date	Notes

How to Use the Contact Record Form

Fill out one Contact Record form for each contact you make.

Line 1   Write down the name of the company, ad agency, studio, and the phone number.

Line 2   List the address. This is necessary for finding your way there the first time and will be useful for follow-up visits. Get into the habit of using a contact record, rather than looking things up on a list or asking your agent.

Line 3   List the person you are to see. Knowing his or her name and establishing a good contact is vital. It is also better when you call to ask for a specific person. These people change jobs frequently, so it is a good idea to keep abreast of who is working where. Also note the person's position.

Line 4   At the interview, or from your agent, find out all the types of work the company does and how often they use models. In the blank spaces below, note any other information of interest.

In the area below Line 4 you will write notes pertaining to your contact with this company, photographer, client, editor, coordinator, etc. Each time you have contact with this client or individual note the date in the left column. In the "Notes" column jot down whether it was a go-see, audition (and for what), or just a follow-up visit. You might also want to jot down what you were wearing or your "look" that day. Always write down any possible future testings, bookings, opportunities, or advice that may have been mentioned during the course of your conversation with the contact.

Use your contact record also when phoning for appointments. Jot down the date you called and what the contact said. If you are asked to call back in a week, note the date to call back. This information makes it easier to follow up. Use the Contact Record form to jot down written correspondence. List the date you sent your correspondence along with a description of what was sent.

Study the information you collect on Contact Record forms. Share the information with your agent to determine which clients you need to pursue more energetically and how you should approach them. Learn from advice or suggestions contacts may have given you.

Self-Promotion on the Job

This chapter has explained the various ways in which you can get clients to be aware of your looks and abilities. Getting a client to notice you and persuading him to book you requires a considerable effort. However, securing that initial booking with a new client is not the only key to building a successful modeling career. The other necessary key to success is performing well on the job. If you impress a client on the job and produce great results for his or her concern, you will be called back again. A model cannot build a career by obtaining a single booking from every client in a given market. She or he must acquire a group of clients who book her repeatedly. Also, when a client is very satisfied with your performance he or she will tell his or her colleagues about you, which will lead to even more opportunities. In addition, your good work (photos in magazines and catalogs and appearances in television commercials, fashion shows, or live promotions) will be visible to others who are in need of models and constantly on the lookout for new faces.

PART 4 THE FIELDS OF MODELING
Chapter 10 Modeling for Print Media

TYPES OF MODELING FOR PRINT MEDIA

Print modeling refers to modeling for photographs that will appear in printed materials such as magazines, brochures, packaging, newspapers, and catalogs. In addition to photographs, illustrations of models may be used to depict an idea, product, or service. Printed materials fall into four basic categories:

1. Editorial.
2. Advertising.
3. Catalog.
4. Publicity/public relations.

Editorial

Editorial material refers to the parts of a magazine or newspaper that are created by the editors, not the advertisers. Unlike ads, which promote specific products (a dress, or a cosmetic), the editorial pages explain new ideas or concepts and promote images or looks. An editorial photograph may accompany a story or article in the magazine or newspaper, or the photographs themselves may tell the story or present the information with the details supplied by subtitles or copy. Depending on the subject matter and the type of magazine, models of all types may appear. Fashion models appear in fashion and beauty-related editorials.

Modeling for fashion editorials is the most prestigious and glamourous work in print modeling, but it is also the lowest paying. Models for editorial print assignments are most often drawn from the fashion or celebrity group of models, but specialty models are occasionally needed. Selection of the editorial model is based on how well the model represents the image or philosophies the magazine promotes to its readers; how well his or her look expresses current concepts in fashion, beauty, and life-style; and whether he or she can contribute creativity in movement and expression to the photographs.

More than any other type of model, the editorial fashion model must have charisma, uniqueness, style, and projectable personality. For editorial work, the fashions are the latest, the atmosphere exciting, and the talent endless. Top photographers, hairdressers, makeup artists, stylists, editors, and models are in abundance. Although many of the models seen in the editorial sections of magazines are international model stars, these models can have the least experience of any other type of model and still produce a great result; in fact, the freshness, originality, and spontaneity of a relative novice are often exactly the commodities that editors desire. For most models, editorial work is not a steady, year-to-year occurrence. Most of a model's editorial exposure will occur toward the beginning of her career or occasionally for periods throughout. To make it to the top, a model needs editorial exposure; however, it is a rare model who can make a substantial living solely on editorial work. Not only does editorial work offer a lower rate of pay, it is also limiting. This is because successful editorial models have a more identifiable and, therefore, more expendable look than their commercial or catalog counterparts. The look of an editorial model exemplifies current fashion, and as fashion in clothing changes, so does fashion in models.

Advertising

Advertising work refers to pictures used in magazines, newspapers, direct mail literature, product labels and tags, package inserts, sales displays, packages, billboards, and posters used to promote an item. These materials are created by advertising agencies, stores, manufacturers, or anyone who is trying to sell a specific product or service. Photos taken for advertising purposes feature models of all types from character to specialty to high-fashion models. The type of product and the advertising approach used will determine the choice of model. For product ads, the model is usually chosen from the commercial, character, or specialty group. Fashion models are most often used in ads promoting fashion and beauty-related products or such glamourized products as liquor, travel, soft drinks, and cars.

Advertising is the most lucrative of all print work because the model is paid according to the amount of exposure the ad is given. For example, if an ad is run for many months in a magazine, or if the model's picture appears in an area of high visibility (on a billboard, a package, or a point of purchase display), she is paid a bonus. This residual type of payment is referred to as a "print usage fee." Print usage fees are designed to compensate the model for modeling assignments she will not be eligible to do, because she is precluded from modeling for competing products when she agrees to represent one product.

Firms do a lot of research on the demographics of their potential customers and choose models based on how well they appeal to the group most likely to use the company's product or service. Successful advertising models appeal to a large and diverse base of consumers.

Catalog Photographs

Catalog work refers to the photographs taken for retailer's catalogs, mail order brochures, flyers, and other materials used to sell merchandise. The way a catalog looks has a lot to do with the items it contains. Catalogs, like magazines, are produced with a certain type of customer in mind. Retailers using catalogs to sell their wares conduct involved studies of their existing and potential customers and produce catalogs that will appeal to the group they think will draw the greatest profits for the merchandise they are offering. Usually the higher the price of the items the catalog sells, the more elaborate and creative the catalog.

Catalogs for Volume Merchandising

Catalogs that must appeal to a large diverse group of consumers often have a conservative, straightforward appearance. Models possessing a fresh, wholesome, naturally pretty or handsome image are usually prevalent in these catalogs. The ideal model for this type of catalog is the one whose looks are not too extreme. The majority of these catalogs are shot in a studio against seamless backdrop paper or on a very simple set with crisp lighting that clearly shows the details and construction of a garment. Sometimes shootings take place out of doors. To achieve the desired garment lines and proper fit and to make the garment look as good as possible, it may be pinned, tucked, weighted, or stuffed. Although the model's movements should always look natural, not stiff or posed, they tend to be simple and confined because of space, visibility, layout, and other limitations.

Companies that produce volume-type catalogs often display clothes that are not particularly fashionable. They select garments that will sell tens and even hundreds of thousands of pieces, so it is important that the garments chosen appeal in price and style to a large group of catalog shoppers. It is for these reasons that typical catalog modeling is often considered the dreariest. The clothes provide little inspiration, and the situation does not demand a lot of self-expression or creativity.

Catalogs for Specialized Merchandising

Specialized catalogs have a more limited appeal; however, they are targeted to specific types of customers. These catalogs contain high-ticket or trendy items or items made for a single segment of the population, such as large-size women. The aim of a specialized catalog is exclusive rather than volume selling. These catalogs usually have a smaller distribution than the average catalog and often there is a charge to the customer to obtain them. Usually more space is devoted to each garment and more expensive production and printing techniques are employed. These catalogs take a more creative approach to photography, design, and styling. They are often shot on exotic locations or elaborate sets. Because these catalogs often display photographs that look similar to the editorial pages of a magazine, editorial models whose looks range from classic to trendy to exotic are often employed.

Some catalogs exhibit characteristics of both volume and exclusive merchandising. There are a few things that nearly all catalog modeling situations have in common. There is usually a large quantity of merchandise to be shot. Because of costs involved, a lot of time cannot be spent on each garment. Another limitation inherent in catalog modeling is that attention must be paid to the model's movement to avoid unbecoming wrinkles and to highlight the draping of the garment. In other words, the garment must be displayed clearly and optimally because the customer will not view it firsthand before ordering or purchasing it. Finally, because of the high cost of printing and postage, the catalog producer tries to limit the number of pages in the catalog. This is done by limiting the number of garments shown or by photographing models in groups of two or more. Another way might be to display several small or narrow shots of individual models. All three of these methods maximize the number of garments per page.

Although catalog work may not be as glamourous as other modeling assignments, it is lucrative and considered the "bread and butter" of the business. A model who does catalog work earns steady money over a long period of time. In most cases a popular catalog model will earn more than an editorial superstar. Although the cost of catalog production and distribution is high, selling by catalog has proven to be very lucrative for many companies. Because of the number of catalogs that exist, both specialized and general, and the fact that they employ all types of models of varied ages and sizes, modeling opportunities abound in this area.

Publicity/Public Relations Photographs

Publicity and public relations photos are produced by individuals or firms having an idea, product, or service to promote. These photos are distributed to newspapers, news services, magazines, and other periodicals in hopes that the editors will include them in their editorial sections. Publicity or public relations photos often are taken with a newsy or informational approach. These photographs may be taken in an editorial style or against a plain background. Sometimes these photos are taken during the course of an event. For example, a designer may hire a photographer to take pictures during the showing of his or her collections. As another example, a hair salon may have photos taken showing the newest hairstyles being created along with step-by-step photos and explanations of how they are achieved. These photos will then be duplicated as mass-produced glossies and sent with information or a press release to magazines or other printed media that provide such information to readers.

If an editor spots something that is newsworthy, he or she will include the photos along with information about the sender in a column. Although the sender does not have to pay for such exposure, he or she has limited control over how the material will be presented or explained. However, in most cases, the exposure is positive. Positive editorial mention carries more weight with readers than advertisements, and such exposure effectively promotes the sender's business and image.

Modeling for Fashion Illustrations

A fashion illustrator's model poses for commercial artists who sketch fashion drawings for newspapers, magazines, catalogs, and ads. Hand-drawn illustrations are used by editors and advertisers for a variety of reasons. An eye-catching sketch often has greater impact than a photograph. Illustrations add variety when mixed with photos and other illustrations. Because only an artist and model are commissioned, fashion illustrations are cheaper to produce than photos. Also, simple illustrations can be drawn in a matter of hours and inserted in the next edition of a newspaper. A photo shooting requires many time-consuming and intermediary tasks.

Sometimes fashion illustrators do not use models but draw from memory or from magazine photos. However, when accuracy and realism are crucial, a model is employed. Models are used by illustrators in two different ways: (1) the model puts on the garment and assumes a position for as long as 2 hours (with breaks usually at quarter- or half-hour intervals) while the artist sketches or (2) the model puts on a garment, a few photographs are taken, and the artist then draws from these photographs.

PRINT MODELING SKILLS

The ability to move or pose for the camera is the most important skill for obtaining print modeling assignments. There is no step-by-step way to learn how to move or pose for the camera. There are no hard and fast rules or a battery of standard poses to be memorized. Great models have a natural instinct for the moves that look right to the camera, the timing involved in a photographer–model interchange, and for projecting different looks, attitudes, and emotions. Others evolve into good models by learning through trial and error what works and what doesn't.

A beginning model often thinks that when she is in front of the camera, the photographer will inspire her, teach her, encourage her, give her confidence, and guide her every step of the way. However, as a highly paid professional or would-be professional model, you will be expected to know what you are doing and to offer a lot of creativity. New models are surprised to learn that many photographers give no clues or instructions whatsoever. Other photographers give useless instructions such as "move," "do something," "act natural," "be yourself," or "just relax." Very few photographers have the patience or time to draw out a performance from their models by setting up a mood, perfecting the model's pose, or thinking of poses for the model to execute. In fact, some photographers have very little contact with the model. Sometimes a photographer's assistants set up the shooting and the photographer appears at the moment the model steps on the set, expecting to shoot several frames in a matter of minutes.

Other times several models will appear together on the set; in this instance, it is not feasible for the photographer to single out each model and encourage her into the desired movement and expression. A successful model commands a high fee because unlilke the average person he or she knows how to make it easy for the photographer to take a good picture. The model knows which movements and expressions are most photogenic and flattering to him- or herself and the item he or she is modeling. He or she can quickly and effectively become the desired character he or she is to portray and project the desired mood. A good model needs very little direction or coaching to achieve the result that the photographer wants. Time is money in the modeling business, and the models who succeed are those who achieve the desired results effectively, easily, and quickly.

A model has a great deal to do with the success of a photograph. Other than just presenting the design and details of an item, the model must really "sell" it. Of course, some items and situations allow for more creativity than others, so understanding the demands and limitations of each situation is important. However, even the plainest outfit, appearing in the most commonplace catalog, requires a model's contribution. Clients hire models because they make an impact or draw attention. Your good looks may qualify you to model but what will really set you apart from the competition is the contribution you make in movement and expression to the photograph and the items or garments you model.

Learning how to pose is best accomplished by actually doing it over and over. Taking dance lessons in ballet and jazz or exercise classes may get you more in touch with your body and will increase your flexibility and fluidity. Acting classes may help you to feel less inhibited and give you ideas for expressing different emotions. Practicing posing in front of a mirror may help. However, your best training will always be testing—that is, getting in front of the camera and trying new movements and expressions. Testing will also help you to understand how to work with different photographers, products, garments, and situations. After shooting, studying your contact sheets to see what works and what doesn't is the most effective form of instruction.

THE FUNDAMENTALS OF POSING

The most common mistake beginning models make when moving for the still camera is to treat posing as a series of exercises that are done for no particular reason. But a good model allows the situation, the item he or she is modeling, and several other factors to determine the poses he or she will do.

Posing isn't just putting on an outfit and going through the motions of a number of familiar modeling poses such as hand on hip, hand in hair, hand on collar, smile, or don't smile. Posing involves creating a look, adopting an attitude or character, conveying a message or concept. In addition, posing involves assuming different postures, positions, and movements to display an article in an effective, accurate, or artistic way.

Analyzing How to Model an Item

There is no one right or wrong way to wear, hold, stand next to, or represent a product. There is not one technique, pace, or style that will work for all situations. What might be considered a "don't" in one situation would be a "do" in another. Each product and situation will demand a different approach. To help you to understand how to model effectively, you must know how to analyze the item you are modeling and the situation. Modeling effectively requires thought, concentration, and creativity. Each time you put on a garment or are given an item to model, ideas should start coming to mind about how you might show it. Take some time and concentrate. You won't have time to be nervous if you are really thinking about how to show the garment or item to best advantage. Thinking before you step in front of the camera and while you are on the set will yield the most effective results. Use the following questions as starting points to consider how to model an item or garment effectively. Experienced models automatically take these criteria into consideration; however, as a beginner, these points will help you to analyze the situation and the item you are modeling in a thorough, methodical way.

What Are the Characteristics of the Item?

Study the item. Pay attention to its design, construction, and details. For example, if you are modeling an article of clothing, you must determine what its special features are and from what angles it looks best. If it has pockets, you will want to place your hands in them for some of the shots. If the garment is a dress with a row of buttons down the center, you would either position your body straight on for the camera or turn your body at a slight three-quarter angle. When positioning your body at this angle, you'll do so to show the camera the side containing the buttons, rather than the side that shows the gaps between the buttons. If you are modeling a bathing suit with an ornament on one side, you'll turn your body in profile to show that side detail, because this is what makes that garment special.

If you are modeling a product such as a bottle of dishwashing liquid, you will be conscious of holding it so that the label shows clearly.

What Is the Concept of the Shot?

Understanding what the client is trying to communicate about the product will be very important in determining your poses. The overall tone of the shot is usually decided on by the client or advertising agency. The photographer establishes lighting, setting, and other factors that will portray a certain mood. It is the model's job to reflect this tone or mood in his or her movements and facial expressions. The model must ascertain whether he or she is to present the product in a simple, straightforward manner or whether he or she is to act out a fantasy or scenario around the product. The photographer or client will usually explain to the model what type of character he or she is to portray. If he or she does not, and you are unsure, always ask. Another consideration a model may have is his or her contact with the camera and how he or she is to interact with other models or elements that may be present. Understanding what the client is trying to accomplish with the photograph will determine what moods and expressions you are to have.

Finding out what the photo will be used for will help to determine your movements and expressions. When an advertisement is being created, there will usually be a detailed concept for the shot. When a catalog photo is being created, sometimes there is a detailed concept, other times the model is expected to execute standard catalog poses and expressions. When an editorial photograph is being taken, if there is no specific concept, the model is expected to use his or her creativity to present the item. A good model is able to take on the character of the clothes or product and the mood of the situation, whatever it may be.

What Posing Style Is Appropriate?
Editorial Style

When posing for a photograph that will be used for editorial purposes, the model is usually most concerned with artistic presentation and creating an interesting and appealing image. In fashion editorials, the model must project an attitude or concept about what is new in fashion. The essence of a garment as opposed to its threads and construction is what is being communicated. The model has the most flexibility and freedom of expression in editorial work and his or her movements can range from being natural or ordinary to very unusual or dramatic. The model may enact a fantasy or create a scenario around the garment he or she is modeling. In editorial work there is no one set style of posing; how much freedom the model has depends on the guidelines of style and the philosophy of the magazine employing him or her and also on the style of the photographer with whom he or she is working.

Catalog Style

In standard catalog work the model is usually concerned with clearly showing the lines, fabric, fit, and details of an item so that a catalog shopper will be persuaded to order the item from the photograph. Garments are presented to look ideal, that is, wrinkle-free and neat. The model's movements are usually simple and natural and somewhat confined to the body. His or her expressions usually portray happiness, contentment, and confidence. (Consult Figures 9 to 15 on basic physical presentation in Chapter 2 for movements that are used as common catalog poses.)

A model must be aware that all catalog shootings do not follow the standard catalog approach. Some catalogs are photographed in an editorial style. When modeling for a such a catalog, the model uses the editorial style of posing previously described.

Advertising Style

Advertisements are usually created by an advertising agency staff who formulates a concept and draws up a layout. A layout is a sketch of the proposed ad drawn up by the art director showing the model's position, the composition of the shot, and all the various elements that will be present in the proposed ad (Figure 1). In some cases the model strictly follows the layout; in other cases, the layout is used as a springboard for ideas acquired in the course of the shooting.

Figure 1.
An example of a layout.

The type of product and the objectives of the advertiser will determine what approach is used for an ad. For example, a straightforward hard-sell ad might depict a model holding or using the product. On the other hand, a concept ad may look like an editorial page from a magazine.

What Photo Movement Technique Does the Situation Demand?

Even though the style of posing may vary from one situation to the next, there are common techniques that are employed in all photo sessions. Moving for the still camera is usually done in one of four ways. The method used will depend on the concept of the shot, the situation, the photographer's preferences, or other factors. A model should understand and be proficient in each method.

Move–Pause–Shoot

Move–pause–shoot is the most commonly used method of posing; the model moves and pauses momentarily to allow the photographer to capture the pose. The click of the shutter is the model's cue to change his or her movement and pause. Some photographers or situations demand that you change your movement completely each time you pause (this often yields a more spontaneous, unexpected type of feeling), whereas others demand that you repeat the same basic movement but present minor variations for each click of the shutter (this provides greater control over the image). This move–pause–shoot technique works equally well for the model and photographer; however, it is important that the model get in rhythm with the photographer. Note how long he or she takes between shots to wait for the strobe to recover and to compose the picture or focus the lens; synchronize with the tempo he or she sets. The photographer usually has more constraints than you do, so forcing him or her to shoot faster or slower than he or she desires will probably not yield a satisfactory result for either of you.

Continuous Movement in Place

Continuous moving in place is usually done when action or spontaneity is desired but when space is limited, for example, in a small studio or when sharp focus is critical. The model stays in the same spot but shows action by shifting his or her weight. Walking in place is an example of a continuous movement in place that is commonly used in modeling. Here is how to do it: Start with one foot ahead of the other as if you were walking. When shooting starts you will shift your weight from your right to your left foot, rocking back and forth, swaying your hips and shoulders slightly, and moving your arms in the opposite direction to that of your legs. You will be staying in the same spot. Your feet need not even leave the ground, except for a heel-to-toe motion. Beginning models often feel ridiculous when "pretend walking," but it is a movement that is often used and looks natural in still photos. Remember to get your entire body into the action as if you were really walking. Do it fairly rapidly and add variations by changing the direction in which your feet are aimed. Create the look of action by twisting just the upper part of your body, changing the length of your step, changing your arms and hands, and tilting and turning your head. Change your facial expressions too. Just keep moving unless the photographer tells you to stop. Think of what you do when walking down the street. Your eyes move from side to side, you turn your head, you look at your watch, and on and on.

Practice other types of actions while moving in place. Enact different activities in keeping with the outfit you are modeling. For example, try sport movements, such as playing tennis or doing exercises, dancing, or pivoting. When practicing this photo movement technique, don't pause to pose and don't stray off the designated spot.

Continuous Traveling Movement

Continuous traveling movement is a candid type of shooting style that is done when there is ample room, such as at an out-of-doors location, and lots of spontaneity is desired. Usually the photographer will use a motor drive on his or her camera to allow him or her to capture various stages of movement. The model moves continuously, without pausing or posing, but instead of standing on a designated spot, the model moves through the spot while the photographer captures his or her movement. Usually the photographer will "prefocus" to ensure sharp focus. When doing this, he or she will ask you to stand on a spot that he or she designates. He or she will focus and then you will take a few steps backward and begin walking, running, or otherwise moving up to the spot. Don't stop on the spot, keep moving on through. Always try to make sure you are landing on the designated spot, and don't stop until instructed by the photographer. After you have passed through the spot, quickly go back to your starting point and repeat the action. Concentrate on not destroying the lines or appearance of your garment by pulling it out of shape or covering it with your movement. You must also be aware of your facial expressions. Sometimes when engaged in a strenuous action, there is a tendency to forget what your face is doing. It is important to fit your action, gestures, and facial expressions to the activity you are trying to depict. For example, if you are executing graceful, dancelike movements, a facial expression that looks soft and romantic would be in order.

The continuous movement posing technique is used to depict slice-of-life situations and overt action, such as sports and dancing. Often the photographer will prefer that your attention be focused on what you are doing rather than on your contact with him or her for a realistic caught-in-the-action effect.

No Movement or the Static Pose

When the static posing technique is used, the model is positioned in one way and the pose is held for an extended period of time, allowing the photographer to shoot one or more photos. After establishing the pose, the photographer may direct the model to make very slight alterations, such as tilting his or her head or changing his or her facial expressions, but the basic pose remains the same.

Static posing is sometimes used when a layout must be strictly followed, or when technical factors, such as the use of a large format camera or slow shutter speed, are involved. Hand and product models encounter this often. Because in these instances there is little leeway for error, this technique allows for greatest control and precision. Some spontaneity may be lost, but a good model is able to inject life and freshness into a pose that she or he has had to hold for several minutes.

Staying in position and holding still is important. If your face is included in the shot, decide where your eyes will be directed and keep them focused on that spot. Allow the photographer extra time to focus and compose, and shift your eyes or talk to her only after the shot has been taken. Ask before you move. She may want to take more than one shot, and sometimes getting everything just right may take awhile. If she takes a lot of time between shots, ask her to indicate when she is going to shoot so that you won't blink or move. Usually fewer shots are taken when this method is employed, so concentrating on the details and keeping conversation to a minimum are important. If you become too tired to continue so that your muscles tremble or ache, ask for a break.

What Photographic Facts Will Influence the Way I Pose?

Although it is certainly possible to take a good picture knowing nothing about photography, having a basic understanding of lighting and photographic techniques and equipment will make you a better model. Studying the factors that will affect your appearance in the photograph will be advantageous.

A Primer on Lighting for Models

A good model knows how to work with lighting to make it enhance his appearance. Understanding different lighting sources and the way in which lighting is used is helpful. Of course, following the photographer's instructions is always essential. If a photographer asks you to do something that conflicts with the information here, you must do what he says. Only he can see the effects he is trying to create.

Photographers use light in a variety of ways. There are basically two types of light sources: artificial and natural. Strobe light (electronic flash) is an example of artificial light. It is used by most photographers for studio shootings. It can also be used outdoors. Strobe can be anything from a hand-held flash to a complex bank of lights. The flash of the strobe is activated by the camera shutter. Strobe is cool, lights a large area, offers mobility to the model and the photographer, and allows for fast shooting. Strobe power units vary in strength, so sometimes it is necessary for the model to wait a few seconds between shots for the flash to recharge.

Tungsten light is another type of artificial light. Unlike strobe, which produces flashes, tungsten produces a continous source of light. It is used occasionally for studio stills and videotaping. Tungsten requires patience on the model's part, because the lights are warm. In addition, tungsten lights give off less light than strobes necessitating slow shutter speeds. Therefore, the model must hold very still to prevent blurring.

Natural light is light that comes from the sun and is found outdoors or in studios with windows, skylights, or doorways. It can be affected by weather, time of day, season, and location. For example, in the summer around sunset the light is soft and warm (having golden tones), in the winter it is hard and cool (having bluish tones).

Photographers use both natural and artifical light in a variety of ways (Figure 2). In using artificial light in studio, they have a high degree of technical control; lighting can be varied by changing the direction and height from which it comes and its quality or intensity. In using natural light outdoors photographers place the subject at different angles to the light. They manipulate the light and can achieve a great deal of control by using reflector cards, portable strobes, light diffusion materials, and other methods to alter the shadows and highlights produced by the sun.

The quality of the light often has a lot to do with how flattering a photo will be. Soft, diffused light is very flattering. This can be produced in various ways such as with a large box of light or umbrellas or diffusion materials (screens, grids, frosted paper, etc.) placed over the lights. Lighting contrast also plays a part. The brightness of the light is also a factor. A model must be conscious of squinting when working with very bright light in a studio or outdoors. If you have a problem keeping your eyes relaxed and open, ask the photographer to wait between shots, then close your eyes for a second, relax your facial muscles then slowly open your eyes. Don't anticipate the brightness. If you can't tell if you're squinting, feel with your hand. Be careful not to overcompensate by opening your eyes too wide. This will cause an unnatural, staring expression. Experienced models are able to keep their eyes open without squinting in even the brightest light. This is a skill that all models must acquire.

Figure 2. Lighting. These photographs show how lighting may be used to create different moods and to change a model's appearance. In addition, a model can use this information to understand how to work with different lighting styles to enhance her appearance. In a photo session, a model should use the information provided here only when the photographer has not directed him or her to do otherwise. This information can also be applied to other areas of modeling and everyday situations. For example, lighting in offices and in convention centers usually comes from ceiling lights. The lighting on the runway of a fashion show may come from a spotlight placed above the runway. To achieve the most flattering effect in both situations, you would raise your chin slightly and follow the instructions given in part a.

Figure 2a. Light From Above
Light that is cast downward from a source above the model is often employed in classic high fashion photography. It is found outdoors before or after noon when the sun is above the horizon but not overhead. The closer it is to noon the higher in the sky the light is. In studio this lighting is present when the main source of light is placed at an angle higher than the model's face, casting shadows downward. Tilting the chin upward toward the light will usually yield the most flattering result.

Figure 2b. Light From Below
Lighting that is cast upward from a source below the model's face is very flattering when it is diffused and not placed at too low of an angle. If too harsh, it can yield a goulish look. When used in fashion and beauty photography, it yields a sexy, uplifting, warm look similar to very soft candlelight at a dinner table. Tilting the chin downward slightly will usually be most flattering.

Figure 2c. Light From One Side
Lighting that comes from one side of the model gives a dramatic look. It is used for men and to play up textured or difficult-to-photograph garments such as a solid black dress. Facing straight ahead, or working into the light (facing in the direction of the light) is usually most flattering.

Figure 2d. Flat Lighting

Flat lighting is often used in fashion photography. It shows no shadows and smooths and evens out contours. There may be no shadows or small even, local shadows. Flat lighting occurs outdoors when the sun is on the horizon or indoors when a flash is positioned on the camera. It may also be produced by using two or more umbrella lights or reflector boards placed in front of the model. When flat lighting is used, nearly any facial angle can be assumed with flattering results. Photographers often use flat lighting for beauty shots. A little extra contour makeup may be needed to define shapes.

Figure 2e. Light From Behind

Lighting that comes from behind the model is used to highlight the model's hair and separate the model from the background. It is usually used in conjunction with another source of light in front of the model. Outdoors it is created when the sun is behind the model. In studio a light is placed behind the model. Light from behind creates a flattering result however extra care must be taken in arranging the hair so that light does not shine through it making it appear thin.

Figure 2f. Overhead Light

Overhead lighting is usually used in conjunction with another source of light and it is used to highlight the hair. This lighting is present outdoors at noon when the sun is directly overhead. In studio, a light is placed directly over the model's head. If the hair is very light or arranged in a wispy way on top of the head, hair may wash out and not look ideal.

Figure 2g. Three-quarter Light

Three-quarter lighting illuminates three-fourths of the model's face. The source of light may be at a 45-degree angle to the model or it may be placed just to one side of the camera. The height of the light may vary from being at camera height, above, or below. Three-quarter lighting is commonly used in traditional portrait and catalog photography because it reveals textures and shapes well. Turning the face toward the direction of the light always works well. Straight-on facial movements are flattering to full or round faces.

There are basically two types of lighting setups used by photographers: single source and multiple source. Single-source lighting means that all or the majority of the light comes from one source. A single umbrella, a large square of light, or a plain light may be the only source. When this type of setup occurs, the model will usually obtain the most flattering result if she or he works into the light or aims his face in the direction of the greatest amount of light. The photographer will often tell you which is the key or main light. If you are in doubt about where the main source of light is, ask the photographer.

Multiple-source lighting means that there is no single source of light—this light comes from several sources. For example, there may be several lights or reflector cards distributing light in several directions. If this is the case, the model can aim his face in several directions and still achieve a flattering result.

More Photo Facts for Models

In addition to lighting, there are other factors that may influence the way a model poses in a given situation. Use the following information as a guide to enable you to work effectively in all situations.

Composition. Understanding the composition of a photograph is very important for a model. The model will want to know how much of her body will be included in the photograph. For example, if the photograph is a three-quarter length shot, the model need not worry about the position of her feet. She may choose to elevate one foot slightly off the floor to alter the line of her legs or hips to attractively display her garment. If the photograph is to be a closeup shot, the model's makeup must be carefully applied and blended. She must also make sure that she has no obvious facial hair or stray hairs around her face or obstructing her eyes because every detail will show.

The model will also want to consider the shape of the photograph. Sometimes a photograph will be taken that will appear in a very narrow space on a catalog page. In such a case, a model must pose so that her arms will not be cut out of the photograph. For example, instead of placing her arms or elbows outward, she will have to do poses in which her arms are kept down at her sides or close to her body.

Knowing what camera angle the photographer will be using will also be helpful. For example, if the photographer is shooting from a very low angle, the model will be careful to avoid lifting her chin so much that her eyes and the top of her head disappear. Visualizing what the photographer is seeing through the lens is an important key to successful modeling.

Long lenses. Long lenses necessitate that the photographer be 20 feet or farther away from the model, which makes it difficult for the model to see what the photographer is doing or to hear his or her instructions. Sometimes the photographer will use walkie-talkies to communicate with the model. Since you won't be able to hear the shutter click, indicating a pose change, keep moving from one pose to the next. Don't wait for the photographer's approval after each pose.

Short lenses. Short or wide-angle lenses are used when a distinct background or a large subject needs to be recorded. They are rarely used for closeups because they tend to distort the face, making the nose appear larger. If a photographer is shooting full length yet is very close to you, he or she is using a short lens. The shot will be more flattering to your face if you confine your angles to profiles and three-quarter angles. Also avoid extending anything closer to the camera than the rest of you (for example, a hand, an elbow, or a prop), as a short lens will enlarge it out of proportion.

Motor drives. A photographer uses a motor drive (a mechanism on the camera that quickly and automatically advances the film) when doing action shots or when spontaneous, natural-looking shots are desired. With a motor drive the photographer can shoot several frames instantaneously. Obviously you shouldn't try to strike a separate pose for each shot, but you should have continuous movement. Make sure, in the midst of all this movement, that you don't stray out of focus. A few inches may make a difference.

Use of fan or wind. If you are in studio, set the fan on low and aim it from below to get the most attractive result for hair. Brush hair periodically while wind is blowing to increase volume and softness. Look down or close your eyes periodically between shots so that your eyes don't become watery.

Color film. Color films require that the model pay strict attention to color harmony when combining garments and when using makeup. For more information, consult Chapters 3 and 5.

Black and white film. In black and white shots the graphic shapes your body forms are more important than in color. Think a little more in terms of silhouette. If you are modeling a dark or black outfit, it will absorb light, hiding the details. Be aware of how you can emphasize the characteristics of the garment. Turn at an angle toward the light. Make sure your arms are held slightly away from your body so the silhouette or shape of your outfit is easier to see. If you are on set with other models, the darkest outfit should always be closest to the light. If you are modeling a white outfit, you should be farthest away from the light. White is difficult to photograph because it reflects light, making it difficult to see the details. Angle your body away from the light and check that your arms are slightly away from your body so that the shape is easier to see. Refer to Chapter 3 to learn how to effectively apply your makeup for black and white photography. When coordinating clothing and other items, think in terms of contrasts. Consult Chapter 5 for more information.

Bracketing. Sometimes, especially when shooting color slide film, the photographer will "bracket" the shots to make sure he or she gets the correct film exposure. He or she will shoot with three different lens settings or f-stops. The model should do each pose three times to make sure that the photographer gets the pose and the exposure he or she needs.

Seamless or sweep. The seamless backdrop paper or sweep is a mainstay in lots of studios. It is a large roll of paper that comes in various sizes and colors. Always make sure that the soles of your shoes are clean before stepping onto the set. Use a cloth to wipe off bottoms of shoes or if shoes are new or from the client, wear them only in front of the camera. Taping the soles with masking tape can also be done to protect them and the backdrop. Always be careful not to soil, scratch, scuff, or tear the sweep.

Painted backdrops. Some backdrops display a custom-painted design on canvas and can cost hundreds or thousands of dollars. Be extra careful and follow the preceding advice. Also take clues on how to pose from the backdrop. For example, if you are posing on a backdrop that depicts a castle, your movements would probably be elegant and sophisticated.

Infinity wall. Instead of seamless paper or a canvas backdrop, some studios have an infinity wall, which has the same effect but is built into the studio. The infinity wall is painted with the color desired for the background. Follow the advice given under "Seamless or Sweep."

Background projection. With the appropriate equipment, the photographer can project a slide of a scene behind the model for a background effect. This is called "rear screen projection." In most instances, the scene will not be visible to the model; however, the photographer will tell him which scene is being used. If the scene is a beach, you should display motions and expressions in keeping with the scene on the backdrop.

Reference marks. A reference mark or set mark indicates where the model is to stand on the set. This ensures that the model is positioned on the set where the lighting will hit her most attractively. It also ensures sharp focus and ideal composition. The photographer or assistant will indicate with tape or chalk where you are to stand, or he or she may instruct you to stand under a certain light or in line with a certain point. It is important for the model to constantly check that she is on her mark and in line with the camera lens.

Are There Special Instructions?

Photographs are produced by a team of skilled people. Cooperation with them is an important key to any successful photo session.

The Model–Photographer Relationship

Although photographs are conceived and produced by a team of experts, the photographer has the most influence over the outcome of the shot. It is he or she who ultimately creates the image.

For a single shooting, a photographer often spends hours in preparation. The photographer holds a preproduction meeting in which he or she and the client or art director discuss the concept of the ad or catalog. At this time, planning and scheduling of the shooting is outlined. The photographer must be able to understand what the client wants the finished picture to look like and to use his or her creativity and technical knowledge to accomplish results.

The photographer selects and recommends the models, stylists, makeup artists, hairstylists, set designers, and other people who can best accomplish the client's purpose. The photographer may scout for locations, backdrops, and props that are to be used. During the shooting, it is the photographer who orchestrates the total operation (directing models, stylists, and studio assistants) so that all the elements combine to produce the desired result. After the shooting the job is still not finished. At this time the film is turned over to a lab where it is processed according to the photographer's specificiations. When the slides and contact sheets are returned, the photographer edits them and chooses the best ones to go to the client.

Photographers differ from one another just as models do. You may find that one photographer shoots very slowly, making sure that everything is perfect each time he or she clicks the shutter. Another photographer may work very quickly and spontaneously. Some photographers are talkative and will provide you with detailed instructions. Others will give no directions and will expect you to know what you are supposed to do. The more professional a model is, the less important his or her rapport with the photographer becomes. The "pro" can assess the demands of the job at hand and accomplish the photographer's and the client's goals without a lot of instruction or encouragement. The following suggestions will help you when working with photographers.

- Learn how to quickly pick up on the photographer's directions. Each photographer has her own style and terminology for directing models. Some photographers may instruct you to move "camera left" or "camera right." This means the photographer's left or right as she is facing you. Most photographers will tell you to move to "your left" or "your right." "Move up" or "come forward" usually indicates to move toward the photographer. "Move back" means move away from her toward the background. "Hold still," "don't move," or "that's good" means that your head, feet, hands, body, expression, and eyes are to remain exactly as is until the photographer has clicked the shutter.

- Follow directions closely, even if you don't agree. Make sure you allow the photographer to run the shooting. He is in charge and makes the final decisions about how things are done, not you. If anything goes wrong, the photographer is held accountable. Be open and cooperate with all orders he may make regarding makeup, hair, and posing.

- Don't take personally any comment a photographer may make. She sees things according to the demands of the situation.

- Offer a lot of variety in movements, angles, and expressions in each roll of film. Each time the photographer clicks the shutter is your cue to change. But pay attention to the rhythm he establishes. If he wants you to move or hold a pose for a few seconds each time rather than moving continuously, be alert to this. Follow the rhythm he establishes. Don't fuss and delay for too long trying to strike a perfect pose, instead work yourself into it as he shoots. Don't intentionally strike poses that you know will be unusable. However, don't let an awkward movement you may have done throw you off. Go on to the next pose and try to improve.

- Concentrate 100% on the image the photographer is trying to produce. Posing so that you are following the instructions you have been given and creating the desired effect or attitude takes concentration. Don't allow your thoughts to wander. Never make it necessary for a photographer to repeat the same instruction.

- Pick up on the mood and working style the photographer sets. If he is quiet, keep conversation to a minimum. If he is energetic and works quickly, you should follow his lead.

- Don't refuse to do a movement he may instruct you to do because you think it is a bad angle for your face or because you have never seen or tried it before, it feels uncomfortable, or it is difficult to do. Don't be overly sensitive to discomfort or inconvenience. Many times movements that feel awkward or uncomfortable don't appear that way for the camera. Don't be childish when having to deal with less than ideal circumstances, such as very hot or cold weather. Be a good sport and be strong. Overcome minor disturbances by increasing your concentration. Realize that what you may be unwilling to do can easily be done by another more determined and more professional model. You should refuse only if something seriously jeopardizes your well-being.

- Don't tell a photographer how he should set up his lights or what angles to shoot from or anything about how he should do his job. However, you should let him know if his equipment is malfunctioning, for example, if the strobe is not flashing.

- Don't criticize the photographer's equipment, studio, or so on, even if he does.

- Concentrate on making the job easier for the photographer. Try to stay in one plane for a number of poses before you change so he doesn't have to refocus on every shot. If he has marked an X on the floor or has told you to land or stand on a designated spot, be careful that you don't stray from that spot. Staying on the mark helps maintain proper focus, framing, and lighting. If there is no designated spot, stay in line with the camera lens.

- Above everything else, concentrate on your contact with the photographer. Try to shut out the commotion or conversations around you. Get used to being watched by other people when you work because there will usually be assistants, other models, clients, and spectators lingering around the set.

- It is important to realize that the model's attitude can set the tone for the shooting. Being interested and involved and keeping your energy up during the shooting sets a good example for the other members of the team producing the photograph. A model who yawns continuously or who looks bored or anxious doesn't create an atmosphere conducive to obtaining great results.

- Always look for the positive aspects in a photographer and his work. You may not care for a photographer's work or personality, but while you are working together, make your best effort to give him the shots needed.

- Don't be afraid to ask questions. Ask the photographer what type of look he is after. While you are in front of the camera, express yourself, but constantly be aware of his reactions. Verbal instructions are not the only way that communication takes place. Be sensitive to nonverbal clues. For example, if you make a move and he doesn't take the picture (providing he is not focusing the lens or changing film or attending to something else), he probably doesn't like what you are doing and wants you to change. Don't wait for him to say so. If he likes what you are doing, he will tell you to wait. Never stand there expecting him to think of a movement for you to do. Keep moving from one pose to another until he sees something he likes. Don't stop unless you are told to do so.

- Always try to anticipate what the photographer wants. Don't wait until he has to tell you. A good model needs very little or no instruction. Try to do things with a minimum of explanation on his part.

- Be considerate of what the photographer needs for his concentration. Keep conversation to a minimum and be considerate of his wishes.

- Don't get stuck in a routine. Take a fresh, new approach to every booking, realizing that each is unique. Relax and enjoy your work. Always be open to suggestions. Your main objective will always be to help the photographer achieve the image he is after.

Other People Involved in Photo Shootings

It is helpful to understand the functions of the individuals involved in a photo shooting. Some shootings are very simple and involve only a model and photographer. Other shootings are more complex and require the services of several highly skilled specialists. The following is a list of people you may encounter at photo sessions.

Photographer's assistant. The photographer's assistant sets up the lights, moves equipment, loads film in the camera, and, in general, saves the photographer time and effort that he or she needs to apply elsewhere. There may be one or several assistants who are either full-time employees of the studio or hired on an independent free-lance basis. In some studios, the assistant may do everything involved in setting up the shot including focusing the camera. At the last minute the photographer will step in and click the shutter. Most assistants are young men who are trying to gain experience so that they eventually can go out on their own as photographers. Even though the pay is low, there is a lot of competition to become an assistant to a good photographer.

Production assistant/secretary/studio manager. Most photographers have at least one full- or part-time employee who acts as a production assistant/secretary/manager. She or he answers the phone, manages the photographer's time, and may do a variety of other tasks that could include scouting for locations, negotiating bookings for the photographer, booking models, ordering lunch, and organizing the shooting. In smaller studios he or she may even double as a stylist, hairdresser, and/or makeup artist. Learn her or his name and be as courteous to this individual as you are to the photographer.

Makeup artist. Makeup artists are usually independently employed. They may be hired for a few hours to apply the model's makeup at the start of the shooting, then the model is expected to maintain it throughout the day. Usually the makeup artist is hired for the entire length of the shooting to make sure makeup looks good throughout the day or to make changes along the way. When a makeup artist is present, he or she takes responsibility for the way the makeup looks. See Chapter 3 for information on how to work effectively with a makeup artist.

Hairstylist. Hairstylists are usually hired on a free-lance basis. Both makeup and hair stylists may be on the staff of a prominent salon or may be free-lancers who specialize in doing hair or makeup for photo shootings. When a hairstylist is present, he or she is responsible for the way the model's hair looks. See Chapter 4 for information on how to work effectively with a hairstylist on an assignment.

Stylist. Stylists are usually hired independently or through agencies representing stylists. The person doing the styling may also be an editor from the magazine for which you are working. The stylist may do anything from obtaining clothing, accessories, and props to accompany the item being photographed, to ironing and pinning to make sure the garments look right in the photo. The stylist helps develop the image for the shot and coordinates all the elements of the production. A lot of thought must go into the articles he or she selects for the shooting, and he or she must have good contacts with retailers, designers, and other individuals who can supply him or her with these items. See Chapter 5 for information on how to work effectively with a stylist.

Client. The client is the person representing the entity that pays for the shooting. He or she may be an employee of the company that has manufactured the items being shot. The client may also be a magazine editor or an employee from the advertising agency that has been enlisted to create the promotional campaign. The client has the final say about everything at the shooting. You may have met him or her on the audition, or he/she may have selected you based on your composite.

Art director. The art director is usually an employee of the advertising agency or may be hired independently. He or she has conceptualized the look of the campaign or project and has control of the design and layout. The art director works closely with the photographer to obtain the desired result for the finished piece. At the shooting he or she is the one with the layout who may supervise how and where the models will be positioned and how the set will look.

Others. Among the other people who may be present at a photo session are: the set designer who has designed and constructed the set on which the pictures will be shot; the go-fers who run out for coffee, lunch, and make trips back and forth to the lab for processed film during the shoot; spectators who can include the people from the advertising agency who drop in to see how things are going or individuals from the company who want to see models and a photo session up close. There may also be a driver or chaffeur present when the photographer has hired a fully equipped van complete with makeup mirrors, ironing boards, clothing racks, toilets, and power generators for location work.

HOW TO BE MORE PHOTOGENIC

Now that you understand the fundamentals of posing and how to approach each item and situation you may be given, it will be helpful to study some of the following information to refine your performance. The following tips are just suggestions—they are not intended as hard and fast rules. Remember that a good model makes posing look effortless. A spontaneous, natural style is always preferred over an affected, overly camera-conscious approach.

To understand how you can polish your print modeling skills and become more photogenic, tips will be given for the five variables in the way a model moves:

1. Head movements.
2. Facial movements.
3. Body movements.
4. Movements of the legs and feet.
5. Movements of the arms and hands.

Head Movements

There are basically four ways in which a model can vary the position of her head: straight on, side to side movements, up and down movements, and diagonal movements. (See Figure 3.)

The best way to arrive at attractive head and facial angles is to study your contact sheets to determine which ones are most flattering to your face. In general, subtle movements are more effective that exaggerated movements. For example, tilting the head too far to the left or right gives the model an unbalanced, uncomfortable look. Raising or lowering the chin too much may also give an unnatural or strained appearance. Turning the head in an extreme three-quarter angle will make the cheek that is away from the camera appear flat. A general rule of thumb is: A movement is usually too exaggerated if the eyes have to strain in order to be comfortably focused on the lens of the camera. (This does not apply to profile angles.) When executing profile angles, it is usually most photogenic when your chin and shoulder are in line so that only one side of the face is seen. Practicing these concepts is best done by testing.

Facial Movements
The Eyes

The eyes are usually the most important aspect of a facial expression. They must show expression in order to give the photograph impact. The eyes are usually the focal point of a headshot, so communicating with them is important.

There are lots of ways to vary the eyes. Changing the direction in which your eyes are focused is the most obvious way of altering the look of the eyes. To arrive at different ideas, imagine that you are standing in the center of the face of a clock, aim your nose at 12:00, then move just your eyes so that they aim at 1:00 or 2:00, 11:00, or 10:00. To add another expressive variation, subtly raise or lower the focus of your eyes while looking to the side.

369

Slight movements of the eyes are usually more attractive than exaggerated movements. For example, facing straight ahead but aiming the eyes to the extreme right or left usually yields an undesirable strained or bulging look. When looking down, it may be necessary to cheat a little, that is, to aim your gaze a little higher so your eyes won't appear to be closed. When your face is in profile to the camera, shift your eyes slightly back toward the camera, so that the irises, not just the whites of your eyes can be seen.

When executing any eye movements, it is important to really focus on something as if it has captured your interest rather than staring absentmindedly. Stabilize your gaze; don't let your eyes drift around looking vague and unsure.

Figure 3. Head movements. (a) A straight on view with the chin level reveals the full face. (b) Turning the head to the left or right while keeping the chin level shows different facial angles. Turning the head so that one-half of the face (left or right) is shown results in a profile angle. (c) Turning the head so that three-fourths of the face (right or left) is visible to the camera results in a three-quarter angle. (d) Up and down movements of the face can express different attitudes. Raising the chin is shown here. (e) This shows lowering the chin. (f) Diagonal movements of the face involve tilting the head to the left or right. (g) All of these basic movements can be combined to create lots of variations and different looks. Shown here the head is tilted, turned, and raised.

Another way you can vary your eyes is by opening them wider (giving a wide-eyed, innocent look) or squinting them slightly, yielding a more aggressive, sophisticated look. Wink with one eye, and you have another look. Vary your eye contact, but when looking into the lens, confront it directly. Look right into the lens or through it, not just at it. Imagine that you see something of interest in the lens. Don't be shy or self-conscious or your expressions will look untrue. Don't look at the photographer's head or hands, look into the center of the lens.

The Eyebrows   Eyebrows are important expression makers. Lift them and you will have a surprised look. Lower them and you have a serious look. Lower them more and you have an angry look. Try raising just one eyebrow for a lilting or sexy look. Try arching your brows more for a sexy, devilish, or angry look. Unless you are creating a specific effect, you'll want to avoid tense or worried-looking brows.

The Nose   You can change the appearance of your nose by changing your facial angles. To make your nose appear shorter or more upturned, tilt your chin up. Likewise, to make it appear longer, tilt your chin down. A wide nose looks narrower when the face is turned at a three-quarter angle. A crooked nose will seem less so when the face is tilted to one side. Contouring or highlighting the nose using makeup can make a less than perfect nose look ideal for the camera.

The Cheeks   The appearance of the cheeks and cheekbones can also be altered by assuming different facial angles. If your cheekbones are very flat or unpronounced, straight on or tilted head movements will usually be most flattering. If your face is very wide or your cheeks are full, three-quarter angles will give your face more contours. If your cheeks are ideal you can create different looks by puffing them out, or sucking them in slightly for a hollowed-cheek effect. Male models sometimes bite down to give the jaws a strong, masculine look.

The Mouth   Your mouth provides many posing options. To see some of the possible variations, watch yourself in a mirror or photograph yourself pronouncing every letter in the alphabet. To arrive at different mouth expressions you can mouth words for the camera. Pick a word like "personality," and sound each vowel, consonant, and syllable slowly and expressively.

Another way you can study different mouth expressions is to practice different ways of smiling. Think of all the different ways you can smile. You can go from big, laughing, open-mouth smiles to closed-lip smiles in which just the corners of the mouth turn up. Think of all the different emotions that smiles can express such as sarcasm, sexiness, reluctance, shyness, glee, warmth, and on and on.

When executing smiles, always make sure your expressions are genuine. You'll want to avoid a frozen, artificial-looking grin. To achieve a natural-looking smile for the camera, think of something that you like or that makes you laugh. Or try smiling for an instant, then stop smiling, then smile again. Your second smile will usually look most natural. Remember to smile with your eyes. The expression in your eyes should complement the expression of your mouth. Try to keep your eyes open and as large as possible. Take care that the muscles in your face don't move up so much that it causes your eyes to squint and wrinkles (crows feet) to form. Perfect your smiling expressions by practicing in front of a mirror. This will also help you to avoid lopsided smiles as well as smiles that show too much of your gums, or a disappearing upper lip. Remember that in some situations such imperfections may be desirable to lend a natural or unique look to a photograph.

For more ideas on mouth expressions, draw inspiration from actions you do in life, such as blowing a kiss, eating, drinking, pouting, whistling, singing, licking or touching your lips, smoking, applying lipstick, biting your lip, parting your lips slightly, pursing your lips, shouting, exclaiming, crying, frowning, and making a face.

Neck

A long neck is most photogenic so concentrate on elongating your neck when being photographed. Reaching upward with the crown of your head while keeping your chin level will make your neck appear long and straight. You will want to avoid the look of a collapsed neck, which occurs when the head falls slightly back and the chin comes up causing the Adam's apple to protrude. Another common problem to be aware of is holding the head too far back. Many times out of shyness, a novice model will lean her head back away from the camera creating the look of a full throat or double chin. To eliminate such a look and to create an attractive jawline, try projecting your face toward the camera keeping your chin level. This may feel unnatural, but from the camera's perspective it looks attractive.

Body Movements

There are five basic body movements that models use: standing, sitting, kneeling or squatting, and lying. Each movement can be varied using the four basic angles: straight on (entire front of body aimed at camera), profile (one side of body visible to camera), three-quarter (three-fourths of the body aimed at camera), and back (back of body visible to camera).

Standing Positions

Standing is the most common way that models are photographed. Standing indicates that your weight is balanced on one or both feet. The basic standing positions are shown in Chapter 2. They are: symmetrical (hips and shoulders level), assymetrical (one shoulder or hip raised or lowered), inward curve (arched), outward curve (spine is curved outward), and twisted (hips and shoulders turn in opposition). If you want to look slimmer, stand at a three-quarter angle to the camera or try twisting your body. To make your hips look narrower, angle just your hips at a profile or three-quarter angle to the camera. To make your waist look smaller, use an assymetrical posture to make your torso form an S shape. This will exaggerate the indentation of the waist.

Sitting Poses

Sitting is a posing option often used in modeling. Some garments are best displayed when the model stands; others look better when the model sits. The way you sit for the camera will depend on your garment, the object on which you are sitting, the mood you are trying to create, and instructions from the photographer. When sitting, lift the torso out of the hips and elongate the body upward. A straight (not stiff) back usually looks better than a rounded one. You may often find that the most comfortable, natural position doesn't look flattering to the camera. Likewise leaning against the back of a chair can appear ungraceful; if you do lean, do so lightly. Usually legs look better when a longer line is created, so placing the feet farther out than the knees and softening the bend of the ankles looks more attractive. Aiming bent knees or open crotch straight at the camera doesn't work for most photographic situations.

Be creative. There are several different ways to sit whether on the floor, a chair, or stool or anything else. Try sitting in profile or at a three-quarter angle to the camera. Alter positions by sitting on the side of one hip; leaning forward, backward, or to one side; or by changing the position of the legs, arms, and upper torso.

Kneeling or Squatting Positions

A model may kneel or squat to add an interesting movement to the photograph or to create an attractive line for the garment he or she is modeling. When squatting or kneeling, a model is careful to elongate her torso to give the illusion of length. Also most squatting or kneeling positions look best when executed at a profile or three-quarter angle to the camera, rather than straight on. Paying attention to the position of the feet and the placement of the hands is important.

Reclining

A model may lie on the floor, the ground, or a piece of furniture to model an item. The model may rest on one side of her body or she may support herself on one elbow or hand. When reclining a model carefully arranges her garment in an attractive manner and makes certain that the position of her legs, feet, hands, and head are attractive. Often an uncomfortable position is the most photogenic.

Hand and Arm Positions

Regardless of the item you are modeling, understanding attractive hand positions is important. The way in which you hold your hands can indicate your level of experience as a model. Awkward positions can detract from what you are modeling and make an otherwise suitable shot unusable. Always be conscious of the way your hands appear. Think about ways you can make them appear more attractive every time you make a movement. Whether you are in an interview, in front of a still or video camera, demonstrating a product at a trade show, or modeling on a runway, be aware of the appearance of your hands.

Study the way models hold their hands in fashion photographs. Studying ballet to arrive at graceful-looking hands is also helpful. Think of creative ways to use your hands. Perfect your hand techniques by practicing before a mirror, studying your contact sheets from photo shootings, or using videotape. Of course, paying too much attention to your hand movements is not good because an affected rather than natural look will emerge.

A model's hands must always be impeccably groomed. If your hands are unattractive or out of proportion, you will have to create ways to downplay them without looking as though you are trying to hide them. If your hands are attractive, you will have many more posing options, plus, if they are truly perfect, you will be eligible for opportunities for hand modeling.

Beginning models are often at a loss as to what to do with their hands; however, when a model gains experience, he finds many ways to use his hands when posing. When modeling a garment there are several things a model can do with his hands. Review the information on physical presentation in Chapter 2 to determine natural and creative ways of holding your hands. There are four basic ways in which models use their hands: holding them at sides of body; placing hands on a garment, product, or prop; placing the hands so they are touching the body; and moving the hands in a creative way.

Holding Hands at the Sides

This is a good movement for modeling any garment, especially a garment that is constricting, such as a suit jacket. Holding your hands at your sides may also be your only option when a photograph must fit into a narrow space in a layout. If this is the case the photographer will inform you or show you a sketch of how the finished photograph will appear.

To achieve attractive positions when holding your hands at your sides, review the pencil trick explained in Chapter 2. It is also important to keep your elbows slightly away from your body and softly bent, not stiff or rigid. When holding your hands at your sides consider how you can use slight movements to vary your pose. For example, try bending your elbows at different degrees or vary the position of your shoulders. For example, raise or lower one shoulder or place one shoulder forward or back. You might also vary your arms by placing one arm slightly in front of the body, the other arm slightly behind the body.

In some situations, allowing just one hand to show will be desirable. For example, when your body is in profile the hand away from the camera need not show, nor should you appear to be straining to hide it. For a natural look, simply place the hand just out of the camera's view.

Placing Hands on the Body

There are lots of different ways you can place your hands on your body. You may place one or both hands on your hips or waistline to show the shape of a garment's sleeves or bodice. Touching your hair, face, neck, or shoulders are other options. Placing your hands on the outer sides of your upper thighs or hips can be done to create other poses. Usually a gentle, yet deliberate hand movement is best; overly relaxed hands look sloppy or awkward. The opposite extreme, nervous-looking hands can appear clawlike or stiff. It is also important when placing your hands on your body or face that you don't use a position or pressure that will cause wrinkles in your skin or distortions of your features. In addition, assuming a graceful hand position so that the hand itself looks attractive is necessary.

Touching the Face or Hair

One of the options a model has for using her hands is touching her hair or face (Figure 4). Although there are no hard and fast do's and don'ts for posing the hands, a model should consider which angles make her hands look most attractive. Palms are not the most attractive part of the hand, so rotating the hand to a three-quarter or profile angle is usually best.

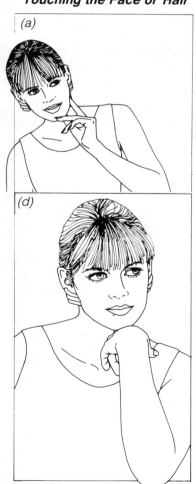

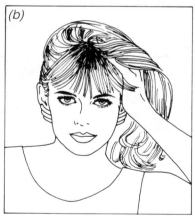

Figure 4. (a) When placing your hand on your face, use a gentle touch. (b) When placing your hands in your hair, do so in a way that enhances your hairstyle. Use a light touch to avoid flattening or distorting the look of your hair. (c, d) When posing, consider how your hand looks to the camera. Notice that the hand position shown in c is visually more interesting than the hand position in d, which appears obtrusive and distorted.

Placing Hands on a Garment, Product, or Prop

If a garment has pockets, this is a desirable feature and the model should emphasize their presence by placing her hands in them for some of the shots. The way in which you place your hands in the pockets will be determined by the mood and construction of the garment. For example, shoving fists into the pockets of a tight-fitting elegant skirt will distort the design and conflict with the mood of the garment. On the other hand, making fists inside the pockets of a big, sporty jacket will contribute to the shot by displaying a relaxed, informal feeling. See the Figure 17 in Chapter 13 for more ideas.

There are lots of ways you can vary your pose even with your hands in your pockets. For example, you may choose to raise one or both shoulders or push one elbow forward or backward. Always pay attention to the construction of the garment to ensure that when you place your hands in the pockets that the lines of the garment and the appearance of the pockets looks attractive.

Models sometimes touch the collar of a garment or flare the skirt of a garment by grasping the hem. Take care when executing these movements that the garments lines look well and that the movements fit with the mood of the shot. Some photographers do not like these types of movements because they often look too posed.

Holding a Product or Prop

Attractive hand positions are also important when holding a product or prop. Hands usually appear best when neither the backs nor the palms are shown flat to the camera. Angling the hands to varied degrees or in profile will usually be the most attractive. Fingers usually appear best when they seem long and tapering. Aiming the ends or tips of the fingers straight at the camera lens will cause foreshortening, so angling them slightly upward, downward, or to the right or left usually looks better. Hands also appear more attractive when the fingers are slightly flexed and evenly spread, rather than concave and held tightly together or unevenly fanned or clawlike. A natural bend to the wrist flowing naturally from the movement of the arm is usually preferred over a sharp downward or upward bend or a stiff wrist. Holding your hands in the same plane as your body will guard against the enlarging effect created when hands are placed closer to the lens.

When holding a prop or product, you will want your hand position to work well with the item. The way you hold the item will be determined by the construction and nature of the item. For example, you would hold an elegant evening bag in a different manner than you would hold a beach bag.

When you are holding a product that is being advertised, the label on the package is the most important element of the shot. Make sure your fingers don't cover the label and that it is aiming straight into the lens. Also be aware of glare. Because the label may be shiny and reflect the photographer's lights, making it difficult to see, it may be necessary to tilt the object slightly to avoid glare. It is also important to know where you are to be in relation to the product. Know exactly how high or low, how near or far from your face or body the item is to be placed. Usually holding the item very close to you or in a certain plane is important for focusing and composition.

Products or props are handled firmly, but gently. When holding a prop, make sure that it doesn't obstruct important details. For example, if you are modeling a garment, you would not hold a prop in front of the garment. If you are standing with other models, hold the prop in a visible spot, but take care that it doesn't obstruct their garments. Usually holding the prop in the hand that is farthest away from the other model is best.

When holding a prop, it is also important to hold it so that the prop itself is identifiable from the camera's perspective. For example, holding a flat, envelope-style purse so that only the end of it is visible to the camera will make it difficult to determine what the prop is. Instead, turn the flat part of the purse slightly toward the camera.

Another option that a model has is touching something on the set or touching another model on the set. Don't plop your hand on another model's shoulder or an object on the set. Instead, place your hand in an attractive position. When leaning or supporting yourself against a wall or chair, do so with grace and purpose. You should be more concerned with making your pose enhance your garment and your body than you are with getting into a comfortable position. For example, don't lean your hips against a chair or desk, causing your skirt or pants to bunch or crease. Instead stand an inch away from the desk or chair rather than actually leaning against it. Also be careful not to stand behind a part of the set such as a piece of furniture, because this will cover your garment. Of course, if the piece of furniture is the item being shown, you would stand in a way to make it, rather than your garment, the focal point of the shot. Having another model or other objects on the set with which you can interact yields lots of posing ideas, so use your imagination and try to think of lots of ways to incorporate your movements and the setting.

Creative Hand Movements

Many times a model will have nothing to hold or interact with. He or she may use gestures that are natural or stylized to create new poses. Study the way models hold their hands in midair and use dance-like hand positions.

Figure 5. Men's hand movements. These illustrations show some of the most common ways men position their hands in photographs. (a) Holding hands down at the sides is a common hand position when walking. Hands are in a relaxed, slightly open fist with the thumbs touching the forefingers. (b) Poised hands usually look best when the fingers are held together and bent. Hands should not look rigid, stiff, or too posed. Hands should not obstruct important details of the item being shown.

(c) Folded hands are often a good option for men with attractive, well-groomed hands. (d) Placing the hands in pockets is one of the most common hand movements used by male models. Usually hands are placed in the pockets of suit pants, rather than the pockets of the suit jacket. When a single-breasted jacket is worn, the sides of the jacket are neatly gathered behind the wrists. (e) Double-breasted suit jackets are usually shown buttoned. Hands are placed in pants pockets under the jacket. (f) Crossed arms give a self-assured, authoritative look. When such a position is assumed, the male model is careful to avoid creating excess bunching or wrinkling in his garment.

(Note: Female models sometimes use many of the men's hand positions shown when modeling casual, sporty or masculine clothing.)

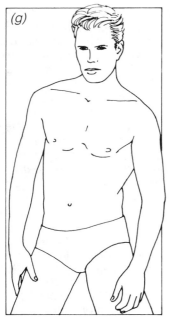

(g) Hands touching the body might be placed on hips or thighs. (h) Hands touching the garment might be done by grasping one side of a jacket to pull it back slightly in order to show the vest being worn underneath. (i) Another example of hands touching the garment is shown here. (j) When the model is accompanying a prop, he holds it naturally. The backs of men's hands, unlike those of female models, are often shown flat to the camera. (k) A male model will often model with a female model. Usually when it is the woman's clothing being featured, the male model stands behind or to the side of the female and places his hand on her shoulder, waist, or arm. When doing so, the man places his hand gently, purposefully, and attractively. He doesn't clumsily, unconsciously plop his hand on the other model. He is also careful to avoid disturbing the lines of the female model's garment when touching it. Usually when it is the male model's garment being featured, the female stands behind him or to his side and places her hands on him. (l) A male model might touch his hands to his face. In most cases, men's hands look best when positioned in a relaxed fist.

Movements of the Legs and Feet

The position of your feet in a full-length photograph can also be an indication of your modeling experience or lack of it. Feet often present posing problems for beginning models. Basically the same information that pertains to hands applies here. Unattractive foot positions can have a negative impact on a shot.

Some of the most common feet and leg positions used by models are shown in Figures 18–21 in Chapter 2. These are the basic closed stance, the basic open stance, feet spread symmetrically, and feet spread asymmetrically. There are several variations of these positions. Study the way models in magazines pose their feet. Always be conscious of perfecting the position of your feet when posing.

Feet usually appear best when photographed at varying angles or in profile rather than when aimed straight at the camera, especially if they are bare. Women's feet and legs usually appear most attractive when wearing shoes that have neither flat nor extremely high heels. It is a good idea to wear heels even when your feet are cropped out of the photograph; heels give your legs a better line and make you stand more gracefully. When bare feet are to be photographed, if you lift slightly on the toes of one or both feet, it will often give you an attractive appearance.

When sitting or standing, maintain an attractive line for the legs and feet. Turning the toes inward is not used in most modeling situations. It is usually reserved for a comical or unique look. Keeping the toes in line straight ahead of you or slightly turned outward will create a more graceful line for the feet, ankles, and legs.

Another technique that works well is to place your weight on one foot. This is referred to as the "base foot." From here you can create attractive leg and foot variations by moving your free foot (the foot your weight is not on) to the left or right, forward or backward, up or down. Creating a longer line for the legs can also be achieved by softening the bend of the ankle. For example, when sitting with crossed legs, point the toe of your free foot slightly downward for a longer, more pleasing line.

PHOTO MOVEMENT INFORMATION FOR SPECIALTY MODELING
Posing in Body-Revealing Garments

Lingerie and bathing suits often present complications not present in other types of modeling. Models who show these items must not only possess good figures but must have excellent skin all over their bodies. Underarm and bikini line hair must be removed. Waxing and cream depilatories are often recommended, as shaving can cause rashes in these areas. The legs, underarms, and bikini line must meticulously be kept hair-free because even the slightest stubble may show up on camera.

When called for lingerie and bathing suit assignments, avoid wearing such garments as tight jeans, pantyhose, and underpants with tight elastic bands to the booking. These will cause red indentation lines that can take an hour or more to disappear and are very difficult to camouflage with makeup. When you arrive at the studio, make sure you remove garments that might create a problem.

A light tan usually looks best when showing bathing suits, but tan lines can pose big problems because they are difficult to camouflage with makeup and expensive to retouch. If you are tanning, do so in a skimpy, strapless, or tan-through suit. Aim for just a slight bit of color by using a high sunscreen and working on your tan gradually. If you don't have a tan, a sun-toned body makeup or pan-stick makeup applied with a sponge may be the answer. Take care that makeup is evenly applied all over (face and body must be perfectly matched) and that makeup does not soil the articles you are wearing.

When modeling any revealing garment, skin should look smooth, so applying a moisturizer, especially to the legs, is a good idea right before shooting begins. Some situations demand the wet look, which is accomplished by coating the body with baby oil and using a spray bottle filled with water frequently throughout the shooting. Wearing pantyhose with a bathing suit rarely looks good because they make the legs look darker and shinier than the skin on the rest of the body. Although it is usually not needed, body makeup would be a better solution.

When posing, always be conscious of not twisting or moving your body in ways that may create bulges or creases in the skin to appear. Since so much of the body is uncovered, you must be extra conscious of avoiding poses that will reveal such problems.

Posing to Enhance the Figure

There are lots of posing tricks that can be used to enhance the figure. Some of the more common ones are described here.

Arching the back. Arching to create an inward bend in the back looks attractive especially when the body is turned in profile or at a three-quarter angle to the camera. Figures 6a, b.

Keeping the arms away from the body. Keeping the arms away from the body so that the indentation of the waist can be seen is always a good idea. This can be accomplished by extending the arms upward or outward or by holding the arms down at your sides and bending the elbows to create a space between the arms and the waist. See Figures 6a, b, and c.

Stretching or elongating the body. Elongating the body is attractive whether sitting, lying down, or standing because it creates a longer, firmer line. Hands and arms can be stretched freely above the head or can be touching the hair. Figure 6b.

Working in profile. Standing with your body in profile to the camera or angling your body slightly away from the lens will give a slimmer look.

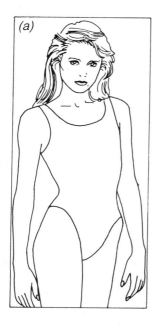

Figure 6. Posing in different positions to enhance the figure.

380

Twisting the body. Twisting the body accentuates the waistline. Stand so that your hips are turned in profile or at a three-quarter angle to the camera, but swing the upper part of your body to face the camera. This is called "turning in opposition."

Hip action. Raising one hip while raising the opposite shoulder will make your body form an attractive S curve. When executing this idea take care not to lean too far over on the weighted side because this can create a bulge in the hip and thigh area. You can also use this position when your body is at a three-quarter or profile angle to the camera. Another way to use the hips and add curves to your body is by rocking the pelvic area forward or back or side to side. Fig. 6c.

Crossing thighs. Whether lying or standing, crossing the thighs by placing one knee slightly over the other gives the thighs and hips a slim, pleasing appearance. When standing this is usually done by keeping one leg straight while bending the other leg inward at the knee. When walking, this slimmer appearance is accomplished by placing one foot in front of the other. Figure 6c.

Using hands effectively. A hand can make a hip appear smaller by being placed so that it obstructs the side of a hip, the buttocks, or a thigh. Figure 6c.

Holding abdominal muscles tight. If you are modeling bathing suits and such body-revealing garments as leotards or dancewear, your abdomen should be firm and flat. You should always be aware of holding in your abdomen. This is especially true when leaning, lying on your side, bending over, or sitting. Holding the abdominal muscles tight while keeping the rib cage in usually looks better than sucking in the abdomen and causing the rib cage to raise and enlarge. Don't eat a big meal or drink lots of fluids (especially carbonated beverages) before modeling such garments because eating and drinking will naturally cause your stomach to expand, enlarging the area.

Hand Modeling

Hand modeling is a specialty that requires a lot of skill. In addition to having attractive hands, the hand model must have several other characteristics. Dexterity is a must. The photographer may direct the model to hold each finger a certain way. This is not only difficult, requiring excellent coordination and flexibility, but it is uncomfortable as well. Regardless of how uncomfortable a pose may be or how awkward it may feel, a good hand model is able to hold poses with grace and ease. In order not to disturb the focus, the product or other elements of the shot, the model will have to hold hands extremely still.

In addition to beauty, hands must have acting ability. They must look as if they belong to the face (which may not be your own) with which they are paired. They must portray an attitude toward a product or situation. Their movements must realistically reflect the character they are imitating. A hand model must know what her approach to the shot will be. She must consider if she is to assume a natural or realistic hand position to display a household product or if her hand position is to be creative and unconventional to display a fashion-related item. If you are after the realistic approach, consider how you would naturally hold, use, or handle the item; however, realize that for the camera you may have to make adjustments that seem neither natural nor comfortable. There are correct ways of holding such items as sporting equipment. A good hand model is concerned with accuracy. If you are to take a more liberal approach, be aware of how much freedom is allowed. Experiment with different ways of holding the item.

Allow your hands to express emotions. Hands are very expressive and can convey a wide range of emotions, attitudes, looks, and personalities. Allow what you are holding to dictate the manner in which you will handle the item. For example, you would hold an elegant champagne glass differently than you would a mug of beer. Know what your attitude toward the item is to be. For example, you can impart value to an item (your client's) simply by handling it in a sophisticated, delicate way. You can make another item (the competitor's) appear cheap and flimsy simply by changing the way in which your hands treat it.

A hand model must also be able to do a variety of tasks that most people would never think of as requiring special skill. For example, a hand model might be required to dispense a specified portion of liquid from a bottle without splashing or spilling. Add patience to the above skills, because it may take several trials to get the right effect, and you will understand how much expertise hand modeling requires.

Hand models must have impeccable hands that are free of dry skin, hangnails, cuts, and other problems that arise from normal, daily tasks. Makeup to improve the appearance of the hands may be necessary. Some male and female models use a nongreasy makeup to lighten or darken the hands to achieve the desired skintone. Sometimes just a light application of powder is needed to make the hands appear smoother and more photogenic. However, great care must be taken when hand makeup is used so that it is not visible around the nails or comes off the hands onto the item or clothing being modeled. To give the skin on the hands a flawless finish, removal of the fine hair on the backs of the hands and wrists may be necessary. This is usually done by salon waxing or use of a mild cream depilatory. In most cases, using just a moisturizer on the hands and no makeup is the ideal.

Foot Modeling

Feet must be perfectly groomed and vein-free. If you have an audition or booking for feet, don't walk, ride to it. Remove your shoes when you arrive to eradicate indentations or lines caused by your shoes and socks. Nails should be polished and shaped to follow the contour of the toes, yet not extend in length beyond them. There should be no blemishes or foot disorders, and hair on legs and ankles should be removed.

USING YOUR IMAGINATION WHEN MODELING

Often times it will be difficult to summon your creativity when on an assignment. Many times the atmosphere in the studio will be uninspiring or even unpleasant. There will always be pressures due to time constraints and the costliness of a photo shooting. However, even when shooting conditions are less than ideal, a good model is able to delve into her imagination to create great results for the camera. Good models know how to draw out their creative energies without having to rely on other sources for inspiration. The following approaches can be used as exercises to stimulate your creativity and inject fun and freshness into your modeling endeavors. Determine which approaches will be most effective based on the item you are modeling and the situation.

The Character Approach

This is the most obvious approach for getting posing ideas for a specific garment. Think about what type of person would wear or use the item and then portray that character. Create a mental picture of the person describing him or her by age, social position, marital status, job, life-style, and so on. Consider how your physical presentation can be varied to reflect the character you are portraying.

The Personal Approach

Recall your own personal experiences to evoke a mood or look that the photographer wants or the garment dictates. Re-enact your experience for the camera. For positive or happy expressions, think of someone you like, something good to eat, something you are looking forward to after the shooting or something funny. For darker expressions, think of a sad experience or something that made you angry. Practice until you can project a wide range of moods and emotions with ease.

The Artistic Approach

Consider yourself as an artist creating different designs with your body. Visualize a black frame around your body in regard to the shot being made. Does it include the whole body or is it cut and where? Is it square or rectangular (horizontal or vertical)? Think in terms of how you can utilize the space, fill out the frame, and create interesting shapes, silhouettes, and lines with your body. Think in terms of how contrasts (lights and darks or colors) placed in different areas of the frame will contribute to the composition of the picture. Think in terms of artistic composition or design as you have seen it in paintings, sculptures, photographs, and other artistic media. Your movements may be ordinary movements from life or they may be borrowed from dance, sports, or even geometric-like shapes. The important thing when using this approach is to think about how your movements utilize the area inside the frame of the picture.

The Situational Approach

Create a scenario or environment around the garment or product you are modeling. If you are wearing an evening dress, imagine yourself at a party. Create an entire situation, complete with an interesting stranger. Study the way people stand, walk, gesture, and interact in various situations, then adapt these ideas for the camera.

The Improvisational Approach

You've seen actors and comedians pick up or stand next to an object, such as a ball, a book, or a wall, and use the object in an imaginative way. To improvise, think of 20 or more different things you can do with a particular object. For example, using a chair, see how many different ways you can think of to sit on it.

The Copy-Cat Approach

Watch and copy other models. Adapt their ideas to your style and preferences. Keep an idea notebook of poses, movements, and expressions. Tear out magazine and catalog pages displaying poses you think are effective for different items and situations and collect the clippings in a three-ring binder. Use this as a source book for copying the poses while adding your own input.

Mimic a Famous Person

Certain clothes often remind us of a famous person. If the garment you are modeling reminds you of a particular celebrity, rock star, movie star, political leader, or businessperson, conjure up that individual's expressions and gestures as you have observed them in news photos, on television, or in films, and act them out for the camera. Even mythical figures, characters in literature, and subjects of well-known artworks will provide inspiration. When you put on a garment, think: Who does this outfit remind me of?

The Historical Approach

Some garments remind us of a specific era. If you are given an outfit that is a throwback to the 1950s, you might try some vintage rock and roll movements or copy the gestures or actions of an actor or actress in a film or television show set in the fifties. Mimic poses you may have seen in 1950s fashion photos.

The Photographer's Approach

Study the photographer's work to understand his or her style and how he or she likes the models to move and look. The client engages a particular photographer because that photographer's work exhibits a certain style. While being photographed, "watch" yourself through the lens to see yourself as the photographer is seeing you. Try to visualize how you will appear on the contact sheet of the film the photographer is shooting. Picture all the elements of the shot, such as the way the light is hitting you, the background, and your garment; then create a mental photo on the contact sheet as you move from one frame to another. Ideally, each pose could be used as the final picture.

The Natural Approach

The natural approach involves using only very basic, everyday movements. Standing with your feet together and your hands folded in front of you is an example of a natural movement, whereas placing one hip out and the opposite shoulder up is an example of a stylized movement. Watching the way people stand, sit, and move in a restaurant, airport, or on the street is the best way to gain inspiration for natural movements.

Change Your Perspective

As the model you may be concentrating on how you appear in the picture. Ideally you should be concerned with how you are fulfilling the needs of the art director, client, and photographer. Consider the expectations of others involved. Consider the client's objectives. He or she is concerned with presenting an image that will attract attention to the item and sell it. Put yourself in the client's place. Determine the reasons why the client hired you, then capitalize on the ability, look, style, and experience that convinced the client to engage you. Also be aware of the budget the client must work within and think about what your expectations would be if you were paying for the shooting. You must present a lot of creativity and skill if you expect to earn the high fee that good models command. A good model is worth every cent of his or her fee. A bad model can ruin a picture and cost the client hundreds or thousands of dollars to reshoot, when the fees for all those involved (other models, photographer, stylist) are added on.

The Dancer's Approach

Think of movements or stances you have seen ballet, tap, jazz, aerobic, or rock dancers perform. These often make beautiful poses. Or just borrow certain aspects from dancers' movements, such as the way they hold their head, hands, or feet.

The Athlete's Approach

Look at sports activities for ideas on body movements that might be right for different garments, products, or situations. Even the exercises you do to keep in shape will provide good posing ideas when modeling workout wear.

Experience the Garment

Feel the texture of the garment. Is it smooth and satiny or rough and coarse? Move around. Does the garment move with you, against you, or not at all. Feel the fit. Where does it strain or sag? Look at the cut. A good model can feel the way a garment drapes, wrinkles, folds, and pulls and knows how to alter his or her posture and movements so that the cut, fit, and fabric looks ideal. Every time you make a move, note what it does to your garment. Study your garment from different angles and in different poses in the mirror to determine what is most attractive.

Movement Isolation Techniques

Good models have flexible bodies and move fluidly and gracefully. They have excellent mind-to-body control like highly trained athletes and experienced actors. Making your body and face express exactly what you want them to is a key to successful modeling. Dancing, sports, and acting classes will help you to understand how to isolate your movements. Here is an example of isolating a movement: Placing your hands in your pockets, stand with your feet firmly planted on the ground as if they are stuck there. Then think of all the different movements you can do just by altering your right shoulder. You might raise it, lower it, bring it forward or put it back. Your head, hips, legs, and feet should stay in exactly the same position—only your right shoulder moves. Movement isolation techniques can be used to perfect a pose or to provide lots of variations in one basic pose. Often one subtle movement can make the difference between a pose that has impact and a pose that does not.

Meditation Techniques

Some models use meditation techniques to get themselves into the desired mood. Meditate on the mood you want to depict and transcend your body and mind into the picture the photographer is trying to create.

Relaxation Techniques

You can use relaxation techniques while you are posing to ease tension or to help you to maintain a difficult pose. Sometimes you will find that your pose is stiff or the photographer may tell you that it is. Taking care not to muss your garment, hair, or makeup, try some of the following little tricks while stylists are arranging your garment or the photographer is changing film. To relax and calm your nerves or to increase your energy, take a few deep breaths, shake your body or your arms, or do a few neck rolls, first to the left, then to the right. Do a few shoulder rolls, backward then forward to achieve a more natural position or posture. To achieve a better hand position, try tensing your muscles by clenching your fist and then relaxing your hand. To relax your facial muscles, try closing your eyes and dropping your lower jaw for a few moments. Or try yawning, licking your lips, laughing, or making a funny face. If an area of your body seems tense, try massaging it lightly or try stretching. If you are nervous, alter your breathing so that you let the air out slowly, or try to release excess energy before an appearance by bouncing softly on your toes or doing a few aerobic exercises.

The Actor's Approach

The next time you watch a movie, study various acting techniques. Note how an actor or actress uses posture, eyes, and movement to convey certain feelings. Store up these "freeze frames" in your memory, and recall them the next time you shoot. Think of some of the methods an actor uses to discover how a character should be presented. For example, rather than try to act out feelings, concentrate instead on reacting to a stimulus. Pretend someone has paid you a great compliment, then react to it.

Another method actors use is to think in terms of a point of view. A model can develop a point of view about the items or clothing he or she is modeling. For example, if you are modeling an item of clothing, you will want to show how great it makes you feel and that you like it. If a female and male model are photographed together, usually a romantic point of view is desired.

Another way to use the actor's approach is to try acting exercises. To overcome shyness and increase your ability to project emotions with your body and face, you might try the following exercise: First, think of an emotion you would like to portray, such as anger or happiness. Begin counting aloud and expressing the emotion with your facial expressions, voice, and body movements as you direct the feeling toward another individual or the camera. As you are counting, you are building the emotion from a subtle expression to its peak. It is as if you were gradually becoming angry and then shouting at someone. To portray happiness, at the count of 1, you'll begin with a contented expression. By the time you reach 15, you will be ending with an open projection of joy. By practicing this exercise, you will soon see how you can turn on your emotions at will for the camera.

The Pantomime Approach

Pantomime is another acting technique that works well for models. Pantomime is telling a story by using only body movements and facial expressions. To pantomime for the camera, you might make a gesture such as pretending to yawn when modeling sleepwear. Next time you are in front of the camera, try playing charades.

The Musical Approach

This is an obvious but effective way to inspire a model and one that is used often. Music can induce different moods or inspire you to move. However, not all situations allow for a stereo to be blasting while a model gets into a mood. Don't insist that you need certain music to get you moving. If music is unavailable, you can play a song in your head while in front of the camera. Singing to yourself also works well, but depending on the sound of your voice, it may not be appreciated by those present! Whether it's playing in your head or out loud, move to the music or try mouthing the words for different facial expressions. Respecting the wishes of others so that they too can best summon their creativity is important. Make sure you use music to elicit movements that work well with the mood of your garment.

The Fashion Show Approach

Treat a print booking as if it were a fashion show. Move fluidly from one pose to the next, making each pose as good as it can possibly be. Any pose should be suitable for use as the final picture. Some of the best models really give a performance as if they were on stage, moving and emoting from one movement and expression to the next. A simple fashion show movement you can do for the camera is to execute one-quarter, one-half, or full turns in place to get your garment moving. While doing this, pretend that you are on stage and that the photographer or camera is your audience.

The Unconventional Approach

Used judiciously the unconventional approach can be very effective. Look at your garment, think about what you would normally do, and then do the opposite. For example, if you were in an evening gown, usually you would move elegantly and in a feminine manner. For a creative switch, do a few movements that you would normally reserve for jeans, such as standing with your feet wide apart and fists on your hips.

The Clock Concept

The clock concept is an easy method of thinking of different ways to move your body. It involves breaking down movements so that you can make minor variations in a pose. This approach is used mainly to perfect or alter a pose. It is important to remember that any pose, whether you are standing next to a lawn mower or modeling an Yves St. Laurent gown by a castle, must project an attitude. The mood or feeling projected may be subtle or overt, depending on the message being conveyed. The clock concept utilizes minor variations in angle to change or improve a pose and therefore a photograph. These ideas will help you to arrive at combinations you can execute to offer the photographer a variety of poses, positions, and expressions to choose from.

The clock concept should not be used as the only way of finding new poses. It should be used in conjunction with your acting ability to express the desired concept. Use this approach when you've exhausted all other ideas or you can't think of any other poses.

You can vary every part of your body by thinking in terms of of the clock (see Figure 7). Visualize a clock painted on the floor. Your feet, face, and body are pointed at 12:00. The camera is in front of you. You can change a simple pose like this just by varying angles. For example, aim just your hips, shoulders, or feet at 1:00, 2:00, 3:00, and so forth. Another way you might want to change your pose is to leave your feet and body aimed at 12:00 but turn your head so that it aims in the direction of 1:00, 2:00, or 3:00 (left profile) or 11:00, 10:00, or 9:00 (right profile). As another variation, try angling parts of your body in different directions. For example, aiming your feet at 3:00 or 9:00, twist and aim your shoulders at 12:00 and your head at 1:00; or aiming your feet at 6:00, turn your shoulders so they aim at 5:00 or 4:00, turn your head to 2:00 and set your eyes at 12:00 (the camera).

Another way to use the clock concept is by leaning your body toward various points of the clock. For example, leaning toward 3:00 and bending at the waist will result in a motion that looks like a side bend you might do as an exercise. Another way of utilizing this technique is to lean parts of your body in different directions. For example, lean with your shoulders toward 3:00, while leaning with your hips toward 9:00. This will result in a curved S-shaped pose that will flatter your waistline.

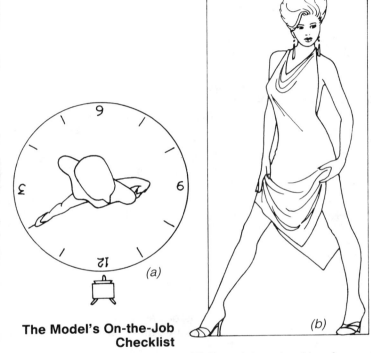

Figure 7. The clock concept. (a) The clock concept is shown here from above. The camera is at 12:00 o'clock, and the model is in the center of the clock facing the camera. She has angled her left foot (base foot) to point between 12:00 and 1:00 and has extended her right foot (free foot) to 2:00. Her right shoulder is pointing to 4:00, and the left shoulder is angled toward 10:00. Her left elbow is positioned slightly back toward 9:00. (b) This is how the pose on the clock looks when viewed through the camera. These two illustrations show how many variations are possible when using the clock concept. Try combining the clock concept with all the other suggestions in order to discover an unlimited number of poses.

The Model's On-the-Job Checklist

Before the Booking
☐ Complete a booking form when your agent calls with information about the job. See Chapter 7.

☐ Make sure you have all garments and accessories or acquire them.

☐ Clean and press clothing, shine shoes, and assemble accessories. Pack totebag, making certain that you have included all standard totebag items.

☐ Wash and set your hair. Do your makeup.

☐ Know whether you are to arrive 15 minutes early or at the start of the booking time. Always allow enough time to get to your destination. If you live outside the city, allow more time.

When You Arrive
☐ Check in with the photographer and coordinator or stylist so they know you have arrived.

☐ Go over the outfits you will be modeling with the coordinator and ask about order, hairstyles, makeup, and accessories needed. Remove your personal jewelry items such as your wristwatch, rings, etc.

☐ Complete makeup and hair.

☐ Put on the first outfit.

☐ Check with the photographer and stylist or client to finalize accessories, makeup, and hair.

☐ Find your position on the set by studying the layout or by asking the photographer.

During the Shooting

☐ Pick up on the tone in the studio, the photographer's shooting style, and other factors to make the shooting productive and pleasant.

☐ Take responsibility for the appearance of your hair, makeup, clothes, and styling when hairstylists, makeup artists, and stylists are not employed. Don't expect the photographer to be aware of these details; he or she needs your help. Be critical because small flaws are exaggerated in photographs.

☐ Follow the photographer's directions closely.

☐ Each time you take off a garment, hang it properly on a hanger. Change accessories with every shot. Put accessories in the proper place.

☐ Observe studio etiquette.

Studio Etiquette

☐ Be time conscious. Always work as quickly as possible. Clothes changes should not take longer than 5 minutes or 10 to 15 minutes if more extensive hair and makeup styling is necessary. Don't keep the photographer waiting. Always be ready and waiting in the dressing room or near the set. The amount of time devoted to each shot will depend on the photographer, the concept or situation, what the picture will be used for, budgets, deadlines, and other factors. Generally 8 to 12 shots may be done per day for catalogs, 1 to 4 shots for advertisements, and nearly any number for editorial shots depending on the photographer and the situation. For example, a concept-oriented photographer who has a strong, detailed idea of the lighting, setting, and movement to be used will take longer to shoot than a photographer who takes spontaneous-looking shots.

☐ Be careful of studio props, equipment, and lights. Don't lean against walls or props on the set.

☐ Help the photographer to keep his or her studio neat and clean. Confine your belongings to a small area in the dressing room. Put clothes you have modeled back on hangers after each shot, clean up makeup, and throw refuse in the wastebasket. At the completion of the assignment, make sure you have all your belongings. Leave the dressing room as you found it; other people will have to use it after you.

☐ Keep conversation to a minumum while on the set. Keep voices low while waiting between shots.

☐ Cooperate with other models to make the shooting run as smoothly as possible. Be helpful to models who may be new to the job. Be cooperative in helping to get the job done. For example, if another model has forgotten an item she was to furnish and you have one, be willing to lend it to her.

☐ Make a special effort for every client and every photographer. Whether you are modeling a $10 dress or a $10,000 dress, or whether you are working for a well-known photographer or a beginning photographer, the high quality of your work, your enthusiasm, and your willingness to give it your all should still be there.

☐ Always maintain a pleasant manner. Don't get into squabbles with stylists or other models. Never leave in a huff in the middle of a shooting. Don't get upset; it is best to save the dramatics for outside of the studio. Keep everything on a business level. You will be expected to change clothing in all sorts of places, but do try to maintain some degree of modesty. If fun and excitement abound in the studio, keep your professionalism in mind. Even if the atmosphere in the studio is relaxed or others are behaving in an outrageous manner, avoid indulging in anything unseemly, such as vicious gossip, profanity, boisterous behavior, drugs, and alcohol.

☐ Always change your hair slightly for each change of clothes (unless otherwise instructed). Fit it to the mood of your garment. Make subtle changes in makeup. Keep a lookout for shiny skin, creased eyeshadow, smudged mascara, lipstick on teeth, and stray hairs. If you have a choice in the order you will model garments, start with sporty or casual looks and work up to dressy looks so you can end with your hair up and more makeup on. Always try to save hats for last. Headshots should usually be done first so that makeup looks ideal.

☐ Don't discuss your fee or how soon you will be finished when you are on the set. Don't talk about other jobs; concentrate on the job at hand.

☐ Don't be difficult. Don't refuse to wear an outfit just because you don't like it. If you are asked to do or wear something questionable (involving nudity, etc.) that the client has not cleared with your agency, make a quick phone call to your agent and explain the problem while the client is present.

☐ Don't make fun of the client's product (even if he or she does). Welcome the challenge. If you genuinely like it, compliment him or her on it.

☐ Don't complain if a shooting runs overtime. Don't forget that the entire staff is working late, not just you. If you must be at another booking, phone your agency. They will handle the problem.

☐ Take extreme care with clothing and other items you are modeling. Consult "Handling Your Client's Clothes with Care" in Chapter 5.

☐ Never bring friends or relatives along to shootings. If you must, get permission in advance.

☐ Don't get into competition with other models. If you are allowed to choose what you will wear, don't hoard the best clothes. Ask the other models first for their preferences, and take turns wearing the unattractive outfits. Wear without protest the garments you are assigned to model.

☐ Don't try to mediate between a photographer and client who are disagreeing about the shot. If they are disagreeing about your movement, try lots of variations in your movement until you come up with one they both like. Never argue with a client.

☐ Don't tell others how to do their jobs. Veterans don't like to be told their jobs by relative newcomers. Make suggestions only when you are asked. Don't draw attention to any mistakes made by others.

☐ Don't waste precious breaktime. If you are on an all-day job, use lunch time wisely by resetting your hair before taking time out, checking in with your agency, or reorganizing your supplies. If lunch is served, eat lightly (e.g., soup and salad). Don't be picky about what you eat. Take what you are offered.

☐ Don't stand behind the photographer watching or directing the model on set. Never look through the viewfinder of the camera unless you are asked to. Stay out of the way until you are to do your shot.

After the Shooting

☐ Clean up after yourself.

☐ Check to be sure that you don't accidentally leave the studio with any of the client's accessories.

☐ Complete your voucher using your booking form for reference and have it signed by the client (if present) or the photographer.

☐ Give designated copy or copies to the client. Thank the client and leave. If this was the last booking of the day, call your agency from a pay phone outside the studio before you head home to get updates in your schedule.

Chapter 11 Modeling For Electronic Media

TYPES OF MODELING FOR ELECTRONIC MEDIA

Television Commercials

Electronic media provides several opportunities for models and actors. Some of the different types of work available are the following.

Most national commercials are filmed or taped in New York, Los Angeles, Chicago, and other major cities and run on network television. These can be very lucrative for the model or actor involved. Many local commercials are also made in these and other cities for local stores, banks, automobile dealers, restaurants, and other accounts. These are run on a limited basis. The majority of this chapter is devoted to television commerical work because it is the most available, and these principles generally will apply to other areas of electronic media work.

Industrial Films

Companies often hire independent filmmakers or production houses to make industrial films for one or many of the following reasons: publicity, recruiting staff, training employees, analyzing working techniques, and keeping staff in offices in other locations informed and enthusiastic. Industrial films may be made solely for in-house use (within the company) or they may be used at trade shows or other exhibitions to promote the company to other businesses. A lot of the people used in industrial films actually work at the company; however, models or actors are employed when the budget allows and when there is scripted dialogue and a professional delivery is required. Models or actors are also hired when a particular look is needed.

Educational Films

Educational films, filmstrips, slide programs, and videos may be sponsored by the government, large corporations, educational materials firms, or other entities and are used in schools and other training programs to inform and instruct. Actors are commonly employed to narrate such films, and occasionally models or actors are needed to appear on camera.

Entertainment or Feature Videos and Films

A model may appear in films and videotapes made by filmmakers for use in cable, subscription, or network television. Soap operas commonly employ models in key roles or as extras in group scenes. Music videos, made-for-TV productions, and motion pictures also use models or actors in the same way. This type of work is obtained through modeling or talent agents, independent casting directors, or film production companies.

Promotional Films and Videos

Promotional audiovisuals are made to promote products, services, and ideas to the public and function as extended commercials. They run from a few minutes to an hour and are usually not intended for broadcast. Such a film can display a range of products more completely than any brochure or display; it can present a company image showing the firm and its products in detail. While providing entertainment, promotional films can outline a proposition and back it up with evidence. For example, a cosmetics company may have a video showing new makeup products and application techniques at the counter in a department store where its products are sold; this draws attention and promotes products. A fashion designer may assemble a fashion video that features new looks in his or her collection to show to buyers or the public. For public relations, multimedia productions may be sent to editors, schools, and other organizations in hopes that the producer will get exposure and publicity for his or her company and products.

Direct Sales Videos

A company may assemble a video catalog of its offerings that shows still and moving pictures and gives information on the merchandise. For example, when clothing is being featured, models may be shown walking down a runway or posing to music. The viewer uses his or her telephone or home computer to order products shown in this form of video merchandising.

ROLES IN ELECTRONIC MEDIA PRODUCTIONS

There are three capacities in which models may be employed in electronic media productions: on-camera principal, extra, and off-camera player.

An On-Camera Principal

An on-camera principal is an individual who appears on camera and either has lines or does not have lines to speak. His or her appearance plays an important part in the production. In a commercial production, he or she is closely identified with the product or service being featured.

An Extra

An extra is an individual who gives atmosphere to a scene but whose role is not vital to the storyline or product. Extras are used in crowd scenes in films or in commercials to lend realism to a particular scene where people other than the main character are present.

An Off-Camera Player

An off-camera player is an individual whose face does not appear on camera. Hand models are off-camera players. Hand models, or product demonstrators as they are sometimes called, not only have attractive hands but also have the dexterity and grace to accomplish a variety of tasks necessary to emphasize a client's product. For example, a commercial may require a hand model to perfectly pour a cup of coffee (no splattering and to just the right level in the cup) using a steady hand and one graceful motion in a designated number of seconds. It is also important that the hand model's hands stay on the mark or spot that is necessary for proper camera focus and composition. This motion may have to be done several times to achieve the desired effect.

Hands of all types and looks are employed in television commercials. Long, elegant-looking hands with beautiful tapering nails are referred to as cosmetic hands and are used to model or demonstrate cosmetics or other glamour-oriented products. Smallish, attractive, more average-looking hands are called noncosmetic hands and may show household products. In addition, hand models are often used to provide the hands for a celebrity or actor who is making a commercial, but whose hands are less than ideal for the camera. In addition to the hands, other body parts such as feet or legs may be used to show or demonstrate a product.

A voice-over artist is another example of an off-camera player. Voice-over work is done by individuals with outstanding voices and the ability to make words come alive. In voice-over work only the voice is heard; the model or actor does not appear on camera. Voice-over artists are employed to narrate entire productions and deliver lines, tag lines, and bulletins in commercials and other productions for radio, television, and films. Basically there are four types of work within the voice-over category:

1. Straight announcing refers to the majortiy of voices heard in commercials. The voice may be heard explaining the product while it is being shown. It may be used at the end of a commercial to tell where the product can be purchased in the area (this is referred to as a "call-to-buy" tag), or the voice may be used for dubbing if the on-camera performer's voice is unsuitable or unavailable.
2. Character voices are funny or unusual-sounding voices heard in commercials and animated cartoons.
3. Industrial/educational voices are used to narrate films, slide presentations, and the like for industrial and educational uses. This is a very conservative, informative, and authoritative voice.
4. Jingle singers sing the songs or lines in commercials.

The majority of voices used in the voice-over field are male. As in other areas, versatility is helpful. Voice-over talents must possess interesting, unusual, or attractive voices that will captivate a listener's attention. They must be able to intepret words and make a script come alive. A strong acting background is helpful. The voice-over artist does not have the benefit of facial expressions and gestures with which to communicate. Everything must be conveyed through the voice.

Vocal skills are also a necessity. Sounds of breathing as well as mouth and lip noises must be absent for a professional presentation. Sometimes the structure of the mouth, the formation of the teeth, or even the size of the tongue can preclude an individual from pronouncing words precisely. These disadvantages may not be noticeable in everyday conversation or even in on-camera appearances where the actor's performance can make less-than-ideal pronunciation undetectable. At other times an unusual speech pattern may add to a performance. For example, a minor speech impediment, such as a slight hiss when pronouncing "s" sounds may not be noticeable in everyday situations and may even enhance an on-camera presentation.

A voice trained to be versatile is so important because the artist must be able to alter his or her presentation. Understanding the concepts that can be employed to make the voice sound different, such as phrasing, intonation, range, and accent, is necessary. Being directable is another important trait for anyone hoping to succeed in the voice-over field. If an individual refuses to take direction or isn't able to understand and implement what he or she is instructed to do, it will be impossible to achieve the desired effect.

Technical considerations, such as the ability to work a microphone, are also important. Overprojection may be great for the theater, but it is a problem in a recording studio. Another plus is the proverbial "clock in the head" that allows the voice-over artist to stretch or shave seconds when interpreting copy so that the commercial is properly timed. Seconds make a big difference in radio and television productions.

It is easy to understand why the voice-over field is made up primarily of individuals with either strong acting, radio, or singing backgrounds. Few models explore the field because they are accustomed to projecting ideas with their looks and movements, not their voices. If a model possesses the necessary voice and talent, the voice-over field can be very lucrative. However, it is also a difficult field in which to get started.

If you think your voice has interesting, attractive, or unique qualities, your first step should be to contact agents specializing in the voice-over field. Some modeling agencies have divisions devoted to voice-over work, but most of this work is handled through talent agencies. You can find the names of agencies in your area that handle voice work by contacting your local SAG and AFTRA union offices. Write or telephone the agency to find out how to apply.

Before you are able to secure an appointment with an agent, you may need to send a cassette that gives samples of your voice or the voices you can create. This cassette need not be professionally recorded. Reading one minute or two of copy taken from commercials or other productions is sufficient. Because the way your voice sounds when recorded is what the agent will be looking for, a voice that is intriguing when recorded like this will be even more impressive when recorded under professional circumstances. A qualified agent will understand this and be able to detect the quality of your voice and your ability to interpret copy. If he or she hears a marketable sound, you will be called to audition in person. If the agent is impressed at the interview, he or she may offer to assist you in assembling a voice-over artist's most important promotional tool—the voice tape. (See Chapter 9 for information.)

The voice-over field can be very lucrative. The majority of work is found in New York, Chicago, and Los Angeles. The reason voice work can be so lucrative is that for continuity and company image reasons, one voice is often selected to do all the commercials, tags, and so forth in a campaign for a product. Also, unless an individual possesses a very identifiable voice, conflicts and overexposure are not problems as they are when the performer's face appears.

HOW TELEVISION COMMERCIALS ARE CREATED

Generally, when a client wishes to promote a product on television, he or she hires an advertising agency to produce the commercials. To begin, the client interviews several advertising agencies to decide which one has the most experience and best ideas for promoting and marketing the type of product being featured. The agency account executive is the individual who sells the client on using the agency and acts as a link between the client and the creative staff.

Upon engaging a particular advertising agency, the agency staff and the client meet to discuss how to best promote the product. After conducting market research and deciding what marketing strategies will accomplish the goals established, two or three important advertising claims or copy points are agreed upon. These are the strongest selling points of the item and are the facts around which the elements of the commercial will revolve. The ad agency's creative supervisor then selects a creative team made up of a writer and an art director, based on their experience and familiarity with the type of product involved, to work on the concept and details of the commercial.

Budget is also an important consideration at this time, with the agency account supervisor outlining the finances. Large budget commercials can include costly special effects, elaborate sets, or exotic locations and employ well-known personalities or numerous actors.

From this point the agency begins work on developing the idea into a proposed commercial. Sometimes this is done by producing demo commercials showing three or four different approaches. From these the client decides on the preferred approach. The client may decide to use all four approaches in four different commercials. Demo commercials are used to give the client a general idea of the proposed commercial and employ simple, less expensive production methods.

After the approach is determined, the writer from the agency (called a copywriter) composes the dialogue to be used. A storyboard is drawn up. It consists of small pictures with the dialogue written alongside the appropriate action. At this stage, several meetings and discussions are held to finalize all decisions before production takes place. Legal clearance is important to be sure that claims made in the spot can be supported and that nothing said about a competitor is libelous. Next, the agency assigns a producer on staff whose job it is to get all parts of the commercial together. The producer, taking into consideration financial and creative concerns, assigns the work to a director and a production house that will do the actual filming and producing. Commercials are not produced at the ad agency but at a production house that supplies all the necessary elements, such as the set, cameras, lighting and sound equipment, technicians, and props. After the production house is hired and the budget is approved, the actual particulars of producing the commercial get under way. This may include scouting for a location to shoot the commercial, selecting props, or designing sets. Casting begins at this point.

Auditions are held at the advertising agency, casting director's office or production house and are recorded on videotape. Sometimes only a few people are auditioned, and the talent will be found after a single casting session. At other times, 20 sessions and hundreds or models or actors may be auditioned before the right faces and talents are found. This all depends on how much time there is to cast, the specific casting requirements, advertising agency politics, and the personalities and preferences of the people making the casting decisions.

Casting for television commericals may be done by an ad agency, a production house, or an independent casting service or by all three simultaneously. The decision on which models or actors will be used in a commercial is made by several people; however, the final decision rests with the client.

To begin the casting process, the producer of the commercial fills out a request-for-casting form for the casting department or director. This form outlines everyone's ideas of what the characters should be like, as defined by their age, size, look or type, coloring, special skills or talents, and special features. Typecasting is a common practice in selecting talent for television commercials and is subjective to a point; often variations of basic types are auditioned. Deciding on which people to invite to audition may be done in several ways. The casting director may have a few specific people in mind that he or she feels will be just right, the casting director may search his or her files of glossies to get ideas or find people, or the director and other creative people from the ad agency are asked to make suggestions. Casting orders might also be placed at modeling agencies asking them to send over all the models who might meet the description.

AUDITIONING FOR ELECTRONIC MEDIA PRODUCTIONS

When your agency informs you of an audition, complete an Audition Form (see Chapter 9) to ensure that you get complete, accurate information. You will more likely have an effective audition if you are fully prepared. Find out what type of role is being cast and dress the part. (See Chapters 5 and 9 for more information.) If you are given no instructions regarding what to wear, look your type; that is, go to the audition looking like the picture on your commercial headshot.

Step-by-Step Guide to Auditioning

Following are some of the most common components of television commercial auditions and recommendations on how to proceed.

Arrival

Interviews or auditions for television commercials are usually set 5 to 10 minutes apart, so it is important that you always be on time or early. Arriving a few minutes early will allow you to check your hair and makeup. Also, you will have to perform a few tasks before auditioning.

Sign In

At most commercial auditions, large auditions, and all SAG-governed auditions, you will have to write your name, social security number, the time you arrive, and the time of your audition on a sign-in sheet. (See the Audition Report form.) This determines the order in

Audition Report Form

Audition Date _____

Casting Rep. _____ Commercial Title _____

Advertiser _____ Product _____ Job No. _____

Advertising Agency _____ City _____

Studio/Production Co. _____

Player's Name	Soc. Sec. No.	Agent	Actual Call Time	Time In	Time Out	Interview 1–2–3–4	Player's Initials

Authorized Signature _____

which you will be interviewed or auditioned and serves as a record for the casting director once the auditions have finished. On jobs governed by performers' unions, for example, SAG, these forms are used by the casting director when checking to find out if you are a member in good standing with the union. Another function of these sheets in this case is to ensure that union members kept at the audition for more than an hour will be paid overtime.

Paperwork   After you sign in, you may be given a casting sheet that acts as an information record for each talent auditioned. (See the Casting Sheet in Chapter 9.) List your name and your agent's telephone number and your answering service number. The casting sheet may also serve as a conflict sheet or you may be given a separate sheet of paper to sign, stating that you are not currently advertising products that are similar in nature to the one for which you are auditioning. These products will be listed on the conflict sheet.

You may also be asked to sign a statement that you have not been photographed in the nude or in any compromising situation. This may be done by a company promoting a conservative or family-oriented product or image.

When you have completed the paperwork, you will hand it to the person in the auditioning room along with your headshot and resume. If models are being interviewed, composites will be accepted.

Polaroids   Polaroids are not taken at all auditions, but when they are taken at electronic media auditions, they are used mostly for purposes of identification or reference. Polaroids are not usually used to determine casting choices. The casting director may use Polaroids to group families together or to match other characteristics.

The Script   You will be handed a script and directed to a studio or waiting room where there probably will be other models. Use this time wisely, don't socialize. Prepare as thoroughly as possible so that you will look professional. Even if you don't get the job, if you can impress the casting director during the audition, you will be asked back again to audition for other jobs.The following are some ways to prepare:

- Read the script over and analyze it carefully.
- Read the lines of the script aloud. They often sound differently when spoken. If the script calls for dialogue between two people, read the lines aloud with another model. Focus on the words and phrases that are important and that you should emphasize. Notice which words are there just to connect key words.
- Think about some ways to add your own input. There is no one right way to act out a script. Interviewers at the audition will be interested in seeing what you can do with the words.
- Run through the script incorporating all these elements. At some auditions you will find that you will have lots of time to study (15 minutes), other times you will be given the script only 30 seconds before you have to audition. Sometimes you will be given a script to study a day or two in advance of the audition.

The Audition   In the next phase you will be ushered into the room where you will audition. You may have to audition before a group of people or for only the casting director and one other person. Get accustomed to auditioning in front of groups. At the first audition for a product, the client usually conducts a "cattle call" or "look see" to screen all the prospects. For call backs or subsequent auditions, more people who make decisions will be involved in the session. Some of those most commonly present at auditions are the following.

Casting director. The casting director is on your side and hopes that you do a good job because he or she has chosen you and is presenting you to the client. If you do well, it's a good reflection on the casting director's ability to pick the right people to audition. If impressed, he or she will keep in you mind for future auditions.

Director. The director is generally in charge of the session and holds the most responsibility for talent selection, along with the client. The director may be a self-employed independent contractor or he or she may work for a film or video production company.

Producers. There are usually two producers. The producer from the advertising agency oversees the whole production, from conception and budgeting, through talent selection and session coordination, to final editing of the tape or film. The producer from the production company makes all the specific arrangements for the shooting, such as finding the location or building the set where it will take place, supervising the technical crew, and so on.

Copywriter, creative director, and art director. These three people work together to create the commercial. They have very specific ideas about the characters, situation, and the like because they have formulated the scenes and action of the commercial. However, they usually do not direct actors during the audition. They attend to check that the models or actors are following the script the way it was intended or written.

Others. The account executive may attend final auditions. He or she is the one who links the advertising agency with the client. The client usually will not be present at the audition unless it is a very small ad agency or the company is doing the commercial in-house. Usually the ad agency selects only the best taped auditions to show to the client for final approval. Employees of the advertising agency who have nothing else to do or are on their coffee breaks may drop in because they like the entertainment of auditions. Video camera operators, the technicians who run the video recording equipment, might also be present.

The following events will take place:

Direction
The person in charge will give you general information about what is wanted or about the character and situation. This person may also tell you where to stand and give instructions on using or holding a prop or how to do a particular movement. These activities are referred to as "blocking." If you have any questions, ask them at this point. Don't criticize; ask only for clarification. In many cases there will be no direction. The people in charge may want to see what you do with what you are given. You may be given the script a few minutes before auditioning and be expected to use your own ideas and interpretation.

Run-Through
This is the rehearsal before the audition is recorded on the VTR (videotape recorder). You should perform the action exactly as you would if the camera were on. If you will be reading from cue cards, ask to read them through before your rehearsal. If you are not offered a run-through and it would make you feel more confident, ask for one.

Recording
Slating is the first thing you will do when recording begins. Slating is done for reference purposes. You will give your name and you may also be asked to state the modeling agency that sent you or to possibly identify the take. You may also have to give other specific information, such as height and age, if it is pertinent to the commercial. It is important to slate every take.

After slating you will begin the reading. This is your chance to show them how well you can make the script come to life. Follow directions and perform when the camera is rolling. A red light indicates that the camera is on. Don't rush through the script, trying to get the audition over with; this is how they will remember you. When reading the script, remember to hold the paper motionless, down and parallel to the floor, so that your face or voice is not obstructed. Try to look up from the script as much as possible.

You may be requested to do something specific to make your performance more impressive. For example, if you are being considered for a commercial advertising a hair product, you may be asked to swing your hair because it may be one of the actions seen in the commercial.

Many of the parts in commercials filled by models do not have lines. The model is just used as an attractive face. If this is the case, you may or may not be given a script. The commercial makers will be most concerned with how you fit the role, whether you are expressive and can take direction, and how you look and move on videotape. Sometimes you may be required to portray a simple action or a certain emotion using a facial expression (for example, tasting a soft drink and smiling). You may be given general or specific directions. They will start the VTR, you will slate and then do the action they have requested, or what they direct you to do from behind the camera. At the very least, you may be asked to look straight into the camera, look left profile, right profile, and smile.

Critique

Sometimes you will be given direction after the recording about how you can improve or change what you did. Accept all suggestions in an amicable, open-minded way. Then concentrate on how to implement the suggestions. If you feel you really failed during the recording, ask for (don't insist) a second chance by suggesting that you have a different approach you would like to try. It is not a good idea to criticize yourself or what you have done. After the critique, you will be retaped or asked to give a revised run-through.

After the Audition

At this point you may be asked a few other questions concerning such things as your experience, availability, and whether you look good in a certain hairstyle. Always leave with a pleasant remark and a smile. Don't forget to mark the time you leave on the sign-in sheet. You will usually not get to see the tape of your audition, and you will usually not be told immediately following the audition if you have gotten the job. They will contact your agent. Don't linger around after the audition, discussing the latest gossip with other models. You should always give the impression that you have places to go and things to do. Also, don't ask to see the Polaroid or videotape that was taken of you. This is unprofessional; the interviewers don't care what your assessment is and are usually pressed for time. Finally, never make excuses for your lack of preparation or less than ideal performance. Never blame your shortcomings on the script or situation.

SKILLS FOR ACTING IN ELECTRONIC MEDIA PRODUCTIONS

Whether you plan to work in television commercials, industrial films, soap operas, or any other type of electronic media production, you will need to acquire acting skills. Although a certain amount of natural talent is necessary it is possible to tap your talents more fully and to gain new ideas and fresh approaches by taking acting classes. There are several types of instruction that can benefit a model or other individual seeking acting work such as studies in improvisation, body movement, and voice. Television technique classes are also valuable and will help the model to increase his or her skills in this area. Seeing yourself acting out a scene on videotape is an excellent way of practicing and honing your skills and talents.

Television Acting Techniques

There are three basic phases than an actor goes through to prepare for a performance: analysis (of the script and instructions), warm up, and rehearsal.

Analyzing How to Act in an Electronic Media Production

The first step in preparation for a performance is to observe and analyze all the information that is available to you. The main points you'll want to consider are covered here.

What Product, Service, or Idea Is Being Promoted?

If possible, try the product prior to the commercial shooting. Or do some informal research. Find out what it is about the product that the commercial maker is trying to play up. Is it the price, design, its convenience, or a new way of using an old product?

Who Is the Character You Are Portraying?

Think about all the characteristics of your character: How old is she? What does she look like? What is her occupation? What is her marital status, economic status, geographic location, and general situation in life and what are her personality characteristics? Take on the physical characteristics of your character such as her posture, voice, and facial expressions. Consider your character's motivations in this situation. In other words, what is the character's objective? What is your character's point of view toward the product, the setting, the activity, the other characters, and the situation in general? Is she happy, disgusted, nosy, worried, sad, annoyed, angry, bored, or efficient?

What Is the Purpose of This Production or Commercial?

If it is a commercial, its purpose is obviously to sell products or services, but it can be taken further than this. Every advertiser has a marketing problem to overcome. There may be some obstacle that inhibits the sale of the client's product or service to every single human being. Maybe the product or the company wants to change its image. In other types of productions the purpose may be public service, educational, public relations, and so forth.

What Is the Overall Mood of the Commercial?

Commercials fall basically into two categories; hard sell or soft sell. A hard-sell commercial has a straight sales pitch; often the spokesperson talks about the product or the offer in a straightforward way; for example, a used car dealer who barks out prices and tells about his inventory or a testimonial where a satisfied customer compares two brands. An example of a soft-sell commercial would be the vignette or slice-of-life spot. This may be a minidrama with a clear beginning, middle, and end; for instance, a worker comes through for her boss and is commended. Soft-sell spots can run the gamut from comedy to drama to tragedy, or they can be educationally oriented.

There are variations in the hardness or softness of hard- and soft-sell spots. Know whether what you are doing is supposed to be entertaining, funny, or serious. Within the commercial there may be different moods or transitions. For example, in the beginning the character may have a miserable cold and look and feel terrible, but after using the product, she is relieved, happy, and ready for action. Notice whether the commercial's mood is high key (high energy), comedic (displaying cartoon-like characters), or low key displaying serious, credible characters.

Where and When Does the Action Take Place?

What is the setting? Where is your character? Why is he there? Is this a familiar or strange place to him? How does he feel about being in this place? What time of day, what season, and what year is it? Does this influence how the character acts?

Are There Other Characters in the Scene?

What is your relationship to the other characters? Who are they and what do they have to do with your character? Does your character know them, are they strangers, are they relatives? What is her attitude toward them? Is your character the one giving or receiving advice? Is your character responsible for the main action or does she react to the main action? Who is your character talking to? Herself, another character, the product, or the audience?

What Is the Basic Storyline?

Ask to see the storyboard. Divide the commercial or scene into a beginning, middle, and end; question and answer; or problem and solution. The beginning will probably be the part that captures a viewer's interest. The middle will contain the name of the product, what it does, why it is better than other products, and what the product can do for the viewer. The end will tell the viewer to buy it, where it's available, what sizes and colors it comes in, and how it can be purchased.

Who Is My Audience?

To whom are they trying to sell this idea? Is the target audience composed of business executives or homemakers? Think about ways you can relate to your viewers and make them want to listen to you and believe what you say.

What Props or Blocking Instructions Are There?

The physical activity you must perform is referred to as "blocking." You will not only have to remember your lines and how and when you are to say them, but you must pay attention to your movements and your marks (where exactly you are to stand, perform a movement, etc.). In addition, you may be given specific instructions for handling a product or prop. What you have to say is as important as what you have to do.

What Can I Do with the Script?

Examine the script for copy points, that is, key words and phrases. Think about how you will emphasize the key words. Punching a word means emphasizing it by increasing or decreasing the volume of your voice (saying selected words louder or softer) or raising or lowering your voice a note or two. It also means pausing a second just before or just after the word. Punching a word might also be done by emphasizing a vowel or consonant within the word. For example, when talking about how smooth and soft a lotion makes your skin feel, you emphasize the word smooth "smo-o-o-o-th" and soften your voice when saying "soft."

Practice emphasizing different words in the sentence to see where emphasis should be placed to best express the meaning. Think about detailed gestures when to blink your eyes or minor facial expressions that will add to your presentation. Effectively using your face, body, and voice as instruments of expression will result in the best presentation.

Are There Specific Instructions from the Director, Client, or Cameraperson?

Follow any instructions to the letter. Determine how you fit into the frame of the shot. Does the camera zoom in on your hands, is it a closeup of your face, or will you be seen only from the waist up? Framing will affect your actions and facial expressions. If the camera sees you from a distance, your actions will be bigger; if close up, a subtle action such as blinking your eyes will be obvious.

What Is the Timing? How much time will you have? How fast does the dialogue or the action have to be? What are the transitions or different scenes within the commercial or production with which you must be concerned? What rhythms are necessary in transitions or dialogue? In successful commercials all the elements fall into place perfectly without the audience's awareness of the timing or cues.

Warm-Up Before you act out a scene it is helpful to do some warm-up exercises to loosen up your body and to stimulate ideas for your character. There are lots of different techniques that actors use to warm up. Many of the techniques for gaining inspiration for print modeling explained in Chapter 10 will work equally well for using your imagination for acting. Some of the most common techniques actors use are covered here.

Visualization Visualization means that you see a mental picture of yourself acting out the scene. This helps to get your physical being and your mind synchronized.

Meditation Meditation techniques can be used to clear any extraneous thoughts or feelings from your mind to allow it to concentrate on the role at hand. Meditation can also be used to get yourself into the mindset or mood of the character you are portraying.

Flashbacks Use flashbacks of your own past experiences to create the emotion your character is to have. For example, if you are to act angry, think of a personal experience that made you angry and relive it.

Physical Exercises Physical exercises can stimulate your body and brain and can also help you to relax. Many actors employ breathing, aerobic, or muscle relaxation techniques to help induce the desired mood.

Acting Exercises Another way to warm up for a performance is to try some of the following simple exercises. For example, try turning around and at the completion of your turn take on the mood of your character. Or, try the same exercise but to shift into the character walk through a doorway or into another room.

Rehearsal Rehearsal is used to combine all the elements together for a performance. When rehearsing concentrate on really getting into your character rather than on just reciting your lines or actions. Be flexible and try actions and dialogue implementing different ideas until you come across the right combination. Remember that to be a good actor or actress you must set yourself and your personal feelings apart from the character and do what is necessary to accurately portray him or her. For example, it does not matter that you yourself would not behave in the way your character is behaving or agree with what he or she says. What matters is that you totally become that character physically and psychologically when called upon to perform. What will set you apart as a good actor is the individual contribution you make to the performance.

ON THE JOB	Understanding on-the-job procedures will make the assignment go more smoothly. It may be helpful to participate as an extra in a variety of electronic media productions when starting your career so that you will know what goes on. The information that follows is a basic guide to on-the-job procedures.

The People Involved in Electronic Media Productions	Cooperation with co-workers is important for achieving the best result. The following is a list of people you will be working with in electronic media productions.

Principals. Principals are actors seen on camera that are very identifiable and do or do not have lines.

Extras. Extras are other people in the commercial who are not identified or involved with the product in any way.

Off-camera players. Off-camera players are hand models or product demonstrators who handle and demonstrate the product. Off-camera players also include announcers who are heard and not seen. Voice-over artists are also off-camera players and usually do their work, such as tagging phrases or giving locations where the product is available, after the commercial has been filmed or videotaped.

Makeup artist. A makeup artist is someone trained in techniques of television makeup. The makeup artist does the actors' or models' makeups from start to finish to create the look desired by the director. The makeup artist also does touchups along the way.

Hairdresser. The hairdresser styles the hair according to the director's instructions and maintains the style during shooting.

Specialists. A wardrobe stylist is responsible for clothing and accessories for the actors. Unlike photo shootings, there will probably be a specialist for each area: one for props, one for wardrobe, and others. For food commercials, one or more food stylists or home economists will be employed to make food look luscious and photogenic. When a hand model is employed, a property person is very important to her performance. One of his or her duties may be to strip the inside of a jar lid so that the hand model can remove it in one graceful turn.

Director. A director is the individual who directs the entire operation, giving blocking and dialogue instructions to the actors. Directors usually are specialized according to the type of commercial or product. A director is hired because his or her work exhibits a certain look or concept, just like a photographer's work exhibits a certain look. Some still photographers also direct electronic media productions.

Working with the Director	Directors, like still photographers, have different working styles. Here are some ways in which they differ in directing style. Depending on the job or situation at hand, one director may encompass several of these variables.

Concept-oriented versus spontaneous. A director who is highly concept-oriented has definite and exacting ideas on every element in the commercial. This director will spend a lot of time getting things exactly the way he or she wants them and may give you detailed instructions about what is going to occur and how it is to be done. The spontaneous director's approach is done in a free-flow way, with little instruction. A spur of the moment candid look is sought. This director also knows exactly what he or she wants but achieves it in a different way. This type of director often works with children who have a short attention span.

Negative versus positive approach. The director with a negative approach elicits what he or she wants from talent by telling them to stop doing certain things. A positive approach capitalizes on the good aspects of a talent's performance and makes suggestions for improvements. The negative approach gets the message across faster but might not work as well for all talent, particularly those with inflated egos or little experience.

Motivational versus imitational approach. A director with a motivational approach puts the talent in the setting and explains how the character feels and why. A director using the imitational approach might say the line of diaglogue the way he or she wants it delivered and have the talent parrot the line. Or the director may assume the posture or movement the actor is to do and have the talent imitate. Often the imitational approach works well for inexperienced actors.

Other Crew Members

Assistant director. The assistant director helps the director by organizing the cast and crew and making sure that they are available to the director when needed. The assistant director takes care of all the details in regard to talent, such as having performers where they should be at all times. In addition, the assistant director sees that contracts are signed and shooting runs smoothly.

Camera person. Usually there are one to three camera persons headed by the director of photography, who determines how the shot is lit and how the cameras will move to get the desired effect. The assistant camera person takes light readings and determines correct focusing. Other than the director, the camera person is the only one who will give talent directions when doing the scene; these may include where to stand and how close the camera will be.

Gaffers. Gaffers are electricians who move lights and equipment.

Grips. Grips are individuals who move cameras and sets.

Set designer. The set designer designs the set and appears at the shooting to make certain that plans have been executed correctly.

Sound person. Sound is handled by one or two engineers who record the dialogue in a filmed commercial.

Property person. The property person is the individual responsible for props and products.

Script supervisor. The script supervisor times each take and makes certain that each successive shot can be properly edited into the final commercial.

Client. The client is the representative from the company that manufactures the product being sold.

Agency copywriter. The agency copywriter is the individual who has formulated the concept and written the dialogue of the commercial. He or she is present to see that each filmed sequence is in keeping with his or her words and concept.

Agency art director. The agency art director deals with all the visual aspects of the commercial and determines the final "look" of it.

Agency account executive. The ad agency account executive acts as a liason between the client and the agency.

Agency producer. The agency producer is the person who casts the commercial and deals with the production company, director, editor, and the like. He or she is responsible for bringing together the various elements of the commercial to produce the desired result.

Studio producer or production manager. The studio producer is part of the production company. His or her job is to coordinate and oversee the mechanics at the shooting. When the agency producer is not present, the production manager or studio producer takes over. He or she ensures that payment, meals, and transportation of the crew is handled correctly.

On-the-Job Checklist
Before the Booking

When you find out that you have gotten the job, either your agent will provide you with all the particulars for the job or you will be instructed to get in contact with the production company, producer, assistant producer, or director of the shooting.

Always find out as much as possible about the booking beforehand. Know what will be expected of you. Find out if you are to get a script and study it prior to the shooting, whether you are to supply wardrobe, or when a wardrobe check or fitting will be scheduled. The other most important facts to know are your "call time," the exact time you are to arrive, and where you are to go. Complete a Booking Form found in Chapter 7 so you will be fully prepared.

When You Arrive

When you arrive at the booking, introduce yourself or report to the person you have been told to contact. Usually you will check in with the production assistant or assistant director. At this point, you may have to complete some paperwork, such as filling out federal and state tax forms, a union contract, and consent and release forms.

You will then be directed to makeup and wardrobe. Don't be determined to do your own makeup. Makeup artists employed for electronic media productions are specially trained and know what will look best for the lighting and the camera. Wear what you are given to wear. Don't complain about the clothes, makeup, or hairstyle; the client and director are trying to create a specific effect. Defer to their decisions. They have the final say. Extras usually do their own makeup and hair. Use makeup and wardrobe time wisely by going over your lines, studying the script, doing a few warm-up exercises, and the like. While you are doing this, the set is being readied.

After you and the set are prepared, the director will call for a run-through or rehearsal. Often you will not see any of the same faces at the shooting as at the audition. Casting directors rarely attend TV commercial shootings.

On the Set

While you're in makeup or when your makeup is finished, the director may give you some preliminary instruction about interpreting the script or action (blocking instructions). Listen carefully to these instructions to avoid repetition once you are under the lights. Know in which segments you are to appear.

Rehearsal is the next phase. Depending on the number of lines or the spontaneity that is needed, you may not have seen the lines you are to speak until rehearsal. You will have plenty of time to learn them, so don't worry about making mistakes. The rehearsal is necessary for everyone, not just you. The director will be checking out the lighting, camera angles, and background. You should use this time to practice your lines and action.

If you are given very little instruction, rely on your own creativity, but adhere to what you did at the audition. The qualities you presented then are probably the ones for which you were hired. Specifics may be worked out later.

Don't criticize the script or suggest changes. These words have been worked over by copywriters and the advertising agency's creative team many times to get them just right. Don't argue with the director about the interpretation of the script in front of other actors and crew. If you feel strongly about something, discuss it with the director in private.

Treat everyone on the set with equal importance. Makeup artists, hairstylists, wardrobe assistants, and technicians can either help or hinder you, depending on your attitude. Be friendly and cheerful to everyone on the set, but don't be a pest who constantly talks and asks questions. Don't try to be helpful by moving things or doing anything other than your job. Everyone is unionized and has his or her specific job.

If you are an extra, you will receive instruction along with a group of other extras. Your part should not demand as much time and attention as the key characters, and you should concentrate on being part of the group or the background.

After the initial rehearsal, there may be a break to iron out minor technical problems or to refreshen your makeup and hair.

Filming   Before the taping begins, you might do a few more run-throughs. This is the time to clarify any questions you might have. Do your run-throughs exactly the way you would perform if the cameras were rolling.

Learn the jargon used in film and video productions. Some of the most common terms are the following.

- "Places on the set" means that everyone involved in the scene being shot is to be present under the lights, ready for direction.
- "Let's do a take" or "let's do a scene" means get ready to do a shooting.
- "Quiet" means the microphones are on and the sound recording will begin. There should be no talking at all.
- "Stand by" means get ready to start.
- "Camera" means the camera is on.
- "Slate it" means the scene to be filmed is identifed on a slate placed in front of the camera and the information is spoken.
- "Speed" means all elements are in place, camera, talent, ID, and sound.
- "Action" means talent is to begin the action, dialogue, etc.
- "Cut" is the cue to stop the action.

The scenes in a commercial are often not shot in sequence so it is important that you are alert to what is happening. Once filming has begun, keep an eye out for what is going on, and listen for your name being called. Don't stray far from the set, and when not on the set, keep quiet. Always bring along a good book or quiet tasks to do while waiting in between shots. In TV, everything is "hurry up and wait." Don't disappear between shots. If you must leave the area, always let someone know where you will be.

When you are on the set under the lights, don't carry on conversations with other models or actors. Always be alert to what is going on and be ready to listen to new instructions.

Don't ask how you look in a shot or if you can see the playback of the tape. Never suggest to the cameraperson how he or she should shoot you or what your best angles are. Get accustomed to being watched by lots of people during production. Concentrate on what you are doing and on your contact with the director. If you are an extra, be as natural and unobtrusive as possible. Don't be determined to get your face on camera.

At the End of the   Don't ask to leave early even if you have finished all your segments.
Booking   Retakes may be necessary. When the director says "it's a wrap," this means that shooting for the day is finished. Once you are dismissed, gather up your belongings, take care of any paperwork, and thank the key people. Don't linger around the set with other models, adding to the confusion.

OTHER CONSIDERATIONS FOR PERFORMERS IN ELECTRONIC MEDIA PRODUCTIONS

If your aim is to make a career of performing in electronic media productions, you will have to deal with performer's unions. It is not necessary to join a union before you start getting television commercial jobs. There are several circumstances in which union membership is not required.

- If you live in a right-to-work state. In these states there is no obligation to hire SAG (Screen Actor's Guild) or AFTRA (American Federation of Television and Radio Artists) talent for commercial productions. Within these states there may be areas or cities that are unionized, and these are called "preference zones."
- If the maker of the commercial is not signatory. Some producers of electronic media productions have no affiliation with performer's unions.
- If the commercial is made outside of a union "preference zone." This may be 100 to 150 miles from the center of any city where a SAG or AFTRA union office is located.
- If the maker of the commercial can get a waiver. Legally, according to the Taft-Harley Law, you cannot be denied employment solely because you are not a union member. However, casting directors who are sanctioned by the unions will be fined if they hire nonunion performers unless they can get a waiver. Modeling agencies and casting directors must be sanctioned by the unions if they want to provide talent for union-governed auditions, which includes most productions. A waiver means an exception to the rules, and it can be obtained by a casting director if he or she can prove that you have special skills or talents that are necessary for the commercial, or if he or she can prove that you are a professional. Representation by an agent, extensive training in acting or television technique, or performance in nonunion situations will qualify you as a professional. According to the waiver, you may do the job at hand and any jobs you can get in a 30-day period, starting on the day you signed the waiver. You are not required to be a union member to participate in a commercial if you are the president, owner, or employee of a company and you appear on camera as yourself, doing what you normally do. If you are a "real person" giving a testimonial and are doing the commercial as a one-time acting job, you are exempt.
- If this assignment is your first union-sanctioned job. The union allows you to do one job (that comes under the union's jurisdiction) before you must join the union.

Although it is possible to obtain many opportunities that do not fall under union jurisdiction, there are many good reasons for belonging to a union if you want to become very involved in radio and TV. When working at union-sanctioned jobs generally you will be provided with better working conditions. You also will obtain benefits and receive more money for the jobs you do. On nonunion jobs you must rely on what the market will bear or whatever you or your agent can get.

The two unions that have jurisdiction over commercials are SAG and AFTRA. The purpose of the unions is to act as a bridge between the creative and business communities and to lend credibility to the business and promote professionalism.

AFTRA. The American Federation of Television and Radio Artists covers live and taped performances on television and radio (all radio commercials). AFTRA is an open union, meaning that anyone can join. There is a one-time initiation fee plus semiannual dues based on how much money you make doing radio and TV work. The more money you make, the higher your semiannual dues.

SAG. The Screen Actor's Guild governs everything that is done on film and most on-camera and voice-over commercials. (Some commercials are produced on videotape and still come under the jurisdiction of SAG.) SAG is more of a professional's union and becoming a member is more difficult.

To qualify for SAG you must have been a member of AFTRA or one of the other show business unions, such as AEA (Actors Equity Association) or AGVA (American Guild of Variety Artists), for a full year and have worked as a principal performer at least once under the jurisdiction of that union. The other way you can join SAG is to secure a job that is under their jurisdiction. There is a one-time initiation fee for SAG, which is about double that of AFTRA. Semiannual dues are also collected and are based on a sliding scale depending on how much money the talent makes. If the talent belongs to another four-A guild, he or she pays a reduced fee.

If you are selected for a videotaped television commercial, you must join AFTRA before your first appearance. If the work you have been hired to do is on film, you will be allowed to appear on one TV film before you must join SAG. However, after 30 days you may not appear in any other TV films without joining SAG.

Functions of Television Unions

Television unions do the following:

- Regulate the rates that commercials pay and monitor work so that performers are paid fairly.
- Provide benefits, such as insurance, pension, and welfare plans, for members. This is true of SAG and applies to members who have been with the union 10 years and have made $2000 or more in each of the 10 years. Pensions are paid beginning at age 55.
- Prescribe the working conditions that must exist on auditions, on the set, and while traveling to and from the set. They also establish requirements pertaining to overtime, meal breaks, and rest periods between days of shooting.
- Provide full-time staff members who are able to answer talents' questions and solve any problems they may have.
- Arbitrate any disputes between the talent and the producer once the commercial has been made.

Important Union Regulations

The following are important union regulations a model might encounter during the course of his or her work. These are not all the rules and regulations but a sampling of the major ones.

- At auditions legible cue cards must be provided for the actor.
- An actor must be paid half a session fee if he or she is asked to memorize copy prior to an audition.
- If an actor is required to improvise during an audition, it is considered a created session, and he or she must be paid accordingly.
- Producers cannot require auditioners to dress the part; they may, however, request a certain look.
- The model or actor must be paid for any time over 1 hour that he or she is required to remain at an audition.
- A model or actor must be compensated for a third audition and all subsequent auditions for the same commercial.
- Union-governed auditions and fittings for children must occur after school hours and prior to 8 PM. Actual bookings are not limited to these hours.
- Once a model or actor is booked for a commercial in SAG cities, the advertiser is committed to pay the actor whether the commercial actually gets shot or not.

- From the time the actor or model is dismissed until the first call the next day, he or she is entitled to a 12-hour rest period.
- A model or actor who must provide wardrobe for a television commercial shooting shall be compensated a union-specified amount per outfit.
- Meal periods must begin within 5½ hours after the time of the actor's call. For every half hour over the designated 5½-hour meal regulation, the actor is paid $25.
- Both SAG and AFTRA contracts stipulate that producers must issue checks to talent within a fixed amount of time. For example, session fees for TV commercials should be paid within 12 working days. Residual payments are due 15 days after the date of the first use of the commercial (Class B or C) or 15 days after the end of the week on which the commercial aired (Class A). If the producer is late with the payment, he or she must make a late payment fee to the talent.
- A modeling or talent agent cannot charge a SAG member who is promoting himself or herself as an actor for television or as a voice-over artist for the inclusion of his or her picture in an agency talent book or master reel of voices. The agent must pay these promotional costs. If the individual is promoting himself or herself as a model for print work, this does not apply.

The Model's Obligations to the Unions

In order to remain in good standing, the model should do the following.

- Keep dues current. For both SAG and AFTRA dues must be paid semiannually on May 1 and November 1.
- Participate in union officer elections and strike votes.
- Carry your union card on all union jobs and auditions.
- Complete member report forms at jobs.
- Refuse to work for any producer who is not signed to a union contract.
- Solve problems in a professional manner. If you have a problem working on the set, call your agency; they will deal with the union. If you don't have an agent, you can call the union for backing and/or advice. If necessary, a "field rep" will be sent to the site and will authorize the action that should be taken.
- Always indicate your union membership on your promotional materials. Displaying SAG or AFTRA indicates to potential clients that you have done TV or radio work, and this adds to your prestige.

Exclusivity and Conflicts

On the day of shooting a commercial, you will usually be asked to sign a contract (see Chapter 8) that states that you will not appear in commercials advertising similar competitive products or services. This is called "exclusivity" and applies only to principals and identifiable voice-overs. Extras, parts models, and unidentifiable voices are exempt. If you have entered into such an agreement and another commercial maker or manufacturer wants you to advertise a product, you must first check to see if the product or service is in competition with the one to which you are under contract. Sometimes there are gray areas in regard to what products or services comprise a conflict. Products or services are not competitive and do not comprise a conflict if

- They are manufactured or offered by the same company.
- They fall into two different categories (however, if they both claim to do the same thing in the advertisements, they will probably be in conflict).

- The advertiser did not stipulate or specifically state in your contract that you could not advertise other unrelated types of products. Sometimes an advertiser will want to prevent you from doing commercials for other products even though they are not in direct conflict with the product in his or her commercial.
- You have a written release from the first advertiser stating that you can participate in the proposed commercial.
- The commercial in which you participated was a nonexclusive type of commercial. Commercials that run to a limited audience or have a limited use, such as seasonal commercials (those related to the Christmas season), test market commercials (those used to test a product's appeal in a specific market before it is released nationally), or a commercial not intended for broadcast (such as a demo commercial made by the ad agency to show the client).

When you are asked to perform in a commercial, always discuss with the casting director and your agent where conflicts might exist between the product you are about to advertise and other products you have previously advertised. Exclusivity agreements are only for a certain period of time, so go back and look at what you have contracted. Not taking responsibility for investigating all these things can involve you in lawsuits, which could cost you anything from your fee to the cost of the entire commercial production.

Chapter 12 Modeling in Live Promotions

INTRODUCTION   National corporations, local businesses, and other concerns promoting products and services often employ promotional models to appear in person to accomplish some or all of the objectives listed below:

- .To attract attention and lend a personal touch to an exhibit, meeting, or promotional event.
- To screen prospects and to secure leads for salespeople.
- To distribute literature or samples.
- To sell a product or service.
- To take orders for a product or service.
- To demonstrate a product or service.
- To give a talk about a product, service, or company.
- To perform an act, such as singing, dancing, or magic, to attract attention to a display, product, or service.
- To field questions about a product or service.
- To direct conventioneers, to steer traffic to a designated area, to usher at a special event, and to perform other administrative tasks, such as signing up participants, filling out application forms, making name tags, etc.
- To model an item informally.
- To be the model on whom a product or technique is demonstrated.

There are several situations in which a promotional model may be employed. The most common are trade shows, promotions, sales meetings, and special events.

Trade Shows   Each year businesses spend billions of dollars to exhibit wares at expositions and trade shows around the world. There are thousands of shows held each year in the United States alone, specializing in areas such as printing, packaging, beauty products and services, home furnishings, sporting goods, textiles, construction, electronics, pharmaceuticals, chemicals, computers, office equipment, restaurant products and services, automobiles, and hardware.

The major trade shows are national and travel from city to city throughout the country. In addition, other shows are conducted regionally through local trade organizations, chambers of commerce, and public concerns.

Trade shows are one of the most effective ways for suppliers and customers in large and complex industries to get together. People who attend trade shows are afforded the opportunity of making contacts with new suppliers, solidifying existing contacts, and gathering crucial industry information on new products, procedures, and personnel changes. Exhibitors (the model's clients) participate in trade shows for different reasons. Usually they participate in order to introduce new products or to show new applications of existing products.

Many times a company will participate in a trade show to provide marketing opportunities such as scouting out potential customers, making contacts with others outside their city, and meeting decision makers in person who are in need of their products or services. Participating in a trade show is also a way of conducting impromptu research and comparing one's company and its offerings to competitors'. Even if none of these reasons exist, a company will participate in a trade show in order to be represented when their competition is present.

An exhibit booth at a trade show represents a sizable investment on the part of a company. A booth can cost from several hundreds to several thousands of dollars, depending on the show, the size, design, and construction (standard size is 10 feet by 10 feet) and whether entertainers (models, actors, dancers, etc.) are employed. The model's client carefully selects the trade shows to participate in on the basis of reaching the greatest number of valuable prospects at the lowest possible cost.

The model is employed to attract attention to the exhibit with her looks and personality, talents, product demonstration, or speaking ability. Although there may be hundreds of exhibits, most people will only visit 30 to 40 exhibits. It is the model's job to make sure that people's attention is drawn to the exhibit.

Trade shows are commonly held in major cities and resort locations usually at large convention centers or hotel exhibition rooms. New York, Las Vegas, Chicago, and Los Angeles host the most shows but many cities are gaining recognition for their excellent trade centers. The average show runs daily over a period of a week; the middle days are the busiest, while the first and last days are less busy. Usually the show is open to the public the last day or two.

Promotions

Models working in promotions perform basically the same tasks as those in trade shows. Increasing sales using person-to-person contact is the objective. However, promotions other than trade shows are an alternative for smaller businesses that cannot afford to participate in large national trade shows. Also many small businesses are strictly local and do not need exposure to sources beyond their geographical location.

Promotions for products or services may be held in a retailer's place of business such as a department store, on the street, or at any location other than a trade show or convention center. In this type of promotional work, the model may be employed to demonstrate a product, pass out literature or samples, or sell special promotional items. Promotions may pertain to anything from charge accounts to perfume and automobile tires, or it may require assisting in conducting contests, prize drawings, or other promotional gimmicks. Promotional models are hired by the retailer, the product manufacturer's regional sales representative, or a company specializing in promotional activities.

Sales Meetings

Often a company or individual participating in a trade show or sponsoring a special event will reserve a suite or meeting room (in a convention center, hotel, or restaurant) in which to entertain their most valuable customers. Here refreshments (cocktails and hors d'ouerves) are usually served. Models are employed to greet people, introduce them, and to see that everyone has refreshments. The main objective is to assist the host or hostess to ensure the success of the occasion.

Special Events   Models are often employed to participate in special events in the performance of a variety of tasks. For example, models may be present at a golf tournament to welcome participants or their families. Models may be requested to present a trophy or award at a special event, such as a competition, or to usher people who are receiving awards onto the stage at a ceremony. An association or other concern may employ a model to participate in a public relations event.

Models used in special events are often individuals who have earned some recognition by being a member of a professional cheerleading team or perfoming troupe or a winner of a beauty pageant.

Specific Capacities   Promotional models are used in the following capacities:

Hostessing/hosting. The model acts as a hostess or host by greeting people, standing at the display to create a friendly and inviting atmosphere. Models also distribute company literature or may take down the names of interested people to whom company literature will be sent.

Demonstrating. The model displays or demonstrates how a product works, giving a brief explanation of procedures and benefits to consumers.

Narrating. The model recites a script or talks about the product. He or she may give a short, basic talk or technical narration, which requires some knowledge, understanding, or experience. The model may be required to learn several paragraphs or pages of script and will be expected to deliver the script without deviating from it or he or she may be given certain facts and told to ad lib.

Performing. When used in a performing capacity, the model may be expected to dance, sing, or act in a skit. He or she might also serve as a company figurehead or symbol that would require developing the character.

Sampling. Sampling includes distributing samples or giving a customer a sample by applying a fragrance or makeup product. This would also include models who conduct wine or food tastings in stores or at exhibits.

Platform modeling. In this type of modeling the model is the person on whom an idea, product, or service is demonstrated. For example, at a cosmetology show the model will be seated before an audience and a makeup artist or hairstylist will use her face or hair to perform a demonstration in utilization of new products, applications, or techniques. The model concentrates on keeping attention focused on that procedure. The model pays attention to what is going on and gives the audience the opportunity to see what has been done from different angles. She takes on the character of the hairstyle, makeup, accessories, or other items she is modeling.

ANALYZING HOW TO PRESENT A PRODUCT OR SERVICE   When you are to present a product, analyze how to present it most effectively.

- What is the product?
- Who am I employed by? What are the basic, important facts about the company?
- What type of image does my client want me to project?
- What does the client hope to accomplish by engaging me?
- Whose attention am I trying to draw?
- What type of selling technique does this product dictate?
- What objections, obstacles, etc. can I anticipate, and how will I handle them? Are there specific facts I should know?

What Is the Product?

Look at the product and think about how you will handle and promote it. Think about the purpose of the product. Is it for entertainment? Does it solve a problem? Think of the product's attributes and be aware of its drawbacks. Read company literature regarding the product. Ask employees of the company questions you may have.

Who Is the Employer?

Do you have basic information about the company you are employed by? This includes history, products, or services offered, names of major competitors, etc. Do you know the names of the people (and their positions) you are working with in the exhibit?

What Type of Image Does My Client Want Me to Project?

Clients hire models for different reasons. One client may want a pretty, shapely girl to attract attention. A more sophisticated or conservative client will select a model who is attractive, yet presents a credible image. Another client may request a model who is an effective public speaker who has some in-depth knowledge of the company she represents. There are clients who may request a model with a specific educational qualification, such as a degree in home economics to demonstrate a food product.

Indications as to the type of image your employer will want you to project will come from the outfit you are to wear or told to furnish, the instructions you are given, and the image of the company.

What Does the Client Hope to Accomplish by Engaging Me?

Has the client hired you to demonstrate the product? If so, what particular aspects does he want you to bring to the attention of his customer? If you are given a narration to recite, think of ways to add your own input. If you are hired to glamourize, draw attention, or lend a personal touch to the exhibit, think about how you might accomplish this with your appearance, actions, and speech. Think how you might alter your approach in each situation and how to accomplish your client's purpose. Your client may have specific ideas.

Whose Attention Am I Trying to Draw?

Ask your client whose attention you will be trying to draw. Distinguish between who is and who is not important. Your client will advise you what types of people he or she wants you to pitch to. Don't waste time on someone who's just sightseeing. Your job is to attract people who will be interested in what your company is promoting. You are a catalyst to the sales force. Generally, people attending conventions are given name tags that are colored coded indicating that they are press people, manufacturer's representatives, etc. Your client will advise you of the colors on which you are to concentrate.

What Type of Selling Technique Does This Product Dictate?

Each product (and client) dictates a different selling technique. If you are employed to sample fragrances and cosmetics in a department store, you should adopt a soft-sell approach. If you are hired for a special promotion to sell a different type of item, you might be more aggressive in your sales technique.

What Objections Can I Anticipate?

You will find that no matter what the product is, people will have objections to buying or even trying it. Think of a positive comment or a solution to their objections. Learn how to screen the people you approach, spending the most time on those who appear to be in the market for your type of product. For example, if you are promoting a glamourous makeup product, you wouldn't approach a girl who is obviously too young to use it or a woman too old to be interested in it. In other words, you attempt to target potential customers.

Are There Specific Facts I Should Know?

In many situations you will have to know specific facts, for example, for an in-store promotion you should know when the special offer you are promoting will close. At a trade show, knowing particulars such as shipping and ordering information may be necessary. It will be important to know details about special promotional gimmicks used by your client for the trade show or promotion, such as reduced prices, incentives, contest rules, and the like.

PROMOTIONAL MODELING TECHNIQUES

In addition to having an attractive appearance, a promotional model's most important asset is a pleasing personality. She must be able to make people feel welcome and engage them in conversations that will help her employer. Her voice must be pleasing and interesting. Some promotional modeling assignments may require other skills. The skills most commonly needed are

- Hosting/hostessing techniques.
- Product demonstration techniques.
- Speaking and narrating.
- Selling.

Hosting/Hostessing Techniques
Greeting Visitors

Attracting visitors is one of a promotional model's most important functions. Promotional models are not employed to stand idly in an exhibit. Instead a model may use facial expressions such as a friendly smile or eye contact to draw a person to the exhibit. She may extend her hand to greet an individual or offer him or her a sample or brochure. She may say something such as asking a visitor if she can show him or her the product or she may say something unrelated to the product to begin a conversation to draw him or her to the exhibit area. A good model makes people feel as if they belong at the exhibit. Greeting people by asking their names or by reading their nametags is a good way to welcome people. Telling them about what they will see or what is planned for them is also a part of welcoming.

Giving Information or Assistance

A model may be instructed to tell something to visitors or she may answer inquiries. An informed model knows the basics of her employer's product (for example, if the product were an appliance, she would know how to turn it on and operate it) and can assist people when they are viewing it. If the model is not expected to know such information, she will be able to introduce the visitor to someone in the booth who does know (usually a salesperson).

Ending Encounters with Visitors

A competent model is able to assess a visitor's interest in her employer's product and make sure that he or she has been given sales literature to take home or that his or her name and address has been taken for the company's mailing list. The model thanks the visitor for attending the exhibit and always ends encounters with visitors on a positive note.

Product Demonstration Techniques

Product demonstrations are an effective way to promote products. The eye perceives more than the ear, therefore, a visual presentation will be retained more accurately and for a longer period of time by the potential customer than an audio presentation. Demonstration may involve actually using the product or service, or it may involve just going through the motions of using the item while giving a step-by-step explanation of its functions or features. When you are called upon to demonstrate or display something, remember these "show and tell" techniques.

- Know your product completely, from its qualities to its quirks. Know what problems it solves and its advantages over the competition.
- If you have instructions on exactly what you are to do and say, follow them to the letter. Often, a certain presentation has already been developed by the company and found to be highly effective. It is a "magic formula" that gets results. In this case, it is suggested that you learn the presentation word for word and not change anything. The only thing you are expected to add is personality.
- Plan your presentation so you know what you are going to do first, last, and always. Anticipate all the things that could possibly go wrong and devise a plan for handling each situation. Practice your demonstration several times before attempting it in front of others. Use a tape recorder or enlist some critical friends to help you.

- If you will be creating your own presentation, stick to a quick, simple format. Don't be intent on showing all your product's capabilities. Your demonstration should not be a rundown of every function of the product but should instead give the customer enough information to capture his or her interest. Choose one or two functions to illustrate, making sure that each can be understood without a great deal of knowledge on your viewer's part. Always try to demonstrate an application that solves a problem that your viewer might have or one that attracts attention. Keep your demo short, simple, and lively. Use humor, interesting facts, and the like to make it memorable.

- Always have attractive well-manicured hands. Make sure the appearance of your hands does not draw attention away from the product. Bitten or jagged fingernails, chapped hands, or long clawlike nails with very deep or unusual nail colors will all detract from what you are showing. Short- to medium-length, nicely shaped nails with a subtle or medium toned nail color and smooth, well-cared-for hands make the best impression.

- Handle the product delicately and gracefully. Impart value and importance by the way you handle it. Treat the product as though it were expensive and fragile. Remember to show your hands attractively, always slightly in profile. Keep your fingers relaxed, slightly flexed, and spaced. Avoid rigid, pointy fingers or awkward, grasping, masculine hand positions. Have a graceful, unexaggerated, natural bend to your wrist.

- Try to keep the product in your hands or on your territory. Avoid handing it over to the prospective customer (unless you are instructed to do so) because once he or she takes the item and begins to examine it, you will lose his or her attention. Hold the product just far enough away from him or her that it will seem rude for him or her to reach over and grab it. If you want to hand the item to the prospect, do so but retrieve it before going on with your talk.

- When you have completed getting your point across, allow the customer to touch and examine the product more closely. Retrieve the item before you transfer the customer to a salesperson or make the close on the sale. This way his or her full attention will be regained.

- Look at your prospect's face while you're talking to observe his or her facial expressions and reactions. Extend your explanation on topics that appear to catch his or her interest, briefly touch on those that lose his attention.

- When giving a demonstration, clean up as you go to give your demo a simple, uncluttered look. Make sure you have everything you started with before going onto your next demonstration. Clean your appliance or product after each demo to remove fingerprints and the like.

- If your demo fails, don't blame the product, blame yourself. Treat the occurrence with humor and either talk to divert attention away from the mishap or proceed to further demonstration. Don't dwell on it.

Presentation Techniques   When giving a presentation or speech a model must concentrate on what she has to say and how she will relate to her audience. Any kind of performance requires preparation, practice, and a way of working. The promotional model's objective is to inform and sell. Whether she is selling ideas, products, or services, specific points must be covered. In this case the model may rely on memory, notes, or a script.

The following 10 rules for giving a presentation should be observed:

1. Think first about your appearance by practicing "executive posture." A confident, direct posture will make you feel more in command and will impart authority to the image you project to your audience.

2. Begin any appearance or presentation with a smile.

3. Make eye contact with your audience. It says you believe in what you are saying and care that you have their attention. Focus on people in the back and along the sides of the room as well as those in the front.

4. Keep smiling unless the subject matter is grim, in which case you should reflect the proper concern. Return to more positive matters as soon as possible.

5. Use brief and meaningful language. Whether making a speech or answering questions, keep your statements short, simple, and to the point. In answering questions, pause for a moment before your reply to capture your listener's attention and to allow a few extra seconds to organize your thoughts. Simplicity always communicates best. Use familiar illustrations and comparisons to make your point. Make sure your comments follow a logical, organized pattern.

6. In a speech or presentation, start with the conclusion, then explain. Use the adage: tell them, tell them what you told them, and tell them again.

7. Always accentuate the positive, and don't be the one to bring up the negative. Anticipate every negative comment and have a ready reply.

8. You will immediately be able to tell how your presentation is going by looking for feedback from your audience. If they are moving around a lot, are not looking at you, or are coughing or talking, you know you are losing them. Speaking in a louder or softer tone, pausing, or saying something aside from what they expect will respark their attention.

9. If you feel tense, concentrate on looking relaxed. Drop your shoulders, take a deep breath, relax your hands and jaws. Slow down and eliminate any gestures that may give your nervousness away.

10. Make sure that with any presentation you transmit your energy to your audience. The energy you relay is directly related to your effectiveness. Use vocal techniques (punch, pause, volume), gestures, and eye contact to emphasize important points. Facial expressions and other acting techniques help to keep your presentation lively and entertaining.

Sales Techniques

In some promotional modeling situations, the model's employer will expect her to sell an item or service. Therefore, a model must understand the basics of selling. A model who is not only attractive but is creative in his or her approach will be an asset to the client. To be successful as a salesperson the model should be aware of the four stages of selling: (1) attract attention to the merchandise or service, (2) hold a potential buyer's interest, (3) kindle the potential customer's desire for what the model is trying to sell or promote, and (4) stimulate the individual to take action that leads to the purchase of the product or service.

The following are techniques a model can use when selling or promoting:

Be knowledgeable. While a promotional model is not expected to be an expert, it is important to have a basic knowledge of your client's company and its products and services in order to talk about them intelligently. It is particularly important to be well acquainted with the product or service that is being promoted at the exhibit. The following are some helpful ways to research a company before doing a show.

- Study the company's advertisements for the product or service, catalogs, sales brochures, and annual report.
- Study the competition. Read the sales literature of competing products to understand the advantages of your product over those of your competitors.
- Ask questions of the client or sales force.

Be enthusiastic. "Salesability" is simply transferring enthusiasm from one person to another. Successful salespeople have an electrifying enthusiasm for their product or services. Being enthusiastic has two effects: it keeps you "charged up," and it stimulates and helps to convince your prospect. Show that you are glad to be working for your client and excited about his or her product or service.

Be a good listener. Listen to your prospect; think about and remember what he or she says. Try to ascertain his or her needs, as well as likes and dislikes, and determine how they might be dealt with by use of your product or service. Use this information to relay the key points to the salesperson when you introduce the prospect.

Be determined. Greet and meet as many people as you can. Try to make every one of those encounters productive. Keep your courage up. Even if several people walk away from you or say they aren't interested, train yourself to keep trying. Even if the situation seems hopeless, you have nothing to lose by trying.

Be gracious. If the individual you are pitching to is obviously not interested or criticizes your product, be friendly and retain a positive attitude. A customer's rejection is not a personal affront.

THE PEOPLE INVOLVED IN PROMOTIONS

When working in an exhibit, it is helpful to know who will be there.

Booth manager. The booth manager is in charge of the exhibit. Large companies sometimes have a convention organizer, whose job it is to travel to different areas for conventions, setting up booths, and conducting exhibits.

Marketing director. The marketing director is often the person in charge of hiring the models. He or she also heads the salespeople, manages the booth, handles inquiries, and supervises activities at the exhibit. There may also be a national and local marketing director.

Sales representative. Sales reps are employed by the company's sales department and will be from the home office as well as from offices located in other cities. They will handle inquiries from distributors, buyers, and others who may attend their exhibit to look at established and new products.

Company personnel. Company personnel including the owner and/or president and managers may be at the show.

Manufacturers. Manufacturers of the product are usually on hand to answer technical questions. They will also be walking around the exhibits to look at the competition.

Buyers. Buyers attend the show and walk around the exhibit floor to look at what is available and to purchase items at special wholesale prices to sell in their stores or businesses.

Distributors. Distributors of a variety of products will be wandering around the show area to examine products they may decide to distribute to their customers.

Public relations people. Sometimes an independent public relations firm is engaged to create promotional events or exhibits for a company. Other times these responsibilities are handled by employees of the company's public relations department. A public relations person may act as a coordinator of events and be the person to whom you report. Essentially this person would be your employer or supervisor.

Department heads. Often for in-store promotions you will be directed by the head of the department that handles the merchandise you are promoting.

DEVELOPING A PROMOTIONAL MODEL'S PERSONALITY

A photographic model learns to express her personality through her movements, poses, gestures, and expressions and tailors them so that they project on film. A fashion show model expresses her personality through her posture, walk, movements, and expressions and learns to project them to her audience within the confines of a fashion show. However, the promotional model must incorporate all these aspects, the voice, and ongoing personal contact as well. The way she looks, acts, speaks, dresses, smiles, reacts, and responds all make up her personality and all determine the impression she makes on a prospect. She must have an engaging personality that wins people over and causes them to like her and (with hope) the product or service she is exhibiting. There are a few ways which may help you to develop the poise and personality a promotional model needs.

1. *Smile.* Smiles spread happiness. Not a self-conscious-looking or, worse, artificial smile, but a genuine, warm, pleasant smile—a smile that comes from really liking people. (If you don't like people, this is the wrong job for you.)

2. *Be positive.* Although you should always give the impression of being intelligent and alert, you should also always be cheerful, positive, and not too agressive. Discuss only positive matters; steer away from negative or serious concerns. Keep your opinions to yourself on everything except your product or service and use discretion in how you advance even those. Look for a positive aspect in everyone you meet. Often times conventioneers do leave something to be desired, but you can always find something to like about a person. Get out of the habit of criticizing others. You will endear yourself to everyone with whom you come into contact and will bring out the similar positive aspects found in your own personality.

3. *Be considerate of everyone.* Greet people you meet with a pleasant hello. You never know who can help you to get a lead or make a sale. Develop the habit of saying "thank you" to everyone. When you thank someone, they feel that they're being appreciated and that's an important feeling for anyone. Treat everyone with equal consideration and respect. Enjoy the people you meet.

4. *Concentrate on the other person.* Psychologists have proven that most of the time people are thinking about themselves. Prospects or customers don't want to hear about your problems, accomplishments, or activities. They'd probably prefer to talk about their own. Get the other person to do most of the talking.

5. *Build up your confidence.* Maintain a balanced combination of getting people to like you, making people believe in you, getting people to act on your recommendations, and getting people to find you literally irresistable. Build up your confidence by reliving successful encounters, not concentrating on failures. When you get into undesirable situations, be gracious and pleasant.

Etiquette for Promotional Models

1. Maintain your sense of humor. Don't be rude to or embarrass visitors who may embarrass or tease you, flirt with you, proposition you, or make off-color comments. To be rude will reflect negatively on your client. Politely ignore offers. Report any offensive behavior to the exhibitor. If undesirable behavior is displayed by the people with whom you are working, report it to your agency.

2. Don't carry on long conversations with other models or exhibit personnel while in the booth. Conduct brief conversations relevant to the job at hand quietly away from the display area. Don't invite relatives or friends for visits to your exhibit while you are working.

3. Don't leave the booth unless you get permission. Take breaks only at the usual 15-minute morning and afternoon, and 1-hour lunch breaks. Go on and return from assigned breaks at exactly the times specified. Don't be a clock watcher. Always notify the individual in charge when you are leaving as well as where you are going and how long you'll be gone. Never leave an unattended exhibit area.

4. Don't smoke, eat, drink, or chew gum while on the job. Alcoholic beverages are not allowed at any time during the show day (this includes during breaks and lunch hours).

5. Don't sit down. Stay on your feet and be active.

6. Don't use the company phone to check in with your agency or to make personal calls. Use a public phone while on your break.

7. Don't arrange to work for your client's competitors while employed by your client. Do not go behind your agent's back and arrange future bookings with your client independently.

8. Don't advance your opinions about the products offered by your clients' competitors. Be diplomatic at all times.

9. Don't ask if you can have items on display in your company's booth. If they are perishables that will be discarded on the last day or other items that your client offers you, accept graciously. Never take items from the booth without permission.

10. Don't fix your hair, makeup, or clothing in the exhibit area in view of visitors. Keep your personal belongings (clothes, purse) out of the visible exhibit area.

11. Don't make dates either with individuals working in your booth or visitors to your exhibit. Be aware that many people who attend trade shows are of the misimpression that models also serve as paid escorts or offer other services. Because of such attitudes, maturity is a necessary characteristic for models engaged in promotional work.

12. Do not ask to change your schedule or to leave early or arrive late unless absolutely necessary. Consult with your agency so they can secure the approval of the exhibit manager.

13. Photos may be taken of you during the show while you are performing your usual duties. If you are asked to pose for photos or go to a studio, you should consult with your agency prior to signing a model's release. If your client instructs you to perform duties that you were not informed of prior to the booking, call your agency.

14. Always keep in mind that you should behave in a way that will represent your client well. Going beyond the guidelines of good taste may attract attention but will not enhance your client's image.

15. Smile. Look and be cheerful at all times. Co-workers and visitors to your exhibit are not interested in your problems or moods.

On-The-Job-Checklist

Before the Booking

☐ Complete the Booking Form (see Chapter 8).

☐ If you are giving narration or a demonstration, memorize and practice beforehand. If possible, use a tape recorder or a videotape recorder to hone your presentation style.

☐ Do some advanced research on the product, service, and company you will be promoting.

☐ Organize the clothes you are to wear. Pack your totebag with makeup, hair items, and anything you may have been told to supply. Remember to leave valuables at home.

☐ Do hair and makeup.

☐ Allow plenty of time to get to your assignment.

When You Arrive

☐ On the first day of the show, arrive early (15 to 30 minutes) to familiarize yourself with the company, exhibit, co-workers, and the layout of the entire show.

☐ Obtain your ID badge.

☐ Check hair and makeup.

☐ Check in with the exhibit manager, marketing director, or the person who hired you. Secure your client's approval for your makeup, hair, and wardrobe.

☐ If there is a training session on the first day, pay close attention. If there is no training session, ask your employer for specific instructions. To get acquainted with the people with whom you will be working, obtain business cards.

☐ To familiarize yourself with the company and the product or service, study their brochures and other promotional materials. Become acquainted with items on display and the whereabouts of other things you may need in the exhibit.

☐ Look over forms you may be asked to complete for visitors to your exhibit, such as request-for-information cards, contest entry blanks, order forms, etc.

☐ Analyze how you will promote your company's product. Secure approval from the individual in charge before deviating from a script.

During the Day

☐ Be alert at all times and put forth a special effort. Approach people, engage in lively, brief conversations, stay on your feet, and find things to do, rather than waiting for someone to tell you what to do. Make your job fun and interesting. Be expressive and cheerful. Don't daydream.

☐ Concentrate on being a help not a hinderance to the store personnel, your client, or exhibit salespeople. Relay prospects to them, and ask if they need extra assistance.

☐ Make certain you look attractive throughout the day. Refresh your makeup and hair during your morning, lunch, and afternoon breaks.

☐ Cooperate with others and make an extra effort. If you see little things that may take away from the appearance of your exhibit area or booth, such as full ashtrays, empty coffee cups, etc., clean them up. Constantly restock the brochure rack.

☐ If there are certain words or sentences that you are to say, think of ways to make the words come alive and how to add your own input. You may want to warm up your audience or ad lib. Always ask your client for approval before you do or say anything that deviates from the script or approach she or he has given you. Discuss how far you can go. Keep the company's image and the theme of the show or promotion in mind.

☐ Perform your demonstration, narration, or act at the specified number of times per hour, with respect to traffic.

After the Booking ☐ Return all wardrobe items in good condition during and at the end of the show as specified.

☐ Stay around a few extra minutes to help your client finish up last minute business and clean up the booth.

☐ Thank your client and have your voucher signed on the last day of the show.

Chapter 13 Modeling in Live Fashion Shows

Live fashion modeling means that the model appears in person to show how the garment looks on a human figure. To best understand the kinds of opportunities available, it is helpful to look at the process of apparel design, manufacture, and merchandising. Models play an important part in each step of the process.

HOW THE APPAREL INDUSTRY WORKS

While not all designers or manufacturers of apparel conduct business in the same way, the information here will give a general idea of the process that results in the clothing that appears in stores.

The first stage is the designing phase, which begins a year or more before the garments actually appear in the stores. A designer will start with a concept that has been inspired by any number of things, such as social trends, the economy, or cultural events. He or she will first decide on the colors to be used, then select the fabrics to be used by working with textile companies. Models are important at this initial stage because the designer drapes various fabrics on models to stimulate ideas for designs. From these ideas, the designer may then draw sketches to establish specific designs. Next a designer or an assistant will make a pattern from which the garment is cut and sewn to create a sample. After this, another sample or duplicate is made that will be used to show to buyers. Fitting models are very important at these junctures because the garment must be adjusted and readjusted until the design is right. When the sample is perfected, a model who may or may not be the one booked to model the garment in the collections show will appear to perform "looks." Here different hair, makeup, and accessory looks are tried with the garment to create a total image.

After the design samples are finished, runway models show them to people who will play an important part in the future of the garments. There are a few ways in which this is done. Each designer has his or her own style; however, most designers plan a formal collection showing in which the samples are shown to wholesale buyers who will place orders for retail stores, members of the press who will feature the garments in their magazines and newspapers, and individuals, such as socialites or celebrities, who will place individual orders for their favorite garments. A designer's collection showing is a showcase of his or her current work that is performed to generate excitement for the new designs. It can be a lavish production in a hotel ballroom complete with music and choreography, or it can be a much simpler setting, such as a designer's showroom, with no music or choreography, just a commentator calling out the garment numbers as the models parade down a pathway.

Some designers do not have a live showing. Instead they may videotape models showing their samples and send this to the buyers and the press to stimulate their interest. Sometimes a designer will host a "two show" in his or her showroom that is a private minifashion show for an important buyer, such as a buyer for a large chain of retail stores.

After the formal showings, showroom models are enlisted to be available at the designer's salon or showroom on a full-time basis during market weeks so that buyers and others can get a closer look at the designs.

Many designers assemble a new collection four times a year. In New York, fall collections occur from the end of April to the beginning of May. Spring collections are shown the first week in October, summer collections at the end of January and holiday or cruise/resort collections in August. Key showings of the collections are in fall and spring. Some designers show twice a year, whereas others show up to five times a year. In general, showings of the collections last two weeks, with the dress houses showing the first week and the sportswear houses showing the second week.

Each fashion center around the world has designated weeks in which native and international designers can conduct their collections showings. The collections take place first in Milan, then London, Paris, and New York. The Alta Moda in Rome and the Tokyo collections showings follow.

After the orders have been placed by the buyers for their stores, the garments must be manufactured. At this point fitting models are used to alter the designs for mass production, because details that look great on the runway are often not practical or desirable for the consumer. Adjustments are made to increase the garment's marketability. After the production sample is established, another set of fitting models are engaged. These models' figures establish the sizes in which the garment will be manufactured.

Once the production of the garments has been completed, they are then shipped to the retailers who have ordered them. These retailers may include local and metropolitan area department stores, large-chain department stores, local specialty stores and boutiques, chain specialty stores, discount and off-price stores, and mail-order houses. Garments may be shown formally or informally to the staff to create enthusiasm for the new merchandise.

At this stage, promotion to the consumer begins. One of the most prevalent types of live fashion modeling is the retail fashion show. The publicity department of the store organizes such events to promote the garments their buyers have selected. This is usually done when stocks are in full supply and the garments are new and selling at their optimum price. Retail shows are also planned around the buying patterns of the consumer, such as back-to-school shows held in late summer and bridal shows held in January.

There are several ways in which retail shows are conducted. Cooperative shows are those in which a group of stores participate, such as is done in mall or shopping center shows. A store may hold its own show or provide garments for a fund raiser or charity benefit. A department within a store may conduct a small show to bring customers to the department. A designer or manufacturer may have a trunk show, which travels from city to city displaying garments from his or her latest collection only at stores that carry his line.

In addition to formal fashion showings, informal modeling is done. This involves a smaller-scale, more personal type of selling. Floor models are employed to circulate among customers in the store, a restaurant, or tearoom to sell the garments they are wearing.

THE FOUR AREAS OF LIVE FASHION MODELING

Now that you understand how the entire process works, looking at each area of modeling in detail will be helpful. There are four basic capacities in which live fashion models work: fit, showroom, informal, and runway modeling.

Fit Modeling

The fitting model on whom a design for a garment is created can have an important influence on the final result. Some designers work with a house model who epitomizes their current philosophy of fashion and use her to gain inspiration, to provide valuable input for the mechanics of the design, and to model the finished garment sample in the collections showing. She may also appear in publicity photos, print ads, and other media to promote the designer's new ideas.

A good fitting model has a strong sense of style, an appreciation of fashion, and an interest in the designing process. Many designers prefer a model who would wear the clothes they design in their personal life. A good fitting model also has a sense of what will and will not work on a runway. Her contribution, when solicited, can be a valuable one to a designer. In many instances, the fitting model does not participate in the formal collections showings.

The typical scenario for a fitting model involves just the designer, the model, and maybe an assistant. The model stands very still while a muslin pattern or fabric garment is created on her by cutting, pinning, and basting. Patience is a prime requirement for any type of fitting model because from the time the first ideas are molded into a finished sample, hundreds of alterations are made. The model must be able to hold very still so as not to disturb or misguide design lines and fit. Most fitting models must stand for fittings during half-hour intervals with short breaks in between. In addition, the fitting model must be able to make valuable suggestions to the designer on how the garment feels on the body.

For some designers, the fitting model on whom a production sample is established need not portray any specific image. What is most important is that she possess the figure type and measurements needed by the manufacturer.

Fitters' models for production samples must be dependable because there will be deadlines to meet. The model must maintain her measurements and size exactly at all times. A half-inch increase in the hips or waist can completely throw off the sizing of a garment. A great deal of the success of a garment, as far as the customer is concerned, is not only in the design but in the fit.

Showroom Modeling

Each designer or manufacturer of apparel maintains a showroom often located in an apparel mart or fashion district. Here buyers and others in the market can view samples or lines all during the year, but especially at market times (weeks preceding and following the collections showings). Showroom models are usually not the same models who have appeared in the formal showing. They can fit perfectly into the samples that were shown but are often found among the ranks of new models. Showroom modeling is one of the few full-time jobs available in the industry. Not all companies are large enough to require the services of a permanent, full-time model. Instead they may hire models by the hour or for a period of weeks or days. Showroom models perform one or more of the following functions.

- To be available to model garments informally when buyers come into the showroom to look and place orders following the collections showings. The busiest times are during market weeks. This is the most common function of the showroom model.

- To participate in small scheduled shows, such as special preview shows, before the collections or "two shows" after the collections to show highlights on a private basis to highly valued buyers. In these cases the showroom is closed and only a buyer is invited.
- To participate in the manufacturer's major collection fashion shows.
- To double as a secretary, assistant, or salesperson.

Showroom models are hired in one of three ways: full-time, part-time, or on an hourly basis. A model may be a year-round, full-time employee of the showroom. In these cases she also usually has other duties such as being a receptionist, secretary, go-fer, or salesperson. A model who is employed part-time may work only around the busy times and then only for a block of hours each day. When this occurs, models may be hired with "outs," meaning that they have flexibility to change their hours should an important print or other type of booking arise. When this happens, the model must always give advance notice. Models are hired on an hourly basis when the showroom needs extra models during market times or when their budget is limited and they cannot afford full- or part-time models.

A showroom model deals primarily with buyers who purchase garments at wholesale prices to be sold in their retail stores. The model's main objective is to impress the buyers with the merchandise. She must have a friendly, helpful attitude that will put the buyer in a buying mood. She deals with buyers on a more personal level than a runway model. Also showmanship is not as important for a showroom model as for a runway model. Buyers, members of the press, and others who attend showrooms are interested solely in the clothes. They are seasoned professionals who are trying to determine how the garments they are being shown can help them in their jobs or businesses. A straightforward approach that enhances and really sells the garment is what is needed.

The typical scenario in showroom modeling involves a buyer coming into the showroom (usually by appointment) to get a closer look at the items that caught his or her interest at the designer's collection showing. The designer or director of the showroom will ask the model to show the individual the garments he or she requests, which are designated by style or garment numbers. The model will appear in the garment, and either she, the director, or a sales representative will tell the stock number, fabric content, design highlights, sizes, and colors in which it is available.

The showroom model will stand close enough for the buyer to see the garment. She will do a few slow pivots enabling the buyer to see the front and back of the garment. She must project how much she likes the outfit, how comfortable it is, and how good it makes her feel. She tries to create an atmosphere of enthusiasm and good will. Sometimes the buyer will also ask the model how the garment feels or will make comments about the garment. In these cases the model's personality and opinion as well as her ability to converse about special qualities of the fabric and how it wears or feels can make or break the sale.

The technical skills required for showroom modeling are not extensive. Taking great care with the clothes to be modeled is very important as is having good carriage, a smooth walk, and a knowledge of a few basic turns. Speed in changing outfits is important because buyers don't like to be kept waiting and the pace in the showroom can get very hectic during market times. Knowing how to show the garment to best advantage is vital. Maintaining enthusiasm and a fresh approach are also necessary. Because the showroom model shows the same line day after day, she must be able to convey the impression that every time is the first time she has put on the dress and that every entrance is as exciting as the first.

TABLE 1 Fashion Terms Showroom Models Should Know

Term	Definition
Sample	A single garment, the first one in a new style made by a designer or manufacturer
Sample size	The size in which a designer makes his or her sample; sample sizes are cut with a model's, not an average person's, figure in mind
Collection	Any group of samples made up to show buyers
Line	All the samples made by one designer or manufacturer for a particular season
Showing	Formatted live modeling held up to four times a year by designers; showings are held for buyers and the press
Original or creation	Another word for sample
Swatch book	A catalog of a manufacturer's garments that displays samples of fabrics in which garments are available as well as other information, such as care instructions
Buyer	An individual employed by a retail store (for example, a department store or boutique) to purchase apparel at wholesale prices and quantities directly from a designer or manufacturer; buyers attend collection showings and showrooms to look at samples and place orders

Showroom modeling is an excellent way to learn the practical aspects of the fashion trade. The model has the opportunity to work with top professionals in the field of fashion design, manufacturing, and merchandising. Showroom modeling is a good first step in any model's career because it provides steady work, modeling experience, and exposure to designers, editors, and other important people who can further her career (see Table 1).

Informal Modeling

Informal, or floor modeling as it is sometimes called, is live fashion modeling that involves no set format of timed appearances and no stage or runway. In this type of modeling, models circulate among a group of people who may be seated in a restaurant, tearoom, or hotel dining room. They may stroll among customers who are shopping in a department or specialty store, or they may mingle among members of an audience who are enjoying cocktails or conversation following a formal fashion show. Informal modeling brings the garment to the attention of potential customers while showing how it looks up close on a human figure.

The right mental attitude as well as good looks are important for a model wishing to do informal modeling. Genuine enthusiasm for people, outgoing friendliness, the ability to chat, and cheerfulness are all necessary qualities for this type of model. Information about the garment she is modeling may be handled in several ways: the model may be required to give a little speech to customers telling the garment's designer, manufacturer, design details, fabric, care, sizes, and availability. Price is usually not mentioned, especially when the garment is from an exclusive store. The model gives the price only when asked. In many situations, the model has no lines to speak but will carry a card listing the designer's name and the store or department where the outfit can be purchased. She may pass out a card or other literature that gives product and availability information.

Basic Guidelines for Informal Modeling

- Maintain an open, friendly attitude at all times; however, keep your contact with the customer short, interesting, and to the point. Don't indulge in a lot of small talk.

- Screen your prospects. Briefly give attention to customers who appear disinterested or who are involved in business discussions or other activities that will preclude their interest in what you're showing. In some informal modeling situations, cards or other symbols will be placed on tables to indicate whether or not you are to model there. In these instances, know what to look for by asking your coordinator.

- When in contact with a customer, always take note of his or her reaction. If he or she looks disinterested, cut your time there short and go on to another customer or table. If the customer seems interested or asks questions, extend your time with the person, telling a little about your garment, such as how comfortable or fashionable it is and where or how it can be purchased. Always keep in mind that the people are there first of all to be entertained. If they are sold in the process, all the better. Remember, though, that this is soft selling.

- While describing your garment, make sure that you are showing it in the most attractive way. Do a turn or two or angle your body in different directions so it can be seen clearly by all. A little grace and style in the way you move will further enhance your garment and the way you appear. Convey a friendly, relaxed attitude. Put your hand in the pocket or on the waist, or lift the fabric of the skirt to make it flow. Don't make it appear that you are trying to think of something to say or do. Speak with a smile, greet people when you approach them, and thank them or acknowledge their attention when you leave (this is especially important at the end of an informal showing). Remember to establish eye contact with each person at a table or in a group to which you are showing your garment.

- Study fashion design and fabrics. As a model, people will expect you to know more about fashion than the average person. Members of your audience may ask you what's going to be in fashion or what is in fashion. When answering always have your client's best interests in mind. The more successful you are in motivating people to go to the department or store for a look, the more often you'll be called by the client.

- Change your garments as quickly as possible. Make minor hair and makeup changes to suit your outfit. Don't talk to other models while modeling or changing. Models can't always count on having an ideal place to change. Changing may be done in a restroom or empty banquet room. To discourage theft, it is a good idea to have someone stay with the clothes while models are away. Floor models are often responsible for picking up and returning the clothes they will model, so it is important that they know how to handle and protect clothes.

- While modeling, if you are criticized or customers make off-color comments, always smile and act completely unruffled. Complete your presentation and move on to the next group.

- Be aware of timing while you are out on the floor. In a tearoom setting that seats 200 people, you might allow 15 to 20 minutes to cover all the tables. On the other hand, in a department store with a smaller audience, you would need less time.

- Spacing is important when there are several floor models employed. Avoid congregating in one area. Don't proceed to the next table until the model ahead of you has completed modeling and has moved on.

Also, don't stand idly waiting to take your turn to approach customers when another model already has their attention. Extend your time at the table where you are already modeling or move to another table if one is available.

- It is important to be aware of your customer's interest and to know when to move on to the next table. The customer will indicate interest by asking questions or indicate lack of interest by having no comments.
- If accessories are not provided, stick to basics in shoes and jewelry to avoid drawing attention away from the garment you are modeling. Always make certain accessories are in top condition and in a current style. If a customer admires your accessories and they are not from your client's store, simply say "thank you." If the customer persists in knowing where you bought the item, give a polite and appropriate answer that will not compete with your client's best interests. For example, if the item is jewelry, you can say that it was a gift. If shoes, you can say you don't remember where you purchased them.
- If you are doing floor modeling in a store, it is important to keep moving and concentrate on areas where there is traffic. Don't be timid about approaching customers. However, do so in a logical way. Don't startle a customer by abruptly beginning your presentation or by approaching from behind. Never interrupt a customer who is talking to a salesperson or in the process of making a purchase. Think of some of the ways you might approach a customer. For example:

  "I'd like to show you our new. . . ."
  "Have you tried (or seen). . . ?"
  "Would you like to try. . .?
  "Isn't this beautiful fabric?" or describe something you are wearing or showing.
  "Please accept this sample of . . . compliments of . . . ."
  "May I help you find something?"

Get acquainted with the store so you can be helpful in directing customers.

- Always be professional and courteous because you represent the store or organization for which you are modeling.

Runway Modeling Runway or formal fashion modeling takes place in a set area, such as a stage or runway, and involves a programmed set of appearances of models wearing different garments. There are basically four reasons why fashion shows are conducted:

1. To introduce new designs to buyers at the wholesale level.
2. To release news to the press.
3. To sell garments to customers at the retail level.
4. To entertain thereby gaining publicity or raising money for a company or idea (for example, shows associated with a magazine or charity benefits).

There is no better way to attract attention or give authority to a new fashion than to have it shown by a model who looks great in it. An attractive face, an excellent figure, and an interesting way of moving all add up to enhancing the garment and making it desirable. Runway modeling must be entertaining to have an impact, so style, flair, and showmanship are important qualities.

A fashion show model uses movement techniques to show, enhance, and express the garment she is wearing on the runway for her audience. There are five basic elements of movement that a fashion show model uses: posture, walk, turns, stances, and gestures. These are described in the following sections.

BASIC SHOW MODELING SKILLS
The Model's Walk

For the basics of walking review Chapter 2. A model's walk differs from a normal walk in that it is more than just a means of getting from one point to another. Although there is no one specific way of walking, a model's walk must have style in order to have impact. The style of the model's walk is influenced by several factors: the type of show in which she is modeling, the construction and character of the garment she is modeling, her client's preferences, and current styles in modeling. A model's walk also usually needs to be quite fast. Walking too slowly on the runway drags the pace of the show and lessens the number of garments that can be displayed.

The Basics of a Model's Walk

- An attractive walk begins with good carriage. The body must be elongated to make it appear tall. You do this by stretching upward to lengthen both your body and neck. Hold your head high with your chin parallel to the floor. Your shoulders should be back and down as far as possible and relaxed. Your arms should also be relaxed at your sides, with your hands held neither stiff nor limp. Keep your lower body balanced so that your hips and pelvis are thrust neither forward nor backward. Also, avoid thrusting your hips to one side as you walk. Your abdomen and derriere should be held in. Knees should be slightly flexed, not rigid. Ankles should be firm and weight should be evenly centered over both feet. Don't hesitate to use creative or different postures if it helps to better express the garment you are modeling.

- As you step, you push into your next step with the foot that is back while reaching with the ball of the other foot into the next step. For smoothness and speed, aim for a continuous motion.

- Step lightly, yet securely. When walking on a runway, there should never be thumping or clumping sounds.

- Although it is important to remember the basic techniques for walking (Chapter 2) with the balls of your feet on an imaginary line, you may want to alter your technique. For example, when walking in a tight skirt, you may place one foot directly ahead of the other on an imaginary line. When doing this, turn your toes slightly outward to achieve a smooth motion.

- When walking, keep the upper body relaxed, but avoid excessive movement. Initiate your movement with the thighs. Keep your knees flexed.

- Although a model's walk is controlled, it should also have style. Try walking toward a full-length mirror to analyze your walking style and how it affects what you are wearing. For example, a slight movement in the hips might be attractive with some garments.

- A good sense of rhythm is crucial to a fluid walking style on the runway. Establishing a rhythm will eliminate jerkiness and extraneous movement. Put on music when practicing or try counting beats. For example, count "one and two and three and four" and so on. Each number count should be a step. Many shows involve music, so being aware of how to move rhythmically with different tempos is important. However, you would not do an actual dance step, unless instructed to do so.

- Pacing is important, so practice walking at both fast and slow paces. In most runway situations, the walk should be as fast and smooth as possible. In many shows the average walking pace is eight or nine steps in 5 seconds.

- The situation in which you are modeling ultimately determines the style of your walk. One designer or coordinator may tell you to walk a certain way, whereas another may prefer another style.

- Walking styles, just like posing styles, change with the times. One season a very staccato type of walk may be in style, at another time a free-form, almost loping gait may be used. Stay current with the times.

- Walking styles may also vary in different locales. Observe models on the runway at fashion shows in your local area so you will not look out of place.

- It is helpful to observe experienced models on television and those from other areas in order to borrow ideas that you might incorporate into your own walking and modeling style. In this way you will be prepared to model anywhere.

- Walking down the runway is somewhat like posing, but in a continuous, traveling motion. Regarding it in this way gives you opportunities to use your imagination, as suggested in Chapter 10. For example, imagine you are wearing a sleek-looking evening gown. Without making your movement overt or comical, think in terms of slinking down the runway like an exotic cat. Take on the character of any garment you model.

- Impact is important and is determined by the setting in which you model. If you are modeling informally in a store and have personal contact with customers, you won't utilize a theatrical approach; a walk that is slightly stylized yet looks natural will be best. In a more dramatic situation, such as on the runway, you will utilize more elements of style and showmanship. You might exaggerate your walk for more dramatic impact.

How to Do Turns for Live Fashion Modeling

As stressed in print modeling, learning or memorizing specific poses or techiniques is not the objective. In fashion show modeling, the same principle applies. Knowing how to do a battery of turns isn't the key to effective show modeling. Your aim should be to "work the clothes," that is, to show them to their best advantage while projecting an attitude or image that completely expresses the designer's intention. Your clients will expect you to be proficient in basic runway modeling skills, so becoming familiar with commonly used turns will be worthwhile.

You should master all turns in both directions. Unless otherwise choreographed, you should always turn toward your audience. When modeling in doubles, models turn facing away from each other.

Another important point is to practice turns on all kinds of surfaces. Runways are usually carpeted, but you may occasionally have to model on wood, tile, or other surfaces. Shoes may also cause problems. Often the shoes you are given to wear will be new with slick soles that make it difficult to control turns. Other soles, such as crepe or rubber, may not allow full turns.

The following are basic guidelines for performing turns on the runway. There are three parts to a turn: the approach, the turn, and the exit.

Approaching a Turn

1. All turns are built around the model's basic stance. (When you are standing still on the runway or on a stage and not in a specific pose, you will use this stance.) When you initiate and complete your turns, your feet should be in the basic stance position.

2. Always move into your turn. Don't stop before turning. Walking into it will give you the momentum you will need to get you turning. Walking up to the place where you plan to turn, then stopping before beginning the turn is one of the most common mistakes made by beginners.

3. Lead into a turn with the foot opposite the direction you will be turning. For example, to turn to the left, lead in with your right foot. To increase the flow of your movement into a turn, establish a rhythm by counting the beats as you approach the turn. Count all the way through your turn and after it.

4. To establish your sense of balance, think in terms of your base foot and and your working foot. The base foot is the foot on which you bear most of your weight. Your working foot (free foot) takes the lead in turns. Concentrate on "digging in" while turning. For example, for a simple turn to the right, place your weight on your right (base foot). This enables you to use your left foot (working foot) to propel you around toward the right. As you turn, transfer your weight so that it is even on both feet.

5. When turning, keep your shoulders and hips balanced over your feet. You don't lead with your shoulders or hips.

Turning 6. When turning, place your weight on the balls of your feet, and lift your heels only slightly off the ground. Do not elevate heels too much, as this will result in a bouncing motion. Turns should appear smooth and effortless.

7. Practice until you can control your feet so that all movements will be smooth. In most runway situations, your feet will be at the eye level of the audience. Do your turns so smoothly that your feet will not look tangled or awkward when you finish turning.

8. Keep knees flexed (slightly bent) when turning. They should not be stiff, nor should they produce a obvious straightening and bending motion.

9. Keep your arms controlled in turns. Don't allow them to fly out haphazardly. Keep arms at your sides, relaxed but not limp. Usually a slight bend at the elbow is best especially for showing the indentation at the waist. To show your garment more effectively, you may want to put your hands in the pockets or on your hips. If you're showing dolman sleeves you may want to hold your arms away from your sides when turning. Turns also provide a good opportunity for removing a coat or jacket.

10. Rather than concentrating on completing your turn, think in terms of getting into the direction in which you want to be headed.

11. When doing turns on the runway, keep your eyes on the audience as long as possible before turning your head. This technique, borrowed from ballet, is called "spotting."

Exiting a Turn 12. Try not to break the continuity of your movement when completing your turn and continuing to walk down the runway. When you complete your turn, your feet should be in the basic stance position, making it easy for you to take your next step. Don't stop at the completion of your turn, instead as you finish the turn, continue to walk smoothly down the runway.

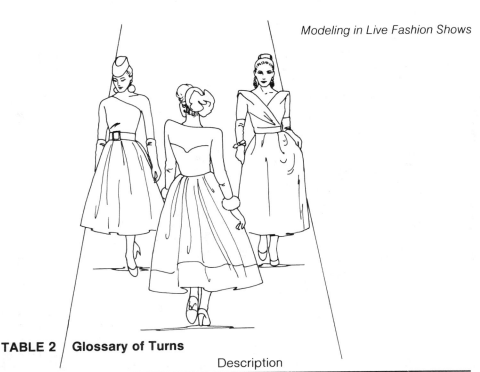

TABLE 2	Glossary of Turns
Turn	Description
Quarter turn or pivot	This turns you around only slightly. You might use it in conjunction with other turns. This turn is not often used on the runway; however, it might come in handy for showroom modeling to give your viewer a good look at the garment.
Stationary half turn or pivot	This is a 180-degree turn, which faces you in the opposite direction. A good way to practice is to start in the basic stance with the right foot forward. Step forward on the right foot (turn the toe slightly to the right). As you step, you will turn to the right, bringing the left foot around behind the right. As you complete the turn, you will be facing the opposite direction in basic stance with your right foot forward. Repeating this movement will bring you back to your original direction. To reverse this turn so that you can show your garment to the other side of the audience, you step back with the right foot, which will place you in a basic stance with the left foot forward. Lead with the left foot, pointing the toe outward, turn placing the right foot behind your left. Repeat this movement leading with the left foot to return you to your original direction. This is a simple, very commonly used turn and it works especially well when modeling on a pivot box or other limited space. Male models use this turn frequently.
Swing or reverse step	This is a step used in conjunction with half pivots. It changes your basic stance to allow you to turn in a different direction. For example, if you have completed half pivots to the right and wish to change direction to the left for variety, swing your right foot slightly outward as you step back. You have now reversed your basic stance so that your left foot is forward. You can now make turns to the left. Keep alternating stances so that it is easy for you to turn in either direction.
Walking half turn or pivot	This is the same turn as above except, rather than being stationary, you are walking into the turn. Begin again in the basic stance with the right foot forward. With the right foot take the first step, left foot second step, right foot third step, and turn to the right. You are doing a right half turn. Repeat these three steps, leading with the

	right foot; turn and you will be facing in your original direction. If you lead with the right foot and take four steps (instead of three), you will be in position to turn to the left.
Three-quarter turn	This is a 270-degree turn. It is very useful when entering at stage left or right and turning at the center in order to face in the direction of an extension on a T-formation. Whether you enter at stage left or right, you will walk to the center and step into the turn with the foot that is away from the audience (base foot). The foot toward the audience (working foot) follows your base foot around to complete your turn. You are now ready to step down the runway.
Basic full turn	This is a 360-degree turn. You will come out of the turn facing in the same direction as you entered it. This is the most commonly used turn. It is sometimes called a Dior turn. To execute this turn, start from a basic stance with the right foot forward, step as you would for a half turn only continue to turn in one smooth motion, turning until you face the same direction from which you started. Practice this turn in both directions.
One-and-a-half turn	This is a 540-degree turn that is often used at the end of the runway to get you headed back into the opposite direction. This is not an easy turn to do. To cheat, you can do a full turn with an immediate half pivot. Practice this turn by leading with the right foot and then the left foot until you are proficient in either direction. In this turn, it may be desirable to finish the turn with your legs intertwined.
Two half pivots	Executing two half pivots will give the same result as a 360-degree turn; however, your movement is broken down into two stages rather than one continuous movement. This turn works well for beginners who are not secure with the full turn. It also works well for showing garments that sway and move well. Male models will find this a useful, casual-looking turn.
Mannequin turn	A slow 360-degree turn.
Carousel turn	This turn can be done in one and one-half revolutions or more. In this turn, your base foot is kept stationary while your working foot takes steps around it. It is similar to the action of a basketball player dribbling a ball and turning. It works well for actionwear and very full skirts. It is sometimes called the paddle turn.
European turn	This is a full turn; however, instead of crossing over in front with your working foot to initiate the turn, you cross your working foot in back to turn. Sometimes several of these turns are done in succession to create a ballet-like effect. This turn is sometimes referred to as the Parisian.
Sport turn	This is essentially a one-fourth pivot or half pivot, with the difference being that your pivot ends with your feet in a wide stance (shoulder width or slightly wider). Your hands are usually on hips. Doing two of these—one right after the other—and shifting your weight from one hip to the other while doing so, yields an attractive swaying motion. It can be used for active wear or billowy garments. Male models will also find it useful; however, they shouldn't sway but rather shift their weight.
Mannequin modeling turn	This combines posing and turning. While doing a very slow paddle turn, the model assumes various poses like a store window mannequin.
Bridal turn	This is a full turn and works well for gowns with very full skirts or long trains. Take several small steps in a circle large enough to accommodate your dress. This will prevent your train from wrapping around your feet.

**ADVANCED SHOW
MODELING SKILLS**

**How to Remove a Coat
or Jacket**

You will often be requested to remove a coat or jacket in order to show the garment being worn underneath. Coats and jackets are sometimes not removed because of timing or other circumstances of the fashion show; however, it is always a good idea to check with the coordinator first. It is important to practice opening a coat or jacket a few times so you will be able to do it smoothly once you are on the runway. (See Figures 1–14.)

Some coats and jackets are nearly impossible to remove gracefully. For example, if you are wearing large bangle bracelets and the sleeves of the jacket are tight, don't attempt to remove the jacket. If the jacket is unlined and you are wearing a garment underneath that will cause resistance, avoid removing the jacket unless it is necessary. You may just want to unbutton the jacket and open it to show the lining or what you have on underneath. On some garments the buttonholes are not the right size and removing the jacket will look clumsy. To avoid fumbling, button only one or two key buttons. Usually it looks more attractive to remove a coat or jacket when you are turning.

Fig. 1

Fig. 2

Fig. 3

Figure 1. Here the model is walking with her jacket still buttoned.

Figure 2. The model begins to unbutton her jacket as she walks down the runway. Note that she uses one hand, keeping it in profile to maintain an attractive hand position. Usually the model will begin to unbutton the jacket with the bottom button to keep the shoulders and collar intact, because these areas have important details. Unbuttoning should be done as quickly and efficiently as possible. When dressing, don't fasten inside closures, such as those on a double-breasted jacket.

Figure 3. To create anticipation on the part of audience, the model pushes back one side of the garment to give them a glimpse of what she is wearing underneath.

Fig. 4

Fig. 5

Fig. 6

Fig. 7

Fig. 8

Fig. 9

Figure 4. For more dramatic effect, she uses both hands to open the jacket on both sides. This is how the model shows the garment underneath when she does not plan to remove the jacket. (In this case, however, she does plan to remove the jacket.)

Figure 5. The model grasps the lapels gently and lifts the jacket off her shoulders while beginning her turn.

Figure 6. The model allows the jacket to slide smoothly downward while holding her arms close to her body. Some jackets will not slide downward easily. When this is the case, the model puts both hands behind her back and uses one hand to tug on the hems of the sleeves.

Figure 7. For dramatic impact, the model fans the jacket outward while turning. This is particularly effective when the garment has an attractive lining.

Figure 8. When the jacket reaches the model's hands, she grasps the top of the jacket at the neckline.

Figure 9. Holding the jacket with both hands, the model folds it with the lining turned inward. This is done to avoid showing labels and to keep the jacket neatly folded.

Fig. 10

Fig. 11

Fig. 12

Fig. 13

Fig. 14

Figure 10. As she completes her turn, the model places the jacket over her arm. If the jacket has a very floppy collar, she might place the hemline toward the audience.

Figure 11. The model has completed her turn, and with the jacket folded, she continues down the runway. She is careful to hold the jacket to the side so as not to obstruct the view of her garment.

Figure 12. The model shows another way to hold the jacket. She places her hand on her hip.

Figure 13. For dramatic effect or when a coat is very long, the model may choose to swing the garment over one shoulder. The model must remember to maintain an attractive hand position while holding the coat firmly.

Figure 14. One of the most dramatic ways to handle a coat or jacket is to hold it with one hand and drag it along the runway. However, the model must always get permission from the coordinator beforehand. Whether the model chooses to sling her jacket over one shoulder, drape it over her forearm, or swing it down along one side of her body, her objectives are to keep the garment looking neat and to avoid obstructing important details on the garment that is being shown.

What to Do with Your Hands

Inexperienced models often feel awkward because they don't know what to do with their hands. Some of the basic ways models hold their hands in live fashion modeling are as follows.

Holding Hands Down at Sides of Body

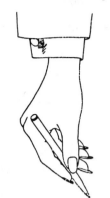

It is not necessary that you always do something with your hands. Too much movement of the hands can look frantic and will detract from your garment. The key is for hands to look poised yet natural at all times. When your hands are at your sides, it is usually best to have a slight bend in the elbows to create a space between your waist and arms. This will give your garment a better silhouette and will make your waist look slender. Also, make certain your arms swing naturally when your walk. To ensure that hands don't look limp, try the pencil trick (Figure 15). Hold a pencil loosely in each hand, and keep hands down at your sides. Drop the pencil, maintaining the hand position. This hand position will look attractive in nearly any modeling situation.

Figure 15. The pencil trick.

Placing Hands in Pockets

Pockets are a great asset on any garment, so in most instances your client will want you to show them to the audience. Note, however, that the way you might normally put your hands in pockets may not be the most flattering to you or the garment. Even a simple movement such as this can be done in many ways (Figure 16). Always place your hands in the pockets to suit the character of the garment. For example, you would put your hands in the pockets of jeans differently than the way you might when modeling elegant silk pants. Also, avoid detracting from the lines of the garment. For example, don't thrust your hands in the pockets of a garment, causing it to stretch or sag.

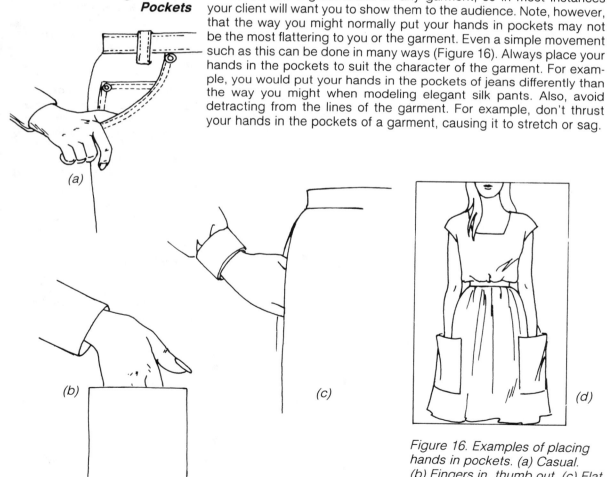

(a)

(b)

(c)

(d)

Figure 16. Examples of placing hands in pockets. (a) Casual. (b) Fingers in, thumb out. (c) Flat side pocket. (d) Deep pockets.

Placing Hands on Hips

Placing hands on hips while walking down the runway or turning adds style and shows off the shape of the bodice and sleeve of your garment. There are different ways to do this, depending on the mood or character of your garment (Figure 17). Concentrate on making your hands appear graceful. Don't tug or otherwise distort the lines of your garment. Place your hands lightly on the garment to avoid wrinkling the fabric. Keep your shoulders back and down to create a good line for your neck and shoulders.

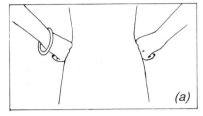
(a)

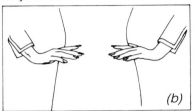
(b)

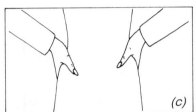
(c)

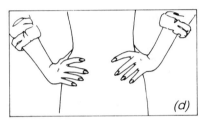
(d)

Figure 17. Examples of placing your hands on your hips. (a) Fists. (b) Poised. (c) Thumbs to front. (d) Fanned fingers.

Handling the Garment or a Prop

There are various ways to handle a garment to show off its lines and details. Some movements go in and out of fashion. In former times it was fashionable to point to the detail of a garment, such as a row of buttons or a piece of jewelry. Recently this has gone out of favor because it appears too contrived. Unless such movements are done for a special effect, current styles in modeling dictate a more natural, unaffected way of moving. If you want to handle the garment in a dramatic way, check first with your coordinator.

Hand props are sometimes used to add interest to an outfit. For example, you may be given a handbag, a piece of sporting equipment, or some other item that would be used with your outfit. When handling props it is important to use graceful hand positions and to keep the prop from obstructing important details on your garment. For example, if you were given a bouquet to hold when modeling a bridal gown with distinctive beading on the bodice, you would hold the bouquet down and to the side. If you are given a prop, such as a tennis racket, that represents a particular sport, carry it as if you know how to play the game.

Gesturing

Gesturing when modeling is movement you might do for emphasis, such as putting a hand on your face, extending your arms outward when showing dolman sleeves, or pantomiming an activity. Gesturing, when done well and used appropriately, can be very dramatic and can add to a model's showmanship. Excessive gesturing should be avoided. For example, you would not use the same distinctive gesture twice within a single appearance or even within a single show. The model's gesture should draw attention to the clothes and not to the gesture itself.

Observe how other models use gestures effectively. See Chapter 10 for ideas on hand and other movements that you could execute on the runway. Practice until you can do gestures with confidence and ease. Gestures should never be done in an awkward, self-conscious manner. There are times when a choreographer may instruct a model to do a certain gesture to emphasize a garment. Even if it makes you feel foolish, you will be expected to perform the movement whole-heartedly and in keeping with the choreographer's expectations. In this case, practice until the movement feels natural.

Facial Expressions and Eye Contact

Confident, attractive facial expressions are important and should be based on the mood of your garment. For example, you may adopt a sophisticated expression for an elegant gown, whereas you may find a bright smile more suitable for modeling sportswear.

Decide on the facial expression you are going to project. Aim for consistency throughout each run, using one mood. In other words, midway through your run, avoid changing from an aloof to a smiling expression.

It is important to be aware of the tone and reaction of your audience. If they respond to your garment by applauding, project that mood yourself by drawing out their emotions as an actress would do.

Keeping your head up and eyes focused ahead is important. Don't look down at your feet or the runway. Study the basic positions of the head explained in Chapter 10 to create interesting visual images on the runway that your audience will remember. Use the information in Chapter 10 on facial expressions to create different looks and moods. Use your eyes to "work" your audience. For example, you might want to establish a personal contact with your audience by selecting faces in different areas of the audience on which to focus. You may choose to do the opposite and ignore your audience by becoming totally absorbed in the character you are portraying. Both methods can add impact to your performance. Remember that head and eye movements usually look best when they are done slowly, smoothly, and purposefully.

Many models use nodding as a way to acknowledge their audience and establish contact. For example, a model may come onto the runway, pause, and lift her chin then bring it down in a slow bowing motion. Or while doing a turn or at the end of her appearance, she may tilt and turn her head slightly over her left shoulder to nod and look to the audience on her left. She will repeat the same motion toward the center, nodding her head directly forward. Turning her head to the right, she will tilt her chin toward her audience on the right.

More Fashion Show Facts for Models

Ascending and Descending Stairs

When walking up or down stairs, models angle their feet slightly in one direction, keeping the knees flexed and close together; this prevents bobbing up and down. It is important to avoid making a clumping noise with the feet. When walking up stairs the entire foot should be placed on the stair so that the heel of the shoe doesn't hang over the edge. This looks unattractive and throws you off balance.

Keep your back straight and your head up. Lower your eyes to see where you are going; don't bow your head or bend at the waist to look down. When ascending stairs in a long skirt, you will need to lift it gracefully to avoid tripping. Never reach down or bend over to pick up the front of the skirt. Instead, pick up the skirt gently where your hands fall at your sides. Lift the skirt only slightly. Keep your elbows down and close to your sides.

The same rules for ascending stairs apply when you are descending. When approaching the stairs, time your steps so you don't break your rhythm. You want to avoid having to pause to look down at the stairs. Your aim when descending stairs should be to look as if you are gliding down. If you are wearing a long, full skirt, it may not be necessary to lift it with your hands as you descend; a slight kicking motion with your foot should be enough.

Stances or Posing on the Runway

There are times when you may be requested to assume a stance while other models show garments. Try to assume a stance that enhances your garment, fits with its mood, and works well with the show. This may be anything from a basic stance to a creative pose you may have seen in a photograph. Sometimes posing on the runway is called "making a picture."

While you are standing on the runway (assuming a stance) avoid looking around the audience. Concentrate on the action on the runway or fix your eyes on something and hold them there. Don't fidget or shift your weight as if you are tired or bored. Don't respond to comments made by people in the audience. Don't talk to other models on the runway.

Modeling in Doubles or Groups

Two or more models may often appear on the runway simultaneously in order to show more garments in a shorter period of time. This is usually done in one of three ways. Models may follow one another, walk abreast of each other, or split the runway. When models are walking in single file, each model should keep an even distance between herself and the model in front of and behind her. Successful fashion show modeling requires teamwork.

There are times when you will be modeling in a group of two or three models abreast. Keep pace with the other models so that you are in one even line. Always be conscious not to cover or upstage another model. Also, practice walking along the edge of a runway to prepare yourself for such a situation.

Splitting the runway occurs when two or more models walk in opposing directions on the runway. For example, one model may walk out to the end of the runway and turn, and another one will enter. They will pass each other at the middle of the runway. When this is the case, stay to your right. This way you and the other model won't have a collision when you meet. Staying to your right also ensures that the audience to the right (walking down the runway) and to the left (walking back up the runway) sees your garment adequately. Remember to angle your body slightly toward the audience when you are covering only one side of the runway or when they are seated on only one side of the runway.

When three models are involved in splitting the runway, two models will be walking together and another model will be walking toward them. In this instance, the singular model walks between the two models (Figure 18).

Splitting the runway is often done on a T-shaped runway. Two models will walk down the runway together and when they arrive at the cross section of the T, the model on the left turns and walks down the left portion of the T while the model on the right, walks down the right portion of the T. At the end of the extension they each turn and trade places. Each model stays to her right to avoid a confrontation. After each model has walked down the opposite extension of the T and turned, they will meet in the center and walk back up the runway together.

When modeling in doubles or groups, if you are given no specific instructions, it is a good idea to huddle with the other models with whom you will be appearing, before going on the runway. You will want to coordinate your moves and expressions. Don't converse with other models while on the runway.

Figure 18. Splitting the runway.

Modeling for Still Photographers

Photographers for the press or other concerns are often present at fashion shows. When this occurs, you should not stop the show to pose for the photographer. Instead, momentarily pause or do a turn or two to allow him or her to get a pleasing shot of you and your garment. If lots of cameras are clicking, extend your appearance for the photographers. If you are behind a model who is getting lots of attention, hold back to allow her more time. Do a turn, or walk a few steps in the opposite direction.

Modeling for Video Cameras

In most situations where a fashion show is videotaped, the objective is to depict an event. Usually the models are not supposed to be conscious of the camera by playing up to it or looking into the lens. In general, the model should proceed as naturally as if there were no cameras present. It is important to avoid quick side-to-side or up-and-down movements with the eyes because they are exaggerated by the camera. Movements look more natural when the model concentrates on her audience and garment rather than whether or not the camera is on her.

Many designers videotape or film their collections showings and then use these tapes or films for promotional purposes in stores where their garments will be sold.

Dancing on the Runway

Styles of movement on the runway change with the times. Previously models would dance down the runways; however, this is not done nearly as much now because it tends to divert too much attention from the clothes. Dancing is sometimes done for special effect. You may be given specific dance steps to perform on the runway, or you may simply be expected to move creatively to the beat of the music. A model should be prepared to dance if instructed to do so; therefore, training in jazz and ballet dancing is helpful.

Showmanship is important but a model shouldn't lose sight of what is happening to the clothes. Too much movement or the wrong type of movement can make it difficult for the audience to see the details and lines of the garment.

Modeling Bathing Suits

A model should never look self-conscious when modeling bathing suits. Put yourself into a setting where you would normally wear a bathing suit. Don't ask to wear anything under your suit. Also, leg makeup looks much better than wearing nylons. To maintain the firm appearance of your legs, keep your steps light and controlled. Refer to the suggestions outlined in Chapter 10 on modeling bathing suits.

Modeling in Commentated Fashion Shows

At a commentated fashion show a coordinator, designer, or celebrity may give a running commentary describing the garments being shown. Commentated shows tend to go in and out of popularity. They are often used for small shows.

A model should remain on the runway during the commentary about her garment, and not leave before the commentator indicates that she is ready for the next model.

If you are modeling in a commentated show, it is very important to be alert to what the commentator is saying about the outfit you are modeling. He or she may request that you open your coat, remove your jacket, or show some detail of the garment.

Your cue to come onto the runway will vary so that the commentator's delivery doesn't sound repetitious or routine. Your cue may be the commentator speaking your name. Mentioning your name again, such as "Thank you, Karen," may also be your cue to leave the runway. A commentator may choose to pause to indicate she is finished, rather than repeating your name. Sometimes the model's cue to exit will be when the commentator starts talking about the next model's garment.

Because shows are often held in restaurants or other locations having less than ideal acoustics, it may be difficult to hear the commentator. A good model knows her garment well enough to show the important details, even if she can't hear what the commentator is saying. She should also be aware of the timing of the showing so as not to remain on the runway too long or leave before the commentator is finished.

There are times when the commentator will deviate from the information on the commentary card to ad lib. For example, the commentator may need to stall to allow the next model enough time to dress. On the other hand, he or she may ad lib to speed up if the show is running overtime. When commentary is extended, the model should slow down her walk and turns and may even pause at certain points.

A good model dresses carefully to be prepared for whatever the commentator may ask her to show. However, if circumstances are such that what is asked is impossible, the model indicates this to the commentator by way of a smile or facial expression. Such a case might be when she has not had time to completely button the back of a blouse worn under a jacket.

Small shows, such as department store shows, trunk shows, and the like, are often simple, commentated shows. These usually do not require a rehearsal; however, there are times when the commentator or others may insist on one. Even when there is no rehearsal, it is helpful if you can read or hear the commentary pertaining to the garment you will be modeling.

Problems and Solutions for Show Modeling

Unfortunately, accidents do occur no matter how thoroughly a fashion show is planned and rehearsed. Models accidentally trip or fall or even walk off the end of the runway. The mark of a true professional is how effectively the model deals with less than ideal or even disastrous circumstances.

In most cases, if a mishap occurs while you are modeling on the runway, the best way to handle it is to act as if nothing happened, maintain your composure, and continue on. An unruffled expression and a smile can go a long way. If you flub a turn, lose your balance, or trip, this is the best course of action. If a small, inexpensive item falls from you while modeling, such as an earring or button, let it go and retrieve it after the show. If something large falls, such as a scarf or jacket, stoop gracefully and quickly and pick it up, then continue on as if nothing out of the ordinary has occurred. Always try to leave as little to chance as possible. Don't hope that something will work on the runway if you haven't tried it beforehand.

If there is a problem with the music, for example, it stops while you are modeling, act as if it were planned and punctuate the pause with a turn. Continue on as if nothing unusual is happening.

FASHION SHOW PARTICULARS

There are several elements that comprise a fashion show. The model must have knowledge of these because they will affect her directly.

Rehearsals

Many fashion shows entail a rehearsal a day or two or an hour or two before the show. At some rehearsals the director or coordinator will simply tell models what will occur and what they are supposed to do. At other rehearsals models are given detailed instructions or sometimes written scripts for the show. Models walk through their parts as they will perform them in the show. This is called a "dry run-through." A dress rehearsal may follow. A dress rehearsal combines all the elements of a show (clothes, music, lighting, etc.). It is important to always listen closely to instructions given during rehearsals.

There will not be any time for the director, coordinator, or commentator to repeat or go over the information right before the show. If necessary, the model should take notes.

Accessories List   An accessories list is a written form outlining everything the model is to wear for each appearance. The list is used when accessories and shoes are provided by the client to ensure that the model wears everything that is necessary. Usually accessories, such as jewelry and other loose items, are placed in a bag and attached to the hanger of the garment. Sometimes they are organized on a table containing all the models' accessories. Other times a list is made of all the accessories for one garment. One copy of the list is pinned to the garment, one is given to the model, and another is given to the starter or show director. Other accessories lists have as many as 10 of one model's garments listed on the same sheet. Usually the garments are listed in the order the model will wear them. Sometimes an accessories list or sheet is called a fitting sheet.

Lineup Sheet   A lineup sheet gives the order in which all the models will appear. It is posted by the entrance to the runway where the starter is seated, and a copy may be given to each model. Occasionally the lineup sheet and the accessories list are combined into one form. Usually each garment or model is assigned a number, and this number appears on the sheet to indicate each appearance.

Lineup Sheet

LINEUP NO.	OUTFIT	SHOES	STOCKINGS	JEWELRY	ACCESSORIES	OTHER

The order in which the models appear in a fashion show must be thought out very carefully. Most shows contain several segments each displaying a collection of garments grouped by fabric, style, and/or overall look. The number of garments each model will show varies from show to show. The higher the budget and the more important the show, the fewer garments each model will wear. In a top designer's collection showing in New York, 100 samples may be shown in little more than half an hour by 30 or more models. Most fashion shows average about 30 minutes. A short show is 15 to 20 minutes. A long show is up to 50 minutes. In less extravagant consumer shows, the following numbers will generally apply.

Number of Garments in the Show	Number of Models
30	5–7
40	6–10
50	8–10
60	10–12
70	12–20
100	20–30

A long runway, a distant dressing room, garments that require more time for changing (for example, bridal gowns), or models appearing in groups on the runway are all factors that may necessitate having more models to keep the show moving. However, in most shows, models appear four to six times on the runway and usually at least five outfits are shown between a model's reappearances to allow her time to change. If it can be avoided, a model usually doesn't appear twice within the same sequence. Of course, the more professional a model is and the more assistance she has dressing, the faster her changes can be made.

The Runway

Runways come in all shapes, sizes, and forms. They may have carpeted, wood, tile, or cloth-covered surfaces. Runways are usually 4 feet wide and 3 to 5 feet high. The length may vary. Many runways that are supplied by hotels and restaurants are designed in sections that are 8 feet long. Several 8-foot sections may be placed end to end to form the length of the runway. A short runway is approximately 8 feet in length, a medium-sized runway is about 16 feet, and a long runway is in excess of 24 feet.

The most common type of runway extends straight out from a stage. A runway can be designed in nearly any shape to add movement or interest to a show or to cover the room more adequately. (See Figures 19 to 26.)

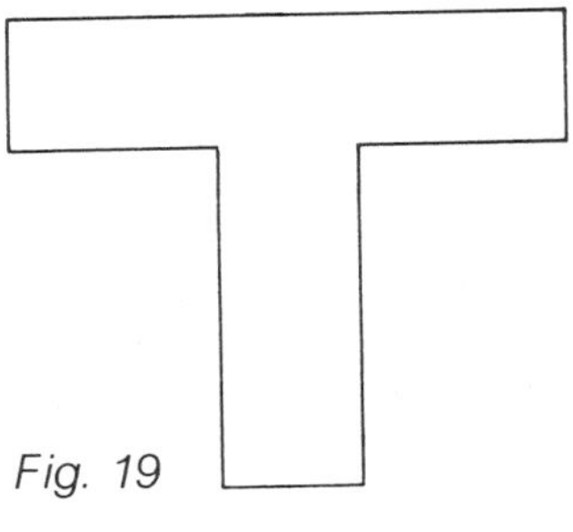

Fig. 19

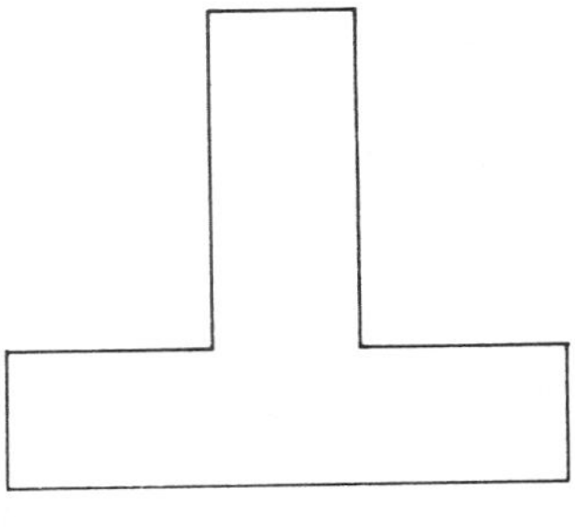

Fig. 20

Figure 19. A T-shaped runway is the most common. It is usually formed by a runway platform extending perpendicularly from a stage. Models usually enter at stage left or stage right. This requires less construction than more elaborate forms.

Figure 20. An inverted T-shaped runway is another popular formation. It lends itself well to team or group modeling.

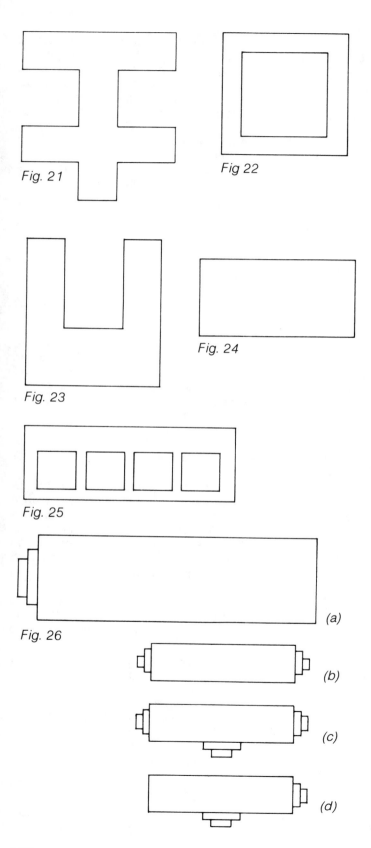

Fig. 21

Fig 22

Fig. 23

Fig. 24

Fig. 25

Fig. 26

(a)

(b)

(c)

(d)

Figure 21. A cross-shaped runway is seen in many forms. Sometimes the end of the runway has a rounded tip, whereas other variations include more than three branches at the end of the runway, which can create a more dramatic presentation.

Figure 22. One example of a "runway in the round" is this square-shaped runway. Guests may be seated in the center and around all sides. This may also be in circular form.

Figure 23. A U-shaped runway, or paserelle, allows for seating on all sides of the runway and adds movement to the showing.

Figure 24. A pivot platform is the simplest type of runway. It is a platform that is usually wider than a runway and ranging in size from 4 x 6 to 6 x 8 feet. It may be just one step (8 inches) or as high as 18 inches off the floor. It is used when there is a small audience. Often models doing informal modeling will come out and model on the platform and then circulate among the audience to give them a closer look.

Figure 25. A pivot box is a small square- or round-shaped platform, one step high, that allows just enough room for a model to stand and turn. Several pivot boxes may be used in conjunction with a runway; models may stand on these and assume poses while other models appear on the runway.

Figure 26. Standard straight runways are another popular formation. There are several variations. Stairs for entrances and exits may appear at the ends or on either or both sides of the runway. (a) One entrance/ exit (b) Opposite entrance/exit (c) Straight with center entrance/exit (d) Stage with center and side entrance/exits.

446

Choreography   Choreography refers to the patterns models follow to cover the runway and the style used in their steps, turns, and other movements. Some shows are not choreographed. A basic retail or consumer show may consist of a simple runway with one entrance. The models will take turns walking down the runway, with each staying out the same amount of time and covering all parts of the runway. The patterns a model uses to cover the runway each time she appears are her choice.

The situation may be more involved, in which case models are instructed where to enter, walk, and exit. They may also be told where to pivot and what to do while walking. Usually the bigger the show and the more money that is being spent, the less things are left up to chance.

Choreographed shows always require a rehearsal. There may be only a run-through or there may also be a dress rehearsal, which is usually held at least 1 hour before the show. At the time of the rehearsal, models may be expected to take notes on the choreography, or each may be provided with a runway choreography form, which is often pinned to her garment on the hanger.

Many of the same principles used in theatre productions are used for runway shows. For example, when a choreographer instructs you to walk *down* the runway, this means downstage or toward the audience. When he or she instructs you to walk *up* the runway, this means upstage or away from the audience.

A runway choreography form is shown in this chapter along with information on how to complete it. When diagramming the action to be performed by the model on the runway, choreography symbols are used. Each choreographer may have his or her preferred choreography shorthand. Usually each turn is assigned a number or letter to indicate the succession in which they are to occur. Many of the common symbols used are shown in Table 3.

TABLE 3   Choreography Symbols

Action	Symbol	Action	Symbol
Quarter pivot	●	One and a half turn	⬥
Half pivot	(	Traveling turn	ℓℓ
Three-quarter turn or French turn	◔	Sport pivot	x͡x
Full turn or Dior	◎	Stance	⌷S
Carousel turn	◎	Remove a coat or jacket	☆
Mannequin turn	ⓜ	Walking	⟹
Bridal turn	ⓑ	Entrance	A
One and a quarter turn	⊙	Exit	X

Runway Choreography

Model _____   Appearance No. _____ of _____

Lineup. No. _____   Segment _____

☐Single   ☐Double   ☐Group   ☐ Other _____

Outfit Description	Shoes	Stockings	Jewelry	Accessories/Other

CHOREOGRAPHY

NOTES: _____

Using the Runway Choreography Form

The runway choreography form is used by models, fashion show coordinators, and choreographers to act as a written reminder of the action to take place on the runway. Models should always bring these forms or paper and pencil to rehearsals and shows for taking notes. Complete one form for each garment change or appearance.

Line 1   List the model's name. If models are assigned numbers, indicate the model's number on this line as well. On the right, indicate the number of each appearance for the model and how many appearances she will have. Using designations, such as first or 1st, instead of a number alone will prevent confusion with the lineup number.

Line 2   Lineup number refers to the model's place in the order of the show. For example, this may be the model's first appearance but the fourth garment shown in the show. Her lineup number is 4. On the right indicate the segment or part of the show. Fashion shows are usually divided into segments, each with a different mood, music, and so on.

There may be six segments in a show, with each segment containing 10 garments. The first segment of a show may feature swimwear, the second, sportswear, the third segment may contain clothing for school or work, and the fourth segment or finale, may feature evening wear.

Line 3   Check the box that applies. If the model will be alone on the runway, check single. If modeling with another model, check double. If there will be more models, check group, and indicate how many will be on the runway together.

Line 4   In this section, write down everything the model is to wear for this appearance.

Space 5   Use this space to diagram the runway. Be sure to indicate the shape of the runway, where the audience will be seated, where there are stairs or other important elements. Use the choreography symbols to indicate where the model is to walk, turn, and stand. Indicate the succession of movements using numbers or the alphabet. Use "A" to indicate the model's entrance, "X" to indicate where she is to exit.

Space 6   Use the bottom of the form for miscellaneous notes.

How to Be Your Own Choreographer

There will be many times when you will be given no direction. Use the following guidelines and ideas to make your performance look as if it were choreographed by a professional choreographer.

- Cover all parts of the runway where guests are seated.
- The length of the runway will determine how many turns you will do. On short- or medium-length runways, perform turns at the ends and in the center. For a long runway, divide it into quarters or fifths, and place your turns accordingly.
- Usually you won't cover the runway more than twice. This is only done when stalling for time.
- Vary your turns and the order in which you execute them so that the show doesn't look routine.

The Fashion Show Finale

Nearly all fashion shows have a finale of some sort to indicate that the show is over. All the models reappear in either their last garment or the most outstanding garment each modeled. During rehearsal the model should ascertain which outfit she is to wear for the finale and also what she is to do. Some finales are intricately choreographed, whereas others employ an impromptu approach. Many times models will appear on the runway with the designer of the clothes that were modeled for the finale.

ANALYZING HOW TO MODEL A GARMENT

A professional model carefully analyzes the garment she is to model in order to show it effectively. There are seven basic points to consider when determining how to model an outfit:

1. What kind of look or mood does this garment dictate? Who is the character I am supposed to be?
2. Who is my audience? What is my purpose?
3. What is the theme or concept of this show?
4. What are the features of this garment that make it special, attractive, or practical?
5. How does the garment move?
6. What elements are present in this show?
7. Are there specific instructions from the designer, client, and choreographer?

449

What Attitude Does This Garment Dictate?

Your movement, attitude, and facial expressioin must take on the character of the garment. Try to create a look or image by isolating the feeling or impression you want yourself and the clothes to express. Use your posture, head carriage, eye contact, walk, gestures, and hand movements to act out the character who would wear the garment. Following are some suggestions to give you inspiration.

You Are Modeling	Your Movement/Expression
A business suit	A look of authority, serene businesslike expressions. Medium strides with controlled movement of the hips and shoulders. Try putting your hands in the pockets of the jacket and/or skirt and remove the jacket.
A bridal gown	Happy expressions, graceful, simple movements. Walk slower than usual, no turns if the train is long. Touch your veil or hold your bouquet out to one side.
Sportswear or jacket, sweater, and pants	Smiles and casual movements. Medium to wide strides with a slight spring in your step. Put hands in pockets of pants. Remove jacket and drape it over your shoulder.

Who Is My Audience?

Identify the audience attending the show. If you are doing informal modeling, your contact with customers should be natural and personal. If you are modeling on a runway before a large audience, you will have to be more theatrical in your presentation to communicate your image. Determine where your audience or key members of the audience are seated, and play up your presentation to them or establish eye contact. Consider the background of the members of your audience. If they are sophisticated fashion show goers, your presentation will have to be polished and professional. If you are modeling for a very conservative audience, you should tone down your actions.

What Is the Theme or Concept of the Show?

Consider the reasons for staging the fashion show. Is the show being given to release news to the press? If so, determine exactly what is newsworthy about the designer's collection and what concept he or she is using to obtain the interest of the press. If you are showing to buyers, ascertain what type of look or garments the designer is trying to promote, then reflect these ideas in your performance. If you are showing to consumers at the retail level, you will want to entice them to visit your client's store for a closer look at the garment you are modeling. If you are modeling at a charity benefit show, your objective will be to entertain. Many times fashion shows are planned around a theme, such as a back-to-school show. This would indicate to you that you will portray students and try to appeal to the students in your audience. Often a show is given a name that will give you clues as to how you should act.

What Are the Features of the Garment?

When you put on the garment, check that you have all the correct accessories and that you are wearing the garment correctly. Look for features that will be of interest to your audience, such as pockets, a fur- or satin-lined jacket, a full skirt, or a slit skirt. Approach your garment as if you were the one who designed it. Then think of ways to bring these characteristics to your audience's attention without being obvious about it.

How Does the Garment Move?

It is very important to move around a little in your garment before going onto the runway. Place your hands in the pockets to make sure they have not been sewn closed or to ensure that hands go in easily. Also, you will get used to where they are on your garment. Put your hands on your hips to see if this enhances your garment. Some garments pull or look bunchy when hands are placed on hips. Sway in the garment to see how much it moves and to gain ideas for walking. Practice unbuttoning and removing a jacket to see what possible problems are present and how you can overcome them. Do different turns to see how your garment swirls. If possible, try these moves in front of a full-length mirror to determine how your garment appears at its best.

What Elements Are Present in the Show?

Consider the type of music, lighting, commentary, runway and the like that are used in the show. How do these factors affect your presentation?

Are There Specific Instructions?

Listen closely for specific instructions from the commentator, coordinator, director, or designer. Follow any instructions from the client to the letter. Implement the instructions with confidence and logic. Study your runway choreography form, if there is one. Make sure that you clarify anything that is not clear at the rehearsal, not right before the show. Listen for directions in regard to changes in lineup or choreography right up to the last minute you are to appear.

On-the-Job Checklist

What to Do before the Booking

☐ Complete the booking form.

☐ Attend all fittings, rehearsals, and so forth. If you will be unable to attend preshow assignments, notify the agent or client at the time you audition or are booked. Make sure that you have all the standard totebag items. Don't bring a lot of money or expensive jewelry to a show.

☐ Know whether there is a makeup artist or hairdresser. If both are employed, arrive with clean hair and clean, moisturized skin. If neither are employed, arrive with only finishing touches to be added to your hair and makeup.

☐ Usually it's a good idea to arrive at fashion shows from 15 to 30 minutes before the show starts. If the rehearsal is to be held half an hour to 2 hours before the show (as is often the case), arrive 5 to 15 minutes ahead of the time you are given. Usually you will have a short break between rehearsal and the show. Allow for traffic, parking, or other unexpected delays.

When You Arrive

☐ When you arrive, check in with the show staff so they know you have arrived.

☐ Take a minute or two to go to the restroom, take care of phone calls, or anything else of a personal nature, so you won't have to worry once the show begins.

☐ Go over the clothes you will be modeling. If there is a dresser, check over the clothes together. Review what you are to wear and where you are on the lineup sheet. Line your clothes up on the rack in the order you will model them. Group garments together with proper accessories and shoes. Unzip zippers and unbutton buttons of all your garments. Make sure any tags are removed (an envelope may be provided for each garment to store tags) or concealed. Don't remove tags without prior permission.

☐ Look very carefully for stains, rips, and the like on the clothes you will be modeling, and bring them to the attention of the coordinator immediately, so you won't be held responsible for them later.

- ☐ Discuss makeup and hair changes with the coordinator.
- ☐ Lay out any items you will need during the show, such as antiperspirant, extra stockings, proper undergarments, comb and brush, hairpins, elastic bands, and makeup. If you are to make slight alterations in makeup, uncap lipsticks, dip a few cotton swabs in baby oil for removing lip and eye colors, put proper eyeshadow colors on cotton swabs for changes, and arrange things in the order you will use them.
- ☐ Remember to keep all your personal belongings such as coat and umbrella, in one place away from all the confusion. Confine your modeling supplies to the area you've been assigned.
- ☐ Put on proper undergarments and your changing robe. Complete hair and makeup. Apply antiperspirant. Put on accessories and shoes.
- ☐ Put on your garment. Always put the garment on last.
- ☐ Take your place in the lineup.

During the Show
- ☐ Make sure you wear the garments in exactly the way you were instructed. Be sure you haven't forgotten a belt or other accessory.
- ☐ Dress quickly. Changing your garment should not take longer than a minute. When hair and makeup changes are involved, usually extra time is allowed.
- ☐ Line up promptly for cues. Always know who is ahead of you in the lineup.
- ☐ Observe dressing room etiquette.

Dressing Room Etiquette
- ☐ Don't ask to borrow items from other models. Don't use things that belong to other models.
- ☐ Don't talk. Talking adds to the confusion and slows everyone down. If it is necessary to say something, do so in a low tone so that voices are not heard by the audience.
- ☐ Don't let backstage pressure and confusion affect you. Always be pleasant and calm.
- ☐ Make cooperation your motto. Teamwork is essential for a successful fashion show. Help other models who may need assistance.
- ☐ Don't expect help from others. Take care of yourself first. Stay out of other people's way. Respect the lineup and cues of others. Don't hoard the mirrors.
- ☐ Never bring food or drink backstage. Don't smoke, sit, or lean on anything once you are dressed.
- ☐ Never bring friends or relatives backstage.
- ☐ Don't leave the dressing area during the show. If you must leave, notify the coordinator, starter, or other person in charge.
- ☐ Be alert to changes in lineup or other occurrences.

Handle the Clothes with Care
- ☐ Protect the clothes from perspiration by applying antiperspirant frequently (always allow it to dry completely before putting on the garment). Use tissue under arms until just before going on the runway.
- ☐ Wear the client's shoes as briefly as possible so they won't stretch, get out of shape, or get damp from perspiration. Never walk on uncarpeted surfaces unless the soles are masked. Be very careful when stepping into a garment that the heel of your shoe doesn't catch in the hem.

☐ Put clothes on over your head whenever possible to prevent them from being dragged on the floor. Protect necklines from getting soiled by cosmetics by placing a "change scarf" or other cover over your face when pulling the clothes on or off.

☐ Don't be hasty when changing. Don't force zippers, pull buttons apart, pull tags off clothing, or handle garments in a hurried, careless way.

☐ Always put the dress on last, that is, after makeup and hairstyling, jewelry, and shoes. Garments must stay wrinkle-free. Avoid bending over to put on shoes and bending arms to rearrange hair. Every movement can cause a wrinkle.

☐ Don't throw garments on the floor after you've modeled them. Hang them up or hand them to a dresser.

On the Runway ☐ When in lineup, mentally go through what you are going to do on the runway.

☐ Always check all garment fastenings before going out on the runway.

☐ Follow instructions to the letter. Spend the designated time on the runway, but be flexible if circumstances require otherwise. Follow choreography and other instructions given during rehearsal; don't expect anyone else to know what you are supposed to do. Listen to and follow the commentator.

☐ Be careful not to collide with another model when entering or exiting or while on the runway. Observe equal or designating spacing between yourself and other models when several are on the ramp simultaneously.

☐ The moment you are out of the audience's view (and not before), begin unbuttoning your dress, taking off gloves, and so forth while en route to your own dressing area backstage. Use every precious minute wisely.

☐ Don't lose your composure no matter what happens on the runway. Smile and quickly and gracefully ease yourself out of the problem. Don't try to blame anything that occurs on anyone else.

After the Show ☐ Put the clothes back into stock after the show. Hang up garments properly and make sure accessories are grouped together in their proper spots and that shoes are replaced in boxes. If dressers are employed, assist them in putting things away and thank them for their help during the show. Make sure any tags that were removed are matched with the clothing.

☐ Do follow-up checks by noting stains, lost buttons, or other mishaps that may have occurred during the show. Realize that you are responsible for bringing such wear to the attention of the coordinator and that you must pay for damages, cleaning, or replacement. Expenditures for repairing or cleaning problems that were clearly your fault might also be deducted from the fee on your voucher.

☐ Clean up after yourself. Don't leave used tissues and refuse lying around.

☐ Have your voucher signed, usually by the fashion coordinator. Thank your client and/or the individual who employed you.

TABLE 4 People Involved in Live Fashion Shows

Title	Function
Show coordinator	The show coordinator is the individual who probably auditioned and hired you and is responsible for bringing together all the elements of the show.
Designer or manufacturer	If all the garments are from one designer or manufacturer, he or she or a representative may be backstage to see that everything goes according to plan.
Dressers	At a large show, there is a dresser for every model. In smaller shows, one dresser will handle up to three models. For small shows and most informal and showroom modeling, no dressers are employed. Dressers are responsible for detaching garment tags and retagging, taping soles of shoes, and having the clothes and accessories ready for the model to put on for his or her next run. They make sure garments are unfastened and unzipped. Dressers also check that all appropriate accessories are worn and that there are no styling errors, such as hanging threads, loose buttons, and uneven hems. When the model takes off the garment, the dresser is to hang it up immediately. After the show, the dresser is responsible for putting all clothes back on hangers, accessories in bags, and shoes in boxes.
Fitter/stylist/checker	The fitter/stylist/checker is responsible for checking each model before he or she leaves the dressing room for the runway. The stylist/checker usually has attended or supervised the fittings and knows exactly how the garments are to be worn. Usually he or she is stationed in the lineup area and is equipped with a list of garment, hair, and makeup instructions plus last-minute changes. The stylist checks the model to see that he or she has the total look and, if not, recommends necessary changes.
Starter	The starter sees that each model is on the runway at the right time. He or she knows the cues and is equipped with a script of the show.
Makeup artist	The makeup artist does each model's makeup. The makeup artist may be a free-lancer, a representative of a cosmetic company, or on the staff of a salon. The makeup artist usually has his or her own station where he or she does each model's makeup before the show. During the show the makeup artist checks to see that makeup is intact and that needed changes, such as color adjustments, are made for the garment being modeled.
Hairdresser	The hairdresser is usually stationed near the makeup artist and may be a free-lancer or from a salon. He or she styles each model's hair in advance of the show and makes certain that hair is intact throughout and that style changes are made according to garments. If a model is to wear a hat in one sequence and not in another, the hairdresser takes care of it. He or she must work fast, creating a hairstyle in a matter of minutes. Sometimes models are instructed to go to a specific hair salon prior to the show to have their hair done.
Alteration hands/pressers	These individuals may be seamstresses from the store's alteration department, members of the fashion show staff, or free-lance stylists. They are at hand to unstick a stubborn zipper or make quick repairs. They also press garments that may have become wrinkled on the way to the show. Ironing boards with clean covers, steam and dry irons, and press cloths are the tools these individuals use.
Security	Dressing rooms are filled with expensive merchandise and are easily subject to loss and theft. Therefore, guards may be employed to watch over items while the show is going on or during breaks.

PART 5 MODELING INTERNATIONALLY

Chapter 14 Modeling in New York

New York is the foremost city in the world in terms of modeling opportunities. No other city offers as much variety, vitality, opportunity, or challenge. The most money can be made in New York City, and, therefore, the competition is the keenest. The most attractive and talented young men and women from around the world flock to New York to fulfill their dreams of high incomes and international recognition. Offices of the big advertising agencies are located in New York, as are most European and American fashion designers and nearly all the national magazines. For a model to get the important recognition needed to be a success he or she needs exposure in one or several of the national publications found in New York City. Nearly every aspiring model at one time or another considers "hitting the big time" or trying to make it in New York. Each year agencies are beseiged by thousands of applicants making the pilgrimage to be seen by the biggest and best in the modeling business.

If you are considering a trip to New York, first arm yourself with realistic expectations, a clear plan, adequate money, a basic knowledge of the city, and some modeling experience. Although it is possible that you can go to New York and be discovered and signed by a top agency as a complete novice, it is unlikely. Most of the models competing in New York become top models in their hometowns or have extensive portfolios and experience in European, Japanese, or other foreign markets. Before you get the idea that you can rush off to New York to take the town by storm, sit down and do some research. You can test your possibilities by sending your snapshots to agents for an evaluation. If New York agents like what they see, they may invite you to New York for an interview or will schedule an appointment with a representative from their agency in your locale. If you are rejected but still want to make the trip because you feel that your great looks or talents need to be presented in person in order to be fully appreciated, then do some preparation. If the snapshots you sent didn't impress the agents, professional photographs may be in order. Spend some time at home testing with several photographers and gaining some modeling experience before going to New York.

Having enough money is a very important factor as the cost of living in New York is much higher than you may expect. Save your money and do some planning as to what it will cost. Research places to stay by looking at travel guides or by contacting the New York City Chamber of Commerce for hotels and residences of varying rates. If you have a friend or relative to stay with, it will help, but be prepared to offer something in exchange for their hospitality. You should plan on spending at least a week to interview with the agents.

PLANNING AND PREPARING FOR YOUR TRIP TO NEW YORK

Write or call the agents you want to see to find out when they conduct open interviews or whether you can make a definite appointment. You will find that most agents in New York are quite accessible and are always on the lookout for new faces and talent.

Book your airline ticket well in advance. Although it is possible to get very reasonable air fares to New York, your chances of getting a bargain are greater when you book in advance, as airlines often have certain stipulations or restrictions on inexpensive fares.

Make your living arrangements well in advance. New York is a very busy city and getting a hotel room is often difficult. Check with contacts you have there and tell them your plans along with specific dates.

Assemble all your pictures and put them in your portfolio. A composite is not necessary to get an interview with most agencies; however, having a few extra prints that you could leave behind with agents is a good idea. Write your name, measurements, and phone number on the backs of photographs.

GETTING AROUND NEW YORK

There are three airports that service New York: Newark in New Jersey, La Guardia, and Kennedy International. La Guardia is often the most convenient.

Obtain a city map. New York is divided into five boroughs: Manhattan, the Bronx, Queens, Brooklyn, and Staten Island. Manhattan is where the modeling business is concentrated. It is divided into the East and the West Sides with the dividing line being Fifth Avenue, and the upper and lower parts with 42nd Street (midtown) being the divider. Grand Central Station, which is located at 42nd Street on the East Side, is a hub for the subway system.

Getting around New York is easy because everything is fairly centralized, and the subway and bus systems are efficient. Avenues run north and south, streets run east and west. Avenue address numbers do not coincide from avenue to avenue in New York. To find at which cross street an address is located, refer to the New York Street Chart.

Many of the major advertising agencies are located on Madison Avenue, as are several of the major magazine publishing headquarters. Several photographers' studios are located in what is called the "photo district," which is an area extending from 14th Street to 30th Street along Fifth Avenue. It gradually extends south and west of this vicinity. The fashion district, where the offices and showrooms of designers and clothing manufacturers are headquartered, are concentrated on Seventh (or Fashion) Avenue.

New York, like other major cities, can be a city full of perils for the uninitiated. Be careful and alert at all times. Use common sense and don't wear expensive-looking jewelry that will attract attention to you. Don't carry a lot of cash.

Models must be very careful. You may find yourself in some undesirable and unsafe places. High rents force photographers and other businesses you may deal with into less than desirable areas of the city. Carrying your portfolio in a softsided briefcase or totebag is a good idea, as it will cut down on harassment you may receive from being identified as a model. Don't venture into areas where no other people are present, such as the middle of Central Park. Be cautious of where you go alone after dark. Be guarded with people who may approach you and those you encounter on the street.

NEW YORK CITY STREET CHART

West   **East**

Cross Street	CPW	B'wy	7th	6th	5th	Mad.	Park	Lex.	3rd	2nd	1st	Cross Street
86	262	2362			1050	1171	1038	1283	1528	1654	1654	86
79	200	2220			975	1037	900	1141	1388	1522	1512	79
72	125	2081			907	901	760	1003	1250	1388	1342	72
71	115	2061			885	865	730	983	1230	1344	1320	71
70	101	2039			800	840	718	963	1210	1330	1306	70
69	91	2020			878	831	690	945	1186	1312	1280	69
68	80	2000	CENTRAL PARK		870	813	680	921	1164	1296	1264	68
67	75	1990			855	795	660	901	1146	1276	1240	67
66	65	1966			847	773	640	889	1128	1260	1220	66
65	53	1936			837	753	610	869	1110	1242	1200	65
64	41	1926			825	733	600	841	1080	1222	1168	64
63	33	1895			816	711	570	825	1068	1202	1152	63
62	25	1888			807	691	550	803	1046	1180	1130	62
61	14	1860			800	673	540	783	1020	1160	1114	61
60	1	1834			795	654	521	767	1010	1140	1102	60
59	8th Ave		990	1441	781	635	502	742	990	1118	1084	59
58	990	1800	925	1420	765	625	480	722	970	1104	1064	58
57	970	1776	901	1401	741	595	460	701	954	1084	1036	57
56	950	1751	881	1381	720	572	440	677	938	1066	1022	56
55	930	1730	860	1361	707	555	420	656	912	1044	1006	55
54	910	1710	842	1340	691	534	400	636	894	1024	984	54
53	890	1691	821	1335	675	515	390	617	879	1004	968	53
52	870	1674	808	1301	653	501	360	595	858	984	946	52
51	850	1657	799	1285	642	477	341	575	845	961	930	51
50	830	1631	768	1260	626	452	320	560	830	846	886	50
49	810	1619	745	1250	610	431	300	540	800	924	874	49
48	790	1595	723	1220	595	415	280	518	776	902	860	48
47	770	1576	700	1200	579	401	270	501	757	884	844	47
46	750	1552	Times Square	1180	562	380	230	480	741	862	820	46
45	720	1540		1160	548	360	200	466	720	846	802	45
44	700	1516		1140	530	341	Grd.	411	711	824	786	44
43	680	1493		1120	516	334	Cen.	415	685	806	778	43
42	660	1472	601	1100	500	330	Ter.	405	666	786	752	42
41	640	1451	582	1081	479	300	117	375	640	768	726	41
40	620	1440	563	1065	465	285	100	355	620	748	702	40
39	600	1412	550	1040	444	270	90	335	600	730	694	39
38	580	1400	525	1020	424	260	67	315	580	710	662	38
37	560	1372	501	1000	411	232	49	303	560	692	644	37
36	540	1359	482	980	389	218	40	275	542	664	628	36
35	520	1333	462	960	372	200	20	254	524	638	616	35
34	500	1314	450	Hrld.	360	185	7	239	509	622	598	34
33	480	1286	421	Squ.	334	171	1	221	488	602	580	33
32	460	1256	405	885	318	153	Park	201	466	584	558	32
31	440	1238	391	871	300	135	Ave. S	179	448	562	536	31
30	420	1216	363	853	276	119	443	161	430	542	514	30
29	400	1200	335	831	264	99	423	139	414	520	496	29
28	380	1178	321	811	250	79	403	121	392	500	478	28
23	260	956	225	713	200	1	301	23	300	402	396	23

Note: Address numbers in New York City may seem confusing to a newcomer because address numbers are not consistent on all streets the city. This chart is designed to enable you to find an address by checking cross streets. For example, if you want to find 200 Madison Avenu check the top of the chart, then by going down the chart, find the number (or nearest) of the address you want. Next, check the outermo column to find the nearest cross street. The address on Madison would be closest to 35th Street.

THE RESULT OF YOUR NEW YORK EXPERIENCE

If several agents have expressed an interest in you, try to get commitments from them, and then decide with which agency you will be affiliated. Once you have decided, do some in-depth planning with the agent. Determine the right time of year to return. If possible, try to arrange a few testings with photographers that the agencies recommend while you are in New York. New York has a number of excellent photographers who do test photos at reasonable prices, and your pictures will have that "New York" look, which may help you in your hometown.

If you get enough good photos, you can have a simple composite made in the interim. That way when you return to New York you'll be ready to begin meeting prospective clients. Even if you are an established model planning to make the move to New York, or if you have a place to stay at no charge, you will need money just to get around. You may need to consider some kind of income or job ability to tide you over. Because of the intense competition and the high stakes of this market, you will find making a name takes longer than you may have thought. Even models who have gained experience in other cities find it can take several months to a year or longer before they are established and earning a good enough income to support themselves adequately in New York.

On the other hand, if things didn't work out during your first try, and no one expressed an interest in representing you, act on the advice you were given. Return to your hometown to gain more experience or consider working in Europe to gain experience and to acquire tearsheets. Plan a return visit to New York in the future.

Chapter 15 Modeling Opportunities Outside the United States

TYPES OF FOREIGN MODELING OPPORTUNITIES

Specific Assignment

Modeling is a job that can involve worldwide travel. There are two ways in which models may work in other countries: specific assignment and extended stay.

A model may have a U.S. client who decides to shoot an assignment on location outside of the country. The client may choose an exotic location to draw attention to his or her product, or it may be necessary because of seasonal characteristics. For example, if the client wants to photograph bathing suits at the ocean in January, a warm, sunny environment will be needed. Editorial shootings often take place in exotic locations around the world.

Another way a model may have a specific assignment abroad is to be booked by a foreign client, who books him or her for a shoot to take place in the client's country.

Extended Stay

Models move from one modeling marketplace to another. European models try their luck in New York, whereas American models travel to Europe and Japan. A model will stay in a particular country for a minimum of 3 weeks up to several months. The average length of stay is about 2 months. The model is represented by an agency and works there as she would on a daily basis at home. Modeling in Europe or Japan is often used as a stepping-stone in a career. A model will travel to gain experience, polish, and tearsheets, all of which will give her an edge over the competition. Or an experienced model who needs a change of pace to improve or to make a fresh start with a new look may choose to travel. Usually it takes less time for a model to get editorial exposure away from home because she is a foreigner and her stay will be limited. This distinguishes her from the other models populating the area, and agents and editors are quick to pick up on a model who has the right look and qualifications for their assignments.

Each model is different, and it is difficult to predict how one will fare in Europe or Japan. Some models work from the day they arrive, others find no work after a month. Many models trying to build a reputation and a portfolio have found that it takes from 6 months to a year to do so. Even when the model returns to her home country with an excellent portfolio, it is no guarantee for future success. In New York, very few models who are successful have not at some time worked in Europe.

The Countries and the Competition

There is hardly a market existing today that is not swarming with models trying to get work. New York, Paris, Milan, London, and Tokyo are the most competitive. Aside from the fact that American models flock to these cities to work, there are also many extraordinary models already there from all over Europe (particularly the Scandinavian countries) offering tough competition. Other cities where models commonly go to gain experience and see the world are: Zurich, Switzerland; Barcelona and Madrid, Spain; Munich and Hamburg, Germany; Amsterdam, the Netherlands; Copenhagen, Denmark; Sydney and Melbourne, Australia; and Ontario, Canada. Modeling fees vary but generally the rates are lower than in the United States. In Japan, rates are often comparable to New York rates.

THE QUALIFICATIONS FOR MODELING ABROAD

Physical qualifications are basically the same everywhere. Females must be at least 5'8" for photography work and 5'9" and up for fashion show work. A size 8–10 is the standard size (European size 38) for female models. Male models must be 6'0" to 6'2" tall and wear a size 40R suit (European size 50). Of course, there are exceptions, but most of the models who do not meet these requirements are usually natives. In Europe the looks that are in demand tend to be more editorial or extreme than those predominating here. Also fashion concepts and therefore the types of looks that may be in are usually slightly ahead of those found currently in the United States. Slightly smaller models (5'6" or 5'7", sizes 4–6) are sometimes preferred in Japan for print work.

One of the most important nonphysical characteristics a model must possess for working abroad is the ability to survive just about any situation. A model usually will not have a traveling companion. She must be adept at living out of a suitcase and finding her way around unfamiliar places. Models who travel internationally must also be able to cope with unfamiliarity in languages and customs. Fluency in foreign languages will make things a lot easier, however it is not necessary for a model working in foreign countries to speak the languages. English and French are the languages spoken by most of the agents, photographers and prospective clients with whom the model will have contact. Most important is that the model have a willingness to communicate and an ability to understand a few key, often-used words.

Most agents require that you have some modeling experience. An excellent composite and portfolio will increase your chances of getting work. Also most agents are interested only if you are affiliated with a good agency in a major city in your home country. Be aware that you may have to remake your composite and reedit your portfolio to make it more effective for a foreign market.

This leads to another important prerequisite—money. Don't go to Europe or Japan or any other part of the world without money; you cannot survive on promises. You will have more flexibility, less stress, and an all-around better time if you have money to spend on necessities and other things of your choice. The cost of living is higher in Tokyo than in New York. Parts of Europe are comparable to New York. If you will be spending American dollars, your buying power will depend on their current monetary value. Usually when you work through a foreign agency, you are paid in their currency.

Having contacts in Europe, such as friends or relatives that you can socialize with and depend on, will be helpful. When you meet foreign agents, their concern for their models will be an important criteria on which to judge which agent to select.

HOW TO MAKE CONTACTS ABROAD

Most of the models who work abroad are affiliated with agencies who have connections with foreign agents. Either the agency has offices around the world or agents from these countries come to the United States and other countries to scout for talent that they can take home with them. In advance of the busy seasons (usually in May through July for fall and in December and January for spring), agents make excursions to select a number of models who will travel to their country when the season starts. A model can also contact a foreign agent by referral or through her own research. To do this, the model would send a letter (see Chapter 7) and enclose a few composites, tearsheets, and color photocopies of prints from her portfolio. If a foreign agent is interested in a model, he or she will do one of the following.

- Offer the model a contract with his or her agency that guarantees advance bookings or a certain amount of money. A round trip air ticket and lodging may also be included. This occurs usually when the model is a star.
- Advance an airline ticket. This occurs when the agent is convinced you will be successful in his or her market. He or she advances you the money for transportation, which will be deducted from your earnings once you begin to get bookings through the agency. If you don't get bookings, you will be sent home and owe nothing for the transportation costs.
- Extend an invitation to work with his or her agency. This is not a promise of anything specific. If the model decides to make the trip at her own expense, she will have an agent to represent her.

How to Deal with a Foreign Modeling Agent

Your criteria for judging which foreign agent to select will be similar to that you would use to judge any agent. In addition, you should ask the agent the following:

- What kind of work will I be doing mostly? (catalog or editorial print, fashion shows, etc.)?
- Are there other American models in the agency?
- How much money do the other American models in the agency earn?
- How much commission does the agent take? How much money will be subtracted from my earnings for taxes? (In Europe, between these two things, as much as 50% may be deducted by some agents.)
- Will I have to sign a contract and/or what are the terms of our agreement (for example, length of stay)?

If you want to work in Europe or another foreign country and have received invitations from agents, here are some important points you should consider:

When is the best time to come? Busy seasons seem to correlate around the world. Also check that there are no extended holidays around the dates you will be staying.

Will a work permit be needed and how is this arranged? Find out if a work permit is needed, if the agent can arrange one for you, what documents or information you will need to provide, how long the permit is valid for, and how it is renewed.

Find out if any medical procedures, vaccinations, etc. are needed.

What will the accommodations be? Find out if accommodations will be arranged for you by the agent, the cost and the location in relation to the agency. If they will not be arranged for you, ask the agent for suggestions or research inexpensive weekly hotels, apartment-hotels, and pensions. There are several excellent guides for travelers that list such information.

What is a reasonable amount of money to bring? Ask your agent or contact about the cost of living in the city and what amount of money she or he would suggest you bring with you.

Find out what the climate will be at the time you will be there. Find out prevailing weather conditions so you can pack accordingly.

Find out if you will be required to bring certain items. Ask if you will have to provide wardrobe, shoes, or accessories for bookings and the like and know what style, season, etc. Ask what type of clothing the agent prefers for attending modeling appointments.

Find out about promotional tools. Ask the agent if your composite will be satisfactory and find out how many you should send prior to your arrival so the agent can begin sending them out. Bring your portfolio plus other prints, slides, and tearsheets you may have so the agent can sift through them and make his or her selections for your portfolio so it is tailored to his or her market.

PREPARING FOR YOUR TRIP ABROAD

Once arrangements have been finalized, begin preparing right away. In some instances, an agent may give you only a few weeks' advance notice. It is always a good idea to telephone or send a telegram to the agent in the weeks preceding your arrival to confirm all particulars.

Checklist of Items for Modeling Abroad

☐ Valid passport.

☐ Round trip flight ticket.

☐ Work permit, visa.

☐ Portfolio.

☐ Composites.

☐ Money, traveler's checks, and foreign currency.

☐ Addresses and telephone numbers of agents to whom you've confirmed your exact arrival. In many instances, models are not met at the airport, so the model will need to know the address and telephone number of her destination or hotel.

☐ A list of American Express offices and American consulates.

☐ A foreign language dictionary.

☐ Items the agent has requested you to bring.

☐ Lightweight canvas luggage, including a totebag.

☐ Travel convenience items such as an electrical currency adapter for using American appliances in Europe, wind-up alarm clock, vitamins, and preferred medications for colds, skin problems, irregularity, allergies, and food sickness.

To obtain a passport, you will need three forms of identification and your birth certificate (the original, not a photocopy) or an expired passport if you have one. You must also have a regulation black and white or color passport photo. It may take a few weeks to obtain your passport under normal circumstances; however, if you need one in a hurry you can usually get one if you have proof of your departure date (your flight ticket) or a letter from the modeling agent.

A few more tips: Do as much research and preparation at home as possible. Study fashion magazines of the places you'll be visiting, buy a map of the continent and country; read travel guides and make notes of the customs and specialties. Make an effort to learn a few words in the language. This will ensure that your trip will be enriching and enjoyable.

Don't change your hair or alter your appearance in any way between the time you met with the agent or sent your pictures. Don't ever misrepresent your qualifications or intentions to an agent.

Appreciate your stay for all the unfamiliarities it has to offer. Do not consider modeling abroad if you are the homesick type, undependable, physically frail, have a lot of responsibilities at home, or are not open-minded when it comes to new and different experiences.

Also, approach modeling abroad as a business trip, not a pleasure trip. Don't expect your foreign agent to entertain you. Conduct yourself in a professional manner. Be aware that your foreign agent will be giving periodic reports of your progress and conduct to your home agent.

TRAVEL TIPS
- Always carry identification with you wherever you go. Label the inside and outside of your luggage with your name and the addresses of both your home and foreign agent.
- Always have a name and telephone number of someone to contact in case of emergency, both in your hometown and the place where you are going.
- Carry tickets and important documents (passport, etc.) with you, rather than packing them in your luggage. Carry your portfolio and composites with you, rather than packing them in a suitcase.
- Carry only credit cards essential for your trip. Carry traveler's checks instead of cash. Keep a list of numbers of these checks in a separate place and the address and telephone numbers to contact to receive replacement checks.
- Carry some money with you at all times in a place (on your person) other than your purse, so that you will be safe should your purse or belongings be lost or stolen.

WORLD MAP

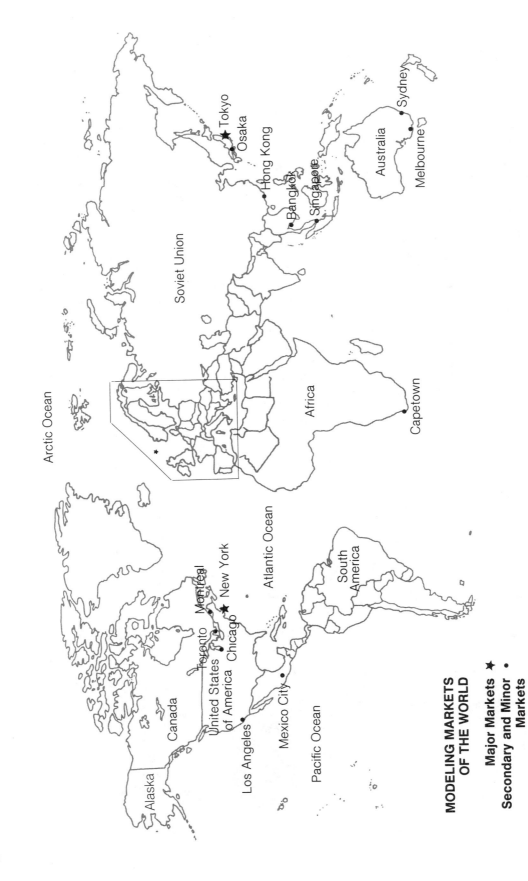

464

Arctic Ocean

Alaska

Canada

United States
of America

Los Angeles

Mexico City

Pacific Ocean

South
America

Atlantic Ocean

Toronto
Montreal
Chicago ★ New York

Soviet Union

Tokyo ★
Osaka

Hong Kong

Bangkok

Singapore

Australia

Sydney

Melbourne

Africa

Capetown

**MODELING MARKETS
OF THE WORLD**

Major Markets ★

Secondary and Minor •
Markets

*Enlarged on Next Page

MAP OF EUROPE

To obtain a list of modeling agencies abroad contact MPC Educational Publishers, 3839 White Plains Road, Bronx, New York 10467. This list gives names and information regarding agencies in Australia, Austria, Belgium, Brazil, Canada, China, Denmark, England, Finland, Italy, Japan, Mexico, Netherlands, South Africa, Spain, Sweden, Switzerland, West Germany, and many others.

PART 6 RELATED CAREERS
Chapter 16 Exploring Fields Related to Modeling

There are many jobs related to the modeling field that are challenging and that require skills and talents similar to those needed for modeling. If you have tried modeling and your experience has not met your expectations, you may want to redirect your professional pursuits. Even if you have enjoyed success as a model, you must realize that for the majority of people, it is a short-lived career. Keeping an open mind and exploring all kinds of opportunities can lead to success in other areas.

Many models have ventured into new fields and found lucrative and exciting careers. The assets necessary for success in modeling, such as interpersonal skills, personal style, aesthetic awareness, creativity, and perserverance, are important for the related careers listed here. The information you have read in this book in regard to professional conduct will apply equally well to these professions.

One of the most important things you will have to realize, though, is that entering into these jobs may take just as much, and usually more, effort, money, and time as entering into modeling. You may find you will need a college education or formal training even for the entry-level jobs. The jobs listed here are not like modeling where an individual can begin with little or no training or experience and progress to the top in a short amount of time.

You may also encounter a prejudice against your former career as a model. Many of your future employers may think that models are spoiled, lack ambition, and rely on their good looks rather than their brains and personalities. For every advantage that being a former model has afforded you, there may be a disadvantage in the way others regard you. In other words, you'll have to prove yourself all over again.

The careers listed here are all associated with glamour. As you may discover in your modeling endeavors, glamour jobs are often not all that glamourous. To attain any level of achievement, a lot of hard work is necessary. Whenever something appears glamourous, you can be assured that there will be a lot of competition. The money-making potential of several of the careers listed here is also a dubious factor. Many of the people competing for such careers are very young and eager to toil endlessly for little or no pay, just to obtain opportunities. This makes it difficult for anyone but those well established to derive an adequate income. Also because of their nature, these jobs are unstable. Unlike businesses that provide for the basic necessities of life such as food and medicine, a career in fashion or entertainment is highly subject to economic downturns and even social trends.

The most important task for anyone contemplating a career change is to assess his or her assets and liabilities. It is also important to try to establish long-term goals. There are so many different paths in life from which to choose, and each requires an investment in time that you can never recover. When considering the following careers, your most important concern is not how much fun they might be, but how they might best utilize your own special blend of talents, skills, ideas, and ambitions.

JOBS RELATED TO THE MODELING FIELD

Makeup Artist

Artistic talent, an eye for color, and the ability to apply makeup on all types of faces to create different looks is necessary if you want to become a makeup artist. A complete understanding of makeup technology and how makeup relates to the medium (television, print) in which you are working is also a must. Most makeup artists are self-taught; however, art courses in portraiture, sculpture, etc. can be very helpful.

For some jobs within the makeup artistry field, you may need to have a cosmetologist's license. This will require attending a cosmetology school to earn a state-approved license. State requirements vary but in most cases you can expect to attend school for a minimum of 1000 hours. Most cosmetology schools include makeup artistry as a minor part of their regular hairstyling curriculum. Other states have separate or specialty licenses, for example, a license for people who demonstrate makeup application. A cosmetologist's license may not be a requirement for makeup artists who apply makeup for photo shootings in many locations; however, states vary in legislation.

In most cases if you want to do makeup for television and films you will have to have a cosmetologist's license in addition to membership in a union for makeup artists. Sometimes it is necessary to serve a lengthy apprenticeship.

To obtain work as a makeup artist for still photography and fashion shows, you will have to assemble a portfolio of photos of models and nonmodels demonstrating your makeup artistry skills. You will also need a promotional card similar to a model's composite, showing the best samples from your portfolio. These cards will be distributed to photographers and other potential clients who use makeup artists. Some makeup artists represent themselves, whereas others are represented by agents. Modeling agencies sometimes represent makeup artists as well as hairstylists and stylists. Makeup artists are usually paid by the hour or may negotiate a flat fee. Another way to get started is to become a makeup artist on the staff of a well-known salon and to build your reputation.

You may also want to consider other areas that are related to makeup artistry, such as skin care (esthetics) and nail care. An esthetician administers facials and other treatments for the skin. He or she may also work in connection with a dermatologist or cosmetic surgeon. A nail specialist gives manicures, does nail sculpturing, and provides other treatments for the hands. In some states you will need a regulation cosmetologist's license, whereas in others you may only need a separate, less extensive license.

Hairstylist

Artistic ability and hairstyling skills as well as an understanding of the human face and its variations are necessary for work as a hairstylist. In addition, it will be important to understand the medium for which you are styling hair.

For photo sessions and fashion shows, a cosmetologist's license may not be necessary. However, if you intend to work in a salon and will be cutting hair or applying chemical preparations, such as color and perms, to the hair, possessing a license is required by law. Attending a state-accredited cosmetology school and passing a state-regulated exam are necessary to obtain a license. As with makeup artists, hairstylists wishing to do hair for photo shootings, fashion shows, and electronic media must assemble an impressive portfolio and composite.

Stylist A fashion stylist can be self-taught or may have a background in fashion design, textiles, and art. A stylist must have a innate knack for combining garments, accessories, and props as well as an eye for overall concept and strict attention to detail. Also important is having contacts for sources of wardrobe, accessories, and props. Stylists perform a variety of duties, so organizational skills are also vital.

To obtain styling work for fashion shootings, the aspiring stylist must assemble a portfolio of photographs for which he or she has done the styling and a promotional card to show to photographers and potential clients. Unless a stylist has established credibility by working in the fashion department of a magazine, or similar job, it may be difficult to obtain items for shootings or secure assignments from photographers and other clients. In addition to magazine work, it is possible to break into the field through a staff position at a photo studio or catalog house.

A food stylist usually has a degree in home economics or has taken formal instruction in cooking, cake decorating, and similar activities. He or she must be able to make food look delicious. He or she must understand lighting and photography and how they relate to the appearance of food. Knowing tricks of the trade and being inventive are also important. For example, specially designed plastic ice cubes are often used when photographing drinks because they look more appetizing and they won't melt. Glycerin or corn syrup is often used to coat vegetables and other foods that must appear wet for a photograph; water evaporates too fast and is absorbed by the food, resulting in a changed appearance.

Instruction in art is a plus. For obtaining work as a food stylist, an individual must present a portfolio of test shots of different types of foods in various arrangements. This portfolio is shown to table-top photographers who specialize in shooting food and to companies in the food business.

Stylists are paid on the same basis as hairstylists and makeup artists. Representation is also the same. In large cities there are also agencies solely devoted to representing hair and makeup artists and stylists.

Set or Theatrical Designer A set designer designs the set on which a photograph will be taken, an electronic media production will be shot, or a live promotion or fashion show will take place. For a fashion show, this individual decides where there will be entrances and exits, different levels, stairs, or other elements that will set the scene for the clothes or other items to be shown. He or she will decide on how the runway will be formed, what color carpet will be used, and other particulars.

A television commercial, a fashion photo shooting, or other type of assignment can require any type of set, from one that simulates a beach setting to one that looks like the lobby of an elegant hotel. For these assignments, the set designer will consult with the photographer or director as to the lighting used, the concept of the shot, and other particulars of the production. Sketches of the proposed set are drawn and approved, and then carpenters are brought in to construct the set.

A career in theatrical design with an emphasis on fashion is extremely competitive, so versatility in all areas of set design is recommended. Studies in theater design, scenery, costumes, art, lighting, and photography are helpful for this career. Working by trial prior to a paid assignment is often a way to break in. Testing with photographers to assemble a portfolio of photos depicting sets created by the individual that can be shown to potential clients is another way to gain opportunities. Working as an apprentice or assistant for an individual or firm specializing in producing shows of all kinds is also a good way to get started.

Fashion Show Producer/ Director

A fashion show producer/director is hired by a designer, store, apparel company, or other concern to create a show by coordinating the efforts of the client, the models, the set and lighting designers, stage crew, choreographer, and music programmer. In some instances, this individual may be responsible for employing all the talent needed for the show (including models) as well as establishing the script detailing the run of the show.

An understanding of show business and a knowledge of fashion are necessary for this type of work. Although a formal degree may not be necessary, training in dance, acting, theatrical design, fashion design, and human relations will be helpful. Fashion show producer/directors are usually employed for large charity shows, large budget shows, and important collections showings. These individuals might promote themselves by producing showcases to exhibit their work to potential clients. Working as an apprentice or assistant for an individual or firm specializing in producing shows of all kinds is also a good way to get started.

Fashion Show Coordinator

Free-lance fashion show coordinators do much of the same work as the fashion show producer/director, but usually on a smaller scale. Many times a fashion show coordinator is responsible for assembling the clothes to be shown and will also engage the models, the place the show will be held, and other particulars. He or she may even be responsible for promotion. In addition, a fashion coordinator may be expected to do all the commentary for a show. A background in fashion and theater production is helpful, as are excellent organizational skills. Fashion education is helpful, but many fashion coordinators learn by experience.

Breaking in as a free-lancer is difficult, because many clients will expect the fashion show coordinator to work for very little or no money. Newcomers in this field are constantly undercutting fees, making it difficult for everyone but those who are established to remain.

Free-lance fashion show coordinators promote themselves by staging showcase fashion shows and inviting potential clients. In addition, they usually assemble a promotional piece that outlines their services, which can be distributed to boutiques, department stores, and other concerns in need of fashion show coordinators.

A fashion show coordinator may also be an employee of a retail store, apparel company, or other concern. Coordinating shows may be his or her only duty or he or she may have additional responsibilities. At a large concern, the position may require coordinating shows for a chain of stores in different locations.

Fashion Writing

Fashion writing encompasses careers such as fashion editor, editorial assistant for a magazine or newspaper, and free-lance writer. There are many different types of jobs on a fashion magazine. To study the possibilities, look at the masthead of a fashion magazine

470

listing the jobs and the people who occupy them. Not all of the jobs require writing skills. For example, a fashion magazine's model editor is responsible for researching, selecting, and booking the models who appear in the publication. Magazine jobs are not particularly well paid; however, there are lots of advantages that go along with these positions. Competition for such jobs is heavy. A college degree in journalism is usually helpful. One way to break in is through a magazine internship program or by starting as a secretary and working up.

Writing as a free-lancer is also a possibility. However, submitting unsolicited samples of your writing is a very difficult way to obtain recognition or assignments. Having a literary agent and previous experience with a publishing or advertising firm is usually necessary. Writing for your school or local newspaper is a good way to obtain published samples of your work.

Fashion Photographer

Fashion photography is a highly competitive field. In order to succeed, a fashion photographer must have technical skills, artistic talent, and the ability to deal with people. More than anything else a consistent, individual photographic style is the factor that will set him or her apart from other photographers. Acquiring this style is done in many ways. Although many successful photographers are self-taught, attending college or art school photography classes as well as workshops will help to establish a solid base of skills. To increase his or her skills and to promote his or her talents to potential employers, the aspiring photographer will need to assemble an impressive portfolio of test shots or sample photos. In addition, promotional pieces displaying highlights of the portfolio should also be developed for distribution to potential clients.

Many photographers start their careers by assisting an established photographer. However, these jobs are difficult to come by and pay very little. Well-known photographers are deluged by people offering to assist for no pay. Also many photographers prefer male assistants because a great deal of the work involves carrying and setting up heavy equipment. Some photographers begin by working on the staff of a large catalog photography studio or in the photography department of a newspaper.

Other photographers work independently to establish their own photography studios. Acquiring a backlog of established clients is crucial to success. Although some photographers acquire jobs on their own, most obtain work through a photographer's representative who receives a commission from the assignments he or she procures. When self-employed, a photographer will need a substantial amount of money for equipment, a studio, and property and liability insurance to protect valuable equipment and the people he or she works with should accidents occur while shooting. The photographer also must have money for assembling a portfolio, self-promotion, and other business necessities.

Fashion Designer

Fashion designers work in basically two ways. Many are employed in full-time staff positions in large apparel companies and are responsible for creating new garment designs. Others are independent and establish their own design companies.

Independent designers work out of a main office near a showroom and may have several employees including assistant designers, administrative personnel, and salespeople. In addition, a designer may own and operate a factory that manufactures the items; however, many designers have an arrangement with a contractor who handles production.

Some designers also preside over retail operations that sell their designs, such as a chain of boutiques. Many designers have licensing agreements with companies handling designer linens, eyeglasses, jewelry, or home furnishings. In these cases, a manufacturer of such merchandise will purchase the right to use the designer's name on a product. The designer receives royalties on each item sold. The designer may not actually design the item but will usually will have input.

The path to success in fashion design varies. Some designers begin their own design firms by making garment samples at home. The aspiring designer will show these samples to buyers at local stores with hopes of making sales. The next step usually involves making a trip to New York to meet buyers and make sales at prominent department and specialty stores. When orders exceed what the designer is capable of producing, he or she will contract out the work. This is where a large monetary investment is needed.

To prepare for a career as a fashion designer, a broad background and education in a variety of areas are helpful. The ability to sketch design ideas as well as perform technical fashion designing skills, such as sewing, patternmaking, and draping, are important. Also important are courses in business and merchandising. A model's experience, particularly if she has worked in a showroom, is helpful. A good place to start is as a designer's assistant or through a fashion school or college internship program.

Other Design Careers

A person with a talent for fashion and art may also be interested in fields involving textile, accessories, and jewelry design.

Visual and display merchandising encompass designing window and in-store displays. Creating scenes by assembling props, dressing mannequins, and designing sets can be very interesting work.

Artist's Representative

An artist's representative procures assignments for a photographer, designer, or other type of artist. The representative does this by calling on potential clients and showing them the artist's portfolio, promotional pieces, and work samples. An artist's representative may work independently and represent as few as 3 artists, or he or she may be employed by a firm that represents several. The representative receives a commission from the assignments he or she procures and negotiates for the artist. Excellent sales, negotiating, and interpersonal skills are vital for this profession. Perserverance is also necessary.

Many reps begin by working with new, unestablished talent who are unable to secure representation by a prestigious agent or representative. When the representative is able to obtain recognition and prestigious assignments for the artists he or she represents, he or she is able to build a more lucrative business. Established artists begin to approach the representative, and he or she is able to assemble a group of high-income artists.

Model's Agent

A career as a model's agent usually begins with applying to an established agency and working up through the ranks. To work as a booker in a modeling agency requires a pleasant voice and personality on the phone. In representing models, it is also important to have excellent interpersonal skills, loads of patience, and a great deal of understanding. Being able to spot modeling potential in others as well as knowing how to develop that potential are strong assets. Expertise in couseling models in regard to fashion, makeup, and hair and a basic understanding of photography are pluses. Sales and negotiating skills are also musts for selling the talent to potential employers.

Bookers are usually salaried employees of an agency. For outstanding work a booker may receive bonuses or commissions in addition to a salary. Most bookers do not make a lot of money; in fact, most do not make nearly as much as a reasonably successful model, even though the booker may put in more hours.

Broadcasting

Many models have the necessary looks to become a television anchorperson or talk show host; however, the competition for the limited number of on-camera positions is fierce. To get into this field, you will need a well-trained voice and stage presence as well as knowledge in a number of areas. You will usually begin working in an off-camera job, such as writing, so skills in journalism and other areas will be useful. The majority of people holding these jobs have college degrees. One of the best ways to get started is to work at a television station through a college internship program.

Public Relations

Public relations deals with promoting and enhancing a company's image in the eyes of the public in order to increase sales or popularity. Basically advertising and public relations are similar; however, a more indirect approach is used in public relations. Instead of creating ads, public relations involves writing press relases, holding press conferences, and staging or sponsoring promotional events, such as receptions, shows, parties, or contests. Videotapes highlighting a company or its products or services might also be produced and distributed to the media in order to gain quality exposure.

Opportunities exist in independent public relations firms that represent several companies or in large companies having their own in-house public relations departments. Public relations jobs require a variety of skills, most important of which are communications skills (writing, speaking) and the ability to deal with people. Creativity is also an important asset. One of the most common ways of entering the field is by having good secretarial skills.

Advertising

There are many facets to the advertising field, many of which may be of interest to the former model. The business aspect, coordinated by account executives, deals with selling an advertising agency's services to manufacturers or other concerns possessing a product or service needing improved sales. The business side also employs researchers who conduct market and product surveys.

The creative side of an advertising agency employs the art directors, creative directors, and copywriters who develop the words and images used to promote the item. Working as a casting director in an advertising agency or department involves selecting the models and talent to appear in the ads.

The production facet of advertising deals with implementing the creative side's ideas into the finished form, whether it be a print advertisement, a television commercial, or some other form of promotion. Production people are responsible for contracting the work out to printers, video producers, photographers, and several other firms or individuals whose expertise and services are needed to create the finished product.

Advertising is a high-pressure, fast-paced industry known for its fierce competition and high turnover of talented individuals. Most of the people employed in advertising have college degrees. Those on the business side may also have MBA's. For jobs in the creative areas, unique artistic or creative talents are always in demand, and college degrees aren't always necessary when an individual has a lot to offer.

Those in search of art and copywriting jobs will have to submit samples of their work when applying for such positions and will usually need previous professional experience. One way to break into advertising is through a college internship program.

The Performing Arts

If you have talent and ambition, you may be interested in a career in dancing, singing, or acting. The greatest opportunities still exist in New York and Los Angeles, although it is becoming more feasible to obtain opportunities regardless of your home base. Auditions are often videotaped and delivered to the firm or individual casting a production. Finding the right person to motivate, guide, and represent you early in your career is important. Hard work and luck are important for achieving success.

Behind-the-Scenes Glamour Careers

You may want to consider becoming an assistant or personal secretary to a celebrity or high-powered executive. Many of these jobs involve travel, meeting interesting people, and many other advantages. Often these jobs are obtained through connections or exclusive employment representatives. Because the competition for such jobs is intense, you will need special skills, such as organizational and time-management abilities. Such positions also require you to be an exemplary representative for your employer.

Flight Attendant

Becoming a flight attendant is a career that often interests models. It is a glamourous way of life that involves travel to interesting places and meeting people. A good flight attendant must be friendly, mature, attractive, and resourceful. Like any other business, it is routine to a certain extent and has disadvantages. To obtain a flight attendant job, you must apply to an airline, and if accepted, you will be trained for the job.

Business Owner

If you have an idea that you think is unique and very marketable, you may consider opening your own business. Your first task will be to research the demand for your idea and the cost of producing and marketing it. Your other major task will be to obtain capital to start your business. Any business requires an investment. Raising the money to start and operate your business, through loans or through savings, is absolutely necessary. Very few lucrative ventures, contrary to what you read or hear, were actually started with little or no investment. A lot of dedication, long work days, plus a lot of creativity and knowledge in regard to your product, marketing, and business operation is required.

RULES OF PROFESSIONAL CONDUCT FOR MODELING AND RELATED FIELDS

Whether you are in the modeling field or have chosen a related career, the following list of personal qualities and professional attributes will help you to succeed. Study each of these principles carefully to be sure you are applying them.

1. *Be honest.*
   - Don't lie about your physical characteristics, product conflicts, experience, qualifications, abilities, or availability.
   - Don't withhold information about an appearance change or problem from agents or clients.
   - Be honest with yourself. Being honest with others is not the only important point. Be realistic about your assets and liabilities. When you know yourself and your limitations, you are better able to cope with setbacks more effectively. If your modeling endeavors should fail, being honest with yourself will help you to pursue other opportunities.

2. *Be prepared.*
   - Always do your job with a knowledge of who you are working for and what will be expected of you.
   - Research the client and photographer by looking at samples of ads and other work they have done to get a basic idea of their approach and ideas.
   - Arrive at bookings with the basic items you need and with the items you have been asked to provide, in camera-perfect condition.
   - Always have more than you think you will need. When in doubt, bring it along.

3. *Be dependable.*
   - Always keep appointments. If missing an appointment is unavoidable, call and cancel as far in advance as possible.
   - Be on time for assignments or appointments. If you are going to be late, call the studio or agency to notify them; once you arrive, apologize, then get to work.

4. *Maintain a professional model's appearance.*
   - Always present a totally professional appearance. As a model, you are expected to be clean, perfectly groomed, and healthy.
   - Diligently and consistently maintain your ideal looks and weight.
   - For bookings, hair should always be freshly shampooed. It must be in good condition. Ends must be kept trimmed and hair kept in a manageable cut.
   - Skin and nails are expected to be in excellent condition with no irregularities, such as bitten nails or unhealthy cuticles.

5. *Be a good business person.*
   - Always have a voucher and know how to complete it correctly. Vouchers should be turned into the agency within 24 hours after the job.
   - Always know your rate and what you are to charge for the job at hand.
   - Do not negotiate fees with clients. Allow your agent to do this.
   - Do not discuss rates on the set.
   - Do not try to cheat clients or agents out of services, money, or commissions owed them. Live up to agreements, promises, or contracts you have made.
   - Always have a clear understanding between yourself and an individual or company as to reimbursement in the form of cash or favors. Realize that whenever someone provides you a service, something is expected in return. Do not enter into one-sided arrangements.
   - Do not expect to get into business without making some investment. Don't expect others (parents, photographers, agents) to make the investment for you. Becoming a model is your choice.
   - Strive to be an effective money manager. Modeling is a seasonal business and a short-lived career; you will be wise not to spend all of your money. Make a short-term and a long-term budget and adhere to it.
   - Planning is one of the most important tasks any smart business person does. It will help you to establish goals and to keep track of your progress.

6. *Market yourself well.*
   - Have a clear, realistic idea of the type or types of work for which you are best suited and then aim for that market. If you want to succeed, realize that you may have to change your look and your approach in order to be more marketable. Often models must go on diets and get bad skin, teeth, or unsuitable hair corrected or even have minor cosmetic surgery or cosmetic dentistry performed. Speech classes are often necessary to overcome accents or impediments. Television performing or acting classes are necessary to eradicate shyness or to train for modeling in electronic media.
   - Assemble a professional portfolio and composite and don't attend any appointment without them. Continually update them. Don't display pictures older than 1 or 2 years. Keep your clients and agents supplied with current composites. Most important, be able to reproduce the looks exhibited on your composite for any client at any time. Follow the guidelines set forth for composites and portfolios.
   - Carefully select an agent who is right for you and then take full advantage of his or her services and expertise. Listen to your agent. Trust and follow his or her advice and instructions. The agent is there to help you and to act as the link between you and the market. The information the agent transfers to you has been gathered through daily contact with clients, photographers, advertising agents, and others in the profession.

7. *Know your profession.* Develop the basic skills necessary for all models who want to succeed. These are to:
   - Produce a makeup that is in fashion, flattering to your features, and suitable for each type of modeling situation (photography, fashion show, electronic media, and live promotion).
   - Work with your hair. You should be able to arrange it in several different, current, and suitable styles.
   - Ascertain the demands of the job and produce the expressions, movements, or looks required.
   - Be adept at moving in front of the camera. Be able to offer a photographer a wide variety of poses, movements, angles, and expressions in each roll of film.
   - Perfect your runway walk so that it shows the garments you model to best advantage. Be aware of current choreography styles used in fashion shows. Know how to relate to the audience.
   - Develop acting ability, whether for a still camera, a television camera, or on the runway.
   - Speak well. Speaking ability and a pleasant voice are important for all models; they are essential for electronic media and promotional models.
   - Develop a fundamental knowledge and a basic appreciation of photography, lighting, styling, clothing construction, and design.
   - Know how to present and sell the garments or products you are wearing, holding, or representing. Know the framework in each type of modeling situation. Know your limitations and responsibilities.
   - Make speedy clothes changes. This includes minor hair and makeup changes (unless directed otherwise). Changes should not take longer than 3 to 5 minutes. More time will be needed if

hairstylists and makeup artists are involved. In fashion show modeling, you may have as little as 30 seconds to change a garment.

- Keep abreast of current trends in modeling and fashion and take instruction in areas that may help you as a model. Have your hair and makeup done by the professionals who work with your potential clients.

8. *Be a professional on the job.*

- Be a good listener and get instructions right. Know how to take direction and respond quickly. Ask questions if you don't understand. Be able to perform activities with a minimum amount of instruction.
- Don't smoke, eat, or drink at interviews or on the job unless you get permission.
- Be pleasant to work with. Don't argue or complain during bookings. Never argue with a client.
- Don't refuse to wear something you are given to model. Don't refuse to do movements or actions that you may be instructed to do. Exceptions are dangerous or immoral activities. Should you be faced with something of this nature, contact your agent to clear any misunderstanding.
- If any questions or problems arise during a booking that you are not able to handle, call your agency when the client is present and explain the situation.

9. *Be considerate.*

- Be considerate of other people's time, needs, efforts, talents, and property.
- Work at the pace demanded by the situation. Don't unnecessarily take up the time of agents, clients, photographers, and others. Accomplish your purpose quickly and efficiently.
- Understand and appreciate the needs of others. Each person must operate under certain restraints. The client must show certain garments and details in order to make a sale. The photographer has certain limitations inherent in photography, and everyone has certain time restrictions.
- Don't be selfish. Consider other people's needs before you own, and don't make unnecessary or unreasonable demands.
- Each person employed on a booking is vital to the final outcome. Each is skilled and has a certain knowledge and aptitude for his or her particular field, just as you do for yours. Be concerned about performing your own job successfully. Don't instruct others as to how they should do theirs. Don't offer suggestions unless you are asked.
- Be respectful of the property of clients. Protect their garments from wrinkles, stains, and damage. Always handle their clothing or product with care. Be extremely cautious in studios where there is a lot of valuable equipment. Be careful with props and sets, and stay clear of cords on the floor. Leave dressing rooms neat and clean. Do not take items from the studio that do not belong to you.

10. *Make an extra effort.*

- Don't limit yourself to performing the bare minimum that is expected of you. Be willing to extend yourself.
- Make a contribution to the job by inspiring creativity and enthusiasm in others. Continually try to learn, to improve, to experiment, and to be creative. Have alternative ways of doing things and maintain an open mind.

THE PSYCHOLOGY OF SUCCESS

If you have read all the chapters in this book you may be thinking, "I just couldn't do all that." Most successful models had the same feeling when they were beginning. Few people can start at the top in modeling or any other worthwhile profession. Modeling is a demanding profession, and it is not for everyone. However, if you really have the desire to make modeling your career, and if you feel that you have the ability to meet the requirements and challenges the modeling profession offers, then visualize what you want and how you will achieve it. Keep your vision of success fresh in your mind.

Be assured that you will encounter disappointments. You will be able to cope with them if you remind yourself that all great accomplishments were the end result of many attempts and failures on the part of people just like you. Many of the top people in the modeling or any other profession had some of the same obstacles to overcome as you may be facing now. Keep in mind that even when you don't succeed in the way that you had hoped, the lessons that you learned while trying will be valuable experience for future endeavors.

Glossary

A

Abroad: Pertaining to work outside one's own country.

Accessories: Items worn to enhance clothing, such as jewelry and scarves.

Acting glossy: A mass-produced glossy photograph displaying a headshot of an individual seeking acting work in industrial, educational, feature, or other types of filmed or videotaped productions and television commercials.

Action: A term used in film or videotape production by the director indicating that cameras are to begin filming or taping.

Advance: Money made available to the model before a job is completed and later deducted from her pay. An agent will advance money to a beginning model for test photos and other modeling expenses.

Advertising: To call attention to a product or service in order to increase sales. Advertising may be done through various media. The advertiser must pay a fee to have his message presented. For example, a company wishing to place an advertisement in a magazine must pay the rate that the magazine charges for a page.

Advertising agency: A company that is hired by a manufacturing, distributing, or design firm to promote a product or service. The ad agency coordinates all the elements to create a print ad, television commercial, brochure, or catalog.

AFTRA: American Federation of Television and Radio Artists, a union of television performers.

Age category: The age a model is or is capable of appearing to be; also referred to as 'age range.' An age range usually encompasses a five-to-seven year span.

Agency: A company devoted to finding and promoting models or talent, scheduling bookings and negotiating terms and fees for talent or models. The agency receives a percentage of the payment a model is given for completing an assignment.

Agent: A person working individually or for an agency who arranges contacts and assignments between a talent or model and a company or other entity in need of a talent's or model's services.

AGVA: Actor's Guild of Variety Artists.

Alteration hand: A person who makes certain that clothing to be modeled is in good repair and is properly altered to fit the model.

Alum: An aluminum salt having astringent properties.

Appointment book: A book the model uses to record time, place, and other information about interviews, auditions, bookings, and other activities. The appointment book may also be used to record expenses for income and tax records.

Art director: A person working as a freelancer or employed by an advertising agency, magazine or other concern to develop the look for an ad, editorial, or other visual presentation.

Assignment: A term used interchangeably with booking, indicating a situation in which the model is paid for her services.

Audition: A method used in selecting models and actors for specific commercials, advertising campaigns, fashion shows, and photo shootings. At an audition a model or actor will usually have to perform an activity relevant to the job.

Audition form: A form used by an agent and model to record information pertaining to an audition.

Audition report form: A sign-in sheet used by casting directors or other individuals conducting auditions for an assignment. It is used as a record of those interviewed and as a means to ensure that talent is compensated, if necessary.

B

Base foot: A ballet term meaning the foot on which you are standing or on which the majority of your weight is carried.

Bathing suit model: A model with an attractive figure who models bathing suits and active sportswear.

Beauty: Anything that is pleasing to the eye; in modeling, beauty is an area of specialization focusing on skin, hair, and makeup.

Beauty shot: A headshot that focuses on hair and makeup.

Big and tall men: Male models who wear a size 44 suit and up.

Billing form: A form used by models to record names of clients, job description, hours worked, fees, and expenses.

Black and white photo: Photograph taken with film that produces an image in black, white, and variations of gray.

Book: (1) to assign a model. (2) Jargon used for a model's portfolio.

Book, agency presentation: A 16 x 20 or larger portfolio containing pictures and tearsheets of the models the agency represents. The agent will make calls on prospective clients to show the presentation book.

Book, model agency: A loose-leaf notebook or spiral-bound printed book ranging in size from 6 x 8 to 9 x 14 issued yearly (or more often) by an agency to display photos of models the agency has chosen to promote. Clients use this as a reference guide or catalog from which to select models for auditions and assignments. Model books are sometimes referred to as talent books or promotional books.

Booker, agency: A person employed by an agency to schedule appointments and assignments for models.

Booking: A modeling job; a paid modeling assignment.

Booking conditions: Factors that may exist in a booking and for which the model may be paid more. An agency establishes booking conditions that outline fee specifications for cancellations, weather permitting bookings, overtime or weekend fees, or bonuses for a variety of other conditions.

Booking form: A form used by a model and agent to record information pertaining to a specific job.

Booking out: When a model books out he or she makes specific hours or days unavailable for assignments. This is done well in advance.

Bookkeeping: The practice of keeping records of business transactions.

Bookkeeping department: The department in a modeling agency which keeps track of the money earned by models. Also called accounting department.

Briefing: A company-sponsored class given by the model's client to give her or him information about the company and product to be represented.

Brochure: A printed promotional piece used by companies to give information about its products or services.

Budget: The allotment of money for a specific purpose.

Business manager: One who advises a model on career and money matters.

Buy-out: An arrangement in which a client will issue a model a one-time payment for a commercial instead of residuals.

Buyer: The person who is responsible for buying merchandise from a designer or manufacturer at wholesale quantities and prices to be sold to consumers at retail prices in stores or other outlets.

C

Call back: A second audition for a product and an indication that the model is seriously being considered for the job. This term is usually used in connection with television commercials.

Camera operators: People who operate the cameras in a video or film production and are directed by the director or director of photography.

Camera ready: When used to refer to models or items to be photographed, this means that they are in ideal, optimally photogenic condition. When used to refer to items to be printed, this means that they are ready for the printer. All print sizes are correct, retouching and other photographic print finishing techniques have been completed.

Career: A profession or other endeavor that one trains for and pursues over a period of time.

Casting: The act of selecting a suitable model or actor for an electronic media production, fashion show, photo session, or other promotional reason. This term is most often used in connection with video and film work.

Casting director: An individual who works independently or in connection with an advertising agency or other firm to select talent or models for television commercials, films, print ads, or other promotions.

Catalog work: Modeling for pictures to be included in a catalog produced by a manufacturer or distributor to sell items.

Cattle call: A mass interview or audition where several models or actors report in hopes of being selected for a job. Cattle calls are usually done to find a new face or talent.

Celebrity model: A superstar in arts, sports, television, or business who is hired to model an item or to endorse products or to make appearances to attract attention to a product; a model who has achieved celebrity status.

Change sheet: A cloth or large sheet of plastic placed on the floor for models to stand on while dressing in less than ideal environments. This protects clothes and shoes from soiling.

Character model: A model who is neither a straight commercial type or an attractive fashion model type. Character models usually have very individual or unusual looks or skills. Children character models are also found.

Chart: A sheet or poster used as a reference. Agencies use charts to schedule and record a model's activities.

Checker: The person responsible at a fashion show for checking to make sure that models appearing on the runway have on the right garments and accessories and are appearing in the correct order.

Checklist: A list used as a reminder of items or activities.

Cheekcolor: A cosmetic used to contour or color the cheeks. Also called blusher or rouge.

Child model: A model who is or appears to be between the ages of 2 and 12 and promotes items such as children's toys, furnishings or clothing in print, electronic media, live promotions and fashion shows.

Class A commercial: The most lucrative type of program commercial. Class A commercials are aired in over 20 cities. The other types of program commercials are Class B, which run in 6 to 20 cities, and Class C, which are shown in 1 to 5 cities. This is a system devised for the payment of residuals on television commercials.

Client: The entity paying the costs of a shooting, or the individual representing the concern paying the model's fee.

Clientele: A group or body of clients or customers.

Closed set: A photography or television set that is occupied only by the individuals directly involved in the production, such as the photographer, model, makeup and hair artist, and assistant. Closed sets are usually requested by the model's agent for lingerie and nude modeling assignments.

Cold reading: Reading a script without having the benefit of preparation.

Collection: A group of samples made up by a designer.

Coloring: A term applied to the coloring of one's hair, skin, and eyes.

Colorist: A licensed hairdresser who specializes in using chemicals and other substances for coloring, permanenting, or straightening the hair.

Combination skin: Skin that exhibits more than one condition, such as oily, dry, and normal areas.

Commentary: A narration giving information about what is being shown or done.

Commentator, fashion show: A person who describes and comments on fashions modeled in a show.

Commercial: The advertising of a product.

Commercial art: Art used in advertising.

Commercial glossy: A mass produced 8 x 10 glossy photograph used by models and actors promoting their looks and talents for television commercials.

Commercial look: A look that appeals to a large and diverse group of consumers.

Commercial model: A model who represents or sells non-fashion related products.

Commission: The percent of a model's fee paid to his or her agency.

Competition: People who are vying for the same position.

Composite: A 6 x 8 or 8 x 10 mass-produced sheet or card upon which the model's best photos showing a variety of moods, angles, clothing styles, and information are reproduced. Also called a comp, card, or Sed card.

Composite glossy: A mass-produced 8 x 10 black and white or color photographic reproduction that displays more than one photo of the model along with her statistics.

Conflict: Products, ideas, or services that are in direct competition with each other.

Contact: An acquaintance or connection who is influential in helping one's career.

Contact sheet: A sheet that displays all the exposures from a single roll of film and from which photo selections are made. Contact sheets are made when black and white or color negative films have been used.

Contour makeup: The shading of areas of the face with a makeup product that is darker than the skin to create more interesting planes, or to correct or balance facial features.

Contract: An agreement signed by an agency, company, or union and a model to outline in writing the obligations of each for a given situation.

Coordinator, fashion: A term that has several meanings. In a fashion company a coordinator may help to plan a design line and coordinate all the elements to produce the desired result. In a department store, a fashion coordinator may act as an adviser to customers seeking fashion assistance.

Coordinator, fashion show: The person who selects the models, handles the fittings, conducts rehearsals, and performs a variety of other tasks associated with putting together a fashion show.

Copywriter: The person who writes the words actors will speak in a commercial or the words (copy) to appear in a print ad.

Cosmetic checklist: A chart used by models to list cosmetic products, types, brands, colors, and other information.

Cost: Purchasing a garment at cost means purchasing it at its wholesale cost, before it is marked up to be sold at retail outlets.

Cove: An infinity wall built into a photo studio; also called a cyc.

Cover try: A photo session to try out a model and concept for a magazine cover. Often several different models and/or concepts are tried for a single cover. The one winning the approval of the magazine's editors and/or the publisher is the one that will be used.

CU: Meaning close-up. Noted on a video or film script to indicate that the camera lens will be focused on the model from the waist up. ECU means extreme close-up.

Cue cards: Large cards which contain large handprinted words that the on-camera person is to read or to refer to if he or she forgets the lines.

D

Day rate: The fee the model charges for an eight hour day during business hours.

Decollete: To bare the neck and shoulders.

Demo tape: Another name for voice tape.

Demonstration: To describe the qualities of an item or product and show how it is used.

Derriere: The buttocks.

Designer: The person who designs fashions, accessories, etc.

Designer, set: People who design sets or scenes for theatrical, exhibition, or photographic purposes.

Direct mail: Advertising to individuals by mailing ads, catalogs, and other promotional pieces directly to private homes or businesses to solicit orders for a product or service. See mailing lists.

Direct sales: Selling direct to a consumer through a catalog, show or exhibition, video presentation, or other method.

Director: The person in charge of a production who coordinates all the talent, technical people, and other elements to achieve the desired result.

Dressers: Persons who assist models backstage during a live fashion show and who are responsible for putting clothes back in order following a show.

Dressing room: A room in a studio or production facility reserved for models to dress and apply makeup.

Dry skin: Skin that is lacking sufficient oil, moisture, or both and may be characterized by scaly areas.

Dubbing: Substituting a voice for the on-camera person's voice.

Dye transfer: An effective, involved, and expensive technique for altering a photo. It is done by a lab and requires that the photo be broken down into negatives in which adjustments are made. This process can enliven, subdue, or change colors in a photo so they more closely represent the merchandise or subject matter.

E

Ear: A device consisting of a small earphone and tape recorder, hidden in the model's ear and clothing, used to record and play back a script that has not been memorized.

Editorial: An opinionated way of making a statement by way of photographs, words, television, and film.

Editorial print work: Pages of magazines produced by the magazine staff not the advertisers to promote a philosophy of current fashion or events.

Electronic media: Work that appears on radio, television, videotape, film, slides, and other audio visual presentations made for commercial, industrial, entertainment, or public relations purposes.

Etiquette: Established rules of proper conduct.

Exclusive: Belonging only to a select group, not shared by the masses. Exclusivity or an exclusive arrangement with a client or agent means that the model works only for that agent or client during a given period of time.

Exhibit work: A type of modeling where products or services are displayed by a model in person.

Expense form: A form used by models to record expenses related to jobs and for tax purposes.

Exposure: The amount of publicity a model receives and the type and quantity of his or her visibility in various media.

Expressions: Various emotions or messages portrayed through face, body, and voice.

Extras: People in a commercial who are not identified with or involved with the product. People used on films or television shows for crowd or group scenes. They either have no lines or only incidental lines and do not play a prominent role in the plot. They are used to add atmosphere or realism. Extras are sometimes referred to as "under fives," meaning under five lines.

F

Facial features: Pertaining to the structure of the face.

Fashion awareness: A consciousness of current trends in fashion.

Fashion illustration: A sketch or drawing of fashionable clothing and other items.

Fashion model: An individual who has the qualifications to fit into specific size ranges and to show fashions for buyers, designers, manufacturers, and consumers.

Fashion photographer: A photographer whose main business is photographing fashions for ads, magazines, trade papers, newspapers, and other media.

Fashion shot: A photograph of a model from head to toe concentrating on fashions being shown.

Fashion show: A presentation involving formatted appearances of different fashions.

Fashion terms: Words or phrases particular to the fashion business.

Fashion videos: An entertaining and informative videotaped production showing a designer's collection or taken from a designer's collection fashion show. This is sent to buyers to obtain orders for the clothing shown. This is sometimes done instead of, or in addition to, a formal collections fashion show.

FAX: Photographs and information about a model sent instantaneously by a facsimile machine between agencies and clients.

Feature films: Film and videotape productions, such as soap operas, motion pictures, and syndicated productions.

Fee: The amount of money an agency charges for a model depending on the job.

Figure model: One who models unclothed or partially clothed.

Fitting: The trying on and selection of clothing the model is to wear for an assignment, such as a live fashion show, photo session.

Fitting model: A model on whom clothes are designed or a model on whom the standard sizes for a design line are established.

Flat fee: A set amount for one particular job.

Form: A printed sheet with blank spaces to be filled in, such as an expense form.

Formal fashion showing: A fashion show involving a set format taking place on a runway or specified local area.

Format: A plan or arrangement.

Free foot: The foot that is not carrying your weight; also called the working foot.

G

Gaffers: Electricians who move lights and equipment in television and film production.

Galley: A printer's proof.

Garment district: An area of a city in which the majority of apparel showrooms and businesses are located.

Glossy: A mass-produced 8 x 10 shiny black and white or color photograph to which the model's or actor's resume may be attached. It is distributed to clients particularly for securing television and acting work.

Go-fer: An individual who runs errands and completes minor tasks.

Go-see: A type of activity that requires a model to go on rounds of studios and clients to further job possibilities.

Grips: People who move cameras and sets in television production.

H

Hairdresser (hairstylist, hair designer): The person who cuts, styles, or arranges a model's hair.

Hair supplies kit: A bag containing the items, products, and equipment a model needs for various assignments.

Halftone: A copy of a photograph, made up of fine dots in varying shades of gray, used by a printer for reproduction.

Handbook: A guidebook or book of instructions.

Hand model: A model who possesses hands that are ideal for showing products. A male hand model has ideal hands and nails suitable for showing products, jewelry, etc.

Hand modeling: The use of well-groomed hands to show products in commercials and other areas of modeling where hands are on view.

Hard sell: An aggressive, high pressure sales approach in which the basic facts about a product are given and the procedure for purchasing it is outlined.

Haute couture: The French word for high fashion.

Headsheet: A poster-sized sheet or brochure onto which a headshot of each model represented by the agency is reproduced along with his or her name, height, etc.

High fashion: The most current fashion concept.

Highlight: In photography the lightest or most prominent part of a scene or picture.

Highlighting, makeup: The application of lighter makeups to create interesting effects, correct balance, or enhance features.

Hospitality suite: A suite of rooms in a hotel or convention center where a model may host or assist at a party or meeting attended by a client's most valuable contacts.

Hostessing: A type of live promotional modeling job in which models are hired to attract attention to an exhibit or direct people at various special events.

House model: One who models designs within a designers salon or place of business.

I

ID polaroid: A polaroid photograph taken to identify a model auditioning for an assignment.

Illustration photography: A nonfashion related type of photography that yields a photograph that tells a story or describes a situation. Character types are most often used in illustration photography.

Illustrator's model: Posing for a photo or in person for an artist to draw an illustration that may be used for advertising or other purposes.

Image: A representation of a look. A concept of a person or a visual impression.

In character: A term meaning that the model assumes the attitude and actions of the individual he or she is to portray.

Income form: A form used by models to record dates, sources, and descriptions of and amounts received.

Income tax: A tax on your income after business-related expenses have been paid.

Industrial films: Films made to instruct, recruit, etc. by companies for in-house use or for exhibitions. These films usually cover the subject matter in detail and last from five minutes to one hour.

Infant model: An infant usually between 6 and 18 months of age who models such items as baby foods and furniture or appears in family situations in television commercials or print ads.

Informal modeling: A type of modeling where a model strolls through a store, tearoom, or restaurant giving potential customers an opportunity to see various garments.

In-house: Within a company.

Insurance: A system of protection against misfortune for which a person pays. This is a guarantee for himself and his property.

Interview: A meeting to determine an individual's qualifications for a job.

J

Jingle: A catchy tune sung in radio and television commercials or other productions.

Jingle singer: Individuals who sing songs for radio and television commercials. Jingle singers must be able to sight read music, harmonize with other singers, and know how to interpret music to add impact.

Junior model: A model who fits into junior-size apparel and has a young look. Usually she wears a size 7. Junior models weigh between 105 to 116 pounds with approximate measurements of bust 32-33, waist 23-24 and hips 32-34.

K

Kit, makeup: A small bag in which a model carries his or her makeup and grooming supplies.

L

Large size models: A model (female) who wears size 12, 14, 16 or up.

Layout: The positioning of photographs, type, rules, etc. on a composite, ad, catalog, or other printed piece to catch the eye and draw attention to the most important elements.

Leg model: A model who has ideally proportioned legs for showing hosiery, beauty products for legs, etc.

Level: A word used in audio and audio-visual productions to determine setting of controls for the talent's voice.

Liability insurance: Insurance that protects an individual or company that is responsible for other people. For example, a photographer has liability insurance to cover medical bills, etc. for a model who is injured in his studio.

Light meter: A mechanism used to determine how much light is falling on a scene so that the camera can be set accordingly and the desired effect obtained.

Lighting: The various uses of light to create desired effects in photography or live modeling situations.

Line: All the samples made for a particular season.

Liner: Pertaining to specially designed pencils or brushes used to outline lips and eyes.

Lingerie model: A model who specializes in modeling intimate apparel.

Live modeling: A term used to indicate that models will be showing the clothing or demonstrating products in person.

Live promotion: A type of promotion that employs models to appear in person at trade shows, sales meetings, stores, or exhibits to demonstrate or help promote products in other ways. Also called live industrial modeling.

Location: Any place other than a studio where photos are taken.

Loft: A large open space usually in the upper part of a building that is often a location for photography studios.

Look: An image.

Looks: Models are booked for 'looks' in which a fashion designer, stylist, or other individual will pair different accessories, hairstyles, and other elements with the clothing the model will wear at a photo session or fashion show to determine which combination looks best.

Look-see: A term used when a model calls on a client so he can have a look at the model and his or her portfolio.

Loupe: A small magnifying glass used to magnify slides and contact sheets to determine how the images will look when enlarged as photographic prints.

LS: Meaning long shot, noted on a script to indicate that the camera will show the model full length.

M

Madison Avenue: A major street in New York City where much of the advertising business is centered.

Mailing list: A list of names and addresses of potential employers to whom composites will be mailed by the model or her agency; a list of names and addresses of potential customers used by department stores, manufacturers, or any company to send promotional pieces, catalogs, free samples, and similar items. Large companies may purchase these lists of names from companies who specialize in assembling very demographically pinpointed lists.

Major markets: The most populated cities. In the United States there are three major markets: New York City, Los Angeles, and Chicago. Advertising and television commercials that appear in major markets are paid on a higher scale because of greater exposure.

Makeup artist: A man or woman who specializes in the application of makeup for models, actors, speakers, and others who appear before the public in person, on television or in photographs.

Makeup artistry: The art of applying makeup to enhance, change, or correct a person's appearance.

Male model: A man who models in one or various areas of the modeling field. Generally, he wears a size 40 regular suit and is 6'0 tall with approximate measurements of: Shirt 15-15½/34/35, Chest 38-40, waist 32-34, and inseam 32.

Mannequin: Originally derived from the Dutch word *manneken*, meaning man and related to the anatomy. The French derivation is *mannequin*, meaning fashion model or inanimate human figure. Sometimes it is used to refer to fashion show or house models.

Mannerism: A distinctive trait of speech, gesture or facial expression.

Market: Pertaining to the location of an agency and number of clients in the area.

Master reel: An audiotape made by an agency representing voiceover talent containing the best voices it has to offer clients.

Mini-portfolio: A smaller (e.g. 5 x 7) duplicate of the model's portfolio, which is messengered or mailed to prospective clients. Also called a mini-book.

Model: One who is employed to attract attention by wearing, holding, or standing next to, demonstrating, or representing products and fashions; an individual who presents an image or trait worthy of imitation.

Model agency: An employment agency for models.

Model editor: The individual on the staff of a magazine who is responsible for researching, selecting, and booking the models to be featured in the publications. Also called a model or talent coordinator.

Model type: This term refers to a model's appearance classified by age, size, sex, look or type, special features, and skills.

Modeling field: The range of jobs related to modeling.

Model's agent: An individual who works on a model's behalf to find the best opportunities for the model and to negotiate the best arrangements and fees.

Model's guild: An organization of models that helps to establish working conditions, procedures, and fees for models in an area. To belong to such guilds, models must usually apply and be accepted for membership. Model's guilds are often present in large modeling centers.

Model's release: A form signed by a model that gives a photographer or client the right to sell or publish the pictures obtained from a session.

Model's wardrobe: All the garments a model may need to wear or supply.

N

Narration model: A model who gives a short talk explaining a product and its uses.

Negatives: Film that has been processed to render an image opposite in tone and coloration to the subject.

New York City: Manhattan is considered the heart of New York City and known as the modeling capital of the world.

Newsletter: A brief, informative periodical that is mailed to readers. Model agencies sometimes use newsletters to promote models by including the latest information and pictures of each model.

"Ninety-one day out" clause: A stipulation in SAG contracts stating that if the talent does not earn a certain amount of money from commercials (e.g., $2,000) within 91 days after signing the contract, he or she can terminate the contract without incurring legal action.

Nude model: A model who is hired to pose unclothed.

O

Off-camera players: Hand models, voiceover artists, and others who are involved but whose faces are not seen on camera.

Oily skin: A skin that is excessively oily and is usually characterized by larger follicles (pores).

On-camera principal: One of the main characters in a television commercial.

Optical illusion: An effect created by lighting or photographic techniques that tricks the eye into perceiving reality differently.

Original: One of a kind; in fashion used to refer to a designer's sample.

Outgraded: When an actor's performance is completely cut from a commercial during the editing process.

Overscale: In television commercials, payment that is higher than the amount established by the television performers unions.

Overtime: Work that occurs before or after normal business hours and on holidays.

P

Parts model: An individual who models certain parts of the body, such as hands.

Payment upon publication: This means that the model or photographer is paid only when a picture is published. This very rarely occurs for models; however, it is a common procedure for the photographer shooting editorial photographs for a magazine.

Penalty fee: A fee imposed on a model by an agency or union for misconduct or an infraction of a rule.

Personality: The distinctive qualities or characteristics of a person.

Petite model: A model who wears smaller sizes, usually in junior petite sizes 3-7, petite sizes 3-5, or junior sizes 1-3. The petite model's weight is between 98 and 110 pounds. Measurements are approximately: Bust 31-32, waist 20-23, and hips 32-33.

Photo movement: Movements or poses done for the still camera.

Photo session: A time designated to take pictures. Also called a shoot, shooting, sitting.

Photo template: A group of cut out squares or rectangles corresponding proportions to sizes of film and photographic paper to enable the model to visualize on a slide or contact sheet photo, how a picture will be cropped when enlarged.

Photographer: One who makes a business of photography or who takes photographs. There are several different areas of specialization within photography.

Photographic testing record: A form the model uses to record information pertaining to a photographic testing session.

Photography assignment: A job involving photography.

Photography, color: Photographs taken with film that reproduces colors.

Physical: Relating to the human body as distinguished from the mind; matter or material.

Physical presentation: The model's presentation of herself by way of facial expressions, mannerisms, movements of arms, legs, torso, and feet.

Pivot: A movement or turn done by models to show an item from different angles.

Places, places on the set: The spot where the model or actor is to stand while being photographed, filmed, or videotaped to ensure that she or he is framed correctly and in proper focus. When a director says "places on the set" all the talent involved in the scene being filmed or taped are to take their positions on the set.

Platform model: A model on whom a product, service, or technique is demonstrated while on a stage or small platform.

Portfolio: A professional scrapbook of the model's best photos from testings and bookings.

Pose: A stance or position the model assumes when modeling.

Poster: An 11 x 14 or larger printed piece containing a photograph or illustration. Model agencies sometimes promote models by sending to clients posters containing a group shot of the agency's best models.

Posture: The position and carriage of the body and its parts; a position assumed in modeling.

Potential: Possible but not actual; having the capacity to succeed.

Presentation: A formal showing of an item or technique.

Presser: A person who sees that clothing is pressed before being modeled.

Principals: Actors seen on camera who may or may not have lines to speak but who are important in the commercial.

Print: A photographic print. Prints are available in many sizes: 3 x 5, 5 x 7, 8 x 10, 11 x 14, and 16 x 20.

Print work: Refers to photographs or illustrations in printed materials, such as newspapers, magazines, catalogs, brochures, weeklies, flyers, package inserts, product tags or labels, posters, billboards, or packages.

Printing: A process involving a printing press that produces copies of an item.

Producer: The person who oversees the entire production and is often concerned with adhering to the production's budget.

Product demonstration: Showing and explaining how a product works. This term usually applies to live promotional modeling.

Product demonstrator: A hand model or other model who shows how a product is used.

Professional: One who pursues as a business some vocation or occupation.

Progress report form: A form used by models to record the efforts the model has made to secure assignments and improve her chances at career success.

Promotional: Anything done to increase the sales or popularity of a product or service.

Proof sheets: Another word for contact sheets. Sometimes just called proofs.

Property person: The person responsible for props and products used in a television or other type of production.

Props: Items placed on a set to add interest to a scene. A prop might be an animal, piece of equipment, or an accessory.

Public relations: Activities concerned with creating a favorable image with the public.

Public relations photos: Photographs distributed to news services, newspapers, editors, and magazines documenting an event, new product, or technique that are issued by the maker and sent in hopes of getting publicity.

Publicity: Events or materials that call attention to a person or product.

Public relations: Activities performed to enhance a company, event or product in the eyes of the public. Also called PR.

R

Rag business, rag trade: Jargon for the garment business.

Rate: An established amount of money charged by a model, photographer, or other professional at hourly or daily periods for his or her services. Models have three types of rates: established, negotiated, and client mandated.

Rate list: A sheet that lists rates models charge per hour, half day or day. European lists often show a sliding scale in which models receive the most money the first hour. For two hours of work they receive a slightly lower amount, than double the amount of the first hour.

Reading: The reading of script to show one's ability to interpret words and act them out.

Recording: The act of taping action or sound.

Red Book: The Standard Directory of Advertising Agencies. A reference book listing the names, addresses, and telephone numbers of thousands of advertising agencies and the accounts each one handles. It is issued three times a year.

Release: A form signed by a model and his guardian (if underage) giving the photographer or client the right to publish the photograph.

Reshoot: An additional attempt to get the right shot, necessitated by an unsatisfactory initial shooting. A reshoot may be required due to technical problems, unsatisfactory modeling or other factors. If the model's performance or selection requires the reshoot, she is usually replaced by another. If the model was not the cause of the problem, she will usually be booked again and will be paid for the reshoot at her regular rate or rate determined by her agency.

Residual: The payment to a model or actor for work in a commercial that is aired more than once.

Resumé, model's: A data sheet containing information about the model's qualifications, training, and experience.

Right-to-work law: A state law that prohibits unionization. Local offices for unions cannot be maintained in right-to-work areas. In such states persons do not have to join a union in order to obtain employment.

Rounds: "Making the rounds" means seeing all the people who may be in a position to employ the model.

Rounds list: A list of all the model's potential employers in a given area. Included on the list are photographers, stores, designers, manufacturers, and advertising agencies.

Run-through: The rehearsal before an audition or performance.

Runway: An elevated stage or other designated area where models walk and stand to show fashions. Also called a catwalk or ramp.

S

SAG: Screen Actor's Guild.

Salon or house model: A model on whom designers, hairstylists, etc. try out new ideas and exhibit them for customers. The model usually models in the designer's salon but may also participate in traveling trunk shows and publicity events.

Sample: A single garment, the first one in a new style made by a designer or manufacturer.

Sample size: The size in which the designer makes his or her sample. This is usually tailored to a model's figure not the average figure.

Sampling or distributing model: A model hired to walk through a store or convention center to give free samples of products, literature, or to conduct product surveys.

Scale: The amount of money an individual is paid for performing various activities for an electronic media production established by the union.

Scheduling: Setting up appointments for models.

Script: The written commercial or part which the model learns before a performance.

Script supervisor: A person who supervises each take and sees that each shot fits in the final commercial.

Security: Guards who watch over clothing and expensive items during a show.

Sed card: (pronounced Zed) Another name for composite named after the German modeling agent who invented it.

Set mark: The place on a set designated for the model to stand.

Shoe model: A model who wears and shows sample shoes. A male usually wears size 10, a female usually wears sizes 6-7 narrow or medium.

Shooting: Photographic session. Also called a shoot.

Show modeling: A person or a group of people in a live formal or informal structured presentation.

Showing: Formatted, live modeling.

Showing, collections: The clothing designs created for each season and held up to five times per year.

Showroom: A room maintained by a designer to show clients his samples.

Showroom model: A model who shows garments to buyers or the press in the designer's or manufacturer's showroom.

Sitting: A word used in place of shooting. This is more often used by magazine editors especially when referring to beauty or cover shootings.

Skin disorders: Any condition of problem, blemished skin, skin disease, or allergy.

Slating: Identifying a film or videotape segment (take) when a talent gives his name, the number of the take, the name of the production, or scene or other particulars so viewers of the tape will know what they are seeing.

Slice of life: A type of commercial that depicts everyday or common events.

Slides: 35 mm film that has been processed to yield an image, which is encased in plastic or cardboard for ease of handling. Also called chromes.

Sound person: The person who handles the recordings of dialogue in a film or commercial.

Spec, speculation: Shooting on speculation means that a model and photographer do a shooting and are paid only upon acceptance by the person or company needing the picture. Model releases are not signed for shootings done on speculation until the model is paid.

Specialty model: A model who specializes in modeling only one or two parts of her body, such as hands, feet, legs, or face.

Spokesmodel: An attractive individual who represents and speaks for a product or service.

Spokesperson: An individual who represents and speaks for a product or service.

Spread: Two or more pages containing photographs or illustrations devoted to one concept or topic.

Starter: The person responsible for seeing that a model is on the runway at the right time.

Statistics: A model's statistics are his or her height, clothing sizes, measurements (female's bust, waist, hips), (males shirt size, waist, inseam), haircolor, and eye color.

Storyboard: Small illustrations combined with a script to show how a television commercial should appear. A story guideline.

Street casting: The selection of non-models from the streets or public places to appear in photographs and other productions to achieve a natural, realistic effect.

Stylist: A person who assists fashion coordinators, photographers, and models by selecting accessories, props, or clothing to be shown with the merchandise being modeled. The stylist also attends the booking to make certain that everything is worn correctly by the models and is pressed and in good condition. During a shooting the stylist will adjust garments of the models on the set to make certain they look perfect for the camera. There are different areas of specialization for stylists.

Stylist's kit: A bag or other container that holds numerous items, such as sewing, grooming, and repairing items often needed to enhance the clothing or merchandise during a fashion show or photographic session.

Swatch book: A catalog of manufacturer garments that give the sample of the fabric and instructions for its care.

T

Take: The shooting of a scene for films and videos.

Talent: Pertaining to a person who performs an activity well.

Talent agent: A representative for an individual who can act or perform another activity for commercial reasons.

Tax deduction: Any item or service that is a necessary business expense and therefore is not subject to income tax.

Tearsheets: Actual pages from a magazine, catalog, or other printed material in which the model appears. Also called cuttings, clippings, tears, or documentation.

Teleprompter: A machine that has a screen displaying the words of a script for the on-camera person's reference.

Template, photo: See photo template.

Test job: A trial shoot to test an idea or model prior to an actual photographic assignment and for which the model and photographer are paid. Usually the fee for test jobs is less than for actual jobs. No model releases are signed for test jobs, and therefore the results cannot be published.

Testing: Taking photographs for which a model is not paid.

Tools: Items needed for a model's job.

Tonality: The contrast and overall lightness or darkness of a photograph.

Totebag: A large bag in which a model carries makeup and hair supplies commonly needed for modeling assignments. Sometimes called a tote or model's bag.

Trade: Work or line of business.

Trademark: A distinctive or identifying face or body feature or other characteristic, such as a particular style of clothing, jewelry, hairstyle, or makeup.

Trade show: A show usually held at a convention center to display a wide range of products or services of a similar nature, such as a boat show, accessory show, and jewelry show.

Travel packing chart: A chart used by models when packing for various assignments that require travel.

Trunk show: A fashion show, usually featuring one designer's garments, that travels to different cities. Trunk shows are usually held in stores carrying the designer's clothing. Garments are carried in large trunks.

Turning in opposition: Turning one part or section of the body opposite to another.

Type: (1) A category of people displaying common characteristics that distinguish them as a group. (2) The printed words, letters, or numbers on a composite. Type is available in several styles, called typestyles, that display different moods, sizes, etc.

Typecasting: Assigning roles in print, video, film, or other modeling or acting assignments based on one's appearance.

U

Union: The joining or uniting for some mutual interest or purpose.

Union card: A card certifying that the person named on the card is a member of a specific union or group.

Upscale: A word pertaining to a well-bred or sophisticated individual.

Upstage: Toward or at the rear of a stage. Also pertains to one individual trying to gain more attention or obtain a more advantageous position than others on the stage.

Usage fees: Additional fees paid to a model when his photograph is exposed to a large number of consumers.

V

Video: The picture portion of a telecast.

Voiceover talent: People who deliver lines for radio productions. They also speak lines for video and film productions but do not appear on camera.

Voicetape: A reel-to-reel or cassette tape giving samples of a voiceover talent's vocal abilities that is used as a promotional tool and sent to potential clients.

Videocassette: A cassette containing recorded videotape.

Videocomposite: A videotape displaying a collection of a talent's commercial credentials or mock commercials.

Videodisc: A disk similar to a phonograph record on which sounds and images are recorded and played back on a home television screen.

Videotape, agency: A videotape made by an agency of their models for promotional and advertising purposes. Videotapes are often used to promote the best models for television commercial work.

Voucher: A form that serves to verify that a job has been completed; an invoice. When signed by the client or photographer and model, the voucher documents the hours worked, fee the model is to be paid, and rights to the photograph. Also called a fiche.

W

Wardrobe: All the garments belonging to any one person or a collection of clothing to be worn by a model.

Weather permit: A type of job dependent on the condition of the weather.

Wholesale: Material or goods sold at less than retail prices. Generally the selling of goods in large quantities for resale.

Working foot: A ballet term indicating the foot on which you are not placing the majority of your weight, your free foot.

Index